THE CAMBRIDGE COMPANION

SOCRATES

The Cambridge Companion to Socrates is a collection of essays that provides a comprehensive guide to Socrates, the most famous Greek philosopher. Because Socrates himself wrote nothing, our evidence comes from the writings of his friends (above all Plato), his enemies, and later writers. Socrates is thus a literary figure as well as a historical person. Both aspects of Socrates' legacy are covered in this volume.

Socrates' character is full of paradox, and so are his philosophical views. These paradoxes have led to deep differences in scholars' interpretations of Socrates and his thought. Mirroring this wide range of thought about Socrates, this volume's contributors are unusually diverse in their background and perspective. The chapters in this volume were authored by classical philologists, philosophers, and historians from Germany, Francophone Canada, Britain, and the United States, and they represent a range of interpretive and philosophical traditions.

Donald R. Morrison is Professor of Philosophy and Classical Studies at Rice University. He has also been a Rockefeller Fellow at the University Center for Human Values at Princeton University, a Junior Fellow of the Center for Hellenic Studies, and a visiting professor at the University Paris I–Sorbonne. His publications have appeared in edited collections and scholarly journals, including *Polis, Ancient Philosophy*, and *History of Political Thought*.

CAMBRIDGE COMPANIONS TO PHILOSOPHY

OTHER VOLUMES IN THE SERIES

(Continued after the Index)

The Cambridge Companion to
SOCRATES

Edited by
Donald R. Morrison
Rice University

CAMBRIDGE
UNIVERSITY PRESS

CAMBRIDGE
UNIVERSITY PRESS

University Printing House, Cambridge CB2 8BS, United Kingdom

One Liberty Plaza, 20th Floor, New York, NY 10006, USA

477 Williamstown Road, Port Melbourne, VIC 3207, Australia

314-321, 3rd Floor, Plot 3, Splendor Forum, Jasola District Centre, New Delhi - 110025, India

79 Anson Road, #06-04/06, Singapore 079906

Cambridge University Press is part of the University of Cambridge.

It furthers the University's mission by disseminating knowledge in the pursuit of education, learning and research at the highest international levels of excellence.

www.cambridge.org
Information on this title: www.cambridge.org/9780521541039

© Cambridge University Press 2011

First published 2011

A catalogue record for this publication is available from the British Library

Library of Congress Cataloging in Publication data
The Cambridge companion to Socrates / edited by Donald R. Morrison.
    p.   cm. – (Cambridge companions to philosophy)
    Includes bibliographical references and index.
    ISBN 978-0-521-83342-4 – ISBN 978-0-521-54103-9 (pbk.)
    1. Socrates.   I. Morrison, Donald R., 1954–   II. Title.   III. Series.

    B 317. C 35   2010
    183´.2–dc22   2010039160

ISBN 978-0-521-83342-4 Hardback
ISBN 978-0-521-54103-9 Paperback

Contents

Contributors

HUGH H. BENSON is Professor and Chair of the Department of Philosophy at the University of Oklahoma. He was a Samuel Roberts Noble Presidential Professor from 2000 to 2004. He is the editor of *Essays on the Philosophy of Socrates* (1992) and *A Companion to Plato* (2006) and author of *Socratic Wisdom* (2000). He has also published various articles and book chapters on the philosophy of Socrates, Plato, and Aristotle, and he has been the recipient of ACLS and Howard Foundation fellowships.

RICHARD BETT is Professor of Philosophy and Classics at Johns Hopkins University. His scholarly work has focused particularly on the ancient skeptics. He is the author of *Pyrrho, His Antecedents and His Legacy* (2000) and has translated Sextus Empiricus's *Against the Ethicists* (1997, with Introduction and Commentary) and *Against the Logicians* (Cambridge, 2005, with Introduction and Notes). He is editor of *The Cambridge Companion to Ancient Scepticism* (2010). He has also published articles on Plato, Socrates, the Sophists, the Stoics and Nietzsche.

CHRIS BOBONICH is Professor of Philosophy at Stanford University. He has written a number of articles on Greek ethical and political philosophy and psychology. He is the author of *Plato's Utopia Recast: His Later Ethics and Politics* (2002) and coeditor, with Pierre Destrée, of *Akrasia in Greek Philosophy: From Socrates to Plotinus* (2007).

KLAUS DÖRING is Emeritus Professor of Classics at Otto-Friedrich University, Bamberg. His publications include *Die Megariker* (1972); *Exemplum Socratis: Studien zur Sokratesnachwirkung in der kynisch-stoischen Popularphilosophie der frühen Kaiserzeit und im frühen Christentum* (1979); *Der Sokratesschüler Aristipp und die Kyrenaiker* (1988); *Sokrates, die Sokratiker und die von ihnen begründeten Traditionen* in H. Flashar (ed.), *Die Philosophie der Antike 2/1* (1998); [Platon] *Theages: Übersetzung und Kommentar* (2004); and *Die Kyniker* (2006).

LOUIS-ANDRÉ DORION is Professor of Philosophy at the University of Montreal. He is the author of *Socrate* (2004) and of various French translations of Aristotle (*Les réfutations sophistiques*, 1995), Plato (*Lachès and Euthyphron*, 1997; *Charmide and Lysis*, 2004), and Xenophon (*Mémorables, livre I*, 2000). He is currently working on the second (and last) volume of the new edition of Xenophon's *Memorabilia* (Les Belles Lettres), which will appear in 2011.

CHARLES L. GRISWOLD is Professor of Philosophy at Boston University. He is the author of *Self-Knowledge in Plato's Phaedrus* (1986; paperback, 1988; reprinted with a new preface and bibliography in 1996), a book that was awarded the Franklin J. Matchette Prize by the American Philosophical Association, and the editor of *Platonic Writings, Platonic Readings* (1988), reprinted with a new preface and updated bibliography in 2001. His *Adam Smith and the Virtues of Enlightenment* was published by Cambridge University Press in 1999. His latest book is *Forgiveness: A Philosophical Exploration* (Cambridge University Press, 2007). He is coediting, with David Konstan, *Ancient Forgiveness: Classical, Judaic, and Christian*, forthcoming from Cambridge University Press.

DAVID KONSTAN is John Rowe Workman Distinguished Professor of Classics and the Humanistic Tradition and Professor of Comparative Literature at Brown University. Among his recent publications are *Sexual Symmetry: Love in the Ancient Novel and Related Genres* (1994); *Greek Comedy and Ideology* (1995); *Friendship in the Classical World* (1997); *Pity Transformed* (2001); *Heraclitus: Homeric Problems*, with Donald Russell (2005); *The Emotions of the Ancient Greeks* (2006); *Aspasius: On Aristotle's Nicomachean Ethics* (2006); *Lucrezio e la psicologia epicurea* (2007); and *Terms for Eternity: Aiônios and Aïdios in Classical and Christian Texts*, with Ilaria Ramelli (2007). His most recent book is *Before Forgiveness: The Origins of a Moral Idea* (Cambridge University Press, 2010).

MELISSA LANE is Professor of Politics at Princeton University. Previously, she taught political thought as a member of the History Faculty of Cambridge University, where she received her PhD in Philosophy, having received her first degree in Social Studies from Harvard University. She is the author of a new Introduction to the Penguin edition of *Plato's Republic* (2007); of *Plato's Progeny: How Plato and Socrates Still Captivate the Modern Mind* (2001); and of *Method and Politics in Plato's Statesman* (1998), as well as a number of specialized articles on Greek political thought and the modern reception of the Ancients.

A. A. LONG is Professor of Classics and Irving G. Stone Professor of Literature at the University of California, Berkeley. His recent works include *Stoic Studies*, *The Cambridge Companion to Early Greek Philosophy*, and *Epictetus: A Stoic and Socratic Guide to Life*. Forthcoming works include *Greek Models of Mind and Self* and an annotated translation of Seneca's *Epistulae Morales*, with M. Graver.

MARK L. MCPHERRAN (Simon Fraser University) is the author of *The Religion of Socrates* (1996) and the editor of *Wisdom, Ignorance, and Virtue: New Essays in Socratic Studies* (1997); *Recognition, Remembrance, and Reality: New Essays on Plato's Epistemology and Metaphysics* (1999); and the forthcoming *Cambridge Critical Guide to the* Republic. He has written a variety of articles on ancient skepticism, Socrates, and Plato, including, most recently, "Medicine, Magic, and Religion in Plato's *Symposium*," in *Plato's Symposium: Issues in Interpretation and Reception* (2006); "Platonic Religion," in *A Companion to Plato* (2006); and "The Piety and Gods of Plato's *Republic*," in *The Blackwell Guide to Plato's Republic* (2006). He is also the Director of the Annual Arizona Colloquium in Ancient Philosophy.

DONALD R. MORRISON is Professor of Philosophy and Classical Studies at Rice University. He is the author of numerous articles and *Bibliography of Editions, Translations, and Commentary on Xenophon's Socratic Writings, 1600–Present* (1988). He has published in a variety of fields within ancient philosophy, including Aristotle's metaphysics, Xenophon's Socrates, skepticism, political philosophy in Plato and Aristotle, and late ancient philosophy of science.

JOSIAH OBER is the Constantine Mitsotakis Professor in the School of Humanities and Sciences at Stanford University, where he holds appointments in Classics and Political Science, and in Philosophy by courtesy. He has authored a number of books, including *Mass and Elite in Democratic Athens* (1989), *Political Dissent in Democratic Athens* (1998), and *Democracy and Knowledge* (2008). His current research explores relationships between institutions, values, knowledge, and authority.

DAVID K. O'CONNOR has been teaching at the University of Notre Dame since 1985, where his work focuses on ancient philosophy, ethics, and philosophy and literature. He is a faculty member of the departments of Philosophy and Classics. His recent publications include an edition, with notes and introduction, of Percy Bysshe Shelley's 1818 translation of Plato's *Symposium* (2002) and "Rewriting the Poets in Plato's Characters" in *The Cambridge Companion to Plato's* Republic (2007).

TERRY PENNER is Professor of Philosophy Emeritus, and was, for a time, Affiliate Professor of Classics at the University of Wisconsin-Madison. In spring 2005, he was A. G. Leventis Visiting Research Professor of Greek at the University of Edinburgh. His previous publications include *The Ascent from Nominalism: Some Existence Arguments in Plato's Middle Dialogues* (1986) and numerous articles on Socrates.

CHRISTOPHER ROWE is Emeritus Professor of Greek at the University of Durham; he was Leverhulme Personal Research Professor from 1999 until 2004. His previous publications include commentaries on four Platonic dialogues; he edited *The Cambridge History of Greek and Roman Political Thought* (with Malcolm Schofield, 2002) and *New Perspectives on Plato, Modern and Ancient* (with Julia Annas, 2002), and provided a new translation of Aristotle's *Nicomachean Ethics* to accompany a philosophical commentary by Sarah Broadie (2002).

PAUL WOODRUFF is Darrell K. Royal Professor in Ethics and American Society at the University of Texas at Austin. He has published extensively on Socrates and on various sophists. His recent books include *Reverence: Renewing a Forgotten Virtue* and *First Democracy, the Challenge of an Ancient Idea.*

Editor's Preface

Socrates is the patron saint of philosophy. Although he was preceded by certain philosophical poets and surrounded by some learned sophists, he was the first real philosopher. If you wish to know "What is philosophy?" one good answer is that philosophy is what Socrates did and what he started.

Socrates was a revolutionary. He revolutionized the intellectual method by searching for rigorous definitions of concepts such as "courage" and "justice." He revolutionized values by arguing that what matters most to human happiness is not money or fame or power, but the state of one's soul. He revolutionized ethics by insisting that a good person will never harm anyone. He was a spiritual revolutionary who remained obedient to the law; unjustly condemned to death, he refused his friends' offer to break him out of jail and lead him to exile.

Socrates was a revolutionary who began a tradition. He wrote nothing. What we know of him comes from several sources. He had the good fortune to number among his devoted followers one of the greatest geniuses, and most gifted prose stylists, of all time – Plato. Socrates is the major character in most of Plato's dialogues. The historical person Socrates exerted his greatest influence on history by way of the literary figure "Socrates" in Plato. The greatest of Socrates' followers was Plato; Aristotle was a dissident Platonist; later, the Stoics and Skeptics saw themselves as heirs of Socrates; many of the Church Fathers christianized Plato; and so on through history.

Plato is not our only source for Socrates. Our earliest substantial source for information about Socrates is Aristophanes' comic play *Clouds*. In addition to Plato, other followers of Socrates wrote Socratic dialogues. Xenophon wrote a memoir of Socrates and other Socratic works that have survived intact. From the other followers of Socrates – often described as "the minor Socratics" – we have only fragmentary remains. Aristotle was only one generation removed from Socrates, and so his reports about Socrates' philosophy are important evidence. Among various later sources, the most important is the life of Socrates by the late ancient historian of philosophy Diogenes Laertius.

What do we know about the real, historical Socrates who lies behind this varying literary evidence? The "problem of the historical Socrates" is a famous scholarly crux, akin to the problem of the historical Jesus. Chapter 1 is devoted to this problem. Chapters 2, 3, and 4 discuss the main contemporary sources other than Plato. The concluding essay in this volume, Chapter 15, covers later sources – that is, the reception of Socrates in later Greek philosophy.

The deepest problem facing the editor of a general volume on Socrates is the lack of a single subject-matter. *Socrates is essentially contested territory.* "Socrates" can of course mean the historical Socrates. But some scholars have thought that the historical Socrates is best found in the writings of Xenophon, others in Plato, and others only in certain dialogues of Plato. The portraits of Socrates found in our various sources partially agree: in all our sources, Socrates is intellectually brilliant and (by conventional standards) physically ugly. However, the sources also have clear disagreements: the Socrates in Aristophanes' *Clouds* is devoted to cosmology and physics, whereas the Socrates of Plato's *Phaedo* abandoned such studies in his youth. In other areas, the compatibility of our sources is unclear. Plato's Socrates is known for his biting irony. Does Xenophon's Socrates lack irony, or merely display it more subtly and less often? Can one speak of a "Socratic ethics" common to the dialogues of Xenophon and Plato, or not? These are disputed questions. Despite such complications, since Plato's Socratic writings are the most extensive and philosophically brilliant of our sources, most scholars who write about Socrates have in mind Plato's Socrates, or the Socrates of one or more particular Platonic dialogues.

My own response to this problem has been to invite a diverse group of contributors to define the Socrates who is the subject of their individual chapters differently. For example, Josiah Ober in Chapter 7 is concerned with the "Socrates constructed by the tradition." Like Ober, Paul Woodruff in Chapter 5 and Mark L. McPherran in Chapter 6 draw on multiple sources for their Socrates. Richard Bett in Chapter 10 and Melissa Lane in Chapter 11 concentrate on Plato on the grounds that their topics appear almost exclusively in Plato's writings. Hugh H. Benson in Chapter 8, Terry Penner in Chapter 12, and Christopher Bobonich in Chapter 13 restrict their attention to a range of Platonic dialogues regarded as written early in Plato's career. Christopher Rowe in Chapter 9 focuses on two famous passages in Plato, one from the *Apology*, which may be the earliest of Plato's writings, and one from a much later dialogue, the *Phaedrus*. Charles L. Griswold in Chapter 14 means by Socrates the character Socrates in all of Plato's dialogues where he appears.

I would like to thank the following for kindly granting permission for the use of material appearing in this volume: Chapter 9, excerpts from *Plato and the Art of Philosophical Writing*, by Christopher Rowe, copyright © 2007 Christopher Rowe. Reprinted with the permission of Cambridge University Press. Chapter 11, material drawn from "The evolution of *eironeia* in classical Greek texts: why Socratic *eironeia* is not Socratic irony," Melissa Lane, *Oxford Studies on Ancient Philosophy* 31 (2006): 49–83, copyright © 2006 Oxford University Press; Chapter 15, material drawn selectively from *Stoic Studies*, by A. A. Long, copyright © 1996 Cambridge University Press. Reprinted with permission.

This volume has been many years in preparation. The blame for delay is mine, and I apologize to the contributors. As a result of this delay, the bibliographies to some contributors' essays are not fully up to date.

I thank Beatrice Rehl, my editor at Cambridge University Press, for her patience, goodwill, and expert advice. For their painstaking labors, cheerful encouragement, and expert computer assistance in preparing the manuscript for publication, I am very grateful to Brandon Mulvey and Anthony Carreras, graduate students in Philosophy at Rice.

Abbreviations

I. ARISTOTLE

EN	*Nicomachean Ethics*
Met.	*Metaphysics*
Pol.	*Politics*
Rhet.	*Rhetoric*
Soph. El.	*De Sophisticis Elenchis*

II. PLATONIC TEXTS

Alc.	*Alcibiades*
Ap.	*Apology*
Chrm.	*Charmides*
Cri.	*Crito*
Euphr.	*Euthyphro*
Euthd.	*Euthydemus*
Grg.	*Gorgias*
H. Ma.	*Hippias Major*
Men.	*Meno*
Phd.	*Phaedo*
Phdr.	*Phaedrus*
Phil.	*Philebus*
Prm.	*Parmenides*
Prt.	*Protagoras*
Rep.	*Republic*
Smp.	*Symposium*
Theag.	*Theages*
Tht.	*Theaetetus*

III. XENOPHON

Apol.	*Apology*
Cyrop.	*Cyropedia*
Mem.	*Memorabilia*
Oec.	*Oeconomicus*
Symp.	*Symposium*

IV. DIOGENES LAERTIUS

D.L.	*Lives of Eminent Philosophers*

V. MODERN TEXTS

DK   Diels, H. *Die Fragmente der Vorsokratiker*, 6th ed., rev. W. Kranz, 3 vols. (Berlin, 1952; first ed. 1903).

LSJ   Liddell, H. G. and R. Scott. *A Greek-English Lexicon*, rev. H. S. Jones, 9th ed. with new supplement. Oxford, 1996.

SSR   Giannantoni, G. *Socratis et Socraticorum Reliquiae*. Naples, 1990.

CPF   *Corpus dei papiri filosofici greci e latini*. Florence, 1989–.

VI. JOURNAL ABBREVIATIONS

AGP	*Archiv für Geschichte der Philosophie*
CQ	*Classical Quarterly*
JHP	*Journal of the History of Philosophy*
OSAP	*Oxford Studies in Ancient Philosophy*
RhM	*Rheinisches Museum für Philologie*
GRBS	*Greek, Roman and Byzantine Studies*
PBA	*Proceedings of the British Academy*

THE CAMBRIDGE COMPANION TO
SOCRATES

1   The Rise and Fall of the Socratic Problem

The Socratic problem has quite a history, and is now perhaps only a part of history, since its desperately unsolvable nature does not seem to guarantee it much of a future. It would undoubtedly be presumptuous to claim that the Socratic problem is a closed issue simply because it is not amenable to a satisfactory solution, but it is certainly useful to identify the principal obstacles and pitfalls that render the discovery of a solution improbable, or even impossible.

Socrates, as we know, wrote nothing. His life and ideas are known to us through direct accounts – writings either by contemporaries (Aristophanes) or disciples (Plato and Xenophon) – and through indirect accounts, the most important of which is the one written by Aristotle, who was born fifteen years after Socrates' death (399). Because these accounts vary greatly from one another, the question arises as to whether it is possible to reconstruct the life and – more importantly – the ideas of the historical Socrates on the basis of one, several, or all of these accounts. The "Socratic problem" refers to the historical and methodological problem that historians confront when they attempt to reconstruct the philosophical doctrines of the historical Socrates. Any future stance on the Socratic problem, if it is to be an informed and well-grounded one, presupposes a full understanding of the origins and consequences of the proposed solutions of the last two centuries.[1]

Translated from the French by Melissa Bailar.

[1]   Reviewing all attempts at a solution would be tedious and useless. I will limit myself to those studies I find to be the most representative or the most significant. For an excellent overview of the literature on the Socratic problem, see Patzer 1987, pp. 1–40. Montuori 1992 pulled together a very useful anthology of the principal texts on the Socratic problem.

I. THE GENESIS: SCHLEIERMACHER AND
THE CRITIQUE OF XENOPHON

According to the unanimous opinion of historians,[2] the text that contributed the most to the development of the Socratic problem is Schleiermacher's study entitled "The Worth of Socrates as a Philosopher" (1818).[3] Although certain passages from this seminal work of Socratic studies are often cited, Schleiermacher's work remains largely unappreciated. This lack of recognition is counterproductive because scholars attempting to solve the Socratic problem are often unaware that they are relying on arguments rooted in Schleiermacher that do not stand up to critical analysis.[4]

Schleiermacher starts from the observation that there is a contradiction between the importance of the new beginning attributed to Socrates in the history of Greek philosophy, on the one hand, and the banality of typical representations of Socrates, on the other. According to the latter, Socrates was occupied exclusively with moral questions, concerned himself above all with bettering his disciples, questioned his interlocutors on the best type of life available to mankind, and so on. If Socrates' contribution to philosophy were limited to questions of this sort, we would no longer have any reason, according to Schleiermacher, to see in him the man who was the inspiration for a sort of second birth of Greek philosophy. Schleiermacher thus rejects in their entirety the principal characteristics that constituted the traditional representation of Socrates the "philosopher" at the beginning of the nineteenth century. Because until then scholars had turned primarily to Xenophon to determine the content of the historical Socrates' ideas,[5] it is hardly surprising that Schleiermacher distanced himself from Xenophon's account. In fact, he criticized the author of the *Memorabilia* on two points:

(a) Xenophon was not a philosopher, but rather a soldier and politician, and was thus not the most qualified witness to give a faithful account of Socrates' principal philosophical positions (1818: 56 = 1879: 10). Schleiermacher's criticism presupposes that philosophy

2   See Magalhães-Vilhena 1952, pp. 131, 138, 158, and 186; Montuori 1981a, p. 31; 1981b, pp. 7, 9, 11; 1988, pp. 27–28; Patzer 1987, pp. 9–10.
3   For the English translation of this text, see Schleiermacher 1879. See also Dorion 2001 for an analysis of this text by Schleiermacher.
4   In this way, Brickhouse and Smith 2000, pp. 38, 42–43, discredit Xenophon's account by using two arguments that, although the authors seem unaware of it, could already be found in Schleiermacher.
5   For a study of the importance of Xenophon's accounts before the start of the nineteenth century, see Dorion 2000, pp. VIII-XII.

is essentially a speculative activity. Thus, since Xenophon's Socratic writings are hardly speculative, Schleiermacher naturally concludes that Xenophon was not a philosopher and that he did not do justice to Socrates' profound philosophical positions. This is in a way an unjust attack on Xenophon, whose admitted goal, as he proclaimed at the start of the *Memorabilia* (1.3.1 and 1.4.1), was to show how and to what extent Socrates was useful to others and contributed to the bettering of his companions through both his example and his words. Are not being useful to others and bettering them worthy objectives of a philosophy understood as *a way of life*? In any case, this criticism received great acclaim, and commentators seeking to discredit Xenophon's account have used it ever since.[6]

(b) Xenophon was so zealous in defending his master against accusations regarding his subversive teachings that Socrates figures in his writings as a representative of the established order and the most traditional values. The positions that Xenophon's Socrates defends are so conservative and conventional that it is impossible to understand how such a flat and dull philosopher could attract, captivate, and maintain the interest of naturally speculative thinkers, such as Plato and Euclid, the founder of the Megarian school. In short, if Socrates had resembled the Socrates of Xenophon's writings, he would not have been surrounded by such disciples; he would instead have repelled them.[7] At the start of the twentieth century, Xenophon's detractors followed Schleiermacher's lead and pushed his criticism of the apologetic nature of Xenophon's Socratic writings even further, saying, for example, that Xenophon defended Socrates so well against the accusations against him that it is difficult to understand how Socrates could possibly have been sentenced to death. (See Burnet 1914: p. 149; Taylor 1932: p. 22.)

It is thus clear to Schleiermacher that Socrates must have been *more* than what Xenophon said about him, because if Socrates only amounted to his portrait in the *Memorabilia*, the immense philosophical influence we attribute to him would be incomprehensible: "And not only *may* Socrates, he *must* have been more, and there must have been more in the back-ground of his speeches, than Xenophon represents." (1879: 11 = 1818: 57) This harsh judgment is nevertheless belied by texts

---

6   See Dorion 2000, pp. XC-XCI, where I provide many references.
7   Brickhouse and Smith 2000, p. 43, made the same criticism in the same terms.

and accounts that attest that the *Memorabilia* exerted a considerable influence on the first Stoics.[8] But where does Schleiermacher intend to find this other dimension of Socrates that is presumably absent in Xenophon's text? Schleiermacher intends to find the more philosophical dimension of Socrates – "philosophical" in the modern and speculative sense of the term – in Plato, of course. But whatever is found in Plato should not contradict certain given facts in Xenophon's account that are widely recognized as reliable. Schleiermacher states in the form of a question his suggested method for reconstructing the philosophical content of the historical Socrates' thought:

> The only safe method (*Der einzige sichere Weg*) seems to be, to inquire: what may Socrates have been, over and above what Xenophon has described, without however contradicting the strokes of character (*Charakterzügen*), and the practical maxims (*Lebensmaximen*), which Xenophon distinctly delivers as those of Socrates: and what must he have been, to give Plato a right, and an inducement, to exhibit him as he has done in his dialogues? (1879: 14 = 1818: 59)

This "method" raises more problems than it can possibly hope to resolve. As far as the "practical maxims" or the "rules of life" (*Lebensmaximen*) are concerned, a single example will suffice to illustrate the pitfalls obstructing the application of Schleiermacher's so-called method. Book IV, Chapter 5, of the *Memorabilia* is devoted to the way in which Socrates assisted his companions in regulating their behavior. In reading this chapter, it appears that self-mastery (*enkrateia*) is the surest foundation for behavior and action. If self-mastery is the *sine qua non* condition for all successful practical activity, it is hardly surprising that Xenophon affirms that *enkrateia* is the foundation of virtue (*Memorabilia* 1.5.4). Must we consider, then, that the principal role attributed to *enkrateia* has the value of a "practical maxim"? If so, Xenophon's account would have precedence over Plato's as far as this essential aspect of Socratic ethics is concerned. In fact, since Plato's Socrates grants no theoretical importance to *enkrateia* – the term *enkrateia* is not found in Plato's first dialogues, and the idea that moderation (*sôphrosunê*) is in any sense reducible to *enkrateia* is also not found in the *Charmides* – and because he attributes to knowledge the role that Xenophon attributes to *enkrateia*, his position appears irreconcilable with a practical maxim defended by Xenophon's Socrates and must, in accordance with Schleiermacher's method, be sacrificed. As can be seen, this "method" leads to results that are at times contrary to those that Schleiermacher

---

8   See D.L. 7.2; Sextus Empiricus, *Adversus Mathematicos* 9.92–101; Long 1988, pp. 162–163; Dorion 2000, p. 33 n. 231.

had anticipated. The difficulties raised by this method notwithstanding, it did exert exceptional programmatic influence in as much as it defined the program of research followed by several generations of philosophers in their attempt to determine the philosophical content of the historical Socrates' thought. Schleiermacher's method enjoyed a considerable success, as is demonstrated by the very large number of historians who adhere to or refer to it.[9]

After a considerable time, Schleiermacher's essay eventually led to the full rejection of Xenophon's account. The critical movement he initiated grew over the course of the nineteenth century, and reached its height in 1915 when Xenophon's Socratic writings had become completely discredited. To Schleiermacher's two criticisms, nineteenth- and early twentieth-century historians added eight others.[10] Nearly a century after Schleiermacher's seminal article and in the space of only a few years, scholars in France (Robin 1910); England (Taylor 1911; Burnet 1911 and 1914); and Germany (Maier 1913) published in rapid succession and completely independently from one another studies that were so critical of Xenophon's Socratic writings that it was no longer clear what merit could possibly be attributed to the author of the *Memorabilia*.

The consensus that emerged during this period is neither accidental nor a coincidence, and in fact represents the end result of the movement launched by Schleiermacher a century earlier. From there, it was only a small step to claim that Xenophon is completely worthless to us, as Taylor and Burnet did,[11] and that the historical Socrates completely corresponded to Plato's Socrates. Burnet and Taylor's position thus seems to be the culmination and logical conclusion of Schleiermacher's attack on Xenophon's Socratic writings at the start of the nineteenth century. Even if it is generally agreed that Burnet and Taylor's thesis is too extreme, and that Plato's Socrates cannot be simply equated with the historical Socrates, twentieth-century scholarship has in a sense endorsed their work by ostracizing Xenophon's Socrates and by deeming Plato's Socrates the only one worthy of any interest whatsoever.[12] Although the historical development of the Socratic problem has been

---

9   See the numerous references given by Dorion 2000, p. XIII, n. 2.

10 For a detailed presentation of these critiques, see Dorion 2000, pp. XVII-XCIX.

11 See Burnet 1914, p. 150: "It is really impossible to preserve Xenophon's Sokrates, even if he were worth preserving."

12 See, among others, Vlastos 1971, p. 2: Plato's Socrates is "in fact the only Socrates worth talking about"; Santas 1979, p. X: "It is only Plato's Socrates that is of major interest to the contemporary philosopher"; Kahn 1981, p. 319: "As far as we are concerned, the Socrates of the dialogues [i.e. Plato's] *is* the historical Socrates. He is certainly the only one who counts for the history of philosophy."

far from linear, the overwhelming majority of the scholarly work dating from the beginnings of the Socratic problem until 1915 completely reversed the prevailing situation of 1815 against which Schleiermacher rebelled, to the benefit of Plato. If the disgrace that Xenophon's Socratic writings suffered were the immediate consequence of the birth and development of the Socratic problem, in contrast, the recent renewal of interest in them is largely due to the decline of this problem.

2. THE IMPASSE AND THE FALL: THE FICTIONAL NATURE OF THE *LOGOI SOKRATIKOI*

The nearly unanimous discredit that befell Xenophon's Socratic writings nonetheless did not bring about a solution to the Socratic problem. Historians continued to debate the value of the three other sources, with the majority of them giving priority to Plato, others to Aristotle,[13] and a final few to Aristophanes.[14] In short, if everyone, or nearly everyone, agreed to reject Xenophon's accounts, no one was in agreement over the respective reliability of the three other sources. It is probably impossible to reconstruct the ideas of the historical Socrates from Aristophanes' *The Clouds*, not only because the very genre of comedy lends itself to exaggeration and even excess, but also because there is good reason to believe that Socrates' character in *The Clouds* is really a composite figure whose traits were gathered not only from Socrates himself but also from the *physiologoi* and the sophists.[15] The case of Plato's account especially highlights the absence of consensus; if we consider only those commentators who are inclined to grant priority to Plato's dialogues, we notice that they do not turn to the same dialogues to reconstruct the historical Socrates' theories. Some rely mostly on the *Apology*,[16] many base their work on the entirety of the early dialogues,[17] or on just a few of them, others still call on the apocryphal dialogues,[18] and finally some consider that every word that Plato put in Socrates' mouth, whether in an early, middle, or late dialogue, has a place in the record of the historical Socrates.[19] It is quite surprising that there is

---

13   Joël 1893, I, p. 203.

14   See the numerous references indicated by Montuori 1988, p. 42, n. 36. H. Gomperz 1924 went so far as to claim that the historical Socrates was found not in *The Clouds* but in fragments of other comedies!

15   See Ross 1933, p. 10; Dover 1968, pp. XXXVI, XL; Guthrie 1971, p. 52; Vlastos 1971, p. 1, n.1 and the many authors mentioned by Montuori 1988, p. 41, n.35.

16   See *infra* pp.17–18.

17   See Maier 1913; Guthrie 1975, p. 67; Vlastos 1991, pp. 45–50; Graham 1992; Brickhouse and Smith 2000, pp. 44–49; 2003, pp. 112–113.

18   See Tarrant 1938.

19   This is the position defended by Taylor 1911, p. IX, and Burnet 1911; 1914.

no consensus regarding the number and identity of Plato's dialogues that would allow for the reconstruction of the historical Socrates' ideas, but, in another way, this disagreement among interpreters is inevitable because of the doctrinal heterogeneity of Socrates' character in the *corpus platonicum*.[20]

The lack of consensus and the proliferation of attempted solutions undoubtedly led to the scholarly works running out of steam, but this did not necessarily mean that the Socratic problem was a false problem to which a solution could never be found. The position that would finally evoke a lasting skepticism surrounding the Socratic problem was initiated in Germany in the last quarter of the nineteenth century. This major discovery, credited primarily to K. Joël (1895–1896), is that of the fictional nature of the *logoi sokratikoi*.

The Socratic problem has all the makings of a false problem because it rests on a misunderstanding. This in turn entails an inevitable misinterpretation of the exact nature of the preserved "testimony" about Socrates. For the Socratic problem as it had been debated since the start of the nineteenth century to have meaning, the principal direct witnesses (Xenophon and Plato) must have intended to faithfully reconstruct Socrates' ideas through writings that aimed to transmit at least the spirit and content, if not the exact words, of Socrates' dialogues. If this had been their intention, we would be justified in asking which account best corresponds to the thought of the historical Socrates. Yet everything seems to indicate that neither Xenophon nor Plato set out with the intention of faithfully reporting Socrates' ideas. Xenophon's and Plato's Socratic writings belong to a literary genre–that of the *logos sokratikos*, which Aristotle[21] explicitly recognized and which authorizes by its very nature a certain degree of fiction and a great freedom of invention as far as the setting and content are concerned, most notably with the ideas expressed by the different characters. Yet, since Aristotle sees in the *logoi sokratikoi* a form of *mimêsis* (imitation), would we not be well justified in considering them faithful documents that aim to accurately reproduce the life and thought of Socrates? This is precisely how Taylor interpreted Aristotle's account of the *logoi sokratikoi*: "Aristotle [...] regards the 'Socratic discourse' as a highly realistic kind of composition. You cannot, of course, infer that he holds that the actual Socrates must have really made every remark ascribed to him in such a discourse, but

20 Montuori 1981a, p. 225: "It is important to underline that Plato does not give us a single image of Socrates, coherent and complete, but a disconcerting plurality of images, all of which have been noted by the critics, who in turn have taken one or the other as the most faithful description of the historical person of Sophroniscus's son." See also p. 226.

21 See *Poetics* 1.1447a28-b13; *Rhetoric* 3.16.1417a18–21; fr. 72 Rose (=Athenaeus 15.505c).

it would not be a proper 'imitation' of Socrates unless it were in all its main points a faithful presentation." (1911, p. 55) A lot is at stake in the interpretation of Aristotle's testimony, because if the *mimêsis* is understood as a faithful imitation of reality, in principle nothing keeps us from considering the *logoi sokratikoi* to be a reliable and privileged material aiming to reconstruct the life and thought of Socrates; on the other hand, if the *mimêsis*, as Aristotle understands it, is a creation that authorizes a degree of fiction and invention, the task of reconstructing the thought of Socrates based on the *logoi sokratikoi* seems doomed to fail. According to Joël, then, Aristotle's account establishes that the *logos sokratikos*, classified as a form of *mimêsis*, allows for a substantial amount of fiction and invention, as far as both the setting and the ideas expressed by the characters are concerned. The recognition of the fictional character of *logoi sokratikoi* did not immediately gain acceptance without debate or controversy.[22] It is to Joël's immense credit that he brought this essential dimension of *logoi sokratikoi* to light; it is likewise unfortunate that this important discovery is not always credited to him.[23]

Since *logoi sokratikoi* are literary works in which the author can give his imagination free reign, while remaining within the plausible bounds of a credible representation of Socrates' *êthos*, the degree of fiction and invention inherent in *logoi sokratikoi* means they cannot be considered as accounts written for their historical accuracy. This does not mean, of course, that the *logoi sokratikoi* contain no single authentic trait or accurate detail; but as the historical concern of *logoi sokratikoi* is only incidental, and since we do not have at our disposal the criteria that would allow us to separate invention from authenticity, it would certainly be more prudent to renounce any hope of finding the "true"

---

22 On the debate surrounding the nature and status of the *logoi sokratikoi*, see Deman 1942, pp. 25–33. In the years following the publication of Joël's study, numerous commentators agreed with him and recognized the fictional nature of the *logoi sokratikoi* (see Robin 1910, p. 26; Maier 1913, p. 27, n.1; Dupréel 1922, pp. 457–460; Magalhães-Vilhena 1952, pp. 225, 326, 345, 351, 370, etc.).

23 Momigliano's works 1971, pp. 46–57, are often cited to justify affirming the *logoi sokratikoi*'s fictional nature (see Vlastos 1991, pp. 49, n. 14, 99 n.72; Kahn 1992, pp. 237–238; 1996, pp. 33–34; Beversluis 1993, p. 300, n. 14; Vander Waerdt 1993, p. 7; 1994, p. 2, n. 6). In fact, searching Momigliano's work for a precise argument that attempts to demonstrate the fictional character of the *logoi sokratikoi* is fruitless (see Dorion 2000, pp. CVIII-CXI). Furthermore, Momigliano never refers to Aristotle's account of the *logoi sokratikoi*, even though it is precisely this account that authorizes evaluating the *logoi sokratikoi* as literary creations.

Socrates in these writings. Furthermore, if we consider the fact that many of Socrates' disciples wrote *logoi sokratikoi*,[24] and that there is good reason to believe that the portraits of Socrates differed greatly from one author to the next, and sometimes even within the same author's writing,[25] it is likely that Socrates rapidly became a sort of literary character (*dramatis persona*) endowed with his own existence and placed at the center of the polemics and rivalries that pitted one Socratic against another.[26] Each author of *logoi sokratikoi* in this way created "his own" Socrates, whom he contrasted with the competing Socrates' outlined by the other Socratics. Each laid claim to, and quarreled over, the heritage of their bygone master, as well as faithfulness to his memory and his teachings.

If the *logoi sokratikoi* cannot be read or interpreted as historical documents in the strictest sense, but rather as literary and philosophical works that include a substantial degree of invention, even concerning the ideas expressed, then the Socratic problem seems hopelessly deprived of the "documents" from which the elements of a solution could be unearthed and the key to the enigma found. If our principal sources are already interpretations, we must recognize all that this entails: first, we cannot favor one interpretation over another, since nothing justifies such a bias on the historical level, and second, attempting to reconcile them all would be in vain, because such agreement would be either *impossible* or *superficial*. It is often *impossible* because of the many insurmountable contradictions in Plato's and Xenophon's accounts.[27] It is not the case that

the Socrates of Plato's early dialogues agrees with the versions of Socrates in Xenophon, Antisthenes, Aeschines, and also the spurious Platonic dialogues (see D. Tarrant 1938), e.g. in practicing the style of refutation known as the

24 According to Diogenes Laertius, Antisthenes (6.15–18), Aeschines (2.60–63), Phaedo (2.105), and Euclid (2.108) composed Socratic dialogues. Diogenes Laertius (2.121–125) attributes *logoi sokratikoi* to several other Socratics as well (Crito, Simon, Glaucon, Simmias, Cebes), but this evidence should be treated with caution. It is generally accepted that Aristippus did not compose Socratic dialogues.

25 I am thinking primarily of Plato, whose representation of Socrates evolved so considerably from the early to the middle dialogues that we are really dealing with two Socrateses, irreducible and opposed to one another, as Vlastos clearly demonstrated (1991, pp. 45–80).

26 See Gigon 1947, p. 314: "The Socratic literature is primarily self-presentation of the Socratics, of their own philosophical thought and their literary (*dichterisches*) abilities."

27 See the list of the seventeen major contradictions on the philosophical level (Dorion 2006, pp. 95–96). This list is not exhaustive.

elenchus, professing ignorance of major questions, and having a philosophical mission. (Graham 1992, p. 143 n.9)

This claim reveals a significant misunderstanding of Xenophon's Socratic texts, for Xenophon's Socrates hardly ever practices the *elenchus*, never acknowledges his ignorance regarding the most important questions, and in contrast to Plato's Socrates, never identifies a philosophical mission. And when agreement is possible between Plato and Xenophon, it is more often than not *superficial*. Not only does such agreement not necessarily guarantee an objective fact; it is usually nothing but a superficial concordance that might mask more fundamental discrepancies. There are, of course, many Socratic themes common to Xenophon and Plato, but such overlapping does not indicate a common theory that could be attributed to the historical Socrates. To "demonstrate" a fundamental agreement between Plato and Xenophon, Luccioni (1953, pp. 48–56) was naïve enough to believe that drawing up a list of several dozen common themes (the divine sign, virtue as science, piety, self-knowledge, the dialectic, his rejection of the study of nature, etc.) would suffice. In fact, it is easy to demonstrate that Xenophon's treatment of any one of these themes cannot be assimilated with Plato's treatment of it. The differences in the treatment of these common themes are so important that the least common denominator amounts to very little in most cases. For example, self-knowledge is a privileged theme in the reflections of both Plato's and Xenophon's Socrates, but their respective conceptions of self-knowledge are so different from one another that it is impossible to tease out any features of a common theory. Furthermore, the sporadic agreements between Plato and Xenophon are not as significant as some might suggest. Take the case of the Delphic oracle: both Plato (*Apology* 20e-23b) and Xenophon (*Apology* 14–16) certainly attest to it, but this nevertheless does not mean that it constituted an actual episode in Socrates' life. In fact, there is nothing to say that it is not a myth first invented by Plato and later taken up and reinterpreted by Xenophon. It would be a mistake to believe that an agreement between two texts allowing the use of fiction is indicative of an objective fact (see Joël 1895: 478). Moreover, the existence and significance of the many differences between these two versions are not really apparent without an exegetic study that would seek to understand them in light of the respective and consistent representations that Plato and Xenophon created of Socrates and the fundamentals of his ethics. The oracle's response in Xenophon's *Memorabilia* appears as a sort of condensed or concentrated version of the ethics defended by Socrates, which justifies the claim that, "Xenophon has reformulated Plato's account of the oracle's response in the service of his own understanding of Socratic ethics." (Vander Waerdt 1994, p. 39)

Rather curiously, K. Joël did not explore all of the consequences of his valuable discovery. If it is futile to attempt to resolve the Socratic problem on the basis of texts that do not aim to faithfully reproduce the historical Socrates' teachings, how is it that Joël himself did not give up the hope of finding a solution to this problem? This apparent paradox is explained by the fact that Joël believed he was in a position to resolve the Socratic problem by turning to an account that is not itself a *logos sokratikos*, in this case that of Aristotle (see 1893, I, p. 203). Yet if Aristotle's account is not an independent and objective source, as it is essentially dependent on Plato's Socratic writings, as Taylor would later demonstrate,[28] then the Stagirite's account of Socrates cannot provide the solution to the Socratic problem. Furthermore, even if Aristotle's account at times appears independent of Plato's Socratic writings[29] and of other *logoi sokratikoi*, its extremely narrow scope would not allow us to progress far at all. What Aristotle has to say about Socrates is extremely limited, and in fact his silence on a host of subjects means that his account cannot provide the infallible arbitration that Joël had hoped for. For example, in regards to Socrates' *daimonion*, the importance of *enkrateia*, his understanding of piety, his conception of the *elenchus*, the nature of his political *engagement*, his interpretation of the statement "know thyself," and his attitude toward the *lex talionis*, all of which are subjects that are irreconcilable in Xenophon's and Plato's accounts, Aristotle is of no help because he provides no pertinent information. Furthermore, we cannot rule out the possibility that Aristotle's account of Socrates more often than not has an "ulterior motive," in the sense that the Stagirite interpreted Socrates to fit with his own priorities, so that it would be erroneous to consider it an objective and impartial account.[30]

Let us put all of this in perspective. If we have strong reasons to be skeptical of the possibility of resolving the Socratic problem – that is, of reconstructing the philosophy of the historical Socrates, just as he explained and defended it in front of different audiences in Athens during the second half of the fifth century BCE – there are certain facts about Socrates of which we have no good reason to be suspicious. First, there is information concerning Socrates' biography and appearance.

---

28 See Taylor 1911, pp. X, 40–90; 1932, p. 17, n. 1; Burnet 1911, pp. XXIII-XXV.
29 The source of the passages in the *Metaphysics* (A 6.987b1–6; M 4.1078b17–32; M 9.1086a37-b5) that attribute the paternity of the theory of intelligible forms to Plato and not to Socrates could not possibly be Plato's dialogues. This is an important but purely negative piece of information: Socrates did not develop the theory of intelligible and separate forms.
30 This is a common criticism of Aristotle, most notably in Kahn 1992, pp. 235–239; 1996, pp. 79–87.

We know, for example, that Socrates was born in Athens in 470, that he came from the deme of Alôpekê, and that he was sentenced to drink hemlock after he was judged guilty in 399 of each of the three charges that Meletus, Anytus, and Lycon accused him of: corrupting youth, introducing new divinities, and not believing in the state gods. On the other hand, scholars still debate over the exact reasons underlying and motivating the three charges. As far as Socrates' appearance is concerned, Plato (*Theaetetus* 143e) and Xenophon (*Symposium* 2.19, 5.5–7) do not paint a flattering picture: Socrates has a broad nose, bulging eyes, thick lips, and a large belly – in short, his physique seems so unappealing that his two disciples do not hesitate to compare him to a Silenus.[31] Second, the textual evidence provides some insight into Socrates' philosophical interests. Because Xenophon's and Plato's accounts of Socrates share many common themes, it is almost certain that they are Socratic themes – that is, philosophical positions that the historical Socrates explained and defended. But it is important to remember that we are often forced to affirm that Socrates supported one position or another without being able to reconstruct with any certainty the full details of these positions, because the reasons and arguments that underlie them are often quite different if we turn to Plato or to Xenophon.

Just as several decades passed before the critical movement initiated by Schleiermacher's article was carried through to its conclusion, the ultimate consequences of Joël's discovery were not reached until the first half of the twentieth century. It was a Belgian scholar, E. Dupréel, who was the first to adopt a resolutely skeptical position concerning the Socratic problem (1922, pp. 398, 412–413, 426). But it was undeniably O. Gigon who contributed the most to establish the fact that because the Socratic problem was predicated on erroneous assumptions, it was a false problem whose solution could not be found. His book on Socrates (1947) is a vibrant manifesto in favor of abandoning the Socratic problem and a stimulating illustration of another type of research into Socrates and the Socratic tradition. If, because of the conventions of the genre, Socratic literature always involves an irreducible element of fiction, invention, and creativity (*Dichtung*), then it must be studied in and of itself as such. In other words, we should be attentive to the variations that we can find among the different versions of a single Socratic theme in order to throw light on the significance and the scope of the variations on the philosophy and the representation of Socrates.[32] This is a rich field of research that has still not yielded all that it promises.[33]

---

31   See Plato, *Symposium* 215a-b; Xenophon, *Symposium* 4.19, 5.7.

32   See 1947, pp. 34, 68, and the chapter titled "Die Sokratesdichtung" (pp. 69–178).

33   If the work of Joël, Dupréel, and Gigon has, in certain respects, become dated, it is above all due to the gratuitous hypotheses they constructed in

Joël's works allowed us to rediscover in the *logoi sokratikoi* a truth that had already been well known to the Ancients themselves. One of the reasons the Ancients never debated the Socratic problem is because they fully recognized the fictional nature of the *logoi sokratikoi*. This is demonstrated by the aforementioned passages from Aristotle as well as by several anecdotes and accounts expressing a profound skepticism regarding the historicity of the subjects and theories that Socrates expresses in the dialogues in which he figures as the protagonist. The following anecdote related by Diogenes Laertius is quite instructive: "They say that, on hearing Plato read the *Lysis*, Socrates exclaimed, 'By Heracles, what a number of lies this young man is telling about me!' For he has included in the dialogue much that Socrates never said." (3.35; trans. Hicks) This anecdote is misleading insofar as the composition of the *Lysis* likely occurred after Socrates' death, but, on the other hand, it also contains an element of truth in that it fully acknowledges the fictional nature of *logoi sokratikoi*. Athenaeus (11.507c-d) also recounts an amusing anecdote with an analogous meaning. Socrates relates one of his dreams: Plato, transformed into a crow, was perched atop his bald head, where he hopped about while looking around. To Socrates, this dream meant that Plato would tell many lies about him.[34] Likewise, Cicero (*Republic* 1.10, 15–16) did not allow himself to be deceived by the setting and characters of Plato's dialogues: he was convinced that Plato attributed to Socrates theories that were actually of Pythagorean origin.[35] In addition, the presence of many anachronisms in the *logoi sokratikoi* of Plato, Xenophon, and also Aeschines[36] likewise serves to demonstrate that the authors of Socratic dialogues treated historical truth lightly and that their poetic license was probably recognized because of the conventions of the genre. Finally, it would be a mistake to think that the fictional nature of the literary Socrates was a phenomenon posterior to the first dialogues written out by Socrates' disciples, because the existence of at least two portraits of Socrates within Plato's

---

the framework of "source research" (*Quellenforschung*). However, a legitimate criticism of the *Quellenforschung*'s excess does not necessarily lead to a complete rejection of Joël's accurate and profound intuition that a *logos sokratikos* must be interpreted as a philosophical work in which the character named Socrates is often the spokesman of the author's theses and arguments, which are themselves in opposition to other theses and arguments that a character named Socrates formulated in other *logoi sokratikoi*. The thesis of fictionality does not necessarily lead to the extreme positions of the *Quellenforschung*.

34 See also 11.505d-e.

35 See also D.L. 2.45; Proclus *in Alcibiades* 18.15–19.12 Creuzer.

36 On the many instances of historical implausibility in the settings and characters of Aeschines' dialogues, see Kahn 1996, pp. 27–28.

works confirms that the fictional dimension of Socratic literature dates back to its very origins.

The position of those who recognize the fictional nature of the *logoi sokratikoi* but who nonetheless hope to resolve the Socratic problem is methodologically untenable, and raises more problems than it can possibly solve. Two recent and quite different examples serve as proof that we have reached an impasse with the Socratic problem. My first example comes from G. Vlastos. Although he recognizes the fictional and creative nature of the *logoi sokratikoi* (1991, pp. 49–50), he believes nonetheless in the historicity of the Socrates depicted in Plato's early dialogues (1991, pp. 1 n. 2, 53, 81, 90–91, etc.). This position seems at first to be belied by another thesis that Vlastos develops in his work–namely, the presence of two Socrateses – the Socrates of the early dialogues (Socrates^E) and the Socrates of the middle dialogues (Socrates^M) – who uphold diametrically opposed positions on ten specific subjects. In fact, if Plato, as Vlastos admits, believed that he was authorized to have Socrates^M be the spokesman of theses that were actually Platonic, is this not proof that the fictional nature of the *logoi sokratikoi* extends to the content of the theories attributed to Socrates? And if Vlastos readily recognizes that the ten theses that Socrates^M developed are not Socratic, how can he be sure that the positions Socrates^E expresses belonged to the historical Socrates and are not positions Plato felt authorized to attribute to his character of Socrates by virtue of the poetic license allowed by the conventions of the literary genre of the *logos sokratikos*? Vlastos himself raises this possibility,[37] and his argument against it consists of affirming that on several important points, the portrait of Socrates^E is confirmed and corroborated by Aristotle's and Xenophon's accounts.

The way in which Vlastos treats Xenophon is rather singular: when his account agrees with Plato's, Vlastos is quick to mention it and to view it as a guarantee of the truthfulness of the Platonic account (1991, pp. 99–106), but when it is irreconcilable with Plato's account, Vlastos strives to discredit it by using arguments that are in fact nothing more than old biases pulled from the arsenal of objections that Schleiermacher and the nineteenth- and early-twentieth-century critics of Xenophon had already formulated.[38] To cast doubt on the strictly philosophical

37   See 1991, p. 81: "For there is no intrinsic reason why both of these philosophies, despite their polar differences, could not have been Plato's own original creations at different periods of his life." See also Graham 1992, p. 144.

38   Of the ten criticisms regularly directed toward Xenophon, Vlastos draws on four – namely, Xenophon was not an actual disciple of Socrates (see 1991, p. 103); he was not an eyewitness of the conversations he reports (see 1991, pp. 49, n. 14, 99 n.72); he is excessively zealous in his apologetics (see 1988, p. 92); he did not have the necessary philosophical aptitude to faithfully

value of Xenophon's account, Vlastos strives to highlight supposed contradictions whose very presence in the text of the *Memorabilia* would,
he claims, justify a wary attitude toward Xenophon. To choose one
example, Vlastos suggests this would be the case with the account of
the impossibility of the weakness of will, or *akrasia* (1991, pp. 99–101);
yet it is possible to demonstrate that Xenophon's account is in fact perfectly coherent and that its supposed contradictions can actually be
attributed to errors in Vlastos' interpretation (see Dorion 2003).

All evidence suggests that Vlastos grossly overestimated the agreement between Xenophon and Plato. Keep in mind that the positions
that Vlastos examines are the following: (1) The philosophy of Socrates^E
is *exclusively* a moral philosophy. (2) Socrates^E did not develop a metaphysical theory of intelligible and separate forms. (3) Socrates^E searches
for knowledge through refutation, and professes over and over that he has
no knowledge. (4) Socrates^E did not develop a tripartite conception of the
soul, which would have undermined his theory concerning the impossibility of *akrasia*. According to Vlastos (1991, pp. 99–106), Xenophon's
account would confirm positions (1), (2), and (3), while its confirmation
of (4) would be only partial in light of the (supposedly) contradictory
nature of his account. The agreement between Xenophon and Plato on
all of these points would thus guarantee the historicity of the positions
supported by Socrates^E. Yet, contrary to what Vlastos claims, Xenophon
only confirms positions (2) and (4). In fact, although Xenophon's Socrates
(see *Memorabilia* 1.1.16) is primarily concerned with questions relating
to ethics (= 1), he is also interested in religion (see *Memorabilia* 1.4,
4.3, 4.6.2–4); education (see *Memorabilia* 4.1–3, 5–7; *Apology* 20); and
art (see *Memorabilia* 3.10), which are, as Vlastos himself admits (1991,
p. 48), three of Socrates^M's favorite subjects. As far as (3) is concerned,
Vlastos goes beyond the evidence when he claims (see 1991, p. 105),
on the basis of *Memorabilia* 4.4.9, that Xenophon's Socrates recognizes
his ignorance and seeks knowledge through the *elenchus*, a claim that
is unfounded. Xenophon's Socrates never acknowledges his own ignorance on the moral level,[39] and the *elenchus*, which he uses in only one
dialogue,[40] offers no assistance in the quest for knowledge but only in

report Socrates' ideas (see 1991, p. 99). I showed elsewhere that most of
these objections do not stand up to a careful examination (see Dorion 2000,
pp. XXII-XXX, XXXIX-LII, LXV-LXX, XC-XCIX, respectively).

39 Socrates acknowledges his ignorance as far as economics and agriculture are
concerned (see *Oeconomicus* 2.11–13), and in those fields where he acknowledges his ignorance, he encourages his interlocutors to seek instruction from a
competent master (see *Memorabilia* 1.6.14; 4.7.1). But Socrates certainly never
views himself as ignorant when it comes to questions pertaining to ethics.

40 See *Memorabilia* 4.2 and Dorion 2000, pp. CLXIX-CLXXXII.

the revelation of his interlocutor's ignorance. The agreement between Xenophon and Plato in the end concerns only points (2) and (4), which are purely negative positions: they boil down to stating that Socrates did not develop the metaphysical theory of separate forms, nor did he set up a tripartite conception of the soul. In brief, this agreement gives us absolutely no insight into the content of the historical Socrates' ideas. Furthermore, as I stressed earlier, such points of agreement often conceal doctrinal divergences; for example, Xenophon's Socrates and Plato's Socrates affirm the impossibility of the weakness of will[41] for different reasons, and although neither develops a tripartite conception of the soul, Socrates[E] and Xenophon's Socrates do not ascribe the same importance to the soul at all, since the former equates it to the "self" or to the essence of what man is, whereas the latter never suggests such an equality and insists just as much on caring for the body as on caring for the soul.

Regarding Aristotle, the vast majority of positions that he attributes to Socrates can be traced to Plato's dialogues, so it is difficult to concede that Aristotle's account of Socrates constitutes an independent source. In suggesting that Aristotle's account is a guarantee of historical accuracy because it confirms Plato's account, Vlastos falls prey to a circular argument.[42] If in fact Aristotle's account has no independent value, and Xenophon's does not provide the desired confirmation, Vlastos is deprived of the one and only argument that would have allowed him to escape from the hypothesis that he himself mentioned – that Socrates[E] is just as much the fruit of Plato's philosophical imagination as is Socrates[M].

My second example is taken from C. Kahn. Since he fully recognizes the fictional nature of Socratic literature as far as the setting, characters, and content are concerned,[43] it is hardly surprising that he adopts a resolutely skeptical position:

41   See Dorion 2003, pp. 662–664.
42   According to Vlastos 1991, p. 97, n. 69, more than a third of the forty-two accounts Deman 1942 selects from Aristotle do not stem from Plato's dialogues. Yet the only example Vlastos provides – that Aristotle could not have learned that Plato had been Cratylus's student from the dialogues – is not very conclusive because it has nothing to do with Socrates. The way in which Vlastos uses Aristotle's account was severely criticized by those who, following Taylor's lead (1911, pp. 40–90), regard the Stagirite as entirely dependent on Plato and thus not an independent source (see Kahn 1992, pp. 235–240; 1996, pp. 79–87; Beversluis 1993, pp. 298–301; Vander Waerdt 1994, p. 3, n. 7).
43   See, among others, 1996, p. 88: "Plato has deliberately given himself almost total freedom to imagine both the form and the content of his Socratic conversations."

Our evidence is such that [...] the philosophy of Socrates himself, as distinct from his impact on his followers, does not fall within the reach of historical scholarship. In this sense the problem of Socrates must remain without a solution. (1992, p. 240)

[I]t is a fundamental misunderstanding of the nature of Socratic writings to see them as aiming at a faithful portrayal of the historical Socrates. [...] the Socratic literature, including the dialogues of Plato, represents a genre of imaginative fiction, so that [...] these writings cannot be safely used as historical documents. (1996, pp. 74–75)

One would thus think that the issue was settled and done with: the Socratic problem is by definition unsolvable. Yet Kahn almost immediately backs away from this conclusion and asserts that the Platonic *Apology* is a separate case since it is the text that has the best chance of corresponding to a "quasi-historical document" (1996, p. 88) and a "historical account" (1992, p. 257; see also 240 n. 9) of Socrates' philosophy. This position is not unique to Kahn; numerous commentators[44] do not in fact consider the *Apology* to be a *logos sokratikos* because in it, Plato reports a speech that has the status of a historical event witnessed by several hundred people. This would have prevented Plato from straying too far from historical accuracy and would have forced him to recount – if not the exact words – at least the spirit of Socrates' defense before the court. If in fact the *Apology* were not a work of fiction like Plato's *logoi sokratikoi*, it would be possible, at least in theory, to reconstruct Socrates' philosophy based on the *Apology*.[45] However, such a position is subject to the following objections:

(1) We have no reason to exempt the *Apology* from the status of a *logos sokratikos*[46] and to believe that it does not contain a degree, and perhaps a considerable degree, of fiction.[47] The existence of

44 See Taylor 1932, p. 28; Ross 1933, pp. 15, 22–23; Guthrie 1971, p. 158, n.1; and the references Montuori indicates in 1981a, pp. 42–43.

45 On the basis of the *Apology*, which he presents as "our measure for the historical Socrates" (1996, p. 95), Kahn (pp. 88–95) proposes a "minimal view" of the historical Socrates. For more recent attempts at reconstructing the historical Socrates' ideas on the basis of the *Apology*, see Döring 1987, 1992, pp. 2–4.

46 See Joël 1895, p. 480, and Morrison 2000b, p. 239, whose work is a methodical refutation of those – notably Kahn and Döring (see n.45) – who regard the Platonic *Apology* as a viable "document" for reconstructing the historical Socrates' philosophy.

47 Thus it cannot be ruled out that the Delphic Oracle story, which plays a fundamental role in the *Apology*, was invented by Plato to serve as the founding myth of Socrates' philosophical mission (see Montuori 1981a, pp. 57, n. 6 and 8, 140–143; 1988, p. 52 n.81).

several *Apologies* by different authors further confirms that the theme of Socrates' trial and defense was no less a subject of rivalry among the Socratics than other themes that they debated among themselves through the medium of the dialogues (Dorion 2005). If the Platonic *Apology* were a faithful report of Socrates' trial, it would then be necessary to deem other rival versions on Socrates' trial, including Xenophon's *Apology*, unfaithful, which brings us back to the argument from the heyday of the Socratic problem that Plato's account is superior to Xenophon's. Could we in all seriousness affirm that the Platonic *Apology* is a faithful report and that the other *Apologies* are fiction?

(2) Plato's *Apology* is a report not only of Socrates' trial, but also of the very fundamentals of his philosophy; this implies that the supposed faithfulness of the account must cover everything from the theories Socrates developed to the actual progression of the trial. But because the philosophical positions developed in the *Apology* are also present in other dialogues, it follows that we must also consider the philosophical theses of the other dialogues that conform to those of the *Apology* to be historically accurate. Yet we have already established that it is impossible to reconstruct the thinking of the historical Socrates on the basis of the *logoi sokratikoi*, since the very nature of their genre authorizes a considerable freedom of invention. If we follow this line of thinking through, Kahn's position thus leads to the acceptance of the possibility of what it denies at the start. And it follows that since Socrates' philosophy, to the extent that we can reconstruct it on the basis of the *Apology* and the early dialogues, differs on several points from the philosophy established in Xenophon's Socratic writings, Plato's *logoi sokratikoi* should thus take precedence over those of Xenophon, without any possibility of justifying such a preference.[48] And thus we are yet again mired in the quicksand of the Socratic problem.

3. THE FUTURE OF SOCRATIC STUDIES

Recognizing the unsolvable nature of the Socratic problem represents neither a loss for interpretive studies nor an impoverishment of exegesis; on the contrary, it is an opportunity, an exceptional occasion for

48 Kahn disqualifies Xenophon's account on the pretext that it relies on Plato's dialogues (see 1996, pp. 75–79). However, Kahn greatly exaggerates Xenophon's dependence on Plato (see Morrison 2000b, p. 262 n. 42; Dorion 2000, p. LVIII, n. 2).

enriching our understanding of Socratism. In truth, it is the Socratic problem that caused an impoverishment of exegesis because a direct consequence of limiting the scope of Socratic studies to only the Socratic problem was the exclusion of entire sections of accounts relating to Socrates – in particular Xenophon's Socratic works – under the pretext that they did not conform to what were believed to be the historical Socrates' ideas.[49] Let us take the recent example of the Delphic oracle. The exegetic choices are the following: either we prefer Plato's version to Xenophon's for reasons that have more to do with bias than the possibility of ruling in favor of one over the other (Vlastos 1991, pp. 288–289); or, rather than keeping one and disqualifying the other, we conserve both versions and strive to note their differences and most importantly interpret them in the framework of the philosophical convictions specific to each of the authors (Vander Waerdt 1993). It seems quite likely that this type of comparative exegesis, because it revives the pertinence of positions hitherto discarded by the Socratic problem, will considerably enrich our understanding not only of the reception of Socratism but also of the authors who express themselves through the intermediary of Socrates.

If we must abandon the project of faithfully reconstructing the historical Socrates' ideas, so desperately out of reach, interpreters of Socrates and Socratism will certainly have their work cut out,[50] since a triple task awaits them:

(1) Analyze each extant *logos sokratikos* independently in order to reconstruct those of Socrates' doctrines that can be teased out of its narrative. As far as Plato's Socratic writings are concerned, this research, which underwent considerable invigoration following the work of Vlastos, is already quite far along. On the other hand, Xenophon's Socratic writings and fragments from other Socratics are virtually untouched territory.

---

49 See Vander Waerdt 1994, p. 4: "An impoverishing, if unsurprising effect of the recent scholarly preoccupation with the Platonic Socrates has been the exclusion of rival portraits of Socrates from serious study."

50 In a recent article that attempts to defend "Socratic studies," Brickhouse and Smith 2003 understand this expression in such a way that it designates only those works that endeavor to reconstruct the historical Socrates' ideas on the basis of Plato's early dialogues. If this is the only object of *Socratic studies*, it is hardly surprising that Brickhouse and Smith take to task those who challenge the notion that the historical Socrates' ideas can be reconstructed because it would deprive Socratic studies, as they understand the term, of its sole object and *raison d'être*. As the reader will shortly see, I understand by *Socratic studies* a far broader and diversified program of study.

(2) Pursue comparative studies of the different portraits of Socrates left to us by his principal direct and indirect witnesses. In comparing and contrasting these different portraits, we will be better able to grasp how, and eventually why, a single theme spawned multiple interpretations more or less compatible with each other. Without going to the extremes of the *Quellenforschung*, we should push the analysis of the common themes in the *logoi sokratikoi* as far as our sources will allow, because it is precisely this intertextuality that allows us to grasp an echo of the debates that caused such a frenzy in Socratic circles. This exegetic program has been very eloquently defended by commentators who share our skepticism concerning the possibility of resolving the Socratic problem on the basis of the *logoi sokratikoi*:

I suggest that this comparative study of the Socratic literature can be a useful substitute for that old but ultimately fruitless attempt to define the relationship between the Platonic and the historical Socrates. The historical Socrates certainly existed, but to a very large extent the fifth-century figure escapes our grasp. What we have instead is the literary Socrates of the fourth century, in a diversity of portraits. (Kahn 1990, p. 287)

Plato and Xenophon were not the only authors of Socratic dialogues. Many of Socrates' followers contributed to this genre. The conventions of the genre seem to have allowed authors considerable freedom to reshape Socrates, idealize him, and put their own views in Socrates' mouth. Therefore the cautious and reasonable view is that certainty about the historical Socrates is lost to us – and, in a way, not very important. The most important fact about Socrates was his influence: the extraordinary fertility of his ideas and the moral example he set for his followers. (Morrison 2000a, p. 780)

Some might accuse comparative exegesis of being a sort of literary pastime that abandons any aspiration to a historical understanding of Socrates' texts and character. We can respond to this objection by pointing out that comparative exegesis is rather, on the historical level, the most appropriate approach given the nature of the *logoi sokratikoi*. If the various Socratics composed the *logoi sokratikoi* not only from an apologetic perspective but also in order to promote their own respective representations of Socrates in opposition to representations put forth by other Socratics, only comparative exegesis, freed from the Socratic problem, is really up to the task of grasping and interpreting the differences among the *logoi sokratikoi* that are, in a way, the very reason for their existence and diversity. If the historical Socrates' philosophy is out of our reach, the *logoi sokratikoi* only offer us a "diffraction" of Socrates' character and ideas, or, in other words, the different and often conflicting interpretations that his disciples have given of his life and ideas.

Only comparative exegesis seems in a position to identify the Socratic themes that were the subject of such diffraction and, above all, to give a comprehensive account of each divergent interpretation of each theme found in the Socratic literature.[51]

> (3) As for Socrates' posterity within ancient philosophy, we should pursue the already numerous studies that attempt to show how, on the one hand, the majority of later philosophers (Stoics, Academics, Neo-Platonists) appropriated the figure of Socrates, and for what reasons, on the other hand, certain others (notably the Peripatetics and the Epicureans) were opposed to him.

Gigon's skepticism has often incited profound hostility, no doubt because such a position was feared to lead inevitably to the disappearance of Socrates.[52] This fear is unfounded since the type of exegesis that Gigon recommended in fact allows for a better evaluation of the actual historical breadth of the Socrates' character and his numerous portraits. Paradoxically, it is the Socratic problem that leads to a double denial of history: by chasing an elusive Socrates hopelessly out of reach, it finds only a pseudo-historical Socrates all while ostracizing accounts reputedly irreconcilable with this simulacrum of the historical Socrates; by doing so, the Socratic problem obstructs a fair historical understanding of the efficiency of different representations of Socrates in the history of philosophy. Historians of Socrates and Socratism thus have their work cut out, and this is why bothering with the useless and cumbersome Socratic problem is no longer of interest to them.

WORKS CITED

Beversluis, J. "Vlastos's Quest for the Historical Socrates." *Ancient Philosophy* 13 (1993): 293–312.
Brickhouse, T. C., and Smith, N. D. *Socrates on Trial*. Oxford, 1989.
Brickhouse, T. C., and Smith, N. D. *The Philosophy of Socrates*. Boulder, 2000.
Brickhouse, T. C., and Smith, N. D. 2003. "Apology of Socratic Studies." *Polis* 20 (2003): 108–127.
Burnet, J. *Plato's Phaedo*. Oxford, 1911.
Burnet, J. *Greek Philosophy: Thales to Plato*. London, 1914.
Deman, T. *Le Témoignage d'Aristote sur Socrate*. Paris, 1942.
Döring, K. "Der Sokrates der Platonischen Apologie und die Frage nach dem historischen Sokrates." *Würzburger Jahrbücher für die Altertumswissenschaft* 14 (1987): 75–94.

---

51   Vander Waerdt (1993, pp. 4–5) also makes the case for this exegetic project.
52   See Montuori 1981a, p. 45; 1988, pp. 1, 33; 1992, p. 241; Graham 1992, p. 143, n. 11.

Döring, K. "Die Philosophie des Sokrates." *Gymnasium* 99 (1992): 1–16.

Dorion, L. -A., and M. Bandini. *Xénophon: Mémorables*, vol. 1: *Introduction générale et Livre I* [Introduction, translation, and notes by L.-A. Dorion. History of the Greek text by M. Bandini]. Paris, 2000.

Dorion, L. -A. "A l'origine de la question socratique et de la critique du témoignage de Xénophon: l'étude de Schleiermacher sur Socrate (1815)." *Dionysius* 19 (2001): 51–74.

Dorion, L. -A. "Akrasia et enkrateia dans les *Mémorables* de Xénophon." *Dialogue* 42 (2003): 645–672.

Dorion, L. -A. 2005. "The *Daimonion* and the *Megalêgoria* of Socrates in Xenophon's *Apology.*" In *Socrates' Divine Sign: Religion, Practice, and Value in Socratic Philosophy*, eds. P. Destrée and N. D. Smith. Kelowna, B.C., Canada, 2005, pp. 127–143.

Dorion, L. -A. 2006. "Xenophon's Socrates," In *A Companion to Socrates*, eds. S. Ahbel-Rappe and R. Kamtekar. Oxford, 2006, pp. 93–109.

Dover, K. J. *Aristophanes' Clouds*. Oxford, 1968.

Dupréel, E. *La légende socratique et les sources de Platon*. Brussels, 1922.

Gigon, O. *Socrates. Sein Bild in Dichtung und Geschichte*. Bern, 1947.

Gomperz, H. "Die sokratische Frage als geschichtliches Problem." *Historische Zeitschrift* 129 (1924): 377–423, repr. in Patzer 1987: 184–224.

Graham, D. W. "Socrates and Plato." *Phronesis* 37 (1992): 141–165.

Guthrie, W. K. C. *Socrates*. Cambridge, 1971.

Guthrie, W. K. C. *A History of Greek Philosophy*, vol. IV. Cambridge, 1975.

Joël, K. *Der echte und der xenophontische Sokrates*, 3 vol. Berlin, 1893–1901.

Joël, K. "Der logos Sokratikos". *AGP* (1895–1896): 466–483; 9: 50–66.

Kahn, C. H. "Did Plato Write Socratic Dialogues?" *CQ* 31 (1981): 305–320.

Kahn, C. H. "Plato as a Socratic." *Hommage à Henri Joly. Recherches sur la philosophie et le langage* 12 (1990): 287–301.

Kahn, C. H. "Vlastos's Socrates." *Phronesis* 37 (1992): 233–258.

Kahn, C. H. *Plato and the Socratic Dialogue*. Cambridge, 1996.

Long, A. A. 1988. "Socrates in Hellenistic Philosophy." *CQ* 38 (1988): 150–171; repr. in *Stoic Studies*. Cambridge, 1996.

Luccioni, J. *Xénophon et le socratisme*. Paris, 1953.

Magalhães-Vilhena, V. de. *Le problème de Socrate: le Socrate historique et le Socrate de Platon*. Paris, 1952.

Maier, H. *Sokrates, sein Werk und seine geschichtliche Stellung*. Tübingen, 1913.

Momigliano, A. *The Development of Greek Biography*. Cambridge, 1971.

Montuori, M. *Socrates: Physiology of a Myth*. Amsterdam, 1981a.

Montuori, M. *De Socrate iuste damnato. The Rise of the Socratic Problem in the Eighteenth Century*. Amsterdam, 1981b.

Montuori, M. *Socrates: An Approach*. Amsterdam, 1988.

Montuori, M. *The Socratic Problem. The History, the Solutions*. Amsterdam, 1992.

Morrison, D. "Xenophon." In *Greek Thought. A Guide to Classical Knowledge*, eds. J. Brunschwig and G.E.R. Lloyd. Cambridge, MA, 2000a.

Morrison, D. "On the Alleged Historical Reliability of Plato's *Apology.*" *AGP* 82 (2000b): 235–265.

Patzer, A. 1987. "Einleitung," In *Der historische Sokrates*, ed. A. Patzer. Darmstadt, 1987, pp. 1–40.

Robin, L. "Les *Mémorables* de Xénophon et notre connaissance de la philosophie de Socrate." *Année philosophique* 21 (1910): 1–47, repr. in *La Pensée hellénique*. Paris, 1942.

Ross, W. D. "The Problem of Socrates." *Proceedings of the Classical Association* 30 (1933): 7–24.

Santas, G. X. *Socrates: Philosophy in Plato's Early Dialogues*. London, 1979.

Schleiermacher, F. "Ueber den Werth des Sokrates als Philosophen," *Abhandlung der philosophischen Klasse der königlich preussichen Akademie aus den Jahren 1814–1815*. 1818: 51–68; repr. in Patzer 1987 : 41–58. English trans.: "The Worth of Socrates as Philosopher," *PLATON: The Apology of Socrates, the Crito and part of the Phaedo*, ed. W. Smith. London, 1879.

Tarrant, D. "The Pseudo-platonic Socrates." *CQ* 32 (1938): 167–173.

Taylor, A. E. *Varia Socratica*. Oxford, 1911.

Taylor, A. E. *Socrates*. London, 1932.

Vander Waerdt, P. A. "Socratic Justice and Self-sufficiency. The Story of the Delphic Oracle in Xenophon's *Apology of Socrates*." *OSAP* 11 (1993): 1–48.

Vander Waerdt, P.A., ed. *The Socratic Movement*. Ithaca, 1994.

Vlastos, G. "The Paradox of Socrates," In *The Philosophy of Socrates. A Collection of Critical Essays*. ed. G. Vlastos. Garden City, NY, 1971, pp. 1–21.

Vlastos, G. "Socrates." *PBA* 74 (1988): 89–111.

Vlastos, G. *Socrates: Ironist and Moral Philosopher*. Ithaca, 1991.

2   The Students of Socrates

INTRODUCTION

At the end of the Socrates chapter in his *Lives of Eminent Philosophers*, Diogenes Laertius asserts that out of all the friends and students of Socrates, seven have to be regarded as the most important ones. These are the four Athenians – Antisthenes, Aeschines, Plato, and Xenophon – as well as Euclides from Megara (who must not be confused with the well-known mathematician with the same name, who lived in Alexandria about 100 years later), Aristippus from Cyrene, and Phaedo from Elis. All seven wrote books, but only Plato's and Xenophon's are still preserved. Thus, when we talk about the Socratics, we have Plato and Xenophon primarily in mind. The other five were students of Socrates, as much as Plato and Xenophon were. So their writings, if they had been preserved, would stand on an equal footing with those of Plato and Xenophon, and would deserve the same attention as representations of the influence of their common teacher, Socrates. Since these writings have been lost, their place will have to be taken by what can be learned from the texts of various other authors who referred to their writings and doctrines. How much this broadens the spectrum of Socrates' influence is clear from the very different views that Antisthenes, Aristippus, and Plato hold on the issue of pleasure (*hêdonê*).[1]

For the presentation of their philosophical views, the Socratics created their own literary genre – namely, the Socratic dialogue (*Sôkratikos logos*). These are texts in which Socrates discusses a wide variety of philosophical problems with one or more conversational partners. Of the Socratics mentioned earlier, Aeschines, Antisthenes, Euclides, Phaedo, Plato and Xenophon wrote Socratic dialogues. Only Aristippus seems not to have done so. We do not know who was the first Socratic to write

Translated from the German by Stan Husi

1   I document in detail what we can learn about the lives, writings and philosophies of the seven Socratics, apart from Plato, in Döring 1998.

a Socratic dialogue.[2] There is no evidence to corroborate the widespread assumption that it was Plato. It is also controversial as to whether the first Socratic dialogues had already been written while Socrates was still alive, or whether this type of dialogue was originally created only after the occurrence of his violent death in 399 BCE. Some think that Plato wrote his dialogues *Ion* and *Hippias Minor* before 399.[3] As already mentioned, only Plato's and Xenophon's dialogues are preserved; about most others nothing is known except for their titles. There are only a few dialogues of which we can at least roughly reconstruct the plot.

Ancient literary theory distinguishes three types within Plato's dialogues (cf. D.L. III.50): (1) the "dramatic" dialogue, in which only the conversation as such is reproduced (an example is Plato's *Euthyphro*); (2) the "narrative" dialogue ("dihegmatic"), which reports a conversation (examples are: Plato's *Republic* and the dialogues of Aeschines; (3) a mixed form, in which the dialogue starts out with a directly displayed conversation and continues with a report of a conversation in which Socrates took part (an example is Plato's *Phaedo*). A special type of the narrative dialogue that is not especially distinguished by the ancient literary theorists is one in which the author pretends to report a conversation that he himself has overheard. We know of this type only from Xenophon, who was also perhaps its creator. What all forms of the Socratic dialogue share is that the setting, the situation, the topic, and the course of the conversation are purely fictional. Even in cases where the dialogue makes reference to concrete historical events, or where the author asserts to have been present at the particular conversation, this is only part of the literary fiction. Thus these details must not be interpreted as indicating that the conversation has in fact taken place in this or a similar manner. The intention of the Socratics in writing these dialogues was not to document a conversation that Socrates actually conducted in some way or at some time.[4] Their prime goal instead was to discuss philosophical issues in the same manner in which Socrates discussed them. In subsequent generations, however, the Socratic dialogue

---

2   A quote from Aristotle's *On Poets* (Arist. fr. 72 Rose, fr. 15 Gigon) that survived in Athenaios (XI.505bc) remains puzzling. It is claimed there that a man named Alexamenos of Teos wrote dialogues or even Socratic dialogues before the Socratics. As the transmitted text seems to be corrupt, we don't know what Aristotle exactly said.

3   Cf. recently Heitsch 2002a and 2002b, pp. 181–189. See also Rossetti 1991.

4   This is already evident from the fact that Socrates' conversations in Plato and in Xenophon not only heavily diverge but are to a considerable extent incompatible. Socrates advances claims in the later dialogues of Plato that the historical Socrates cannot even have thought about. For more on the fictional character of Socratic dialogues, see Dorion's Chapter 1 in this volume.

became dissociated from this aspect, and became a literary genre that was used even by those who had never personally met Socrates or had been able to meet him. People still wrote Socratic dialogues even after Socrates had been dead for over 100 years.[5]

The only Socratic dialogues that have entirely been preserved beside those of Plato's and Xenophon's are the so-called Pseudoplatonica. These are those dialogues that have been transmitted together with Plato's, and were not written by Plato but rather by some unknown authors. Like Xenophon's dialogues, almost all of these dialogues have a comparatively plain structure and are of limited scope. On the basis of the preserved reports, we may suppose that the same is true of the lost dialogues of Aeschines and Phaedo. This is probably also true of the dialogues of the two older Socratics, Antisthenes and Euclides, although one has to keep in mind that we do not have evidence that would permit conclusions about the structure or the scope of their dialogues. In any case, there is strong reason to think that no other Socratic brought the potential contained in the Socratic dialogue to such fruition and full development as Plato did, with respect to both literary form and philosophical breadth and depth. Thus it is not surprising that as far as we know, the Socratic Dialogue first reached, and then burst, its boundaries only in Plato. In many of Plato's later dialogues, Socrates only operates in the background. In the *Laws*, Plato's last work, Socrates does not appear at all. There is no shred of evidence that any comparable development occurred in the work of any other Socratic.

Besides Aeschines, Antisthenes, Euclides, Phaedo, Plato, and Xenophon, several other Socratics are supposed to have written Socratic dialogues. Diogenes Laertius (2,121–125) mentions the titles of numerous works by Socratics known from Plato's dialogues (Crito, Glaucon, Simmias, and Cebes) as well as by the cobbler Simon.[6] It is doubtful, however, whether those works really existed. A surviving work titled *Pinax* (*Painting*), supposedly written by Cebes, certainly originates from a much later time. The same might be true of the dialogues by the Socratic authors Crito, Simon, and Cebes mentioned in a catalogue of books dating from the beginning of the third century CE, parts of which are preserved on a papyrus found in Memphis.[7] Through the recovery of papyrus texts, other remains of unidentified dialogues have been revealed, some of which very likely (in one case, even certainly) belong to the category of Socratic dialogues. The most important discovery

---

5   Some of the spurious dialogues contained in the Platonic corpus certainly are from later times.

6   About Simon, cf. next section.

7   CPF I 1, 85–93.

contains a fragment of a dialogue in which Socrates justifies to another person why he refused to defend himself in court, or at least not in any way likely to result in an acquittal. There he argues that if one regards pleasure and pain as what above all else must be striven or avoided in life, life is not to be preferred to death. Unfortunately we do not know what role this argument played in that dialogue.[8]

In addition to writing Socratic dialogues, the Socratics wrote dialogues of other sorts as well. It appears that at least one of the *Herakles* writings by Antisthenes was a dialogue taking place in a *mythical* setting.[9] Perhaps the same is true of the *Phoenix* by Euclides.[10] Xenophon's dialogue *Hiero* contains a conversation between Hiero I, tyrant of Syracuse between 478 and 467/6, and the poet Simonides. The issue discussed is whether and under what conditions a tyrant can be happy.[11] In addition to writing dialogues, Antisthenes also composed writings that have the form of philosophical treatises. Whether the writings of Aristippus included dialogues of some kind is beyond our knowledge. In any case, it seems certain that Aristippus was the only one among the seven Socratics who did not compose a Socratic dialogue.

Looking at the surviving evidence concerning the five Socratics Aeschines, Antisthenes, Aristippus, Euclides, and Phaedo, one can draw the conclusion that while some things can be ascertained about the writings of Aeschines and Phaedo, very little is known about their philosophical views, perhaps because they did not propagate specific teachings of their own. With respect to the three other Socratics, the opposite is the case. While some facts can be ascertained about their philosophical views, next to nothing is known about their writings.

AESCHINES OF SPHETTUS[12]

Aeschines (430/20 – after 375/6) wrote seven Socratic dialogues, entitled *Miltiades, Callias, Axiochos, Aspasia, Alcibiades, Telauges,* and *Rhinon* (D.L. II.61). Only a few decades after Socrates' death, the story arose that Socrates was the author of these dialogues and that Aeschines

---

8   PKoeln 205 = SSR I C 550; cf. Barnes 1991/92), Spinelli 1992.

9   For issues pertaining to the *Herakles* texts of Antisthenes, cf. Giannantoni, SSR IV 309–322.

10   This assumes that the titular figure of the dialogue (of which we know nothing except the title) is indeed the Phoenix of the *Iliad*.

11   We would have a similar case here if the titular figure of Antisthenes' dialogue *Cyrus Minor* (D.L. II.61 = SSR V A 43) were Cyrus I, the founder of the Persian empire. Cf. Giannantoni, SSR IV 295–308.

12   For Aeschines, see Dittmar 1912 and Doering 1998, pp. 201–206. The surviving testimonies: SSR VI A.

had received them as a gift from Xanthippe after Socrates died. This allegation warrants the conclusion that Socrates figured as the narrator in all seven dialogues, just as he did in Plato's dialogues *Lysis*, *Charmides*, and the *Republic*. All the dialogues of Aeschines have been lost. It is possible, however, to reconstruct the plot of *Alcibiades* and *Aspasia* in at least a rough fashion, as a result of quotations found in later authors as well as in papyrus discoveries.[13]

In the *Alcibiades*,[14] Socrates reported on a meeting with the "enfant terrible" Alcibiades. In the dialogue, the reader encountered in Alcibiades a young man who exhibited virtually unlimited self-confidence and who believed himself to be superior not only to all of his contemporaries but also to the great Athenian politicians of the past, including Themistocles. Here, Socrates' argument began. Socrates used the example of Themistocles in order to make Alcibiades aware of the truth about himself and his talents. First, Socrates forced Alcibiades to acknowledge that Themistocles' extraordinary cleverness was not the result of some innate skill but rather acquired through time. Then Socrates drew Alcibiades' attention to the two greatest deeds achieved by Themistocles' cleverness. When Xerxes, the king of the Persians, went off to subdue Greece with his enormous army, Themistocles, through his victory at the battle of Salamis, proved superior in cleverness even compared with the most powerful man in the world. Shortly thereafter, Themistocles provided another spectacular proof of his superior cleverness. Once the battle of Salamis was over, Themistocles tried to persuade the Athenians to destroy the bridge of ships built by the Persians over the Hellespont. By doing so, they would have been able to thwart Xerxes' return to Asia. The Athenians, however, declined to follow his advice. Themistocles then sent a secret message to Xerxes in which his and the Athenians' roles were reversed. By this clever chess move, Themistocles gave Xerxes the impression that he owed his safe return to Asia to Themistocles. Later, when Themistocles was banned from Athens, Xerxes offered him his warmest hospitality as a sign of his gratitude for the alleged rescue. In addition, Xerxes richly rewarded him with gifts. In conclusion, Socrates drew Alcibiades' attention to the fact that even Themistocles' superior sagacity ultimately did not protect him from disfranchisement and expulsion by the city. Directly addressing Alcibiades, Socrates added the following: "How do you think, then, things go for bad people who do not take much care for their own

---

13   For the dialogues *Alcibiades* and *Aspasia*, see Ehlers 1966, Döring 1984, Kahn 1994 and 1996, 18–29; Giannantoni 1997.
14   The testimonies for Aeschines' *Alcibiades*: SSR VI A 41–54.

affairs? Isn't it quite remarkable if they can even be successful in their small matters?"

Those words of Socrates had their effect: Alcibiades was deeply shaken. Until then, Alcibiades had thought he was endowed with such unique talent that without giving much care to his own affairs, he could do much better than all others. Now he placed his head on Socrates' knee and began crying. He was full of dismay that he didn't even come close to a man like Themistocles, and that he, the aristocrat Alcibiades, was no different from the least of his fellow citizens. He then begged Socrates to lead him to virtue (aretê) and dispel his pitiful shame. At the end of the dialogue, Socrates concludes that while he was indeed able to help Alcibiades, this was not due to his own skill (technê), but rather due to divine destiny (theia moira). With the physically ill, Socrates continued, there are healing processes brought about by divine destiny besides those caused by medicine alone. And the same thing holds for ethical improvement: "And so although I know no skill which I could teach to anyone to benefit him, nevertheless I thought that in keeping company with Alcibiades, I could by the power of love make him better."

Once we look at the dialogue in its entirety, as we are able to reconstruct it from the fragments, we will realize that there are three distinct senses of improvement discussed in the dialogue. Themistocles illustrates the results of improvement. Then Alcibiades pleads with Socrates to improve him and to lead him to virtue. And at the end, Socrates claims to have improved Alcibiades. The question is, then, what is meant by improvement in each of these cases?

As far as Themistocles is concerned, the result of improvement consists in the fact that he surpasses everyone else in practical cleverness. His cleverness, however, does not reach so far as to protect him from all kinds of failure: it does not protect him from disfranchisement and expulsion. Yet ultimately these failures confirm his cleverness, by showing how well-prepared Themistocles was for such a scenario. When Alcibiades pleads with Socrates to lead him to virtue, what he has in mind is the cleverness and the knowledge to which Themistocles owed his success. He seeks to become as good as Themistocles. The greatness of Themistocles' knowledge was shown by Themistocles' ability to prepare for his future welfare by reversing the facts. Yet this ability is certainly not the one Socrates has in mind at the end of the dialogue when he speaks of having improved Alcibiades. What Socrates means is that he has helped Alcibiades to become at least partly aware of his enormously foolish self-regard, and thereby to acquire better knowledge of himself. Thus, when Alcibiades begs Socrates to lead him to virtue, and when Socrates talks about having improved Alcibiades – that is, brought him further on the path toward excellence – then what each has in mind is something completely different. Alcibiades asks for knowledge in Themistocles' sense, a teachable and learnable practical expertise that helps him to deal with all sorts of problems with great success and benefit. In contrast, what Socrates has in mind is taking the first small steps toward a correct self-understanding. Yet by conducting his conversations in the way he does, Socrates can only give a push in the right direction. Only those who themselves feel the call for this kind of wisdom have a real chance of acquiring it.

By now it should be clear enough what Socrates means by talking about having improved Alcibiades, despite not having any knowledge that he could pass on to others. There is one exception: we have not yet considered the essential role Socrates assigns to his love for Alcibiades. One might think that what Socrates says about love means nothing more than this: apart from his special affection for Alcibiades, Socrates does not have any reason to look out for him. This, however, understates the significance of love. One major theme of the *Aspasia* is the important role love plays in facilitating improvement. Further, Socrates in the dialogue calls himself a student of the famous courtesan Aspasia especially with respect to matters of love (*ta erôtika*).

Aspasia[15] started out with Callias – an affluent Athenian – asking Socrates to recommend a teacher who would be capable of forming his son into an able citizen and politician. Socrates recommended the famous Milesian Aspasia, whom Pericles married some years after the death of his first wife. In the main section of the dialogue, Socrates attempts to make his suggestion plausible to a puzzled Callias. Three basic arguments can be reconstructed from this part of the dialogue: (1) Using the example of two queens – the Persian Rhodogyne and the Thessalian Thargelia – Socrates proved that women can be important politicians and hence experts on that subject. (2) Using two additional examples, he illustrated Aspasia's outstanding talent as a teacher of political affairs. Not only did she form Pericles into an excellent politician; she also did so with Lysikles, whom she married after Pericles' death, and who had formerly been a completely unimportant sheep merchant. She accomplished this partly by teaching them rhetoric, in which she herself excelled, but mostly by arousing their love for her, which in turn unleashed unanticipated powers in both men. (3) Finally, Socrates reported a conversation that Aspasia once held with Xenophon and his wife in his presence. Aspasia began: "Tell me please, wife of Xenophon, if your neighbor had a more beautiful golden ornament than you have, would you then prefer to have hers or yours?" – "Hers," she

---

15   The testimonies for Aeschines' *Aspasia*: SSR VI A 59–72.

replied. – "And if her clothing and other furnishings were of greater value than yours, would you prefer yours or hers?" – "Hers, of course," she answered. "Well," Aspasia said, "and if she had a better husband than you, would you then prefer your husband or hers?" – Here the woman blushed and turned silent. Then Aspasia began to talk to Xenophon. The questions she asked him were analogous, and so was the ending. Embarrassed, Xenophon also turned silent when asked whether he would prefer his neighbor's wife, in case she turned out to be better than his own. Hereupon Aspasia remarked: "Since neither of you answered the very question I most wanted you to answer, I'm going to tell you what each of you is thinking. You, woman, want to have the best husband, and you, Xenophon, desire above all things to have the most excellent wife. Therefore unless you can contrive that there is no better man and no more excellent woman on earth (i.e. than you are), you will certainly ardently strive for what you regard best: you, that you are the husband of the best conceivable wife, and she, that she is married to the best conceivable husband."

In all likelihood, the conversation between Aspasia, Xenophon and his wife was prefaced by Socrates' remarking that he occasionally went to Aspasia himself, together with his friends and their wives, and that he was instructed by her in matters of love (*ta erôtika*).[16] Thus there is an intimate connection between the conversation between Aspasia, Xenophon, and his wife, and Socrates' remark that he was Aspasia's student in matters of love. When Aeschines makes Socrates say that he was a student of Aspasia's, then what he is suggesting is that there is a particular Socratic aspect "concealed" in the very manner in which Aspasia conducts her conversation with Xenophon and his wife. Put differently, the suggestion is that Aeschines projects a Socratic aspect on Aspasia. This is rather obvious, and has long given Aspasia here the reputation of a female version of Socrates.

Let us try to be a bit more precise. What immediately grabs one's attention is the fact that Aspasia uses Socrates' famous methodological tool, the argument by analogy, with which she corners her conversational partners in good Socratic fashion. To what end? Her goal is twofold. First, Aspasia seeks to make Xenophon and his wife aware that they are caught in an inconsistency. This inconsistency arises between (1) their belief that they love no one else as much as the other, and (2) the admission that they would favor a superior spouse in case one came along. The result is that they do not in fact love their spouses in the way they think. Second, Aspasia wants Xenophon and his wife to realize that they are capable of ending this inconsistency by trying to become

16   Cf. Ehlers 1966, p. 97.

as virtuous as possible. Evidently, they have already made a first step by becoming aware of the inconsistency. A sign of this is their blushing embarrassment and silence.

The conversation between Socrates and Alcibiades, as reported by Socrates in the dialogue *Alcibiades*, appears to have had, on a larger scale, the same structure as the conversation between Aspasia and Xenophon and his wife. Alcibiades also has to acknowledge an inconsistency in which he finds himself, between his foolish self-assessment and his actual self. And he also has to recognize that only he can liberate himself from this inconsistency by beginning to care for himself – that is, for becoming better. In the *Alcibiades*, the first step in the process of self-improvement is already achieved by becoming aware of the inconsistency. A sign of this is Alcibiades' despairing tears.

If this conceptual correspondence between Aspasia's conversation with Xenophon and his wife and Socrates' conversation with Alcibiades is correct, then when in the *Aspasia* Socrates says he has been instructed in matters of love by Aspasia, and when in the *Alcibiades* Socrates says that his love for Alcibiades enabled him to help Alcibiades improve himself, then Socrates in both cases has the same thing in mind: his peculiar skill of conducting conversations so as to bring others to reflect upon themselves. He makes them realize that they need to take care of themselves (*epimeleisthai heautou*), as he likes to put it, and so to take the first steps toward virtue. In short, as Aeschines sees it, Socrates' skill in matters of love (*erôtikê technê*), and his argumentative skill (*elegktikê technê*), which he uses to help others gain better self-knowledge and a better sense for what is good for them, are only the two sides of the same coin.

Like Aeschines, Antisthenes wrote a dialogue with the title *Aspasia*. Our knowledge concerning this dialogue, however, does not go much beyond the title (SSR V A 142–144). In Plato's dialogue *Menexenus*, Socrates claims that Aspasia was his instructor in rhetoric (235e-236a), and recites from memory a speech about the fallen from 386, which had been delivered extemporaneously by Aspasia in his presence the day before. This shows the literary freedom authors of Socratic dialogues had, since by 386 the historical Socrates had already been dead for thirteen years. At two places in Xenophon's oeuvre, Socrates claims to have participated in conversations conducted by Aspasia, and to have found Aspasia to be an enormously skillful educator (*Mem.* II.6.36. *Oec.* 3.14). An even more interesting aspect, however, is this: in Plato's *Symposium*, Socrates also claims to have been instructed in matters of love by a woman (201d5). The woman in question, however, is not Aspasia, but Diotima. What she taught Socrates, in sum, is the doctrine of Eros as the longing for the beautiful and the good, which, together with the awakening of such a longing in the beloved one, ascends from the realm of the corporeal and the mortal to the realm of the incorporeal and eternal. What Socrates means when he talks about being instructed in matters of love by Diotima, then, is that he owes to her his ability to awaken in others a striving for the beautiful and the good, and hence for knowledge and excellence.

Alcibiades was a central figure in the Socratic dialogues. Antisthenes (SSR V A 198–202) and Euclides (D.L. II.108) made him a titular figure in their dialogues. Among Plato's writings we find two *Alcibiades* dialogues. However, one of these certainly (*Alcibiades Minor*) was not written by Plato, and the other (*Alcibiades Major*) may not have been. Alcibiades also participates in the conversation in the *Protagoras* and *Symposium*. One of the most famous ancient texts is the speech of praise Alcibiades delivers for Socrates in the *Symposium* (215a4ff.). From a note in Cicero's *De fato* (10) we can conclude that Alcibiades also appeared in Phaedo's *Zopyros* (cf. the following section).

In one of Aeschines' dialogues – we do not know which – there is the following tale about Aristippus's conversion to philosophy. Once at the Olympic games Aristippus met one of Socrates' students, Ischomachus, and asked him, "What is the reason for the enormous impact that Socrates made with his conversations?" After Ischomachus related a few examples of those conversations, Aristippus was so shaken that it made him pale and drawn. He immediately travelled to Athens in order to personally experience Socrates and his conversations, which aimed at the recognition and removal of one's faults.[17] The central theme of Aeschines' dialogues appears to have been the process Socrates set in motion of acquiring self-knowledge and the willingness to better oneself.

PHAEDO OF ELIS[18]

One of Plato's most famous dialogues was named after Phaedo (˙418/16 BCE, year of death unknown). Phaedo himself wrote two dialogues, *Zopyros* and *Simon*.

In a quote from *Zopyros* – preserved word for word in the *Progymnasmata* of the rhetorician Aelius Theon – it says:[19] "They say, Socrates, that somebody gave a lion to the youngest son of the king of Persia. [Here Theon omits a passage] And the lion, who grew up with

---

17 Plut. *De curios.* 2.516c. D.L. II.65 = SSR IV A 1+2 = VI A 91.
18 For Phaedo see Döring 1998, pp. 238–241. The surviving testimonies: SSR III A.
19 Theon *Prog.* 3 pp. 33–34 Patillon = SSR III A 11.

the boy, apparently followed the boy up to his maturity at every turn, so that the Persians said of the lion that he loved the boy." No additional explicit information concerning the content of the dialogue has been preserved. There is reasonable agreement, however, that the story about a meeting between Socrates and the oriental magus Zopyros, who was an expert in physiognomy, originates from this dialogue. The story of this meeting is reported in Cicero and other authors.[20] The story goes that Zopyros once came to Athens and offered his expertise in reading anyone's innate character from his appearance. When Zopyros met Socrates and diagnosed stupidity, intemperance, and lewdness in him, the bystanders – and especially Alcibiades – burst out laughing. Socrates reassured Zopyros that he did indeed possess those traits; however, he was able to overcome them by virtue of insight and discipline. If this story was a central theme of the dialogue (and there is no reason to doubt this), then Phaedo, in a quite original manner, connects three themes found in the Socratic literature that as far as we can see appear elsewhere only scattered and in isolation: (1) The theme of physiognomy must also have played a role in Antisthenes' work. At any rate, his text *About the Sophists* has been labelled a 'treatise in physiognomics.'[21] (2) The contrast between Socrates' appearance and his quite different inner self, as expressed in his actions, was also thematized in Plato and Xenophon, most notably in their *Symposia*. (3) Finally, Socrates met oriental sages in other dialogues as well. For this we have no explicit testimony, though the fact that such meetings are occasionally mentioned elsewhere[22] is best explained by assuming that those passages reflect Socratic texts. It is also relevant that Socrates in the *Charmides* (156d-157b) presents a medical teaching that he claims to have learned from a doctor of the school of the famous Thracian, Zalmoxis. Phaedo's intention in his dialogue *Zopyros* was evidently to show how far serious education, and especially self-education, can turn man toward the good.

For the dialogue *Simon*, it is remarkable that we do not have a single surviving testimony about its content. Hence we must rely on inferences. The titular figure of the dialogue can only be the philosophizing cobbler Simon. Simon is said to have taken notes of the conversations Socrates conducted with him in his workshop, from which he produced his "cobbler dialogues" (D.L. II.122–124). Incidentally, we can determine, with reasonable confidence, the location of Simon's workshop. An excavation of the Agora in Athens carried out in the 1950s found,

---

20   The testimonies are collected in Rossetti 1980, pp. 183–198.
21   D.L. VI.15; see Ath. XIV.656f.
22   Arist. ap. D.L. II.45, Aristox. fr. 53 Wehrli, [Pl.]Ax. 371a-372b.

near the ruins of a comparatively modest house in the southwest corner, some cobbler's nails and bone eyelets for laced boots, as well as the foot of a drinking cup engraved with the name "Simon." Naturally the excavators immediately supposed they had hit on the ruins of the house of that very cobbler with whom Socrates had philosophical conversations.[23]

The collection of *Letters of the Socratics*, written by an unknown author about 200 CE, mentions Simon several times.[24] Three things stand out here: (1) that Simon, despite being forced to make a living by doing mundane work, was seriously and ardently dedicated to philosophy. (2) that Simon, like Antisthenes, advocated a simple life style as appropriate for philosophy. (3) that Simon therefore firmly rejected the idea of receiving subsidies (as Aristippus had done) from a powerful ruler like Dionysius, tyrant of Syracuse, because this would make him dependent. Simon is said to have rejected an offer from Pericles to pay for his living expenses. The reason Simon gave for this was that he was unwilling to sell his freedom of speech (D.L. II.123). It is very possible that much of this material derives from Phaedo's dialogue *Simon*; unfortunately, we are in no position to decide. Only one detail can be settled with sufficient confidence. The famous sophist Prodicus originally invented the story of Hercules at the crossroad in one of his writings (DK 84 B 1). The thirteenth letter of the Socratics[25] indicates that in Phaedo's dialogue *Simon*, a participant reports that Simon forced Prodicus to admit that he had "disproved" Prodicus's version of the story. How Simon carried out this disproof is not said. We can presume that Simon forced Prodicus to replace the aristocratic-military virtue (*aretê*) he advocated with Socratic virtue, which can be achieved by everyone, including common craftsmen like himself.

The cobbler Simon, being a poor craftsman, occupies an exceptional position among the persons encountered by Socrates in the Socratic dialogues. Craftsmen such as the artist Parrhasius, the sculptor Cleiton, and the blacksmith Pistias, whom Socrates visits in their workshops in order to have a conversation (Xenophon, *Memorabilia* III.10), cannot be compared to Simon, for they occupy a significantly higher social status than the cobbler.[26] Further, though a man like Antisthenes is poor, he has voluntarily chosen to be poor, rather than being poor because of his social position. Granted, we cannot in principle rule out that another

23 Cf. Thompson 1960.
24 9,4. 11. 12. 13. 18,2 = SSR IV A 222. IV A 223. III A 16. IV A 224. VI B 91.
25 See von Fritz (1935).
26 About the low reputation of cobblers cf. Headlam and Knox 1922, XLVIII-XLIX.

person of low social status like Simon appears in one or another of the lost Socratic dialogues. There is not a shred of evidence for that, however, and the known titles of the dialogues rather speak against it.

As far as we can tell, the central theme of Phaedo's dialogues was that philosophy is not only available to those with good inborn talent and first-rate education. To the contrary, philosophy can help everyone improve himself ethically, regardless of native gifts, social status, and personal circumstances. In the dialogues *Zopyros* and *Simon*, Phaedo developed this thought in two directions. First, by using Socrates, who by his own admission was endowed by nature with plenty of negative traits, and Simon, the modest cobbler, he presents two persons in whom philosophy has demonstrated its full potential for improvement. Hence Socrates and Simon testify to the power of philosophy. Second, he shows how philosophy exerts its power on others through the influence of wise persons such as Socrates and Simon. According to Seneca's testimony (*Letters* 94.41 = SSR III A 12), Phaedo described this influence in one of his dialogues in the following manner: "Certain tiny animals [think of mosquitoes and other insects] do not leave any pain when they sting us; so subtle is their power, so deceptive for purposes of harm. The bite is disclosed by a swelling, and even in the swelling there is no visible wound. That will also be your experience when dealing with wise men: you will not discover how or when the benefit comes to you, but you will discover that you have received it." (trans. R. M. Gummere).

EUCLIDES OF MEGARA[27]

Euclides (̔450/435 – c. 365) wrote six dialogues. Unfortunately we know nothing more about them than their titles (*Lamprias, Aeschines, Phoenix, Crito, Alcibiades, Eroticus*).

In the center of Euclides' philosophy stood the Socratic question, "What is the good?" Euclides' answer was that the good is *one*. On this, all surviving testimonies concur. On other points, the accounts diverge. We need to differentiate two traditions. On one side, there is the claim – found explicitly in Cicero, but also covertly in other authors – that Euclides belongs to the Eleatic tradition of Xenophanes, Parmenides, and Zeno, because his teaching was that "only what is one, alike, and always the same is good." (Cic. *Academica* II.129 = SSR II A 31). On the other side, there is the testimony of Diogenes Laertius, who says this: Euclides "held that the good is *one* though called by many names. Sometimes wisdom (*phronêsis*), sometimes God, sometimes reason

---

27 For Euclides see Döring 1998, pp. 208–212. The surviving testimonies: SSR II A.

(*nous*) and so on. But all that is contradictory to the good he rejected, declaring it has no existence." (D.L. II.106 = SSR II A 30,2–4).

For a long time, modern accounts of the history of philosophy more or less uncritically accepted the ancient tradition that grouped Euclides with the Eleatics. This changed, however, in 1931, when in a seminal and influential work, Kurt von Fritz reassessed all the evidence pertaining to Euclides.[28] He arrived at the following conclusions, which are now widely accepted:

(1) The tradition that classified Euclides as a successor of the Eleatics is a doxographic construct by ancient historians of philosophy. Since Eleatic philosophy and Euclides both assigned a special role to the *One*, these historians effectively reformulated Euclides' philosophy – while purging its Socratic characteristics – so as to subsume it under the Eleatic tradition.

(2) If any of the ancient sources can claim authenticity, it is the testimony of Diogenes Laertius. Yet this source clearly shows Socratic coloring, as is evident from the following. The majority of current Socrates scholars agree that the philosophy of Socrates revolved around three convictions: (1) Those who live according to virtue are happy. That is why there can be no more important activity for a man than to continually strive to realize a life of ethical virtue in all its aspects: justice, piety, and so forth. (2) Anybody who has achieved true knowledge of the good will, by necessity, do what is good. Thus, virtue is knowledge. (3) Hence those who do what is bad do so only because they are mistaken, and erroneously assume the bad to be good. All three doctrines can be found in one or another form in the teachings of Euclides, as reported by Diogenes Laertius. The first doctrine is contained in the thesis that the good is one; the second in the thesis that insight and prudence are but different names for the good; and the third in the thesis that what is opposed to the good does not exist. This last claim must obviously be understood in a Socratic sense, which interprets the bad as a misconception of the good, and hence not as something real but rather as a form of deprivation of the good. These correlations can hardly be disputed. So far, Kurt von Fritz's interpretation is on firm ground, but anything going beyond that is less certain. This applies even to the question as to what Diogenes Laertius meant by "and so forth." Here there is some reason for thinking of the particular virtues, or at least for thinking of them *as well*. As for what Euclides meant

28   von Fritz 1931.

when proposing God as an additional name for the good, it is possible that Euclides interpreted the good in a teleological sense as
divine and all-regulating reason aiming at the good.

The rest of what we know about Euclides' philosophical views
concerns the domain of logic. The source for this is again Diogenes
Laertius. Diogenes reports (D.L. II. 107 = SSR II A 34) that Euclides
"attacked proofs not by disputing their premises, but rather their conclusion." Assuming that this refers to the dialectical procedure in
Socratic dialogues – and we have to assume this, since Euclides didn't
write texts of other sorts – then "premises" in this testimony can only
mean those claims or assumptions from which the Socratic refutation
departs. Likewise, the "conclusion" can only be the result at which the
argument arrives. Thus what Diogenes Laertius means is that the criticism was not applied until the conclusion had already been reached.
Diogenes further reports (II.107 = SSR II A 34) that Euclides rejected
argument by analogy – which Socrates liked to use and which is well
known from the Socratic dialogues – as an unsuitable tool for argumentation. Euclides' reason is reported to have been this. In the argument by analogy, the similar will be compared either to the similar
or to the dissimilar. If what is compared is similar, then it is better to
focus on the things themselves rather than on those to which they are
compared. If what is compared is dissimilar, then the comparison is
misleading.

Thus we can learn two things about the dialectical praxis of
Euclides: (1) his method of refuting the arguments of others, and (2) that
he declared his teacher Socrates' favorite form of argumentation to be
useless. Unfortunately we do not know what Euclides' general thoughts
were on the possibility of proving anything, nor how he argued for his
teaching of the good, as it is ascribed to him by Diogenes Laertius.
This may be due to the extraordinary scarcity of surviving testimonies.
More probably, however, this is due to another reason. Consider that
100 years after his death, Euclides was denounced as being the prototype of an Eristic (controversialist) by the satirist Timon of Phleius
(D.L. II.107 = SSR II A 34), and further, that his students and even his
students' students were infamous for their destructive logic. From this
we can conclude that Euclides did not defend his teachings in a positive way, but rather negatively, by showing that opposing views were
indefensible. Thus he utilized the same method that Zeno of Elea used
to show the correctness of the views of his teacher Parmenides (Either
A or not-A is true. Then we prove that assuming not-A leads to absurd
conclusions. Since not-A has to be false, A must be true). As is well
known, Plato used this method throughout his dialogue *Parmenides*.

ARISTIPPUS OF CYRENE[29]

As far as we can tell, Aristippus (c. 430–c. 355) travelled a great deal. At least once, but more probably numerous times, he stayed at the court of Syracuse. As already mentioned, Aristippus was the only one among the seven prominent Socratics who did not write Socratic dialogues, but only other kinds of text. We are told that one of his writings was titled *To Socrates* (*Pros Sôkratên*; D.L. II.85). Of course, we should very much like to know what was written in that text. Unfortunately we do not have any hint of its content; indeed, we cannot even be certain whether the text existed. Since the evidence concerning Aristippus's writings is extraordinarily cojnfused,[30] we cannot rule out the possibility that the title is fictitious. Furthermore, it is possible that the name "Socrates" is a corruption of the name of the rhetor "Isocrates." There certainly is one such corruption at another place in Diogenes Laertius (II.55). It is not implausible that Aristippus could have written a text addressing Isocrates. There was a famous rivalry between the Socratics and their contemporary Isocrates, as a result of their contrasting conceptions of education. Plato and Isocrates referred to each other critically in their works, and the same must have been true for Antisthenes and Isocrates.[31] Besides writing philosophical texts, Aristippus is said to also have written a three-volume history of Libya. In all likelihood, this was a local chronicle concerning his birthplace, Cyrene.[32]

In a conversation with Socrates in Xenophon's *Memorabilia*, Aristippus describes his goal in life. He sides with those who desire to "live as easily and comfortably as possible." He believes he will best be able to realize that desire by eschewing any sort of attachment and living a life of unrestrained freedom (*Mem.* II.1.9,11,13). This is consistent with what we can read in the surviving testimonies (often anecdotes) about Aristippus's way of life. There he is described as a dandy who seeks luxury and amusement wherever he resides, even though he is not dependent on it. He is a master of every situation, even the most awkward, because of his independence from all people and all things. He also knows how to exploit the favor of the powerful, like the tyrant of Syracuse, while at the same time avoiding the danger of becoming obsequious. Characteristic of his relations with other people and things

---

29 For Aristippus, see Döring 1988 and 1998, pp. 246–257; Tsouna 1994, pp. 377–382; and Mann 1996. The surviving testimonies: SSR II A.

30 See Döring 1998, pp. 249–250.

31 See Eucken 1983. The inventory of writings of Antisthenes in Diogenes Laertius contains at least one, perhaps even two writings whose titles contain the name Isocrates. (D.L. VI.15; cf. Patzer 1970, pp. 228–238.)

32 Cf. Zimmermann 1999, pp. 137–138.

is a famous saying he used to describe his relationship with the courtesan Lais: "I possess her, but am not possessed by her" (D.L. II.75 = SSR
IV A 95. 96).

Whether and in what form Aristippus provided a theoretical justification for his way of life is controversial. We cannot definitely answer
this question for two reasons: (1) While there are many detailed reports
about the philosophical views of those who "adhered to the path of
Aristippus and were called Cyrenaics [after his birthplace]" (D.L. II.86),
it is not anywhere stated whether Aristippus himself already advocated
those teachings, or parts of them. (2) A note in Eusebius[33] states that,
while in his remarks and way of life Aristippus gave the impression he
held that human happiness consists solely in pleasure, he did not in fact
explicitly advocate hedonism: this was only done by his grandson with
the same name.

Commentators interpret this evidence in various ways. Most believe
that Aristippus did not himself present a theoretical justification for
his way of life, but only his students did, and most prominently his
grandson with the same name. Yet there are reasons to think that the
teachings ascribed to the Cyrenaics do date back to Aristippus, at least
in their essentials. Since this issue cannot decisively be settled, the
teachings attributed to the Cyrenaics can be at least briefly described.

Sextus Empiricus describes the basis of Cyrenaic teaching thus:[34]
"The Cyrenaics assert that the affections (pathê) are the criteria, and
that they are alone apprehended and are infallible, but of the things that
have caused the affections none is apprehensible or infallible. For, they
say, that we feel whiteness or sweetness is a thing we can state infalli-
bly and incontrovertibly; but that the object productive of the affection
is white or is sweet it is impossible to assert." (trans. R. G. Bury) The
reason we don't recognize this is – so the Cyrenaics argue – primarily
that we have learned to name the affections things arouse in us by certain common words. However, this does not mean that the affections
are the same. Everyone knows only his very own affections. We must
take seriously the idea that the affections individual people have may be
quite different, in virtue of the different structures of their sense organs.
Thus, we can only issue reliable statements about our affections, not
about the nature of things (S. E. M VII 191–198 = SSR IV A 213).

Like their contemporaries, the Cyrenaics explain the genesis of
affections as a mind-body interaction, in which, through the impact
of external objects on someone's body, certain movements or changes

---

33   Eus. *PE* XIV.18.31–32 = SSR IV A 173 + IV B 5.
34   For the epistemology of the Cyrenaics see Döring (1988), pp. 8–32; Tsouna
      1992 and 1998, Brunschwig 1999 and 2001.

(*kinêseis*) occur, which are then transported through the sense organs into the soul, where they register as this or that affection. This is the key to Cyrenaic ethics.[35] If everyone can only be certain of his own affections, then good and bad for him can ultimately only consist in this. Since, when it comes to affections, the good must be the same as the agreeable or the pleasurable (*hêdu*) and the bad must be the same as the disagreeable or the painful, this implies that the good consists in pleasurable affections and the bad consists in painful affections. Consequently, the Cyrenaics regarded the pleasurable as the highest good and the goal of all our actions and the painful as the greatest evil. And because they assumed that we experience soft movements as pleasurable and rough ones as painful, they determined the pleasurable to be soft movements and the painful to be rough movements. Besides these, they recognized a third, intermediate condition, in which one experiences neither of the two movements and hence no pleasure or pain.[36] Because every movement sooner or later must come to a rest, experiences of pleasure can be of different intensity or duration, but are necessarily limited in time. What a Cyrenaic strives for is momentary bodily mediated sensory pleasure; this is the goal of all his actions.[37] Anything else can have only relative value, if any, which is determined by how much it contributes to the sensation of pleasure. The job of reason is to size up the situation and carefully calculate at each moment how we can obtain pleasure and avoid pain. One of the most important lessons is that we must as far as possible avoid all affects that bring with them pain and stand in the way of pleasure. For some affects, this can be accomplished fully. One example is envy, which is based on the illusion that, in order to be happy, we must acquire something that someone else has. For others, the natural ones such as elementary fright, this is not possible (D.L. II.91 = SSR IV A 172). One must guard against these by mental and bodily training.[38] Through this training one may hope to learn the art at which Aristippus himself is said to have excelled: the art not to subject oneself to things, but to subject things to oneself, as the famous admirer of Aristippus, Horace, has formulated it (*Letters* 1.1.19 = SSR IV A 100).

To what extent Socrates' student Aristippus already advocated these teachings is, as mentioned earlier, uncertain. What we do know is that if Aristippus did not teach those things himself, then he at least evoked such teachings by his way of life.

35 Concerning the ethics of Cyrenaics see Tsouna 2002 and O'Keefe 2002.
36 S. E. *M* VII.199. D.L. II.85,86. Eus. *PE* MIV.18.32 = SSR IV A 213. 172. B 5.
37 Ath. XII.544ab. D.L. II,87–88 = SSR IV A 172. 174.
38 Cic. *Tusc. Disp.* III.28–31 D.L. II.91 = SSR IV A 208. 172.

ANTISTHENES[39]

Antisthenes (c. 445–c. 365) was a son of an Athenian and a Thracian. According to some testimonies, he studied with Gorgias, and then taught rhetoric himself. As A. Patzer has shown, however, we may not be able to rely on these testimonies.[40] By his early twenties at the latest, Antisthenes associated with Socrates. From the polemics that Isocrates wrote in his two speeches *Against the Sophists* (written c. 390) and *Helen* (written c. 385) against the Socratics and their teachings, we can conclude with high probability that Antisthenes was the most prominent Socratic in Athens in the first ten to fifteen years after Socrates' death.[41] He taught in the gymnasium Kynosarges. The catalogue of Antisthenes' writings contained in D.L. VI.15–18 reports about sixty titles of works of varied scope. In these works, Antisthenes treats topics in epistemology, logic, ethics, interpretation of Homer, and rhetoric. The only works that have survived are the declamations *Ajax* and *Ulysses*, in which Antisthenes lets both opponents justify their claim to the weapons of the dead Achilles.

In epistemology, Antisthenes was a declared opponent of Plato's.[42] The difference between them is nicely captured in an ancient anecdote. Once, in a debate with Plato, Antisthenes objected: "I see a horse, Plato; what I do not see, however, is horsehood." And Plato replied: "You only have the eye with which one sees a horse. The eye for seeing horsehood you do not have." (Simp. *in Cat.* p. 208,29–32 = SSR V A 149) Plato firmly believed that his hypothesis of the Ideas, as eternal self-identical objects as the target of knowledge, provided the means for establishing definitions. For Antisthenes, this was a serious mistake. Aristotle presents Antisthenes' view in this way: "One cannot define what a thing is (*to ti estin*). However, one can explain what it is like (*poion ti estin*); for instance, one cannot say what silver is, but one can say that it is like tin (*Met.* H 1043b23–28 = SSR V A 150). All that Antisthenes believed possible was to describe the characteristics of things by a process of comparison, and so to attempt to understand their nature at least approximately. How Antisthenes further developed and defended his views, or how he tried to disprove Plato's position, cannot be ascertained with certainty, due to the scarcity of and the disparities between

---

39   For Antisthenes in general, see Patzer 1970; Rankin 1986; Blaise, Cherki et al. 1986; Döring 1998; pp. 268–280; Tsouna 1994, pp. 369–377; Kalouche 1999, and Eucken 2000. The surviving testimonies: SSR V A.

40   Patzer 1970, pp. 246–255.

41   Patzer 1970; pp. 238–246; Eucken 1983; pp. 25–27, 45–47, 101–105.

42   For Antisthenes' epistemology, see Döring 1985, Celluprica 1987, Brancacci 1990, and Giannantoni, SSR IV 365–385.

the surviving evidence. This topic thus remains controversial, and to say much more about it would exceed the scope of this chapter. Let me only say this. When Diogenes Laertius tells us that Antisthenes was the first who defined what a definition is, – that is, "that which indicates what something is or was" (D.L. VI.3 = SSR V A 151) – this does not imply that Antisthenes believed that as a matter of fact there are such definitions. The testimony merely states what, according to Antisthenes, is required of definitions, and what consequently all those who believe they can provide definitions must fulfill. Antisthenes' paradoxical thesis that contradiction is impossible (*ouk estin antilegein*) is correctly located by the ancient tradition in the context of the debate with Plato.[43] What exact role the thesis played in that context is controversial.

Diogenes Laertius describes the heart of Antisthenes' views on ethics by using the following shorthand (VI.11 = SSR V A 134, 3–4). "Virtue is sufficient for happiness, and in addition needs only the strength of Socrates." This formula contains a contradiction when it first describes virtue to be sufficient for happiness, and then adds that one needs the strength of a Socrates for it. What Antisthenes meant must be this: He who lives in accordance with virtue is happy. In order to achieve that goal, however, it is not enough to know what virtue is. What is needed is to realize that knowledge in action, and for this one must have the strength of a Socrates. With this view, Antisthenes both follows and distances himself from Socrates. He agrees with Socrates that ethically good action leads to happiness. He disagrees with Socrates, however, that those who know the good necessarily do the good. He rather thinks that in addition to knowledge of the good, one also needs the strength of a Socrates in order to consistently act on and realize what one regards as good. By "the strength of Socrates" Antisthenes evidently meant Socrates' capacity, so admired by his contemporaries, to maintain the greatest modesty with respect to bodily wants, and to stay completely independent concerning his external reputation. In order to acquire such strength, Antisthenes recommended purposefully seeking out stresses and strains. By doing this, one will become immune against the many unknown and artificially produced desires, and will learn to satisfy the remaining elementary needs such as nutrition, clothing, and dwelling in a most simple manner. One will then not regard that as a deficiency, but rather as an advantage, because it enables one to fully concentrate on living in accordance with virtue and so to reach happiness.

---

43   Aristotle, *Met.* Δ1024b32–34. D.L. III.35, IX.53 = SSR V A 152. 148. 154.

In the *Symposium*, Xenophon lets Antisthenes describe in what ways and how successfully he realized those principles in his own life (4.34–39 = SSR V A 82,3–28).

It is because I think, gentlemen, that people don't keep wealth and poverty in their houses but in their hearts. I see plenty of private citizens who have plenty of money but who are so poor in their own estimation that they undertake any task and any danger provided they can make more by it, and I know of brothers who receive an equal share of the inheritance, and one of them has plenty, more than he spends, while the other is short of everything. I know of some tyrants, too, who are so hungry for money that they do things far worse than the poorest of men do, some turning to theft and some to burglary and some to the slave trade because of their neediness, presumably, and there are some tyrants who destroy whole households and kill the whole family and often enslave whole cities for the sake of money. I really do pity these people; their disease must be so painful. I think they've got the same problem as a man who's got plenty and eats plenty and never gets to be full. I've got so much I can scarcely find it all myself; and yet the net result is that I can eat and reach a point of not being hungry, and I can drink and not be thirsty, and I can clothe myself so that I'm no colder out of doors than millionaire Callias there, and when I'm at home my walls are a warm tunic, my thatch is a thick mantle, and my bedding is so adequate that it's quite a task to rouse me. If ever my body wants sex, my present means are so adequate that because no one else is willing to approach the women I approach they greet me with enthusiasm. All of this seems to me so pleasurable that in each bit of it I wouldn't pray for more pleasure but less: some of it seems so much more pleasurable than is appropriate. (trans. A. J. Bowen)

The catalogue of Antisthenes' writings contains numerous titles clearly indicating that those writings dealt with problems concerning Homer's *Iliad* and *Odyssey* (D.L. VI.17–18). If the surviving testimonies are representative, then what Antisthenes sought to establish was that Homer in his epic presented models of right life and conduct. How Antisthenes argued may be shown by an example. A detailed account has survived of Antisthenes' interpretation of the attribute *polytropos* ascribed to Odysseus in the first verse of the *Odyssey*. *Polytropos* means "much-turned" – that is, much-travelled, or turning many ways, versatile, wily. The sophist Hippias in Plato's *Hippias Minor* argues for the view (365bc) that this attribute is used to characterize Odysseus negatively, declaring that it is to be understood in the sense of deceptive (*pseudês*). Antisthenes objects to this view. He declares that Homer called Odysseus this because he was smart (*sophos*). His argument amounts to this: Homer calls Odysseus *polytropos* because in virtue of his knowledge he knew (1) the multifarious *tropoi* (turns = kinds) of the human character, and (2) the multifarious *tropoi* (turns = forms) of linguistic expression, and hence was capable of using the appropriate form of expression regarding every person (Porph. *Sch. ad Od.* 1,1 = SSR V A 187).

Antisthenes hence interprets the attribute *polytropos* so that it characterizes Odysseus as the perfect speaker. Antisthenes possibly developed the philosophical/rhetorical theory he uses here in his book *On Style or On the Different Sorts of Style*[44] (D.L. VI.15 = SSR V A 41,3). The same theory might help one to find an answer to the question what goal Antisthenes tried to achieve by his two declamations, *Ajax* and *Odysseus*. He probably sought to illustrate his theory with a lively example by contrasting, in the form of a debate, the plain warhorse Ajax with the wise and eloquent Odysseus.

WORKS CITED

Collection of Primary Sources

CPF: *Corpus dei papiri filosofici greci e latini.* Florence, 1989–2002.
Decleva Caizzi, F. *Antisthenis fragmenta.* Mailand and Varese, 1966.
Döring, K. *Die Megariker.* Amsterdam, 1972.
Mannebach, E. *Aristippi et Cyrenaicorum fragmenta.* Leiden and Cologne, 1961.
SSR: Giannantoni, G. ed., *Socratis et Socraticorum Reliquiae.* Collegit, disposuit, apparatibus notisque instruxit, 4 vols. Naples, 1990.

Secondary Sources

Algra, K., J. Barnes, J. Mansfeld, and M. Schofield, eds,. *The Cambridge History of Hellenistic philosophy.* Cambridge, 1999.
Barnes, J. "Socrates the hedonist." In *The Philosophy of Socrates,* ed. K.J. Boudouris. Athens, 1991/92, pp. 22–32.
Blaise, F., Cherki, Ch. et al. "Antisthène: sophistique et cynisme." In *Positions de la sophistique* ed. B. Cassin. Paris, 1986.
Boudouris, K. J., ed. *The Philosophy of Socrates,* 2 vols. Athens, 1991/92.
Brancacci, A. *Oikeios logos. La filosofia del linguaggio di Antistene* Naples, 1990. French edition: *Antisthène. Le discours proper.* Paris, 2005.
Brunschwig, J. "Cyrenaic Epistemology." In *The Cambridge History of Hellenistic Philosophy,* eds. Algra, K., J. Barnes, J. Mansfeld, and M. Schofield. Cambridge, 1999, pp. 251–259.
Brunschwig, J. "La théorie cyrénaïque de la connaissance et le problème de ses rapports avec Socrate." In *Socrate et les Socratiques,* eds. Romeyer Dherby, G., and J.-B. Gourinat Paris, 2001, pp. 459–479.
Celluprica, V. "Antistene: logico o sofista?" *Elenchos* 8 (1987): 285–328.
Clay, D. "The origins of the Socratic dialogue." In *The Socratic Movement,* ed. P. A. Vander Waerdt. Ithaca, 1994, pp. 23–47.
Dittmar, H. *Aischines von Sphettos.* Berlin, 1912.

---

44 The title could also be translated: *On Style or On the Different Characters of Men.* It must remain an open question as to which version of the title Antisthenes intended.

Döring, K. "Der Sokrates des Aischines von Sphettos und die Frage nach dem historischen Sokrates." *Hermes* 112 (1984): 16–30.

Döring, K. "Antisthenes: Sophist oder Sokratiker? " In *Gorgia e la sofistica. Siculorum Gymnasium* XXXVIII 1–2 L, eds. Montoneri and F. Romano. Catania, 1985, pp.229–242.

Döring, K. "Der Sokratesschüler Aristipp und die Kyrenaiker." In *Abhandlungen der Akademie der Wissenschaften und der Literatur Mainz. Geistes – und sozialwissenschaftliche Klasse.* Wiesbaden and Stuttgart, 1988.

Döring, K. "Sokrates, die Sokratiker und die von ihnen begründeten Traditionen." In *Die Philosophie der Antike* 2/1, ed. H. Flashar. Basel, 1998, pp.139–364.

Ehlers, B. *Eine vorplatonische Deutung des sokratischen Eros. Der Dialog Aspasia des Sokratikers Aischines.* Munich, 1966.

Eucken, Ch. *Isokrates. Seine Positionen in der Auseinandersetzung mit den zeitgenössischen Philosophen.* Berlin and New York, 1983.

Eucken, Ch. "Antisthenes." In *Philosophen des Altertums.* eds. M. Erler and A. Graeser Darmstadt, 2000, pp.112–129.

Fritz, K. von "Megariker." In *Realencyclopädie der classischen Altertumswisseschaft* Suppl. 5 (1931): 707–724. Shortened version in K. von Fritz. *Schriften zur griechischen Logik.* Stuttgart, 1978, vol 2, 75–92.

Fritz, K. von "Phaidon von Elis und der 12. und 13. Sokratikerbrief." *Philologus* 90 (1930): 240–244., repr. in K. von Fritz. *Schriften zur griechischen Logik.* Stuttgart,1978, vol.2, 171–174.

Giannantoni, G. "L'*Alcibiade* di Eschine e la letteratura socratica su Alcibiade." In *Lezioni Socratiche*, eds. Giannantoni and Narcy. Naples, 1997, pp.349–373.

Giannantoni, G., and M. Narcy eds. *Lezioni Socratiche.* Naples, 1997.

Headlam, W., and A. D. Knox *Herodas: The mimes and fragments.* Cambridge, 1922., repr. New York, 1979.

Heitsch, E. "Dialoge Platons vor 399 v. Chr.?" In *Nachrichten der Akademie der Wissenschaften zu Göttingen* I, Philologisch-Historische Klasse. Göttingen, 2002, pp. 303–345.

Heitsch, E., trans. and commentary. *Platon: Apologie des Sokrates.* Göttingen, 2002.

Kahn, C. H. "Aeschines on Socratic eros." In *The Socratic Movement*, ed. P.A. Vander Waerdt. Ithaca, 1994.

Kahn, C. H. *Plato and the Socratic dialogue.* Cambridge, 1996, pp.87–106

Kalouche, F. "Antisthenes' ethics and theory of language." *Revue de Philosophie Ancienne* 17 (1999): 11–41.

Long, A. A. "Aristippus and Cyrenaic hedonism." In *The Cambridge History of Hellenistic Philosophy*, eds. Algra, K., J. Barnes, J. Mansfeld, and M. Schofield. Cambridge, 1999, pp. 632–639.

Mann, W. -R. "The life of Aristippus." *Archiv für Geschichte der Philosophie* 78 (1996): 97–119.

O'Keefe, T. "The Cyrenaics on pleasure, happiness, and future-concern." *Phronesis* 47 (2002): 395–416.

Patzer, A. *Antisthenes der Sokratiker*, dissertation. Heidelberg, 1970.

Rankin, H. D. *Antisthenes Sokratikos* Amsterdam, 1986.

Romeyer Dherby, G., and J.-B. Gourinat eds. *Socrate et les Socratiques.* Paris, 2001.

Rossetti, L. "Ricerche sui ‚dialoghi socratici' di Fedone e di Euclide." *Hermes* 108 (1980): 183–200.

Rossetti, L. *"Logoi Sokratikoi* anteriori al 399 a. C." In *Logos e logoi.* ed. L. Rosetti. Naples, 1991, pp.21–40.

Rossetti, L. "Le dialogue socratique in statu nascendi." *Philosophie Antique* 1 (2001): 11–35.

Spinelli, E. "P. Köln 205: Il 'Socrate' di Egesia?" *Zeitschrift für Papyrologie und Epigraphik* 91 (1992): 10–14.

Thompson, D. B. "The house of Simon the shoemaker." *Archaeology* 13 (1960): 234–240.

Tsouna McKirahan, V. "The Cyrenaic theory of knowledge." *OSAP* 10 (1992): 161–192.

Tsouna McKirahan, V. "The Socratic origins of the Cynics and the Cyrenaics." In *The Socratic movement,* ed. P.A.Vander Waerdt. Ithaca, 1994, pp. 367–391.

Tsouna, V. *The epistemology of the Cyrenaic school.* Cambridge, 1998.

Tsouna V. "Is there an exception to Greek eudaemonism?" In *Le style de la pensée: Recueil de textes en hommage à Jacques Brunschwig,* eds. M. Canto-Sperber, and P. Pellegrin. Paris, 2002, pp. 464–498.

Vander Waerdt, P. A., ed. *The Socratic Movement.* Ithaca, 1994.

Zimmermann, K. *Libyen. Das Land südlich des Mittelmeers im Weltbild der Griechen.* Munich, 1999.

3   Xenophon and the Enviable Life of Socrates

Socrates had the amazing good fortune of having Plato, one of the great literary figures of the West, to tell his story. Xenophon the Athenian (c. 425–354 BCE) is not Plato's equal, but his substantial writings about Socrates are second only to Plato's for our knowledge of Socrates.

A most unusual man, Xenophon was as capable of leading hard men as he was of writing subtle books. As an adolescent, he knew Socrates, who was then nearing sixty, though it isn't clear that he was among Socrates' more devoted companions. While still in his mid-twenties, Xenophon was thrust into the command of a desperate troop of Greek mercenaries, stranded 1,000 miles from home before the gates of Babylon. Xenophon proved to be a charismatic and successful military leader. After many adventures, he led this famous band, known as "The Ten Thousand," back home to Greece.

Exiled from Athens because of his Spartan connections, Xenophon in later life was a striking innovator in prose literary forms. His writings about Socrates, about one-sixth of his complete works, include two shorter pieces, the *Symposium* and the *Apology of Socrates*, that appear to recast Plato's works by the same titles.[1] The *Oeconomicus* ("The Artful Estate Holder") is a reflection on wealth and virtue, set mostly as a conversation between Socrates and a wealthy gentleman. His longest Socratic work, known as the *Memorabilia* ("Memoirs of Socrates"), tells of a wide variety of Socrates' conversations and actions, with a special emphasis on the good influence Socrates had on his friends in both word and deed. His other major works are focused on political and

My thanks to Alexander Duff, Matthew Holbreich, Debra Nails, C. D. C. Reeve, and especially Donald Morrison for their comments on this chapter. I gratefully acknowledge the support of this work by a special leave sponsored by the Dean's Office of the College of Arts and Letters at the University of Notre Dame. Unless otherwise credited, all translations are my own.

1   Most readers of the Socratic writings of Plato and Xenophon find more compelling those interpretations that read Xenophon as recasting Plato rather than the other way around. But we have no direct confirmation that Xenophon worked this way.

military affairs. His *Hellenica* ("Affairs in Greece") is a political history of the half-century after Sparta defeated Athens in the Peloponnesian War. He also wrote an account of his own youthful military exploits in Asia Minor, the *Anabasis* (which means "The Ascent," an expedition from the coast to the interior). His most extensive theoretical work is the *Cyropaedia* ("The Education of Cyrus"), Xenophon's fictionalized account of Cyrus the Great, founder of the Persian Empire.

For 2,000 years, from Cicero to Rousseau, distinguished readers held Xenophon in very high esteem. His reputation collapsed in the nineteenth century, and it has never really been recuperated, despite the efforts of a persistent minority of scholars.[2] This is an essay in persistence. Perhaps Xenophon's literary accomplishment and the quality of his mind can best be compared to Machiavelli. Machiavelli owed a special debt to Xenophon, and he was far more deeply engaged with him than with Plato and Aristotle combined.[3]

Socrates does not dominate Xenophon's writings the way he does Plato's. Xenophon sees Socrates within a horizon that is, of course, philosophically much narrower than Plato's. But Xenophon's horizon is in another way broader than Plato's. Xenophon is more open to the ways that politically ambitious men see their own aspirations. Plato is rather quick to moralize, to criticize politics and its attractions.[4] It is useful to look at Xenophon to compare him to Plato,[5] but this perspective can diminish or distort Xenophon's own achievement. Xenophon is more interested in what makes politics and political leaders work, and in improving politics in ways that politicians can actually find credible. When Alexander the Great conquered the Persian Empire, half a century

---

2   For an extended account of the collapse of Xenophon's reputation, and an answer to many of the charges made against him, see Dorion and Bandini 2000, pp. vii-cxviii. See also Dorion's contribution to this volume, Chapter 1. Pomeroy 1994, pp. 22–26, gives a useful brief overview of the history of the scholarship. The influential dismissal of Xenophon's intellectual importance in Vlastos 1971 has been vigorously answered by Morrison 1987. I share the view of Vander Waerdt 1994, p. 11, n.34, that the response to Morrison's criticisms in Vlastos 1991, pp. 99–106, "tends to be selective and unsympathetic."

3   The importance of Xenophon for Machiavelli was made especially prominent in Leo Strauss 1991 [1948], pp. 24–25; see also Strauss 1989, p. 147. For a more recent account along these Straussian lines, see Nadon 2001.

4   Wood 1964, pp. 41–51, is an excellent discussion of how Xenophon's appreciation of military leadership leads to systematic differences between his account of politics and those of Plato and Aristotle.

5   For a compact account emphasizing the differences between Plato and Xenophon, unusually sympathetic to Xenophon, see Dorion 2006. For a compact account emphasizing the similarities, see Pomeroy 1994, pp. 26–29.

after Xenophon had exposed its military weaknesses, he carried with him as a kind of handbook Xenophon's account of his own campaign against the Persians, the *Anabasis*. Whatever good the reading of Plato's *Republic* may do for an aspiring political leader, it will not do the same good as reading Xenophon's major works on political leadership.

Xenophon understood Socrates' life as exemplary, but he did not see it as the only exemplary life. In particular, he always considered lives of political leadership as alternatives to the Socratic life.[6] At their best, suggests Xenophon, such political lives are not obviously inferior to the Socratic life. Xenophon compares these ways of life by focusing on the tension between achieving self-sufficiency and avoiding envy. It may be fair to say that this tension is his central preoccupation. Great achievement, Xenophon believed, brings with it the risk of great envy, and this risk is one of the fundamental challenges to a successful life.

With this theme, Xenophon was continuing an old tradition in Greek wisdom literature. One stock topic of this wisdom literature is the comparison between an idealized sage and an idealized political ruler or king. In the centrality of this theme, and in his treatment of it through historical anecdotes focused on both Greeks and Persians, Xenophon is more akin to Herodotus than to any other classical author, including Plato.[7] Xenophon organizes his contribution to this tradition around two themes. The first is his analysis of benefaction and patronage. Xenophon sees benefaction as the preferred way to exercise power while minimizing envy. The second theme is his meditation on the limitation of human self-sufficiency by the divine. This essentially tragic theme explains Xenophon's special interest in divination. Xenophon's general strategy is to show the life of Socrates, his ideal sage, as a more intensive accomplishment of self-sufficiency than any merely political life, even the life of an ideal king such as Cyrus the Great. In this respect, the Socratic life seems to exceed the political life. But the intensity of Socrates' self-sufficiency exposes the Socratic life to destructive envy, a force that Xenophon's best political life is designed to control. Only Socrates' peculiar intimacy with the art of divination can make this exposure an acceptable risk.

6   This point is emphasized in Pangle 1994, pp. 127–128.
7   See especially Herodotus 1.32, where Solon warns Croesus of the threat of divine envy to happiness, especially in a public life. For an account of this aspect of Xenophon's writing that packs much insight into few pages, see Gray 1989, especially pp. 3–6 and 178–182. Hermann 1987 brings out very well the analytic similarities between Herodotus and Xenophon, with a particular focus on the politics of gift-exchange and benefaction, though Socrates does not figure in his project.

BENEFACTION AND POLITICAL POWER

Xenophon stages the purest form of a conversation between a sage and a political leader neither in his Socratic writings nor in his historical works, but in the short dialogue titled *Hiero*, a conversation between Simonides, the Athenian poet, and Hiero, tyrant of Syracuse.[8] The pivotal place of envy in this dialogue brings into focus the distinctiveness of Socrates' enviable life.

Once upon a time, Simonides visited Hiero in Syracuse. The poet asked the tyrant to compare the private life to the tyrant's life with regard to their pleasures and pains (*Hiero* I.1). Hiero tries to convince Simonides that the tyrant's life has no advantages, and many disadvantages. The tyrant's life is particularly burdened, complains Hiero, by failures of trust. Simonides scoffs at Hiero's complaints. For example, surely tyrants receive many praises and honors. Simonides would know about this, since he was made famous, not to mention rich, by writing such praises, especially in victory odes for wealthy clients, among whom was Hiero himself. The poet even says that honor is "nearer the divine" than any other human pleasure (*Hiero* VII.4). But the tyrant, retorts Hiero, cannot trust the honor and praise he hears. True honor, he says, comes

> when people think a man is a capable benefactor, and believe they enjoy good things from him, ... and crown him because of his public virtue and benefaction. ... I deem him blessed who is so honored. For I perceive that ... without fear, without being envied, without danger, with happiness, he passes his life. (*Hiero* VII.9–10)

For similar reasons, the tyrant cannot have satisfying erotic relationships. "The private person has direct proof," says Hiero, "whenever his beloved does something to please him, that the beloved gratifies him out of love, since he knows that the favor wasn't forced. But the tyrant can never trust that he is loved, since we know that people who do something for us out of fear try to make themselves look like they are pleasing us as lovers" (*Hiero* I.37).

---

8   In the introduction to the second Platonic Letter (*Letter* II.310e-311a), the author mentions Simonides and Hiero as one illustration of the relationship between wisdom and power, and correctly predicts that Plato's own anxious relationship with Dionysus, tyrant of Syracuse, will go down in history as another exemplary case. (Many scholars dispute whether this Letter was actually written by Plato, but it is certainly interesting evidence of an ancient Greek view of the topic.) The Letter also lists famous conversations between other pairs of wise men and rulers that are mentioned in Plato and especially in Herodotus. See Gray 1986, pp. 119–122.

Hiero's despairing portrait of the unhappy tyrant –Hiero had gone as far as to say that the tyrant might profit from hanging himself (*Hiero* VII.13) –prompts Simonides to give him advice about how to manage his affairs better. The poet, though, sees the issue in exactly the same terms as the tyrant himself. The dialogue concludes with this guarantee from Simonides:

Strive to conquer everyone with benefaction. For if you control your friends with benefaction, your opponents will be unable to stand against you. And if you do all these things, know well that you will possess the finest and most blessed of all the possessions of human beings: you will be happy without being envied. (*Hiero* XI.14–15)

Power and preeminence will, Simonides concedes, attract envy. Hiero is right to see this as the central threat to his happiness. But, the poet suggests, the intelligent political leader can use his power to control others without their resenting him. The key is to "conquer" them with kindness, or more precisely to put them in his debt with benefaction. By manipulating public benefits and patronage, the prudent tyrant will cloak the iron fist of his power in the velvet glove of his favors. Even the tyrant's mercenary bodyguard, which he needs to keep the citizens cowed, can be made acceptable. Simonides suggests that Hiero use his foreign mercenaries as a police force against the citizens' slaves. Help the citizens to play the master in their homes, and they will be more accepting of your mastery in the city (*Hiero* X.4).

The manipulation of patronage and benefaction that Simonides recommended to Hiero is practiced to perfection by Xenophon's ideal king, Cyrus the Great. Xenophon presents mastery through benefaction as the key to Cyrus's rise to power. "Wouldn't we show ourselves to be noble by immediately trying to conquer our benefactors with our own benefactions?" he asks his officers, explaining his own approach to distributing the spoils of a victory (*Cyrop.* V.3.2). It is, of course, the same principle that Simonides recommended to Hiero. It will also be a central part of Socrates' life. Xenophon presents Socrates as an alternative realization of the cultural ideals embodied in the perfect king or the idealized tyrant.

Cyrus's gradual take-over of power from his uncle Cyaxares reveals the competitive or antagonistic aspect of benefaction. Cyrus does not usurp the throne simply by attacking Cyaxares. Instead, he establishes his dominance over him by doing Cyaxares favors that Cyaxares is in no position to reciprocate. This comes to a head when Cyrus "borrows" some of his uncle's troops without telling him, and returns with a brilliant success from a daring raid. Cyaxares burst into tears of anger at Cyrus's triumphant return, and he accuses Cyrus of treating him unjustly. "That you think I've done you an injustice," replied Cyrus, "I find hard to bear. How, by trying to do as much good as I can for my friends, could I instead be thought to have accomplished the very opposite?" Cyaxares' reply shows he is beginning to understand how Cyrus is manipulating the soft power of benefaction: "Cyrus, I don't know how anyone could say that the things you've done are *bad*. But surely it's exactly these *good* things that are a heavier burden on me the more of them there are. ... Since I did not share in accomplishing these good results, I am left to accept them like a woman, as your benefactions. To everyone, especially my subjects, you'll look to be the real man, while I appear unworthy to rule" (*Cyrop.* V.5.12, 25, 33–34). Cyaxares' difficulty finding the right way to complain about Cyrus shows how powerful a tool of domination benefaction can be. Even when Cyrus provokes a restless dissatisfaction in others, he is more likely to move them toward emulation and rivalry than to destructive envy.

While Xenophon developed a more extensive analysis of benefaction and power than any other ancient writer, the theme is hardly limited to him. Thucydides, for example, makes clear the veiled threat behind expectations of gratitude in the famous Funeral Oration of Athens' greatest statesman, Pericles:

In our virtue, we Athenians are different from most. For we obtain our friends not by receiving benefits, but by doing them. The doer of the favor forms a more secure attachment, because through continued aid he keeps the other in his debt. The one who owes is less keen, knowing that when he reciprocates it will not be a favor, but merely a repayment for the other's virtue. (Thucydides, *History of the Peloponnesian War*, II.40.4)

Do not be fooled by Pericles' gentle talk of "friends," nor his mild complaints about their "less keen" gratitude. He is talking about the subordinate allies in Athens' empire, and warning them that if they don't do what Athens wants, they will be punished as ingrates.

Aristotle is full of passages that reflect the issues of benefaction. Indeed, he appears to have had this very passage from Thucydides in mind in his own discussions of goodwill and benefaction (*EN* IX.5 and IX.7). The dynamics of competitive benefaction are also at play in his account of noble self-love, where he analyzes the friendly rivalry among ambitious men to do more good than others (*EN* IX.8). He gives a particularly clear statement of the connection between benefaction and domination in his discussion of magnanimity:

The magnanimous man is the sort to be a benefactor, though he is ashamed to be a beneficiary, since superiority belongs to the first, but subordination to the second. He also reciprocates more benefits than he receives, so that the one repaid will both owe him something and be the receiver [rather than the agent] of benefaction. Magnanimous men seem to remember the benefits they confer, but not the ones they receive, since the one who receives a benefit is subordinate to the one who confers it, and the magnanimous man wants to be superior. (*EN* IV.3.1124b9–14, 17–18)

Aristotle's magnanimous man is so intent on being a benefactor that he appears to be a bit of an ingrate when he has been a beneficiary.[9]

BENEFACTION AND SOCRATIC FREEDOM

Xenophon makes it clear that intense political ambition character- ized some of Socrates' most prominent admirers. This was especially the case with a pair of notorious admirers, Critias and Alcibiades, who became the greediest, most outrageous, most violent men in Athens

---

9   Aristotle's analysis of the dynamics of benefaction (in Greek, *euergesia*, or the verbal phrase *eu poiein*) had a decisive influence on modern anthropologi- cal theory about so-called "gift-exchange" economies. This influence is espe- cially prominent in the tradition that originates in the classic essay of Marcel Mauss, *The Gift* [1924; Cunnison trans. 1954]. For example, when describing how gift exchange in the Trobriand Islands shows "one's freedom and auton- omy as well as one's magnanimity," Mauss comments, "This morality [of gift- exchange] is comparable with the fine paragraphs of the *Nicomachean Ethics* [IV.1–2] on *megaloprepeia* [magnificence in expenditure] and *eleutheriotes* [liberality in expenditure]" (21n.24). Mauss also emphasized the very prin- ciple of control that Xenophon's Cyrus pursued through benefaction: "The prestige of an individual [is] closely bound up with expenditure, and with the duty of returning with interest gifts received in such a way that *the creditor becomes the debtor.* ... The principles of rivalry and antagonism are basic" (35, emphasis added).The distinguished classical scholar Paul Veyne was fol- lowing in Mauss's footsteps (as pointed out by Oswyn Murray in his introduc- tion to Veyne 1990 [1976], pp. xv-xvi) in his influential analysis of benefaction (which he calls "euergetism") in the ancient world. Veyne gives an extended account of the very passage from Aristotle on magnificence and liberality referred to by Mauss (pp. 14–18). Veyne also sees (pp. 71–72) that Socrates focuses on the necessity for a public man to spend "magnificently" and to be a "benefactor" in his advice to Critoboulos: Xenophon, *Oeconomicus* II.4–6.
    The most influential modern ethical theories in Anglophone philosophy, whether Kantian, utilitarian, or the newer theories of "virtue ethics," are ill designed to capture this subtle morality of benefaction, gratitude, and envy. (Approaches to ethics that are heirs to Hegel and Nietzsche fare bet- ter.) Gratitude in these modern theories is reduced to something close to mere etiquette, like sending thank-you notes for wedding gifts, and loses the centrality and the sometimes oppressive moral weight identified by Thucydides, Xenophon, and Aristotle. Thus it is easy for modern readers to overlook the moral depth of the ancient analyses. Perhaps this blindness has something to do with Xenophon's fall into disrepute during the 200 years such ethical theories have been regnant.

(*Mem.* I.2.12).[10] How could such men ever have found Socrates attractive? The key is that they saw in Socrates something they wanted to emulate, or at least appropriate. Critias and Alcibiades wanted "to do everything for themselves and become more famous than anyone." They associated with Socrates because they saw in Socrates' apolitical self-sufficiency, self-control, and power in speech an image of the political capacity for speech and action to which they aspired (*Mem.* I.2.14–15).

That Socrates attracted the emulative energies of two such notorious men raised suspicions that he pandered to undemocratic political ambitions (*Mem.* I.2.9). Xenophon did not attack this suspicion as directly and thoroughly as one might expect. He does provide a detailed account of how Socrates tried to chasten Critias (*Mem.* I.2.29–37), but no examples at all of any chastening of Alcibiades. Since Socrates emphatically treats Critias and Alcibiades as a pair, this difference is striking. On the contrary, Xenophon reports a conversation that does not put Socrates' influence in a very good light, between the teenaged Alcibiades and the statesman Pericles, who was one of his legal guardians (*Mem.* I.2.39–46). This conversation seems to illustrate the sort of influence Plato's Socrates himself says he has on "the young men who have the most leisure and wealth": they "enjoy hearing people questioned, and often imitate me by trying to question others" (Plato, *Apol.* 23c).[11] Using dialectical skills that certainly appear to be imitating Socrates, Alcibiades quizzes Pericles about the nature of law, and concludes by questioning the legitimacy of the laws of the democracy. Xenophon reports this suspicious conversation as evidence of Alcibiades' early and enduring political ambition. But it also leaves the impression that Alcibiades' ambition was fed by a skill in speech he picked up from Socrates.[12]

10   Xenophon emphasizes that he considers Critias and Alcibiades a pair grammatically, by using the dual forms throughout this section.

11   There has been a lively scholarly debate about how Xenophon understood Socrates' dialectical questioning, with particular interest focused on how different his picture is from Plato's. A central issue is whether dialectical refutation (in Greek, *elenchus*) was understood by Socrates, Plato, or Xenophon to be merely destructive of false opinion, or constructive of true belief. To address this topic would require a detailed comparison between texts of Plato and Xenophon beyond the scope of this chapter. For orientation to the debates, see Benson's contribution to this volume, Chapter 8; Carpenter and Polansky 2002 and Brickhouse and Smith 2002, who are skeptical that a general account can be given of Socrates' dialectical method in Plato; and Morrison 1994 and Dorion 2000, pp. cviii-clxxxii, who give compelling accounts of the place of dialectic refutation in Xenophon's Socratic writings, with a special emphasis on the conversations between Socrates and Euthydemus in *Memorabilia* IV.

12   Morrison 1994, pp. 181–182; Gray 1998, pp. 50–51; and Johnson 2003, pp. 277–279 all portray Alcibiades in this passage as misusing Socratic

Xenophon also allows the reader to see that Socrates offered some sort of praise for kingship, a position that someone with Alcibiades' ambitions might find hard to distinguish from a defense of tyranny. Socrates, it was charged, "selected passages from famous poets ... to use as evidence in teaching his associates to be unscrupulous and tyrannical" (*Mem.* I.2.56). Xenophon quotes from one of these passages at some length (*Iliad* II.188–206). It is a speech by Odysseus, encouraging the nobles to obey their king Agamemnon, and chastising the common people for their lack of deference. Odysseus caps his speech with a line that would have fit well with the ambition "to do everything for themselves" that characterized Critias and Alcibiades: "Lordship for many is no good thing. Let there be one ruler, one king." If, as Xenophon concedes, Socrates regularly quoted from this passage, it is not surprising that some of his admirers looked for a political interpretation, or perhaps we should say a political appropriation, of his self-sufficiency.

Xenophon emphasizes this political appropriation rather more than Plato does. This difference of emphasis shows up immediately in a memorable story that each reports in his *Apology*. At his trial, Socrates claimed that a friend of his, Chaerephon, consulted the Delphic Oracle about Socrates. In both versions, the oracle makes a pronouncement on Socrates' distinctive virtue. But in Plato's version, the oracle says only that no one is wiser than Socrates. In Xenophon's version, the oracle says Socrates is of human beings the most free, most just, and most sane (Plato, *Apology* 20e-21a; Xenophon, *Apology* 14). To be sure, Plato's version of Socrates' wisdom makes ample room for his freedom and justice, as Xenophon's version of his freedom makes room for his wisdom. But it is more immediately obvious why Socrates' superlative freedom would be politically attractive than why his wisdom would be.

dialectical skills, especially by contrast to Socrates' own use of these skills elsewhere, especially with Euthydemus in *Memorabilia* IV. I think they protest too much on this point. Xenophon creates a sharp contrast between Socrates' chastening of Critias and his silence toward Alcibiades. When Xenophon does show Socrates' dialectical skill at its most constructive with Euthydemus, I believe the reader is invited to notice a difference from Socrates' relationship with Alcibiades. In Plato's *Symposium* (222b), Alcibiades names Euthydemus as, like himself, a lover of Socrates; and the conversation between Socrates and Alcibiades in Plato's *Alcibiades I* appears to have been the model for much of the Euthydemus conversation in *Memorabilia* IV. (For a compact, effective argument for the connection between *Alcibiades I* and *Memorabilia* IV, see the introduction to Denyer 2001.) If one accepts these intertextual references, Xenophon's relative silence, compared with Plato, about Socrates, chastening Alcibiades becomes especially provocative. See Johnson 2005, pp. 46–48.

Xenophon's Socrates seems to understand freedom, on which he puts a very high value, to involve two rather different disciplines. To be free, one must control one's desires. This is the ascetic aspect of freedom. But he pairs this ascetic freedom from desire with the freedom one maintains by being owed gratitude by others while owing others nothing. This we might call the exchange aspect of freedom. Like Cyrus, and like the Athenian Empire, Socrates stands at the head of a chain of benefaction relationships.[13] Socrates, it turns out, is as much a master of the strategy of control through benefaction as is Cyrus. Xenophon presents this perhaps surprising aspect of Socratic self-sufficiency as a part of Socrates' superlative freedom.

When Socrates interprets the oracle, he boasts that he is the freest man in Athens. He mentions how he avoids "slavery" to desires, but he also emphasizes his exchange freedom:

Whom do you know who is less a slave to the desires of the body? And what human being is more free than he who takes neither gifts nor pay from anyone? ... Many citizens who aim at virtue, as well as foreigners from everywhere, choose to associate with me. Why is it, even though everyone knows I don't have any money at all to reciprocate a gift, that many people still desire to give me gifts? How can it be that not a single person expects a return benefaction from me, but many acknowledge owing me a debt of gratitude? (Xenophon, *Apol.* 15–17)

We see here, too, how Xenophon understood Socrates' refusal to take money for teaching. By "taking neither gifts nor pay from anyone," Socrates maintained his position at the head of the benefaction chain. "He held that by refraining from taking money he was watching out for his freedom, and called those who took pay for their company 'enslavers of themselves,' since they had to converse with anyone who paid" (*Mem.* I.2.6). He scoffed at those who took money for teaching precisely because they did not appreciate the far greater benefit they would derive from a gift-exchange relationship, between a benefactor and a beneficiary, than from a market relationship. "Do they not believe the greatest profit is simply to obtain a good friend," said Socrates, "or do they fear that one

---

13   For a different account of benefaction in Xenophon's *Apology*, see Vander Waerdt 1993. Following a lead from Strauss 1989, pp. 130 and 138, Vander Waerdt argues that Socrates' universal benevolence is a translegal form of justice, and so brings Socrates into at least potential conflict with his city. This approach tends to obscure the potential of benefaction to be an instrument of domination, and makes it harder to see in Socrates' exemplary benefaction something of particular interest to the politically ambitious. Pangle 1994, pp. 147–150, focuses on Cyrus as an alternative to Socrates, and sees the importance of gratitude to Cyrus.

who has become truly virtuous might not have the greatest gratitude to the one who has done him the greatest benefactions?" (*Mem.* I.2.7).

The ascetic and exchange aspects of Socrates' superlative freedom are also linked to his abject poverty. He is indifferent to money because his desires are so controlled; this is his ascetic freedom applied to wealth. And because he refuses to accept gifts, not to mention outright pay, he remains in control of the people he benefits, his exchange freedom. Socrates' companions are burdened with a gift that cannot be repaid. It is just the situation Aristotle mentions when he says, "The worth of our associates in philosophy cannot be measured in money, and no honor would be of equivalent weight. But perhaps it is enough, as with gods and parents, to do what we can" (*EN* IX.1.1164b2–6). Socrates is to his grateful friends what gods and parents are to their offspring: his friends are his creatures.

A distorted, political image of Socrates' freedom, including his exchange freedom, centered in benefaction and its soft power, is what attracted Alcibiades and Critias. But they were incapable of the ascetic discipline of Socratic freedom. The attraction these men felt for power had too much of an admixture of licentious desire. The true king needs a rigorous self-control, a type of asceticism, that distinguishes him from the tyrant. In this crucial respect, even a new, improved Hiero, enlightened by a Simonides, would fall short of being a political Socrates.

The deficiency of Hiero's enlightened tyranny is brought out by the asceticism of Xenophon's Cyrus. From his youth, Cyrus disliked the loss of control that came with sensual indulgence (*Cyrop.* I.3.11). He taught his troops to control their own desires for food and drink while on campaign, and his own practice gave them an example of this restraint (see especially *Cyrop.* IV.2.38–45). Once he had succeeded in securing the empire he sought, he urged his troops to maintain that empire by preserving all the discipline they embraced in order to conquer it, as he himself gave the example (*Cyrop.* VII.5.77–78, VIII.1.30–32). Cyrus constantly urges asceticism on himself and others primarily for its political usefulness.

But Socrates lived an essentially private life, not one of political engagement, a point stressed by Xenophon. (Stressed by Plato, too, for example, in Callicles' speech in the *Gorgias* (484c-486c) and in Socrates' own description of his life in the *Apology* (23b and 31c) and *Republic* (VI.496a-497a).) Cyrus' political argument for asceticism cannot explain what sort of ascetic Socrates was himself. An especially revealing consideration of these two types of asceticism comes in an exchange that Xenophon reports between Socrates and one of his admirers, Aristippus. (For Aristippus, see Döring in Chapter 2 in this volume.) Now, Aristippus was the opposite of a politically ambitious man. He thought political involvement a waste of one's freedom. And so he defended a radically apolitical way of life, devoted to a special kind of hedonism. To be free, he said, "I do not close myself in to any political community. I am everywhere an alien" (*Mem.* II.1.13). His alienation made possible his hedonism; he did not need to keep his nose to the grindstone as a man like Cyrus did. In this escape from political entanglements, he probably thought he was imitating the privacy of Socrates' own life. So it is surprising and a bit comical to see Socrates pressing on Aristippus an argument for asceticism, based precisely on its necessity for a political ruler. Aristippus happily concedes that *if* a man is interested in political rule, he cannot allow himself the sort of freedom Aristippus values. But Aristippus is not such a man, since he resists the notion that political leadership is anything to strive for. In exasperation when Socrates continues to push the point, he exclaims, "Socrates, you seem to hold that happiness is nothing but the art of kingship!" (*Mem.* II.1.17).

We might sympathize with Aristippus, who is so obviously an unreceptive candidate for this particular conversation. The tenor of Socrates' argument here for asceticism depends on an undefended assumption about the intrinsic attractions of the kingly life. But the point of this conversation becomes clearer when we see that it was not directed solely, and perhaps not even primarily, at apolitical Aristippus himself.[14] Xenophon introduces the conversation (*Mem.* II.1.1) by reporting that Socrates noticed that one of his companions was "rather licentious," and the conversation with Aristippus is meant to benefit this companion. This companion, we may expect, accepted Socrates' undefended assumption about the value of the political life. By exposing the radically apolitical assumption behind Aristippus's hedonism, Socrates is able, with gentle indirection, to provoke his more politically ambitious companions to develop habits of self-control that would have pleased Cyrus himself. But of course such politically motivated self-control is not the same as Socrates' own asceticism. Aristippus is in one respect more like Socrates than the unnamed companion must be, because his goals are more private. But in another respect, the political companion is more Socratic, since there is some continuity between what attracts him to asceticism and what attracts Socrates to it. Aristippus's utter rejection of politics is a partial imitation of Socrates' freedom, but so

14 Xenophon shows Socrates having a conversation with one person for the benefit of someone else in the audience several times. In particular, when in a later conversation Aristippus tries to get back at Socrates by refuting him just as he has been refuted, Xenophon says that Socrates answered, not with a view simply to defending himself, but with the intention of being useful to those present (*Mem.* III.8.1).

is the politically obsessed appropriation of Socrates' self-sufficiency attempted by men of the ilk of Alcibiades and Critias. Xenophon's true Socrates, the whole Socrates, inspires both types of passionate partiality, but is captured by neither.[15]

SOCRATES' EROTIC INTENSITY

Socrates, ideal sage, and Cyrus, ideal king, are both monsters of benefaction. A politically ambitious man, we can now understand, would see something well worth imitating in Socratic self-sufficiency. But Xenophon reveals a crucial distinction between Socrates and the king. Socrates' benefactions take place in an erotic context, where the subordination of his beneficiaries is deeper than in the political context, and indeed would be considered abject enslavement outside an erotic relationship. Socrates intensifies the domination that is produced when one "conquers one's friends with benefaction." This eroticized intensity also runs a much greater risk of provoking envy than its political imitation.

Xenophon focuses on Socrates' erotic intensity in some sharp banter he records with Antiphon the Sophist. Antiphon attacked Socrates and tried to attract away some of his companions. He jeered at Socrates for not accepting money. "At least you're being fair, Socrates," he said, "when you charge for your teaching at a price that fits its value: nothing!" Socrates' response goes to the heart of his own relationships:

Among us, it is held that the bloom of youth and the flower of wisdom are offered on like terms, whether in a beautiful or an ugly way. If you sell youth's bloom for money to whoever is willing to pay, they will call you a whore. But if you see someone truly virtuous is in love with you, and make him your friend, we hold that you are temperate and prudent. Likewise, those who sell the flower of wisdom to whoever is willing to pay are called sophists, just like whores. (*Mem.* I.6.13)

Here Socrates analyzes his own exchange freedom in extremely harsh language. Hard as it may be for those who "converse with anyone who pays" to hear Socrates say they are "enslaving themselves" (*Mem.* I.2.6), it is surely worse to be told they are prostituting themselves.

---

15 For a fuller discussion of Aristippus and Alcibiades as partial imitations of Socrates' self-sufficiency, see O'Connor 1994, pp. 155–163. The issues surrounding the difference between philosophical privacy rooted in hedonism and Socratic privacy are at the heart of Strauss 1991, especially in the "Restatement" pp. 177–212, in response to Alexandre Kojeve's criticism in "Tyranny and Wisdom" pp. 135–176.

How did Socrates maintain such erotic relationships without becoming debauched? Xenophon tells us he had both natural and preternatural supports. First, Socrates educated his body and soul in a regimen that allowed him to live as "boldly and securely" as one can "without some divine intervention" (*Mem.* I.3.5). Second, Socrates did in fact have "divine intervention" in addition to this regimen, in the form of the famous "divine sign" that came to him. Socrates playfully expressed these two aspects of the bold security of his erotic life, one divine, one human, by comparing himself to Odysseus. When the temptress Circe enchanted all his men and turned them to swine, Odysseus escaped, "partly through the warning of Hermes, partly through his own self-control" (*Mem.* I.3.7). It is worth remembering that Odysseus did not flee from Circe's erotic pleasures. He managed to sleep with the beautiful goddess for a year without any ill effects.

Socrates' unusual self-control seems to have been especially remarkable with regard to erotic desire. He had trained himself so that he could have an erotic life that would have been foolishly risky for his companions. To them, because they were not "secure" in their desires, he recommended great caution. But he himself, says Xenophon, "was evidently so well prepared that he could as easily hold back from the most beautiful and youthful erotic objects as others can from the ugliest and most over-the-hill" (*Mem.* I.3.14). Unlike his companions, he could run the risk of beauty with impunity, and did not heed the cautionary advice he gave to others.

Xenophon gives a charming illustration of Socrates' security in erotic matters in a conversation with a famous courtesan, Theodote. (Xenophon emphasizes Theodote's name, which means "divine gift.") Theodote "consorted with whoever persuaded her" – that is, with whoever offered her sufficiently lavish gifts. One of Socrates' associates, mentioning that she was in town, claimed that "the beauty of this woman is beyond description," or more literally "stronger than *logos*." This ineffable beauty was especially manifest when "she displayed herself, as much as she could without vulgarity, for the painters who visited to take her image." Socrates suggested they all go and contemplate her for themselves, since "what is stronger than *logos* can't be comprehended by hearing about it." When they arrive, they are lucky enough to find her with a painter, and they contemplate her as she poses (*Mem.* III.11.1–2). In banter with a serious point beneath its playful exterior, Socrates suggests that Theodote's attractions can be exploited to obtain friends. More specifically, she can bind her admirers to her by manipulating the benefactions she exchanges with them (*Mem.* III.11.4, 11–12). Theodote is impressed by Socrates' understanding of the subtleties of erotic control, and asks Socrates to visit her often and become her helper in hunting for friends. Socrates then inverts the usual relation between the courtesan and her contemplators: he tells her he will help her "only if, by god, *you* persuade *me*." With this response, Xenophon makes it clear that Theodote is something of an image of Socrates. His advice to her is a description of himself. It turns out he will never have time for her. He already has too many admirers of his own –he names his philosophical companions Apollodorus, Antisthenes, Cebes, and Simmias – whom he has captured with potions and charms (*Mem.* III.11.15–18). Socrates manages always to provoke admiration and service, even when confronted with a beauty such as Theodote's, so enthralling to other men.

To see how striking Socrates' erotic self-control is, we should compare him to Xenophon's Cyrus. Cyrus is unerotic on principle. He sees in erotic attraction nothing but an occasion of enslavement, inconsistent with his superlative freedom. In an episode that seems to have in mind Socrates' encounter with Theodote, Xenophon considers Cyrus's anti-eroticism. When Cyrus and his troops defeated the Assyrians, they captured the beautiful wife of one of the Assyrian commanders. Her name was Pantheia, which means "utterly divine." Pantheia was put under the guard of Cyrus's old friend Araspas. Pantheia was informed she would be taken from her husband and made the wife of Cyrus, and in her grief she rent her veil and mourned aloud, exposing her face and shoulders. Araspas was astonished, and he urged Cyrus to come see the lady. This vision of her body convinced Araspas that "there has never been in Asia a woman of mortal birth of such beauty" (*Cyrop.* V.1.6–7).

Socrates did not deprive himself of the contemplation of beauty. Cyrus does. Pantheia's beauty, he says, might cause him to become indifferent to what he should be doing, simply to contemplate her. Araspas laughs and tries to convince Cyrus that erotic attachment can be rationally controlled, so that he will be in no danger (*Cyrop.* V.1.8–9). Cyrus disagrees. Erotic love, he says, is a most extreme slavery, and leads people to do things they would never do otherwise (*Cyrop.* V.1.12). "I do not willingly touch a flame, nor gaze on people of beauty. Beware, Araspas! Fire burns only those who touch it, but beautiful people touch off even those who contemplate them from afar, making them burn with erotic desire" (*Cyrop.* V.1.16). Of course, Araspas does fall in love with Pantheia. Now it is Cyrus who laughs, but he sympathizes with his friend's plight: "I concede of myself, that I would not be strong enough to consort with things so beautiful and be indifferent to them." So little does he trust his own erotic resistance that he refers to the beautiful lady only vaguely as a "thing," and he apologizes to Araspas for putting him in close quarters with "this troubling thing that cannot be defeated." Araspas was relieved to be forgiven, and compliments Cyrus for being able to sympathize with "mistakes that are only human" (*Cyrop.* VI.1.36–37).

To preserve his freedom, Cyrus must avoid beauty and its erotic charge. For him, it is nothing but trouble. Eros, it seems, is a force he cannot trust himself to master. In this, Socrates exercises the more complete mastery. Theodote's model body is a divine gift for Socrates. For Cyrus, Pantheia's utterly divine beauty is a forbidden fruit.

In the detail of Pantheia's torn veil, and the erotic impact this unexpected glance of her body has on Araspas, Xenophon probably had in mind Theodote's ineffable unveiling. But he may well also have in mind a passage from Plato's *Charmides* (155d). Socrates caught an accidental glance of young Charmides' beautiful body when his cloak fell open. "I was enkindled, I was no longer myself," he says. But the sequel shows that Socrates, unlike Araspas, did control himself. His erotic attraction to young Charmides becomes part of the energy of their conversation. In a similar vein, Xenophon shows Charmides scoffing at Socrates' ascetic erotic advice, and mentions that he has seen Socrates sitting close enough to Critobolous to make their naked shoulders touch (Xenophon, *Symp.* 27). Socrates professes not to have known they had touched, and to have suffered dire consequences, unaware of the cause: "Oh no! So that's why for more than five days my shoulder's been aching, as if bitten by some animal, and I've seemed to have some sort of sting in my heart!" (28). So Socrates' own erotic practice was more liberal than his precepts, and his companions noticed. What Socrates should be doing, as opposed to what Cyrus should be doing, is intensified rather than cast into indifference by erotic attachment. From this point of view, the openness to erotic desire of Socrates' life makes Cyrus' asceticism look like a poor second best, a strategy born from weakness.

But Xenophon also gives us a stark lesson in the political dangers of Socrates' erotic intensity. Rather early on in his conquests, Cyrus captured the king of Armenia and his family. The king had acted against Cyrus in bad faith, and Cyrus was considering whether to execute him. The king's son, Tigranes, asked to speak in his father's defense. Cyrus knew that the young man had been a close companion of an Armenian sophist's with a reputation for wisdom, and so he was eager to hear what the young man would say. Tigranes made an impressive case, and Cyrus spared all his family. Then Cyrus inquired, "Where is that man you used so much to admire?" Tigranes was forced to report that his teacher had been executed – by his own father! "My father said he was corrupting me," said Tigranes. Cyrus was shocked, but the king had a

justification that Xenophon must have intended to remind the reader of
the trial of Socrates:

> Surely, Cyrus, men who catch strangers consorting with their women execute
> them. And it's not because they think the strangers have made their women
> less intelligent! Rather, they take away the women's love for themselves, and
> so those strangers are treated as enemies. I thought this sophist made my son
> admire him more than me, and so I envied him. (*Cyrop.* III.1.39)

The charge that Socrates "corrupted the young" exactly by persuading
them to obey him rather than their parents was, Xenophon tells us,
made directly by Meletus at Socrates' trial. In response, Socrates says
it is no wonder that people listen to him about education, just as they
would listen to other experts rather than to their parents (Xenophon,
Apol. 19–21). But this response is disingenuous. Socrates was not just
one schoolmaster among many, and parents are not typically resent-
ful whenever their children learn from teachers. Tigranes, too, must
have had other teachers, but only the Armenian Socrates provoked
the young man's father to feel that his affections had been alienated.
Xenophon has Meletus make the very point made by the king of
Armenia. Socrates' erotic hold over his companions was so intense that
it provoked destructive envy. Socrates' Armenian double shows that the
intensity of erotic envy can happen anywhere. In effect, this confirms
the dim view Socrates takes in Plato's *Apology* of exile as a possible
punishment. How, says Plato's Socrates, could people somewhere else
accept from me the very practices and arguments that have provoked
the hostile envy of my fellow citizens? "For I know well that wherever
I would go, the young men would listen to what I say just as they do
here" (Plato, *Ap.* 37d-e).

   Though Cyrus joined Tigranes in admiring the young man's wise
teacher, he accepts the king's justification for executing him. In the same
language later used by Araspas, Cyrus said to the father, "I think your
mistake is only human," and advised the son, "and you, Tigranes, have
sympathy for your father" (*Cyropaedia* III.1.40). As Cyrus humanely
tolerated Araspas's erotic fall, so he tolerated the Armenian king's
erotic envy. But Cyrus does not allow this humane erotic vulnerability
into his own life. He rigorously preserves his freedom at the cost of eros,
thinking the pleasures of beauty are not worth the price of passion and
envy. Socrates' preternatural self-control allows him to run the risk of
beauty's passion, and like his Armenian double, he is willing to run the
risk of being envied, even unto death.

   There could hardly be a clearer confrontation between political and
erotic benefaction. Cyrus can recognize Socratic wisdom, but he cannot protect it. Insofar as one identifies Xenophon's own judgment with

the judgment of Cyrus, one would have to say that he does not simply refute Meletus's capital charge. If the highest form of political prudence achieves self-sufficiency while avoiding envy, Socrates did not have it.

SOCRATES' ENVIABLE PIETY

As Xenophon tells the story of Socrates' trial, his penchant for provoking envy was the central cause of his conviction. "Socrates incurred envy by exalting himself in the courtroom, and so made the judges more disposed to convict him" (Xenophon, *Apology* 32). Plato's Socrates also mentions the envy directed against him (at *Apology* 18d, 28a, and 37d). Both also have Socrates directly comparing himself to Palamedes, whose unjust execution was arranged by Odysseus (Xenophon, *Apology* 26; Plato, *Apology* 41d), and Xenophon elsewhere identifies Odysseus' motive as envy (*Mem.* IV.2.33). This deadly envy had two aspects, corresponding to the two parts of the formal charge against Socrates, "corrupting the young" and "introducing novel divinities." We have seen that Socrates' wisdom did not protect him from the envy provoked by the erotic intensity of his relationships, especially with the young. Similarly, the claims he made for his special relationship to the divine outraged his judges.

Xenophon and Plato make it clear that Socrates provoked his judges with his boastfulness, his "big talk," in the lovely Greek idiom, and explained that this "big talk" is the focus of Xenophon's *Apology* (see *Apol.* 1). By seeming to exalt himself and contemn his audience, Socrates touched off angry shouts from the crowd at the trial. These outbursts of indignation track Socrates' most enviable claims. Xenophon and Plato both use these flashpoints of envy to point us to the most mysterious aspect of Socrates' self-sufficiency: his privileged relationship to the divine. This privilege is revealed in the public pronouncement of the Oracle at Delphi, which confirms Socrates' distinctive virtue, and in the essential privacy of Socrates' "divine sign," the silent voice that gave him sure guidance whenever he started toward an inappropriate action. The indignation at these two claims to divine privilege provoked an envy as deadly as the erotic sort.

Plato prefaces the oracle story with Socrates' admonition to the judges, "Gentlemen of Athens, do not shout me down even if I seem to you to be talking big. ... I present to you as a witness to the sort of wisdom that is mine: the god in Delphi!" (20e). Socrates knows he will provoke an outcry, and he has to repeat the admonition against creating a disturbance as he gets to his punchline:

Chaerephon once went to Delphi and dared to inquire of the oracle – now, as I was saying, do not shout me down, gentlemen –for in fact he asked whether anyone is wiser than I. And the Pythia replied that no one is wiser. (Plato, *Ap.* 21a)

Plato does not connect this public affirmation of Socrates' divine privilege with the private divine sign. But later, when Socrates mentions the sign, it is clear that he expects it to be provocative. Socrates does not bring it up until he has already insulted the judges by claiming to be a "gift of god" to Athens, in the form of a stinging gadfly, a remark that Socrates also introduces with a warning against the outburst he expects to provoke (Plato, *Apology* 30c and e). He says that his accuser Meletus has "made a comedy" of his habitual guidance from this private oracle. Socrates is linking Meletus's ridicule back to his "first accusers," the comic poets, especially Aristophanes, the source of the charge that he introduces novel divinities, the poets who, Socrates had said, accused him "with envy" (Plato, *Apology* 18d).[16] In particular, Socrates cautions the judges not to be angry if he tells them the truth: the sign has always kept him out of politics, for justice can be pursued only in private, not in public (Plato, *Apology* 31d-e).

Xenophon rewrites this story with a somewhat different emphasis, and with an explicit connection to envy. We have already noticed that Xenophon's version of the Delphic Oracle story focuses on Socratic virtue more broadly than Plato's does, and emphasizes freedom at least as much as wisdom. Xenophon also connects the private and public divine privileges. His Socrates tells the Delphic Oracle story only after first boasting about the sure guidance given by his divine sign. "I have made pronouncements to very many of my friends of what the god recommends," he says, "and never yet have I turned out to be wrong." (Plato's *Apology* had not mentioned any advice that the divine sign may have given to anyone besides Socrates himself.) The immediate result of this boast is envy:

The judges shouted Socrates down when they heard him say this. Some did not believe his claims, others were envious that he should get more even from the gods than they did.

Only then does he provoke them the more with the oracle story:

Come, listen to something else you can disbelieve about my being honored by the divine, if you're so inclined. Once Chaerephon made an inquiry concerning me at Delphi. Apollo gave the reply that compared to me, no human being was more free, more just, or more sane. (Xenophon, *Apol.* 14)

16   See *Philebus* 48a-50b, where ridicule in comedies is linked to envy. Strauss 1989, p. 105, points out the relevance of this passage to Plato's understanding of Aristophanes' *Clouds*.

Xenophon offers a laconic comment: "On hearing this, the judges shouted him down all the more, as would be expected." They see this arrogant claim to be god's favorite as either an unbearable lie, or an even more unbearable truth.[17]

Xenophon's Socrates is always pressing on his companions the human need for divine guidance. He counseled them to concern themselves with divination "if any of them wanted to prosper beyond the limits of human wisdom" (Mem. IV.7.10). In particular, the need for divination revealed the limits of the political achievement of self-sufficiency.[18] "People who are going to govern households and cities well," says Socrates, cannot rely solely on becoming skilled in ruling human beings, nor on any other art under the control of human judgment. To find out whether or not you will benefit from employing any of these merely human kinds of knowledge, you need divination as well (Mem. I.1.7–8). We see, then, how Socrates exaggerated the connection between kingship and happiness in his conversation with Aristippus (Mem II.1.17). Divination rather than kingship proves to be the indispensable means to control over one's own happiness.

If this is true, no wonder Socrates was envied and pursued by the politically ambitious. He seemed to have a unique gift for divination, utterly more secure than the dark signs of sacrificial entrails, birds of prey, or riddling oracles wreathed in smoke.[19] And his uncanny divinatory gift is

17   Both Plato and Xenophon mitigate somewhat Socrates' apparent boastfulness in the story about the Delphic oracle, by contrasting the excellence the oracle ascribed to Socrates with some type of divine excellence. Plato has Socrates contrast the "human wisdom" the oracle apparently meant to ascribe to him – namely, that he knows he knows nothing – to divine wisdom (20d-e, 23a). Xenophon has Socrates contrast what the oracle said about his (clearly human) superlative freedom, justice, and sanity, to the oracle's doubt about whether to address Lycurgus, lawgiver of Sparta, as a human or a god (15, quoting Herodotus, I.65). This is another instance of the way Xenophon broadens Plato's focus on Socrates' wisdom to take in a wider range of virtues connected to self-sufficiency.

18   This is a central theme of Xenophon's historical and political works. Gray 1989, pp. 179–80, aptly summarizes how Xenophon selects historical events for his narrative in the Hellenica: he makes "the choice of the philosopher, intent on making the ultimate statement about the limits of human achievement." Many contemporary scholars take this emphasis on human limitation and the necessity of pious divination to be evidence of Xenophon's superstition, rather than as a consistent reflection on a tragic theme.

19   Lefkowitz 1989 makes this point in a telling criticism of the reductive account of Socrates' divine sign in Vlastos 1989: "It was revolutionary (and dangerous) [of Socrates] to claim that the gods spoke directly to him and told him what was right"(p. 239); for "in saying that the god sends him frequent, but private negative signs that no one else hears or sees, Socrates implies that he has a

also, in Xenophon if not so clearly in Plato,[20] at the service of Socrates' friends. So in the end, Socrates' erotic intensification of control through benefaction is connected to his private prophetic endowment.[21]

Socrates' divine sign had a strong influence on his erotic relationships with his companions, as Antisthenes complained (Xenophon, *Symp.* 8.5). This link between Socrates' eroticism and his divine privilege is especially important in Socrates' relationship with Euthydemus (*Mem.* IV). In Plato's *Symposium*, Alcibiades names Euthydemus as one of the other young men who know what it is to suffer from falling in love with Socrates (222b). It is very curious how closely related Xenophon's account of Socrates and Euthydemus is to the account of Socrates and Alcibiades presented in the Platonic dialogue *Alcibiades I*.[22] By choosing Euthydemus rather than Alcibiades, Xenophon does not hide Socrates' eroticism, but he somewhat mutes its political riskiness.

There is a striking aspect of Euthydemus that has no parallel in Plato: he is an avid *reader*, who prides himself on his library. This means Euthydemus is precisely the sort of man that Socrates tells Antiphon he most seeks in his friendships (*Mem.* I.6.14). (The contrast with Plato is made particularly pointed because in this passage, Xenophon virtually quotes Plato, *Lysis* 211d-e about Socrates' eagerness for friends. By this means, Xenophon indicates that he is rewriting Plato with a different emphasis.) Socrates himself is an avid reader, who says he has no greater pleasure than to find the treasures of the wise men of the past in common

---

closer relationship to the gods than even the sons of the gods and goddesses in traditional myth" (p. 245). The revision of Vlastos 1989 in Vlastos 1991, pp. 157–178 and pp. 280–287, does not respond to Lefkowitz's point. See also the discussions of Socrates' divine sign in McPherran 1996, pp. 194–208.

20   If one accepts the dialogues *Alcibiades I* and especially *Theages* as authentically Platonic, there are much more direct and stronger links between Xenophon and Plato on the erotic and political importance of Socrates' unique prophetic endowment. For an attempt to work this out, see O'Connor 1998.

21   At the conclusion of the *Oeconomicus* (XXI.5 and 11–12), Ischomachus, a gentleman who has been teaching Socrates how to rule a household, completes the lesson by emphasizing that a successful leader needs more than a good natural endowment and the right education. A leader must have the charisma that allows him to inspire his subordinates, and this charisma is not a matter of being naturally talented or well educated. It is, Ischomachus says three times, something "divine" that exceeds any "human good." The divine charisma that defines the leader is a diminished political version of the charisma of the divine sign for Socrates' companions.

22   Denyer 2001 documents the close relationship between Plato's dialogue and Xenophon's account of Euthydemus in *Mem.* IV (see the list of references on 83, note to *Alcibiades* 103a1). The introduction also gives a vigorous defense of Plato's authorship of *Alcibiades I*, which many scholars have disputed.

reading with his friends. Indeed, such common reading is portrayed in this passage as Socrates' exemplary activity with his friends, and the high point of his erotic life. When Socrates had rubbed naked shoulders with Critobolous, they too had been reading a book together (Xenophon, *Symp.* 27). One did not need Dante's Paolo and Francesca or the young man reading over the other's shoulder in Raphael's "School of Athens" for portrayals of the erotics of books. This erotic activity, Xenophon shows, complements the extraordinary self-sufficiency Socrates boasts of to Antiphon, which allows him to approximate the independence of a god (*Mem.* I.6.10). Socrates' complementary self-sufficiency and eroticism, Xenophon says, made Xenophon think him "blessedly happy" (*Mem.* I.6.14; in Greek, *makarios*).²³

Euthydemus "aspires to that virtue which makes human beings adept at politics and household management, capable of rule, and beneficial to other human beings and themselves, the finest virtue and the greatest art, ... namely kingship" (*Mem.* IV.2.11). Out of his erotic interest in the young man, Socrates tries to make Euthydemus aware of what sort of wisdom would really be required to fulfill these "kingly" aspirations. Of course, the young man is soon thrown into perplexity by Socrates' questions. He will be in no position to exercise the kingly art with any guarantee of profit until he can recognize "what is expedient for himself and what he can and cannot do" (*Mem.* IV.2.26).

Socrates goes on to convince Euthydemus of just how problematic this sort of knowledge of "the good and the bad" really is (*Mem.* IV.2.31–35). Even such apparent blessings as health, wisdom, and prosperity can sometimes turn out to be disadvantageous. For example, health may permit someone to make an unsuccessful military campaign, which sickness would prevent; or wisdom may make one the object of desire and envy by the powerful.²⁴ This is the same argument Socrates uses

23 Strauss 1989, p. 140, sees the significance of this statement of Socrates' blessed happiness, but mistakenly takes Xenophon to be referring only to the erotic activity of shared inquiry. Johnson 2005, pp. 50–55, sees the significance of these passages about reading, and makes an interesting application of them to how Xenophon conceived of his own readers.

24 Socrates gives two examples of men undone by their wisdom through the desire and envy of the powerful, Daedelus by Minos and Palamedes by Odysseus (*Mem.* IV.2.33). As Johnson 2005, p. 68, points out, both victims are elsewhere in Plato or Xenophon images of Socrates. For Daedelus, see Plato, *Euthyphro* 11b-d and *Alcibiades I* 121a; for Palamedes, see Plato, *Apology* 41d and probably *Republic* VII.522d, and Xenophon, *Apology* 26. I take it that Xenophon wanted the reader to see this, and to consider how we know Socrates was not undone by the envy of the powerful, despite his conviction and execution. For Xenophon, the ultimate confirmation comes

elsewhere for the necessity of divination. Here, he urges Euthydemus to acquire "self-knowledge" so that he will not unwittingly fall into disaster when he fulfills his political ambitions.

Euthydemus goes away, "holding himself in contempt" for his ignorance and "believing that he is in fact slavish" (*Mem.* IV.2.39). But unlike some who refused ever again to associate with Socrates after being reduced to this perplexity, Euthydemus became deeply attached to him. Xenophon tells us that from that time, "Socrates explained directly and clearly to him what he thought one should know and what one would be best to do" (*Mem.* IV.2.40).[25] But we hear no more of Euthydemus's pursuing his grand ambitions.

The first thing Xenophon shows Socrates explaining is how to have a proper respect for divination. After Socrates piously exhorts Euthydemus to a pious dependence on signs of divine purpose, the young man replies, "The gods seem to treat you more lovingly than anyone else, if, without even being asked, they really do give you a sign of what you should and shouldn't do!" (*Mem.* IV.3.12). This is the same impatient response to Socrates' pious exhortations that Xenophon gives to another young lover of Socrates, Aristodemus (*Mem.* I.4.15). These ambitious young men are driven to this exclamation with some frustration and resignation. Happiness, Aristippus was told, needs kingship. Kingship, Euthydemus was told, needs self-knowledge. But now, it turns out, self-knowledge needs something divine. Only Socrates can be this pious and still be self-sufficient, for only he has his own transparent oracle.

Euthydemus desires the knowledge that kingship requires. Socrates teaches him that this knowledge is not humanly available – it depends on divination. But divination is neither sure nor under our control. Euthydemus will have to rethink his ambitions in light of this chastening understanding of the divine. The chastening of political ambition when it confronts divination turns out to be a central feature of Socrates' erotic relationships.

XENOPHON'S SOCRATES AND XENOPHON'S XENOPHON

It is amusing to move from this rather sobering, not to say somber, view of the influence of Xenophon's Socrates to his influence on Xenophon's

---

from the veracity of Socrates' divine sign, which never impeded him in the "big talk" and other provocative actions that led to his execution. (*Mem.* IV.8.1 and 5; see also Plato, *Ap.* 40a-b.) For a more detailed discussion, see O'Connor 1994, pp. 167–171.

25 Morrison 1994 gives an especially rich account of how this picture of Socrates gently leading Euthydemus contrasts with the dominant picture of Socratic dialectic in Plato's dialogues.

Xenophon. As it happens, Xenophon tells of just two of his own conversations with Socrates, one about erotic affairs, and one about divination. These two anecdotes show Xenophon as an affectionate admirer
of Socrates but a less docile disciple than Euthydemus. He maintained a
certain distance from Socrates despite his affection and admiration. This
rather comic reception of Socrates rounds out Xenophon's portrait.

Xenophon's own attitude toward the choice between Socrates' erotic
but private life and the political asceticism of Cyrus is the topic of the
only conversation between Xenophon and Socrates in the *Memorabilia*
(*Mem.* I.3.8–13). Socrates had noticed that Critobolous, a young man
Socrates was trying to make more serious, had kissed an attractive
boy. He tells Xenophon that Critobolous is as rash as a man somer-
saulting through knives, or – repeating an image of Cyrus' – jumping
through fire (*Mem.* I.3.9). Xenophon seems much less worried than
Socrates. He says he would be pleased to be running the same risks
that Socrates worries poor Critobolous is facing. This sends Socrates
into an ascetic speech worthy of Cyrus himself. If you kiss an attractive person, "won't you immediately become a slave rather than free,
a spendthrift for bad pleasures, a man without time to devote to any
true virtue, forced to be concerned with things even a madman doesn't
care about?" (*Mem.* I.3.11). Xenophon suggests this is an awful lot of
risk to ascribe to one kiss. Socrates does not let up. "Young beauties
are worse than scorpions: a scorpion must touch you to do harm, but a
beauty can do it from a distance, when all you do is contemplate him!"
He completes the screed by suggesting that Xenophon run away, and
Critobolous go into exile for a year (*Mem.* I.3.13). Cyrus was proved
right to warn Araspas not to underestimate the long-distance destruction of contemplating the beautiful Pantheia. But the comic tone of
this passage does not invite the reader to find Socrates very convincing.
No doubt Xenophon was impressed by the old man's performance, but
it is clear that he plans to grant himself rather more erotic latitude than
Socrates recommends.

Perhaps Xenophon planned to imitate something of Socrates' own
"bold and secure" erotic practice rather than simply listening to his
advice. Xenophon has fun with this in his *Symposium*. This work,
clearly an imitation of Plato's great erotic dialogue by the same title, is
the story of a dinner party, complete with after-dinner entertainment by
a dancing troop. The audience is dismayed by some dangerous acrobatics
undertaken by a pretty young dancer. But she pulls off the trick, showing how training can make an apparent danger something worth under-
taking. Socrates praises this dancing girl, who has somersaulted through
knives "boldly and securely" (*Symp.* II.11). Xenophon here applies to the
dancer the very descriptions he used for Socrates' erotic self-control and
Critobolous' rash erotic risks (*Mem.* I.3.5 and 9). Xenophon enforces the

connection between Socrates and the bold dancer when Socrates shocks his friends with his interest in taking private lessons so he can imitate the girl's dangerous dances. All of this playfulness is surely intended by Xenophon to remind us of the difference between what is rash in the erotic life of an amateur like Critobolous, and what is acceptable for the well-trained erotic athlete – especially one with some divine help, like Socrates himself.

How precisely Xenophon imitated something of Socrates' erotic "dancing" he does not say. But he is more explicit about how he chose to imitate Socrates' divinatory self-sufficiency.

When still a quite young man, Xenophon tells us (*Anabasis* III.1.3–7), he was invited by his friend Proxenus to join a mercenary force of Greeks being recruited by a rival for the Persian throne, Cyrus the Younger (not to be confused with Cyrus the Great). Before he accepted Proxenus's invitation, Xenophon asked Socrates what he thought of the idea. Socrates feared that Xenophon would be in trouble at home in Athens if he associated himself with this Cyrus, who had given aid to the Spartans against Athens. "Go to Delphi and consult the god about this journey," said Socrates. Well, Xenophon did go off to consult the Delphic oracle. But he did not give the god a chance to tell him not to go. Instead, the intrepid young man asked only, "To which god shall I sacrifice and pray, to best undertake the trip I have in mind?" When he returned from the oracle, Socrates chastised him. "That you would go, you decided for yourself," observed Socrates, "and you only asked the god how best to go." Xenophon here shows he has his own way of combining divine power with human deliberation, Hermes with self-control. His piety does not interfere with his decisiveness. But Socrates did not choose to press the matter further, and told his young friend to do what he intended, with what help from the gods he could get: "Since that's the question you asked, you should do whatever the god commanded you."

Xenophon tells this tale in flashback, at the crucial point in the story of the *Anabasis*. The Greek force under Cyrus's command had just met with two crushing reversals. Cyrus himself had been killed in battle, and their own Greek generals had been treacherously assassinated by the Persians at a parley. Now the Greeks were stranded deep in Asia Minor, without leaders or hope. At this moment, Xenophon ascended from being an obscure companion of the now-murdered Proxenus to becoming the inspirational leader of 10,000 desperate mercenaries. Only at this point in the story does Xenophon look back to how he arrived at such a desperate place, as if the full lesson of how he took Socrates' advice has only now struck him.

His decision to put himself forward as a leader, like his decision in the first place to go on an expedition with Cyrus, resulted in part from his own deliberations and in part from taking the advice of a god. In this case, the divine direction came in what he says was an ambiguous dream. Sprawled in anxious sleep before the walls of Babylon, he dreamed that his father's house was set ablaze by a lightning bolt from Zeus. Xenophon concedes this may not look like such a great omen, but he finds that one way to take it is as a sign of light from Zeus during tribulation. Rather enigmatically, he comments, "What sort of thing such a dream is can be seen by considering what happened after the dream" (*Anabasis* III.1.13). And what came after was his own planning for the way the Greek force could hold together and escape, which of course it did.

The most obvious lesson of this little vignette is that politically ambitious men need humbly to consult the signs of divine favor, whether given by oracles, dreams, or other signs. The less obvious lesson is that a prudent political man will see to it that the divine favor points in directions he wants to go. He will actively seek interpretations that support what reason tells him. Indeed, the accomplished leader will become reasonably skilled in the art of divination himself, since this will protect him when no diviner can be found, or when one is corrupt. Xenophon shows us that he had learned this lesson (*Anabasis* V.6.29), and his fictional Cyrus the Great makes a point of it, too (*Cyrop.* I.6.1–2).

This politic divination need not at all be cynically interpreted, though in the hands of a Machiavelli it could be. Perhaps we could say that it is the political accommodation to Socrates' more stringent advice about submitting oneself to divine purposes. Within the horizon of political ambition, the balance that Xenophon and Cyrus strike between humble piety and decisive deliberation is the closest imitation available of Socrates' own more intensive command of the irruption of the divine into the human.

WORKS CITED

Brickhouse, T. C., and N. D. Smith. "The Socratic *Elenchos*?" In *Does Socrates Have a Method?* ed. Gary Alan Scott. University Park, PA, 2002, pp. 145–157.
Carpenter, M., and R. M. Polansky. "Variety of Socratic Elenchi." In *Does Socrates Have a Method?* ed. Gary Alan Scott. University Park, PA, 2002, pp. 89–100.
Denyer, N. *Plato: Alcibiades*. Cambridge, 2001.
Dorion, L. -A. "Xenophon's Socrates." In *A Companion to Socrates*, eds. Sara Ahbel-Rappe and Rachana Kamtekar. Oxford, 2006, pp. 93–100.
Dorion, L. -A., and M. Bandini. *Xenophon: Memorables*. Tome 1: Introduction et Livre I. Paris, 2000.
Gray, V. *The Framing of Socrates: The Literary Interpretation of Xenophon's Memorabilia*. Stuttgart, 1998.
Gray, V. *The Character of Xenophon's Hellenica*. Baltimore, 1989.
Gray, V. "Xenophon's Hiero and the Meeting of the Wise Man and the Tyrant in Greek Literature." *Classical Quarterly* 36 (1986): 115–123.

Hermann, G. *Ritualised Friendship and the Greek City*. New York, 1987.

Johnson, D. M. "Xenophon at his Most Socratic (Memorabilia 4.2)" *Oxford Studies in Ancient Philosophy* 29 (2005): 39–73.

Johnson, D. M. "Xenophon's Socrates on Law and Justice" *Ancient Philosophy* 22 (2003): 255–281.

Lefkowitz, Mary R. 1991. "Comments on Vlastos' 'Socratic Piety.' " In *Proceedings of the Boston Area Colloquium in Ancient Philosophy* 5. ed. J. Cleary. Washington, DC, 1991, pp. 239–246.

Mauss, M. *The Gift: Forms and Functions of Exchange in Archaic Societies*, trans. I. Cunnison. London, 1954 [1924].

McPherran, M. *The Religion of Socrates*. University Park, PA, 1996.

Morrison, D. 1994. "Xenophon's Socrates as Teacher." In *The Socratic Movement*, ed. P.A. Vander Waerdt. Ithaca, 1994, pp. 181–208.

Morrison, D. "On Professor Vlastos' Xenophon" *Ancient Philosophy* 7 (1987): 9–22.

Nadon, C. *Xenophon's Prince: Republic and Empire in the Cyropaedia*. Berkeley, 2001.

O'Connor, D. K. "Socrates and Political Ambition: The Dangerous Game." In *Proceedings of the Boston Area Colloquium in Ancient Philosophy*, 14. eds. J. Cleary and G. M. Gurtler New York, 1998, pp. 31–51.

O'Connor, David K. 1994. "The Erotic Self-Sufficiency of Socrates: A Reading of Xenophon's *Memorabilia*" In *The Socratic Movement*, ed. P.A. Vander Waerdt. Ithaca, 1994, pp. 151–180.

Pangle, T. 1994. "Socrates in the Context of Xenophon's Political Writings" In *The Socratic Movement*, ed. P.A. Vander Waerdt. Ithaca, 1994, pp. 127–150.

Pomeroy, S. B. *Xenophon: Oeconomicus: A Social and Historical Commentary*. Text, translation, and notes. Oxford, 1994.

Scott, G. A. *Does Socrates Have a Method?* University Park, PA, 2002.

Strauss, Leo. "The Problem of Socrates: Five Lectures." In *The Rebirth of Classical Political Philosophy*, ed. T. Pangle Chicago, 1989, pp. 103–183.

Strauss, Leo. 1991. *On Tyranny*, ed. V. Gourevitch. New York, 1991.

Vander Waerdt, P. A. "Socratic Justice and Socratic Self-Sufficiency: The Story of the Delphic Oracle in Xenophon's *Apology of Socrates*," *OSAP* 11 (1993): 1–48.

Vander Waerdt, P. A., ed. *The Socratic Movement*. Ithaca, 1994.

Veyne, P. *Bread and Circuses: Historical Sociology and Political Pluralism*. trans. Brian Pearce. London, 1990 [1976].

Vlastos, G. *Socrates, Ironist and Moral Philosopher*. Ithaca, 1991.

Vlastos, G. "Socratic Piety." *Proceedings of the Boston Area Colloquium in Ancient Philosophy* 5 (1989): 213–38. Revised version: Vlastos, *Socrates: Ironist and Moral Philosopher*, Ithaca, 1991, Ch. 5, pp. 157–178.

Vlastos, G. "The Paradox of Socrates." In *The Philosophy of Socrates*, ed. Gregory Vlastos Garden City, N.Y, 1971, pp. 1–21.

Wood, N. "Xenophon's Theory of Leadership." *Classica et Mediaevalia* 25 (1964): 33–66.

4   Socrates in Aristophanes' *Clouds*

"Aristophanes has come very close to the truth in his depiction of Socrates."

Kierkegaard 1989

In Plato's *Apology*, a version of the defense speech that Socrates delivered in 399 when he was charged with the potentially capital offense of introducing new gods and corrupting the youth of Athens, Socrates divides his accusers into two groups. On the one hand, there are Anytus and his cronies, who have filed the complaint and hauled him into court. These men are dangerous enough, he says, but he fears another group, much more: "those who have taken the majority of you in from childhood, persuading you and laying the utterly untruthful charge that a certain Socrates is an intellectual, a theorist about the firmament, an investigator of everything that lies beneath the earth, and one who makes the weaker argument the stronger" (*Apology* 18A-B). These antagonists are numerous and have been misrepresenting Socrates for a long while, infecting the minds of the jurors when they were still young and impressionable, with no one on hand to raise objections. But the worst of it is that they are anonymous, "save if one of them happens to be a comic poet" (18C). The influence of these ancient accusers, Socrates asserts, is evident in the indictment that has been brought against him, which mentions just such pursuits on his part. For, Socrates tells the jurors, "you yourselves have seen, in Aristophanes' comedy, a kind of Socrates carried aloft and claiming to walk on air and uttering all sorts of other nonsense, about which I know nothing whatever, neither much nor little" (19C). In the *Phaedo*, Plato refers once more to the attacks on him levelled by comic poets, in connection with his attempt to prove that the soul survives the body: "I do not think, Socrates said, that anyone who hears me now – even if he should be a comic poet – will claim that I am babbling and making speeches about irrelevant matters" (70C). There are less explicit references to comedy in other dialogues as well, especially in the *Euthydemus* (Tarrant 1991: 165).

Aristophanes was not the only dramatist to have ridiculed Socrates on stage. In the same festival at which Aristophanes originally produced *Clouds*, in the year 423, Ameipsias put on a play entitled *Konnos* (frr. 7–11 Kassel-Austin) in which he too caricatured Socrates, who must have done something to attract attention about that time. In a fragment by Eupolis (352–353 Kock = 386 Kassel-Austin), an older contemporary of Aristophanes', a character declares: "I hate Socrates, the babbling beggar, who theorizes about everything else but neglects to think where he can get a meal." The same person or another, presumably in the same play, says: "But teach him to babble, you sophist you." The aside in the *Phaedo* would appear to refer to this play by Eupolis rather than to Aristophanes, especially in light of the word "babble" (*adoleskhein*, cf. Mitscherling 2003; but note the same word at *Clouds* 1480). But the Socrates of the *Apology* clearly pinpoints Aristophanes (whether the real Socrates did so in his trial is moot: he may not have shared Plato's hostility to the theater),[1] and the play he has in mind is, of course, *Clouds* – where Socrates indeed proclaims to "walk on air and contemplate the sun" (225), and his disciples investigate things beneath the earth (188), and he is known for teaching how to make the weaker argument the stronger (112–115).

Aristophanes was a satirist by profession, and it is to be expected that he would deliberately produce a parody of Socrates in a play that centers on him.[2] Socrates was by any account an eccentric personality, who no doubt invited such mockery. But parody, if it is to be effective, must have some basis in reality, and the question that has exercised scholars is to what extent the testimony of Aristophanes, who is our earliest witness to the career of Socrates, can in fact shed light on his character and beliefs. How is one to sort out the truth about Socrates, or even the impression he made on his contemporaries, from the picture of him that Aristophanes presents in this play?

One approach is to compare Aristophanes' portrait of Socrates with what we can learn from Plato, Xenophon, and a few other younger contemporaries, taking as authentic what is confirmed by independent testimony, and dismissing the rest as comic invention. There is

---

1   Plato too may have been more tolerant of the theater, and of comedy, than one might infer from the *Republic*; besides Aristophanes' role in the *Symposium*, Olympiodorus *Commentary on Alcibiades I* 2.65–75 reports (with what plausibility it is impossible to say) that Plato had a copy of Aristophanes with him when he died; cf. Andic 2001, p. 175.

2   Cf. Diogenes Laertius 2.36; Plutarch *On Educating Children* 10C; scholia *to Clouds* 96, reporting an old controversy over whether Aristophanes' send-up was hostile in intention.

some sense in this method, but it discounts the possibility that we have something to learn from Aristophanes. Another angle, complementary to the first, is to see which doctrines ascribed to Socrates in *Clouds* are better attested as pertaining to the thought of other philosophers and sophists of the time, but do not seem compatible with the picture of Socrates that we derive from other sources, above all Plato. Aristophanes' Socrates will thus emerge as a composite figure, representing not a single individual but sophists in general, bearing whatever traits were most striking and likely to amuse, the way Zeuxis is said to have painted Helen of Troy by pooling the features of several different models.[3] The idea, then, is to strip away the extraneous characteristics so as to reveal the Socratic core. Still a third line of attack is to identify Aristophanes' comic style, and compensate for the kinds of exaggeration or distortion that are intrinsic to it. Old Comedy tended to work with simplistic polarities of upright and disreputable behavior, age and youth, wealth versus poverty, though these pairs can be aligned in unexpected, and sometimes contradictory, ways. The image of Socrates will have been adapted to the demands of the genre, and the plot will unfold in ways that are to some extent analogous to the plots of other of Aristophanes' plays (cf. Gelzer 1956: 87). One imagines that the Greek audience was sensitive to such conventions as well, and did not naively suppose that the Socrates they laughed at on stage was identical to the one who sat with them in the audience (an anecdote related by Aelian [*Varia Historia* 2.13], probably apocryphal, records that midway through the comedy, Socrates stood up to show foreign spectators who he really was).[4] Plato's suggestion that Aristophanes' *Clouds* contributed materially to the prejudice against Socrates may be more of a pleader's ploy than an accurate reflection of the play's influence on popular attitudes.

I shall begin by indicating briefly the form of the work, and how Aristophanes' comic purposes shape the representation of Socrates, before discussing the doctrines and practices attributed to Socrates and their likely sources. The premise of *Clouds* is that Strepsiades, a farmer who has married the city-bred daughter of a rich family, is up to his ears in debt because of the extravagant expenses of his wife and more

---

3   Dionysius of Halicarnassus *On Imitation* 31.1; for the view, see Whitman 1964, p. 142; Dover 1968, pp. xxxii-lvi; contra Kleve 1983; Tomin, 1987; Vander Waerdt 1994, pp. 52–61, noting the specificity of Socrates' appearance, (relative) poverty, and method of inquiry.

4   Nor would the audience have imagined that the tragic playwright Agathon actually dressed as a woman when he composed female parts, as Aristophanes has him do in *Thesmophoriazusae* (148–52); comparing Aristophanes' treatment of other historical personalities, such as Cleon, with his representation of Socrates may again serve as a control on his satirical technique.

especially his son, Phidippides, who has cultivated the aristocratic pastime of buying, training, and racing thoroughbred horses. In order to evade payment, Strepsiades conceives the plan of enrolling his son in Socrates' *phrontistêrion* (94) or "theory-joint," imagined as located in a house next door, where for a fee (98, 245, 1146) students are taught about the nature of the heavens and how to win a case in court, whether just or not; this way Strepsiades will be able to escape prosecution by his creditors.[5] When Phidippides refuses to have anything to do with such characters, Strepsiades decides, old and dull as he is, to go to the *phrontistêrion* himself (126–131).

At the school, Socrates' pupils are engaged in ostensibly secret investigations into such deep matters as how far a flea can jump in proportion to its size, and whether gnats emit sound from their mouths or anuses, as well as subterranean explorations, astronomy, and geometry (201–202) by which to map and measure the earth.[6] They are proud too that Socrates has discovered a clever means of stealing cloaks to pay for dinner (177–179; cf. 497, 856). Socrates himself appears suspended in a swing or basket so as better to study the heavens. Strepsiades makes his purpose clear at once (239–245), and Socrates, consenting to accept him as a pupil, summons his patron deities, the Clouds, who form the chorus of the play. Why Clouds? They represent the comic Socrates' interest in meteorology, of course; they serve too as nature deities, like the Vortex which, as Socrates will later explain, has replaced Zeus as the chief divinity in the physicists' pantheon (316–318, 365–382, cf. 423–424, 627, 814–828, 1232–1241, 1468–1477; Strepsiades will misinterpret the word as meaning "Pot," 1472–1474). For it is basic to the characterization of Socrates in *Clouds* that he is passionately interested in cosmology. This apotheosis of natural forces may have lent fuel to the accusation, a quarter of a century later, that Socrates introduced new gods (Plato *Apology* 24B). The Clouds also suggest the airiness of sophistical reasoning, which can assume any shape and take either side of a question.[7] The Clouds approve Strepsiades' plan to defraud his creditors

5   On the term *phrontistêrion*, see Goldberg 1976; Gelzer 1956, p. 69.
6   Vander Waerdt 1994, pp. 60–61, argues that Aristophanes meant these occupations to be associated with Socrates' followers, not with Socrates himself; cf. p. 65. Souto Delibes 1997 argues that not only some of the ideas parodied by Aristophanes (345), but also some of the traits ascribed to Socrates pertain to certain of Socrates' disciples, e.g., Chaerephon's pallor and nocturnal habits (342; cf. *Wasps* 1413, *Birds* 1296 and 1564), Antisthenes' poverty (342; cf. Xen. *Symp.* 3.8 and 4.37), and Simon's thievery (343; cf. *Clouds* 351, Eupolis *Poleis*).
7   Vv. 346–48; cf. Segal 1969; Andic 2001, pp. 179–183; Edmunds 1986 argues that they are a caricature of Socrates' *daimonion* and his ironic manner.

(435–436), and Socrates, though doubtful of his capacity to learn, undertakes to instruct him.

Eventually Socrates gives up on Strepsiades entirely (783). At this point, Strepsiades insists that his son Phidippides enter the school (839), and Socrates accepts him, entrusting his immediate education to personifications of the arguments that Socrates is expert in manipulating – that is, the Stronger and the Weaker Argument. In a debate of the sort that is a regular feature of Old Comedy (called an *agôn*), the Stronger Argument makes a case for traditional education and values, on which the men who repelled the Persians at Marathon were allegedly reared, while the Weaker Argument defends a life of pleasure – eating, drinking, sex, games, and other rascally pursuits (1071–1082). With this, Phidippides is led into the *phrontistêrion*.

Phidippides learns his lessons well, and shows off his skill by teaching Strepsiades how to keep his creditors at bay by exploiting an ostensible ambiguity in the conventional name of the day on which debts fell due. In the finale of the play, Strepsiades runs out of his house howling for help, having been beaten by Phidippides, who revels shamelessly in his father's reproaches, just as the Weaker Argument had done in the face of Stronger Argument's abuse (1327–1330; cf. 908–914). What is more, he ventures to prove that he was right to beat his father, again rendering the weaker argument the stronger, and thereby to demonstrate that Strepsiades had no business preventing him from singing a scandalous song by Euripides (one of Aristophanes' pet targets). If spanking a child is understood to be for its own good, he asserts, then it is equally benign for Phidippides to beat Strepsiades, especially since he is evidently in his second childhood and it is all the more absurd for an old man to misbehave (1410–1419). In the end, Strepsiades recognizes that he has gotten his comeuppance, and he deserves to be chastised if he pursues what is unjust (1437–1439). When Phidippides offers to prove that it is equally right for him to beat his mother, however, it is more than Strepsiades can bear, and he accuses the Clouds of leading him astray. They, in a sudden about-face, reply that Strepsiades himself bears the blame, since he turned (*strepsas*: a pun on his name) to evil deeds (1454–1455).[8] With this, Strepsiades prepares to avenge himself on Socrates and his school, and when his own son declines to assist him, he renounces his belief in Vortex, begs the pardon of Hermes, meditates for a moment on whether to file suit against the scoundrels, and finally, ostensibly in response to Hermes' advice, decides to burn down the *phrontistêrion*. As the

---

8   For the motivation of the Clouds' change of heart, see Segal 1969; Blyth 1994; Redfield 1999, pp. 56–59: Gaertner 1999 argues for a genuine contradiction, which is what makes the scene funny.

building goes up in flames, Socrates and his disciples exit from within and flee in panic.

Comedy has its own license, and the picture of Socrates that emerges from *Clouds* is, as one might have expected, inconsistent. On the one hand, Socrates charges a fee, apparently substantial, for instruction, and has various disciples;[9] on the other hand, he is miserably poor – Strepsiades ascribes the unkempt hair and dirtiness of the disciples to thrift (835–837) – and he needs to filch cloaks, including Strepsiades' own, in order to survive (his disciples, also impoverished, do not seem to be in a position to pay large sums, nor, for that matter, is Strepsiades [Berg 1998: 2]). The sophists contemporary with Socrates were not a notoriously scruffy lot; on the contrary, they were internationally respected figures and generally taught the scions of the rich. Socrates was the odd man out in this company: he did not charge for instruction, he insists in Plato's *Apology* (19D-E), but rather wore simple attire and went about unshod, even in winter (cf. Nussbaum 1980: 71–72). This hardiness is reflected also in his students' comportment: they sleep out of doors, seem immune to cold, and dedicate themselves single-mindedly to learning in a way that is anything but lazy or spoiled; the chorus will instruct Strepsiades that "he mustn't be soft" (727). Nevertheless, they are simultaneously represented as weak and pale, and suited to an indoor life of decadence and luxury of the sort approved by the Weaker Argument. It seems likely that the image of Socrates as poor and tough derives from reality (it is consistent with the portraits drawn by Plato and Xenophon), and is combined with elements of the popular view of professional rhetoricians as rich and idle.

Socrates' beliefs about the gods, like the representation of the Clouds themselves, are likewise a mixed bag; sometimes he personifies natural forces as deities, while at other times he explains these same forces on scientific lines. Some of the more poetically disposed natural philosophers of Socrates' time – for example, Empedocles – might be taken to have deified abstractions such as Love and Strife, but Aristophanes aligns his Socrates principally with the mechanistic views of thinkers such as Anaxagoras and the Ionian cosmologists. If Plato is to be trusted, Socrates did discourse on the cosmos – for example in the myths that conclude the *Phaedo* and the *Republic*, as well as in the account of the

---

9   Vander Waerdt 1994, pp. 60–61, suggests that the ostensible charge for tuition in the *phrontistêrion* is a mistaken belief of Strepsiades', and does not conform to Socrates' actual practice in the comedy; so too Gelzer 1956, p. 92, concludes that Socrates is not actually represented as unjust. Tomin 1987 notes Aristippus' report (fr. 7) that Socrates took food and wine from friends; cf. Andic 2001, p. 165.

heavens in the *Phaedrus* and elsewhere. And if Socrates really spoke like that, it would provide a peg on which to hang the comic exaggerations in *Clouds*.[10]

The theme of Aristophanes' *Clouds* can be described from one point of view as the education of Strepsiades – not in the wisdom purveyed in the *phrontistêrion*, but rather in the value of conventional morality, to which he implicitly subscribes even as he seeks to get round it by mastering rhetoric in order to renege on his debts. Strepsiades is not by nature a lawbreaker; he is driven to desperate remedies by his son's extravagance. But neither is he deeply averse to a little chicanery.[11]

Strepsiades, in turn, learns that the new sophistic logic is a two-edged sword, and can be turned against him and the values he holds dearest, just as well as against his creditors. His son does not start out more clear-headed than his father. He rejects the teachings of the *phrontistêrion* out of aristocratic bias: his passion is for horses, not for intellectual study, and he regards the pallid and disheveled scholars next door with contempt.[12] Nevertheless, it is just youths of his class who were in a position to pay for what the sophists had to teach, and once he is exposed to their pursuits, he abandons his equestrian zeal in favor of sophistical disputation (1399–1407). Phidippides is, then, the kind of rich young man of distinguished family who was susceptible to the influence of the sophists and Socrates alike, and whom Plato and Xenophon represent as attracted to their teachings, if not always for the best of motives. When Strepsiades gets a good look at the consequences of such views, he reacts the way the majority of the jurors did in Athens in 399.

Some scholars have judged the violence of the final episode to be out of tune with the spirit of Aristophanic comedy. Thomas Hubbard, for example, writes (1991: 88): "Critics have often commented upon [*Clouds'*] atypical plot structure and lack of a sympathetic comic hero. One is also struck by the absence of the 'happy ending' and communal

---

10 Note too that in Plato's *Protagoras* (356D-357D), Socrates appeals to an "art of measurement" (*metrêtikê tekhnê*); and in Plato's *Theaetetus*, he is represented as conversing with the most distinguished mathematician of his time. Cf. Xenophon *Memorabilia* 4.7.2, where Socrates observes that one may easily learn enough geometry to measure land without thereby becoming a professional mathematician.

11 In this, he resembles Philocleon, the protagonist of Aristophanes' *Wasps*, which was produced the year before *Clouds*; see Konstan 1995, pp. 15–28; for comparison with other plays of Aristophanes, especially *Birds*, see Gelzer 1956, pp. 80–86.

12 After studying with Socrates, Phidippides becomes so pale as to be unrecognizable; cf. Konstan 2006.

festivity which we usually find at the conclusion of a comedy; instead we have an ending that is violent, discordant, unforeseen, and far more at home in Tragedy than in Comedy." I myself do not find the ending so shocking, nor incompatible with the satirical as opposed to utopian type of comedy that Aristophanes seems to have cultivated early in his career (in *Knights*, *Wasps*, and *Clouds*; see Dover 1968: xxiv). *Knights*, after all, which immediately preceded *Clouds*, "is little more than two hours of character assasination" of Cleon (Redfield 1999: 52; it may be worth noting that it did not impede Cleon's election to office). Besides, there is a possible allusion here to the deliberate conflagration in which many Pythagoreans were said to have been killed in Southern Italy.[13]

The question is complicated, however, by the fact that the version of *Clouds* that we possess is a second edition, as Aristophanes himself indicates (518–526), which he partially revised out of pique at its coming in last in the competition. Internal evidence suggests that the amended version may be dated to four or five years after the original production in 423, though it was apparently never staged in its new form (argument for a later date in Kopff 1990; contra Storey 1993). An ancient preface attached to the play reports that Aristophanes made changes in the parabasis, in the contest between the Weaker and the Stronger Argument, and in the burning of Socrates' establishment, and it is possible, though not certain, that the entire last scene should be assigned to the revised version (for *Clouds* I, see Dover 1968: lxxx-xcviii; Tarrant 1991). It is, under the circumstances, vain to speculate about whether Aristophanes introduced the scene – if indeed it was not already present in the first version – in order to appeal to the sentiments of the Athenian public, or perhaps because he had hardened his view of Socrates in the interim.

Socrates avails himself of various pedagogical methods in *Clouds*. He conducts experiments and has his students assist in carrying them out – for example, measuring the leap of a flea. Sometimes, his teaching takes the form of a dialogue, with Strepsiades interposing questions and remarks, as when Socrates explains the nature of rain, thunder, and lightning. This is perhaps attributable to the genre, which favors dramatic exchange over long speeches, but it resembles Socrates' method as we know it from Plato and Xenophon. Socrates affirms that he will demonstrate how rain occurs with "weighty proofs" (*megalois sêmeiois*, 369), and argues that it never rains when there are no clouds; hence they, rather than Zeus, are the cause of rain. More remarkable in this

---

13   Diogenes Laertius 8.38; Iamblichus *Life of Pythagoras* 35.249-53, citing Nicomachus of Gerasa (2nd c. CE.). Cf. Taylor 1911; Kopff 1977; Mignanego 1992, p. 85; Andic 2001, p. 169; contra Harvey 1981; cf. Davies 1990.

same passage is the explanation of thunder, which Socrates illustrates with reference to Strepsiades' rumbling digestion. Socrates announces, "I shall teach it to you from you yourself" (385), which perhaps suggests for a moment Socrates' dialectical method of eliciting the answer to a problem from the interlocutor, as in Plato's *Meno*.[14] Again in the lesson concerning the genders of nouns, Socrates proceeds by question and answer, and he draws upon analogies from proper names to illustrate his argument (658–693); in fact, however, he is simply imparting knowledge rather than engaging in a genuine elenchus.

It is clearly crucial to Aristophanes' Socrates that his pupils be equipped with good memories (482–483, 785–790; Mignanego 1992: 75); indeed, it is just his forgetfulness that disqualifies Strepsiades for the program. But when he is all but exasperated with Strepsiades, Socrates instructs him to lie down on his cot, cover himself with his cloak, and think through his troubles (695). The chorus adds the advice that he consider carefully and "as soon as you encounter a difficulty [*aporon*], leap to another idea in your mind" (702–705), which sounds like a parody of the Socratic procedure of driving deliberation to the point of aporia (the scholia – marginal notes found in some manuscripts, which go back to ancient commentators – already noted the resemblance). A little later, Socrates orders Strepsiades to "let your thinking become subtle and consider your affairs bit by bit, properly dividing them up and examining them" (*orthôs diairôn kai skopôn*, 739–741); while it would be stretching it to see here an allusion to the technical procedure of *diairesis* that Socrates elaborates in Plato's later dialogues, such as the *Statesman*, it is not implausible that the lines reflect something of Socrates' demand for precision in conversation with his friends.

Finally, Socrates believes that Phidippides, at least, can learn from listening to the debate between the Weaker and the Stronger Arguments (886); these, at all events, are delivered chiefly in the form of speeches. Too little is known of the pedagogical techniques of the sophists and natural philosophers for one to be confident that the apparently more dialogic and dialectical of the methods to which Socrates resorts reflect his specific style of teaching, but it may be that the audience would have associated such approaches with the Socrates they knew.[15]

---

14 His method has been compared with Socratic maieutic or midwifery; cf. Nussbaum 1980, pp. 73–74; Mastromarco 1983, ad v. 137; Mignanego 1992, p. 80; Andic 2001, p. 171; contra Tarrant 1988.

15 Cf. Nussbaum 1980, pp. 48–49, 79; Sarri 1973, pp. 534, 548–50; Mignanego 1992, p. 98; Andic 2001, p. 163: Socrates is "the *same* person that we find in the Platonic dialogues" (163; cf. 170); Edmunds 1986, p. 210, concludes that "we are facing the same Socrates known to us from Plato and Xenophon."

Some scholars have seen an allusion in *Clouds* to a new conception of the soul (*psukhê*) or self, which they have attributed to the historical Socrates (Havelock 1972; Sarri 1973, 1975). *Psukhê* in the popular language of the time commonly signified a ghost (cf. *Acharnians* 375), or simply life (*Acharnians* 357, *Knights* 457) rather than a psychic faculty, and this is how Strepsiades at first employs it (94), though even here Aristophanes may be punning on a more abstract sense.[16] Over the course of the play, the term acquires a more intangible significance (319, 415, 420, 712, 719, 1049). Correspondingly, Aristophanes' Socrates subordinates care of the body to care of the soul (cf. *Birds* 1553–1564; Sarri 1973: 541). Eric Havelock (1972: 15) has argued that along with *psukhê*, one can see a new use of the reflexive pronoun ("himself," "herself") in *Clouds*: "So much of the humor relies on the device of parodying a verbal syntax which, if contemporary and posthumous record are compared, can be identified in all probability as Socratic. The same roles are assigned to the reflexive pronoun, the same verbs of intellection recur connecting the subject with itself as object" (15).[17] If we acknowledge paratragedy – that is, mock-tragic passages that parody real tragedies – Havelock reasons, why deny "the composition, with equal skill, of 'paraphilosophical' passages?" (16–17). It may well be that Aristophanes has employed *psukhê*, and other terms as well, to parody the language of Socrates or of the intellectual elite in general (in particular, perhaps, Diogenes of Apollonia).

We have seen that, although Socrates has various scientific interests, Strepsiades is concerned exclusively with instruction in duplicitous or tricky speech, and it is to learn this that he turns to the *phrontistêrion*.[18] The kind of sophistry he wishes to acquire resides not in rhetoric as such, understood as the ability to compose long and persuasive orations, but in quick and clever repartee that leaves an opponent at a loss for words. It is easy to imagine how such a view of Socrates' verbal skills would have arisen, given the nature of his cross-questioning as Plato and Xenophon portray it; Plato's Socrates acknowledges in the *Apology* (23A-C) that the elenchus did in fact irritate his interlocutors and amuse young onlookers. To this extent, the image of Socrates in *Clouds* may correspond to the way he appeared to his contemporaries.

There is no indication in Plato or Xenophon that Socrates was interested in metrics or the kind of grammatical analysis that concerned

16 See Adkins 1970, p. 19; Sarri 1973, p. 538; contra Handley 1956; Dover 1986: ad loc.
17 Cf. Mignanego 1992, pp.74, 78, who notes too the special use of *phrontizô*.
18 For the distinction between Socrates' principles and those of Strepsiades, see Vander Waerdt 1994, 75; Andic 2001, p. 179.

itself with inconsistencies in morphology and gender, and proper (*orthôs*, 659) usage in this regard. But Socrates did, like most learned men, venture to interpret poetry and apply it to life, and this may have given Aristophanes a nail on which to hang the more abstruse, and at the same time more ridiculous, linguistic fussiness he ascribes to Socrates in *Clouds*. Plato, in the *Protagoras* (338E–42A) represents Socrates as debating with Protagoras the deeper meaning of a poem by Simonides, and Xenophon (*Memorabilia* 1.2.56–57) relates the charge that Socrates "would select the worst bits of the most reputable poets, and using these as testimony would teach those who associated with him to be criminals and tyrannical."

According to Plato (*Phaedo* 96A), Socrates as a young man (*neos*) was fascinated with natural philosophy. Some scholars have seen in the cosmological and other scientific interests of Aristophanes' Socrates a reflection of this early enthusiasm, even while acknowledging that various doctrines ascribed to Socrates are drawn from other thinkers – for example, Damon the Athenian or Diogenes of Apollonia (Gelzer 1956: 68–69, 83–84; Morales Troncoso 2001). Paul Vander Waerdt (1994: 61) maintains that "Socrates is consistently represented in the *Clouds* as an adherent of the views of Diogenes of Apollonia," and takes this to be true of the historical Socrates at the time *Clouds* was composed (62–75), when he was still principally concerned with physical philosophy rather than with ethics. On this view, Plato's *Apology* and some other early dialogues (cf. Xenophon *Symposium* 6 and *Oeconomicus* 11) deliberately refute Aristophanes' characterization by overstating Socrates' indifference to physical philosophy. When *Clouds* was produced, Socrates was almost forty-five years old, well beyond the age at which he could be described as a youth, and if we are to credit Aristophanes, it is necessary to dismiss the explicit witness of Plato (Plato and Xenophon, let it be recalled, were five or six years old at this time). To me, the question seems undecidable. It is clear that Aristophanes assembled a hodge-podge of intellectual pursuits, from eristic argumentation to speculation about the gods, astronomy, meteorological phenomena, biology, poetry, and grammar, and combined them all in Socrates.[19] Socrates wrote nothing, but it is conceivable that he engaged in discussions on a wide range of issues, and that this made an impression on his older contemporaries.[20]

---

19   Vander Waerdt 1994, p. 65, however, sees them all as compatible with his principal interest, at this time, in natural philosophy, especially as represented by Diogenes of Apollonia; cf. Gelzer 1956, p. 84.

20   Epictetus 2.1.32 affirms that Socrates wrote extensively, as a substitute for conversation when interlocutors were not at hand; but this is undoubtedly a fiction.

The *phrontistêrion* is certainly an Aristophanic invention (contra Barzin 1968; cf. Rossetti 1974), just as much as the swing in which Socrates hangs suspended so that he can better contemplate the heavens. The inspiration for it might have been the gymnasia that Socrates frequented, where he enjoyed engaging young people in conversation (as in Plato's *Lysis*), but such encounters were casual; there was nothing like matriculation for a fee. What is more, the establishment that Aristophanes describes is not so much a school as a center of esoteric knowledge. The model is in part that of a cultic association, and the wisdom that is imparted there is described by one of Socrates' disciples as "mysteries" (143; cf. 824). Before beginning his instruction, Strepsiades undergoes a formal induction, in which he is seated, crowned with a garland, sprinkled with water, and ordered to maintain a reverent silence as he listens to the prayer invoking the Clouds (254–266), a procedure, as Socrates explains, that is employed with all initiates (258–259). Some of these rites are paralleled in what is known of other cults;[21] it is likely too that Aristophanes is lampooning esoteric philosophical societies like the Pythagoreans.[22] Here we may detect another inconsistency in Aristophanes' characterization of Socrates: if he wished to conceal his insights rather than disseminate them, it is difficult to see why he should have seemed to pose so great a threat to the community as to require the razing of his academy – or why he should have admitted a character like Strepsiades into his confidence (Berg 1998: 3). There is no suggestion that Socrates himself used his skill at argument for illicit purposes (cf. Guthrie 1971: 39–55; Andic 2001: 170).

Aristophanes' Socrates was a compound figure, combining characteristics of Protagoras (grammar), Damon (metrics: cf. Plato *Republic* 400A), Hippo of Elis (sky as lid), and Diogenes of Apollonia, who made air the arch-principle of all things.[23] Anaxagoras had been charged with atheism for his doctrine that the sun was merely a stone, and it is not unlikely that this was a brush with which to tar any ostensible freethinker. In Plato's *Apology* (26D), Socrates explicitly distances

---

21 Demosthenes 18.259; cf. Dieterich 1893; Gelzer 1956, pp. 67–68; Dover 1968: ad v. 254; Nussbaum 1980, pp. 73–74; Byl 1980; Marianetti 1992, pp. 41–63; Janko 1997.

22 Cf. *Theaetetus* 155E, *Symposium* 209E. Adkins 1970 argues that the parody of the mysteries casts Socrates as blasphemous, analogous to "holding the Black Mass" (15); cf. Marianetti 1992, pp. 64–75; Marianetti 1993; Patzer 1993; contra, de Vries 1973.

23 Note the prominent role of clouds, and of deities such as Air, Breath, and Aether, in the comedy; cf. Vander Waerdt 1994, pp. 71–75; cf. Sarri 1973, pp. 543–545.

himself from this opinion and denounces Meletus's wanton conflation of his own ideas with those of Anaxagoras. In addition, Strepsiades claims to have learned that Vortex has cast out Zeus from "Socrates the Melian" (830), and it is reasonable to suppose that the reference here is to Diagoras of Melos, who was widely regarded as impious or an atheist (Lana 1959; Mignanego 1992: 87). As for the school's investigations into biology, Diogenes (fragments 6, 9) and Democritus are known to have been interested in human physiology. The hostility to Socrates in *Clouds* may, then, represent Aristophanes' way of capturing the popular anxiety aroused not just by Socrates himself but by the entire intellectual movement that we denote by the terms "presocratic" and "sophist," though Greeks of the time would have seen little or no difference between them.

But if Socrates is a stand-in for new currents of critical thought generally, why did Aristophanes and Ameipsias concentrate specifically on him? Surely he must have been an apt and conspicuous object of fun and derision in a way, perhaps, that other contemporary thinkers were not. Several explanations come to mind for Socrates' suitability as a scapegoat in 423 – before, that is, his association with radical political figures such as Alcibiades and Critias tarnished his reputation and no doubt provoked the trial and condemnation in 399, although the amnesty declared in 403 forbade explicit mention of the bloody class warfare that had divided Athens since 411. For one thing, Socrates seems to have been odd-looking, always a good qualification for being the butt of humor (Karavites 1973–74), though it must be acknowledged that, as Dover points out (1968: xxxii), there is no mention of his appearance in *Clouds* (whether this was conveyed by a grotesque mask is a moot question). Besides this, Socrates was a native Athenian, whereas the great majority of natural philosophers and rhetoricians were foreign; it is better to attack a figure who is local and known to many than to pick on a visitor like Gorgias or Protagoras, who might be good for a laugh but hardly would sustain an Athenian audience's interest for an entire play (Whitman 1964: 142; Henderson 1992: 12). Finally, and perhaps most important, Socrates was a character and even a bit of a public nuisance – that is, he was not simply an elite scientist or dialectician who hobnobbed with the rich, but a busy-body, as the Athenians would perceive it, who went round confronting people in the streets and squares, arguing with them and exposing their exaggerated opinion of their own intelligence. At least, this is the way Plato's Socrates describes the effect of his open-air interrogations. And the effect of his interrogations, along with the absence of any positive educational program, may well have been, or been perceived as, corrosive to traditional values (Nussbaum 1980: 81–85; Vander Vaerdt 1994: 79).

In Plato's *Apology*, Socrates seems to suggest that this practice of seeking out interlocutors among the people was inspired primarily by the response that his friend Chaerephon received from the Delphic oracle – Chaerephon inquired whether anyone was wiser than Socrates, and the Pythian priestess replied that no one was (20E-21A). Socrates claims that he was so incredulous at this response that he decided to investigate its meaning by questioning all who had a reputation for wisdom. The *Apology* leaves the impression that prior to the oracle, Socrates did not make it his practice to interrogate his fellow citizens at large.[24]

Two questions pose themselves. First, what did Socrates do before the oracle set him on this path? Second, when did Chaerephon put his fateful query? As to the latter, there is no external evidence for even an approximate date. It is curious, however, that there is no allusion to the oracle in *Clouds*, even though Chaerephon is several times mentioned there as either an associate or a pupil of Socrates' (104, 144–147, 156, 503, 831). Does this warrant the inference that the episode occurred some time after 423 (or later even than the revised version)? Even before the oracle, Socrates must have gained a reputation for cleverness, or else both Chaerephon's question and the response would be strange. It is not necessary to assume that he was at this stage still engaged in natural science, as opposed to ethical inquiries (contra Vander Waerdt 1994: 79). Indeed, while the oracle's response might have caused him to put its meaning to the test for a while, Socrates' account in Plato's *Apology* does not imply that he did so for any length of time. Once he had satisfied himself that the ignorance of others lay in the belief that they knew what in fact they did not, Socrates presumably went back to discussing matters with friends and acquaintances as he had done before.

It is fair to assume that something about Socrates had caught the Athenians' attention in or shortly before 423, for him to be the subject of a spoof in two comedies that year. Very possibly there is an allusion to such an event in *Clouds*, but if so, it is opaque to us. Whatever it was, Socrates provided a good target for a satire on the new learning and rhetoric, for he was typical enough to represent the movement as a whole and at the same time sufficiently idiosyncratic to be readily identifiable as a unique personality.

WORKS CITED

Adkins A. W. H. "Clouds, Mysteries, Socrates and Plato." *Antichthon* 4 (1970): 13–24.
Andic, M. 2001. "Clouds of Irony." In *International Kierkegaard Commentary: The Concept of Irony*, ed. R. L. Perkins. Macon, GA, 2001.

24 On the oracle, see West 1979, pp. 104–126; Brickhouse and Smith 1989, pp. 87–108; Stokes 1992; Holland 2000: ch. 4.

Barzin, M. "Sur les Nuées d'Aristophane." *Bulletin de la Classe des letters de L'Academie Royal Belgique* 54 (1968): 378–388.

Berg, S. "Rhetoric, Nature, and Philosophy in Aristophanes' Clouds." *Ancient Philosophy* 18 (1998): 1–19.

Blyth, D. "Cloud Morality and the Meteorology of Some Choral Odes." *Scholia* 3 (1994): 24–45.

Brickhouse, T. C., and N. D. Smith. *Socrates on Trial*. Princeton, 1989.

Byl, S. "Parodie d'une initiation dans les Nuées d'Aristophane." *Latomus* 80 (1980): 5–21.

Davies, M. "'Popular justice' and the end of Aristophanes' Clouds." *Hermes* 118 (1990): 237–242.

de Vries, G. J. "Mystery Terminology in Aristophanes and Plato." *Mnemosyne* 26 (1973): 1–8.

Dieterich, A. "Ueber eine Scene der aristophanischen Wolken." *Rheinisches Museum* 48 (1893): 275–283

Dover, K. J., ed. *Aristophanes Clouds*. Oxford, 1968.

Edmunds L. "Aristophanes' Socrates." *Proceedings of the Boston Area Colloquium in Ancient Philosophy* 2 (1986): 209–230.

Gaertner, J. F. "Der Wolken-Chor des Aristophanes." *Rheinisches Museum* 142 (1999): 272–279.

Gelzer, T. "Aristophanes und sein Sokrates." *Museum Helveticum.* 13 (1956): 65–93.

Goldberg S. M. "A note on Aristophanes' Phrontistêrion." *Classical Philology* 71 (1976): 254–256.

Guthrie, W. K. C. *Socrates*. Cambridge, 1971.

Handley, E. W. "Words for 'Soul,' 'Heart' and 'Mind' in Aristophanes." *Rheinisches Museum* 19 (N.F. 99) (1956): 205–225.

Harvey, F. D. "Nubes 1493ff.: Was Socrates Murdered?" *GRBS* 22 (1981): 339–343.

Havelock, Eric A. "The Socratic Self as It Is Parodied in Aristophanes' Clouds." *Yale Classical Studies* 22 (1972): 1–18.

Henderson, Jeffrey, trans. *Aristophanes' Clouds*. Newburyport, MA, 1992.

Holland, G. S. *Divine Irony*. Selinsgrove, PA, 2000.

Hubbard, T. K. *The Mask of Comedy: Aristophanes and the Intertextual Parabasis.* Ithaca, 1991.

Janko, R. "The Physicist as Hierophant: Aristophanes, Socrates and the Authorship of the Derveni Papyrus." *Zeitschrift für Papyrologie und Epigraphik* 118 (1997): 61–94.

Karavites, P. "Socrates in the Clouds." *Classical Bulletin* 50 (1973–1974): 65–69.

Kierkegaard, Søren. 1989. *The Conception of Irony, with Continual Reference to Socrates: Together with Notes of Schelling's Berlin Lectures*, ed. and trans. H. V. Hong and E. H. Hong. Princeton, 1989.

Kleve, K. "Anti-Dover or Socrates in the Clouds." *Symbolae Osloenses* 58 (1983): 23–37.

Konstan, D. *Greek Comedy and Ideology*. New York, 1995.

Konstan, D. "'This is that Man:' Staging Clouds 1142–77." *Classical Quarterly* 56 (2006): 595–598.

Kopff, E. C. "Nubes 1493ff.: Was Socrates Murdered?" *GRBS* 18 (1977): 113–122.

Kopff, E. C. "The date of Aristophanes, Nubes II." *American Journal of Philology* 111 (1990): 318–329.

Lana, I. "Diagora di Melo." *Atti dell'Accademia delle Scienze di Torino* 84 (1959): 161–205.

Marianetti, M. C. *Religion and Politics in Aristophanes' Clouds.* Hildesheim, 1992.

Marianetti, M. C. "Socratic mystery-parody and the issue of asebeia in Aristophanes' Clouds." *Symbolae Osloenses* 68 (1993): 5–31.

Mastromarco, Giussepe, ed. *Commedie di Aristofane.* Vol. 1: *Nubes.* Turin, 1983.

Mignanego, P. "Aristofane e la rappresentazione di Socrate." *Dioniso* 62 (1992): 71–101.

Morales Troncoso, D. "El Sócrates de Aristófanes en la parodia de Las nubes." *Diadoche* 4.1–2 (2001): 35–58.

Nussbaum, M. 1980. "Aristophanes and Socrates on Learning Practical Wisdom." *Yale Classical Studies* 26 (1980): 43–97.

Patzer, A. "Die Wolken des Aristophanes als philosophiegeschichtliches Dokument." In *Motiv und Motivation,* ed. P. Neukam. Munich, 1993.

Redfield, J. "Poetry and Philosophy in Aristophanes' Clouds." In *Literary Imagination, Ancient and Modern: Essays in Honor of David Grene,* ed. T. Breyfogle. Chicago, 1999.

Rossetti, L. "Le Nuvole di Aristofane. Perchè furono una commedia e non una farsa." *Rivista di cultura classica e medioevale* 16 (1974): 131–136.

Sarri, F. "Rilettura delle Nuvole di Aristofane come fonte per la conoscenza di Socrate." *Rivista di Filosofia Neo-Scolastica* 65 (1973): 532–550.

Sarri, F. *Socrate e la genesi dell'idea occidentale di anima.* 2 vols. Rome, 1975.

Segal, C. "Aristophanes' Cloud-Chorus." *Arethusa* 2 (1969): 143–161. repr. In *Aristophanes und die alte Komödie.* Darmstadt, 1975.

Segal C. "Protagoras' orthoepeia in Aristophanes' Battle of the Prologues." *RhM* 113 (1970): 158–162.

Souto Delibes, Fernando. 1997. "La figura de Sócrates en la comedia ateniense." In *Sociedad, política y literatura: Comedia griega antigua.* Actas del I Congreso Internacional, Salamanca, noviembre 1996, ed. Antonio López Eire. Salamanca, 1996.

Starkie, W. J. M. *The Clouds of Aristophanes.* London, 1911.

Stokes, M. C. 1992. "Socrates' Mission." In *Socratic Questions: New Essays on the Philosophy of Socrates and its Significance,* eds. Barry S. Gower and Michael C. Stokes. New York, 1992, pp. 26–81.

Storey, I. C. "The Dates of Aristophanes' Clouds II and Eupolis' Baptai: A Reply to E. C. Kopff." *American Journal of Philology* 114 (1993): 71–84.

Tarrant, H. "Midwifery and the Clouds." *CQ* 38 (1988): 116–122.

Tarrant, H. "Clouds I: Steps towards Reconstruction." *Arctos: Acta Philologica Fennica* 25 (1991): 157–181.

Taylor, A. E. 1911. "The *Phrontisterion*." *Varia Socratica,* First Series. St. Andrews University Publications 9 (1911): 129–177.

Tomin, Julius. 1987. "Socratic Gymnasium in the Clouds." *Symbolae Osloenses* 62: 25–32.

Vander Waerdt, P. A. "Socrates in the Clouds." In *The Socratic Movement,* ed. P.A. Vander Waerdt. Ithaca, 1994, pp. 48–86.

West, T. G. 1979. *Plato's Apology of Socrates: An Interpretation with a New Translation.* Ithaca, 1979.

Whitman, C. H. *Aristophanes and the Comic Hero.* Cambridge, 1964.

5   Socrates and the New Learning

Socrates' life coincides with a period in which various intellectual movements seemed, to conservatives, to mount a concerted attack on traditional values.[1] These movements I will gather under one name, "the new learning," without meaning to imply that any one person subscribed to all of them. The two elements in the new learning that seem to have troubled traditionalists the most were natural science and forensic argument. Socrates was associated in the public eye with the new learning; this association is one of the few things we know about him with historical certainty. Probably he was part of the movement in his own unique way, although he had little to do with science and was opposed to the teaching of public speaking.

I. SCIENCE AND ARGUMENT

The natural science of the day differed from modern science in many ways, but it has this similarity: it sought to displace traditional supernatural explanations with natural ones, and in so doing it encountered resistance (though not so fierce as the modern American resistance to the teaching of evolution). Early cosmologists proposed accounts of the beginnings of things in terms of familiar natural processes,[2] while early anthropologists explained culture as produced by human invention,[3]

1   Our main evidence for this is Aristophanes' *Clouds*, which shows that he or his audience were troubled by various aspects of the new learning (421 BCE).
2   Early cosmologists include such figures as Anaximander (whose process may have been a vortex) and Anaximenes (condensation and rarefaction), who antedate the new learning by a century (flourishing in the mid-sixth century BCE), but cosmological speculation continued in the fifth century with Anaxagoras (who did posit a vortex), and evidently provoked a response from traditionalists. Aristophanes' *Clouds* shows Socrates' school replacing Zeus with Vortex (line 828).
3   Early anthropological texts include the *Anonymus Iamblichi*, the Ode to Man in Sophocles' *Antigone*, the *Prometheus Bound*, Protagoras' great speech in Plato's *Protagoras*, and Thucydides' *Archaeology*. See Guthrie 1971, pp. 79–84, and, on the origins of this part of the new learning, Cole 1967.

and one historian explained human events in terms of an empirical theory of human nature.[4] Taken together, these theories leave no room for traditional explanations that appeal to action by the gods. The new learning offered the ancient Greeks cosmology without creation, human progress without divine teaching, and human history without divine intervention. True atheism is elusive in this period, and we do not know for certain of any thinker who denied the existence of the gods.[5] Denying that the gods take action falls short of atheism in the full sense, but this was revolutionary enough to arouse a strong reaction. "Why should we dance," a chorus of Sophocles asks, in effect, "if the gods do not make the oracles they give come true?"[6] Why, indeed, take part in any religious practices? If the gods take no actions that might affect us, why seek to influence them through sacrifice, ritual or prayer? There is an answer, of course, that appeals to the ethical effect of ceremony on individuals and community, but this would have been too subtle for the defenders of tradition (as it is now for current defenders of creation myth).[7]

4   For Thucydides' view on human nature, see Reeve 1999. Thucydides holds that human behavior follows general patterns, familiar to the historian, that are affected in different ways by different circumstances: "Civil war brought many atrocities to the cities, such as happen and will always happen as long as human nature is the same, although they may be more or less violent or take different forms, depending on the variety of circumstances in each case. In peace and prosperity, cities and private individuals alike are better minded because they are not plunged into the necessity of doing anything against their will; but war is a violent teacher: it gives most people impulses that are as bad as their situation when it takes away the easy supply of what they need for daily life" (3.82). This and all other translations used in this chapter are my own, either from Gagarin and Woodruff 1995, or, as in this case, from Woodruff 1993.

5   The speaker in the Sisyphus fragment, probably by Euripides, is an atheist in the full sense, but we do not know of any historical figure who held this view. See Kahn 1997. Prodicus belongs to those who explained religious belief, but it is not obvious that he was therefore an atheist: "The sun and the moon and rivers and springs and everything else that benefited our lives were called gods by early people because they are beneficial. The Egyptians, for example, deified the Nile" (Fragment 5).

6   This is the burden of the second stasimon of *Oedipus Tyrannus*; the famous lines (895–896) are: "But if gods give honor to a life like that, / Why should I dance in prayer and praise?"

7   As practiced, the religion of ancient Greece was hard to distinguish from practices designed to influence or even (as in magic) manipulate the gods. But the deeper meaning of sacrifice, as represented in the poets, has to do with the exchange of honor across the divide between the human and the divine, and exchange that did not necessarily place gods under obligation to humans. Reverence is primarily an ethical virtue, expressed but not

Forensic argument was one of a number of subjects taught by traveling teachers who later came to be called sophists. These partners in the new learning taught a number of subjects under the title of "the art of words." These included display speeches for intellectual entertainment, as well as techniques for presenting arguments in deliberative and forensic contexts. In addition, various sophists taught such subjects as mathematics, astronomy, history, literary criticism, anthropology, ethics, and political theory. Whether any sophist taught what is now known as rhetoric is controversial.[8]

Athenians singled out forensic argument from this catalogue of offerings because of its role in the people's courts of Athens. Prominent citizens feared being prosecuted by someone who had mastered the art – any citizen could prosecute – and ordinary people were afraid that criminals who had mastered the art could talk their way to freedom, no matter how guilty they were. Both fears were summed up in the expression, supposed to capture the Sophists' principal teaching, "to make the weaker argument stronger." In itself, it would appear harmless to teach students to strengthen weak arguments, but the expression was taken to imply that a successful student of the sophists could make the wrong side win. The fear this engendered was more real than the threat; the greatest master of forensic argument in the period was Antiphon, who was executed (probably with justice) in spite of having given a famously brilliant speech in his own defense.[9]

2. THE CASE OF SOCRATES

Popular opinion held that Socrates was heavily tainted by the new learning, while his defenders – Xenophon and Plato – showed him resisting certain innovations.[10] But Socrates' resistance was evidently far from

---

embodied in the practices that appeared to serve the interests of the gods. On the topic, see for example Woodruff 2001.

8　On sophists, see Guthrie 1971, Kerferd 1981. For relevant texts, see Sprague 1972, which translates the relevant parts of Diels-Kranz; also Gagarin and Woodruff 1995. Plato's representations of sophists dominated the intellectual arena before Hegel reevaluated them; the groundbreaking work in English is the famous chapter Grote about them in his history (1869), but the spell of Plato still hangs over this subject. For recent views on the sophists, which differ from what has been widely taught in the past, see Bett 1989, Woodruff 1997, and Gagarin 2001. For the controversy about rhetoric, see Cole 1991 and Schiappa 1990 and 1999.

9　Antiphon's defense speech was admired by Thucydides (8.68.2); a fragment of it has survived and is translated in Gagarin and Woodruff 1995, p. 219.

10　Modern opinions of Socrates derive mainly from Plato and Xenophon, with two results: first, sophists have been viewed as moral dangers (until Hegel

a defense of tradition. Even as he is shown by his defenders, he was affected by the new learning, like other thinkers of his time, so that his resistance to the new learning consisted in developing alternatives to the intellectual fashions of the day that were no less revolutionary than were the fashions he opposed. Socrates' trial does not admit of a single explanation; for all we know, the majority of the 501 judges on the panel had many different reasons for voting to convict. But Socrates' reputation as a teacher of the new learning surely gave him a bad odor.[11] This reputation had been spread far and wide by a popular play produced about twentytwo years earlier.

In his comic play, *The Clouds*, Aristophanes imagined a school, run by Socrates, that promotes both natural science and persuasive argument; thus Aristophanes conveniently painted one human target for the conservative wrath that both of these trends aroused. Plato's *Apology of Socrates*, however, shows the philosopher claiming in his defense that the play's informal accusations against him are false. As to evaluating this defense, we must admit some measure of ignorance; our sources will not allow us to claim that we know precisely what the historical Socrates taught and thought. But for the purposes of this chapter, Plato will suffice. If Plato does not detach Socrates from the new learning – as I will show he does not – then probably the historical Socrates had something of the new learning in him. Just how closely Socrates belonged to the new learning is the question of this chapter.

3. THE NEW LEARNING

There is more to the new learning than science and forensic argument. In order to evaluate Socrates' place in this family of intellectual movements, we need to review its main elements in more detail. The contributors to the new learning include the traveling teachers who became known as sophists, and who had a wide repertoire of subjects to teach – Protagoras, Gorgias, Hippias, Prodicus, and Antiphon are the main figures. We should also include the historians, of whom the most famous are Herodotus and Thucydides, for their interests in the origins of culture and the explanation of human events. To these we should add fifth-century philosophers such as Democritus and Anaxagoras, for their interest in explaining the natural world. Democritus was interested also

and Grote, and still by many writers); second, Aristophanes' evidence for Socrates tends to be set aside. This chapter starts from a fairly positive view of the sorts of things that sophists taught, and looks for similar elements in our main philosophical sources for Socrates.

11   Plato's *Apology* explicitly responds to the *Clouds*. Xenophon's *Memorabilia* takes pains to show Socrates as differing from the sophists.

in human subjects, and he may have been the founder of the new movement in anthropology that surfaces in a number of surviving texts.[12] In
natural science, the main figures of the new learning are the medical
writers whose work survives in the Hippocratic Corpus, and who favor
naturalistic explanations for medical phenomena. The influence of the
new learning shows plainly on the major Athenian poets of the period as
well: the author of *Prometheus Bound* (possibly Aeschylus), Sophocles,
and Euripides, all of whom show an interest in debate, and disputation,
as well as in the human explanation of human events.

Why make a group of these disparate thinkers? Because they were
all engaged in the sort of thing that seems to have upset the audience
for Aristophanes' *Clouds*. Because what they were doing was new in
the fifth century BCE, though building on ideas that were as old as we
can trace in Greek thought. And because they shared certain features –
a willingness to question traditional ideas and customs, a fascination
with what it is to be human, and a delight in the effective use of words.
There are five main themes, which I will treat at greater length next.

3.1. *Displacement of the Divine*

In this period, educated people increasingly sought natural explanations
for events of all kinds. Traditional stories explained things by appeal to
actions of the gods, conceiving of them as personalities on the human
model. Such stories were displaced by the new nature-based explanations. I have already discussed this as a kind of natural science, but we
should distinguish it from modern science. All the explanations that
displaced gods appealed in some way to nature, to natural processes or
to something like human nature, and many of them appealed to observation. But few of them were supported by the sort of empirical study
that modern science demands. Little experimentation occurred, and
none of it in this period used anything like controls. The whole enterprise was highly speculative, and, indeed, it seemed to depend heavily
on its propounders' mastery of the art of words, rather than on a mar-
shalling of evidence.[13]

Thucydides' example is instructive for the case of social science.
Although he appears to support his views from the empirical evidence
given in his narrative, the narrative itself is not well grounded in

---

12 Cole 1967.
13 So Gorgias on astronomy, in his *Encomium of Helen*, 13: "To see that
    persuasion, when added to speech, indeed molds the mind as it wishes,
    one must first study the arguments of astronomers, who replace opinion
    with opinion: displacing one but implanting another, they make incredible,
    invisible matters apparent to the eyes of opinion."

evidence. Thucydides' famous realism consists in his underlying thesis that human beings are more affected by fear, greed, and ambition than they are by religious considerations. His story, indeed, bears this out. But he has selected certain parts of the story to tell prominently, others to bury in what amounts to his fine print, and still others to pass over in silence. In particular, he has neglected to bring out the events that would have shown to a less biased historian that religious consider-ations were indeed operative in history.[14]

The general point is that the naturalistic explanations of the new learning were far less powerful than those of modern science. A critical thinker could conscientiously reject many of them as too speculative and too dependent on clever speech to be entirely credible.

3.2. Consistency Concerning the Gods

Also, in this period and even earlier, many thinkers rejected an obvious inconsistency at the center of storytelling about the gods: On the one hand, the gods were depicted as superhuman beings who used their pow-ers to get away with doing things we humans would condemn on moral grounds (but would perhaps secretly like to get away with ourselves). On the other, the gods were supposed to be champions of justice and other virtues, even, sometimes, to be moral exemplars in themselves. But they cannot really be both. Rather than reject the moral-exemplar model, thinkers who desired consistency would deny (or at least not believe) the storytelling about the gods.[15]

3.3. Respect for Human Wisdom

The growing humanism of the period colored the arts and fed the drive for democracy.[16] This humanism is reflected in the new anthropology

---

14   Hornblower 1992 shows "What Thucydides does not tell us" concerning religious factors in the war between Sparta and Athens.

15   On the role of the gods in ethics, see especially Lloyd-Jones 1983; on discomfort felt over this inconsistency during our period, see, for exam-ple, Euripides *Ion*, lines 436–451 (Gagarin and Woodruff 1995, pp. 67–68). "Those who teach such things" in the last line may refer to the poets who tell stories of divine immorality:

  For when you [the gods] chase pleasures without a thought for the future,
  you commit injustice. It will no longer be just to call men bad
  if we are only following the 'good' examples set by gods;
  only those who teach such things are rightly called bad.

16   Democracy in this period meant primarily the rotation of positions among the citizens by lot, the stringent accountability of magistrates, and the

(Section, 3.1 and n. 3), which sought human causes for human progress. Confidence in human judgment is reflected in the moral criticism of the gods as shown in poetry (discussed in Section 3.2). But the most striking display of humanism was the rise of democracy in Sicily, Athens, and many other parts of the Greek world. Traditional Greek governance probably always involved an assembly of military-age male citizens, as depicted in Homer and practiced in Sparta; such assemblies voted on issues placed before them, but the right of speaking before the assembly was reserved for men of high rank. In democracy, however, every citizen had the right to speak in the assembly, and the man-in-the-agora cherished the right to speak in the assembly, although he was unlikely to exercise it in practice.[17]

The importance of this development is underlined by the howls of protest against it from aristocrats such as Plato, who countered with the ship-of-state metaphor: Who would want to pause for a meeting during a storm at sea? And who would even listen to an ordinary seaman when the captain is an expert navigator?[18] This anti-democratic metaphor is designed to make the point that ordinary people do not know enough to take part in their own governance. But the point would not need to be made unless a great many people disagreed – unless, as the facts of democracy indicate, many believed in the wisdom of the common man.

To an elitist philosopher, the wisdom of the common man would threaten to justify appeals to common opinion, and thus support the practice of presenting issues to a large audience for debate and decision – a practice widely honored in Greece and developed into a fine art by some teachers of the new learning (3.5).

right of adult male citizens to speak in Assembly. For further details, see Hansen 1991. For the connection with the new learning, see Farrar 1988 and Woodruff 2005.

17 People who spoke regularly in Assembly, and were skilled at doing so, were called *rhetors*. For the importance of the right of speaking in Assembly, see Euripides, *Suppliant Women*, pp. 438–441, where Theseus is speaking for ordinary Athenians, defending democracy:

> This is freedom, to ask "Who has a good proposal
> he wishes to introduce for public discussion?"
> And one who responds gains fame, while one who wishes
> not to is silent. What could be fairer than that in a city?

18 Plato's use of the metaphor is prominent at *Republic* 6.488bc; see also *Protagoras* 319de on the issue. The image is misleading: In a boat, all truly depend for survival on working together under good leadership, and leadership in a boat can be learned. In a city, it is not clear that leadership can be learned (as Socrates goes on to show in the *Protagoras*), and the rich or powerful may be able to arrange privately for their own survival.

A further development of this idea is the relativism Plato attributes to Protagoras, that what an individual believes is true, at least for that person.[19] Protagoras was probably not that sort of relativist, but he did say, "A human being is the measure of all things, of those things that are that they are, and of those things that are not that they are not" (Fragment 1). What he meant is not certain, but it seems at least to express confidence in the minds of human beings to get things right – "all things" says Protagoras, implying that if something is not apparent to the human mind, it is not there at all. And this is no doubt a response to the natural philosophers who appeal in their explanations to that which is neither seen nor seeable.[20]

Plato's criticism of Protagoras' relativism has blurred the historical picture. Protagoras was certainly not a consistent relativist, and he may not have been a relativist at all.[21] As we shall see in the next section, the most common theme among teachers of the new learning was not relativism, but something incompatible with that – the criticism of the role of custom in culture. Democracy does not assume that the will of the people is always right; indeed, the Athenians' experience taught them the necessity of placing certain checks on the power of the Assembly.[22] One may urge respect for the wisdom of ordinary people without teaching relativism.[23]

3.4. Criticism of Custom and Law

Teachers of the new learning recognized the enormous power of custom in human life, and they sought grounds to challenge it. A famous anecdote from Herodotus shows how clearly Greek intellectuals of the period understood the way custom varies in its demands, requiring a certain type of funeral in one culture while making it abhorrent in another:

During his reign, Darius called in some Greeks who were in Persia, and asked them how much money would make them willing to eat the dead bodies of

19   *Theaetetus* 152a6–8, cf 167c4–5.
20   Gorgias, *Helen 13*, quoted in n. 13.
21   Protagoras' doctrine of the correctness of words is not compatible with relativism, nor is his idea (if it is his) that justice and reverence are gifts from Zeus to humankind. On the general issue of sophists and relativism, see Woodruff 1997 and Bett 1989.
22   After the trial of the generals in command at Arginusae, Athenians took care not to let the Assembly triumph over law again. The trial was an anomaly, and in the early fourth century the democracy evolved in ways that checked the power of the assembly (Woodruff 2005, p. 56).
23   For a modern defense of the idea that, on specific kinds of issues, crowds can be wiser than experts, see Surowiecki 2004.

their fathers; and they said they would not do this for anything. After that, Darius called in some people from India called Callatians, who do eat their parents. (The Greeks were there, and understood what they said through an interpreter.) Then Darius asked the Callatians what sum of money they would take to burn their fathers on a pyre after their death; the Callatians gave a great shriek and told him not to speak sacrilege. So we see that these things are set by custom; and Pindar, in my opinion, was right when he called custom "king of all."[24]

Recognizing the power of custom is the first step in taking a critical attitude toward it. If a type of funeral were actually grounded in the nature of things, or in divine commandment, then everyone would have to use that type or suffer serious consequences. But a little travel showed the Greeks that this was not the case. Different funerals seemed to work equally well for different peoples, and the gods did not plainly punish a people for not being Greek in their way of life. It follows that the grounds supporting each way of life are roughly equal.

Two contrary responses to this discovery are possible. One is the relativistic conclusion that there are no objective grounds for choosing a type of funeral, so that a custom is right for those who follow it, and no more is to be said. All are governed by custom, and this is the true ruler in human affairs: "Custom is king"; *nomos basileus*, as Pindar famously had it.[25] This leaves us with a cultural relativism that allows no grounds for criticizing or reforming traditions.

Individual relativism is the view that a proposition is true for you if you believe it; and cultural relativism says that a custom is right wherever it is the custom. Individual relativism is absurd and easily refuted, but cultural relativism might be satisfactory for funerals. It is less attractive, however, for the laws that define justice and injustice for a society. Not all teachers of the new learning accepted the inference from observations of cultural difference to the strong conclusion that custom ought to be king (not the same as "custom *is* king"). And, indeed, the inference is false. The different laws might imperfectly express a common principle of justice that could itself be objectively grounded. This would be so if, as Protagoras and other teachers of the new learning believed, justice is essential to the survival of society, as a result of certain features in human nature or, at least, to common features of the human condition.[26]

24 Herodotus, *History* 3.38.
25 On Pindar's "custom is king," see the translation and comment in Gagarin and Woodruff 1995, pp. 40–41.
26 For Protagoras, see Plato's *Protagoras*, 320c-22d; for Plato, who builds the argument of the *Republic* on this assumption, see *Republic* 433a, cf. 369.

If there is any way to ground a conception of justice in nature, then we should be prepared to question the customs that are supposed to express justice. Some teachers of the new learning rejected custom-based justice altogether and sought to replace it with nature-based laws and conceptions of justice.[27] This is, of course, antithetical to relativism, as it seeks a common objective standard for morality. But it is equally threatening to traditional morality. Both relativism and the criticism of custom leave tradition in a weakened state; it should be no surprise that traditionalists reacted against the new learning with violent defensiveness.

Law and custom are related through a common Greek word, *nomos*, which is used for both. Some thinkers who criticized customary ideas about justice also criticized the laws of the city and did not always distinguish the two. (I use this term to distinguish laws of the city from divine law or the law of the Greeks, an unwritten inter-city code of conduct.) The ancient concept of law seems always to have been normative – that is, law was never understood in a purely positive way as the command of those in authority. When teachers of the new learning came up with the idea that law was the product of a social contract, they intended by that proposal to undermine the moral force of law. If law has no more hold on us than an agreement negotiated out of weakness, then it would seem that people ought to disregard it in favor of guiding principles that are better grounded, in the nature of things, as Callicles proposes.[28]

3.5. The Art of Words

Most teachers of the new learning taught the arts of *logoi*, and these included theories of language (such as speech-act theory), the art of display oratory (a form of entertainment), skill in disputation, and what we would now call rhetoric for forensic and deliberative purposes. Plato implies that Gorgias and others taught rhetoric as a distinct art, separable from all other divisions of knowledge, and devoted exclusively to persuasion.[29] But some scholars argue that this conception of rhetoric is an invention of Plato's. Be that as may be, no teacher of the new learning, with the possible exception of Gorgias, set himself up as a teacher of rhetoric in this sense, and even Gorgias seems to have been more

---

27 Callicles' rejection of *nomos* (custom, law) in favor of nature is given at Plato's *Gorgias*, 482e–483d. Callicles may be a product of fiction, but Antiphon was real enough, and he seems to have criticized *nomos* from the standpoint of nature (Fragment 44, Gagarin and Woodruff 1995, pp. 245–47; on the interpretation, see Woodruff 2004).

28 The main texts are: Plato, *Republic* 358e3–359b5 and *Gorgias* 483a7–484c3.

29 *Gorgias* 452e, cf. 459c; *Phaedrus* 260a.

interested in displays of oratory than in successful persuasion.[30] Gorgias did say, in a display speech, that language is as powerful as a drug, but he raised doubts as to whether communication is possible at all.[31]

Late in the fifth century, there developed a profession of logography, or speechwriting. Experts in this field, such as Lysias, Antiphon (who was probably also a teacher of the new learning), and the young Demosthenes, wrote speeches for Athenians to use in legal cases, and these were meant to persuade. The speaker's life might depend on his ability to win a debate, so that the arts of words developed in the new learning were put to serious use in these written speeches. Rich people who could afford logographers, or, for that matter, could pay for private lessons with a teacher like Gorgias, were thought to be at an advantage in court. But, as we have seen, the art did not save Antiphon.

We know a fair amount about display speeches, because a number of them have survived. Forensic rhetoric we know from late in the period through the speeches of Lysias and the fragment of Antiphon's defense speech. We do not know as much about the art of disputation, however, because we depend mainly on Plato's reports and fictional examples, most notable of which is the set of disputational fireworks in the *Euthydemus*. These show sophists making clever and interesting use of fallacy, but they belong to historical fiction.

Protagoras was interested in the classification of speech acts and in something he called either "correctness of words" or "correctness of diction", and this apparently covered such matters as the avoidance of contradiction and the appropriate assignment of gender to words.[32] Prodicus was evidently interested in fine distinctions and the precise choice among words with similar meanings.[33] These teachers of the new learning appear to have had an interest in language as an object of study for its own sake, and not merely as a tool for persuasion.

4. SOCRATES' RESPONSE

Socrates was part of the new learning in many ways, but he parted company with its principal teachers on crucial points. He did not claim to

---

30 For the thesis that Plato invented rhetoric, see Cole 1991 and Schiappa 1990 and 1999; for the point about persuasion, see Gagarin 2001.

31 On the paradox of Gorgias' views on language, see Mourelatos 1987.

32 For Protagoras on correctness, see Plato, *Protagoras* 338e7–339a1 in its context, which concerns contradiction, as well as *Cratylus* 391c3 and *Phaedrus* 267c6. For the idea of correctness in argument, see Plutarch, *Life of Pericles* 36.3, 172. For the point about gender, see Aristotle, *Sophisticis Elenchis* 14, 173b17. For Protagoras' interest in classifying speech acts, see Aristotle, *Poetics* 19, 1456b15.

33 Prodicus on words: *Charmides* 163d, *Cratylus* 384b, *Laches* 197d.

be a teacher, as they did, and he did not expect payment from those who kept company with him for the sake of learning. He did have an effect on young men, however, and he was in some sense a teacher. This was fatal for him. Plato is not helpful for evaluating Socratic teaching because he rarely shows Socrates with his most Socratic followers, such as Chaerephon, preferring instead to represent him in failed discussions with figures such as Charmides, who plainly miss the point.

4.1. Displacement of the Divine

The *Clouds* accuses Socrates of trying to displace the gods from explanations of natural events, as we have seen, but Plato vigorously defends him on this charge, both in the *Apology* and in other dialogues. In the *Phaedo*, Socrates says that he was dissatisfied with the kind of explanation sought by Anaxagoras (96a-99d) because it overlooked the real cause of things – why it is good for things to be as they are. Philosophers such as Anaxagoras, he implied, were offering merely necessary causes – what later came to be called material and efficient causes – in place of teleological ones, which, he implied, must figure in any genuine explanation.

In the *Phaedrus*, Socrates briefly adverts to natural explanations for stories about the gods. There he says that he cannot take time to explain away all the stories about the gods; he is too busy trying to know himself, and so he "accepts what is generally believed" (229d-230a).

Socrates held back from the displacement of the divine by natural explanation, not because he was a traditionalist but because he had thrown himself into new projects that lay outside the boundaries of the new learning. Either the inward journey toward self knowledge or the drive to understand the world teleologically would suffice to pluck Socrates out of the mainstream of the new learning and set him down as the source of an entirely new river, which grew to flood height in the period after Aristotle.

There is one niche, however, from which Socrates did displace the gods, although on this point he is not plainly at odds with traditional teaching. Socrates does not assign to any god the role of moral arbiter. He seems committed in the *Euthyphro* to the view that it is not divine approval that makes an action virtuous; rather, the gods approve the action because it is virtuous (11ab).

Probably writing much later, Plato has Socrates assign human and divine souls to the same position with respect to the Form of Justice. Both species – both gods and humans – depend on being able to see the Form where it rests in the space beyond heaven. If they fail to see it, they wear out their ability to remain in heaven; the only difference is that gods are better able than human beings to fly high enough to see the Forms over the rim of the heavenly theater (*Phaedrus* 246a-249c).

Socrates' general view seems to be that the reasoning which grounds ethical judgment is more accessible to gods than to men, but that such reasoning is independent of most facts about the gods; "a god desires it" could never figure in ethical reasoning.[34] The gods of the *Phaedrus* are exemplars for us only because they have their eyes on the Forms. Socrates never at any point in the Platonic corpus proposes to settle a question of ethics by reference to divine will or divine revelation, not even by appeal to his personal divine voice. The ethical displacement of gods is in line with the new learning, but its clear articulation seems to have been unique to Socrates.

4.2. *Consistency Concerning the Gods*

On this, Socrates simply subscribes to the position widely taken by fifth-century intellectuals: that stories of unethical behavior by gods cannot be true. Indeed, Socrates attributed the charge of impiety against him to his refusal to subscribe to such stories (*Euthyphro* 6ab).

Socrates therefore does not do exactly as he says in the *Phaedrus* at 229d-230a. Plato may be inconsistent on the matter, but it is more likely that the *Phaedrus* passage has to be read under a Socratic sort of interpretation. Instead of simply accepting what was generally believed about the gods, whatever that may be, Socrates accepted a belief-system that is defined under the *elenchus* (Socrates' method of testing for consistency). If challenged to defend his claim to accept the going beliefs, he would answer that he subscribes to what is left of traditional beliefs after elenchus – that is, to a consistent subset of them, specifically, the subset of common beliefs about the gods that are consistent with the central premise that the gods are moral exemplars, a premise he would not expect any of his partners to reject under cross-examination.

In this way, Socrates contrives, not without irony, to claim allegiance to common views while proposing a radical rewriting of stories about the gods. The program outlined in the *Republic* at 2.379a, ff. is Socratic

---

34   The Socratic dialogues that investigate ethical questions pursue definitions of ethical terms, mostly with no reference to the gods. The attempt to define reverence with respect to the gods in the *Euthyphro* fails. Socrates' decision to refuse Crito's offer of escape from prison, in the *Crito*, is based on reasoning that makes no mention of gods. The one exception is Socrates' promise not to obey the city if it requires him to give up his mission; there he seems to justify his decision by appeal to his claim that he has been assigned by the god to work as he does (*Apology* 29d).

in essence, and may, as Socrates suggests in the *Euthyphro*, have been partly responsible for his reputation as a dangerous innovator. The accusers were right: in this respect, Socrates is as revolutionary as any teacher of the new learning.

4.3. Respect for Human Wisdom

As we saw, Socrates understood Protagoras to mean that each person's perceptions or judgments are true for that person (*Theaetetus* 152b); it follows for Protagoras that anyone should be safe in relying on his own judgments. Now, it appears that Socrates' position is similar: Socrates can rely on his own judgments if they have survived the testing of the elenchus (*Gorgias* 508d-509a); and what goes for Socrates should go for anyone else. Indeed, a striking feature of the elenchus is its universality: anyone who knows Greek has the resources to participate in elenchus and learn from it,[35] and therefore anyone could find himself with judgments on which he could rely. This tribute to the common wisdom of humankind is moderated by the requirement of elenchus, but it is breathtaking nonetheless. Socrates did subscribe to this crucial tenet of the new learning, but under a qualification.

Among teachers of the new learning, Protagoras apparently supported democracy on the basis of his commitment to the common capacity of human beings to acquire the political expertise represented by justice and reverence (*Protagoras* 322d, cf. 327b-e).

Not all teachers of the new learning would have agreed; Antiphon was executed for plotting to undermine democracy in favor of oligarchy, although he did believe in a common human nature.[36] Socrates could, like Antiphon, accept some premises of the new learning without acknowledging the virtues of democracy. Indeed, democracy as practiced in Athens depended on a process of reasoning antithetical to the elenchus. While the elenchus puts an individual person's beliefs on trial, with that person as both witness and judge, the deliberations and trials of democracy take place in a public forum, and the crowd that is present

---

35 About Meno's attendant, a slave, Socrates only asks whether he speaks Greek before launching into a successful elenctic lesson (*Meno* 82b).

36 I accept the ancient view that there was one Antiphon, both sophist and politician. See Woodruff 2004 on both the identity issue and the interpretation of Antiphon's view about human nature: "We all breathe air through our mouths and our nostrils, and we laugh when we are pleased, or weep when we are grieved. We see by the light with our sight; we work with our hands and walk with our feet"; "We know the laws of communities that are nearby... At birth nature made us completely equal in our capacity to be either foreign or Greek." – Antiphon, in Gagarin and Woodruff 1995, p. 244, 7.

acts collectively as judge. But no crowd can submit to the elenchus. The elenchus reasonably assumes that there is an answer to a question such as "what does Callicles really believe about shame and justice?" Indeed, it presses Callicles to work toward that answer, but no one would suppose that the same question could be answered for a crowd. Different members have different views, and perhaps none of them, sequestered as individuals, would remain committed to the position taken by the crowd of which they had been part.

Socrates' version of the new-learning's commitment to human wisdom is startlingly new. Socrates is the first thinker in this tradition to allow an appeal to individual conscience. In the *Crito*, Socrates appears to have nothing to go on but his conscience, on which he is prepared to rely only when it has been tested in discussion with his friend. There are no experts on the soul available to consult, no ways to ascertain the gods' views on the matter. Socrates must simply examine his own beliefs, evaluate the arguments that support them and, after suitable reflection and discussion, make or confirm his own decision (*Crito* 46b, 48e).

On one view of elenchus, its main goal is to stimulate the reflection necessary before one makes a judgment of conscience.[37] Of course, many of the ethical discussions that developed in the new learning presupposed that individual members of the audience would make up their own minds, but the main idea here had not been given a clear voice before Socrates; it could not have been articulated at all before the invention of elenchus. The main idea is that each individual has the resources needed for making a good judgment of conscience under pressure from a Socratic questioner. Socrates himself did not make the point as clear as we could wish, but many readers have seen it lurking between the lines in Plato's dialogues.

4.4. Criticism of Custom and Law

Socrates was no traditionalist, although he did sometimes set himself against people who try to undermine traditional values. He challenged Euthyphro's innovations on the subject of piety, for example. The principle underlying the challenge seems to be that one must have expert knowledge of virtue before attempting to replace traditional ideas with new ones (*Euthyphro* 4e). For all that, Socrates never claimed expert knowledge of virtue, but he was an innovator in ethics, as we have seen, in many areas; his enlarged concept of courage (*Laches*), his appeal to

37 Woodruff 2000.

individual conscience, and his method of elenchus all seem to have
been new with him.

Socrates was a critic, or at least a challenger, of conventional democratic principles in Athens, especially the idea that ordinary people
should be heard in the Assembly (*Protagoras* 319d); moreover, he did not
admire any of the heroes of Athenian democracy such as Pericles and
Themistocles (*Gorgias* 514a, 515d-517c). And he was critical of principles that seem to have been fundamental to Greek culture, most notably
of the rule that one should help one's friends and harm one's enemies.[38]
Rather, one should do harm to no one; but if someone is acting badly,
one should administer punishment not as harm but as a means of moral
improvement. Socrates shared with other new thinkers the radical idea
that the aim of punishment should be to educate or improve people in
virtue, never to harm them (*Republic* 1.335d, *Protagoras* 324c).

On the subject of law, Socrates is especially interesting. He adopted
the new-learning account of the basis of law in social contract, but
he turned this around. When teachers of the new learning, such as
Callicles, used the account, it was to undermine law as resting on a
mere agreement among human beings. When Socrates used the account
in the *Crito* it was to explain the moral hold that the law had on him
personally by appeal to his personal contract with the laws. Socrates
transformed the social contract argument by focusing on the personal,
while treating the laws as actual partners to the contract. These laws
he understood as fundamental normative principles, independent of the
decisions of the people of Athens and defined by the goal of imparting
virtue to citizens (*Crito* 54bc, *Hippias Major* 284a-e). Otherwise, his
defense of the obligation to obey law would sit oddly with the critical
attitude he showed toward the institutions of democracy (*Apology* 29d).
The law is one thing, and good; decrees of the people are another thing,
and may be very bad indeed.

In short, Socrates was no less critical of common ideas than were the
teachers of the new learning, but he was nevertheless an opponent of
ignorant innovation and a champion of law as an ideal.

4.5. The Art of Words

Socrates was adept at the art of words in two arenas. He was capable
(so Plato represented him) of using fine rhetorical technique, as in the
Apology, and in the art of disputation, to judge from Plato and Xenophon,
he never failed to score.

---

38   For example, at *Republic* 1.335d.

Socrates made formal speeches on a number of occasions, according to Plato. The speech he made in his own defense is the only one given through his own persona, and this is the most refined. Indeed, it is the most elegant defense speech that has come down to us, and, at least in structure, it follows the model established by the teachers of the new learning. In other cases, however, Socrates tends to disclaim responsibility for what he says in speech format. For example, he attributes his speech in the *Symposium* to Diotima, although it is too closely related to the earlier discussion to be anything but Socrates' own work. Even if the basic ideas were Diotima's, most of their expression, tightly as it is linked to Agathon's speech and to Socrates' dialogue with him, must belong to Socrates. In the *Crito*, Socrates casts his argument for obedience to the law in the form of an impassioned speech by the Laws themselves. And in the *Phaedrus*, Socrates composes two formal speeches extemporaneously for which he does not take credit.

Why did a thinker who eschewed rhetoric practice it with such elegance and refinement? And why did he disclaim his speeches? These two questions have one answer: when Socrates gave a formal speech he did not have the standard rhetorical aim of persuasion. For all their intoxicating beauty, Socrates' speeches in the *Symposium* and *Phaedrus* are plainly not intended to bring us over to Socrates' point of view. Instead, they represent sources that are not present and cannot explain themselves or defend their views. They throw brilliant ideas and images up for discussion, they challenge their readers to hard thought, but they are not persuasive of either Socrates' audiences or of Plato's readers. The defense speech comes closer to the usual intent of rhetoric, but this too is deviant. Although Socrates wants to be exonerated by means of what he says in this speech, he plainly does not want to free himself by the elegance or pathos of his rhetoric.

The story about disputation is similar: Socrates appeared to show mastery of an art taught from the new learning, but he used his mastery in a new way. People who studied disputation in that period learned to confound their sparring partners in the same way tennis players today want to dazzle and confuse their opponents. What looks like disputation on Socrates' part in Plato, however, does not aim simply at confounding a sparring partner, although this is often the result. True, Socrates appears to his enemies to be a disputant who would say anything to win, and indeed Socrates was never bested in argument according to the reports we have of him. But Socrates' method of disputation had the goal of shaming his partners into taking the quest for knowledge and virtue more seriously. Like his method in the formal speeches, it was designed to make people think more deeply about growing in virtue, and at the same time to care about what they think. Socrates was explicit about his goal in the defense speech (*Apology* 29d-30b), and nothing we find in other contexts suggests that he was deceiving his panel of judges.

A confounded partner of Socrates might well think that he had been humiliated by a professional wordsmith, by a magician with words, and in a sense he was (*Euthyphro* 11b-d). Socrates' skill with words is immense, and it is more frightening than anything we know of from other teachers of the new learning. But Socrates uses his skill above all for a very serious invitation to philosophy, and this use has no parallel in the surviving works of the new learning.

5. SOCRATES' TRANSFORMATION OF THE NEW LEARNING

Plato was the most severe critic of the new learning among ancient philosophers, yet he is the source for the story I have told in Section 4. Socrates brought new ideas and new intensity to all five of the main areas touched by the new learning. Unlike most teachers of the new learning, however, he was not a generalist. He focused, to the exclusion of all else, on ethics. He joined in the general displacement of the gods, but not through natural or social science; he displaced them as moral arbiters, and put in their place a kind of moral knowledge that he believed the gods have in an exemplary way. A consequence of this (with other beliefs he has about the gods) is that the gods are unanimous and consistent on moral matters; here he joins a mainstream of new-learning thinkers and poets who set the less moral myths to one side. Plato's Socrates went further, however. In both *Euthyphro* and *Republic*, he rejected outright the old stories, an action that must have required considerable courage.

His view of the gods leaves human beings in a perilous state. There is moral knowledge to be had, and gods have it, but we, evidently, do not. What we have instead is a resource for responding well to Socratic questioning on moral matters, a resource that resembles what we call a conscience.[39] In this unique way Socrates joins the mainstream of the new learning, celebrating a capacity of ordinary human beings that would have been news to the rest of the new learning.

His criticism of the role of custom in culture is trenchant, as befits the new learning, although focused on moral issues above all others. His defense of law implicitly separates law from custom, making moral assumptions about the law that parallel those he makes about the gods: like the gods, law must be good, and customary beliefs on both subjects must be subjected to tough questioning.

39   Woodruff 2000.

And, of course, in everything he does, he employs his majestic skill in the art of words. The art belongs to the new learning, but his use of it is like no others' – in speeches and in short questioning he has the same goal, to jog the individual conscience and prompt its owner to devote himself to the quest for moral knowledge.

Socrates swam in the river of the new learning, but he redirected it to purely moral ends, and in the process transformed it into the seed of the august Platonic tradition of philosophy. Through Socrates, Plato was no more critic of, than he was heir to, the new learning.

WORKS CITED

Translations are my own or are drawn from Gagarin and Woodruff 1995. Fragment numbers refer to the "B" sections in DK, translated in Sprague 1972.

Bett, R. "The Sophists and Relativism." *Phronesis* 34 (1989): 139–169.

Cole, T. *Democritus and the Sources of Greek Anthropology* American Philological Association Monographs no. 25, 1967.

Cole, T. *The Origins of Rhetoric in Ancient Greece.* Baltimore, 1991.

Diels, H., and W. Kranz. [DK] *Die Fragmente der Vorsokratiker*, 6th ed. Berlin, 1951.

Dillon, John, and Gergel, Tania. *The Greek Sophists.* London, 2003.

Farrar, C. *The Origins of Democratic Thinking: The Invention of Politics in Classical Athens.* Cambridge, 1988.

Gagarin, M. "Did the Sophists Aim to Persuade?" *Rhetorica* 19 (2001): 275–291.

Gagarin, M. *Antiphon the Athenian: Oratory, Law, and Justice in the Age of the Sophists.* Austin, 2002.

Gagarin, M., and P. Woodruff, eds. *Early Greek Political Thought from Homer to the Sophists.* Cambridge, 1995.

Grote, G. *A History of Greece*, 2nd ed. London, 1869.

Guthrie, W. K. C. *The Sophists.* Cambridge, 1971.

Hansen, Mogens German. *The Athenian Democracy in the Age of Demosthenes; Structure, Principle and Ideology* trans. J. A. Crook. 2nd ed. Norman, OK, 1999.

Hornblower, S. "The Religious Dimension to the Peloponnesian War, or What Thucydides Does Not Tell Us." *Harvard Studies in Classical Philology* 94 (1992): 169–197.

Kahn, C. "Greek Religion and Philosophy in the Sisyphus Fragment." *Phronesis* 10 (1997): 247–262.

Kerferd, G. B. "The First Greek Sophists." *Classical Review* 64 (1950): 8–10.

Kerferd, George B. *The Sophistic Movement.* Cambridge, 1981.

Lloyd-Jones, H. *The Justice of Zeus*, 2nd ed. Berkeley, 1983.

Meineck, P., and P. Woodruff. *Sophocles: Theban Plays, with Introductions by Paul Woodruff.* Indianapolis, 2003.

Mourelatos, A. P. D. M. "Gorgias on the Function of Language." *Philosophical Topics* 15 (1987): 135 – 170.

O'Grady, Patricia. *The Sophists: An Introduction.* London, 2008.

Reeve, C. D. C. "Thucydides on Human Nature." *Political Theory* 27 (1999): 435–446.

Schiappa, E. "Did Plato Coin rhêtorikê?" *American Journal of Philology* 111(1990): 457–470.

Schiappa, E. *The Beginnings of Rhetoric in Ancient Greece*. New Haven, 1999.

Segal, C. P. "Gorgias and the Psychology of the Logos," *Harvard Studies in Classical Philology* 66 (1962): 99–155.

Sprague, R. K. *The Older Sophists*. Columbia, SC, 1972.

Surowiecki, J. *The Wisdom of Crowds: Why the Many Are Smarter than the Few and How Collective Wisdom Shapes Business, Economies, Societies, and Nations*. New York, 2004.

Woodruff, P. *Thucydides on Justice, Power, and Human Nature*. Indianapolis, 1993.

Woodruff, P. "Eikos and Bad Faith in the Paired Speeches of Thucydides," *Proceedings of the Boston Area Colloquium in Ancient Philosophy* 10 (1994): 115–145

Woodruff, P. "Rhetoric and Relativism: Protagoras and Gorgias." In *Cambridge Companion to Early Greek Philosophy*, ed. A. A. Long. Cambridge, 1997, pp. 290–310.

Woodruff, P. "Paideia and Good Judgment." In *Philosophy of Education. Volume 3 of the Proceedings of the Twentieth World Congress of Philosophy*, ed. D. M. Steiner. Boston, 1999, pp. 63–75.

Woodruff, P. "Socrates and the Irrational," In *Reason and Religion in Socratic Philosophy*, eds. Smith, N. D. and Woodruff, P. Oxford, 2000, pp. 130–150.

Woodruff, P. *Reverence: Renewing a Forgotten Virtue*. New York, 2001.

Woodruff, P. "Antiphons, Sophist and Athenian; A Discussion of Michael Gagarin, Antiphon the Athenian and Gerard J. Pendrick, Antiphon the Sophist." *Oxford Studies in Ancient Philosophy* 28 (2004): 323–336.

Woodruff, P. *First Democracy; The Challenge of an Ancient Idea*. New York, 2005.

Yunis, H. *Taming Democracy: Models of Political Rhetoric in Classical Athens*. Ithaca, 1996.

6 Socratic Religion

Socrates is acknowledged to have been a moral philosopher of the first order: the founder of virtue ethics and the chief exponent of the Socratic Method (the elenctic method of question-and-answer cross-examination).[1] It is, however, also common to underplay the idea that he was very much a man of his own time in respect of the supernatural, assuming in his speech and thought the existence of gods vastly superior to ourselves in power and wisdom, and other such conventional Greek religious commitments. Of course, Socrates' trial and execution on a charge of impiety further indicates that he did not insulate his religious beliefs from those many other novel ones he had arrived at philosophically. Rather, our texts indicate that Socrates understood his religious commitments to be integral to his philosophical mission of moral examination and rectification; conversely, he used the rationally derived convictions underlying that mission to reshape the religious

A previous version of this chapter appears as part of the chapter "Socrates and Plato" in Oppy, G., and N. Trakakis, eds. *The History of Western Philosophy of Religion*. Acumen, 2009.

1   Aristotle *Metaphysics* 1078b7–32, *Eudemian Ethics* 1216b3–1216b26; Cicero, *Tusculan Disputations* 5.4.10–11. See Hugh Benson's Chapter 8 in this volume. This chapter does not attempt to identify the views of the historical Socrates, but rather, those of the cross-dialogue, literary figure that emerges from the Socratic dialogues of Plato in concert with the recollections of Xenophon and others (e.g., Aristotle). These portraits constitute a mosaic of the characteristics, methods, views, and activities of a Socrates who manifests distinctly different philosophical attitudes from those expressed by the Socrates of Plato's *Republic* and other such constructive and, arguably, later dialogues. This qualification permits me to avoid the difficult issue of how we might accurately arrive at the views of the actual teacher of Plato, yet still allows us to confront many of the most interesting questions Plato's works provoke. There is not sufficient space here to address the complex issue of whether and how we might legitimately use the testimony of Aristotle in conjunction with that of Plato's dialogues and Xenophon's work to triangulate to the views of the historical Socrates in the manner of Vlastos 1991, chs. 2 and 3; but see, e.g., McPherran 1966, ch. 1.2.

conventions of his time in the service of establishing the new enterprise of philosophy. The direct legacy of that project is the rational theology of Plato, the Stoics, and others. That, in any case, is the overarching thesis of this chapter. My goal in what follows is to delineate and justify it by offering a sketch of the religious dimension of Socratic philosophy – one that illustrates the way that Socrates both challenged and renewed the religious conceptions of his time.

I. GREEK RELIGION

The distinct phenomena we designate by using terms such as 'religion' and 'the sacred' were, for Socrates and his contemporaries, seamlessly integrated into everyday life. Moreover, no ancient text such as Homer's *Iliad* had the status of a Bible or a Koran, and there was no organized church, trained clergy, or systematic set of doctrines enforced by them. What marked out a fifth-century BCE Greek city or individual as pious (*hosios; eusebês*) – that is, as being in accord with the norms governing the relations of humans and gods – was therefore not primarily a matter of belief, but rather, correct observance of ancestral tradition. The most central of these activities consisted in the timely performance of prayers and sacrifices.[2] Such sacrifices ranged from an individual's libation of wine at the start of a meal to the great civic sacrifices of cattle held on the occasion of a religious festival, culminating in a communal banquet that renewed the ties of city-protecting deities with the citizenry through the mechanism of the shared meal (a portion of meat being set aside as a burned offering for the gods; see, e.g., *Odyssey* 3.418–72). Besides such activities designed to ensure the favor of a divinity, however, we must also set those other rituals that aim to harm, not help, others; in particular, curses (see, e.g., Pindar *Olympian* 1.75–115; *Iliad* 3.299–301; *Odyssey* 2.134–145; Sophocles *The Women of Trachis* 1238–40). Whatever the ritual, the actions composing it were typically aimed at a specific deity and were tied to the community, ranging from households to more complex groupings such as the *deme*. The most obvious organizing principle, however, was the city and its religious officials, who exercised final authority over all religious functions and which oversaw the most prominent displays of public piety provided by the city's numerous festivals.[3]

---

2   For examples of prayer, see *Iliad* 1.446–58 and Aeschylus *The Seven Against Thebes*, pp. 252–260.

3   For discussion, see Burkert 1985, chs. 2 and 5; Cartledge 1985; and Zaidman and Pantel 1992, part 2.

It should be clear that ancient Greek religion presupposed a notion of divinity rather different from modern traditions. Socrates and his peers were brought up on the portrait of the gods drawn in the works of Homer and Hesiod, and – to begin with – these gods did not create the cosmos or humankind, but rather were themselves created. Their power was often gained through duplicity and violence, they were neither omniscient nor omnipotent nor eternal, and it was assumed that they regularly intervened in human affairs for good or ill (inflicting, for example, famine, war, and plague).[4] Here on earth, then, there is no clear separation of the religious from the secular, and thus every human action, every facet of nature, had what we would call a religious dimension. But although the ancient Greek world is permeated by the divine, its most potent expression is in beings distinctly different from perishable, mortal creatures: gods, *daimones*, and heroes.[5]

Even though these ancient conceptions of divinity were not elaborated or enforced by an official theological body, religious education was not left entirely to chance. Both Homer and Hesiod were recognized as having established for the Greeks "a kind of canonical repertory of stories about the Powers of the Beyond."[6] It was on the basis of this repertory that "the elegiac, lyric, and tragic poets drew unstintingly while simultaneously endowing the traditional myths with a new function and meaning."[7] Thus, for example, the dramas of Aeschylus and Sophocles (e.g., *Antigone*) juxtapose some present situation against the events represented in Homer's texts, extending that mythology while also calling into critical question some facet of the human condition and contemporary society's response to it. By the time of Socrates, some of this probing of the traditional stories was influenced by the speculations and skepticism of those thinkers working within the new intellectualist traditions of nature philosophy (e.g., Heraclitus) and sophistry (e.g., Protagoras). As a result, in the work of such authors as Euripides and Thucydides, even the fundamental tenets of popular religion concerning the efficacy of sacrifice and

4   See, e.g., Zaidman and Pantel 1992, ch. 13.
5   *Daimones* were sometimes thought of as "intermediary powers," but since "every god can act as *daimon*", the term is better understood as referring to the "veiled countenance of divine activity" (Burkert 1985, p. 180). A hero was a long-dead individual about whom epic adventures might be told. As much as any god, a hero had attained the status of divinity, and thus could respond to prayers and sacrifices by providing protection, retribution, and so forth. On *daimones*, see Burkert 1985, ch. 3.3.5; on heroes, see Burkert 1985, ch. 4; and Zaidman and Pantel 1992, ch. 13.
6   Vernant 1980, p. 193.
7   Zaidman and Pantel 1992, p. 144.

prayer became targets of criticism.[8] Although it is beyond the scope of this chapter to trace the influences of such thinkers on Socrates, I will make brief allusions to some of them as we proceed.

2. THE PUZZLES OF 'SOCRATIC RELIGION'

Socrates' philosophical reputation rests on his adherence to the highest standards of rationality, one given its clearest expression in the *Crito*:

T1   **Rationality Principle**: Not now for the first time, but always, I am the sort of man who is persuaded by nothing except the argument (*tô logô*) that seems best to me when I reason (*logizomenô*) about the matter. (*Cri.* 46b4–6)

Socratic reasoning commonly employs the Socratic Method, and we are encouraged to believe that for many years Socrates subjected a wide variety of self-professed experts on the topic of virtue to this form of examination (*Ap.* 20d-23c). The result of this long effort, however, appears to be not a body of knowledge, but the meager payoff of moral skepticism:

T2   **Ignorance Principle**: I am aware of being wise in nothing, great or small...(*Ap.* 21b4–5)....[except that]...I am wiser in that what I do not know, I do not even suppose that I know....(21d6–8)

This would not be so surprising an outcome were it not that Socrates represents this awareness as resulting from a quest performed at the behest of Greece's preeminent religious authority, the Delphic oracle. For as Socrates sees it, the god Apollo, speaking through the oracle, has stationed him in Athens as though he is a warrior, ordering him to philosophize by elenctically examining himself and others (28d-29a, 30e-31a). As he summarizes the matter:

T3   **Divine Mission**: I...go around seeking and investigating in accordance with the god....I come to the god's aid....because of my devotion to the god (*Ap.* 21e5–23c1)....the god stationed me...ordering me to live philosophizing and examining myself and others.... (*Ap.* 28e4–29a2)

Socrates also emphasizes that his interpretation of Delphic Apollo's pronouncement that "no one is wiser" than he as an order to philosophize has been confirmed through other extrarational sources:

---

8   For Euripides, see, e.g., *Bacchae* 216–220, *Trojan Women* 1060–1080, *Andromache* 1161–1165. For Thucydides, see, e.g., *The Peloponnesian War* 2.8.2.

T4   **Extrarational Information**: To do this [philosophizing] has been commanded of me ... by the god through oracles and through dreams and by every other means in which a divinity has ever commanded anyone to do anything. (*Ap.* 33c4–7; cf. *Ap.* 30a; *Cri.* 43d-44b; *Phd.* 60c-61c)

In addition, Socrates tells the jurors at his trial that he has been assisted in his philosophical mission through the frequent warnings of his divine sign, the *daimonion*:

T5   ***Daimonion***: ... a sort of voice (*phonê*) comes, which, whenever it does come, always holds me back from what I'm about to do but never urges me forward. (*Ap.* 31d2–4)

Our texts – Divine Mission (T3), Extrarational Information (T4), and *Daimonion* (T5) – should now prompt us to ask how it is that Socrates can also subscribe to his Ignorance Principle (T2): for, lacking wisdom, how can Socrates be confident that gods such as Apollo even exist, let alone be assured that Apollo always speaks the truth (21b) and that his divine dreams and signs are not mere delusions? Moreover, since he also endorses the Rationality Principle (T1), we can expect him to justify the claims implied by these texts; but it is hard to see how the Socratic Method could provide that sort of warrant (since it appears to only reveal the inconsistency of interlocutors' beliefs; hence, their lack of expert knowledge).[9] Texts such as Extrarational Information (T4) and *Daimonion* (T5) also make Socrates appear to be far more superstitious than the average Athenian: not the sort of behavior we expect from the paradigm of the rationally self-examined life. After all, if enlightened contemporaries such as Thucydides could stand aloof from comparable elements of popular religion, and if even traditionally minded playwrights such as Aristophanes could poke cruel fun at seers and oracle-mongers (e.g., *Birds* 521, 959–91), how could Socrates not do so as well? Worse yet, it is hard to see how the Socrates who accepts the Rationality Principle (T1), Divine Mission (T3), and Extrarational Information (T4) claims as he investigates the religious assertions of his interlocutors can be self-consistent when he goes on to criticize such interlocutors for acting on ungrounded religious judgments:

T6   **Euthyphro Principle**: ... if you [Euthyphro] did not know clearly the pious and the impious, there is no way you would ever have attempted to prosecute an elderly man, your father, for murder on behalf of a hired man. Rather, as to the

---

9   For a recent discussion of whether the *elenchos* can also be used to establish positive conclusions (e.g., that an interlocutor's definition is actually false), see Benson's Chapter 8 in this volume, and G. Scott 2002.

gods, you would have dreaded the risk that you would not do it correctly, and as to human beings, you would have been ashamed. (*Euphr.* 15d4–8)

Here a rational principle of morality is implied: actions that are morally ambiguous ought not to be performed in the absence of a full understanding of the relevant concepts involved. So we are then left to wonder how the epistemically modest Socrates of the Ignorance Principle (T2) would respond if pressed to defend his risky conduct of challenging the moral and religious views of his fellow Athenians. The mere citation of divine authority instanced by the Divine Mission (T3), Extrarational Information (T4), and *Daimonion* (T5) texts would appear inadequate in view of the demands of the Rationality Principle (T1); such a citation would also open up to interlocutors such as Euthyphro (a self-professed diviner) the possibility of replying in kind that they too, like Socrates, have been commanded in divinations and in dreams to contest conventional norms.

The preceding texts exemplify the way that Plato presents us with a puzzling, street-preaching philosopher who is both rational and religious, and whose relationship to everyday Athenian piety is anything but clear. To begin to make sense of that relationship, and thereby resolve the tensions between these and related texts, it is useful to examine Socrates' own examination of a self-professed expert in Greek religion: Euthyphro.

3. SOCRATIC PIETY AND PHILOSOPHY

The *Euthyphro*'s discussion of the virtue of piety makes it a key text for determining the religious dimension of Socratic philosophy.[10] It also provides vivid examples of the Socratic Method through its portrayal of Socrates' relentless interrogation of Euthyphro's five attempted definitions of piety.[11] Definition (1) – piety is proceeding against whomever does injustice (5d-6e) – is quickly dispensed with because it is too narrow: Euthyphro holds there to be cases of pious action that do not involve proceeding against wrong-doers (5d-e). Socrates also reminds Euthyphro that he is seeking a complete account of the *one* characteristic (*eidos*) of piety: that unique, self-same, universal quality the possession of which makes any pious action pious and which Euthyphro had earlier agreed was the object of their search (6d-e; cf. 5c-d; *M.* 72c).

10 Not everyone agrees with this assessment: whether the *Euthyphro* is a source of positive Socratic doctrine or merely an aporetic inquiry is a much debated issue; see. n. 14.

11 For a more complete account of Socrates' examination, see Geach, 1966; Heidel 1900, and McPherran 1996, ch. 2.

Definition (2) – piety is what is loved by the gods (6e-7a) – is next rejected on the grounds that since Euthyphro's gods quarrel about the rightness of actions, a god-loved, hence pious action could also be a god-hated, hence impious action; thus, definition (2) fails to specify the real nature of purely pious actions (7a-9d). Note, however, that by presupposing without restriction in his definitional search that the definition of piety must apply to *every* pious action – and given his apparent rejection of divine enmity and violence (6a-d, 7b-9c) – Socrates is committed to the claims that (i) there is but one universal moral canon for all beings, gods and humans alike, and thus must reject the tradition of a divine double-standard of morality (cf., e.g., *Rep.* 378b). Socrates' examination also suggest that (ii) his gods are perfectly just and good, and so (iii) they experience no moral disagreements among themselves.

Socrates' rebuttal of Euthyphro's third attempt at definition (3) – piety is what is loved by all the gods (9e) – constitutes the most logically complex section of the *Euthyphro* (9e-11b).[12] Socrates' apparent rejection of this definition comes at the end of a long and complex passage (10e-11b) where he first drives home his conclusion that Euthyphro's various concessions undercut this third definition of piety and then explains the apparent source of Euthyphro's confusion – namely, given Euthyphro's claim that something is god-loved because it is pious, his purported definition 'god-loved' appears to designate only a non-essential property of piety (a *pathos*) rather than specifying piety's essential nature (its *ousia*). With this, Socrates makes it evident that he is no Divine Command Theorist–that is, unlike gods modeled after Homeric royalty, his gods do not issue morality *establishing* commands such that a pious action is pious simply because it is god-loved; rather, it seems, his gods love things that are independently pious because they themselves are by nature wise, virtue-loving beings. By tacitly allowing that the gods are *of one mind* on the topic of virtue, Socrates here lays the groundwork for the view that there is ultimately only one divinity (see Section 5).

Socrates assists Euthyphro in producing a fourth definition of piety by confronting him with the question of piety's relation to generic justice: is all the just pious, or is justice broader than piety such that piety is then a part of justice (11e-12e)? Subsequent to his adoption of the part-of-justice view, Euthyphro attempts to differentiate pious justice from the remainder ('human justice') by stipulating that piety involves the *therapeutic tendance* of gods (*therapeia theôn*) (12e6–9). This differentia, however, is rejected by reference to a craft analogy comparing those

---

12 For analysis of this argument, see Cohen 1971 and Benson 2000, pp. 59–62. McPherran 1996, p. 43, n. 43, provides a bare bones version of the argument.

who would tend the gods in this fashion to those who tend horses, dogs, and cattle (13a-d). Such therapists possess the sort of expert knowledge that includes the capacity to benefit their particular kind of subjects substantially by restoring or maintaining their health, or by otherwise meeting their essential needs and improving the way in which they function. Obviously, then, since mere mortals cannot benefit gods in these ways the virtue of piety cannot be a form of therapy (13c-e). By contrast, *skillful service* (*hupêretikê*) along the lines of assistants to craftspeople contributes to an acceptable differentia of generic justice; assistants to a shipwright, for example, serve the shipwright by satisfying his desire to receive assistance in building ships but do not restore or improve upon the shipwright's own nature or functioning. Socrates has thus brought Euthyphro to the point of agreeing that:

P Piety is that part of justice that is a service of humans to gods, assisting the gods in their primary task to produce their most beautiful product (*pagkalon ergon*). (12e-14a)

Within the constraints of this account, Euthyphro is then asked to specify precisely the nature of that most beautiful product of the gods' chief work in whose production the gods might employ our assistance (13e-14a). Euthyphro, however, tenaciously avoids answering this question (13d-14a), citing instead a fifth definitional attempt: (5) piety is knowledge of sacrificing and praying (14b-15c).[13] To this, Socrates emphatically responds that Euthyphro is abdicating their search just at the point where a *brief* answer – one analogous to "food," the product of the craft of farming (14a) – might have finally given Socrates all the information that he really needed to have about piety (14b-c). Many scholars have found this good evidence for ascribing something like P to Socrates.[14] The question then becomes how Socrates would

---

13 See McPherran 2000b.
14 Among those "constructivists" willing to do so are Brickhouse and Smith 1994, ch. 6.1; Burnet 1924, pp. 136–137; McPherran 1985; Rabinowitz 1958; Reeve 1989, ch. 1.10; Taylor 1982; and Vlastos 1991, ch. 6. Those who do not think a Socratic account of piety is implied by the text ("anticonstructivists") include Allen 1970, pp. 6–9, 67; and Grote 1865, pp. 437–57. Beckman 1979, ch. 2.1; Calef 1995; and Versényi 1982 are qualified anticonstructivists, since they argue that no definition of piety *involving reference to the gods* may be culled from the dialogue's explicit statements, and that in fact the notion of piety toward which Socrates directs Euthyphro is a secular one that identifies it with the whole of virtue (Reeve 1989, pp. 64–66, seems to head in this direction as well). For additional references, see McPherran 1985, ch. 2, nn. 2, 3, and 4, and 1996, p. 30, nn. 4 and 5.

have answered the question as to the identity of the gods' beautiful, chief product?

First, we can expect Socrates to maintain that although we humans cannot have a complete account of the gods' work, since the gods are wholly good, their chief project and product must be superlatively good. But what reasons, per the Rationality Principle (T1), does Socrates have for holding that the gods are entirely good? His thinking would seem to run roughly as follows. Since gods are perfectly knowledgeable, they must be entirely wise (*Ap.* 23a-b; *H.Ma.* 289b3–6); but because wisdom and virtue are mutually entailing (and since there is but one moral realm), it would follow that a god must be at least as good as a good person; but then since the latter can only do good, never evil (*Cri.* 49c; *Rep.* 335a-d), the same goes for the former (cf. *Rep.* 379a-391e).[15]

Socrates' moral reformation of the gods indicates that his gods cannot be fully identified with those of popular tradition. For Greek popular thought assumed as a fundamental principle from Homer on that justice consists in reciprocation, in repayment in kind: a gift for a gift, an evil for an evil (the *lex talionis*).[16] Even among the gods the principle of *lex talionis* is assumed as basic (e.g., Zeus suggests that Hera might allow him to destroy one of her favorite cities in return for abandoning Troy [*Iliad* 4.31–69]; cf. Sophocles *Ajax* 79).[17] In respect of this venerable principle, Socrates must be ranked a self-conscious moral revolutionary (*Cri.* 49b-d): as he sees it, since we should never do injustice, we should never do evil, and from that it follows that we should never do an evil in return for even an evil done to us (*Cri.* 48b-49d, 54c; cf. *Grg.* 468e-474b; *Rep.* 335a-d). For Socrates, then, not even Zeus (rather, least of all Zeus) can return one injury for another.[18]

Next, the Socratic view that the only or most important good is virtue/wisdom (e.g., *Ap.* 30a-b; *Cri.* 47e-48b; *Grg.* 512a-b; *Euthd.* 281d-e) makes it likely that the only or most important component of the gods' chief product is virtue/wisdom. But then, since piety as a virtue must be a craft-knowledge of how to produce goodness (e.g., *La.* 194e-196d, 199c-e; *Euthd.* 280b-281e), *our* primary service to the gods – the one

---

15   For further discussion, see McPherran 1996, chs. 2.2.2–6, 3.2; and Vlastos 1991, pp. 162–165.

16   Cf., e.g., Aeschylus *The Libation Bearers* 306–314, *Agamemnon* 1560–66; Aristotle *Nichomachean Ethics* 1132b21–1133a6; Hesiod fr. 174 Rzach; Pindar *Pythian* 2.83–5; and Plato *Men.* 71e.

17   Yunis 1988, chs. 1 and 3.

18   Cf. Xenophanes, who testifies that "Homer and Hesiod have attributed to the gods everything that is a shame and reproach among humans, stealing and committing adultery and deceiving each other" (Sextus Empiricus *Adversus Mathematicos* 11.193).

we are best suited to perform – would appear to be to help the gods to produce goodness in the universe via the protection and improvement of the human mind/soul. Because philosophical examination of oneself and others is for Socrates the key activity that helps to achieve this goal via the improvement of moral-belief-consistency and the deflation of human presumptions to divine wisdom (e.g., *Ap.* 22d-23b), philosophizing is a preeminently pious activity.[19]

Finally, Socrates' treatment of Euthyphro's fifth definition – (5) piety is knowledge of sacrificing and praying – makes evident that he rejects the idea that piety consists in traditional prayer and sacrifice motivated by hopes of a material payoff (14c-15c).[20] In addition, Socrates' view that the only real good is virtue means that one ought not to pray for any particular material payoff, since any such payoff could in fact diminish one's happiness. Nevertheless, from his perspective, the sacrificial gifts of time, pride, and conventional goods offered up in the pursuit of philosophical activity do please the gods to a greater extent than any burnt offering might (e.g., *Ap.* 23b-c, 31b-c, 37e-38a; *Mem.* 4.3.17–18).

This appropriation and reconception of piety as demanding of us philosophical self-examination would, however, seem to be a direct threat to everyday piety. For now it would appear that for Socrates, time spent on prayer and sacrifice is simply time stolen from the more demanding, truly pious task of rational self-examination *per* the Rationality Principle (T1). More threatening still, Socrates' theology of entirely just, "relentlessly beneficent" gods in conjunction with his moral theory would seem to make sacrifice and prayer (and especially curses) entirely useless.[21] For such practices appear to rest on the traditional and fundamental assumption that justice consists in reciprocation, in repayment in kind (i.e., the *lex talionis*): a principle of returning evil for evil that Socrates rejects (*Cri.* 49b-d). To what extent, then, is Socrates at odds with the ritual bedrock of Greek religion?

I think it is clear that Socrates does not reject conventional religious practices *in general*, but only the narrowly self-interested motivations underlying their common observance. Xenophon, for example, portrays him as "the most visible of men" in cult-service to the gods (*Mem.* 1.2.64) and has him testify that he often sacrificed at the public altars (*Ap.* 10–12; cf. *Mem.* 1.1.1–2, 4.8.11). It seems unlikely that Xenophon would offer as a defense a portrait of Socrates that simply no Athenian could take seriously.[22] There is, in addition, some corroborating Platonic

19 See McPherran 1996, ch. 2.2 and 4.2.
20 See McPherran 2003b.
21 Vlastos 1989, p. 235. But see McPherran 2000.
22 Some modern critics dismiss Xenophon's categorical affirmations of Socratic piety as instances of telltale overkill; e.g., Vlastos 1971, p. 3.

evidence on this point.[23] Although it would not seem that Socrates could consider prayers or sacrifices alone to be *essentially* connected to the virtue of piety (since, independent of the right intention, such actions in themselves do not necessarily serve the purpose of the gods *per* P), their performance is nonetheless compatible with the demands of piety reconceived as philosophizing. After all, since Socrates embraces the positive side of the *talio* – the return of one good for another – we should reciprocate as best we can the gods' many good gifts (see, e.g., *Euphr.* 14e-15a) by honoring the gods in fitting ways through performing acts with the inner-intention to thank and honor them (*Mem.* 1.4.10, 18; 4.3.17). While, again, serving the gods via philosophical self-examination has pride of place in providing such honors, there is no reason why such actions cannot include prayers and sacrifices (cf. *Mem.* 4.3.13, 16). Socrates may well hold that prayers and sacrifices that aim to honor or thank the gods, or that request moral assistance from them, serve both ourselves and the gods: they help to induce our souls to follow the path of justice (thus producing god-desired good in the universe) by habituating us to return good for good. These actions also help to foster and maintain a general belief in the existence of good and helpful gods and an awareness of our inferior status in respect of wisdom and power, something that Socrates is clearly interested in promoting (see, e.g., *Mem.* 1.4.1–19, 4.3.1–17; *Ap.* 21d-23c). Of course, no such action can be expected to establish a claim on any deity that would give us a right to expect any specific or immediate return.

Nevertheless, Socrates appears to think that the gods aid those who do what is virtuous. Xenophon, for example, represents Socrates as accepting the view that he receives goods from the god(s) (e.g., his *daimonion*) *because*, apparently, of the piety of his mission to the Athenians (*Mem.* 1.1.9, 1.1.19, 1.3.3, 1.4.15–19, 4.3.16–17, 4.8.11; *Symp.* 47–49). Hence, since petitionary prayers and sacrifices that offer honor to the gods *are* virtuous by attempting to offer good for good, Socrates will expect that good things will be returned to us for such efforts in some fashion (*Mem.* 1.3.2; 2.1.28): just as a master craftsman offers guidance, nourishment, and tools to his assistants when they ask, Socrates would have thought, so the gods may be expected to aid us in a similar way. Again, however, although for Socrates the gods are always pleased in some sense by the

---

23 For example, Plato is willing to put twelve prayers into the mouth of his Socrates (see B.D. Jackson 1971; *Euthd.* 275d; *Phd.* 117c; *Smp.* 220d; *Phdr.* 237a-b, 257a-b, 278b, 279b-c; *Rep.* 327a-b, 432c, 545d-e; *Phil.* 25b, 61b-c). *Euthd.* 302c-303a, *Menexenus* 243e-244b, and *Phdr.* 229e testify to Socrates' orthopraxy, and note the stage-setting of the start of the *Republic* (327a), where Socrates has traveled down to the Piraeus in order to pray to the goddess Bendis and observe her festival.

honor such sincerely motivated practices display toward them, they – unlike the gods entertained by some Athenians – are not responsive to the material basis of the sacrifice or the specificities of the request (since any particular item requested might not be conducive to our real good; *Mem.* 1.3.2) (especially Socratically unjust petitions – e.g., unjust curse-imprecations).

It appears, then, that with the perfectly wise and just deities of Socrates we have few specific, materially rewarding imprecations to make: beyond the sincere, general prayer that one be aided in pursuing virtue, there are few requests or sacrifices to which all-wise deities can be counted on to respond (since in our ignorance, we can never know if any specific request would be virtue-aiding, and since the gods have no need of our sacrifices; see, e.g., Socrates' prayer at *Phdr.* 279b-c). This implication of Socrates' moral theory cuts straight to the root of everyday self-interested motivations underlying many particular instances of cult-practice. But if Socrates rejected the efficacy of improperly motivated requests, then he was a threat to popular piety – whether he was recognized as such by any of his jurors. After all, to many Athenians, the assistance of a Heracles would have meant, above all, help against the unseen, non-human forces bearing down on one (e.g., plague), and for most of them this meant material help against oppressive *other deities*. By taking away the enmity of the gods and conceiving of them as fully beneficent, then, the need for and the efficacy of *this* Heracles is also removed.

It seems clear that those jurors able to recognize the implications of Socrates' views for sacrificial cult would have seen him as threatening the stability of the state: for if one takes away the conflicts of the deities and the expectations of particular material rewards and physical protections in cult, one disconnects the religion of everyday life and the state from its practical roots. To those not already centered on the development of their inner lives, the substitute of the difficult, pain-producing activity of philosophical self-examination would seem to offer little solace in the face of life's immediate, everyday difficulties. Socrates therefore raised the stakes for living a life of piety considerably by making its final measure the state of one's philosophically purified soul.

4. SOCRATIC REASON AND REVELATION

As our Divine Mission (T3), Extrarational Information (T4), and *Daimonion* (T5) texts demonstrate, Socrates is portrayed as a man who gives clear credence to the alleged god-given messages and forecasts found in dreams, divinations, oracles, and other such traditionally accepted incursions by divinity.[24] But the degree of trust Socrates places in such sources appears to put him at odds with the Rationality and Ignorance Principles (T1 and T2): what is the rational justification for heeding them, and in doing so, must one not regard them as sources of wisdom? The natural response is to hold that while Socrates accepts the everyday notion that the gods provide us with extrarational signs, and so does not pursue a form of the intellectualist rejection of divination's efficacy,[25] he also does not take the operations of traditional divinatory practices at face value. Rather, he insists in accord with the Rationality Principle (T1) that conventional methods of oracular interpretation must give way to a rational method for evaluating such phenomena. These extrarational sources, however, do not supply Socrates with general, theoretical claims constitutive of the expert moral knowledge he seeks and disavows having obtained per the Ignorance Principle (T2). Rather, they yield items of what we might call non-expert moral knowledge (e.g., that his death is good [*Ap.* 40a-c]).[26] Let us consider a few examples.[27]

Early in his defense speech, Socrates explains that his reputation for wisdom can be best understood by attending to the testimony provided by the god who speaks through the Delphic oracle: Apollo (*Ap.* 20d-23b).[28] As Socrates relates the tale, his friend Chaerephon traveled to Delphi to ask the oracle if anyone was wiser than Socrates, and the response was "No one is wiser" (21a5-7). This report, however, was at odds with Socrates' own conviction that he possessed no real wisdom (namely, full comprehension of virtues such as piety), and so – given that "it is not lawful (*themis*) for the god to speak falsely" (21b5-7) – he was provoked to discover an interpretation that would preserve Apollo's veracity. He does this by going from one self-professed expert to another in hopes of finding someone wiser than himself so as to refute the apparent meaning of the oracular pronouncement (and so uncover its real meaning). After continually failing to find such a person, Socrates concludes that what the god actually meant is that Socrates is wisest by

24   Zaidman and Pantel 1992, pp. 121–128.
25   For example, in the manner of the characters of Euripides, who challenge both the abilities and honesty of traditional seers (e.g., *Philoctetes* fr. 795) and the existence of the gods who allegedly provide foreknowledge (*Bellerophon* fr. 286; *The Trojan Women* 884–887; Fr. 480; Sextus Empiricus *Adversus Mathematicos* 9.54). See Ostwald 1986, pp. 279–290, for discussion.
26   For discussion of how Socrates can endorse the Ignorance Principle (T2) but also know (or justifiably believe) things, see Brickhouse and Smith 1994, ch. 2; Vlastos 1994.
27   For a comprehensive discussion, see McPherran 1991, and 1996, ch. 4.
28   On the oracle, see Fontenrose 1978; Parke and Wormell 1956.

best grasping his own lack of real wisdom (this is "human wisdom"). This, in turn, is taken to mean that Apollo has stationed Socrates in Athens ordering him to philosophize and *examine* himself and others (28d-29a). Thus, since one ought always to obey the command of a god at all costs, Socrates is obliged to philosophize regardless of any dangers (29d; cf. *Rep.* 368b-c). His jurors should therefore understand that the oracle's pronouncement marked a turning point in his life so profound that he now philosophizes under a unique and divine mandate (Divine Mission [T4] and *Ap.* 29c-30b). Socrates also continually interrogates others because he has come to believe that the god is using him as a *paradigm* to deliver the virtue-inducing message that that person is wisest, who – like Socrates – becomes most cognizant of how little real wisdom he possesses (*Ap.* 23b).[29]

This account, despite its complexity, suggests that Socrates takes it to be obligatory to subject extrarational signs to rational interpretation and confirmation whenever possible, and especially if they urge him to act in ways that appear to run counter to tradition or prudential considerations. That postulate dissolves two of our initial puzzles. First, the conflict between reason per the Rationality Principle (T1) and revelation per the Divine Mission (T3), Extrarational Information (T4), and *Daimonion* (T5) texts is mitigated by noting how Socrates allows *rationally* interpreted and tested revelations to count *as reasons* in the sense of the Rationality Principle (T1).[30] The second tension between revelation and the Euthyphro Principle (T6) is dissolved as well: this principle can be understood to claim that actions traditionally held to be unjust ought to be refrained from in the absence of compelling rational or *rationally* interpreted and tested divinatory evidence to the contrary. Euthyphro himself threatens traditional filial piety with his suit, but cannot, under examination, defend his conduct; and his purported mantic abilities manifestly fail to give him any revelations whose meaning he could decipher or rationally justify. Socrates, on the other hand, has engaged in few activities that actually violate the traditional code, and has never violated the essential dictates of traditional piety (especially once these are rightly understood). And although he has run some moral risk in pursuing his life of philosophical examination, his belief in its

---

29 For discussion of the problem of how Socrates is able to derive a prescriptive claim that he *ought to* philosophize from the merely descriptive claim of the Pythia that he *is* the wisest, see Brickhouse and Smith 1983; McPherran 2002b; M.C. Stokes 1992, pp. 29–33; Vlastos 1989, pp. 229–230 and 1991, pp. 166–173.

30 Vlastos 1989 and 1991, ch. 6, opposes this view, and is replied to by Brickhouse and Smith 1994, chap. 6, and McPherran 1991, and 1996, ch. 4.

overriding moral worth has survived a lifetime of such testing. He has, in particular, labored at great length to derive his understanding of the Delphic Oracle's pronouncement, and has received varied and consistent extrarational indications that back up his interpretation (that are, in turn, subject to philosophical testing). Finally, Socrates has secular justification and confirmation of this via his conception of the virtues for believing that his mission to the Athenians is a great good (*Ap.* 30a, 30d-31a). To confirm this account of Socrates' treatment of extrarational indicators, let us consider his reliance of his divine sign, the *daimonion*.[31]

Socrates' *daimonion*, we are told, is an internal, private admonitory "sign" (*sêmeion; Ap.* 40b1, c3; *Euthd.* 272e4; *Phdr.* 242b9; *R.* 496c4; *Mem.* 1.1.3–5) and "voice" (*phonê; Ap.* 31d1; *Phdr.* 242c2; Xen. *Apol.* 12.) caused to appear within the horizon of consciousness by a god (probably Apollo).[32] It has occurred to few or none before Socrates (*R.* 496c) and it has been his companion since childhood (*Ap.* 31d). The *daimonion's* intervention in his affairs is frequent and pertains to matters both momentous and trivial (*Ap.* 40a-b, *Euthd.* 272e-273a). That Socrates receives and obeys these monitions is well-known in Athens (*Ap.* 31c-d; *Euphr.* 3b), and they are understood to be apotreptic signs that warn him *not* to pursue a course of action that he is in the process of initiating (*Ap.* 31d; *Phdr.* 242b-3; *Theag.* 128-131a).[33] These interventions are regarded as unfailingly correct in whatever they indicate (*Mem.* 1.1.4–5), just as we would expect the gift of an unfailingly good divinity to be. The *daimonion's* generosity perhaps even extends to warning Socrates of the inadvisability of the actions intended by others (*Tht.* 150c-151b; cf. *Theag.* 128d-131a; *Mem.* 1.1.4; *Apol.* 13), but in no case does it provide him with general, theoretical claims constitutive of the expert moral knowledge he seeks and disavows having obtained per the Ignorance Principle (T2). Neither does it provide him with ready-made explanations of its

31 For discussion of the *daimonion* – and opposition to Vlastos 1996, ch. 6, and Nussbaum 1985, who both downplay the epistemic significance of the *daimonion* – see Brickhouse and Smith 1994, ch. 6.3; and McPherran 1991, 1996, ch. 4.1, and 2005.

32 See *Ap.* 40b1 together with 26b2-28a1. See also *Ap.* 31c8-d4, 40a4-6, 40c2-3, 41d6; *Euphr.* 3b5-7; *Tht.* 151a2-5; *Theag.* 128d1-131a7; Xen. *Mem.* 1.1.2-4, 4.8.1; *Apol.* 4-5, 8, 12-13; *Symp.* 8.5. What evidence there is (see esp. *Ap.* 27c10-28a1) suggests that Socrates is uncertain as to the nature and identity of the divinity behind his "sign," but Apollo is surely a prime candidate since it is Apollo who has charged him with his philosophical mission to the Athenians, one that exposes him to the sort of danger that would warrant a god's help.

33 Although in Xenophon (e.g., *Mem.* 1.1.4; 4.3.12; 4.8.1; *Apol.* 12), the *daimonion* offers positive advice.

opposition. Rather, its occurrences yield instances of non-expert moral knowledge of the inadvisability of pursuing particular actions because those actions are disadvantageous to Socrates and others – for example, the knowledge that it would not be beneficial to let a certain student resume study with him (see, e.g., Xen., *Symp.* 8.5; *Tht.* 150c-151b; *Alc.* I 103a-106a). Finally, these divine "signs" always target *future* unbeneficial outcomes, and especially those whose reasonable prediction lies beyond the power of human reason (*Ap.* 31d; *Euthd.* 272e-273a; *Mem.* 1.1.6–9, 4.3.12). It is, in short, a species of the faculty of divination, true to Socrates' description of it as his "customary divination" (*Ap.* 40a4) and himself as a "seer" (*mantis*) (*Phd.* 85b4–6; cf. *Phdr.* 242c4).

One important example that displays Socrates' reliance upon and rational confirmation of a daemonic warning is found at *Apology* 31c-32a. Here, Socrates notes his obedience to the *daimonion*'s resistance to his entering public partisan politics (cf. *Rep.* 496b-c) and then offers an explanation for its warnings – namely, that such political activity would have brought him a premature death, thus curtailing his vastly beneficial mission to the Athenians (cf. *Phdr.* 242b-243a; *Alc.* I 103a-106a). This account is introduced in the manner of one wholly convinced of not only that explanation but of the extrarationally indicated truth that prompted that explanation – that the *daimonion* opposes now, as it has in the past, his every attempt at going into politics. Socrates never doubts that the *daimonion's* warnings are utterly reliable, although *how* or *why* it is that the result of his obedience will be good-producing is opaque to reasoned calculation (*Tht.* 150c-151b; *Mem.* 4.3.12; 1.1.8–9). But this trust is in no way *irrational* – and so does not contradict the Rationality Principle (T1) – for it may be rationally confirmed in its wisdom and so given credence on an inductive basis; since (1) in Socrates' long experience of the *daimonion*, it has never been shown not to be a reliable warning system (Xen. *Apol.* 13; *Ap.* 40a-c), and (2) the reliability of its alarms has been confirmed by the good results that flow from heeding it (i.e., we should suppose that from an early age Socrates observed subsequent to the *daimonion*'s warning that he would most likely have experienced a harm had he not heeded its advice).

Since Socrates' trust in the accuracy of the *daimonion* has been achieved inductively, the resulting beliefs that various intended plans of action are unbeneficial are not so secure that they amount to certain knowledge (thus, they do not threaten the Ignorance Principle [T2]). That would seem to be why he goes on to confirm his argument from daemonic silence at *Apology* 40a-b with the argument of 40c-41d.

The *daimonion*, then, appears to be compatible with Socrates' profession of his Rationality and Ignorance Principles (T1 and T2): if during or after a process of deliberation the *daimonion* should oppose his action, then given the prior rationally established reliability of the *daimonion*, it would seem that an occurrence of the *daimonion* would count in a perfectly straightforward way *as a reason* for not performing that act. For if one had very frequently in the past always obeyed the promptings of an internal warning that one has reason to believe come from all-wise gods, and this had always been judged to have resulted in the best outcome, then one has good reason for letting this internal warning trump one's merely human judgment (although this does not provide the sort of complete account of the virtues that would contradict the Ignorance Principle [T2]).

5. SOCRATIC THEOLOGY

Socrates' claims to receive guidance from the gods brings us to our last puzzle: how can Socrates satisfy the rational demands of the Rationality Principle (T1), the skeptical restraint marked by the Ignorance Principle (T2), and yet affirm that gods exist and that they have characteristics such as wisdom (*Ap.* 41c-d; *Euphr.* 14e-15a; *G.* 508a; *H.Ma.* 289b; *Mem.* 4.4.25)? Unfortunately, Plato's texts show Socrates simply assuming and never proving the existence of gods (although Plato's Socrates might perhaps take the *daimonion* as evidence that its god exists). However, in Xenophon we are given an innovative teleological cosmology and theodicy grounded on an argument for the existence of an omniscient, omnipresent God: the Maker of an orderly and beautiful universe, a deity who also now governs it in a fashion analogous to the way in which *our* minds govern *our* bodies (1.4.1–19; 4.3.1–18; cf. Sextus Empiricus *Adversus Mathematicos* 9.92–94).

The primary teleological argument contained in the *Memorabilia* holds that since individual beings in the universe are either the products of intelligent design (*gnomê*) or mere dumb luck (*tuchê*), and since human beings are clearly products of intelligent design, we then ought to be persuaded that there exists a vastly knowledgeable and powerful God, a God who is moreover a "loving and wise Maker (*dêmiourgos*)" (1.4.2–7; cf. 4.3.1–18). The argument – with a bit of interpretive polishing – can be given this formal structure:

(1) Everything that is clearly purposeful (*ôphelia*; a beneficial adaptation of means to ends) is the product of intelligent design (*gnômê*; i.e., art [*technê*]) (and not mere dumb luck [*tuchê*]).

(2) Human beings (and other features of the universe, living and nonliving [1.4.8]) exhibit "signs of forethought" (1.4.6); for example, eyes have protective eyelids and lashes, teeth are adapted to cutting, and the anus is far removed from the nostrils.

(3) Things that exhibit signs of forethought are clearly purposeful.

(4) Thus, human beings are the product of intelligent design.

(5) The existence of products of intelligent design implies the existence of an intelligent designer-creator (one possessing the intelligence and power necessary for producing its products; cf. 1.4.2–4).

(6) Thus, an intelligent designer-creator of the cosmos exists.

This is a fairly impressive piece of philosophy to find in any section of fourth century text, since the argument is no mere prototype but close to being a full-fledged version of the classic Argument From Design.[34] Socrates, then, conforms to his Rationality Principle (T1) when he affirms the existence of god. It also appears that because of the analogical relationship Socrates postulates between this Maker-god and the human soul (e.g., both are invisible), his conception of this god is an extrapolation from his own understanding of the human soul. This explains why he is confident that the Maker-god has many human mental characteristics raised to the level of perfection. We are told, for example, that this being has – unlike the divinities of popular imagination – complete knowledge of the present, possessing an awareness of all things at once by being present everywhere (*Mem.* 1.4.17–19). The Deity also has knowledge of the past thanks to Its possession of an all-encompassing divine memory, and It has sufficient knowledge of the future to allow It to send us reliable portents of the things to come (cf. *Symp.* 4.47–49). Vast power, as well, must be ascribed to this Being: Power sufficient to allow It to implement Its cosmic plans (*Symp.* 4.48). Finally, as we saw earlier in Section 3, the wisdom of this god ensures its complete goodness.

   Given this extrapolated characterization, it is not surprising to find that Socrates' Maker has desires and affective states. Indeed, here Socrates shows himself to be a bolder theologian than many modern teleological philosophers: the actual argument goes beyond conclusion (6)'s mere assertion of existence by characterizing the Demiurge as 'loving' (1.4.7).[35] This appellation, naturally, does not strictly follow from the argument, but Socrates offers support for it later on when

34   This inference was adopted by the Stoics as their main theological proof; see, e.g., J.G. DeFilippo and Mitsis 1994; Long 1996. For further discussion and the argument that Xenophon's testimony ought to be accepted, see McPherran 1996, ch. 5.2.

35   The attribute of "loving" marks a new and startling development, for the traditional attitude held that it would be beneath the dignity of Zeus for him to love mere mortals; Burkert 1985, p. 274.

he responds to Aristodemus's postulation of an indifferent Demiurge (*Mem.* 1.4.10.19; cf. 4.3.2–14): we appear, says Socrates, to have been not only designed, but designed to the *greatest advantage* in respect of other living creatures. First, we exhibit a superior adaptation of means to ends in our physical being – for example, our versatile hands, our capacity for speech, and the fitness of our bodies for housing the kind of soul we have been given (1.4.11–12, 13–14; cf. 4.3.11). In addition, the rest of the material Universe also exhibits a solicitous design insofar as it appears to be especially constructed with the requirements of human happiness in mind; for it offers light, seasons, and food crops adapted to those seasons. Furthermore, when our reason is unable to discern the future adequately, the gods send portents to our aid (1.4.15, 18; cf. 4.3.12). So generous does Socrates' theodicy become in the *Memorabilia*'s Book Four account – and so seemingly neglectful of earthquakes, tyrants, and plagues – that Socrates even claims that *everything* in the Universe is "fair and good" (4.3.13; cf. 1.4.13).[36]

The relation between this omniscient, omnipresent Deity and the other gods is left entirely obscure. Socrates speaks at one moment of that singular Deity as responsible for our creation and aid, and in the next breath depicts the plural gods as doing the same (e.g., 1.4.10–11, 13–14, 18). Next, he distinguishes this one Deity *from* the other gods by characterizing It as that particular god who "coordinates and holds together the entire cosmos" (4.3.13), but also treats that Deity as fulfilling *all* the functions of the gods. To reconcile such oddities with what evidence there is that Socrates would affirm a belief in Delphic Apollo and plural Greek gods, we might credit him with being a henotheist – that is, he may understand the Maker-god to be a supreme Deity overseeing a community of lesser deities in the manner of Xenophanes' "greatest one god" (DK 21 B23). Alternatively, it is also possible that

36 Although we never see Socrates grapple directly with the problem of reconciling the existence of good and wise god(s) with the existence of natural disasters and moral evil, his view that piety involves serving the gods by improving our souls via philosophical examination, and his seeming view that we are – qua human beings – constrained from fully possessing the knowledge of virtue constitutive of divine wisdom (*Ap.* 20d-e, 23a) suggest that he might have held something akin to a traditional "soul-building" response to the problem. On this sort of account, there really are no natural evils: ocean storms, diseases, and death are not in themselves evil, but assume value only in relation to the moral development of a person's soul (see, e.g., *Euthd.* 277d-282e; *Grg.* 511c-512e). Moral evils, on the other hand, are a consequence of our having imperfect human souls, an imperfection that is a necessary condition of non-divine human beings having been created in the first place, a creation that is – all things considered – a good thing.

Socrates shared the not-uncommon view that understood the gods to be manifestations of a singular supreme Spirit.[37] In any event, we may expect that Socrates holds that his reasons for affirming the existence and nature of his Maker-god do not constitute the sort of complete and certain account that would give him the kind of theological wisdom he disclaims with his Ignorance Principle (T2).

6. SOCRATES ON TRIAL

According to the report of Diogenes Laertius (D.L. 2.40) and Xenophon (*Mem.* 1.1.1), and as Socrates himself recounts at *Apology* 24b-c (cf. *Euphr.* 3b-d), Socrates was prosecuted on a charge of impiety that consisted of three distinct specifications: (I) Socrates does not recognize (*nomizein*) the gods recognized by the state; (II) Socrates introduces new divinities (*kaina daimonia*); and (III) Socrates corrupts the youth by *teaching* youths the notions specified by the other two allegations.[38] Socrates takes up these claims in reverse order, beginning with III, but he first addresses the informal concerns that he takes to motivate them: these are the old rumors that Socrates investigates natural phenomena in the style of Anaxagoras and is a crafty practitioner of sophistical argument like Protagoras, and teaches others his results and methods in these areas (18b-c, 19b-c, 23c-d). These allegations are especially dangerous because popular opinion holds that such intellectuals "do not recognize the gods [to exist]" (18c2-3). Later, when Socrates addresses the formal accusations by interrogating Meletus as to the precise nature of charge I, atheism again becomes the chief allegation (26a-e). But as our Divine Mission (T3), Extrarational Information (T4), and *Daimonion* (T5) texts – and now the teleological argument of the *Memorabilia* (section V) – indicate, Socrates is no atheist; moreover, Socrates has no trouble showing that Meletus's allegation II of introducing new divinities is inconsistent with a charge of atheism (26a-28a).

However, as discussed earlier in Section 3, it would not seem possible to fully identify the gods of Socrates with either the civic deities of Athens or those of the poets. For example, in response to Euthyphro's mention of the story that Zeus bound his father Kronos for committing an injustice, Socrates exclaims:

Is this, Euthyphro, why I am a defendant against the indictment: that whenever someone says such things about the gods [e.g., that Zeus bound his own father,

37   Guthrie 1971, p. 156; Zaidman and Pantel, p. 176, "As the Greeks saw it, the divine simply manifested itself in multiply diverse aspects."
38   *Ap.* 26b7; a reduction paralleled at *Euphr.* 3b-4e; Reeve 1989, pp. 75–76. See also Brickhouse and Smith 1989, p. 30; Versnel 1981, p. 124, n. 122.

that gods quarrel], I receive them with annoyance? Because of this, as is likely, someone will assert that I am a wrongdoer. (*Euphr.* 6a; cf. 6b-d, 7a-9b)

This piece of pre-trial speculation, however, is not decisive, and later on Socrates affirms his belief in the civic gods at *Apology* 35c-d. Nevertheless, the evidence we saw regarding Socratic theology in Sections 3 and 5 argues that while Socrates is committed to the existence of gods, and is willing to "recognize" them both intellectually and through traditional sacrificial practice under their civic names, they cannot be fully identified with the civic or poetic gods insofar as those gods are conceived of as being at variance with other gods, or given to retributive justice, or as lacking in wisdom or power.[39] Again, Socrates' conception of the gods as thoroughly good does appear to undermine the everyday motivations underlying conventional conceptions of prayer and sacrifice. But if so, then Socrates would have been associated with the sorts of criticisms of popular religion found in Xenophanes, natural scientists, and those of the sophists who followed a similar revisionary line.[40] To what extent, then, is Socrates actually guilty of non-recognition of the civic gods (allegation I)?

Although his revisionary theology puts Socrates at variance with some of his fellow Athenians, it does not seem by itself sufficiently problematic to warrant a conviction on charge I. After all, Socrates' practical, legal guilt before the court on this allegation would be very much a matter of the meaning each juror placed on the phrase "gods of the state": but for most Athenians at the end of the fifth century, it would have been no great shock to hear expressions of doubt or outright denial concerning the poets' tales of divine capriciousness, enmity, immorality, and lack of response to sacrifice. They had been exposed to such criticisms for years by thinkers such as Solon, Xenophanes, Heraclitus, and Euripides, none of whom appears to have suffered from religiously based persecution.[41] Moreover, others such as Pindar could speak plainly of "Homer's lies" (*Nemean* 7.23) without incurring legal sanctions, and we have no evidence of anyone being prosecuted for disbelieving the stories of Homer or Hesiod.[42] Hence, although there may be problematic

---

39 Plato makes the same point, in a clear reference to the *Euthyphro* at *Rep.* 377e-378e; cf. *Laws* 886c-d; *Clouds* 1079–84 and 904.

40 For example, Democritus, a probable contemporary of Socrates, declared that the gods are the source of all good and that man is responsible for the evils he suffers (DK B 175); while the speaker of the Sisyphus fragment (probably authored by Euripides) held the gods and their justice to be the false invention of a certain "shrewd and cleaver-minded man" (DK 88B.25).

41 See, e.g., Euripides, *Heracles* 1340–1346.

42 Lloyd-Jones 1971, p. 134; Burnet 1924, p. 114; Dodds 1951, pp. 141–143; Yunis 1988, p. 39.

implications for traditional religion in Socrates' conception of divinity, charge I does not seem able to bear the entire explanatory weight of Socrates' conviction. Let us consider charge II then.

So far as we know, Socrates was the first person in the history of Athens to be formally accused of the crime specified by II,[43] but despite the lack of precedent, there is every reason to think that the allegation is legally permissible. The Athenian polis took an active role in overseeing all religious activity; in particular, it had the power to exclude or allow forms of worship, and those wishing to introduce new cults into Athens had to seek official sanction.[44] Since such representations to the polis implied privileged access to the divine were in the last analysis unverifiable, presented competition to the established cults, and could easily be based on self-interested or political motives, a significant burden of proof would have been borne by the petitioner. Even then, however, "new gods and their sponsors were by no means assured of a warm welcome when they petitioned for entry into a Greek community."[45]

What sorts of *daimonia*, then, did Socrates and his jurors take the *"kaina daimonia"* of allegation II to refer to? Although it is possible that the term targets the morally purified gods of Socrates, there are a number of reasons for taking the view that the *daimonion* was central to the allegation. Primary among these is Euthyphro's suggestion (to which Socrates does not object) that Socrates has been indicted because of his *daimonion*.[46] It seems, then, that all Socrates' prosecution needed to do was suggest to the jurors that the source of Socrates' *daimonion* has not been formally "licensed" by the state, and thereby incite the natural suspicions Athenians had toward foreign religious imports.[47] There are, then, at least three areas of potential danger the prosecution might have pointed to: (1) the source of the *daimonion* may be an unlicensed deity to whom Socrates pays unlicensed cult; (2) his characterization of this

43 Garland 1992, p. 136, p. 146; Versnel 1981, p. 127.
44 For detailed discussion of this procedure, see, e.g., Parker 1996, chs. 9 and 10; Garland 1992, esp. pp. 14–22, 137, 149. Cf. *Laws* 738b-739a.
45 Garland 1992, p. 146.
46 *Euphr.* 3b5–9; cf. 5a7–8. Xenophon also claims that count II derives from Socrates' talk of the *daimonion* (*Mem.* 1.1.2–3; *Apol.* 12), and the Socrates of Plato's *Apology* reports that "Meletus wrote about it [the *daimonion*] in the indictment" (31d1–2). Add to this the fact that Xenophon feels the need to defend Socrates against this sort of understanding of the second allegation (*Mem.* 1.1.3–4; *Apol.* 12–14; cf. *Mem.* 4.3.12–13), and we have solid grounds for supposing that Socrates' *daimonion* was indeed its primary target. Cf. Burkert 1985, p. 317; Garland 1992, p. 149.
47 Versnel 1981, pp. 121–22, notes that foreign cults tended to be associated with private rituals, which in turn fostered all sorts of suspicions.

sign puts him on special, private terms with a deity; and (3) this sign and the deity behind it may be illusory or the deity may have hostile intentions towards Athens.[48] Although the first concern (1) is the explicitly actionable one, items (2) and (3) can also be understood to generate the sort of ill will that Socrates cites as the true causes of his conviction (28a). Socrates must have only deepened such fears in some of his jurors when he claimed that it was the *daimonion* that kept him from entering public politics (*Ap.* 31d-32a), and then threatened to disobey any order they might concoct to discontinue his *daimonion*-assisted mission on behalf of Apollo (29b-d).

As Socrates surely realized, he was not in an ideal position to soothe these sorts of reactions to the *daimonion* (e.g., the time allotted for his defense speech was inadequate to the formidable task of removing by reason what are very much emotional responses; cf. *Ap.* 18e-19a). Socrates could not deny that the *daimonion* gave him a unique advantage in life, and other sorts of denials unaccompanied by adequate proof are all he had time to offer in response to suspicions that his voice offered evil counsel (e.g., by noting that its content was always dissuasive, never proscriptive; 31d). Moreover, once Meletus opted for his allegation of complete atheism (26b-c), Socrates was obliged to focus most of his defense against that claim, and not on all the other suspicions that the jury might still be weighing against him. Thus, here in the second specification I think we find one potent source that Meletus might have called upon in pressing an allegation of non-conformity and one source for the jury's actual vote for conviction: Meletus's invocation of the *daimonion* may well have inflamed the prejudices of the jury, leading a good number of them to vote for his conviction on the specification of introducing *kaina daimonia*.[49]

While certain jurors might have been discerning enough to see or intuit the danger to traditionally motivated cult in Socrates' philosophical revisioning of the gods and the virtue of piety, the attention of the jurors who voted for conviction was most likely to have been drawn to his apparent introduction of a new dispensation without seeking the sanction of the polis: *that* will have seemed his most obvious and glaring violation of accepted norms.[50] Naturally, given the over-determining

48 McPherran 1996, p. 135; cf. R. Kraut 2000, p. 17.
49 Cf. Garland 1992, ch. 7; and Kraut 2000.
50 Although Socrates himself never names the *daimonion* as a source of the "first accusations" that led to the formal specifications, it may be alluded to when he speaks at *Apology* 23a of unspecified slanders connected with the allegations that he possesses wisdom, and when he notes at 23d-e the allegation that he teaches about 'the things aloft'. In fact, since it is clear that the *daimonion* *was* the source for the formulation of one of the formal

constellation of factors working against Socrates, jurors who believed him guilty of illegally introducing a new divinity may well have made further damning inferences concerning his teachings.

We should not be surprised, then, that Socrates' defense ultimately failed. In the end, the prejudices and allegations ranged against Socrates proved so numerous and broad-ranging that he was in effect put on trial for the conduct of his entire life. His strange, provocative, street-preaching conduct, purportedly commanded by a divinity and exemplifying the new intellectualist conception of piety that Socrates had forged, proved all too prone to misrepresentation before an undiscerning crowd. From outside the circle of Socratic philosophy, that revised piety looked all too similar to the newfangled impiety that Aristophanes had lampooned in his *Clouds* long before (423 BCE), an impiety that Socrates himself would have condemned (*Ap.* 19c-d). It is, then, part of the drama and irony of Socrates' martyrdom that the sign of his god is also the sign of his demise. But, on my account, it is also natural that even with his last words,[51] Socrates gave thanks to a god for the extra-rational assistance that gave him a life of extraordinary rationality.

WORKS CITED

Allen, R. E. *Plato's 'Euthyphro' and the Earlier Theory of Forms.* London, 1970.
Beckman, J. *The Religious Dimension of Socrates' Thought.* Waterloo, 1979.
Benson, H. *Socratic Wisdom.* Oxford, 2000.
Brickhouse, T. C., and Smith, N. D. "The Origin of Socrates' Mission." *Journal of the History of Ideas* 44 (1983): 657–666.
Brickhouse, T. C., and Smith, N. D. *Socrates on Trial.* Oxford and Princeton, 1989.
Brickhouse, T. C., and Smith, N. D. *Plato's Socrates.* Oxford, 1994.
Burkert, W. *Greek Religion.* Cambridge, MA, 1985.
Burnet, J. *Plato's Euthyphro, Apology of Socrates and Crito.* Oxford, 1924.
Calef, S. "Piety and the Unity of Virtue in Euthyphro 11e-14c." *Oxford Studies in Ancient Philosophy* 13 (1995): 1–26.
Cartledge, P. "The Greek Religious Festivals." In *Greek Religion and Society*, eds. P.E. Easterling J.V. and Muir. Cambridge, 1985, pp. 98–127, 223–226.
Cohen, S. M. "Socrates on the Definition of Piety: *Euthyphro* 10a-11b." In *The Philosophy of Socrates* ed. G. Vlastos. Garden City, NY, 1971, 158–176.
DeFilippo, J. G., and Mitsis, P. T. "Socrates and Stoic Natural Law." In *The Socratic Movement* ed. P. Vander Waerdt. Ithaca, 1994, 252–271.
Dodds, E. R. *The Greeks and the Irrational.* Berkeley, 1951.

specifications, it seems likely that Meletus would try to use a formulation that *does* pick up a preexisting prejudice and that the *daimonion* – as the source for the second specification's formulation (II) – was, then, a source of pre-trial prejudice.

51   Namely: "Crito, we owe a cock to Asclepius: please pay the debt and do not forget" (*Phd.* 118a7–8), on which see McPherran 2003a.

Fontenrose, J. *The Delphic Oracle*. Berkeley, 1978.

Garland, R. *Introducing New Gods*. Ithaca, 1992.

Geach, P. T. "Plato's Euthyphro: An Analysis and Commentary," *Monist* 50 (1996): 369–382.

Grote, G. *Plato and the Other Companions of Sokrates*, vol. 1. London, 1865.

Guthrie, W. K. C. *Socrates*. Cambridge, 1971.

Heidel, W. A. "On Plato's *Euthyphro*," *Transactions of the American Philological Society* 31 (1900): 164–181.

Jackson, B. D. "The Prayers of Socrates," *Phronesis* 16 (1971): 14–37.

Kraut, R. "Socrates, Politics, and Religion." In Smith and Woodruff 2000, ch. 1, pp. 13–23.

Lloyd-Jones, H. *The Justice of Zeus*. Berkeley, 1971.

Long, A. A. 1996. "Socrates in Hellenistic Philosophy." In *Stoic Studies*, ed. A.A. Long. Berkeley, 1996, pp. 1–35.

McPherran, M. L. "Socratic Piety in the *Euthyphro*," *Journal of the History of Philosophy* 23 (1985): 283–309. Repr. in H. Benson, ed., *Essays on the Philosophy of Socrates*, Oxford, 1992, 220–241; and in W. Prior, ed., *Socrates: Critical Assessments*. v 2. London and New York, 1996, 118–143.

McPherran, M. L "Socratic Reason and Socratic Revelation," *Journal of the History of Philosophy* 29 (1991): 345–174. Repr. in W. Prior, ed., *Socrates: Critical-Assessments*. v 2. London and New York, 1996, 167–194.

McPherran, M. L. *The Religion of Socrates*. University Park, PA, 1996.

McPherran, M. L. "Does Piety Pay? Socrates and Plato on Prayer and Sacrifice." In Smith and Woodruff, 2000. Repr. in T.C. Brickhouse and N.D. Smith, eds., *The Trial and Execution of Socrates: Sources and Controversies*. Oxford, 2002, 162–190.

McPherran, M. L. 2002. "Elenctic Interpretation and the Delphic Oracle." In Scott 2002, ch. 7, pp.114–144.

McPherran, M. L. "Socrates, Crito, and Their Debt to Asclepius." *Ancient Philosophy* 23 (2003a): 71–92.

McPherran, M. L. "The Aporetic Interlude and Fifth *Elenchos* of Plato's *Euthyphro*." *Oxford Studies in Ancient Philosophy* 25 (2003b): 1–37.

McPherran, M. L. "Introducing a New God: Socrates and His Daimonion." In *Socrates' Divine Sign. Religion, Practice, and Value in Socratic Philosophy*, eds. P. Destrée and N. D. Smith, Apeiron 38 (2005): 13–30.

Nussbaum, M. 1985. "Commentary on Edmunds." *Proceedings of the Boston Area Colloquium in Ancient Philosophy*, 1 (1985): 231–240.

Ostwald, M. *From Popular Sovereignty to the Sovereignty of Law: Law, Society and Politics in Fifth Century Athens*. Berkeley, 1986.

Parke, H. W., and Wormell, D. E. W. *The Delphic Oracle*. 2 vols., Oxford, 1956.

Parker, R. *Athenian Religion: A History*. Oxford, 1996.

Rabinowitz, W. G. "Platonic Piety: An Essay Toward the Solution of an Enigma." *Phronesis* 3 (1958): 108–120.

Reeve, C. D. C. *Socrates in the Apology*. Indianapolis, 1989.

Scott, G., ed., *Does Socrates Have a Method? Rethinking the Elenchus in Plato's Dialogues and Beyond*. University Park, PA, 2002.

Smith, N. D., and Woodruff, P. eds., *Reason and Religion in Socratic Philosophy*. Oxford, 2000.

Stokes, M. C. "Socrates' Mission." In *Socratic Questions: New Essays on the Philosophy of Socrates and Its Significance*. eds. B.S. Gower and M.C. Stokes. London and New York, 1992, pp.26–81.

Taylor, C. C. W. "The End of the *Euthyphro*." *Phronesis* 27 (1982): 109–118.

Vernant, J. -P., trans. J.L. Lloyd. *Myth and Society in Ancient Greece*. Atlantic Highlands, NJ, 1980.

Versényi, L. *Holiness, and Justice: An Interpretation of Plato's Euthyphro*. Washington, DC, 1982.

Versnel, H. S. 1981. "Religious Mentality in Ancient Prayer." In *Faith, Hope and Worship: Aspects of Religious Mentality in the Ancient World*, ed. H.S. Versnel. Leiden, 1981, pp. 1–64.

Vlastos, G., ed. *The Philosophy of Socrates*. Garden City, NJ, 1971.

Vlastos, G. "Socratic Piety." In *Proceedings of the Boston Area Colloquium in Ancient Philosophy* 5 (1989), 213–238.

Vlastos, G. *Socrates, Ironist and Moral Philosopher*. Ithaca, 1991.

Vlastos, G. "Socrates' Disavowal of Knowledge." In *Socratic studies*, ed. M.F. Burnyeat Cambridge, 1994, pp. 39–66.

Yunis, H. A New Creed: Fundamental Religious Belief in the Athenian Polis and Euripidean Drama. Hypomnemata 91. Göttingen, 1988.

Zaidman, L. B., and Pantel, P. S. (trans. P. Cartledge). *Religion in the Ancient Greek city*. Cambridge, 1992.

FURTHER BIBLIOGRAPHY

Brickhouse, T. C., and Smith, N. D. *The Philosophy of Socrates*. Boulder, 2000.

Brickhouse, T. C., and Smith, N. D., eds., *The Trial and Execution of Socrates: Sources and Controversies*. Oxford, 2002.

Brickhouse, T. C., McPherran, M. L., and Smith, N. D. "Socrates and His *Daimonion*: Correspondence among Gregory Vlastos, Thomas C. Brickhouse, Mark L. McPherran, and Nicholas D. Smith." In *Reason and Religion in Socratic Philosophy*, eds. N.D. Smith and P. Woodruff, Oxford, 2000, pp. 176–204.

Burnyeat, M. F. "The Impiety of Socrates." *Ancient Philosophy* 17 (1997): 1–12.

Buxton, R. *Oxford Readings in Greek Religion*. Oxford, 2000.

Connor, W. R. 1991. "The Other 399: Religion and the Trial of Socrates." In *Georgica, Greek Studies in Honour of George Cawkwell*. Bulletin Supp. 58 of the Institute of Classical Studies, eds. M.A. Flower and M. Toher. London, 1991, pp. 49–56.

Dodds, E. R. 1973. "The Religion of the Ordinary Man in Greece." In *The Ancient Concept of Progress*, ed. E.R. Dodds. Oxford, 1973.

Dover, K. J. 1971. "Socrates in the *Clouds*." In *The Philosophy of Socrates*, ed. G. Vlastos. Garden City, NY, 1971, pp. 50–77.

Dover, K. J. *Greek Popular Morality in the Time of Plato and Aristotle*. Berkeley, 1974.

Festugière, A. -J. *Personal Religion Among the Greeks*. Berkeley, 1954.

Furley, W. D. "The Figure of Euthyphro in Plato's Dialogue." *Phronesis* 30 (1985): 201–208.

Gerson, L. P. *God and Greek Philosophy*. London, 1990.

Gould, J. "On Making Sense of Greek Religion." In *Greek Religion and Society*, eds. P.E. Easterling and J.V. Muir. Cambridge, 1985, pp.1–33.

Guthrie, W. K. C. *The Greeks and Their Gods*. Boston, 1950.

Joint Association of Classical Teachers, eds., "The Metaphysical Environment." In *The World of Athens*. Cambridge, 1984.

McPherran, M. L. "Piety, Justice, and the Unity of Virtue." *Journal of the History of Philosophy* 38 (2000): 299–328.

Mikalson, J. D. *Athenian Popular Religion*. Chapel Hill, 1983.

Morgan, M. L. *Platonic Piety*. New Haven, 1990.

Morgan, M. L. "Plato and Greek Religion." In R. Kraut, ed. *The Cambridge Companion to Plato*. Cambridge, 1992, pp. 227–247.

Parker, R. "The Trial of Socrates: And a Religious Crisis?" In *Reason and Religion in Socratic Philosophy*, eds. N.D. Smith and P. Woodruff. Oxford, 2000, pp. 50–54.

Price, S. *Religions of the Ancient Greeks*. Cambridge, 1999.

Sourvinou-Inwood, C. *Tragedy and Athenian Religion*. Lanham, MD, 2003.

Weiss, R. "Virtue Without Knowledge: Socratic Piety in Plato's Euthyphro." *Ancient Philosophy* 14 (1994): 263–82.

7   Socrates and Democratic Athens

In 399 BCE, the Athenian citizen Socrates, son of Sophroniscus of the deme (township) Alopece, was tried by an Athenian court on the charge of impiety (*asebeia*). He was found guilty by a narrow majority of the empanelled judges and executed in the public prison a few days later. The trial and execution constitute the best-documented events in Socrates' life and a defining moment in the relationship between Greek philosophy and Athenian democracy. Ever since, philosophers and historians have sought to explain troubling aspects of the case: Why was Socrates, the philosophical model of a good man, charged with public wrongdoing? Why was he convicted and why on such a close vote? Was he guilty of impiety or other crimes? Why did he undergo trial and execution, rather than leaving Athens to pursue his philosophical investigations elsewhere? Were his loyalties owed to Athens, to himself, or to the world? And, perhaps most pressing: how did a democratic community, committed to the value of free speech and public debate, come to convict and execute its most famous philosopher-citizen? Because there are no simple answers to these questions the ancient tradition and modern scholarship on the trial and its aftermath are rich and of enduring interest.[1]

1   The "Socrates and democratic Athens question" was a primary concern of Gregory Vlastos, a very influential classical philosopher who devoted much of his career to Socrates: see especially Vlastos 1983 (reprinted as Vlastos 1994) and Vlastos 1991. From different perspectives, the same question motivated the life's work of the conservative political philosopher Leo Strauss (see esp. Strauss 1964) and became the culminating project of the left-wing political commentator, I. F. Stone (Stone 1988). Recent book-length treatments by classical philosophers, centered on Plato's account of the trial, include Reeve 1989, Brickhouse and Smith 1989. Colaiaco 2001 is a detailed and well-informed introduction. Schofield 2002 focuses on the implicit debate between Vlastos and Stone over Socrates' attitude towards democracy and his "quietism". Nails 2006 discusses the trial and death in detail, with special emphasis on the atmosphere of religious fundamentalism in 399, and with considerable detail on the biographies of Socrates' accusers. Wilson 2007 assesses ancient and modern accounts of

LEGAL NARRATIVE

The chain of events that began with legal charges being lodged against Socrates and that culminated in Socrates' death proceeded according to the established judicial practices of the democratic polis. Meletus, a voluntary prosecutor (*ho boulomenos*: "he who chooses to act"), brought his case before the Basileus ("King-archon"), a lottery-chosen public magistrate responsible for preliminary investigation of religious crimes (inter alia). Meletus's charges against Socrates were as follows: "Socrates does criminal wrong (*adikei*) by not recognizing (*ou nomizon*) the gods that the polis recognizes (*nomizei*), and furthermore by introducing new divinities (*daimonia*); and he also does criminal wrong by corrupting (*diaphthairon*) the youth (*neous*)."[2] The Basileus summoned Socrates to his office in the Athenian *agora* (public square) for a preliminary hearing; Plato's *Euthyphro* imagines a conversation that took place there just before the hearing.[3] Having interrogated both Meletus and Socrates, the Basileus remanded the matter to an Athenian "people's court" (*dikasterion*). The case was tried in the course of a single day by a panel of 501 judges who had been selected randomly from a pool of Athenian citizens over age thirty. The judges listened to a carefully timed speech of accusation by Meletus who, following ordinary Athenian prosecutorial practice, yielded part of his allotted speaking time to two associates (Anytus and Lycon). Next, Socrates, as defendant, was allowed an identical period of time in which to speak in his own defense. He used part of his time in a rare but legally unremarkable cross-examination of Meletus.[4]

The 501 Athenians who heard the case should be thought of as judges rather than jurors because they made substantive decisions about the meaning and applicability of the law itself, rather than merely determining matters of fact. Athenian written law, while very specific about

and responses to Socrates' death. The main primary sources are assembled in Brickhouse and Smith 2002 and Reeve 2002.

2   Cited in full in Diogenes Laertius 1.5.40, this is consistent with the main ancient accounts (Xen. *Mem.* 1.1.1; Xen. *Apol.* 11–12, 19; Plato *Ap.* 24b, *Euthyphro* 2c-3b), although these may not be the exact words of Meletus's indictment. The most difficult term here is the Greek *nomizein*, which can mean either "believe in" or "appropriately recognize" (by performance of right actions). The most likely scenario is that the prosecutor played on the two senses of the word: claiming that Socrates acted wrongly (in respect to religious practice) out of a wrong belief (in respect to the gods recognized by the state).

3   See Camp 1992 for details of the Athenian *agora* and its buildings.

4   Athenian legal procedure: MacDowell 1978; Lanni 2006. Athenian lawcourts: Boegehold 1995.

procedural rules meant to ensure fairness (e.g., equal time for speeches by prosecutor and defendant) tended not to include definitions of the abstractions upon which the law's application hinged. It was up to the judges to decide on their own, without expert assistance, the meaning of relevant terms as well as their applicability to particular cases. The best-documented example is the Athenian law on outrage (*hubris*): The law carefully specified the categories of persons against whom outrage may not be committed, the procedure to be followed in the case of trial, and the range of penalties that might be inflicted upon a guilty individual. Yet the law did not define *hubris* – it did not specify what behaviors or actions were outrageous. This meant that it was open to prosecutor and defendant to debate both the facts (what the defendant purportedly did) and their legal meaning (whether what he did constituted a breach of the law). Precedent offered no firm guidance: Athenian judicial bodies were not bound by earlier decisions, although litigants often cited wise past judgments.[5]

The Athenian law on impiety appears to have been similar in form: detailing the legal procedure to be followed, but silent on the range of beliefs, behaviors, or acts constituting impiety.[6] There was a strong consensus among Athenians that certain actions were impious and therefore merited prosecution: performing mock religious rites, defacing sacred objects, stealing goods stored in a temple, placing an olive branch upon an altar at an improper time, or removing the stump of a sacred olive tree from private land.[7] Yet Socrates was accused of nothing of the kind. Meletus's charges of failing to properly recognize state gods, improperly introducing new gods, and corrupting the youth were vaguer, and we lack detailed evidence for Athenian impiety prosecutions on similar grounds.[8] In light of the close vote, there is no reason to suppose that a strong normative consensus pertained about what

---

5   Law against hubris: Fisher 1992. Procedural focus of Athenian law: Todd 1993. Precedents: Lanni 2004; Rubinstein 2007.

6   MacDowell 1978, pp. 197–202; see Parker 1996, ch. 10, n. 63, for further discussion.

7   Parker 1996, ch.10.

8   Plutarch (*Life of Pericles* 32.2) mentions a state decree against atheism passed on the motion of one Diopeithes in 432 BCE. No other ancient author cites this decree; if it ever existed, it may have passed out of existence in the course of the late fifth-century revision of the Athenian lawcode. In any event, we have no evidence for prosecutions under the decree; see, further, Reeve 1989, pp. 79–82. The ancient stories regarding other Athenian trials for "thought crimes" have been shown to be spurious: Dover 1975, Wallace 1994. On the scanty evidence for three later charges of "introducing new gods" see Parker 1996, ch. 10, nn. 62, 63.

constituted proper "recognition" of state gods, or what sort of actions would constitute improperly "introducing" new gods, or what counted as an "impious" sort of corruption.

DIGRESSION: RED HERRINGS

Meletus had to demonstrate to the judges that the things he accused Socrates of doing or failing to do were *normatively* impious, as well as showing *factually* that Socrates had done or not done them. This legal burden bears directly on the question of Socrates' innocence or guilt. Given the apparent failure of the law to define impiety, and in the absence of evidence for an Athenian consensus about what constituted improper recognition, introduction, and corruption, it is not possible to answer the question "was Socrates guilty or innocent, according to Athenian law?" in any straightforward way – other than to assert, tautologically, that after the judgment he was certainly guilty, because the court's judgment legally constituted him a guilty man. If (as seems likely) impiety remained undefined in Athenian law and there was no Athenian normative consensus on what constituted impious non-recognition, introduction, and corruption, the central question in much scholarship on the trial – "was Socrates (whether it is Plato's Socrates or the historical Socrates) *actually guilty*?" – is unanswerable.[9] I address instead a question that is perhaps as interesting and certainly more answerable: "How and why did the early Socratic tradition seek to prove Socrates innocent – in respect to absolute justice and in the eyes of a 'reasonable' Athenian judge?"

Plato's *Apology* and Xenophon's *Apology* and *Memorabilia* approach the task of exculpating Socrates differently: both acknowledge, either implicitly (Plato) or explicitly (Xenophon), that Socrates' speech appeared extraordinarily boastful and unconvincing to the judges. Xenophon explains this by the assumption that Socrates, although innocent of any impious thought of behavior and of corrupting anyone, intended to commit a sort of judicial suicide and so intentionally infuriated the jurors with a boastful speech. Plato's approach is more subtle: his Socrates presents a speech of outstanding rhetorical sophistication and filled with dazzling logical gambits. Socrates repeatedly lulls the judge/reader into thinking that the defense is developing according to the standard protocols of Athenian forensic rhetoric, and then suddenly inverts those

9   Guilty of impiety (qua harming the polis by undermining traditional religion): Burnyeat 1997; guilty of harming the democracy: Stone 1988. Innocent of impiety: Reeve 1989; innocent of any anti-democratic tendencies: Vlastos 1983.

protocols in ways that are clearly intended to be shocking – to sting the listener/reader into wakefulness. His sarcastic cross-examination of Meletus seeks to show that Meletus's views on politics and education are both incoherent and typical of most Athenians. Socrates is critical of the underlying assumptions of the democratic culture of Athens: that ordinary citizens were capable of making important decisions and that the public institutions of the polis were adequate to train the youth in good civic values. Plato's Socrates claims to seek acquittal, but is very pessimistic about the likelihood of this, and for good reason: he reveals his own commitments to truth-telling and moral value to be fundamentally at odds with the attitudes of most Athenians – and his life's work to be the painful process of bringing his fellows to acknowledge their individual and collective failings. And yet for all that, Plato urges his reader to suppose that a thoughtful and fair-minded judge *should* have voted to acquit: both on the substance of the case and in his own interest and that of his city.[10]

The question of the *actual arguments* used by the prosecution and the defense leads to another interpretive dead end. Since no version of the prosecution speeches survives, we can only guess at their main arguments. It is quite possible that Meletus accused Socrates of outright atheism, as Plato asserts (*Apology* 26e). Meletus probably claimed that Socrates failed to participate in the ordinary round of state-sponsored religious practices (sacrifice, procession, cult ritual) – an argument that Xenophon sought to refute in his *Memorabilia*.[11] Meletus presumably accused Socrates of improper attention to a deity unrecognized by the state (Socrates' famous *daimonion*).[12] If Meletus charged Socrates with corrupting specific Athenians (by name or implication), these likely included Alcibiades (an Athenian leader during the Peloponnesian War, whose treason contributed to Athens' loss in the war) and Critias (Plato's uncle and leader of an anti-democratic government established in Athens by the Spartans in 404 BCE). Meletus may have implied that Socrates corrupted young men by teaching them to behave as he did, thereby making it more likely that they would willingly harm their fellow citizens (as Critias and Alcibiades had).[13] In developing his impiety

10   For a more detailed analysis of the rhetoric of Plato's *Apology*, see Ober 1998, pp. 166–179.
11   Discussed in detail in McPherran 2000.
12   The Athenian state did in fact allow the introduction of new gods according to a formal, state-approved procedure; see Garland 1992; Parker 1996, ch. 9. Plato, *Apology* 26b-c, points out that the practice of introducing new gods is incompatible with thorough-going atheism.
13   This charge of "educating in badness" is a key part of the hostile portrait of Socrates in Aristophanes' *Clouds*. A half-century after the trial, the orator

case, Meletus was likely to have hinted at sundry other crimes and misdeeds, including a generalized hostility to the democracy itself. The jurors were probably told that Socrates was arrogant (Xen. *Apol.* 32), a diabolically clever speaker (Plato, *Ap.* 17a-b), and an unpatriotic scofflaw with an inherently vicious character (Xen. *Mem.* 1.2.9). Meletus may have claimed that he was prosecuting only reluctantly, as a patriot performing a public service, and that a failure to convict would put the city at grave risk. To prove his case, he may have cited the sworn testimony of witnesses (Xen. *Apol.* 24), but he could also have called upon the jurors themselves as informal witnesses, claiming that it was common knowledge that Socrates acted impiously.

My guesses about Meletus's rhetorical *exposition* are based on the commonplaces used by other Athenian prosecutors. My guesses about the *substance* of the prosecution case against Socrates are based on the charges and the philosophical Socratic tradition regarding the trial.[14] That tradition consists of two quite different *Apologies* (Defense Speeches) *of Socrates* written some time after the trial by Socrates' followers, Xenophon and Plato; various remarks about the trial in the extensive body of "Socratic conversations" written by those two authors; and a miscellany of off-hand, fragmentary, and much later testimonies.[15] Plato's *Apology* is the most important single item in the tradition. It takes the form of three sequential speeches: Socrates' defense proper (for which we have many near-contemporary *comparanda* in the corpus of Athenian legal orations), a speech at the sentencing phase of the trial, and a final address to the jurors who had voted to acquit. The main defense speech resembles real Athenian defense speeches; the other two are *sui generis*. Xenophon's *Apology of Socrates* is not modeled on actual Athenian defense speeches; it takes the form of a secondhand report of the trial and its aftermath. Xenophon's *Memorabilia* was written in response to a literary version of a prosecutor's indictment of Socrates.[16]

Aeschines (1.173) reminded jurors that "you" convicted Socrates for having educated Critias, and Xenophon, *Memorabilia* 1.2.12, claims that Socrates' association with Critias and Alcibiades was brought up by the prosecutors.

14 See Ober 1989 for an analysis of Athenian courtroom rhetoric. Hansen 1995 is a recent and historically well-informed attempt to work out the trial of Socrates "from the Athenian point of view."

15 Besides the *Apologies*, the most important near-contemporary works for our purposes are Plato's *Euthyphro*, *Crito*, and *Gorgias*, and Xenophon's *Memorabilia* (on which, see Gray 1998). The later ancient tradition on Socrates is collected in Calder 2002. Two references to the charges by the Athenian orators Aeschines and Hypereides are considered later.

16 Probably by the Athenian political orator Polycrates, a text to which the famous speech writer, Lysias, offered to write yet another *Apology of Socrates*: *Scholion in Aristidem* 3.480 (Dindorf).

No document surviving from antiquity can be regarded as anything like a transcript of Socrates' actual remarks at the trial – the texts that constitute the early Socratic tradition about the trial were written for philosophical or rhetorical purposes, rather than for historical or forensic purposes. As a result, we do not know what the historical Socrates said in his own defense. Since guesses about the prosecution's substantive arguments depend on the same tradition, it is impossible to reconstruct what the prosecutors *or* the defendant actually said.

The trial of Socrates was, however, a notable and memorable event for the Athenians. It was a definitive moment for the Socratic tradition and for writers who responded to it, quickly generating a substantial literature. The trial took place in a well-documented period of Athenian political and legal history; we can say much about the context of the trial, and about the contexts in which the texts constituting the Socratic tradition about the trial were written. We must keep in mind that the "Socrates" who takes part in "the story of the trial" is, like a character in a historical novel, a conglomerate: in some part modeled on the real Socrates, in some part a fictional being invented by the authors of the tradition. Despite the ink spilled on the subject, there is no way to quantify objectively how much of Plato's or Xenophon's Socrates is historical, how much invented; thoughtful scholarly opinion on this subject covers a broad spectrum.[17] My approach here is to seek to place the events as portrayed in the tradition (especially Plato but taking account of Xenophon) in their Athenian legal and historical context. The result will not be "the real, historical Socrates," but I hope to show that the Socratic tradition engaged creatively with the Athenian context, and that "Socrates on trial and in prison" was constructed by the tradition as a plausible Athenian character, one deeply concerned with the values and practices of the democratic city.

LEGAL NARRATIVE (CONTINUED)

Following the speeches of Meletus and his associates, Socrates delivered his speech of defense. In Plato's account of the trial, Socrates' defense hinged on two substantive claims: First, negatively, Meletus

17   Vlastos 1991, esp. chs. 2 and 3, argued that it was possible to recover, mostly from Plato's early Socratic dialogues, the views and arguments of the historical Socrates. Morrison 2000 carefully reviews the question of the historical accuracy of Plato's account of the trial, concluding that it reliably reports the basic historical facts about the trial, but that there is no reason to suppose that Plato's *Apology* (any more than any other ancient account) gives us anything close to Socrates' actual arguments.

was incapable of recognizing impiety because he had no understanding of piety. Nor did he understand how the youth were either corrupted or benefited. His ignorance was demonstrated by his incapacity to avoid self-contradiction on these subjects under Socrates' cross examination. Since Meletus could not explain what piety or education were without contradicting himself, he could not make a coherent case that Socrates had behaved impiously or had miseducated anyone. Second, positively, in accord with the beliefs of other Athenians, Socrates regarded piety as a virtue. Socrates' ideas about piety were, Plato argues, both internally consistent and fell within the range of reasonable Athenian opinion on the subject.

The tradition's argument for innocence is grounded in these claims: Socrates conducted his life in accordance with his moral commitments. Because he regarded piety as a virtue and his conception of piety conformed to reasonable Athenian opinion, Socrates would not have, and so did not, engage in actions that a reasonable Athenian would regard as impious. Socrates had no motive to corrupt others, since by so doing Socrates would have harmed himself. There was no evidence for corruption of the youth, since neither Athenian youths nor their parents testified that Socrates had corrupted them. These arguments for Socrates' innocence might have convinced some of the judges, but they did not directly answer the prosecutor's charges. A reasonable judge listening to the speech of Plato's *Apology* could hardly be blamed for concluding that the logic lesson given Meletus was a cover-up, and that Socrates actually disbelieved in state-approved gods, and for that reason avoided participation in state religious rituals, promoted a personal deity unrecognized by the state, and corrupted entire families so thoroughly that they failed to recognize the harm they suffered and did. That judge might accept Meletus's argument that such behavior was impious. Plato sets Socrates' logical refutation of Meletus's conceptions of piety and education within a speech that challenged Athenian assumptions about what constituted a proper legal defense. And so the sympathetic reader is given to understand that Socrates was innocent, but also that many of the Athenian judges would have had reason to vote for conviction. A sympathetic reader of Xenophon's *Apology* was likely to reach a similar conclusion.

Plato's "Socrates on trial," like many actual Athenian litigants, spent a relatively small part of his allotted time answering the prosecution's charges; like other Athenian defendants, the bulk of his defense speech was devoted to a discussion of the conduct of his life and an assessment of his behavior and attitudes in respect to the democratic culture of the polis. The choice to use much of the water in the clock on self-presentation was not inherently peculiar. Yet Plato presents Socrates as diverging radically from the standard practice of Athenian litigants in the *substance* of his self-presentation. Ordinary defendants sought to present their lives and attitudes as conforming closely to democratic norms. By contrast, Socrates presented himself as a long-standing and open critic of Athenian mores and as decidedly critical of certain core principles and practices of democratic political culture. Socrates' goal in self-presentation was not that of the ordinary Athenian defendant – that is, persuading the judges to vote for acquittal on the grounds of his sound character and democratic way of life, whether or not they believed a law had been broken. Socrates' actual rhetorical goal was a matter of debate in antiquity: Xenophon suggests that because he was tired of life he portrayed himself in a way intended to assure his own conviction. I will argue that in the philosophically richer account given by Plato, Socrates' goal in presenting himself as a social and political critic was the education (in its distinctively Socratic sense of "stinging into moral wakefulness") of the judges.

Following Socrates' speech, the judges immediately voted on the verdict, by secret ballot and without formal consultation. Because the majority (according to Plato, some 280 of 501) of the judges voted for conviction, Meletus and Socrates each gave another timed speech, offering alternative penalties. Lacking discretionary sentencing authority, the judges were legally required to choose between these alternatives. Meletus proposed death. Plato's Socrates proposed a bizarre conglomerate "penalty": a substantial fine (30 minas: roughly 10 years' wages for a craftsman) paid by his wealthy friends, conjoined with the extraordinary honor of taking meals in the public dining hall (*prytaneion*) for the rest of his life. A majority of the judges voted for death, and Socrates was incarcerated in the public prison (*desmoterion*). A delay of several days ensued because of a religious prohibition (a sacred ship was en route from Delos). Socrates' friends sought to have Socrates smuggled out of prison (Xen. *Apol.* 23). Plato's *Crito* tells the story of Socrates' refusal, on ethical grounds, to cooperate with the escape plan. Socrates received visitors in his prison cell, some of whom stayed with him until the end (see Plato's *Phaedo*). The death sentence was carried out, via hemlock poisoning, as soon as the religious prohibition was lifted.[18]

The story of the trial is set in a compressed and dramatic narrative frame very familiar to Plato's and Xenophon's Athenian readers. Socrates is the protagonist of this story, but the antagonist is not just Meletus, but the polis of Athens: its citizens (qua judges), its established laws, and its democratic political culture. The stark confrontation between the moral philosopher and the democratic city in the dramatically

---

18   Todd 2000 reviews methods of capital punishment at Athens.

satisfying narrative of the legal trial became a foundation story for Western civilization – and especially for moral philosophy. It is difficult to overestimate its impact. According to the *Seventh Letter* (325a-26a, a product of the early Academy if not by Plato), the trial and execution of Socrates was the decisive event that turned young Plato away from an engagement in democratic politics and toward the philosophical project that resulted in the composition and circulation of Socratic dialogues and the foundation of the Academy. The events of 399 cast a long shadow across Plato's oeuvre; the trial theme notably recurs in the *Gorgias*, where Socrates' interlocutor, the aspiring Athenian politician Callias, predicts that Socrates will be unable to defend himself in court when unjustly charged with a crime.

The trial of Socrates spawned a new kind of Athenian literature: speeches of defense (*Apologiai*) and of accusation (*Kategoriai*) written for and against Socrates – the former by Socrates' followers and the latter by their intellectual opponents.[19] The trial was sufficiently notorious a half-century later to be cited in an Athenian courtroom by the politician and prosecutor Aeschines (1.173), who argued that the conviction of Socrates would be rendered unfair in retrospect if the judges were to allow the defendant's supporter, Demosthenes, to use the trial as a sophistical showcase. About a decade earlier (in c. 352 BCE), the Athenian rhetorician Isocrates, whose school rivaled Plato's Academy, wrote an immense and fanciful super-*Apology*. In that speech (*Antidosis*) Isocrates cast himself in the role of an intellectual, falsely charged with "corrupting the youth," who faced capital charges if his defense failed to convince the judges: Isocrates' reader was obviously meant to recognize Plato's *Apology of Socrates* as the literary model that Isocrates sought to surpass in his lengthy and ornate legal fiction.[20]

Notably, in the trial scene in Plato's *Gorgias*, as in both Aeschines' and Isocrates' citations, the themes of the dissident intellectual confronting democratic political culture and the corruption of youth are prominent, but impiety as such has dropped from the picture. The specifically *religious* aspect of the trial proved to be its least enduring feature, at least for the classical tradition. This is perhaps because Athens had no independent religious establishment. The aspect of religion relevant to the trial was a facet of civic life, and so the trial of Socrates is relevant to the question of the compatibility of philosophical dissidence with democratic civic norms. The story of Socrates and Athens remains salient in

19 The most famous *kategoria* was by the fourth-century BCE sophist Polycrates, who is apparently the butt of Xen. *Mem.* Book 1 and Isocrates, *Busiris* 4. See further, Brickhouse and Smith 2002, pp. 5–8.

20 Isocrates and Socrates: Nightingale 1995; Ober 1998, ch. 5; Ober 2004.

modernity – in an era in which "democracy conjoined with law," as originally defined by the ancient Athenians, and "critical ethical inquiry," as originally defined by Socrates, are both regarded by many people as primary goods and basic to human flourishing. Although no retelling can ever hope to be definitive, by taking into account the relevant contexts – cultural, social, political, and legal as well as intellectual and philosophical – we may begin to make better sense of the story of the confrontation between philosophical Socrates and democratic Athens.

SOCRATES' CIVIC DUTIES

We can best understand the story of the trial by starting with its aftermath, at a key moment for the Socratic tradition, with Socrates in prison, awaiting execution. According to Plato's *Crito* – a dialogue that, like the *Apologies of Socrates*, puts Socrates into an active conversation with democratic norms and practices – Socrates refused to go along with an escape plan because escaping from prison meant breaking the law: It would violate a legal order issued by competent public authorities. Escape, as Plato's Crito admits, would constitute a substantive harm to the edifice of Athenian law.[21]

Socrates of the *Crito* considers the harm consideration decisive. He brushes aside counter-arguments regarding the bad effects of Socrates' death upon his friends and sons, and on the reputations of those who might have saved him but failed to do so. This carelessness about morally irrelevant conditions of life is typical of Socrates as portrayed in the tradition. More surprisingly, however, Socrates also refuses to take into consideration the substantive fairness of the judgment against himself. Both Crito and Socrates (and presumably Plato's intended reader) accept that the Athenian judges erred in convicting Socrates of impiety. As we have seen, in Plato's *Apology* Socrates had attacked the coherence of Meletus's conception of piety and sought to establish his own commitment to piety as a virtue. The philosophically inclined reader assumed by Plato's texts was likely to conclude that Socrates had been wrongly convicted in respect to absolute justice. Yet Socrates had been rightfully convicted in respect to Athenian law. That is to say, the Athenian jury had made no procedural error in coming to its legal judgment. Because the trial had been legally (i.e., procedurally) correct, the decision of the court had legal standing. If the verdict had been based on the judges' acceptance of a logically flawed definition of piety, that was unfortunate,

---

21   For thoughtful book-length discussions of the *Crito*'s philosophical arguments see Allen 1980, Kraut 1984, and Weiss 1998.

but strictly irrelevant in terms of the law. In Athenian legal process, there was no presiding magistrate who might declare a mistrial, no provision for legal appeal to a higher court, and certainly no provision for appeal to the authority of "absolute justice." The escape was proposed by Crito in the absence of any obvious options for legal redress.[22]

Having discounted Crito's concerns about the negative effect of Socrates' death on individuals and reputations (harms without moral relevance), Socrates weighs the assumed *injustice of the conviction* against the potential *harm to the polis's laws* and comes to an unambiguous conclusion: The consideration that escape would entail (morally relevant) harm to the laws decided the matter and so he refused to cooperate in the escape plan. But in Plato's dialogue, Socrates comes to this conclusion in two stages: harming the laws is initially rejected as an ethically acceptable course of action on the grounds that doing morally relevant harm is impermissible.[23] Socrates reminds Crito that they had previously agreed (in a conversation unavailable to Plato's readers) on the impermissibility of doing harm. If doing morally relevant harm is impermissible, and harming the law is morally relevant, then harming the laws is impermissible. So the discussion about what Socrates should do seems, philosophically, to be decided quickly and decisively.

Yet the dialogue moves on to a second stage, taking the form of an imagined conversation between the "laws (*nomoi*) of Athens" and a Socrates who is (counterfactually) seriously contemplating breaking the law by escaping from prison. This "dialogue within a dialogue" continues the conversation between Socrates and the jury in Plato's *Apology*. The difference is that now Socrates' interlocutor is the law of Athens as he himself has come to understand it, rather than fallible and educable Athenian citizens.

The imagined laws of Athens make what Socrates takes to be a powerful case regarding Socrates' duty of obedience in respect to themselves: obedience to Athenian law is demanded on the grounds that Socrates, as a citizen, like his forefathers, is the "son and slave" of the

22 On Athenian "legal positivism", see Ober 2005. Convicted Athenian defendants could challenge a court's decision by various roundabout means (e.g., indicting one of the prosecution's witnesses for perjury: see Osborne 1985, but it is not clear that there was time to launch such a challenge in Socrates' case, nor that Socrates would have had any interest in doing so.

23 It is important to distinguish between harm simpliciter and morally relevant harm. Socrates must have willingly accepted the possibility that he might inflict physical damage upon his opponents when he fought in Athenian wars; this sort of harm evidently falls out of the category of moral relevance, even though the wars in which Socrates fought would be regarded as indefensible according to modern "just war doctrine."

laws (50e). This argument, with its unexpected introduction of fundamentally unequal social positions (a father or master may do things to a son or slave that the son or slave may not do to the father or master), is concerned with harms (to the laws) and with what actions are permissible. It does not, however, hinge on the general impermissibility of doing morally relevant harms. It rests instead on the value of reciprocity within a civic/political context: Were Socrates, a citizen of Athens, to harm the laws of his polis, he would be returning evils for the goods he had previously received from the laws. Doing so would be analogous to the behavior of a son who struck his father (a common trope in Athenian literature) despite the goods he had received in the past from his parent. The strengthening of the paternal trope implied by the reference to Socrates as son *and slave* of the laws rests on the claim that Socrates, qua citizen, had received benefits from the laws of Athens that exceeded even the benefits a son received from a parent. To wit: Socrates had received from the laws his birth (*genesis*), his upbringing (*trophe*), and his education (*paideia*).[24]

The tricolon "birth/upbringing/education" was not an idiosyncratic or distinctively "Socratic" group of human goods – the imagined laws of Athens present the benefits they conferred upon each citizen as a simple and commonly accepted "moral fact," well known to any morally attentive Athenian. The tricolon reproduces what was probably a canonical list of goods received from parents.[25] What is remarkable in this case is that the relevant goods are transferred from the parental realm to the civic realm: they are provided by the laws themselves qua "super-parent." In the *Crito*, the provision of birth, upbringing, and education defines the formation of the individual Athenian citizen by, through, and in relationship to his polis: the citizen is quite literally a product of the laws. In this account, the law of the polis qua "state" takes on a role that is substantially different from the legal role of the modern liberal state – that is, something other than a morally neutral guarantor of inalienable individual rights (centered on pursuit of individually defined happiness) within a stable regime of constitutionally mandated and transparent rules. Rather, as the direct provider of both an individual's original being and subsequent becoming, and thus of the entirety of his fundamental identity, the law stands in a paternal and "masterful" relationship to each and every citizen.[26] Although Socrates

---

24 Parent-striking as an Athenian trope with special salience in the era of Socrates: Strauss 1993.

25 Cf. Aristotle, *EN* 1162a4–7.

26 The public discourse of the Athenian polis employed various parental tropes (*patris*: fatherland; *patrios nomos*: ancestral law), but the "state as father"

of the *Crito* equates the goods received by the citizen from the state *only* with the "paternal" trio of birth, upbringing, and education, the general conception that the citizen was eternally indebted to the polis and its law due to the receipt of a basket of goods was, as we shall see, common in normative Athenian political thought.

The relationship between citizen and polis law is characterized by Socrates as paternal and masterful (inter alia) because there is no meaningful chance of the individual citizen's repaying the debt: as Aristotle notes in the *Nicomachean Ethics* (1161a), sons and fathers remain on grounds of inequality (and thus sons owe their fathers obedience, and not vice versa) because of the impossibility of full reciprocity. Yet the impossibility of repayment does not free the son or citizen from an obligation to pay to his parent or polis, to the extent that he was able, interest on the unrepayable capital loan.[27] Borrowing from various sources for Athenian cultural-political attitudes, we may break down the "citizen's payment schedule for goods received" as follows:

First and foremost, the polis requires *obedience* to the written laws and unwritten customs of the polis (the term *nomoi* includes both) and to the orders of legitimately appointed public magistrates. This form of legal obedience included obeying the call to military service: when summoned, the good citizen served the polis with his body – most often as a cavalryman, heavy-infantry man (hoplite), or rower in the fleet. And when in the field he obeyed the orders of his commanders, who were themselves elected or appointed magistrates of the state. Obedience to laws and magistrates, especially in the context of military service, might entail grave physical danger, and might ultimately require the individual to sacrifice his life: among the most important annual ceremonies of the democratic state was the "ancestral (or paternal) law" (*patrios nomos*), which specified collective public burial and public commemoration (via speech and inscribed monument) for the Athenian soldiers who died in that year. In Thucydides' history of the Peloponnesian War, Pericles' Funeral Oration, delivered in the first year of the war (431 BCE), offers an eloquent testimony to the deep Athenian cultural assumption that the goods offered by the polis to each citizen rendered it fitting, indeed glorious, for an individual citizen to give his life in battle for the good of the polis. Likewise, according to the argument offered to

---

was ordinarily obscured by the "fraternal" connection of male citizens as warrior/political actor equals who collectively constituted the polis: see Loraux 1993.

27 So the question is: does the obligation create a virtuous circle of mutual benefit, or a vicious relationship similar to the gangster's "offer you can't refuse" and "debt you can't repay."

Socrates by the laws of Athens in the *Crito*, the sacrifice of one's life could be justly demanded in (partial) repayment for having been given the trio of basic goods. In the *Apology*, Plato's Socrates alludes prominently to his active military service as a heavy-armed infantry man, and he comments specifically on his willing obedience to the orders of elected Athenian military commanders. The later Socratic tradition also celebrated the courage and steadfastness of "Socrates the citizen soldier."[28]

In addition to obedience, the polis expected a certain amount of civic *participation* from each individual citizen: the state required his time and presence in order to operate the institutions of the democratic community. Civic participation ordinarily included political as well as military service. Rather than resting upon the efforts of a few political experts (like Plato's "philosopher-kings"), the democracy depended upon the occasional service of a mass of "dedicated amateurs" to serve as Assemblymen, as councilors in the agenda-setting Council of 500, as judges in the people's courts, as lotteried magistrates, as public arbitrators, and as voluntary prosecutors (like Meletus) of public malefactors. The account of fourth-century BCE Athenian democracy in the Aristotelian *Athenaion Politeia* gives a vivid sense of the large number of citizen-days of public service that were required each year in order for the democracy to operate. Although Socrates' political service is less prominent in the Socratic tradition than is his military service, the tradition acknowledges that Socrates did indeed answer this participation demand: In Plato's *Gorgias*, Socrates mentions that he attended the Athenian Assembly and listened carefully to the debates there. He served a year on the Council of 500 in 406 BCE – and happened to be one of the magistrates in charge of running an especially contentious meeting of the Assembly, at which Athenian generals were charged en masse with dereliction of duty. On this occasion, Socrates sought to restrain the Assemblymen from acting outside the established legal norms of the polis.[29]

With respect to the duties of obedience and civic participation, Athenian citizens were regarded as more or less interchangeable. Obedience and civic participation were demanded of all Athenians, irrespective of their particular and individualized capacities. But the Athenian was also expected to repay the "interest" on the unrepayable "debt principal" represented by the goods he had received from the polis

---

28 Plato: *Apology* 28e; Diogenes Laertius 1.5.23.
29 Socrates in the Assembly: *Gorgias* 455d-e, cf. 503a-d; on the Council: Plato *Apology* 32c-d, *Gorgias* 473b-74a; Xen. *Mem.* 1.1.18. See further, Ober 1998, pp. 193–197.

by freely offering to the polis whatever individual and personal excellence he might possess. In the case of the wealthy individual, this meant paying periodic special taxes based on total family property holding (*eisphora*). For the very wealthy it meant substantial material contributions in the form of periodic festival liturgies (e.g., as chorus-producers for a series of tragedies) and naval liturgies (to defray the expense of maintaining a fleet of warships). Fine singers and dancers performed in one of the fifty-man (and fifty-boy) tribal choruses during major festivals. A victorious athlete, demonstrably strong of body and beloved of the gods, might take a leading place in military formations. The citizen who had relevant expert knowledge and was a capable public speaker would be expected to offer advice at public meetings of democratic bodies.[30]

The citizen's excellence-based contributions were different from his duties of obedience and participation in that, under the right circumstances, he might claim that these special services placed the polis in *his* debt. Athenian litigants who had voluntarily performed more than their allotted share of financial liturgies, might, for example, claim that the judges owed them a sympathetic hearing. Those whose personal excellence greatly benefited the polis expected public honors, potentially including decrees of thanks, the award of a gold wreath, statues in public spaces – or the privilege of taking their meals in the public dining hall. It was because Socrates believed that his own special excellence had been the source of substantial benefits to the polis that he included free public meals in the "penalty" he proposed after being found guilty of impiety. But, as we have seen, in the *Crito* Socrates also claimed that he owed to the laws of Athens an unrepayable debt for goods he himself had received. Although some Athenians (like Alcibiades) may have felt that their debt to the polis for goods received was more than repaid by their special services, both standard Athenian thinking and Socratic thinking was more complex: The performance of outstanding services deserved public acknowledgment in the form of outstanding honors, but those honors did not indicate the full repayment of the individual's underlying debt to his polis. Rather, the indebtedness of excellent citizen and polis was reciprocal, and the reciprocity was expressed in a language of mutual honoring and mutual obligation.[31]

Unlike his overall conventional responses to the obligations of obedience and civic participation, in the area of duty based on individual

---

30   *Eisphora*: Thomsen 1964; festival liturgies: Wilson 2000, naval liturgies: Gabrielsen 1994; choruses: Wilson 2000; athletes: Kurke 1993; knowledgeable speakers: Ober 1989, pp. 314–27.

31   Reciprocity and mutual obligations of gratitude as key aspects of democratic culture: Ober 1989, pp. 226–230; Domingo Gygax, forthcoming.

excellence Socrates developed a distinctive conception of his responsibility to the polis. He was not wealthy. He was no athlete, and we are not given to suppose that his singing and dancing were up to Athenian choral standards. While knowledgeable and politically astute after his own fashion, he was not a public speaker. Indeed, in Plato's *Apology* (31c-32a) Socrates makes a point of his unwillingness to "speak out in public debates" – and this is sometimes mistakenly taken as evidence that Socrates refused to perform the ordinary civic duties of participation. But, in fact, relatively few Athenians spoke in public meetings. This sort of "quietism" was not exceptional and was in no sense incompatible with an active record of public service; indeed, it was structurally essential to democratic governance: had even a substantial minority of Athenians actively sought to exercise their equal right of public speech (*isegoria*) at major public meetings, the polis would be rendered ungovernable.[32]

Many Athenians who lacked the specific "excellence" required to serve as, for example, liturgists or public speakers, contented themselves with repaying their debt to the polis by fulfilling the duties of obedience and civic participation. But Socrates imagined he did have a particular area of excellence in which he could serve Athens: as an educational public gadfly. Plato's *Apology* assumes that his philosophical conversations, carried out in the public spaces of the Athenian agora, were a form of public service. In Plato's *Apology* (30e-31b), the service of waking the Athenians from their moral slumber is famously compared to the service a biting gadfly performs for a large and well-bred but lazy horse. It is precisely on the basis of his "public benefactions" as a gadfly that Socrates made the seemingly audacious proposal during the sentencing phase of his trial that he be offered free meals by the city (36d-e), an honor ordinarily reserved for victorious athletes who, as we have seen, might be asked to take positions of extraordinary risk in war. Although that honor (had it been offered) would not have ended Socrates' obligations in respect to public service, it would have been, he supposed, a reasonable and appropriate acknowledgement of the special educational benefits he provided, and of the risks he incurred in the process.

Of course, like proposing an extraordinary honor as a "penalty," Socrates' gadfly analogy is deliberately paradoxical: No one who has watched a real horse responding to the persistent attack of biting flies – switching its tail, shivering its flanks, shaking its head and mane – will imagine that the horse appreciates the "service" done by the flies in preventing it from sleeping. Given the opportunity, the horse will kill

32 Varieties of Athenian quietism: Carter 1986. The question of Socrates' alleged political quietism is a key element in Vlastos's and Stone's accounts: Schofield 2002, pp. 277–281.

the gadfly – and likewise Socrates recognized that his fellow citizens were unlikely to acknowledge as benefits his own practice of making them uncomfortable with their own moral laziness. Unlike a wealthy litigant's allusion to a solid record of public liturgies, Socrates' allusion at the trial to his well-known "gadfly" behavior certainly did nothing to help him win the sympathy of the jurors and thus secure acquittal; nor, Plato implies, was it meant to.

We should not allow Socrates' distinctive interpretation of his public responsibilities with respect to "special excellence" to obscure his largely conventional interpretation of his duties in terms of legal obedience and civic participation – it is the mix of conventionality and originality that makes Socrates so complex and so interesting. It also makes him extremely difficult to grasp, in that Socrates seems at once to borrow from and yet diverge from a series of ancient Athenian character types: these include the sophists and scientists with whom Socrates was conflated by Aristophanes and other comic poets; Plato and his various philosophical rivals and successors, sequestered in private schools; and Diogenes the Cynic, famous for outrageous behavior and lack of attachment to material goods. But the primary Athenian type against which we should imagine the Athenian jurors of 399 struggling to compare Socrates, and to which he both conformed and diverged in vertiginous ways, was the "standard good citizen" vividly represented in the idealizing portrait offered by Thucydides' Pericles.

The comparison between Socrates and the "Periclean citizen" is apt. In the speeches he gives Pericles, Thucydides expresses clearly the dependence of both the communal flourishing of the polis and the individual flourishing of each citizen upon the patriotic willingness on the part of each and every citizen to work hard and consistently for the common good. Like the Athenian laws that Socrates of the *Crito* imagines as chastising a lawbreaker, Thucydides' Pericles emphasizes the catastrophic harm that will come to the polis if individual citizens or social sub-groups place private interests above the common good. Likewise, in their legal orations, delivered before mass audiences of judges and spectators, Demosthenes, Lycurgus, Aeschines, and other Athenian political orators equate the flourishing of the polis with the active willingness of the citizenry to obey the law, to defend the laws by their voluntary public service, and to offer whatever personal excellence they might possess whenever it is called upon. Like Thucydides' Pericles, these fourth-century Athenian speakers equated the failure to obey, to participate, and to offer personal excellence to the community with the catastrophic incapacity of the polis to ensure its own continuous existence.[33]

33 Thucydides' Pericles: Thuc. 2.37.1, 2.60.2–5. Athenian orators: Ober 1989, pp. 295–304.

There was, in sum, a general agreement between Socrates (as portrayed in Plato's *Crito*) and the democratic political culture of Athens that the citizen had a substantial duty to his polis: obedience to the laws, customs, and magistrates of the polis; public participation in support of the institutions of governance; and voluntary contributions on the basis of whatever special excellence he might possess. These duties were justly demanded by the polis on the basis of a conception of reciprocal exchange that could be analogized as a just (although unequal) contract: the citizen's duties were an (inadequate) repayment for fundamental goods received by each citizen from the polis and its laws.

Yet if Socrates and political Athenian culture agreed on the general principle of the just social contract, the list of "goods received by the individual from the polis" that they emphasized were different. As we have seen, in the *Crito* Socrates emphasizes the "parental" triad of birth, upbringing, and education. By contrast, Thucydides' Pericles focuses heavily on national glory and wealth. Fourth-century Athenian orators, for their part emphasized the freedom, political equality, and security enjoyed by each citizen. In juxtaposing Socratic ethics with the normative views of his fellow Athenian citizens, we must not lose sight *either* of the fact that the principle of a contract between citizen and polis was shared, *or* that the basket of goods each regarded as relevant to the civic contract was different.[34] As we have seen, the reader of the *Crito* learns that Socrates was required to obey the law by a conviction about the impermissibility of doing morally relevant harm. But the amount of time he subsequently spends in laying out the contractual relationship between citizen and laws suggests that the implied contract is a key to understanding the relationship between Socrates and Athenian democracy.

It is impossible to demonstrate that the *historical* Socrates was committed to the contractual conception of citizen duty that Plato's Socrates lays out in the *Crito*. Yet assuming that the real Socrates had such a conception does help explain the ethical basis for a few seldom-disputed facts about the historical Socrates: his record of military and civic service; his habit of engaging in philosophical conversations with ordinary people in public (rather than limiting himself to private conversations with the educated elite); his willingness to answer the Basileus's legal summons and then to report to the people's court as ordered (rather than

---

34 It is important to note that these Greek conceptions of "social contract," with their attention to participation and diverse individual excellence, as well as obedience and the common good, are very different from the early modern social contract theories of, for example, Hobbes and Rousseau. See further, Ober 1996, chapter 11.

ignoring the magistrate's order and going home, as he did when ordered by a magistrate of the oligarchic Thirty to arrest Leon of Salamis); his choice of making a speech of defense at the trial (rather than remaining mute, as Maximus of Tyre later claimed he did);[35] his decision to drink the hemlock (rather than escape from prison); and his decision to continue living in Athens (rather than moving to somewhere with "better laws," e.g., Sparta). We will return to these decisions at the end of this chapter.

The goods that Socrates of the *Crito* acknowledges having received from the laws of the polis were his birth, upbringing, and education – rather than national glory, power, and wealth, or individual freedom, equality, and security. The argument of the Athenian laws in the *Crito* suggests that collectively the three "parental" goods constituted the core civic formation of the individual citizen. While most Athenian citizens had a more capacious conception of the goods offered by the polis, there is no reason to suppose that they would disagree with the positive argument made by the laws in the *Crito*: the parental goods underwritten by the laws provided each citizen with his primary identity; his birth, upbringing, and civic education taught him how to conduct his life.

There is obviously much to Socrates' ethical formation and identity that *cannot* be attributed to this standard civic formation. But Socrates of the *Crito* believed that the formation he had received from his birth, upbringing, and civic education was *consistent with* the distinctive moral and ethical commitments he subsequently developed in the course of philosophical study and conversation. At such time as Socrates perceived a conflict between who he was as a citizen and who he was as a self-consciously ethical subject, he was free to leave the polis – as the laws of Athens pointed out to him in the *Crito*. The tradition emphasizes that Socrates never left the polis except on military orders, and thus supports the validity of the claim of the imagined laws of the *Crito* that Socrates was satisfied with Athenian laws. The implication is thus that his civic formation and ethical formation remained compatible throughout his life.[36]

Socrates rejected the notion that he might believe one thing and act otherwise, and claimed that his inner voice, his *daimonion*, consistently prevented him from acting wrongly. Thus we must suppose that the actions and behaviors demanded by Socrates' "Athenian formation" – the duties he took on qua citizen – were fully consistent with his conception of ethics and morality. And to that extent, despite his critical response to certain principles and practices of the Athenian democracy,

---

35 Maximus of Tyre, *Oration* 3.7 and passim.
36 Socrates' home-boundedness: *Crito* 52b.

we may say that Socratic philosophy and Athenian democracy were compatible.[37] Yet if this is so, then the series of events that resulted in Socrates' death by hemlock in the prison of Athens were historically contingent rather than being the predictable result of a deep underlying conflict between Socratic ethical philosophy and democratic political culture. The Platonic strand of the Socratic tradition that we have been following here thus opens a common ground that Socrates and Athens might jointly inhabit.

GOODS RECEIVED

In order to test the compatibility of Socrates' ethical commitments with democracy, we should look more closely at the three "parental goods" that he acknowledged (in the *Crito*) having received from the laws of Athens. Were these goods a fair exchange, in and of themselves (that is, without the addition of morally problematic "goods" such as national glory, power, and wealth), for the duties demanded of Athenian citizens? What was the relationship of the parental goods to the oft-cited (by Athenian public orators and modern democrats) goods of freedom, equality, and security? Was the contract described by the laws in the *Crito* a fair one, and was it presented by Plato in a way that accurately represented Athenian normative commitments?

By looking briefly at how Athenian law and custom regulated birth, upbringing, and education, we can see how freedom, equality, and dignity were integrated in the formation of citizens. Furthermore, cross-referencing Spartan law and custom will help to clarify Socrates' debt to the laws of Athens. The *Crito* (52b, 53c) suggests that Socrates regarded Sparta (as well as Crete, Thebes, and Megara) as having better laws than Athens; yet Socrates chose to live in Athens, subject to Athenian law. Did Socrates receive goods from "inferior" Athenian laws that he would have lacked under the "superior" Spartan legal regime? This legal/historical exploration gives us a starting point for assessing the historical circumstances that allowed Socrates to live a civic and ethical life in Athens as well as the circumstances that brought Socrates and Athenian political culture into a collision course in 399, ending in the untimely death of the philosopher and a permanent stain upon the record of the democratic community.

37 Kraut 1984, ch. 7, and Schofield 2002, pp. 271–277, review evidence for Socrates' critical stance toward democracy; see, further, Ober 1998, pp. 184–185 and passim, for the essential distinction between criticism and hostility.

BIRTH

Socrates imagines that the laws ask him, "Did we not bring you forth? Is it not through us that your father married your mother and begat you? Now tell us, have you any fault to find with those of us who are the laws of marriage?" (*Crito* 50d). The laws in question concern legitimate marriage. In contrast to Homeric marriage custom, which recognized the full inheritance rights of bastards, Athenian law defined legitimate marriage as constituting the monogamous nuclear family as an inheritance group and thus as a descent group.[38] By canceling one of the privileges of wealth (the begetting of an unlimited number of legitimate heirs: cf. Priam's fifty sons in the *Iliad*), Athenian marriage law placed Socrates' father, Sophroniscus (and eventually Socrates himself), on a more equal footing with wealthier Athenian men. Socrates would also have a limited number of siblings and could thus expect to inherit a substantial share of Sophroniscus's property. This base-line equality of birthright among Athenians enabled Socrates' voice to be attended by the Athenian elite, in a way that contrasts sharply with the treatment of another famously ugly and low-born character in Greek literature: Thersites of Homer's *Iliad* (book 2), who is summarily thrashed when he criticizes the behavior of superiors.

Socrates was born in 469 BCE, which means that he came of age (turned eighteen) in 451, the year in which the Athenians passed a new law requiring that Athenian citizens have both an Athenian father and an Athenian mother (that is, a woman with an Athenian father).[39] Sophroniscus probably brought young Socrates before the citizens of his home deme (township) of Alopece at their very first meeting held under the new law to scrutinize the descent of Athenians. Sophroniscus and his wife, Phaenerete, were accepted by the men of Alopece as native-born Athenians and Socrates was enrolled among the citizens of the deme and the polis.[40] The laws of marriage defined Socrates' "civic being" as an equal inheritance from both his parents and made of the Athenians a closed body – a demotic aristocracy. The laws of marriage defined the subsequent conditions of Socrates' upbringing and education, as well as

38 Lape 2002–3; note, however, that Diogenes Laertius 1.5.26 claims that Socrates had two wives during a short interval in which this was allowed by special wartime law.

39 Patterson 1981, Boegehold 1994, with literature cited.

40 There is a debate among scholars about whether or not boys born to foreign mothers before the passage of the law were "grandfathered." Hansen 1991, p. 53, follows Humphreys 1974, in supposing those born of non-Athenian mothers pre 451/0 were excluded from citizenship. Ogden 1996, argues for grandfathering.

limiting his own future options for marriage. In sum, the laws of marriage did a lot of work in bringing Socrates, qua Athenian citizen, into being in a social and political sense. They provided Socrates with a complex inheritance in that they made civic unequals of persons who might well be regarded as moral equals (e.g. the citizen Glaucon and the metic Polemarchus), and made civic equals of men who might be regarded as moral unequals (e.g. Socrates and Meletus). Yet Socrates' reference (in Plato's *Apology* 30a) to his special relationship to other Athenian citizens on the basis of kinship suggests that it was an inheritance that he willingly embraced.

UPBRINGING

Socrates' upbringing was not specified by formal Athenian law, as it would have been, for example, had he been born to Spartan parents. But the *nomoi* that Socrates of the *Crito* imagines as addressing him included established Athenian customs as well as written law. In contrast to Sparta, Athenian custom specified that the fundamental choice of *whether* to bring up a child or whether to kill it (by exposure) shortly after birth was made by the family rather than by the state. Had Socrates been born to Spartan parents, he would have been examined as an infant by officials charged with exterminating babies who appeared malformed. Although we do not know what criteria the Spartan officials employed, in light of the ancient tradition about his very peculiar appearance, it is at least conceivable that Socrates owed his survival past infancy to Athenian customs regarding upbringing. Shortly after his birth, Socrates was displayed to family members and later presented to the members of Sophroniscus' phratry (a regional/kinship group); at age eighteen he was formally introduced to the demesmen of Alopece. To the extent that Socrates' identity was based on kinship and locality, it was a product of his upbringing according to established Athenian custom.[41]

A second aspect of Socrates upbringing was his paternal inheritance. According to Athenian custom, a father was expected to teach his son a craft and a father who survived into middle age was expected to turn over his estate to his legitimate sons in a timely manner: The estate would be evenly divided amongst the sons, who might then take wives of their own.[42] An Athenian father with a legitimate son lacked the legal authority to disinherit him: even if Sophroniscus (like Aristophanes' Strepsiades in the *Clouds*) had disapproved of his son's pursuits, Athenian

41   On standard Athenian upbringing practices, see Golden 1990.
42   Athenian customs regarding inheritance: Strauss 1993.

law and custom demanded that Socrates be his heir. Although we know none of the details, Socrates evidently inherited a property sufficient to allow him to enroll in the ranks of the heavy-armed hoplite infantry, to marry twice, and to raise three sons. One marriage (the order is disputed by the ancient sources) was to a woman with the aristocratic name Xanthippe. The other marriage, according to tradition, was without dowry, to a daughter of the distinguished Athenian statesman Aristides (nicknamed "the Just").[43] The two connections suggest that his inherited financial position was relatively secure – secure enough, perhaps, to allow him to spend substantial time upon philosophical investigations rather than worrying about starvation. Socrates was not a rich man, and once his philosophical career commenced in earnest his estate declined (*Ap.* 31b-c). But it is undeniable that his conventional Athenian upbringing made it possible for him to become a philosopher.

EDUCATION

When Socrates acknowledged that he had received his education (*paideia*) from the *nomoi* of Athens, he must have been referring to both written law and custom. The imagined laws of the *Crito* ask Socrates if he was dissatisfied with those laws that "told your father to educate you in music (*mousike*) and gymnastics" (50d). Here the reference is to custom: the tradition assumes that Sophroniscus could afford to give his son not only a basic primary education (thus the capacity to read and write), but also a more advanced cultural education offered by private tutors in poetry, musical performance, and athletic endeavor. This sort of education was regarded by Athenians as appropriate to a young man from a comfortable background. Socrates, as presented by both Xenophon and Plato, had a deep and easy mastery of poetry and music, and was very much at home in the gymnasium. The contrast with Sparta is instructive. Had Socrates survived a Spartan infancy, his education (after age seven) would have been highly regulated and provided by the state: he would have been assigned to an age-based "herd of boys" and put through an extraordinarily rigorous physical training aimed entirely at making him into an effective member of Sparta's highly professional land army. Each Spartan was taught to be "similar" (*homoios*) to every other Spartan; his attitudes toward the world, his public and private comportment, and his conditions of life were, at least in principle, standardized by the state. The model against which the young Spartan was formed was also meant to be timeless: change, difference, innovation, and novelty were systematically suppressed as

43 Socrates' marriages: Diogenes Laertius 1.5.26.

inimical to the preservation of Spartan society. In sum, Sparta's legally mandated education would have provided no space for Socrates to develop or pursue his distinctive intellectual and ethical interests. By contrast the "musical and gymnastic" education that Athenian custom demanded that Sophroniscus provide for him clearly did.[44]

Although Athenian law mandated nothing like Spartan training, the democratic political culture and the participatory practices of Athenian governance nonetheless provided each Athenian with a civic education. Athenian civic education may seem haphazard in comparison with Sparta, but it was recognized by the Athenians as essential to the perpetuation of the democratic regime. Athenian public speakers emphasize the educational aspect of public decisions: decrees of the Assembly, judgments of the people's courts, and the laws themselves. The goal of this Athenian civic education was clearly "building citizens" – that is, making those young Athenians who had met the double-descent birth qualification into courageous and patriotic members of a democratic community.[45] It was through the everyday operations of democratic culture and practices that each young citizen was taught that he owed a duty to the polis because of the good things he had received from the polis. Although Socrates of the *Apology* is scornful of Meletus's belief that Athenian judges, Assemblymen, Councilmen, and other officials were effective teachers of the youth, while Socrates alone corrupted them, the normative Athenian position on good citizenship was quite close to the things Socrates imagines he hears the laws saying in the *Crito*, and to which he has no demur.

Plato, in the *Republic*, made special note of the effectiveness and pervasiveness of Athenian-style "civic education by public practice." Yet far from regarding it as a good received, he depicts Athenian civic education as ideological in the worst sense – as training in conformity to popular attitudes and detrimental to the emergence of a genuinely philosophical perspective.[46] The great distance between the position on the proper education of the citizen implicitly accepted by Socrates in the *Crito* and that developed in the *Republic*, may be taken as a measure of how far Plato had to go in order to solve the ethical problem left to him by Socrates' accommodation with Athenian democratic culture.[47] It appears that as Plato worked out his "Socrates and Athens" problem, his

---

44   On traditional education in Athens, Sparta, and elsewhere in Greece, see Griffith 2001.
45   On "rational courage" in Athens, see Balot 2004.
46   On the distinctions between civic education in Plato's Callipolis and in Athens, see Ober 2001.
47   See, further, Ober, 1998 chapter 4.

literary Socrates became both less civic and less "Athenian." Socrates is difficult to grasp in part because much of the early Socratic tradition (Xenophon and Plato of *Apology* and *Crito*) saw him as simultaneously a "self-created" philosopher, who lived his life according to unrefuted moral positions arrived at in uncoerced philosophical conversations, *and* as an Athenian citizen, possessing a polis-given civic identity. In the *Republic*, Plato simplifies the picture by stripping Socrates of most remnants of a civic Athenian identity.

In sum, Socrates of the early tradition believed that he had received a great deal from the laws and customs of his native city: the circumstances of his early life and his early formation were profoundly affected by the distinctive Athenian legal and customary regime under which he was born, raised and educated; under other circumstances, his life-circumstances might not have allowed him to pursue philosophy. Given that Socrates was satisfied with who he was and who he had become, and given that his being and becoming was provided (in some part) by the polis, he did indeed owe Athens a substantial debt. Socrates fulfilled his part of a fair contract by living a life compatible with many (if not all) elements of Periclean "standard good citizenship." There is no reason to believe that the early tradition misrepresented this fundamental point.

THE CRITICAL INTELLECTUAL IN PUBLIC AND PRIVATE

If he had no fundamental quarrel with the laws of Athens, how did "good citizen Socrates" come to be tried and executed by his fellow citizens? There is no single answer to that question, either historically or in terms of the philosophical tradition. Scholarly answers can be roughly grouped into the *political* (an ambitious prosecutor mobilized popular anger at Socrates' anti-democratic behavior and/or that of his students, Critias and Alcibiades) and *cultural* (post-war Athenian attitudes toward intellectual non-conformism hardened and concern with piety grew).[48] Both political and cultural factors certainly played a part, but these should be set alongside the context of civic obligation: the trial was made possible by Socrates' idiosyncratic interpretation and persistent fulfillment of his "duty to contribute to the polis through his personal excellence." Rather than using his unique capacities to benefit the polis in obvious and conventionally acceptable ways (e.g., through material contributions or good advice on state policy), he consistently sought to

48 Political explanations: Stone 1988, Wood and Wood 1978. Cultural explanations: Connor 1991, Parker 1996, ch. 10.

benefit his fellow Athenians educationally by publicly criticizing democratic culture and its associated habits of thought, speech, and action.[49] The Athenians were used to political criticism; indeed, they recognized criticism as essential to democratic flourishing. Socrates managed to be critical in ethical terms that were new, powerful, and ultimately profoundly disquieting to his fellow citizens. His stings were genuinely painful and sometimes untimely. Yet only in the special political and cultural circumstances of the era after the Peloponnesian War did the Athenians decide to take a slap at their troublesome gadfly.

By the 420s, Socrates was well-known enough as a "public intellectual" to stand in for the standard "mad scientist/conniving sophist," in the comedies of Aristophanes and other comic poets. But Socrates diverged from his contemporary intellectuals in that he saw his relationship to himself, to others, and to his community in explicitly ethical terms and in that he initiated critical conversations with ordinary people in public places. Because Socrates, unlike other Athenian intellectuals, carried on much of his critical work openly in public, he was known to the Athenian public at large – and was thus a convenient butt of comic poets used to mocking public figures.[50] Socrates was also remarkable for conjoining his critical enterprise with his duties as a participatory citizen. As we have seen, as Councilor in charge of an Assembly meeting at which several generals were accused en masse of malfeasance, Socrates refused – over the vocal objections of the assembled citizenry – to put the procedurally irregular matter to a vote. There can be little doubt that Socrates' reputation as an outspoken critic of the status quo was securely established well before 399 BCE.

Socrates was renowned in elite circles as well. Plato and Xenophon each wrote a *Symposium*, suggesting that Socrates was in great demand at exclusive gatherings of Athenian intellectuals. Socially, this was a heterogeneous society, composed of aristocratic citizens (like Crito, Alcibiades, Critias, and Charmides), wealthy metics (like Cephalus and his sons Polemarchus and Lysias), and distinguished foreign visitors (like Protagoras, Gorgias, and Thrasymachus). Some of these people came to regard themselves as Socrates' "students" – but that certainly does not mean that they took on all of Socrates' attitudes and

49 Much of the scholarship is polarized around whether Socrates was a friend (Vlastos 1983) or an enemy (Stone 1988) of democracy; see further Schofield 2002, pp. 271–277; I am suggesting that the question is misconstrued: that Socrates was a critic and that being an engaged critic need entail neither friendship nor enmity.

50 Socrates in public: Xen. *Mem.* 1.1.10: Plato, *Ap.* 17c, 19d, 33a-b; Maximus of Tyre 3.7.

behaviors. Whereas certain of Socrates' elite friends and interlocutors (like the citizen Chaerephon and the metic family of Cephalus) were loyal supporters of the democratic regime, others (notably Alcibiades and Critias) came to despise the democracy and worked to overthrow it. The latter group clearly did not buy into the conception of the citizen's "debt to the laws of the polis" that Socrates of the *Crito* subscribes to. Revolutionary anti-democrats eventually overthrew (with Spartan help) the democratic regime and the laws that supported it in favor of an oligarchy: the regime of "The Thirty."

Socrates denied that he had students, since he took no money for teaching. Nor did he accept that it would have been possible for anyone to have been corrupted by his public or private conversations. To the extent to which Athenian anti-democrats did actually learn from Socrates, they evidently focused on his critical view of democratic governance as grounded in a mistaken belief that ordinary persons, as opposed to experts in moral education, were fully capable of making public policy that could make people better. This was grist for the mill of anti-democratic revolutionaries, but it is not incompatible with the assumption that Socrates himself remained an obedient and participatory citizen of the democratic polis: Socrates may well have believed that no moral education experts existed, or that it was impossible to identify them, or that their authority could not be established without doing ethically impermissible harm to the laws. In any event, there is no necessary contradiction between being a critic of democratic ideology and a good citizen of the democratic community. Athenian politicians, for their own part, were often sharply critical of Athenian political habits.[51]

Like a democratic Athenian politician, although for somewhat different reasons, Socrates came to live in two worlds – in the open world of the public square, where his intellectual acumen and critical attitudes were on public view, and in the private world of exclusive elite gatherings. Yet, like an Athenian politician, Socrates insisted that he always remained homogeneously himself – that he was the same over time and that there was no distinction between his "public self" and his "private self."[52] In Socrates' case, there is no reason to doubt that this claim to "always be the same" was sincere. Moreover, Socrates' contentions that he was a good citizen and "consistently at one with himself" in public and private were evidently accepted by most Athenians through most of his life. Despite his association with Alcibiades, and despite Alcibiades' (and others of Socrates' acquaintance) entanglement in the

51   Ober 1989, pp. 318–324.
52   Pericles as "always himself": Thuc 2.61. See further, Connor 1971.

notorious "Affairs of the Mysteries and Herms" in 415 BCE, there is no evidence that Socrates was accused – as they were – of impiously mocking the sacred Eleusinian Mysteries in a private house or of defacing the sacred statues of the god Hermes erected in private and public spaces around the city.[53] By contrast, the Athenian politician Andocides, who was also prosecuted in 399 BCE on a charge of impiety, spent much of his defense speech (On the Mysteries) addressing the question of why he could not legitimately be prosecuted for his part in the events of 415. Socrates was evidently not regarded, in 415 or in the years thereafter, as the sort of politically discontented malefactor likely to be associated with anti-democratic activity. In sum, although he was very well known, and although any number of Athenians, as victims of his public interrogations, may have had reason to dislike him, there is no evidence that most Athenians regarded Socrates as a dangerous malefactor in the decades before 399.

"Socrates in Athens" – famous as a sophist, scientist, public philosopher, and all-around contrarian; friendly with the notorious, and conversation-partner with the ordinary man on the street; an obedient dissident; a critic of democratic culture who takes up public office and is a stickler for the legal rules – may appear to modern readers to be a mass of contradictions. But Athenian democratic ideology and discourse thrived on such apparent contradictions: Political leaders were expected to present themselves as at once extraordinary and ordinary, as at once the spokesmen for what "everybody knows" and as the fonts of highly original policy advice. Famously wealthy litigants could offer themselves in court as incapable of dowering their daughters. Athenians delighted in individual freedom of speech and thought, yet they also honored consensus as public ideal. So, if "Socrates in Athens" is paradoxical, he nonetheless fit within an Athenian culture based on a capacity among the citizenry to embrace contradictions.[54] The question of why Socrates was tried and executed in 399 must be set in the context of his long career as a famous critical intellectual in a famously litigious community. We need to confront both the trial of 399 and the fact that it happened only after decades of public notoriety.

EXPLAINING 399: WHY PROSECUTE? WHY DEFEND?

I have argued that there was no fundamental incompatibility between Socrates, as we know him from the tradition, and Athenian democratic

---

53 Socrates' associates and the Affair of the Mysteries: Ostwald 1986, pp. 537–550.
54 Contradictions: Ober 1989, ch. 7.

culture. Despite the many aspects of Athenian culture that Socrates found worthy of critique, he regarded the implicit contract he had made with the laws as a fair one and compatible with his ethical commitments. Despite the discomfort and confusion some Athenians experienced in Socrates' company, the peculiarities of behavior and expression entailed by Socrates' philosophical commitments were adequately balanced by his sincere and convincing self-portrayal as an obedient and participatory citizen. The balance held until Socrates was seventy years old. What tipped the balance?

In 404 BCE, Athens had surrendered to Sparta, ending the Peloponnesian War. Socrates' associates Critias and Charmides, along with twentyeight other anti-democratic Athenians, were soon installed as Athens' new governors by the victorious Spartans. The reign of the Thirty was short and brutal, featuring arbitrary arrests, judicial murder, property confiscation, and large-scale exile. Plato writes in the *Seventh Letter* (324d) that the former democratic era appeared to be a golden age by contrast. Some Athenians abandoned the city to join a pro-democratic army, based first at the Athenian border village of Phyle and then in the port town of Piraeus. In 403, the government of the Thirty was overthrown by the democratic insurgency: Critias was killed in battle and others fled. The Spartan-brokered peace that followed allowed the reestablishment of a democratic government in the city, with a new oligarchic polis to be founded at the Athenian town Eleusis by the surviving supporters of the Thirty. Meanwhile, the democrats in the city proclaimed an Amnesty, protecting all but the Thirty themselves and a few of their closest associates from politically motivated legal prosecution. Two years later, in 401, following another battle, the polis was reunited under a democratic government.[55]

According to Socratic tradition (especially the *Seventh Letter* and the two *Apologies*), Socrates himself paid scant notice to this dramatic sequence of events. He remained in the city after the takeover of the Thirty, apparently continuing his ordinary round of philosophical engagements. Yet the Thirty were not content to leave him uninvolved: According to Xenophon (*Mem.* 1.2.29–38), Critias hated Socrates for having called attention to his personal and political failings and promulgated a special law forbidding Socrates from holding philosophical conversations with anyone under age thirty. Plato focuses on the attempt of the Thirty to implicate Socrates in judicial murder: Along with four other Athenians, Socrates was ordered to report to the Tholos, a public building in the agora. When the five men arrived, they were told to go to Salamis (an Athenian island off the west coast of Attica) to

55   On this difficult period in Athenian history, see Krentz 1982, Wolpert 2002, Carawan 2002.

arrest a certain Leon and to bring him to Athens for execution. Plato's *Apology* (32c-d) states that the other four obeyed the magistrate's order, but Socrates himself simply returned to his home, refusing to be frightened by the Thirty into doing something unjust. Socrates' principled refusal to cooperate did not save Leon, or the other victims of the Thirty. Actively aiding an unjust act was morally impermissible, but heroic action aimed at saving other men from injustice was evidently not required.[56]

The Leon incident might, on the face of it, seem to have presented Socrates with a hard choice between impermissible legal disobedience and doing an unjust act. In the *Crito* he asserts that it is impermissible to break the laws, and he clearly regarded ignoring orders issued by legitimate authorities (e.g., the execution ordered by the court in 399) as lawbreaking. Yet Socrates deliberately ignored the order issued to him by the magistrates of the Thirty, and there is no hint in the tradition that his choice was a difficult one. Socrates' decision to go home rather than to obey the order to arrest Leon suggests that he did not believe that the Athenian lawcode under which he had grown up had been nullified by the establishment of a new government under the Thirty. If Socrates regarded the Athenian laws that had been in force before 404 as remaining in force after the coup of the Thirty, and not superseded by laws the Thirty sought to put in their place, then Socrates' refusal to obey the magistrate's order to arrest Leon of Salamis is fully consistent with a stance of steadfast obedience to the laws of Athens under which he had been born, raised, and educated. Socrates surely accepted that the established law could be modified by legitimate legislative action (e.g., the new citizenship law of 451 BCE). But he evidently did not accept that the ad hoc legal practices of the new oligarchic government constituted a code of law that he was obliged to obey.[57] Unlike the *nomoi* of Athens under which Socrates was born and raised, the ad hoc legal proclamations of the Thirty failed to constitute an entity that would suffer morally relevant harm as a result of his disobedience. Moreover, only

56   Socrates' passive response to the Leon affair is regarded by Stone 1988 as proof of his fundamentally anti-democratic disposition. Stone's book helped to reopen the question of the political background to the trial, without demonizing the Athenian democracy, but in my view it errs in making Socrates into a simple oligarch whose views were genuinely pernicious and actively destructive to democratic persistence.

57   Xen. *Mem.* 1.2.34 humorously presents Socrates in a dialogue with Critias and Charicles over their new law forbidding him to discourse with the youth, and as open to the argument that he should obey. But Xenophon's Socrates is clearly being ironic, and the reader is not led to suppose that Socrates is given good reason to obey.

the democratic law code that pertained during his youth could demand Socrates' obedience on the basis of its paternal role in providing him with birth, upbringing, and education.

In the aftermath of the democratic restoration the city of Athens was freed from the Thirty, but remained in dire straits: The population was devastated by the effects of the long war; the economy was a shambles; the great fleet and impregnable walls that had protected the city had been destroyed by the Spartans. Athenians who had survived the war and the Thirty had lost much: In many cases, their ancestral property was gone forever. Once proud and wealthy families were now destitute and struggled to make ends meet.[58] The Athenians did what they could. They held civic celebrations stressing national unity. They honored the heroes who had initiated the democratic resistance to the Thirty. And they completed the arduous task of recodifying the laws. But these measures were carried out in an uneasy political environment; Athens would not recover full political stability for some years. In the Assembly, there were rancorous debates about the most fundamental questions of civic membership. Proposals were advanced, and ultimately defeated, that would have radically altered the composition of the citizen body, on the one hand to disenfranchise the poorest Athenians, on the other to enfranchise all non-Athenians who had participated in the anti-tyrannical resistance. Meanwhile, the Amnesty meant that people's anger and pain at the terrible losses suffered during the reign of the Thirty could not be satisfied by gaining what must have seemed to many as just revenge through the legal apparatus. It was an agonizing era; everyone's life was thrown into disarray.

Everyone, that is, but Socrates. His response to the order to arrest Leon of Salamis, as reported in Plato's *Apology* "going away from there, I went on home," might be taken as summing up his lack of concern with the chaos around him: That day was not, as it turned out, a good one for philosophical conversation in the agora, so he went home; but there would be other days and other conversations. The Socratic tradition seeks to make much of Socrates' bravery in ignoring the arrest order: In Plato's *Apology*, Socrates claims that he might have been executed himself had the regime of the Thirty not fallen soon afterward. But to Athenians who had risked their lives and lost much else in order to bring about the fall of the murderous oligarchy, Socrates' easy willingness to stay in the city during the worst of the oligarchic excesses, and his close relationship with some of the oligarchic leaders, were of greater moment than his principled refusal to collaborate in an

58 Xenophon's *Memorabilia* sets Socrates in this milieu, and in its latter books, makes him a source of practical financial and military advice.

arrest. Then again, many Athenians had connections with members of the Thirty and many others had stayed in the city during their reign. The Amnesty was intended to avoid implicating the institutions of the restored democracy in acts of private revenge upon those Athenians whose collaboration with the Thirty had been essentially passive – or even upon most of those who had actively collaborated. Although as Critias's putative teacher, Socrates was no doubt a target of anger, that anger was blocked by the Amnesty from employing the law as its legitimate instrument.

We cannot know the actual motives of Meletus, or those of his associates, for the prosecution of 399. But we can say for certain that in deciding to prosecute Socrates, Meletus was constrained by both the conditions of the Amnesty and by the legal risk to which he was subject as prosecutor. The Amnesty meant that Meletus could not openly prosecute Socrates on the charge of being an oligarch's teacher and collaborator: one Athenian had already been put to death for violating the proscription against seeking to prosecute in defiance of the Amnesty. Meanwhile, Athenian law mandated severe penalties for Athenian prosecutors who failed to secure one fifth of the jury's votes.[59] There was no reason for Meletus to suppose that Socrates would be a particularly easy target. Aristophanes' Clouds shows that Socrates was renowned for his verbal cleverness, and Meletus necessarily faced the possibility that Socrates would mount a rhetorically sophisticated and convincing defense.

Meletus's choice of the grounds of "impiety" ensured that he would not fall afoul of the Amnesty. And impiety might, on the face of it, seem a safe charge for a prosecutor. Whether or not the late fifth and early fourth century was an era of "religious crisis" at Athens, as it is sometimes portrayed, there were a number of successful post-war prosecutions on the legal grounds of impiety. In at least some cases, political concerns hovered in the immediate background.[60] Yet the other well-known impiety trials concerned behavior that most Athenians were likely to recognize as unambiguously impious. In Socrates' case, there was no "smoking gun" of Mystery-mocking, herm-smashing, olive-tree-uprooting, or the like. If he were to convince a jury of Socrates' guilt, Meletus would need to expand the ordinary legal horizon of impiety. As we have seen, impiety was probably not defined in the written law, and so Meletus was free to seek to define impiety as failing to recognize the gods recognized by the polis and introducing new gods. But this would

---

59 Execution for violation of the Amnesty: [Aristotle] *Ath. Pol.* 40.2. Penalties for exceptionally weak prosecutions: MacDowell 1978, p. 64.
60 On the "religious crisis" see Connor 1991; Parker 1996 ch. 10.

be unfamiliar legal ground for the judges; as we have seen there are
no securely attested prior prosecutions under the impiety law employing Meletus's definition. Even given the old and familiar association
of Socrates with possibly atheistic scientists and sophists, as exemplified by Aristophanes' *Clouds*, Meletus could not have been confident
that the judges would vote against Socrates on the basis of the actual
charges. Nor could Meletus count on enough of the randomly selected
judges having deep enough personal reasons to vote automatically for
conviction. In brief, Meletus certainly must have counted on political
factors to tilt the decision in his favor.

The political factors most commonly adduced by the Socratic tradition, and especially by Xenophon, are the charges that Socrates was
the teacher of Alcibiades and Critias and that he was personally anti-
democratic. Xenophon was eager to dispute both charges, and there has
been much scholarly discussion about their actual weight in the trial
and their legitimacy.[61] While it seems indisputable that some Athenian
judges would indeed have been fatally prejudiced against Socrates on the
basis of those charges, it is also the case that others would be alive to
the spirit of the Amnesty and respectful of their oath to judge according
to the written law and according to justice when the law was silent.[62]
Athenian dissatisfaction with Socrates stemmed, at least in part, from
the fact that Socrates seemed unaffected, in his attitudes and in his public behavior, by the momentous events of the late fifth century. Yet
I would suggest that Meletus counted less upon the "low politics" of
resentment and revenge than upon the "high politics" of normative
conceptions of public duty and accountability.

The two extant *Apologies* give us strong reason to suppose that following the fall of the Thirty, Socrates went about his ordinary philosophical
round: earnestly seeking conversation partners in the public space of the
agora as well as in private and elite gatherings, humiliating those who
failed to avoid self-contradiction, and in the process, gathering about
himself a group of young men eager to be known as his students. In the
years preceding the political crisis of the late fifth century, these young
men had included Alcibiades, Critias, and other well-known enemies
of democracy. Plato's Socrates emphasizes that his conversations were
aimed at benefit, to himself and his interlocutors, and that he had no
intention of corrupting anyone. Given that he was doing good and not
harm, Socrates saw no reason not to pursue exactly the sort of life after
the fall of the Thirty that he had pursued during and before their reign.
But many Athenians had come to see things differently.

61   See Schofield 2002.
62   Athenian jurors' oath: MacDowell 1978, p. 44.

Socrates was famous for carrying out remarkable conversations about justice and responsibility (inter alia) in public places and before admiring audiences. The Athenians, for their part were deeply disposed by their political culture to associate speech with action.[63] They believed that citizens should accept responsibility and pay for the consequences of their speech, even if those consequences were not intended or predictable. The Athenians accepted *parrhesia*, frank speech, and *isonomia*, the equal right to public speech, as cornerstones of their democracy. Yet free speech did not, for them, mean freedom from the consequences attendant upon speech: Citizens could say pretty much whatever they wished, but by the same token they were held responsible for the public consequences of their speech.[64]

That conviction ordinarily concerned speech in the context of public institutions. For example, he who employed his powers of frank and equal speech by successfully passing a resolution in the Athenian Assembly was held personally responsible for that resolution. The individual sponsor of a resolution that turned out to have negative public effects could be held legally liable on the grounds that he had proposed something *paranomon* – that is, contrary to the *nomoi* of the Athenians.[65] It was well known that various of the young men who hung around Socrates during the war years subsequently went on to commit crimes against other citizens, and against the public order itself. Whereas Socrates renounced the idea that he was a teacher or intended to harm others, there was prima facie reason to relate the criminal actions of Socrates' followers to things that Socrates said in public and, by implication, in private. Although after the Amnesty Socrates could not be prosecuted for the crimes committed by those who listened to him, his unwillingness to accept that he was in any sense liable for the effects of his speech was deeply troubling to Athenian sensibilities – indeed it appeared indicative of a lack of concern with justice and evidence for personal irresponsibility. In brief, Socrates had come to look like a particularly dangerous sort of public hypocrite.

Many Athenians, convinced by the necessity for Amnesty, were probably willing to give Socrates what was, in effect, a pass for what they regarded (rightly or wrongly) as the negative effects of his prior speech – that is, for his role in the formation of Alcibiades, Critias, and

---

63 Thuc 2.40.2–3 with Ober 1998, ch. 2.
64 The Athenian orator Hyperides [F 44 (Jensen)] claims that Socrates was convicted "for words"; see discussion in Parker 1996, ch. 10 with n. 19. Markovits 2008, chapter 2, surveys Athenian conceptions of accountability, with special reference to *parrhesia* in both public and private contexts.
65 *Graphe paranomon*: MacDowell 1978, pp. 50–52.

other enemies of democracy who had been suppressed by 403. But then, after the restoration of the democracy, Socrates blithely returned to his familiar practices. He acted as if nothing had happened in the meantime, carrying on exactly the same sorts of conversations in the same public spaces as he always had. He brushed aside criticism, asserting that his speech simply could not have had negative consequences. And he thereby made himself vulnerable to the charge that he was perversely and dangerously unwilling to accept responsibility for either the past or (potential) future effects of his own behavior. In such circumstances, his claim to be a public benefactor was likely to be taken by many as evidence of bad faith.

Socrates' behavioral constancy, the fact that he was indeed "always the same" in circumstances that had become very different, made him vulnerable to Meletus's prosecution. As we have seen, Socrates believed that he was ethically required to put his unique personal excellence to the service of his polis in the form of beneficial "stinging"; nothing in the new external circumstances of the city changed that. And so it was that his unswerving and peculiar interpretation of his own public duty ultimately brought him into a fatal conflict with Athenian law. Although Socrates' philosophical convictions and the underlying values of Athenian democracy remained compatible, the special circumstances of the post-war years tipped the balance against him. His reputation as an obedient and participatory citizen was no longer enough to convince enough of his fellow citizens that his distinctive public behavior fell within the expansive parameters established by Athenian democratic culture: because he would not accept any connection between his speech and others' actions, Socrates, who had devoted his life to acting justly, seemed unwilling to accept his own responsibilities in respect to justice.

By 399 BCE, the immediate political crisis had passed, but so had public euphoria at surviving the war, averting endless civil war, and reuniting the polis under a reestablished code of law. The realization sunk in that reunification was only the beginning of a costly and uncertain rebuilding period, and that Athens remained fragile and vulnerable to its enemies. The Athenian willingness to tolerate potentially dangerous behavior and apparently irresponsible public attitudes reached a low point. And so, for Meletus the time was ripe: he could prosecute Socrates for impiety on relatively novel grounds with little concern of incurring the penalty for failing to gain a fifth of the votes.

As it turned out, Socrates' idiosyncratic defense enabled Meletus to gain a guilty verdict. The Socratic tradition holds that he could not have given any other sort of defense and yet remain true to his own convictions, and recognized that it was unlikely to secure his acquittal. But the question remains: Why did Socrates choose to defend himself in the first place: Why not go elsewhere? Or, if he refused to leave Athens, why say anything at all at the trial? The Socratic tradition was bothered by these questions: In Plato's *Gorgias* (521c-22c), Callicles predicts that Socrates will be legally prosecuted by some evil man, and that (lacking Gorgias's training in rhetoric) he will fail to defend himself, and so will be killed. Socrates of the *Gorgias* concurs with this prediction. In his metaphor of the doctor being tried by a pastry-cook before a jury of children, he seemingly predicts that the irrationality of the proceeding would leave him with nothing to say in his own defense. Maximus of Tyre's claim that Socrates stood silent at the trial translates this prediction into fact. Yet the historical Socrates certainly did address the Athenian judges. Perhaps he did so because he believed that even if the chances of acquittal were slight, he owed it to himself (that is to the continuation of his philosophical project) to make the effort. But surely there was another reason, just as compelling: Socrates believed that it was his civic duty to seek to educate (by stinging awake) his fellows – and especially his fellow Athenian citizens. Although the conditions of the trial – speaking at length before a mass audience and with time constraints – were not optimal, Socrates owed it to his polis to offer his last, best sting. And thus, when Socrates claimed that he could not have offered any other defense, he must have meant (inter alia) that his duty to his polis demanded a speech that was at least as much of a "sting" as it was a defense.

CONCLUSION: WHY SOCRATES LIVED IN ATHENS

Finally, it is worth asking why Socrates chose to continue living in Athens in the years before the trial, when he was under no moral obligation to do so and when, according the tradition, he believed that Sparta (at least) had better laws. A full answer is beyond the scope of this chapter, but one part of the equation must be that the Athenian regime of law allowed him to live as a philosopher and as an obedient citizen. As we have seen, the Athenian regime provided Socrates with conditions of birth, upbringing, and education that were compatible with the demands of a philosophical life, whereas the Spartan regime, for example, would not have. Moreover, had he lived under a legal regime in which legal abstractions such as "piety" were carefully defined, Socrates might have developed a conception of pious behavior that contradicted the legal definition. He would therefore have confronted a hard choice between his moral responsibility to act according to his philosophical convictions and his responsibility for obeying the law. In Athens, Socrates had no need to choose, because Athenian procedural law was concerned with establishing fair rules for legal practices, rather than with defining legal terms in an attempt to achieve consistently good outcomes. Since Athenian law apparently forbade impiety without defining it, Socrates need only accept that impiety (properly so understood) was indeed worthy of punishment.

By the lights of the Socratic tradition, the Athenian jurors were wrong to accept Meletus's definition of impiety. Yet Socrates accepted the authority of a legal system that gave the defendant a chance to confront his accuser directly and to argue for a better definition. Like a Socratic dialectical conversation, Athenian legal process allowed for debate over morally relevant terms. Both Socrates and the Athenian legal system assumed that better definitions of contested evaluative terms could be arrived at, and worse definitions rejected. Because Athenian legal process did not, in Socrates' view, consistently settle upon good definitions, it could hardly be regarded as "good": indeed the legal definitions used in Sparta (for example) were evidently, on the whole, better in Socrates' terms. But a law code based on established definitions of moral abstractions was not subject (as were Socrates' working definitions of moral terms) to constant philosophical examination and refinement. Thus, such a system was eventually likely to employ a definition that philosophical inquiry had demonstrated to be seriously flawed. The "better" Spartan regime was, ironically, likely to confront Socrates with a hard choice between his duty to philosophy and to citizenship. So Socrates chose Athens, despite what he saw as its flaws and despite the chance that by remaining the same in the face of radically changed circumstances he would face prosecution.[66]

Athenian-style democracy was, to the very end, the best real-world regime for Socrates. That may not be particularly surprising for modern readers, who take for granted a close relationship between democracy, the rights of the individual, and the rule of law. But it was deeply puzzling to Plato. Plato's great accomplishment, as a political theorist, was in designing imagined regimes in which his literary creation, "Socrates," could truly flourish – in which the laws would provide him with a birth, an upbringing, and an education worthy of his philosophical capacities. I have suggested that one way to unite the historical Socrates the son of Sophroniscus of the deme Alopece, and "Plato's Socrates," is by

---

66   See further Ober 2000, which also seeks to resolve (by reference to Socrates' commitments and fundamental principles of Athenian law) the apparent contradiction between Socrates' statement in Plato's *Apology*, to the effect that he would have to disobey a law forbidding him to philosophize, and his statement in the *Crito* to the effect that it was impermissible to disobey the law.

recognizing the ways in which Socrates was a product of both his philosophical self-fashioning and of Athenian civic culture. That conjunction set a challenge for all those claiming to be Socrates' intellectual heirs: the demand that we live at once as philosophers and as citizens.

WORKS CITED

Allen, R. E., and Plato. *Socrates and legal obligation.* Minneapolis, 1980.

Balot, R. K. "Courage in the Democratic Polis." *Classical Quarterly* 54 (2004): 406–423.

Boegehold, A. L. "Pericles' Citizenship Law of 451/0 B.C," pp. 57–66 in *Athenian identity and civic ideology*, eds. Alan L. Boegehold and Adele C. Scafuro. Baltimore, 1994.

Boegehold, A. L. *The lawcourts at Athens: sites, buildings, equipment, procedure, and testimonia.* Princeton, 1995, pp. 57–66.

Brickhouse, T. C., and N. D. Smith. *Socrates on trial.* Princeton, 1989.

Burnyeat, M. F. "The Impiety of Socrates." *Ancient Philosophy* 17 (1997): 1–29.

Calder, W. M. 2002. *The unknown Socrates: translations, with introductions and notes, of four important documents in the late antique reception of Socrates the Athenian.* Wauconda, IL, 2002.

Camp, J. McK. *The Athenian Agora: excavations in the heart of classical Athens.* New York, 1992.

Carawan, Edwin. "The Athenian Amnesty and the 'Scrutiny of the Laws'." *Journal of Hellenic Studies* 122 (2002): 1–23.

Carter, L. B. *The quiet Athenian.* Oxford, 1986.

Colaiaco, J. *Socrates against Athens: Philosophy on Trial.* New York and London, 2001.

Connor, W. R. *The new politicians of fifth-century Athens.* Princeton, 1971.

Connor, W. R. "The Other 399: Religion and the Trial of Socrates." In *Georgica: Greek studies in honor of George Cawkwell.* London, 1991, pp. 49–56.

Domingo Gygax, Marc. *Benefaction and rewards in the ancient Greek city: The origins of euergetism.* Forthcoming.

Dover, K. J. "The Freedom of the Intellectual in Greek Society." *Talanta* 7 (1975), pp. 24–54.

Fisher, N. R. E. *Hybris: a study in the values of honour and shame in ancient Greece.* Warminster, 1992.

Gabrielsen, V. *Financing the Athenian fleet: public taxation and social relations.* Baltimore, 1994.

Garland, R. *Introducing new gods: the politics of Athenian religion.* London, 1992.

Golden, M. *Children and childhood in classical Athens.* Baltimore, 1990.

Griffith, M. "Public and Private in Early Greek Institutions of Education." In *Education in Greek and Roman antiquity*, ed. Yun Lee Too. Leiden, 2001, pp. 23–84.

Hansen, Mogens Herman. *The Athenian democracy in the age of Demosthenes: structure, principles, and ideology.* Oxford, 1991.

Hansen, Mogens Herman. *The trial of Sokrates – from the Athenian point of view.* Copenhagen: Kongelige Danske Videnskabernes Selskab: Commissioner Munksgaard, 1995.

Humphreys, S.C. "The Nothoi of Cynosarges." *Journal of Hellenic Studies* 94 (1974): 88–95.

Kraut, R. *Socrates and the state.* Princeton, 1984.

Krentz, P. *The thirty at Athens.* Ithaca, 1982.

Kurke, L. "The Economy of *Kudos.*" In *Cultural poetics in archaic Greece: Cult, performance, politics,* eds. Carol Dougherty and Leslie Kurke. Cambridge, 1993, pp. 131–163.

Lanni, A. M. "Arguing from "Precedent": Modern Perspectives on Athenian Practice." In *The Law and the Courts in Ancient Greece,* eds. Edward M. Harris and L. Rubenstein. London, 2004, pp. 159–172.

Lanni, A.M. *Law and justice in the courts of classical Athens.* Cambridge, 2006.

Lape, S. "Solon and the Institution of the Democratic Family Form." *Classical Journal* 98 (2002–3):117–139.

Loraux, N. *The children of Athena: Athenian ideas about citizenship and the division between the sexes.* Princeton, 1993.

MacDowell, D. M. *The law in classical Athens.* Ithaca, 1978.

MacDowell, D.M. *Andocides. On the mysteries.* Oxford, 1989.

McPherran, M. K. "Does Piety Pay? Socrates and Plato on Prayer and Sacrifice." In *Reason and Religion in Socratic Philosophy,* eds. Nicholas D. Smith and Paul Woodruff. Oxford, 2000, pp. 89–114.

Morrison, D. "On the Alleged Historical Reliability of Plato's Apology," *Archiv für Geschichte der Philosophie* 82 (2000): 235–265.

Markovits, E. *The politics of sincerity: Plato, frank speech, and democratic judgment.* University Park, PA, 2008.

Nails, D. "The Trial and Death of Socrates." In *A companion to Socrates,* eds. Sara Ahbel-Rappe and Rachana Kamtekar. Malden, MA, 2006, pp. 5–20.

Nightingale, A.W. *Genres in dialogue: Plato and the construct of philosophy.* Cambridge, 1995.

Ober, J. *Mass and elite in democratic Athens: rhetoric, ideology, and the power of the people.* Princeton, 1989.

Ober, J. *The Athenian revolution: essays on ancient Greek democracy and political theory.* Princeton, 1996.

Ober, J. *Political dissent in democratic Athens: intellectual critics of popular rule.* Princeton, 1998.

Ober, J. "Living Freely as a Slave of the Law: Notes on Why Socrates Lives in Athens." In *Polis and politics: studies in Greek history,* eds. P. T. H. Neilsen Flensted-Jensen and L. Rubinstein. Copenhagen, 2000, pp. 541–552.

Ober, J. "The Debate over Civic Education in Classical Athens," pp. 273–305 in *Education in Greek and Roman antiquity,* ed. Yun Lee Too. Leiden, 2001.

Ober, J. "I, Socrates... The Performative Audacity of Isocrates' *Antidosis.*" In *Isocrates and civic education,* eds. Takis Poulakos and David Depew. Austin, 2004, pp. 21–43.

Ober, J. "Law and Political Theory." In *Cambridge Companion to Ancient Greek Law,* ed. Michael Gagarin. Cambridge, 2005, pp. 394–411.

Ogden, D. *Greek bastardy in the classical and hellenistic periods.* Oxford and New York, 1996.

Osborne, R. "Law in Action in Classical Athens." *Journal of Hellenic Studies* 105 (1985): 40–58.

Ostwald, M. *From popular sovereignty to the sovereignty of law: law, society, and politics in fifth-century Athens*. Berkeley, 1986.

Parker, R. *Athenian religion: a history*. Oxford, 1996.

Patterson, C. *The family in Greek history*. Cambridge, Mass, 1998.

Reeve, C. D. C. *Socrates in the Apology: an essay on Plato's Apology of Socrates*. Indianapolis, 1989.

Reeve, C. D. C., Peter Meineck, James Doyle, Plato, Aristophanes, and Xenophon. *The trials of Socrates: six classic texts*. Indianapolis, 2002.

Rubinstein, Lene. "Arguments from Precedent in Attic Oratory," *Oxford Readings in the Attic Orators*, ed. by Edwin Carawan. Oxford and New York, 2007, pp. 357–391.

Schofield, M. "Socrates on Trial in the USA." In *Classics in progress*, ed. T.P. Wiseman. Oxford, 2002, pp. 263–284.

Stone, I. F. *The trial of Socrates*. Boston, 1988.

Strauss, B. S. *Fathers and sons in Athens: ideology and society in the era of the Peloponnesian War*. Princeton, 1993.

Strauss, Leo. *The city and man*. Chicago, 1964.

Thomsen, R. *Eisphora; a study of direct taxation in ancient Athens*. Copenhagen, 1964.

Todd, S. C. *The shape of Athenian law*. Oxford, 1993.

Todd, S.C. "How to Execute People in Fourth-Century Athens." In *Law and social status in classical Athens*, eds. Virginia J. Hunter and J. C. Edmondson. Oxford, 2000, pp. 31–51.

Vlastos, G. *Socrates, ironist and moral philosopher*. Ithaca, 1991.

Vlastos, G. "The Historical Socrates and Athenian Democracy." In *Socratic studies*. Cambridge, 1994, pp. 87–108.

Wallace, R. W. "Private Lives and Public Enemies: Freedom of Thought in Classical Athens." In *Athenian identity and civic ideology*, eds. Alan L. Boegehold and Adele C. Scafuro. Baltimore, 1994, pp. 127–155.

Weiss, R. *Socrates dissatisfied: an analysis of Plato's Crito*. New York, 1998.

Wilson, E.R. *The death of Socrates: hero, villain, chatterbox, saint*. London, 2007.

Wilson, P. *The Athenian institution of the Khoregia. The chorus, the city, and the stage*. Cambridge, 2000.

Wolpert, A. *Remembering defeat: civil war and civic memory in Ancient Athens*. Baltimore, 2002.

Wood, E. Meiksins, and N. Wood. *Class ideology and ancient political theory: Socrates, Plato, and Aristotle in social context*. New York, 1978.

8 Socratic Method

Plato's Socratic dialogues repeatedly exhibit a distinctive feature of the main character of those dialogues – the so-called Socratic method.[1] Plato highlights this feature of Socrates when he has his main character in the *Apology* blame his prosecution on his customary method (27b2). Aristotle highlights this feature of Socrates when he limits the two things that can fairly be attributed to Socrates to "inductive arguments and defining the universal" (*Metaphysics* 1078b27–29).[2] Nevertheless, the nature of this so-called Socratic method has been subject to a variety of questions, puzzles, and problems. Indeed, two prominent Socratic scholars have recently been led to proclaim "that there is no such thing as 'the Socratic [method].'"[3] I maintain that such a response to these questions, puzzles, and problems is neither necessary nor desirable. Plato's Socratic dialogues coherently present Socrates practicing a distinctive philosophical method featuring a common form, a common strategy, and a common epistemological presupposition.

1   The Socratic dialogues are the following (in alphabetical order): *Apology, Charmides, Crito, Euthyphro, Euthydemus, Gorgias, Hippias Major, Hippias Minor, Ion, Laches, Lysis,* portions of the *Meno, Protagoras,* and *Republic* I. These dialogues have often been classified together as a consequence of their imagined position in the chronological ordering of Plato's composition of the dialogues. They have frequently been taken to make up the earliest of Plato's compositions. Nothing in what follows, however, depends upon such a chronological thesis.

2   If one takes Aristotle as a relatively independent source for the historical Socrates, then we may suspect that a characteristic feature of the historical Socrates was his method. If, however, one takes Aristotle's account of Socrates to be dependent on Plato, then my discussion should be understood as restricted to the characteristic method of Socrates as portrayed in Plato's Socratic dialogues. For more on the issue of the historical Socrates, see Chapter 1 in this volume.

3   See Brickhouse and Smith 2002, pp. 147 and 154–156, and more recently, Wolfsdorf 2003, pp 301–302.

A COMMON FORM: THE ELENCHOS

In Plato's *Apology*, Socrates explains at length why he is being prosecuted. Socrates begins his explanation by doubting that he is being
prosecuted because he is believed to be guilty of the official charges
brought forward by Meletus, Anytus, and Lycon. Rather, he suggests
that the jurors will convict him of older accusations brought forward
by a variety of individuals to the effect that he "is guilty of wrongdoing in that he busies himself studying things in the sky and below the
earth; he makes the worse argument into the stronger argument, and
he teaches these same things to others" (19b4-c1; Grube trans.).[4] But
Socrates even doubts that these accusations explain his prosecution.
Instead, he suggests that he is being prosecuted because of a certain
practice he has engaged in at least since Chaerephon visited the Delphic
oracle and received the response that no one was wiser than Socrates.[5]
This practice that Socrates and his young imitators have employed
has angered and embarrassed many men who were reputed to be wise.
Consequently, these men have leveled accusations against Socrates
that could be leveled at any philosopher. These latter accusations are,
however, trumped up as a result of the anger and embarrassment that
Socrates and his young imitators have engendered by exposing the ignorance of these men.

Notice that Socrates does not suggest that he is being prosecuted
because he advocates unpopular and controversial positions. He does
not think he is being prosecuted because he believes and encourages others to believe, for example, that one should harm neither one friends nor
one's enemies, that one's leaders should be determined by knowledge,
not popular election or lot, or even that the sun is a fiery ball of iron.
Though Socrates does not explicitly say so, prosecutions on the basis
of unpopular beliefs could be brought against any philosopher, and so
this would not explain why Socrates, in particular, is being prosecuted.[6]
Rather, Socrates believes he is being prosecuted because of a certain
practice or manner of philosophizing that is peculiar to him and those
who imitate him.[7] Thus, Socrates believes that at least a portion of his

4   All translations are my own unless otherwise noted.
5   I am not suggesting that Socrates only began practicing his characterisistic
     method after Chaerephon's visit to the Delphic oracle. See Benson 2000: p.
     19 n. 6.
6   See Diogenes Laertius (*Life of Anaxagoras* IX), who tells us that Anaxagoras
     is one philosopher – the only other one we know of – who may have been
     prosecuted for the unpopular and impious belief that the sun is a fiery ball
     of iron.
7   Socrates here explicitly recognizes that his distinctive practice can be
     employed by others, although they may be less proficient than he. See

philosophizing can be characterized as peculiarly associated with him – that is, as Socratic. It is this portion of his philosophizing that explains his prosecution. He describes this distinctive practice in relating his response to the Delphic oracle's answer to Chaerephon.

As Socrates describes it, when Chaerephon informed him that the oracle had declared that no one was wiser than Socrates, Socrates was at a loss at what the oracle could mean. For he was "aware of being wise about nothing great or small" (21b4–5) and yet the god could not lie. In order to understand the oracle, Socrates performed the following investigation. He sought out those reputed to be wise either by themselves or others, thinking that he could thereby refute the oracle – saying "this man is wiser than I am, but you said I was wiser" (21c2; Grube trans.). However, after going through the politicians, poets, and craftsmen, Socrates discovered that he was unable to refute the oracle in the manner he had anticipated. Instead he discovered that all of those whose reputed wisdom he examined suffered the same fault. They all thought they knew (or were reputed to know) certain things that they did not. Consequently, his investigation led him to conclude that the oracle meant that "This man among you, mortals, is wisest who, like Socrates, understands that his wisdom is worthless" (23b2–4; Grube trans.) thereby commanding Socrates to "go around seeking out anyone, citizen or stranger, whom I think wise. Then if I do not think he is, I come to the assistance of the god and show him that he is not wise." (23b4–7; Grube trans.).[8]

In the course of describing this distinctive manner of philosophizing that Socrates takes to be responsible for his prosecution, two features become immediately apparent. First, it consists in examining the reputed wisdom of anyone Socrates happens to meet. Socrates likely began his testing of the oracle by presuming that those he examined had the wisdom they were reputed to have, although one suspects that in time the presumption faded. Nevertheless, the distinctive Socratic practice begins with an examination or test of an individual's reputed wisdom, whatever Socrates presumes the test will show. Second, he performs this examination not only to relieve his ignorance of the meaning of the oracle, but also to persuade those reputed to be wise of their

Brickhouse and Smith 1994: pp. 27–29. That Socrates takes this distinctive practice to be a manner of philosophizing is made clear in his response to the jury's hypothetical offer to find him innocent if he will promise to cease philosophizing (*Apology* 29c-30b).

8   See Brickhouse and Smith 1983 and Brickhouse and Smith 1989: pp. 87–100 for a plausible account of how Socrates derives a divine command or mission from the oracle's pronouncement. See also McPherran 2002.

ignorance, if they are not wise (*Apology* 23b7), and to learn from them, if they are wise (*Apology* 22b5).[9] Here, then, we have something like the identity conditions of a distinctively Socratic manner of philosophizing – at least distinctively Socratic by Socrates' own lights. Those episodes in the Socratic dialogues in which we find Socrates examining the reputed wisdom of interlocutors in order to persuade them of their ignorance (if they are revealed not to be wise) or to learn from them (if they are revealed to be wise) can be identified as instances of Socrates' distinctive practice. So identified, this distinctive Socratic practice is the Socratic *elenchos*.[10] It is not, however, the only manner of philosophizing that Socrates employs. Consider, for example, most of the argument of the *Apology* for which no reputedly wise interlocutor whatsoever is present,[11] or the speech of the Laws in the *Crito* during which the eponymous interlocutor has very nearly disappeared following his admission of his ignorance at 50a5,[12] or the myth of the afterlife in the *Gorgias* during which the self-professed wise Callicles has in fact disappeared.[13] Nevertheless, Socrates does frequently engage in his distinctive practice.

Throughout the Socratic dialogues, Socrates can be seen engaging in short question-and-answer exchanges with interlocutors reputed to be wise either by themselves or by others. Of the thirty-four interlocutors[14]

---

9   See also *Hippias Major* 287a6–7 and *Hippias Minor* 369d1-e2. These two motivations for examining the knowledge of others are related. Socrates' overriding goal even prior to the oracle's response is knowledge of the most important things. Attempting to learn this from others who have it is an obvious way to achieve this goal, and attempting to encourage others who lack it to join him in the search is another. Socrates is convinced that no one will seek the knowledge he lacks until he first recognizes that he lacks it.

10 See Wolfsdorf 2003: p. 306 against employing the *Apology* in this way.

11 The exchange with Meletus at *Apology* 24b-28 resembles a genuine *elenchos*, but I maintain that it is not. Socrates is neither genuinely examining Meletus's wisdom (he has no doubt that Meletus fails to be wise), nor is Socrates concerned to persuade Meletus of his ignorance (he is concerned to persuade the jurors of Meletus' ignorance). But I will not argue the point here. The key is that Socrates is not always practicing the *elenchos* in the Socratic dialogues, whether or not he is during his exchange with Meletus.

12 Once Crito admits his ignorance at *Crito* 50a 4–5, he responds to a Socratic question only three times during the course of the next four Stephanus pages.

13 One may object that myth is not an argument, but it is hard to deny that myth does not constitute part of Socrates' method of philosophizing in the elenctic dialogues; see, for example, McCabe 1992.

14 Meletus, Charmides, Critias (twice), Crito (twice), Dionysodorus, Euthydemus, Cleinias, Crito, Ctesippus (twice), Euthyphro, Gorgias, Polus,

in the Socratic dialogues twenty one have some claim to wisdom that
Socrates goes on to examine.[15] In no case is the interlocutor's wisdom
uncovered and in only seven cases is the interlocutor persuaded of his
ignorance.[16] Nevertheless, in nearly every case, Socrates appears to be
prepared to learn from the interlocutor should his wisdom be confirmed,
and attempts to persuade the interlocutor of his ignorance once Socrates
recognizes it.[17] Thus, while we should not take every Socratic argument

    Callicles, Hippias (thrice), Eudicus, Ion, Melesias, Lysimachus, Laches,
    Nicias, Hippothales, Lysis, Menexenus, Meno, slave-boy, friend, Hippocrates,
    Protagoras, Callias, Alcibiades, Prodicus, Cephalus, Polemarchus, and
    Thrasymachus.

15   Charmides (*Charmides* 154e5–155a1); Crito (*Crito* 45a3 & 46a7–8 together
    with the argument at 47a–48a); Critias 162d4–e5; Dionysodorus (*Euthydemus*
    271c5–272b4, 273c2–274b4); Euthydemus (*Euthydemus* 271c5–272b4,
    273c2–274b4); Euthyphro (4e4–5a2); Gorgias (*Gorgias* 449c9-d2); Polus
    (*Gorgias* 462a5–7); Callicles (*Gorgias* 487a-488a); Hippias (*Hippias Major*
    281a-c, 286d-284–7b); Hippias (*Hippias Minor* 364a-b); Ion (*Ion* 530c1-d3);
    Laches (*Laches* 184e11–187a1, 190c4–5); Nicias (*Laches* 184e11–187a1,
    196c); Menexenus (*Lysis* 211b6-d4); Meno (*Meno* 71d5–8, 71e1–72a2); slave-
    boy (*Meno* 82e5–6); Hippocrates (*Protagoras* 311a8-b2, 312c4–5); Protagoras
    (*Protagoras* 316c-317c, 320c-d); Polemarchus (*Republic* I 331e7–8, 335e1–4);
    and Thrasymachus (*Republic* I 338a1, 344d-e).

16   Charmides (*Charmides* 162b9–10 & 176a6-b4); Crito (*Crito* 50a4–5); Ion
    (*Ion* 541e1–542b); perhaps Nicias (*Laches* 199e11–200c1); Hippocrates
    (*Protagoras* 312e6–313c4); Meno (*Meno* 79e7–80b4); and slave-boy (*Meno*
    84a1–2). These last two are unique in that only in their case does the
    exchange between Socrates and the interlocutor continue following their
    recognition of ignorance. Euthyphro (11b6–8), Laches (*Laches* 194a6-b4),
    and Menexenus (*Lysis* 213c9) all admit to being unable to say what they
    know, but not to ignorance. Finally, Lysis never appears to be wise, and was
    not counted among the twenty-one whose reputed wisdom Socrates goes
    on to examine. Nevertheless, Socrates does indicate that his exchange with
    Lysis is meant as a model of how one should engage one's beloved. The
    goal of such an exchange should be to force the beloved to recognize his
    ignorance or eliminate his high-mindedness, which apparently Lysis does
    at *Lysis* 210d4–8.

17   Of the twenty-one interlocutors whose wisdom is examined, Socrates explic-
    itly announces his desire to learn from them in twelve cases (*Euthydemus*
    272b, 272d5–6, 273c2-d9; *Euthyphro* 5a3-c8; *Gorgias* 447c1–3, 461d, 487e-
    488a; *Hippias Major* 286d-287b; *Hippias Minor* 369d-e, 372a-d; *Laches* 191c-d,
    196c; *Lysis* 212a4–7; *Protagoras* 348c5–349a6; *Republic* I 337d-338b, 344d-e,
    344e). In three others, this motivation is implied (Critias in the transition
    from Charmides, Crito by argument, and Meno by the sting-ray analogy). The
    motivation to persuade the interlocutor of his ignorance is never explicitly
    expressed. This is to be expected given Socrates' desire for the interlocu-
    tor to permit his wisdom to be examined. Nevertheless, this motivation is

as an instance of Socrates' distinctive practice, he repeatedly engages in his distinctive practice throughout the Socratic dialogues.

In those exchanges in which Socrates does examine the reputed wisdom of his interlocutor, a pattern begins to emerge. Socrates begins by asking the interlocutor a question, the answer to which is an indication of the interlocutor's reputed wisdom. This is often, though not always, Socrates' 'What is F-ness?' question.[18] Following the interlocutor's answer to this initial question, a series of other questions elicit answers from the interlocutor that are used by Socrates to derive the negation of the original answer. At this point, the interlocutor either revises his initial answer (e.g., *Euthyphro* 10d1–2), offers an entirely new answer (e.g., *Hippias Major* 289e2–4), admits to being unable to say what he knows (e.g. *Laches* 194b1–4), professes his ignorance (e.g., *Charmides* 162b9–10), is replaced by another interlocutor whose wisdom is examined (e.g., *Gorgias* 461e5–462b2), or marches off in a huff (e.g., *Euthyphro* 15e3–4). Consequently, typical instances of Socrates' distinctive practice have roughly the following formal structure:

> First, (1) Socrates asks the interlocutor a question the answer to which is meant to exhibit the interlocutor's wisdom usually, but not always, concerning the definition of some moral concept. (I will refer to this initial answer, *p*, as the **apparent refutand**.)
> Next, (2) the interlocutor provides answers, *q*, *r*, and *s* to a series of other Socratic questions. (I will refer to these answers as the **premises** of the *elenchos*.)
> Third, (3) Socrates goes on to show that these answers entail the negation of the original answer.
> Thus, (4) the conjunction *p* & *q* & *r* & *s* is false.[19]

Thus we have found a distinctive Socratic practice of philosophy displaying a common form. We have found, that is, the Socratic *elenchos*. We have also, unfortunately, only just begun to face the questions, puzzles, and problems that it raises.

evidenced by the fact that Socrates never takes a single elenctic episode to suffice (except perhaps in the case of Crito who admits his ignorance). A single elenctic episode may suffice for Socrates to recognize the interlocutor's ignorance, but will seldom be enough to disabuse the interlocutor. Consider those passages in which the interlocutor admits to being unable to say what he knows but not to his ignorance, cited in note 16.

18 For the connection between the 'What is F-ness?' question and wisdom, knowledge, or expertise, see the next section.

19 See Vlastos 1994: p. 11 for a similar characterization of the form of what Vlastos refers to as the 'standard elenchus.'

A COMMON STRATEGY: DOXASTIC COHERENCE

In his now-classic essay, Gregory Vlastos maintained that *the* problem with the Socratic *elenchos* is "how Socrates can claim ... to have proved that the [apparent] refutand is false, when all he has established is its inconsistency with premises whose truth he has not tried to establish in that argument." (Vlastos 1994 p.3.) This alleged "problem of the *elenchos*" depends upon maintaining that Socrates concludes from the false conjunction at (4) that *p*, the apparent refutand, is false and that not-*p* is true. To resolve it one must explain what would justify Socrates in so concluding. A variety of scholars have followed Vlastos in understanding the *elenchos* in this way. They agree that Socrates sees his *elenchos* as establishing the truth or falsity of individual answers, although they do not all agree about what justifies Socrates in understanding his method in this way.[20] Such an interpretation of the *elenchos* has been called a constructivist interpretation since it understands the *elenchos* as establishing the truth or falsity of individual answers. The *elenchos*, on this interpretation, can and does have constructive or positive results. This interpretation, however, has been challenged. According to what has been called the non-constructivist account, Socrates neither takes his *elenchos* to establish the truth or falsity of individual answers, nor would he be justified if he had.[21] Rather than rehearsing the details of this debate, I want to focus on what I take to be its essence – the relative credibility of the premises of the *elenchos* – *q*, *r*, and *s*.

If the *elenchos* fails to establish the truth or falsity of individual answers, it is not because of its form. Anyone who sought to show that an opponent's thesis was false or that one's own position, denied by an opponent, was true would seek to obtain premises from which the negation of one's opponent's position could be derived. Doing so would not in any way hinder the establishment of the truth or falsity of the relevant thesis. Indeed, it is difficult to imagine how else one would proceed. What hinders the establishment of such truth or falsity is not the form of the *elenchos*, but the relative credibility of its premises. If the premises obtained are not better known, more evident, more justified, or in some way more credible than the thesis whose falsity one aims to establish, then the argument cannot establish the falsity of that thesis. Moreover, even should the premises of the *elenchos* be more credible than the apparent refutand, Socrates must recognize that they are, and take such an epistemic distinction to be relevant to the

---

20 See, for example, Kraut 1983, Polansky 1985, Reeve 1989, Adams 1998, and Woolf 2000,

21 See, for example, Stokes 1986 and Benson 2000, ch. 2–4.

intended result of the *elenchos*. Otherwise we should not understand Socrates' use of the *elenchos* as intended to show the falsity of the alleged refutand. But an examination of the strategy Socrates employs in practicing his distinctive method shows that he recognizes no relevant epistemic distinction between the premises of his *elenchos* and the apparent refutand. As far as Socrates is concerned, the premises and the apparent refutand are equally credible. According to Socrates, they are all – the premises and the apparent refutands – merely the beliefs of the interlocutor. It is for this reason that the *elenchos*[22] can do no more than establish the falsehood of the conjunction of the alleged refutand and the premises of the *elenchos*– that is, of the conjunction $p \& q \& r \& s$.[23]

The argument that Socrates recognizes no epistemic distinction between the premises of the *elenchos* and the apparent refutand is simple. Let us call it 'The Argument Against Constructivism.'

(1) The only property that Socrates requires that the premises of the *elenchos* to have is that they are believed by the interlocutor.[24]

(2) The property of being believed by the interlocutor is also required of the apparent refutand.[25]

---

22   At least an individual elenctic episode. See Brickhouse and Smith 1994: pp. 3–29 for a defense of the view that repeated elenctic episodes may be capable of more constructive results.

23   Given Socrates' commitment to the view that knowledge entails doxastic coherence, Socrates can conclude from the results of an individual elenctic episode that the interlocutor fails to have the knowledge he is reputed to have. But Socrates' ability to draw this conclusion derives not from successfully establishing the truth or falsity of an individual answer, but from sucessfully establishing the interlocutor's doxastic incoherence – that is, from establishing the falsity of the conjunction.

24   This premise is similar to the variously named 'say what you believe requirement' (Vlastos 1994: p. 7), or 'rule of sincerity' (Irwin 1993: p. 11), which has become a common place of Socratic scholarship. See Beversluis 2000: p. 38 n. 3 for an admirably complete list of scholars who endorse this requirement. More recently, one might add Bailly 1999: p. 66, Woolf 2002: p. 242 n. 38, and Blondell 2002: p. 116. While the 'say what you believe requirement' stipulates that being believed by the interlocutor is a necessary condition for premise acceptability, the first premise in the Argument Against Constructivism adds that this is the *only* requirement for premise acceptability. For a recent argument that the premises are also believed by Socrates see Wolfsdorf 2003: p. 280–283. He does not show, however, that Socrates thinks he must believe the premises for the *elenchos* to achieve its intended results.

25   The argument for this premise can be found at Benson 2000: p. 54–55.

(3) Consequently, Socrates fails to recognize an epistemic distinction between the premises of the *elenchos* and the apparent refutand; they are equally credible.

(4) Consequently, Socrates fails to take the falsity of the apparent refutand as established.[26]

The argument may be simple, but the issues surrounding the premises are not.

Scholarly attention has appropriately focused primarily on the first premise – that according to Socrates, being believed by the interlocutor is both a necessary and sufficient condition of premise acceptability. I have previously offered three considerations in its defense.[27] First, Socrates' methodological remarks concerning the premises of his *elenchos* always and only appeal to the beliefs of his interlocutor. For example, when trying to determine whether the premise that the inexpert well-diver is more courageous than the expert well-diver when each dives into a well should be accepted in the *elenchos* aimed at examining Laches' professed knowledge that courage is wise endurance of the soul, Socrates indicates that it should if and only if Laches believes it (*Laches* 193c6–8).[28] Second, a careful examination of the actual premises that Socrates employs in his elenctic episodes in the Socratic dialogues indicates that the only property they all have in common is that they are all believed by the interlocutor. Properties like being believed by Socrates,[29] self-evidence,[30] common sense, or the beliefs of the wise[31] are subject to immediate counter-example. And, finally, being believed by the interlocutor is just the right sort of property for Socrates to appeal to given the universality of his elenctic examinations. It is only the property of being believed by the interlocutor that is likely to be available to any interlocutor he happens to meet, young or old, citizen or stranger,

---

26 Actually, (1) and (2) only entail that there be no relevant epistemic distinction between the premises of the *elenchos* and the apparent refutand, and that the falsity of the alleged refutand is not established. The logic leaves open the question of whether Socrates recognizes these conclusions. In chapter 4 of Benson 2000 (see also Benson 1995), I argue that nothing in the elenctic dialogues requires that Socrates fail to see the force of these conclusions.

27 For a longer version of these three considerations, see Benson 2000: p. 37–55.

28 See also *Protagoras* 331c1-d1, *Gorgias* 495a7-c3, 499b9-c6, and *Republic* I 349a4–8.

29 See Vlastos 1994: p. 1–37 and Wolfsdorf 2003.

30 See Gulley 1968, Nakhnikian 1971, and perhaps Santas 1979.

31 See Polansky 1985 and Bolton 1993.

who professes to care about truth or knowledge or the care of his soul (*Apology* 29e4–30a4). Nevertheless, these considerations presuppose a more orthodox and simplistic conception of belief than the text of the Socratic dialogues allows.

At *Gorgias* 474b2–6, Socrates ascribes to Polus[32] the belief that he would prefer to suffer injustice rather than do it, despite Polus's adamant denial that he believes any such thing[33] – indeed, despite Polus's claim to believe, on the contrary, that suffering injustice is worse that doing it. Here Socrates ascribes a belief to Polus that Polus clearly is not disposed to act on, nor even thinks that he has.[34] But, then, why does Socrates ascribe such a belief to Polus? The answer seems clear. Polus has other beliefs that he is disposed to act on and/or thinks he has, from which the belief that it is preferable to suffer injustice than to do it follows. Socrates is about to show him that this is so. Socrates here includes among Polus's beliefs not only those doxastic phenomena on the basis of which Polus is disposed to act, and that Polus thinks he has,[35] but also those that are deducible (whether Polus recognizes it or not) from those phenomena Polus is disposed to act on or thinks he has. This is a heterodox and expansive conception of belief.[36] It amounts to ascribing to each and every individual an infinite number of beliefs, most of which one will never be disposed to act on or recognize one has. On such an expansive conception of belief, however, the first premise of the argument against constructivism cannot stand. Polus's 'belief' that it is preferable to suffer injustice than to do it does not suffice for accepting it as a premise of the *elenchos*. If it did, the argument at *Gorgias* 474b–479e would not be necessary. Polus's 'beliefs' are immediately inconsistent. To see what other property for premise acceptability

32 And to everyone else. I leave to one side the implications and justification for this additional claim. See Brickhouse and Smith 1994: pp. 79–82.

33 *Gorgias* 474b2–6. See also *Gorgias* 482a6-c3.

34 This rules out both behaviorist accounts of beliefs and straightforward Cartesian transparency accounts. Note that in rejecting the conditional 'if A does not believe that A believes that p, then A does not believe that p', Socrates need not be rejecting the conditional 'if A believes that A believes that p, then A believes that p'.

35 Socrates does not deny that Polus believes that it is preferable to do injustice than to suffer it. Such a belief ascription is relatively familiar – based on a disposition to act in some way or a self-ascription based on introspection. The familiar idea that beliefs are dispositions or capacities (*dunameis*) to behave in various ways (if only verbally) is suggested at *Laches* (190c6) and elsewhere, while the idea that beliefs can be self-ascribed as a result of introspection is suggested, for example, in the *Charmides* (158e7–159a7).

36 Vlastos describes beliefs of this sort as marginal or covert beliefs in Vlastos 1994: p. 23.

Socrates requires, we can turn to another passage often cited against the first premise of the Argument Against Constructivism.

At *Republic* 348d, Thrasymachus claims that injustice is virtue and wisdom and justice their opposites (hereafter 'injustice is virtue' for short). Socrates complains that it will be harder than he had anticipated to persuade Thrasymachus that the life of the just person is more profitable than the life of the unjust person, contrary to his expressed belief that the life of the unjust person is more profitable.[37] Nevertheless, Socrates asserts, he must pursue the argument as long as Thrasymachus really believes what he has just asserted. When Thrasymachus replies by asking what difference does it make, whether he believes it or not, Socrates surprisingly responds – "It makes no difference" (349b1).

As I mentioned, this passage is often cited as a violation of the first premise of the Argument Against Constructivism. Rather than claiming that it is necessary that Thrasymachus believe the premises of the *elenchos*, Socrates appears here to explicitly deny that it matters. But, despite appearances, this is not what the passage suggests. Socrates claims that it does not matter whether Thrasymachus believes that injustice is virtue. But 'injustice is virtue' is not a premise of the *elenchos* from 349b1–350c11. It is the apparent refutand of this *elenchos*. Socrates had hoped to use the premise that justice is virtue and wisdom, and injustice its opposite (hereafter 'justice is virtue' for short) in his examination of Thrasymachus's wisdom – namely, in his attempt to persuade Thrasymachus that the just life is more profitable than the unjust life contrary to Thrasymachus's belief that injustice is more profitable. But Thrasymachus denies believing that justice is virtue, and instead asserts that injustice is virtue. Socrates is about to show that Thrasymachus really does believe justice is virtue, whatever else he thinks he believes. Socrates is about to provide an argument from premises that Thrasymachus recognizes he believes to the belief that justice is virtue (349b1–350c11). Socrates here employs the expansive conception of belief indicated in the *Gorgias*. According to Socrates, Thrasymachus believes that justice is virtue, whether he thinks he does or not.[38] It makes no difference to Socrates whether Thrasymachus

---

37 See *Republic* 348a-b for this explicit goal. Given Socrates' praise (however ironic) of Thrasymachus's reputed wisdom and his desire to be taught by him at 337d-338b and 344d-e, Socrates appears to suggest to Glaucon at 348a-b that they try to persuade Thrasymachus that he also believes that the life of the just person is profitable, as well as that the life of the just person is not profitable, in order to examine his reputed wisdom.

38 We know from the *Gorgias* that his believing that injustice is virtue is no obstacle to his also believing that justice is virtue, even though the two propositions are contraries.

really believes that injustice is virtue. What matters is that he believes justice is virtue. If he also believes injustice is virtue, then, Socrates will have established an inconsistency in Thrasymachus's belief set already by 350d;[39] if he does not, then the subsequent arguments from 350d onward will.

Notice that rather than serving as evidence that the interlocutor's belief is not necessary for premise acceptability, this exchange indicates that such belief is not sufficient. According to Socrates, Thrasymachus believes that justice is virtue whatever else he believes or thinks he believes at 348e, just as Polus believes that suffering injustice is preferable to doing it at *Gorgias* 474b. Thrasymachus's belief that justice is virtue is deducible from other beliefs that Thrasymachus recognizes he has. Nevertheless, Socrates is unwilling to employ such a belief as a premise in his elenctic argument until he has come to show Thrasymachus the deduction. Not only must the interlocutor believe the premise before it can be employed in a Socratic *elenchos*, but the interlocutor must also recognize that he believes it. This is why Socrates is concerned to determine Thrasymachus's sincerity at 349a. If Thrasymachus is sincere in claiming to believe injustice is virtue and not to believe justice is virtue, then Socrates will need to show Thrasymachus that he also believes justice is virtue – that is, provide the argument of 349b1–350c11–in order to employ justice is virtue as a premise in the subsequent *elenchos*. If he is not, then the argument is otiose. What is necessary and sufficient for premise acceptability is not simply that Thrasymachus believe justice is virtue, but that he recognize that he believes it.[40]

---

39   For at least the second time. He had done this previously at 339b-342e.
40   What is not required, however, is that interlocutor admit that he recognize that he believes the relevant proposition. Socrates is concerned to make the interlocutor recognize his cognitive incoherence, his ignorance, not to make the audience of the *elenchos* recognize the interlocutor's cognitive incoherence. This may be the point of two other passages that are often cited as violations of the first premise of the Argument Against Constructivism – *Protagoras* 333c2–9 and 352c-d. In the first case, Socrates apparently accepts a premise which the many believe, but Protagoras claims not to believe, and in the second case, the apparent refutand is ascribed to the many, but Protagoras denies believing it. In both cases, Socrates may feel that the deduction from Protagoras's man is the measure doctrine, and his belief that the many believe that p to p is true is too immediate for Protagoras to plausibly fail to recognize it. Consequently, despite Protagoras's denial, Socrates feels confident in assuming that Protagoras does indeed recognize that he believes – that is, committed to – the premise and the apparent refutand, whatever Protagoras says. Indeed, it is interesting that in both cases, it is not so much that Protagoras denies that he believes these propositions than that he would be ashamed to admit them.

Now that we have seen the difficulties surrounding the nature of belief involved in the first premise of the Argument Against Constructivism, one immediately wonders about the nature of belief involved in the second premise. In what sense, one may wonder, does the interlocutor genuinely believe the apparent refutand, given how quickly he seems to reject it when he sees that it is inconsistent with the other beliefs he recognizes that he has and how quick he is to offer an alternative?[41]

Now we should not overestimate the speed with which the interlocutors abandon their initial answers. Hippias in the *Hippias Minor*, for example, does not quickly abandon his belief (which serves as the apparent refutand for all of the *elenchoi* in that dialogue) that Achilles and Odysseus are distinct because the former is honest, while the latter is deceitful, nor does Protagoras quickly abandon his belief that courage and wisdom are distinct, the apparent refutand of the last quarter of the *Protagoras*. Moreover, Nicias's defense of his answer that courage is knowledge of fearful and daring things at *Laches* 195a-200c, and Critias's defense of his initial answer that temperance is doing one's own business at *Charmides* 162e-164c, both are maintained through multiple *elenchoi*.[42] Nor can we simply discount the evidence that the interlocutors believe the apparent refutand, given that roughly half of the answers offered to Socratic 'What is F-ness?' questions are explicitly propounded as believed or thought by the interlocutor.[43]

Nevertheless, there is something to this concern. It is doubtful whether at the beginning of the *elenchos* with Laches, for example, that he can be determinately said to believe what courage is. Does he believe that courage is endurance of the soul or does he really believe that it is wise endurance of the soul? According to the expansive concept of belief found in the *Gorgias*, he probably believes that courage is wise endurance of the soul. But he thinks he believes that courage is simply the endurance of the soul, and Socrates does not suggest that. In fact, what Laches thinks he believes about the nature of courage is confused, vague, and indefinite. Indeed, this may explain in general why the interlocutor usually (but not always) abandons or modifies his proposed definition or the apparent refutand.

Moreover, it is unlikely that in the *Charmides*, for example, Charmides is as committed to his third answer to the "What is temperance?"

---

41   For an explicit statement of this worry see Brickhouse and Smith 2002: p. 149.

42   See *Laches* 195a2–196c1, 196c1–197d8, and 197e2–200c2; and *Charmides* 162e7–164d3 and 163e1–164c7.

43   See *Euthyphro* 9e8–9, 12e5–8 (see also 15e1–2); *Charmides* 159a9-b6, 160e3–5, 160d5-e1, 162e6; *Laches* 192b9-c1; *Meno* 73d9–10, 78c1–2; and *Hippias Major* 288a3–5, and 293e7–8.

question as he is to his first. By the time Charmides proffers the answer that temperance is doing one's own business, he is grasping at straws. He is giving answers he has heard from others. He is not sure he believes this. He is not even sure he understands what it means, as the subsequent discussion with Critias suggests. But he thinks he believes it, and that is sufficient for Socrates.[44] Nevertheless, even if we do understand this last answer as in someone way expressive of Charmides' belief – although in some vague or indefinite way – we cannot deny that this belief is weaker than his belief in the first answer. Not only are the interlocutors' beliefs often confused, vague, and indefinite; they also come in a variety of degrees.

None of this, however, shows that the Argument Against Constructivism fails. What it does show is that the conception of belief employed in the second premise, as also in the first, is too orthodox and simplistic to capture Socrates' practice.[45] The Socratic *elenchos* does not show that Laches, for example, has an inconsistent set of well-formed determinate beliefs all of the same strength concerning courage. Rather it shows that Laches' doxastic condition concerning courage is confused and indefinite. His beliefs about the nature of courage are not well-formed, determinate, and consistent. But none of this suggests that Socrates requires that the premises of his elenctic episodes be more determinate or more strongly held than the interlocutor's doxastic commitment to the apparent refutand. All that Socrates requires is that the interlocutor recognize or is aware of his doxastic commitment (whether directly or through inference). Socrates' common strategy for examining an interlocutor's wisdom is to test his doxastic coherence evidenced by the interlocutor's sincere attempt to answer Socrates' questions according to what he thinks he believes. Doxastic incoherence, however, may not be a result of inconsistent determinate beliefs all of the same strength, but rather a result of indefinite or confused beliefs or

---

44 I am not here committing Socrates to the principle that if A believes that *p*, then A believes that A believes that *p*, which the Polus passage would appear to violate. Rather, I am committing Socrates to the principle that if A believes that A believes that *p*, then A believes that *p*, which is nowhere, to my knowledge, violated in the Socratic dialogues and which is supported by Socrates' commitment to the notion that simply requires the interlocutor to be sincere in answering his questions.

45 Although it is an open question whether Socrates and/or Plato would have thought it was mistaken. Plato's suggestion that belief is a silent dialogue (*Sophist* 263e and *Theaetetus* 189e-190a) may indicate that he would not. I suspect that the evidence from the Socratic dialogues underdetermines the answer. Nevertheless, this does suggest a valuable research project. See, for example, Brickhouse and Smith 1994: p. 73–83.

acceptances or near beliefs.[46] Evidence of such doxastic incoherence provides no reason to suppose that some allegedly targeted belief is false or that its negation is true. For this we need evidence that Socrates thinks degree of belief or definiteness of belief carries with it some epistemic weight.[47] But no such evidence is to be found.

Of course, a strategy of examining the doxastic coherence of his interlocutors in order to examine their reputed wisdom presupposes a rather robust conception of knowledge or wisdom.[48] Since Socrates repeatedly takes the discovery of doxastic incoherence to reveal the interlocutor's lack of wisdom, he must be presupposing at least that doxastic coherence is a necessary condition of wisdom. Such a robust conception of wisdom is displayed in an additional feature of Socratic method, to which we will now turn.

THE ELENCHOS AS DEFINITION TESTING

Thus far, we have said nothing (except in passing) of what Aristotle highlights as a central feature of Socrates' characteristic method – his concern with definition.[49] While Plato does not highlight this feature of Socratic method in the *Apology*, he certainly does in other Socratic Dialogues. Of the fourteen Socratic dialogues, six are primarily definitional: *Euthyphro, Charmides, Hippias Major, Laches, Lysis*,[50] and *Republic* I, while three others contain substantial definitional sections: *Protagoras* 312c-314d, *Gorgias* 449a-466a, and *Meno* 71d-79e. After briefly rehearsing the primary adequacy conditions of Socratic definition, I will conclude this chapter by discussing the connection between this Socratic concern and Socrates' concern to examine the reputed wisdom of those he happens to meet.

Let me begin with a caveat. While it is traditional to discuss this Socratic interest as an interest in definition, we must be careful. Socrates does sometimes use the Greek word for definition (*horimos*)

---

46 For the distinction between belief and acceptance, see Cohen 1992, and for the notion of near or partial beliefs, see Morton 2002: p. 55–80.

47 Even this would not suffice. We would need evidence that all of the premises of the elenctic episodes are more strongly held or more definite than the interlocutor's commitment to the apparent refutand.

48 Throughout, I have been and will continue to use 'knowledge' (*episteme*), 'wisdom' (*sophia*), and 'expertise' (*techne*) interchangeably following Plato, at least in the Socratic dialogues. See Benson 2000: p. 10–11.

49 I here reserve for another time Aristotle's mention of induction (*epagoge*); see briefly Benson 2000: p. 77 n.82 and now McPherran 2004.

50 There is some dispute about whether the *Lysis* is genuinely definitional. See, for example, Sedley 1989.

in these dialogues, but it is his fascination and preoccupation with a certain form of question that is noteworthy. The question at issue is the 'What is F-ness?' question, where 'F-ness' is a placeholder for something like a property or nature susceptible in principle to multiple instantiations. For example, in the *Laches*, Socrates searches for an answer to the 'What is courage?' question, in the *Euthyphro*, 'What is piety?' in the *Charmides*, 'What is temperance?' in the *Meno*, 'What is virtue?' and in the *Protagoras*, 'What is a sophist?' Socrates illustrates his questions with examples like 'What is a bee?' 'What is shape?' and 'What is color?' in the *Meno*, and 'What is swiftness?' in the *Laches*. I mention this primarily to remind us that in describing Socrates' concern here as a concern for definition is to already interpret the text. What the text displays is a fundamental concern with the 'What is F-ness?' question. To describe this concern as a concern for definition is to understand the 'What is F-ness?' question in a particular way – a way, indeed, that is potentially misleading.

It is nearly certain that in pursuing his 'What is piety?' question, for example, Socrates is not asking for the meaning of the word 'piety' (or better the meaning of the word *hosiotes*). He is certainly not asking a question that could be answered by using a dictionary. He is asking the same sort of question that scientists ask when they ask 'What is water?' and discover that the answer 'Water is H_2O'. We might put this point by maintaining that in asking his 'What is F-ness?' question Socrates is after a real definition as opposed to a nominal definition,[51] but it might be less anachronistic to maintain that Socrates is after the essence or essential nature. Socrates himself explains that in asking the 'What is piety?' question, for example, he is seeking "the form itself by which all the pious things are pious." In asking his 'What is F-ness?' question, Socrates is after what makes F things F. He is seeking what explains why pious actions are pious.

In addition to this explanatory requirement, Socrates requires that answers to his 'What is F-ness?' question be co-extensive with F-things. Socrates puts this by maintaining that answers to his 'What is F-ness?' question must be in (*Meno* 73a1–3), through (*Meno* 74a9), common to (*Meno* 73d1), over (*Meno* 75a4–5), or had (*Meno* 72c6-d1) by all and only F-things. For example, Socrates objects to Euthyphro's answer that piety is prosecuting the wrongdoer on the grounds that according to Euthyphro, prosecuting the wrongdoer is not common to all pious actions. On the other hand, he objects to Gorgias's answer that rhetoric is the craft that uses speech on the grounds that this does not belong to only rhetoricians.

---

51   See Locke 1961: p. 3.3 and, for example, Fine 1992: p. 202.

Finally, Socrates indicates that an answer to his 'What is F-ness?' question must be "what is called F-ness in all and only F things." For example, in explaining his 'What is courage?' question to Laches in the *Laches*, Socrates explains that in asking 'What is swiftness?' he is asking for what is called swiftness in all and only swift things (192a9–10). With this condition we have come nearly full circle. Some commentators take this condition to indicate Socrates' concern with meanings, while others maintain that this so-called semantic condition is compatible with a Socratic concern with so-called real definitions. However this last dispute is to be resolved, we can conclude this brief excursion into the nature of Socratic definition by maintaining that according to Socrates, an adequate answer to his 'What is F-ness?' question must appeal to what is called F-ness in all and only F things, what belongs to all and only F-things, and what makes F-things F.[52]

With this account of Socratic definition in hand, one might wonder what motivates Socrates' concern with definition. Why does Socrates devote so much time to seeking answers to his 'What is F-ness?' questions from his interlocutors? It was once a commonplace to answer this question in part by appealing to Socrates' belief that definitional knowledge – that is, knowledge of the answer to a Socratic 'What is F-ness?' question – was prior to knowledge of anything else about F-ness.[53] Thus, Euthyphro cannot accurately claim to know that prosecuting his father for murder is pious, if he fails to know what piety is, nor can Meno claim to know that virtue is teachable, if he fails to know what virtue is. In the Socratic dialogues, Socrates tests his interlocutors' reputed wisdom by asking them the relevant 'What is F-ness?' question, and our earlier examination of the elenctic method indicates that Socrates takes a minimal condition of the interlocutors' knowledge of the answer to such a question to be the interlocutors' doxastic coherence. If Hippias, for example, is to maintain his reputation for wisdom concerning fine speeches and activities, he must at least maintain his doxastic coherence in the course of an elenctic test of his knowledge of what fine-ness is.

In recent decades, however, a variety of objections have arisen against attributing this view of the priority of definitional knowledge

---

52 For a more sustained discussion of the nature of Socratic definition see Benson 2000: p. 99–111. See also Vlastos 1981 and Wolfsdorf 2003.

53 See Robinson 1953: p. 51, who for a long time got away with the claim that the dialogues gave the 'vague impression' that Socrates was so committed. We might put the priority of definitional knowledge as follows; "If A fails to know what F-ness is, then A fails to know, for any x, that x is F, or for any G, that F-ness is G."

to Socrates in the Socratic dialogues. It will not be my purpose in the remaining pages to respond fully to these objections nor to otherwise defend this attribution. Rather, I will turn to the objection that I take to lie at the heart of the others, and suggest a response that integrates nicely with the account of Socratic method I have been developing.

Most of the objections to attributing the priority of definitional knowledge to Socrates in the Socratic dialogues fall roughly into two groups – first, that there is no compelling textual evidence for attributing to Socrates such a priority view,[54] and second, that there is good textual evidence against attributing this view to Socrates.[55] But at the heart of these first two sorts of objections lies a third objection – that the priority of definitional knowledge is false. It is simply too implausible to be attributed to the likes of Socrates.[56] The implausibility of the view is familiar from Wittgenstein (among others).[57] As Peter Geach succinctly put it in a classic piece: "We know heaps of things without being able to define the terms in which we express our knowledge."[58] It is this implausibility objection that motivates the other two. If Wittgenstein and Geach are correct, we should expect virtually incontrovertible evidence before attributing the likes of this view to Socrates. Moreover, any textual evidence however slight, will suffice to keep from attributing to Socrates a view so obviously implausible. The result is that if Wittgenstein and Geach are correct, we can no longer rest content with Robinson's judgment that the Socratic dialogues give the 'vague impression' that Socrates is committed to the priority of definitional knowledge.

Now, not everyone has opted for this kind of response to the implausibility objection. Neither Geach nor Wittgenstein took the implausibility of the view to be a reason for denying that Socrates held it. Rather, they blamed Socrates for this 'style of mistaken thinking,' which according

---

54 See Beversluis 1987: p. 215, Lesher 1987: p. 285, and Nehamas 1986: pp. 278–291.

55 See Nehamas 1986: p. 292, Woodruff 1987: p. 22, and Vlastos 1994: p. 74.

56 All three of these objections are plausible and have been powerfully defended, but they should not carry the day. For a sustained rebuttal to the first two sorts of objections in particular, see Benson 2000: p. 112–141. A fourth objection maintains that the priority of definitional knowledge is incompatible with Socrates' repeated professions of ignorance of answers to 'What is F-ness?' questions and his infrequent professions to know various things. For a response to this objection see Benson 2000: pp. 223–238, and Wolfsdorf 2004.

57 See Wittgenstein 1965: pp. 19–20 and Wittgenstein 1958: section 70. See also Moore 1962: p. 225.

58 Geach 1966:371.

to Geach, at least, was more influential in the course of post-Platonic philosophy even than Plato's theory of Forms. Moreover, a rather powerful best-explanation argument supports attributing this view to Socrates. While it is true that Socrates never states his commitment to the priority of definitional knowledge explicitly and in full generality, and while there are hints in the text that can be understood as arguing against his commitment, when all of the passages are put alongside one another, interpretations seeking to avoid such a Socratic commitment begin to look ad hoc, partial, and forced. Attributing to Socrates, the fully general priority of definitional knowledge view begins to look like the best explanation of the variety of texts.[59] Consequently, rather than appealing to charity to force a variety of apparently ad hoc, partial, and gerrymandered attributions, we would do better to let charity force us to reevaluate the implausibility of the priority view.[60]

Wittgenstein, Geach, et al. object to the priority of definitional knowledge on the grounds that we know – in the ordinary or justified true belief sense of know – "heaps of things" about F-ness without knowing what F-ness is. But given the frequency of passages that can be explained by appeal to the priority of definitional knowledge, charity might lead one to question whether the knowledge employed in the view is knowledge in the ordinary sense. Rather than thinking that the view implies that one cannot know in the ordinary sense anything else about F-ness prior to knowing what F-ness is, we might be more charitable to Socrates to think that he does not have the ordinary sense of knowledge in mind. What the attribution of the priority of definitional knowledge to Socrates indicates is not that he is committed to an implausible view, but that he is committed to a stronger conception of knowledge than the ordinary one. Socrates might agree with Wittgenstein, Geach, et al. that we can know in the ordinary sense – insofar as Socrates would recognize such a sense of knowledge[61] – heaps of things about F-ness prior to knowing what F-ness is. But Socrates' appeal to the priority of definitional knowledge indicates that he has little, if any,interest in such a sense of knowledge. He is interested in a stronger, more robust sense of knowledge and it is that sort of knowledge, that one cannot have about anything about F-ness prior to knowing what F-ness is. Indeed, finding Socrates committed to such a sense of knowledge should not surprise us in light of everything else

---

59 For a longer, more complete defense of this inference to the best explanation, see Benson 1990: pp. 19–44. For the most sustained rebuttal to this defense, see Brickhouse and Smith 1994: pp. 45–54.
60 For other responses see Prior 1998 and Wolfsdorf 2004.
61 See 'elenctic knowledge' in Vlastos 1994: pp. 39–66.

we have learned about the Socratic method in this chapter. We should remember that Socrates' characteristic method is motivated by his recognition of his lack of knowledge of 'heaps of things' and his desire to rectify that ignorance by examining the knowledge claims of others. Moreover, we should remember that his method of rectifying that ignorance – learning from those whose knowledge claims are confirmed – is foiled by his utter failure to confirm the knowledge claims of those he examines. Finally, we should remember that his method of examining those knowledge claims depends upon examining the doxastic coherence of the one whose knowledge is being examined, and when the individual's beliefs are found to be doxastically incoherent, Socrates concludes that he lacks the knowledge he claims to have. Such a condition on knowledge is hardly ordinary, and suggests a robust conception. Consequently, Socrates' concern with definition so understood fits nicely with the rest of his characteristic method.

CONCLUSION

In this chapter, I have maintained that in the elenctic dialogues Plato presents us with a coherent and distinctive Socratic method. It is not the only method that Socrates practices in those dialogues, though it does tend to predominate. It is the method that Socrates takes to lead to his trial and eventual execution, and consequently it is, a method that he takes to be distinctive of, but not unique to, himself. Further, it is the method by which he seeks to examine the robust knowledge claims of those reputed to be wise. He does this for two reasons. First, he aims to encourage these individuals to seek the robust knowledge they lack, if indeed they are found to lack it. Second, he aims to acquire the knowledge he lacks from them, if they are found to have it. Finally, he examines the robust knowledge of these individuals by testing their doxastic coherence through a series of questions, often beginning with his notorious 'What is F-ness?' question. Such an account of Socrates' characteristic method is coherent and plausible when properly understood. Such an account is the Socratic *elenchos*.

WORKS CITED

Adams, D. "Elenchos and Evidence." *Ancient Philosophy* 18 (1998): 287–308.
Bailly, J. A. "What You Say, What You Believe, and What You Mean." *Ancient Philosophy* 29 (199):65–76.
Benson, H. H. "The Priority of Definition and the Socratic *Elenchos*." *Oxford Studies in Ancient Philosophy* 8 (1990): 45–112.
Benson, H. H. "The Dissolution of the Problem of the *Elenchus*." *Oxford Studies in Ancient Philosophy* 13 (1995): 45–112.

Benson, H. H. *Socratic Wisdom: The Model of Knowledge in Plato's Early Dialogues*. New York, 2000.

Beversluis, J. "Does Socrates Commit the Socratic Fallacy." *American Philosophical Quarterly* 24 (1987): 211–23.

Beversluis, J. *Cross-Examining Socrates: A Defense of the Interlocutors in Plato's Early Dialogues*. Cambridge, 2000.

Blondell, R. *The Play of Character in Plato's Dialogues*. Cambridge, 2002.

Bolton, R. "Aristotle's Account of the Socratic Elenchus." *Oxford Studies in Ancient Philosophy* 11 (1993): 121–152.

Brickhouse, T. C., and N. D. Smith. *Plato's Socrates*. New York, 1994.

Brickhouse, T.C., and N.D. Smith. "The Origin of Socrates' Mission." *Journal of the History of Ideas* 44 (October-December) (1983): 657–666.

Brickhouse, T.C., and N. D. Smith. *Socrates on Trial*. Princeton, 1989.

Brickhouse, T.C., and N. D. Smith. "The Socratic Elenchos?" In *Does Socrates Have a Method?* ed. Gary Alan Scott. College Park, PA, 2002, pp.145–157.

Cohen, L. J. *An Essay on Belief and Acceptance*. Oxford, 1992

Fine, G.. "Inquiry in the *Meno*." In *The Cambridge Companion to Plato*, ed. Richard Kraut. Cambridge, 1992, pp. 200–226.

Geach, P. T. "Plato's *Euthyphro*: An Analysis and Commentary." *Monist* 50 (1966): 369–382.

Gulley, N. *The Philosophy of Socrates*. London, 1968.

Irwin, T. H.. "Say What You Believe." *Apeiron* 26 (1993): 1–16; *Virtue Love and Form: Essays in Memory of Gregory Vlastos*. Vol. 26. eds. Terence Irwin and Martha C. Nussbaum.

Kraut, R. "Comments on Vlastos." *Oxford Studies in Ancient Philosophy* 1 (1983): 59–70.

Lesher, J. H. "Socrates' Disavowal of Knowledge." *Journal of the History of Philosophy* 25 (1987): 275–288.

Locke, J. *An Essay Concerning Human Understanding*. Ed. and intro. John W. Yolton. London, 1961.

McCabe, M.M. "Myth, Allegory, and Argument in Plato." *Apeiron* 25 (1992): 47–67.

McPherran, M. "Socratic *Epagoge* and Socratic Induction." *Journal of the History of Philosophy* 45.3 (2007): 347–364.

McPherran, M. "Elenctic Interpretation and the Delphic Oracle." In *Does Socrates Have a Method?*, ed. Gary Alan Scott. College Park, PA, 2002. pp. 114–144.

Moore, G. E. *Some Main Problems of Philosophy*. New York, 1962.

Morton, A. *The Importance of Being Understood: Folk Psychology as Ethics*. Routledge, 2002.

Nakhnikian, G. "Elenctic Definitions." In *The Philosophy of Socrates: A Collection of Critical Essays*, ed. G. Vlastos. New York, 1971, pp. 125–157.

Nehamas, A. "Socratic Intellectualism." *Proceedings of the Boston Area Colloquium in Ancient Philosophy* 2 (1986): 275–316.

Polansky, R. "Professor Vlastos' Analysis of Socratic Elenchus." *Oxford Studies in Ancient Philosophy* 3 (1985): 247–260.

Prior, W. J. "Plato and the 'Socratic Fallacy.'" *Phronesis* 43 (1998): 97–113.

Reeve, C. D. C. *Socrates in the Apology: An Essay on Plato's* Apology of Socrates. Indianapolis, 1989.

Robinson, R. *Plato's Earlier Dialectic*. 2nd ed. Oxford, 1953.

Santas, G. *Socrates: Philosophy in Plato's Early Dialogues*. Boston, 1979.

Sedley, D. "Is the Lysis a Dialogue of Definition?" *Phronesis* 34 (1989): 107–108.

Stokes, M. C. *Plato's Socratic Conversations, Drama and Dialectic in Three Dialogues*. Baltimore, 1986.

Vlastos, G. "What Did Socrates Understand by His 'What is F?' Question." In *Platonic Studies*. 2nd ed., ed. G. Vlastos. Princeton, 1981, pp. 410–417.

Vlastos, G. *Socratic Studies*. ed. Myles Burnyeat. Cambridge, 1994.

Wittgenstein, L. *Philosophical Investigations*. trans. G. E. M. Anscombe. New York, 1958.

Wittgenstein, L. *Generally Known as the Blue and Brown Books: Preliminary Studies for the "Philosophical Investigations."* New York, 1965.

Wolfsdorf, D. "Socrates' Pursuit of Definitions." *Phronesis* 48 (2003): 271–312.

Wolfsdorf, D. "Understanding the 'What is F?' Question." *Apeiron* 36 (2003): 175–188.

Wolfsdorf, D. "Socrates' Avowals of Knowledge." *Phronesis* 49(2) (2004): 75–142.

Wolfsdorf, D. "The Socratic Fallacy and the Epistemological Priority of Definitional Knowledge." *Apeiron* 37 (1, March) (2004): 35–68.

Woodruff, P. "Expert Knowledge in the *Apology and Laches*: What a General Needs to Know." *The Boston Area Colloquium in Ancient Philosophy* 3 (1987): 79–115.

Woolf, R. "Callicles and Socrates: Psychic (Dis)Harmony in the *Gorgias*." *Oxford Studies in Ancient Philosophy* 18 (2000): 1–40.

Woolf, R. "Consistency and Akrasia in Plato's *Protagoras*." *Phronesis* 47 (2002): 224–252.

9 Self-Examination

There are two texts that may be considered as fundamental for the understanding of the Socratic notion of self-examination: one from the *Apology*, one from the *Phaedrus*. (In this chapter, I shall restrict myself to discussion of the notion as it appears in Plato, without claiming that Plato gives us the authentic, (i.e., historical) Socratic version – although I know of no evidence that would seriously interfere with such a claim.)

1. *Apology* 37E3–38A6: Perhaps someone might say "But Socrates – why shouldn't you be able to leave Athens and keep your mouth shut, living a quiet life?" This is what it's most difficult of all to persuade some of you about. If I say that living a quiet life is dis-obedience to the god, and that therefore it's impossible to do it, you won't believe me because you'll think I'm being ironical. If on the other hand I say that it really is a good of the highest order for a human being to spend each day *in discussions about virtue* [or 'excellence', 'goodness': *aretê*] *and the other things you hear me conversing about, and examining myself and others, and that the unexamined life is unliveable for a human being* – if I say that, you'll believe me even less.

2. *Phaedrus* 229E4–230A6: For myself [it is again Socrates who is speaking], in no way do I have leisure for these things [sc. rational-izing traditional myths like that of Boreas and Oreithuia], and the reason for it, my friend, is this. I am not yet capable, in accordance with the Delphic inscription, of "knowing myself"; it therefore seems absurd to me that while I am still ignorant of this subject I should inquire into things which do not belong to me. So then saying goodbye to these things, and believing what is commonly thought about them, I inquire ... not into these but into myself, to see whether I am actually a beast more complex and more violent than Typhon [a hundred-headed dragon, who was the last obstacle to Zeus' ascent to kingship of the gods[1]], or both a tamer and a

---

1 See Hesiod, *Theogony* 820 ff.

simpler creature, sharing some divine and un-Typhonic portion by nature.

I shall leave passage 2 aside for the moment, and concentrate first on passage 1.

1. "SELF-EXAMINATION" IN THE APOLOGY AND SOME OTHER CLOSELY RELATED PLATONIC DIALOGUES

What is it, exactly, that Socrates "examines" (the verb is *exetazein*), when he talks about "examining myself and others"? The standard view is that what Socrates examines are his own and others' *convictions*.[2] Let us suppose – as many scholars do suppose – that it is Socrates' typical method to start from an interlocutor's *conviction* about what one of the "virtues" is (note the reference in passage 1 to 'discussions about virtue and the other things'), and to go on from there to other things his interlocutors are convinced of, or believe, in order to get them to think about jettisoning that first conviction or belief: then it will be natural to suppose that what he is doing is looking for *consistency in people's belief-sets*.[3] Add in the assumption that everyone has at least some true beliefs or convictions, about the things that really matter, and that Socrates in particular will have succeeded in weeding out all or most of his own false ones, and we shall be well on the way to having a method for discovering actual truths about "virtue and the other [relevant] things" – provided, of course, that one accepts that crucial assumption about there being truth around in people's, or at any rate Socrates', beliefs (so that all one has to do, in principle, is to get those beliefs straight).[4] And this analysis of Socratic "self-examination" might well seem to receive indirect confirmation from the introduction, in *Meno*, *Phaedo* and *Phaedrus*, of the "doctrine," or theory, of

2   See, e.g., Vlastos 1991: p. 134 ("... elenctic argument is the very process on which [Socrates] depends to test the truth of his own convictions about the right way to live, no less than those of his interlocutor").

3   'The method by which Socrates "examines himself and others," which I am calling "the elenchus" ..., involves the form of argument that Aristotle was to call "peirastic": a thesis is refuted when, and only when, its negation is derived *"from the answerer's own beliefs"* (*Soph. El.* 165b3–5)' (Vlastos 1991: p. 111; italics added).

4   Some such view of Socratic method is held by Donald Davidson, following Gregory Vlastos; Davidson thinks that (what I have called) the "crucial assumption" stands a good chance of being true in any case. See Rowe 2005, which discusses Davidson's position.

"recollection," according to which we all – perhaps – have knowledge of eternal truths latent in our souls, waiting merely to be 'recollected.' While the Socrates of the *Apology* is agnostic about at least part of the complex set of ideas about the nature, origin, and fate of the soul that is wheeled in – in those other dialogues – to support the recollection theory, nevertheless there might appear to be a pleasing continuity, and natural kinship, between the proposal that we have only (only!) to interrogate ourselves, and our souls, to get to the truth, and the sort of theory of innate ideas that we seem to find in *Meno*, *Phaedo*, and *Phaedrus*.

So on this account, self-examination will be a way of getting to the truth, on the basis that the truth is somehow in oneself; but it will also, importantly, be a matter of examining, and coming to know, one*self* – that is, one's true self – as this is revealed by the discarding of false beliefs and the identification of the ones that are true. (These are not just one's true, or deep, beliefs, those that one truly or really holds, but such beliefs that one holds that are really true.) From here it might be only a short step to the kind of view that we find in the *First Alcibiades*[5] (whether or not that dialogue is by Plato): that what we need is to get to know ourselves, where knowing ourselves is a matter of knowing that we are identical with our souls, rather than our bodies or the combination of soul and body.[6] At any rate, Plato's Socrates seems generally to think that caring for our souls, and so for ourselves, has everything to do with getting our beliefs straight. On the interpretation in question (self-examination as the examination of one's belief-sets) this process has to do with examining and sorting *one's own individual* beliefs, keeping some and throwing others away – a kind of individual intellectual therapy (even if everyone would, presumably, end up with exactly the same, true, set of beliefs).[7] That – on the same interpretation – is what Socrates helps others to achieve, but also, and more importantly, aims to achieve for himself: "Socrates is more concerned with testing his own soul. And he tests it to see if it has true beliefs, assuming that they [sc. beliefs, presumably] determine character ..."[8] Seen in this way, self-examination is a means of self-improvement, which will – so Socrates hopes – throw up real truths along the way.

This way of understanding the *Apology* fits well enough with another feature of Socratic conversation, the demand that the interlocutor should

5   See Annas 1985.
6   See *Alcibiades I* 124A, 130E-131B, 132C-133E.
7   That is, on the most important subjects, the ones that affect the quality of one's life (cf. passage 2: Socrates will be not much concerned about, for example, the truth or otherwise of the story of Boreas and Oreithuia).
8   Irwin 1979 [= *Gorgias* commentary]: p. 182, on *Gorgias* 486D.

always say what he thinks (see, e.g., *Crito* 49D-E, *Gorgias* 495A). How could anyone examine another person's beliefs without knowing what those beliefs actually were? The same understanding also appears – at first sight – to sit rather happily with a well-known context in the *Gorgias*, when Socrates says, extraordinarily, that "I *and you* [Polus] *and all the rest of mankind consider* that doing injustice is worse than suffering it, and not paying the penalty for injustice worse than paying it" (474B3–5) – when Polus claims actually to believe exactly the opposite, and plausibly suggests into the bargain that everyone except Socrates will agree with him. On the usual interpretation of this interchange, what Socrates proceeds to do is to find something else that Polus believes (namely, that doing injustice is more *shameful* than suffering it) – and to derive what he, Socrates, says about injustice from that. In principle, such a procedure might very well be taken as an inquiry into Polus's own deepest beliefs.

Yet there is also good reason to reject this approach (and also the general interpretation it embodies). The argument that Socrates uses here in the *Gorgias*, to move from "more shameful" (*aischion*) to "worse" (*kakion*), is generally considered a transparently poor one, which succeeds in showing nothing at all: if so, then his claim about what Polus and others *really believe* is likely to seem merely provocative (and even if, as I myself suppose, the argument will work on Socrates' own premises, that will hardly help).[9]

Nor, if we turn to Socrates' motivation for requiring his interlocutors to "say what you think," need that be connected with any desire to investigate their innermost beliefs. Asking that the other person say what he thinks might, surely, just be an elementary precaution against too

---

9   Socrates' claim at *Gorgias* 474 is, I propose, based on the idea that what Polus, and anyone else, will be referring to when talking about justice and injustice will be *what justice and injustice actually are* – which will bring with it all sorts of consequences that are at odds with what Polus and others now want to say about justice and injustice, even though that fact is not currently recognised by them, and though they are at the same time already saying things (e.g., that doing injustice is more shameful than suffering it) that when properly understood do go along with what is really true about injustice. To that degree, Socrates' claim about what Polus (and others) "consider" is almost as teasing as his suggestion in the *Protagoras* that Simonides is really and truly a fully paid-up Socratic (see *Protagoras* 339D-347A). However, the underlying point about reference – that what everyone, or anyone, will be talking about when they discuss justice and injustice will be *the actual things justice and injustice* – is to be taken with absolute seriousness. On the principle involved (the "principle of real reference"), see Part II of Penner and Rowe 2005.

easily being taken in by wrong assumptions, making false steps. (Merely to say "let it be so" will be a matter of seeing which way the argument goes whether this particular premise be true or false – which is a feature of certain types of discourse, whether rhetorical or "eristic,"[10] against which Plato's Socrates repeatedly sets his face.) And, as a matter of fact, what Socrates and his interlocutors discuss is not usually marked off as something to which anyone – whether Socrates or the other person – is particularly *committed*.[11] If it often takes Socrates time to work out what people have in mind when they say something, again that need have nothing to do with finding out what they really believe; what they just happen to have come up with in answer to a question – whether or not that answer is connected with what they would recognize as their beliefs – may itself stand in need of qualification, and in fact will usually turn out to do so.[12] Thus, even if what Socrates and his interlocutor end up deriving from what they first started out with might count in some bare sense as the "belief" of one or other or both of them, that will be far from what would normally count as "conviction."

This is not to deny that there are occasions when interlocutors are to be found defending their convictions: what Thrasymachus defends in the first book of the *Republic* is surely something he is convinced of, indeed is passionate about; and similarly with Callicles in the *Gorgias*. Both men's commitment to their positions is heavily emphasized. But these are the exceptions. Much more common is a situation that Socrates describes in the *Charmides*:

But, I [Socrates] said, "Critias, you bear down on me as if I claimed knowledge of the things I'm asking about, and as if I'd agree with you if only I wanted to; but it isn't like that. Rather, *I investigate with you on each occasion what is put forward* just because I don't know the answer myself." (*Charmides* 165B5-C1)

Socrates, Charmides, and Critias have considered a series of different accounts of *sôphrosunê*, without their showing, severally or together, any great attachment to any of them: they are just accounts that have

10 "Eristic" is a form of verbal expertise that puts winning the argument above any other end: Euthydemus and Dionysodorus in the *Euthydemus* are eristics par excellence.

11 Some parts of the *First Alcibiades* (hereafter merely "*Alcibiades*") may seem to suggest some such interest in the individual self, but on closer analysis this turns out to be an illusion. So, for example, a passage on 'the self itself' (*to auto auto*: 130E-131B) is aimed just at sorting out what it is to examine something (anything) in, or by, itself, and the *Alcibiades* shows no more interest in what individual human beings are than it shows in what an individual *anything* is.

12 The *Charmides* gives numerous illustrations of the point (see below).

been "put forward" – if Critias is inclined to defend his candidates, that is only because he doesn't like to lose.[13]

But what, in that case, should we make of the idea of *self*-examination? The *Charmides*, again, is revealing. Shortly after the passage just cited, Critias accuses Socrates of trying merely to refute him, Critias, without any regard to the subject in hand – to which Socrates responds:

> What a thing to think of me, ... even if I am as much as anything refuting you – to think that I'm refuting you for any other purpose than the one for which I'd be thoroughly investigating what *I* was saying, out of a fear that I'd ever think, without realizing it, that I knew something when I didn't. Just so now: *this* is what I claim to be doing, looking into what's been said mostly for my own sake, though perhaps also for my friends as well; or don't you suppose it to be a good thing for practically the whole human race, that how it is with each of the things that are [sc. the case?] should become clear? (*Charmides* 166C7-D6)

What is clearly at issue here is not what people believe, or are convinced about, but rather whether or not they *know* anything. Self-examination is an extension of the examination of others, or vice versa – and it will be *self*-examination just to the extent that it is an examination of how one stands, oneself, in relation to knowledge. That, for Socrates, is the absolutely fundamental question.

Why so? Because, for the Socrates of works like the *Apology* and the *Charmides*, the only difference between people that matters is whether or not they are wise. "Virtue," or "excellence" (or "goodness": *aretê*) *is* knowledge – that is the theme around which the Socrates of a whole series of dialogues dances, without ever firmly asserting it; but then how could he assert it, when he knows nothing? None of us desires anything but the – real – good, as the *Lysis* tells us,[14] and as Diotima told Socrates, according to his story in the *Symposium* (205E-206A); the difficulty for all of us is to establish just what that real good is, in any set of circumstances. Not even Socrates is bold enough to assume that he will get it right (that is *why* he continually says that he knows nothing). The only way he, or anyone, will reliably get it right is if they acquire knowledge; if they do, they'll be good – "virtuous," "excellent" – people, but until then they'll be no more than neither good nor bad – not good because not wise, and not bad because not terminally ignorant (i.e., given that goodness/"virtue" *is* knowledge: see above). So knowledge

---

13   The term *sôphrosunê* is here virtually untranslatable: traditionally it is "temperance," presumably because of its association with self-control – that is, control over one's desires – but it is emphatically not that in the *Charmides*. "Sound-mindedness" will be a better rendering: see below.

14   See Penner and Rowe 2005.

is all-important; knowledge, that is, of what is really good (which turns out to be knowledge, and the knowledgeable life) and of what is really bad (ignorance, and a life built on ignorance), because only by having what is really good and avoiding what is really bad can we have what we all desire (the real good, also known as happiness). If we start from here, knowing that one knows or does not know will be all one needs to know about oneself. Nothing else matters.[15] (This, too, will be compatible with the treatment of self-knowledge in the *Alcibiades*, insofar as that culminates in the understanding that the only goods are goods of the soul – and insofar as goods of the soul reduce to knowledge.)

All of this lies just below the surface of the *Charmides*. Not long before the first of the two passages from the dialogue cited earlier, Critias proposed that *sôphrosunê* was a matter of "doing what belongs to oneself," which in response to Socrates' questioning he soon emends to "doing what is good (for oneself)." But, Socrates asks, mustn't the person who does what's good for himself know when he's doing that? Exactly, says Critias – and this is the point where self-knowledge comes into the discussion: *sôphrosune* pretty much (*schedon*) *is* a matter of knowing oneself, Critias now claims (164D3–4). That, initially, Socrates converts into a knowledge that is knowledge of itself – that is, an awareness of the presence or absence of knowledge; and this he claims to find distinctly problematical. It is obvious enough why he should be interested in such an expertise, since it is more or less what he claims for himself in the *Apology*, even while having no (other) knowledge – that is, no substantive knowledge. So the question is: is

---

15 That is, for the pursuit of one's life. If I know I know what is good/bad for me (no matter how), I can go ahead and act on what I believe/know; if I know I don't know, then I shall be circumspect about acting on what I believe, and will – if I really am aware of my lack of knowledge about what really matters to me – start looking for that knowledge (doing philosophy). It might be tempting to suppose that knowing what is good/bad *for* me should count as knowledge *about* myself. But that would be to presuppose not only (1) that what is good/bad for me is specific to me, but (2) that the way for me to be happy may be different from the way(s) in which other people will be happy; and while Socrates might agree to (1), insofar as what is practicably happy-making for a person in any one set of circumstances may be different from what is practicably happy-making for another person in a different set of circumstances, we have no grounds for supposing, and good grounds for not supposing, that he would agree to (2). Were he to have accepted (2), it would be hard to understand, for example, why he should have put so much faith in philosophical argument, which seems capable of getting rather little purchase on what makes one person happy as opposed to another – if indeed there is such a thing. (On the notion of "practicable happiness," see Penner and Rowe 2005: pp. 90, 263.)

it possible to have a knowledge (*epistêmê*) that is just of itself and of its absence (non-knowledge, nescience: *anepistêmosunê*), without that knowledge requiring knowledge *of* anything apart from itself? Are there seeings, hearings, sensings of any sort that are just of themselves, and not – at all – of the objects of other seeings, hearings, sensings – that is, objects other than the sensings themselves ... (and so on with other examples)? Surely not! Nevertheless Socrates is unwilling to give up on this kind of analysis of *sôphrosunê*, and is perfectly clear that if *sôphrosunê* were able to offer a capacity to distinguish knowledge from ignorance, then our lives would all be the happier for it. That is, our lives would be happier if there were such a thing as knowledge of knowledge and ignorance (and we could acquire it) – not knowledge of any old knowledge and ignorance, but knowledge of knowledge and ignorance about the good and the bad (174B-C), which is what actually gives all the other kinds of expertise whatever value they may have. So if *that* is what *sôphrosunê* is, it will be every bit as beneficial for us as Socrates is convinced *sôphrosunê* must be. For, since what we all want is to be happy, in possession of the real good, knowledge of our ignorance must motivate us to that sort of inquiry which alone can lead us to an understanding of what that real good is. (Or, in the unlikely case[16] where we know that we already have that understanding, such knowledge will be a byproduct of our having it – and so having what we want.[17])

There is not room enough here for a full treatment of the *Charmides*, and of the sometimes bewildering twists and turns of its arguments. However, it can hardly fail to be significant, for the topic of the present chapter, that Socrates' (Plato's) most extended discussion of self-knowledge[18] should turn out to be a discussion of the principle, and the possibility, of Socrates' own preferred activity, of examining himself and others; even more significant, that the knowledge which *sôphrosunê* or "sound-mindedness" would be able to test for, if it really were capable of what Critias claims for it, would be knowledge of good and bad (identified specifically as what makes us happy, *eudaimones*, or unhappy). Here is Socrates' vision of what *sôphrosunê* could do for us:

---

16 "Unlikely," if only because Socrates himself claims ignorance – and he has spent most of his life in the necessary kind of inquiry.

17 If what is in question is *practicable* happiness (see n. 15), the gap between knowing what one wants and actually having will be no more than notional and/or temporary.

18 "Knowledge of knowledge" in the *Charmides* is rather more than just *self-*knowledge, insofar as it will include knowledge of knowledge in others. But it will at any rate include knowledge of one's own (state of) knowledge.

... what benefit would we get from *sôphrosunê* if it is of this nature [i.e. a knowledge of knowledge and ignorance]? Well, if ... the *sôphrôn* man knew what he knew and what he did not know (and that he knows the former but not the latter) and were able to investigate another man who was in the same situation, then it would be of the greatest benefit to us to be *sôphrones*; for those of us who had *sôphrosunê* would live lives free from error and so would all those who were under our rule. Neither would we ourselves be attempting to do things we did not understand – rather we would find those who did understand and turn the matter over to them – nor would we trust those over whom we ruled to do anything except what they would do correctly, and this would be that of which they possessed the knowledge. And thus, by means of *sôphrosunê*, every household would be well-run, and every city well-governed, and so in every case where *sôphrosunê* reigned. And with error rooted out and correctness in control, men so circumstanced would necessarily fare admirably and well in all their doings and, faring well, they would be happy. Isn't this what we mean about *sôphrosunê*, Critias, I said, "when we say what a good thing it would be to know what one knows and what one does not know?"[19] (*Charmides* 171D1–172A5, tr. Sprague, but with minor modifications)

Of course, at this point in the dialogue, and indeed later on, it still remains to be established that "knowledge of knowledge" is possible, and what exactly its relationship is to the substantive knowledge of good and bad. (These are the issues around which the dialectic of the *Charmides*, and the *aporia* or impasse in which it at least formally ends, are constructed.) But given what Socrates says in that *Apology* passage from which I began (passage 1 above), he is scarcely going to give up on either kind of knowledge: what he wants more than anything is the substantive knowledge in question, and a precondition of his getting *that* will be knowing whether and when he, or anyone, has it.

It is not, I think, too much to claim that the *Charmides* is itself a paramount example of Socratic self-examination: not just because it shows Socrates asking what he should believe (discussing with Critias "out of a fear that I'd ever think, without realizing it, that I knew something when I didn't": *Charmides* 166D1–2), but because it has him asking whether his own fundamental claims will stand up, or how and why

19 The editor of the present volume objected here that any supposed benefit of this kind of knowledge would be dependent on "there [being] people about who *do* know the good and the bad to whom we can turn the matter over" (as there are expert shoemakers around to mend our broken shoes, doctors to cure our illnesses, etc.). To this I respond that what Socrates says may also be read, for example, as a criticism of existing governments (etc.), for acting in pursuit of given goals before having asked whether these are actually worth pursuing. Here one thinks immediately of the political "programme" of the *Republic* (however that is to be read).

they do stand up. But here, once again, there is nothing individual, in the sense of anything *personal*, involved; the subject is not Socrates, with all his peculiarities, his history, his traumas, and his genetic inheritance, but a set of ideas and a programme that, as he has proposed, should be taken up by everybody, because – Socrates claims – that will enable them to live better lives – that is, to achieve the happiness that we all inevitably want. By parity of reasoning, he is only interested in other people's beliefs to the extent that he will want to know whether he should adopt them; "or don't you suppose it to be a good thing for practically the whole human race, that how it is with each of the things that are should become clear?" (*Charmides* 166D4–6, again). If there is "therapy" here, it is the "therapy" of the academic tutorial (run by a friendly, beneficent, but finally research-obsessed tutor, who thinks that finding out what the truth is more important than anything else); it is not at all that of the psychiatrist's – or the psychotherapist's – couch, and anyone who is tempted to assimilate the latter to Socratic practice has simply not understood Plato or, I would hazard, the original Socrates.

One immediate consequence of the reading of Socratic self-examination and self-knowledge just proposed is that it frees Socrates from that assumption that the truth somehow lies within us, if only we know how to look for it.[20] True, the theory of learning as recollection shows that at some point, Plato became interested in the possibility, perhaps even the necessity, of some sort of innate knowledge; but it is not inevitable that we see this as an outgrowth of Socratic inquiry,[21] which seems perfectly well able to manage without it. Socratic inquiry, from the glimpses we have of it in works like *Apology*, *Lysis*, *Charmides*, or *Euthyphro*, seems to feel itself little in need of extravagant hypotheses about the origins of the soul, or even about the nature of learning, insofar as intellectual progress seems to be understood as taking place without them. In any case, it can hardly be said that the success rate of the proposals made by the Platonic Socrates' interlocutors would have given him much encouragement to suppose that the truth somehow lies in all of us. The

20 See above. The assumption is easy enough for anyone who (perhaps like Davidson: see n. 4) is to any degree inclined towards an intersubjectivist notion of truth; rather more difficult for a Plato or a Socrates. See Rowe 2005.

21 "At the same time, in the *Meno* at least [the doctrine of recollection] was ... a theory of the Socratic method, designed to explain how the dialectical process of eliciting an interlocutor's beliefs and testing them for consistency need not be wholly negative and destructive; if the discussion is pursued with sincerity and determination, Socratic inquiry can lead to knowledge": Burnyeat 1992 [1977]: p. 57.

point is not lost on Socrates himself: he reports in the *Apology* that a systematic search for someone wiser than himself has thrown up no one with any significant knowledge at all (so the Delphic oracle is right: he *is* wiser than other people, but only because of his consciousness that he knows nothing). The theory, or 'doctrine,' of recollection seems to be an answer to further questions: if knowledge is possible, as Socrates seems to propose, even while suggesting that no one actually has it, then how would we know it if we came across it,[22] and what would guarantee its status as knowledge?

Is there, then, no more to self-knowledge than knowing whether one knows or not (the question raised in the *Charmides*), and no more to self-examination than discovering the answer to that question? The passage from Burnyeat cited next illustrates an interpretation of self-knowledge that at first sight suggests a sort of compromise between the one this chapter has so far been recommending, and the one that this chapter has so far been at pains to reject (that knowing oneself, for Socrates, as for us, is a matter somehow of knowing ourselves as unique individuals). The immediate reference is to the *Theaetetus*, generally regarded as belonging to a relatively late period of Plato's writing, and certainly not one of those dialogues traditionally called "Socratic." But what it says might in principle be just as applicable to those dialogues:

... Socratic education can only be successful with someone like Theaetetus who is aware of, and can accept, his need for it; that much self-knowledge is an indispensable motivating condition, for always the greatest obstacle to intellectual and moral progress with Socrates is people's unwillingness to confront their own ignorance.

Self-knowledge, then, is not only the goal of Socratic education. It is also, right from the beginning, a vital force in the process itself, which involves and is sustained by the pupil's growing *awareness of his own cognitive resources, their strengths and their limitations....* [Burnyeat 1992 (1977), 60; italics added]

It is, for sure, the pupil's/the interlocutor's "awareness of *his own* cognitive resources ..." that is at issue. However, this needs to be handled rather carefully, to separate it from the view of self-examination as an examination of one's beliefs. There is, as I have suggested, no evidence for the view – and I propose that the same will be true whether we are talking about the *Theaetetus* or one of the earlier 'Socratic' dialogues – that for Socrates

to discover the limits of one's knowledge [i.e. by finding out what one knows and does not know] it is necessary first to find out *what one really believes*. [An]

22 This sort of question, specifically raised in the *Meno* (answer: because learning is just recollecting), is also implicit in the *Charmides*.

opinion will need to be tested, but to have formulated it and *thought through its implications and connections with other beliefs* is already a step towards self-knowledge.(Burnyeat 1992 [1977]: 59; italics added)

Socrates – as I have said – does indeed often have to spend time sorting out what it is that people are really saying – for example, with Critias in the *Charmides,* who in response to Socrates' questioning has to make several attempts at saying what *sôphrosunê* is before getting to the proposal that the two of them finally discuss. Yet, once again, that hardly seems to have much to do with sorting out Critias's beliefs.[23] It has more to do with what Socrates – and no doubt Plato, the author – really wants to discuss. It is my claim in this chapter that what is at stake is something much simpler than what Burnyeat – and others – suggest. Socrates needs to know, and his interlocutors need to know, whether whatever is being put forward – by the interlocutors[24] – on each occasion (*Charmides* 165B8) is true or not: first, because they all need to know the truth, and second,[25] because if they don't have it to hand now, they need to know that they don't, in order to continue the investigation somewhere else.[26]

2. SELF-EXAMINATION IN THE PHAEDRUS

... I inquire ... not into these but myself, to see whether I am actually a beast more complex and more violent than Typhon or both a tamer and a simpler creature, sharing some divine and un-Typhonic portion by nature [from passage 2, quoted at the beginning of this chapter].

23 Cf. text to n. 13.

24 Usually not by Socrates, though he often has a hand in it (if he does put something forward on his own, as at *Lysis* 216C-217A, he makes a song and dance about how unusual that is).

25 I add, for the sake of clarification, that I do not for a moment propose that "there is [to quote the editor of the present volume] nothing interestingly intermediate between knowing the bare fact that one is ignorant, and knowing the truth of the matter: that a self-reflective inquiry into the details of one's progress is not especially helpful." If knowledge of knowledge and ignorance is beneficial, then it will always be beneficial to try to see if one has progressed. Indeed I cannot see what other form "inquiry" should take.

26 Burnyeat claims that "Socrates' earlier interlocutors, once they have grasped what is asked of them, are prompt enough to produce a "definition," whereas Theaetetus requires Socrates as "midwife" (1992 [1977]: p. 58); but this seems to be a false antithesis, especially if "midwifery" can be allowed to extend to helping people to see what they are saying, which covers a large part of what Socrates seems to be doing with his "earlier interlocutors."

This is evidently a quite different kind of self-examination from the first. The reference to Typhon recalls an image in *Republic* IX, which represents the human soul as containing three kinds of creatures: a multicoloured (*poikilos*), many-headed beast; a lion; and a man – the last representing the rational part; the lion representing the part in us that values honour and the rewards of competition; the monster representing the part that contains our multifarious appetites, for food, drink, sex, and so on. (In Book IV, Socrates has already argued at length for the existence of these three parts.) In the *Phaedrus* itself, the three parts are represented differently, and – in the case of the appetitive part – rather more kindly[27]: reason is the charioteer, the other two parts his horses, one white and one black, the second with an inbuilt tendency to go off in the wrong direction, and barely controllable. In any case, what Socrates' question at the beginning of the dialogue seems to amount to is whether he is, himself (and by implication whether we humans are, in general), identifiable with the *appetitive* aspects of the soul, which are deeply irrational, or with its *rational* aspects.

As a matter of fact, the Socrates of the *Phaedrus* seems committed to the idea that all human souls necessarily, and irreversibly, combine irrational elements with the rational. So it is not as if we could somehow slough off the irrational in us. Socrates rather has something different in mind: something, perhaps, along the lines of the following passage, from *Republic* X:

> ... our recent argument and others as well compel us to believe that the soul *is* immortal. But to see the soul as it is in truth, we must not study it as it is while it is maimed by its association with the body and other evils – which is what we were doing earlier – but as it is in its pure state ... We'll then find that it is a much finer thing than we thought and that we can see justice and injustice as well as the other things we've discussed far more clearly. What we've said about the soul is true of it as it appears at present. But the condition in which we've studied it is like that of the sea-god Glaucus, whose original (*archaios*) nature can't be made out ... Some of his original parts have been broken off, others have been crushed, and his whole body has been maimed by the waves and by the shells, seaweeds, and stones that have attached themselves to him, so that he looks more like a wild animal than his natural self. The soul, too, is in a similar condition ... That, Glaucon, is why we have to look somewhere else in order to discover its true nature ... [namely,] to its love of wisdom [its *philosophia*]. We must realize what it grasps and the sorts of things that it seeks to associate with, insofar as it is akin to the divine and immortal and what always is. ... (*Republic* 611B9-D8, tr. Grube/Reeve)

27   At any rate to the extent that the black horse is no monster, and has only one head; but then the *Phaedrus* is in this context only concerned with one aspect of appetite – lust.

According to this perspective, the irrational parts of the soul are not parts of its *essence*. In its essential, true, nature the soul is a rational entity that loves wisdom – and that, if we put together the *Phaedrus* passage (our passage 2 earlier) with this one, will be the ultimate answer to Socrates' question, "whether I am actually a beast more complex and more violent than Typhon, or both a tamer and a simpler creature, sharing some divine and un-Typhonic portion by nature." He really is "a tamer and a simpler creature," as is each of us. But that then means that our *selves* – despite the introduction of irrational soul-parts, whose desires are not directed towards the good[28] – are identical with our *rational* self.[29] And finding out what that is will, perhaps, still be a matter, as it was in the *Apology* and the *Charmides*, of discovering whether, and what, we know and what we don't know. But however that may be, here too there is no trace of that thoroughly modern idea that the key to life lies in identifying our *personal* histories and coming to terms with whatever it is that makes us *uniquely* ourselves.[30] For Socrates, and for Plato, what we uniquely are, or have become, remains a subject of supreme indifference, except to the extent that it may prevent us from becoming what we could be: that is, becoming as like the gods – that is, as wise – as it is possible for human beings to be.

WORKS CITED

Annas, J. "Self-knowledge in early Plato," In *Platonic Investigations* (Studies in Philosophy and the History of Philosophy, vol.13), ed. Dominic J. O'Meara. Washington, DC, 1985, pp. 111–138.

Burnyeat, M. "Socratic midwifery, Platonic inspiration," In *Essays on the Philosophy of Socrates*, ed. Hugh H. Benson (New York, 1992), pp. 53–65; repr. from *Bulletin of the Institute of Classical Studies* 24 (1977): 7–16.

Gerson, L. *Knowing Persons: A Study in Plato.* Oxford, 2003.

Irwin, T. *Plato: Gorgias.* Oxford, 1979.

Penner, T. and Rowe, C. *Plato's Lysis* (Cambridge Studies in the Dialogues of Plato). Cambridge, 2005.

Rowe, C. 2005. "What difference do Forms make for Platonic epistemology?" In *Virtue, Norms, and Objectivity*, ed. C. Gill. Oxford, 2005, pp. 215–232.

Vlastos, G. *Socrates: Ironist and Moral Philosopher.* Ithaca, 1991.

28 On the model presupposed by pre-*Republic* works, what differentiates my self from yours is just the state of our respective *beliefs*.

29 Cf. Gerson 2003.

30 Nor is there any guarantee that any of us has any true beliefs at all; none of us can count on the truth of what any of us is saying. See Section 1.

10   Socratic Ignorance

I

Socrates famously claims to lack knowledge or wisdom. This profession of ignorance seems to raise a number of questions. There is the question of what precisely he takes himself to be ignorant of – or, conversely, what categories of knowledge, if any, he takes himself to have. There is also the question of what precisely it *means* for him to profess ignorance – or, conversely, what conception of knowledge he is presupposing, such that he considers himself not to have knowledge (at least on some subjects). And there is the question of Socrates' attitude toward his supposed ignorance: is it a matter for regret or despondency, or are there, in his view, positive aspects to being in such a state? While I believe that some progress can be made, and indeed has been made, on these questions, the picture that will emerge from this discussion is not as neat and tidy as are the treatments of this topic by some other scholars.

As with all discussions of Socrates, it is necessary to begin by making clear who is meant by "Socrates." I shall be speaking almost entirely of the character Socrates as portrayed in a certain subsection of Plato's dialogues. The Socrates of Xenophon at one point disparages inquiry into the physical world, in part on the basis that neither he nor anyone else can have knowledge of such matters (*Memorabilia* 1.1.12–15). But Xenophon's Socrates never professes ignorance about the matters that he mainly discusses, and that he considers it especially important to study, namely ethical matters. It is true, as others have noted,[1] that Xenophon's Socrates regularly proceeds, as does Plato's Socrates, by the method of question and answer, as opposed to simply lecturing his interlocutors; and this method might seem natural for one who does not claim to know the truth about the

I thank Don Morrison and Mary Berk for helpful comments on a previous version of this chapter.

1   See Guthrie 1971, pp. 122–124; Waterfield 1990, pp. 16–17.

topics in question. But that connection is never made in Xenophon, and in general Xenophon's Socrates seems much more in control of the direction of the conversation – as befits someone who knows very well where he wants to take it – than does Plato's Socrates. In Plato, on the other hand, Socrates' professions of ignorance are both common and frequently important to the way in which the conversation develops. Plato's Socrates does also disclaim knowledge of physical matters, in the *Apology* (19c5–8) and also in a famous passage of the *Phaedo* (96aff.) where Plato has Socrates offer a brief intellectual autobiography. But that is not the ignorance that matters to him, because physical theory is not what matters to him; it is his ignorance of ethical matters that, as we shall see, he considers worth repeatedly highlighting.

The agreement between Xenophon and Plato on Socrates' professed ignorance of physical matters gives us some reason to think that this reflects a stance of the historical Socrates – especially since the *Phaedo* passage is explicitly presented as autobiography. But there is also some reason, despite Xenophon's silence, to think that the same is true of the professions of ethical ignorance that Plato ascribes to Socrates. A fragment of a dialogue *Alcibiades* by the Socratic author Aeschines (fr.11 Dittmar, *SSR* VI A 53) shows Socrates disclaiming any kind of skill or craft (*tekhnê*) of human improvement, and stating that he does not have knowledge of any kind of learning (*mathêma*) that he might teach someone so as to benefit him. Neither of these parallels *proves* that the real person Socrates disclaimed wisdom or knowledge in the areas in question; for all we know, one author may be picking up on a theme introduced by the other. But the traits that it is most plausible to ascribe to the real Socrates are clearly those that are attested by more than one contemporary author, and this seems to be the case here.[2] However, the question of the true characteristics of the historical Socrates is thorny at best. From now on, I leave aside the question of historicity and concentrate on Socratic ignorance as an aspect of Plato's portrait of Socrates in a certain range of dialogues.

I have twice referred to a *range* of Platonic dialogues. The profession of ignorance is not part of Plato's portrait of Socrates across the board.

---

2   Another piece of evidence might be invoked on this subject. In the *Theaetetus* Socrates describes himself as an intellectual midwife, and a line put in Socrates' mouth in the *Clouds* of Aristophanes has been thought to allude to this piece of Socratic imagery. Since, as we shall see, the midwife theme is connected with that of Socrates' professed ignorance, this might seem to amount to evidence that the professed ignorance is historically genuine. But the connection between the line in the *Clouds* and the midwifery in the *Theaetetus* is open to serious question; see Burnyeat 1977; Tarrant 1988.

The most sustained exploration of the theme of ignorance occurs in Plato's *Apology*. Aside from that, the theme arises primarily in those Platonic dialogues that are relatively short and that focus largely, if not entirely, on ethical matters, especially the definitions of ethical terms.[3] These dialogues are sometimes classified as "aporetic" – that is, as not reaching any definite conclusions; but this description does not fit the *Crito* or the *Gorgias* (or, for that matter, the *Apology* itself), even though they are naturally classified with this group on thematic grounds. This group of dialogues is also often regarded as having been composed early in Plato's career. But this picture of the chronology of Plato's dialogues – and indeed, all attempts to pin down such a chronology – have been the object of considerable suspicion in recent years. The general picture of three broad groups of dialogues – early, middle and late – with the group of dialogues under discussion belonging in the early category, still seems to me to make more psychological and philosophical sense than any other proposed chronology. However, I cannot undertake to defend this position here; nor, in fact, is it necessary for the purposes of this chapter. What we can say, regardless of chronological issues, is that these dialogues seem to form a natural group within the Platonic corpus, in virtue of their shared concerns and approaches, and of these, the profession of ignorance is one. In other dialogues, such as the *Phaedo* and the *Republic*, Socrates frequently disclaims certainty about particular difficult topics, but this does not prevent him from propounding ambitious doctrines and it does not cause him to profess any kind of general ignorance.

The one dialogue that does not fit the pattern just described is the *Theaetetus*. This dialogue is indeed aporetic, but it is about the nature of knowledge rather than about ethical matters. And here Socrates' profession of ignorance does play a significant role; indeed, it is here and here alone in Plato that we find the theme of Socrates as intellectual midwife – someone who is himself intellectually infertile, but who can inspire wisdom in others. I shall have a little to say about the *Theaetetus* toward the end, but it belongs in most respects apart from

---

3   The dialogues in this group that I shall mention are (in alphabetical order) the *Apology, Charmides, Crito, Euthydemus, Euthyphro, Gorgias, Hippas Major, Ion, Laches, Lysis, Meno*, and *Protagoras. Hippas Minor* would also typically be assigned to this group, but I will have nothing to say about it here. Book 1 of the *Republic* is often added to the list, and I shall mention it occasionally in footnotes. This has sometimes been thought to have been originally composed as a separate, freestanding dialogue, but there is no need to accept this in order to agree that, taken by itself, it shares the essential characteristics of this group.

the other dialogues in which the theme of Socratic ignorance plays a significant role.

Before we get to the details, one further issue needs to be put to rest. It has sometimes been maintained that Socrates does not seriously mean his professions of ignorance; rather, it has been thought, he is simply being ironic in claiming not to know about the subject under discussion.[4] It is true that Thrasymachus in the *Republic* accuses Socrates of irony in refusing to answer questions (337a4–7). It is also true that Socrates frequently adopts an ironical pose (for example, of mock admiration) toward those who do claim to know about certain subjects. But there is no reason to believe that Socrates does not mean what he says when he professes ignorance of some topic. Such irony would only have a point in a dialectical context in which Socrates was, for whatever reasons, playing with his interlocutor. However, as was noted a moment ago, the work in which the theme of Socratic ignorance is most fully explored is the *Apology*; but in the *Apology*, except for a brief exchange with Meletus that is irrelevant to the current issue, there are no interlocutors – Socrates simply addresses the jury. More than once in the *Apology*, Socrates even describes his own inner reflections about his ignorance (21b2–5, d2–6).[5] Unless we are to understand Socrates in the *Apology* as engaging in a comprehensive pattern of deception about his own motives and activities – an interpretation that has absolutely no basis in Plato's text – we cannot avoid reading these professions of ignorance as sincere. But if they are sincere in the *Apology*, there would need to be considerable evidence for us not to read them as sincere in related dialogues as well; and there is none. I take it, then, that Socrates is portrayed by Plato as really believing that he is ignorant; the question now is what that is supposed to amount to, and what he thinks about this state of affairs.

2

I begin with the *Apology*. Socrates is often said to have announced in this dialogue that he knew that he knew nothing – that is, presumably, nothing *else* besides this one thing. This reading goes back to antiquity. Arcesilaus, the head of the Academy who first took that institution in a sceptical direction, is said to have claimed to improve on Socrates; whereas Socrates professed to know that he knew nothing, Arcesilaus did not even take himself to have this one piece of knowledge that

---

4   See, e.g., Gulley 1968.
5   As noted by Vlastos 1994, p. 42. For the importance of the *Apology* in discrediting claims of irony in this context see also, e.g., Taylor 1998, p. 44.

Socrates permitted himself (Cicero, *Academica* 1.45). But this is not what Socrates says. When confronted with the oracle proclaiming him the wisest person of all, Socrates' initial reaction is indeed one of incredulity. But what he actually says is that he is well aware of not being at all *wise* (*sophos*, 21b4–5) – not of possessing no knowledge whatsoever beyond this one item. After examining the pretensions to wisdom of a number of other people, he qualifies this stance – as, indeed, he always expected he would have to (since the god issuing the oracle could hardly be lying or mistaken); it turns out that he does have a certain kind of wisdom – "human wisdom" (20d8) – as opposed to some form of higher wisdom such as the gods have or these other people claimed to have. Now, this lesser, "human" wisdom is said to consist not in knowing nothing else at all, but in knowing nothing *valuable* (*kalon k'agathon*, 21d4 – literally, "fine and good") and in seeing that one is "worth nothing" (*oudenos axios*, 23b3) when it comes to wisdom. There is, then, no real change of mind here; Socrates simply comes to understand what the oracle actually meant. The wisdom that he discovers that he possesses simply consists in the recognition that he lacks wisdom of any more exalted kind.[6] Yet the way in which he phrases this clearly allows for a distinction between two categories of knowledge; the possibility is open that there are certain kinds of things that Socrates does take himself to know, but does not consider valuable, and a certain other kind of knowledge that he would consider valuable if he had it, but that he does not – for now, at any rate – take himself to have. The question, then, is whether we can find a clear way of drawing the distinction that he seems to permit.

The *Apology* itself offers a few clues in this direction. First, there is one kind of knowledge that Socrates concedes is possessed by a certain group – this is the knowledge belonging to the practitioners of skills or crafts such as carpentry or horse training. However, while this kind of knowledge is not, in his view "worth nothing" – he expects to find that the craftsmen know "many fine things" (*polla kai kala*, 22d2), and discovers that he was right – it is clearly not included within the type of knowledge that he considers truly valuable. For their possession of this kind of knowledge is outweighed, in his opinion, by their ignorance (but pretension to knowledge) about other things of the greatest importance

6   Benson 2000 rightly insists on this point. However, from the fact that Socrates understands his human wisdom "to reside solely in his recognition of his ignorance" (p. 170), it does not follow that he cannot, consistently with this recognition, lay claim to knowledge of various kinds; such knowledge would not be *part* of his human wisdom, but nor would it be incompatible with it.

(22d-e); on balance he takes himself to be wiser than they are, despite his not possessing any craft knowledge, given his recognition of his lack of wisdom about these really important matters. And the beginnings of an answer are also available in the *Apology* about what this really important knowledge might be. He says that he regularly criticizes those who rank trivial matters above those worth the most (*pleistou axia*, 30a1); and what he specifically accuses these people of neglecting is ensuring that their souls are in the best possible shape (29e1–3, 30b1–2). This, in turn, is what he himself attempts to persuade them to do. He also describes this task as that of trying to get them to care about being as good and wise (*phronimôtatos*) as possible (36c7), and as discussing virtue (*aretê*) with them and testing them about this and other things (38a3–5). Virtue and the state of one's soul, then, are the most important matters for Socrates. So it is presumably some kind of knowledge or wisdom in this area, some kind of ethical knowledge or wisdom, that is the truly valuable variety he takes himself and everyone else to lack.

Yet even in the *Apology*, as has often been remarked,[7] Socrates apparently takes himself to know a few ethical truths. In considering the penalties that he might propose for himself as alternatives to the death penalty proposed by his accuser Meletus, he says that it would be absurd for him to choose some penalty that he knows very well to be a bad thing in preference to death, of which he is not sure whether it is good or bad (37b5–8). And earlier, on a somewhat similar topic, he says that he does not know what the afterlife is like, but that he does know it is bad and shameful to do injustice and to disobey one's superior, whether god or human (29b2–9). Neither of these remarks is very specific as it stands, but both can easily be made more specific by attending to the context. The possible penalties that Socrates rejects include imprisonment and exile, and the injustice and disobedience that he is refusing to engage in is that of ignoring the mission that he takes the god to have assigned him. Socrates does not, then, take himself to lack all ethical knowledge. What, then, is the special kind of ethical knowledge of which he takes himself to be currently ignorant, and that he regards as so valuable?

Here the resources of the *Apology* run out, and we must begin the delicate business of supplementing the *Apology*'s picture with ideas suggested elsewhere. Other dialogues besides the *Apology* suggest a similar combination of knowledge, including some ethical knowledge, and ignorance of certain other, really important ethical matters. In the *Euthydemus*, for example, Socrates is actually asked whether he knows anything; he answers that of course he does know many things, but small or insignificant things (*smikra ge*, 293b8). In the same dialogue

---

7   See, e.g., Vlastos 1994, p. 43; Brickhouse and Smith 2000, p. 103.

he professes a piece of ethical knowledge: that the good are not unjust (296e8). Again, in the *Gorgias* Socrates tells us that the captain of a ship knows how to bring passengers safely across the sea, but cannot tell whether he has thereby done them a favor; for if one's body, or still worse, one's soul is in irredeemably bad shape, it is surely better to have drowned at sea than to have made a safe crossing. Expanding on this, he says that the captain "knows that it is better for a bad person not to be alive," since such a person necessarily lives badly (512b1–2). In presenting the matter this way, Socrates clearly implies that he too knows what the captain knows.[8] However, just a couple of pages earlier there is also a disclaimer of knowledge.

This particular disclaimer is worth careful inspection. Socrates has been arguing that one is worse off doing injustice than suffering it. Summing up this discussion, he asserts that this conclusion is held down "with arguments of iron and adamant" (509a1–2), and that, at least in his experience, no one has attempted to refute them without looking ridiculous. Yet in the very same passage he says "I do not know how these things are" (a5, cf. 506a3–4). How can this unequivocal profession of ignorance coexist with an almost unequivocal expression of confidence in the conclusion just attained?

A plausible recent answer lays stress on the words "how these things are."[9] What Socrates takes himself to lack, according to this account, is a *general understanding* of the subject just discussed. He may be very confident – perhaps even justifiably so – of the fact that one is worse off doing injustice than suffering it. But he does not take himself to possess an account of the nature of justice and injustice in general, which would allow him to fit this result into a broader framework and fully see *why* it must hold as it seems to do. If this is correct, it might well be imagined that one could have knowledge of many things, and even some ethical knowledge, and still lack this favored kind of general understanding.

Part of what makes this a plausible answer is that it connects nicely with Socrates' concerns in a number of the other short, ethically oriented dialogues. As is well known, these dialogues are characteristically concerned with what has been referred to as the "What is F-ness?" question – that is, with providing a definition of, or an account specifying the

---

8   As emphasized by Vlastos 1994, p. 47.
9   Here I follow the interpretation of Brickhouse and Smith 2000, p. 108–109. However, I part from Brickhouse and Smith when they speak of different *types* of knowledge, "ordinary" and "expert" knowledge; for reasons given in the next section, I prefer to speak of different subject-matters that Socrates does and does not know about. In this respect, my account is closer to that of Lesher 1987.

nature of, some ethical property. The properties in question are most often virtues – courage in the *Laches*, temperance in the *Charmides*, piety in the *Euthyphro*, virtue in general in the *Meno* – but they sometimes include other ethically or evaluatively relevant qualities such as friendship in the *Lysis* and fineness (*to kalon*) in the *Hippias Major*. Two points here are important. First, Socrates typically expresses ignorance of the nature of these things, and this professed ignorance is not dispelled in the course of the dialogue. Second, Socrates gives numerous indications that knowledge of the nature of these things, if one had it, would be exceptionally valuable. Taken together, these two points suggest that knowledge of the nature of the virtues and other related qualities is, or is at least a prime example of, the wisdom or truly valuable knowledge that Socrates disclaims in the *Apology*. The first point is easily documented; all of the dialogues just mentioned include remarks by Socrates to the effect that he does not know the answer to the "What is F-ness?" question under discussion – and these remarks occur at various different points in the dialogues, including at the end.[10] The second point, however, is less obvious, and will take a little more explanation.

What would be the value in knowing the definitions of the virtues? An answer is suggested in the *Euthyphro*. Socrates presses Euthyphro to tell him what piety is. After Euthyphro's initial failure to give him an answer of the kind he is looking for, he reiterates his demand, and adds something about what he will gain if he comes to know what the answer is: "So that by looking at it [i.e. at the characteristic, whatever it is, that makes all pious actions pious] and using it as a model, I may say that whichever of the things you or someone else does that is like this is pious, and that whichever of them that is not like this is not pious" (6e4–6). The idea seems to be that knowledge of the nature of piety will give one a systematic and reliable guide to which actions are pious and which are not. And there seems to be no reason why this picture should not be generalized, so that knowledge of the natures of all the virtues, and perhaps of virtue in general as well, would give one a systematic and reliable guide to how to live one's life in general.

---

10   *Laches* 200e2–5; *Charmides* 165b5-c1; *Euthyphro* 5a3-b7, 11b1–5, e2–4, 14b8-c6, 15c11-e2 (these passages do not explicitly claim ignorance of what piety is, but, as Benson 2000, p. 173, puts it, "Definitional ignorance concerning piety is clearly implied by Socrates' complexly ironic wish to become Euthyphro's pupil and learn from him what piety is"); *Meno* 71a1-b8, 80d1–3, 100b4–6; *Lysis* 223b4–8; *Hippias Major* 286c8-e2, 304d6-e3. We may add Book 1 of the *Republic*, on justice; see 337d3–4, e4–5 and (at the end of the book) 354b9-c3.

Some related but more pessimistic points appear in other dialogues. The burden of these is that *unless* we know the answer to the "What is F-ness?" question, our knowledge of the subject under discussion will be extremely defective, or even non-existent. Socrates clearly implies some such point at the beginning of the *Hippias Major* in introducing the question "What is fineness?" He apparently equates knowing *what fineness is* with knowing *what things are fine* (and what things are the opposite) (286c8-d2); the implication is that we are not able to say what things are fine without having a definition of fineness. And the same idea is quite explicit at the end of the dialogue, after they have failed to find a satisfactory definition of fineness; Socrates imagines himself being reproached for thinking that he can distinguish fine speeches (or other things) from those that are not fine, without knowing what fineness is (304d8-e2).[11] Similarly, at the end of the *Lysis* (223b4-8) Socrates says that he and his interlocutors have made fools of themselves, seeing that they think they are each others' friends, yet they have been unable to discover what a friend is; the point is clearly that only in light of knowledge of the definition of a friend would assertions as to who is whose friend be secure.[12] And at the beginning of the *Meno*, Socrates answers Meno's impatient question as to whether virtue is teachable by saying that he cannot possibly tell in advance of knowing what virtue is. Here the point is explicitly generalized: one does not know the qualities of a thing in advance of knowing what it is (71b1-8). And later in the dialogue (including at the end, 100b4-6), the failure to discover what virtue is is several times referred to by Socrates as the reason why they have failed to find an acceptable answer to the question whether it can be taught.

Two different principles seem to be in operation here. The principle behind the remarks in the *Lysis* and *Hippias Major* seems to be that if one fails to know what F-ness is, one fails to know what things are and are not F. The *Meno*, on the other hand, seems to presuppose the

11   Brickhouse and Smith 1994, pp. 46–47, claim that the view stated here is compatible with Socrates' having knowledge of individual cases of fineness. But the challenge is "How will you know who devised a speech, *or any other action*, finely or not, being ignorant of the fine?" I do not see how the italicized phrase, which they do not discuss, allows for individual exceptions.

12   Brickhouse and Smith 2000, p. 116, downplay the significance of this passage, saying that it reports "someone else's reaction to his ... inability to provide a definition." However, while the passage does imagine the reaction of other people (Lysis's and Menexenus's attendants and brothers, who have come to bring them home), this imagined reaction is clearly endorsed by Socrates himself.

principle that if one fails to know what F-ness is, one fails to know what features belong to F-ness. These two principles have sometimes been combined into a single principle known as the Priority of Definition thesis – namely, that if one fails to know what F-ness is, one fails to know anything about F-ness. It is a matter of considerable debate how widespread the Priority of Definition thesis, or either of its components, is in the dialogues with which we are concerned.[13] But whether we focus on that thesis (which holds that knowledge of what F-ness is is *necessary* for knowing what things are and are not F, or what features belong to F-ness), or whether we focus on the position suggested in the *Euthyphro* (where knowledge of what F-ness is is held to be *sufficient* for reliably spotting instances of F things), the vital importance of knowledge of definitions, in Socrates' eyes, is clear; on either view, such knowledge really does make a massive difference to one's grasp of the ethical realm in general – and therefore, surely (to return to a theme from the *Apology*), to the state of one's soul.

However, if we focus on the *Euthyphro*'s suggestion – which could, of course, easily be held in conjunction with the Priority of Definition thesis[14] – we can see especially clearly why knowledge of ethical definitions might be thought of as giving us a *systematic understanding* of the ethical realm, and why such systematic understanding would be what, as the *Gorgias* seems to suggest, Socrates took himself to lack. This is already perhaps suggested by the very notion of knowing what something is. But if knowing what F-ness is is regarded as furnishing one with a quite general ability to discern what things are and are not F, the idea that definitions give one an overall grasp of an entire subject-matter seems all the more attractive. As some scholars have emphasized,[15] knowledge of ethical definitions, on this conception, would amount to the kind of comprehensive body of (generally practical) knowledge designated by the term *tekhnê*. This term is regularly translated as "skill," "craft," or "expertise," but it is the last of these that is perhaps most relevant in this context. In the *Gorgias*, Socrates claims even to be a practitioner of "political" *tekhnê* (521d6–8). This is unusual, and (in view of the *Gorgias*'s disclaimers of knowledge) cannot be taken to mean that he has actually mastered this expertise, as

---

13   For opposing positions, see Benson 2000, ch. 6 and Chapter 8 of this volume; Brickhouse and Smith 1994, chapter 2.3, 2000, ch. 3.2. Brickhouse and Smith 1994, p. 52, concede that the second principle is present in the *Meno*, but they argue against any attempts to attribute to Socrates the first principle.

14   It could be, but, as I argue in the next section, there is no good reason to suppose that, in this dialogue, it is.

15   On this, see especially Woodruff 1990.

opposed to being on the road to acquiring it. But it is not hard to see the aspiration toward a *tekhnê* in ethics as present in other dialogues as well – especially given the common use in these dialogues of analogies drawn from recognized *tekhnai* of the day. In any case, it is this kind of knowledge, I suggest, that Socrates means to disclaim, that he devotes his life to trying to acquire, and that he thinks would make all the difference in the world to him if he had it. The *Apology*, with which we began, does not actually say this. But Socrates does say it in other dialogues that seem clearly to be related to the *Apology*, and it is at the very least tempting to combine the resources of these various dialogues so as to yield a single, composite picture. Whether this picture is internally consistent, or consistent with other things said in these dialogues, is another question. The next two sections take up issues in that area.

3

One difficulty is no doubt already apparent. If one takes seriously the Priority of Definition thesis, and one does not take oneself to be in possession of any ethical definitions, how can one think one is in a position to claim any ethical knowledge whatever? We might try to explain this by minimizing the significance of Socrates' claims to ethical knowledge; perhaps he is simply speaking loosely, and really means to claim nothing stronger than true belief.[16] But this would be unconvincing. It is true that explicit claims to knowledge about ethical matters by Socrates in these dialogues are relatively rare, and there are indeed passages (such as the "iron and adamant" passage quoted earlier from the *Gorgias*) in which he claims very strong confidence about something without explicitly claiming knowledge. But the passages in which he claims ethical knowledge in the *Apology*, at least, are not plausibly explained away as the product of mere carelessness. In both of these passages (29b2–9, 37b5–8), as we saw in the previous section, Socrates is very deliberately contrasting something that he does not know with something that he does know; it would make no sense for him to do this if, in the latter cases, he did not really mean "know."

Another possibility, the effect of which would be much the same, is that Plato intends a distinction in the strength or the character of the knowledge-claims avowed and disavowed. On this view, Socrates means something much stronger by "know" when he denies knowledge of ethical definitions than when he claims knowledge of particular ethical truths or of mundane non-ethical topics. One version of this view has it that the knowledge that he disclaims is *certainty*, whereas

16 See, e.g., Benson 2000, ch. 10.2.

the knowledge that he claims is merely the kind of confidence that can be produced by the results of a typical Socratic examination.[17] Another version draws the distinction in terms of expert versus non-expert knowledge: expert knowledge is the systematically integrated kind necessary for a *tekhnê*, whereas non-expert knowledge meets looser (but unspecified) standards.[18] The trouble with either proposal is that Plato gives no indication of wishing to multiply senses of the various words translated by "know," or to draw any systematic distinction between the words for "know" used in these two different contexts. In fact, we can go further. Given that the same terms are used in the two contexts, it would be very surprising if Socrates did mean something different in one context from what he meant in the other.[19] For a recurring assumption in these dialogues (*Euthyphro* 5d1–5, 6d10-e6; *Laches* 191e9–192b8; *Meno* c6-d1), and indeed in other Platonic dialogues (e.g., *Republic* 435a5–8), is that each word stands for some single characteristic; for the sense of "know" to be bifurcated in either of the ways suggested, with no explicit indication in the dialogues, would be a startling contradiction of an apparently stable semantic principle.

It seems better, therefore, to draw the needed distinction not in terms of distinct senses of "know," but in the manner done in the previous section – that is, in terms of distinct subject-matters for the knowledge that Socrates claims and the knowledge that he disclaims. And here, as we have seen, the notion of a *tekhnê* does seem relevant. The knowledge that Socrates disavows is best understood as knowledge of ethical definitions, which would amount to a *tekhnê* of how to live one's life; this knowledge, if he had it, would, he thinks, be much more valuable than the knowledge he takes himself to have – but because of what it is about, not because of some heightened conception of knowledge itself as applied to these cases. There is, in fact, very little attention given, in the dialogues with which we are mainly concerned, to the nature of knowledge itself (unlike the *Theaetetus*, where this is the central topic); Socrates seems simply to assume that what it means to claim knowledge of something is not itself in need of clarification.[20] But if this is so, a distinction between levels or conceptions of knowledge would again be very unexpected.

---

17   So Vlastos 1994.
18   So Woodruff 1990, Brickhouse and Smith 2000, chapter 3.
19   As was pointed out in Lesher 1987, p. 278.
20   Hence there is no precise answer to one of the questions I mentioned at the outset – what Socrates means in professing ignorance and disclaiming knowledge. The question may be one that naturally occurs to us, but it is not one that Socrates himself focuses on.

It has been objected that Socrates does in fact employ different standards for attributing knowledge in different cases, and that this can only be made sense of by means of a distinction between more and less stringent notions of knowledge.[21] But the only evidence offered for this assertion is that at the beginning of the *Euthyphro*, Socrates refuses to accept Euthyphro's claim to know about piety and impiety unless he can supply a definition of each – whereas his own claims to knowledge are issued without his having satisfied any such demand. However, there is a ready explanation of this that again appeals to the subject-matter rather than to distinctions among levels of knowledge. Euthyphro is prosecuting his father for murder, and thus has the potential to be responsible for his father's own death. Standard Greek values of the time would regard this action as an outrageous violation of one's duties to one's parents,[22] duties that were understood as being religiously based; thus the usual reaction to Euthyphro's action would be that it was dangerously impious. For Euthyphro to be sure of the correctness of *this* action clearly indicates that he regards himself as having an exceptional expertise on the subject of piety and impiety. It is only natural, therefore, that Socrates would expect him to be able to deliver definitions of each; Euthyphro is indeed being held to a higher standard, but not because of any vacillation in what Socrates takes knowledge itself to consist in.

The question, then, still remains: how is one to reconcile Socrates' apparent adherence to the two components of the Priority of Definition thesis, and his admission that he lacks knowledge of any ethical definitions, with his occasional willingness to claim ethical knowledge? A third possible way of handling the difficulty is to question how far Socrates' adherence to the Priority of Definition thesis extends in these dialogues. In the previous section, I mentioned three dialogues (*Lysis, Hippias Major,* and *Meno*) in which one or the other component of it seems to be present. But the *Euthyphro*, as we saw, contains instead the point – which is rather different from either of those components – that knowledge of the nature of piety (etc.) is *sufficient* for knowledge of what actions are pious (etc.); although this is certainly compatible with the Priority of Definition thesis, neither it nor anything else in the *Euthyphro* implies it. This has been challenged on the grounds that a commitment to the Priority of Definition thesis would best explain why Socrates is so insistent that finding a definition of piety is the way to discover what actions are pious;[23] but this is highly questionable. One

---

21   Woodruff 1990, p. 64.
22   Especially since the person his father allegedly killed was himself a
     murderer.
23   Benson 2000, p. 124.

might very well think, as indeed Socrates clearly implies, that finding a definition of piety is the only way in which to discover *systematically and comprehensively* what actions are pious – a discovery whose value I tried to bring out in the previous section – without thinking that one cannot know of *any* actions that they are pious without knowing the definition. Socrates does not explain *how* one might come to know of individual actions that they are pious – or, in general, how one can know the various things that he does claim to know – in the absence of the relevant definition. But there is no reason why we should expect him to have an answer to this question; despite his concern with the issue of knowledge and ignorance, nothing in the dialogues where Socrates claims knowledge suggests that he regards every single claim to knowledge as in need of explanation or justification.

We have, then, no need and no basis for concluding that Socrates is committed to the Priority of Definition thesis in the *Euthyphro*. And this seems to open the way for the view that Socrates' commitment to the thesis, or to one or the other component of it, varies from one dialogue to another. Three dialogues show a clear commitment to one or the other component of the thesis, and in these dialogues, a claim to know particular truths in the absence of knowledge of the relevant definitions would be inconsistent; however, the *Lysis*, *Hippias Major*, and *Meno* do not appear to contain any such unguarded claims (on Socrates' part – his interlocutors are another matter). By contrast, the dialogues in which Socrates does claim to know various things do not appear to show a commitment to either part of the Priority of Definition thesis. The dialogues that I have already mentioned as containing knowledge claims by Socrates are the *Apology*, the *Euthydemus*, and the *Gorgias*; others might add the *Crito* (48a5–7), the *Ion* (532d8–e4), and the *Protagoras* (357d7–e1).[24] But of these, only the *Protagoras* and the *Gorgias* have ever been thought to include a reference to the Priority of Definition thesis, and the case is not strong for either one.[25] In the *Protagoras*, Socrates cautions Hippocrates that, if he does not know what a sophist is, he does not know whether a sophist is good or bad (312c1–4); and in the *Gorgias*, he refuses to answer whether rhetoric is

---

24   Benson 2000, ch. 10.2.2, collects all the relevant passages. Besides those just cited, Benson mentions *Republic* 351a5–6; as noted earlier (n.3), Book 1 of the *Republic* can be considered as belonging to our group of dialogues, at least for some purposes. However, the knowledge referred to in this passage is merely conditional knowledge – that *if* justice is wisdom and virtue, then injustice is ignorance – not a piece of free standing ethical knowledge.

25   Benson 2000, ch. 6.7; again, the argument is of the "inference to the best explanation" type.

admirable until he has answered what it is (462c10-d2, 463c3–6). But it is entirely to be expected that Socrates, of all people, would be cautious about making any overall evaluation of something – which is what is at issue in both cases – without knowing what it is; to attribute *this* reluctance to Socrates in no way requires us to suppose that he does not take himself to know *anything* about sophists or rhetoric respectively.

The apparent problem of inconsistency with which we began this section is only a real problem if we insist on treating all the dialogues in our group as attributing to Socrates a single, monolithic position. But there is no reason to do this. One possible explanation of the discrepancy just pointed to is that Plato's thought is developing in the course of these dialogues; perhaps the Priority of Definition thesis is a product of reflection on the enterprise of seeking definitions, and represents a later stage in his thinking than do the dialogues in which it does not appear. This may be supported by the fact that it is the *Meno*, which has often been regarded as marking a transition from Plato's early to his middle dialogues, in which the thesis, or at least one component of it, receives its most explicit articulation.

However, we need not resort to any such developmental hypotheses. Another possibility is simply that Plato depicts Socrates as exploring different, and incompatible, ideas in different dialogues. While the general focus on ethical questions and especially on definitions is consistent throughout this group of dialogues, we have no reason to expect that there is some single and consistent set of theses to which he is shown as adhering throughout all of them. If we can find echoes and common themes among dialogues – as I have been doing in most of this chapter – that is certainly of interest. But there may well be limits to this approach. Socrates does not, after all, expound theories in these dialogues, but engages in discussion – in most cases very tentative and inconclusive discussion. Even if he were a real person with real psychological states, there would be no reason to assume, given the nature of these discussions, that he would not try out distinct and even inconsistent ideas in different discussions. But the Socrates we are talking about here is a literary creation of Plato's (whatever his relation to the historical person Socrates), and Plato could have all sorts of reasons, philosophical and otherwise, for depicting him as trying out these distinct and even inconsistent ideas. There does not appear to be a conflict within any given dialogue on the points with which we have been occupied in this section; but taken as a group, they do appear to point in opposite directions concerning the priority of definition and the possession of knowledge in the absence of definitions. However, there need not be anything extraordinary or untoward about this.

4

In addition to professing ignorance, Socrates in the *Apology* famously claims that "the unexamined life is not worth living" (38a5–6), and this opens up the possibility of another kind of conflict.[26] One would expect, from the evidence presented so far, that Socrates would be overwhelmingly eager to acquire the systematic ethical knowledge that he regards as so valuable. One might also expect that he would at least periodically express disappointment or even despair at his repeated failure to find the ethical knowledge that he purports to be seeking. Now, one can occasionally find remarks along these lines. The most striking is perhaps the suggestion at the end of the *Hippias Major* that, in the absence of knowledge of a definition (in this case, of fineness), one is no better off alive than dead (304e2–3). This comment is put in the mouth of someone else; but this imaginary "someone else," who has played a prominent role in much of the dialogue, is a kind of alter ego of Socrates himself. Socrates may not endorse this sentiment in its full strength – his reaction to it is somewhat joking – but he clearly does not entirely reject it either. However, such remarks are few and far between. Most of the time, Socrates seems quite content in the pursuit of his inquiries, despite the repeated failure of himself and his interlocutors. Indeed, he regularly seems to regard the pursuit as itself a valuable and worthwhile exercise, regardless of the prospects for actually finding the definitions he is seeking. This is generally implicit in the cheerful attitude with which he approaches his inquiries, but it receives explicit expression in the *Apology*; the famous quotation is part of this, but there is more.

Socrates has a considerable amount to say in the *Apology* about the value he confers on others, and on the city in general, by his constant attempts through discussion to get people to care about the state of their souls. Indeed, his conception of the mission imposed on him by the oracle is expanded so as to include this. Despite having come to understand, through many instances, that the oracle is correct, in the sense explained, in saying that he is wiser than everyone else, he continues to look for someone wiser than himself; but this activity also comes to include a protreptic component – once he has found, as he always does, that his interlocutor is *not* wiser. He actually says at one point that there is "no greater good for the city" (30a5–6) than his service to the god. But, still more strikingly, he also says that there is no greater good for *himself* than to engage in this activity. Immediately before the famous remark, and in explanation of it, Socrates says that

26   For the ideas in the first part of this section, I am especially indebted to Alexander Nehamas.

"this is the greatest good for a human being, to engage in discussions every day about virtue and the other things about which you hear me discussing and examining myself and others" (38a2–5). There is no suggestion here that coming to know the *answers* to the questions being discussed would confer still greater value on the enterprise. Rather, the life of inquiry is itself apparently as good as any human life can be, irrespective of whether it yields any definite outcome; and the ignorance that Socrates freely professes is apparently no bar to the achievement of this supremely good life.

There is something deeply paradoxical about this – and in this case, I do not think that we can parcel off different strands of thinking into different dialogues. A number of dialogues attempt to discover definitions of the virtues; we get a sense of the extraordinary value Socrates thinks knowledge of such definitions would have, and yet for the most part, in these same dialogues, he is relentlessly upbeat in the face of consistent failure to achieve such knowledge. And in the *Apology*, he proclaims that he lives the best possible kind of human life, and yet his admitted ignorance, which is apparently not incompatible with the achievement of this best life, is said to consist in not knowing anything valuable or worthwhile. What, one might ask, is so good about this endless search for understanding of the virtues, if the actual attainment of answers to one's questions would make no difference to the quality of one's life – since it is already as good as it can be? And if this is the case, what is the force of the claim that the knowledge that one currently lacks, but is seeking to attain, is (by contrast with the insignificant knowledge that one has) valuable or worthwhile?

Furthermore, if the knowledge that Socrates lacks is, as I have argued, systematic and comprehensive ethical knowledge, how can he have so clear a conception of what the best human life consists in as to announce that he has attained it? There is no formal contradiction here, since he does not claim to *know* that his is the best kind of human life. However, he resolutely asserts that this is so, in the face of the jurors' presumed scepticism (38a7–8). And in any case, conceptions of the best human life (as opposed, say, to particular ethical claims) are the kind of thing one might expect particularly to require some form of systematic ethical understanding in order to be reliably judged. So not only is Socrates apparently happy to be in a state of ignorance; he is so *confident* about the merits of being in this state as to cast doubt on the claim of ignorance itself. To attempt to dispel or at least mitigate these paradoxes, one might point to Socrates' labeling of the wisdom that he has as "human wisdom"; by contrast, one might say, the wisdom that he lacks must be superhuman, and so perhaps it would be hopeless for anyone to expect ever to attain it. But that would again force us to ask why Socrates devotes his whole life to trying to attain it, why this necessarily fruitless inquiry itself constitutes the best possible human life, and how he can be so sure that this is the case.

This tension – a tension in Socrates' attitude towards his own self-confessed ignorance, but also in how seriously he seems to take the confession of ignorance itself – does not seem to me to have been adequately recognized in most recent scholarship.[27] It does not appear to be eliminable, and it raises deep questions about the nature of the Socratic enterprise. It is, of course, perfectly possible that Plato was aware of this tension, and thought it would be valuable, for a variety of reasons, for the reader to reflect upon it. It is also possible that he devised the positive methodologies and doctrines expounded in, for example, the *Republic* or the *Phaedo* in part as a way to move forward from the curious hermeneutical impasse in which the dialogues with which we have been concerned seem to leave us. But in any case, Socrates' status as a seeker of knowledge in these dialogues is mysterious. There is reason to see him as deeply concerned to achieve a certain kind of knowledge, and quite serious and sincere in saying that he lacks it; but it also looks as if he regards his life as not admitting of any improvement whether he succeeds in achieving it or not – and his confidence about this state of affairs is itself hard to distinguish from a pretension to knowledge.

One other dialogue suggests a positive function for Socratic ignorance, but it is notable that this is much more modest than anything suggested in the last few paragraphs. In the *Theaetetus*, as noted earlier, Socrates compares himself to a midwife (which he claims to have been his mother's profession). By ancient Greek convention, the midwife is herself no longer capable of conceiving, but she delivers the offspring of others. Similarly, Socrates claims to be barren of wisdom himself, but capable of eliciting the wisdom of others. The theme is introduced early in the dialogue and is later alluded to numerous times, including at the end. Here, Socrates ascribes to himself a vital role in inquiry despite, or perhaps even because of, his ignorance. But there is no suggestion here that he is wiser than everyone else. On the contrary, the midwife analogy clearly suggests that the other people with whom he interacts are capable, with his guidance, of expressing truths that he himself could not have expressed on his own. It is not suggested that this invariably happens, and in fact in the *Theaetetus* itself it does not happen; the dialogue as a whole, to continue the analogy, is a series of miscarriages. But the analogy clearly holds out the hope of a successful delivery – and clearly implies that this would be preferable to a miscarriage. Nonetheless, the negative results of the dialogue are said to be

27   A notable exception is Nehamas 1998, especially ch. 3.

themselves of some value (210b4-d1). The lessons of this discussion will be useful if Theaetetus ever engages in future discussions of the same topic; and even if he never comes to an understanding of the topic (in this case, the nature of knowledge itself), he will be gentler and less obnoxious to his companions as a result of not thinking that he knows what he does not know.

Clearly there is some connection with themes from the *Apology*. But the role played by Socrates' ignorance, and by other people's recognition of their ignorance, is far less momentous than what the *Apology* suggested. In particular, there is no indication that the life of inquiry, *irrespective of its success*, is the best possible life. The *Theaetetus*, as noted earlier, does not naturally belong with the group of dialogues with which we have been mainly concerned; although it is aporetic, it is about knowledge rather than any of the virtues, and it employs much more sophisticated theoretical apparatus, developed at far greater length, than is contained in any of them. By the same token, despite the thematic importance of Socratic ignorance in the *Theaetetus*, the tension with regard to Socrates' attitude toward his ignorance that we have identified in other dialogues seems not to be present in this one.

5

Socrates is certainly not the only Greek thinker, or even the first, to express doubts about our prospects for achieving knowledge. Of those Greek thinkers who did so, some (the later Pyrrhonists) called themselves sceptics, and others are routinely referred to in modern scholarship as sceptics, whether in something like the Pyrrhonist sense or in some other sense current in modern philosophy. Is Plato's Socrates, in the dialogues in which he professes ignorance, a sceptic?[28]

Nowadays, a sceptic is usually thought of as someone who denies the possibility of knowledge (either globally, or in some specific domain). In the ancient world, by contrast, a sceptic was a person who refrained from beliefs, and suspended judgement. There is no good reason to call Socrates a sceptic in either of these senses. For him merely to declare that *he* lacks knowledge of a certain kind is not at all the same as declaring that knowledge is unobtainable; and, as was noted in the previous section, his unremitting search for knowledge of the kind he considered really important would make little sense if he thought there was no prospect at all of obtaining it. Nor is Socrates plausibly seen as a practitioner of suspension of judgement; on the contrary, his professed lack of significant ethical knowledge does not prevent him from being

28 I have discussed this question in more detail in Bett 2006.

(subjectively, at any rate) very sure of a number of things – including some very extraordinary and controversial things, such as (in the *Gorgias*) that a person is worse off doing wrong than suffering it, or (in the *Apology*) that a better man (such as he takes himself to be) cannot be harmed by a worse one (30c8-d5). The fact is that Socrates' profession of ignorance is one element in a unique concatenation of views and attitudes, including an extreme confidence about a number of things and even, at times, a claim to know certain things; if one looks at the whole package, one will not be inclined to label Socrates a sceptic in any ordinary sense of the term.

There is, nevertheless, one way in which Socrates' attitude is similar to that of the Greek sceptics. The word "sceptic" derives from the Greek word for "inquire" (*skeptesthai*), and the Pyrrhonist sceptics described themselves as perennial inquirers, by contrast with those who thought either that they had discovered the truth or that the truth was undiscoverable. They also recommended this life of perennial "inquiry" over the lives of non-sceptics. Now in the *Apology*, as we saw, Socrates also portrays himself as engaged in a life of constant inquiry, and he also claims that this life is itself the best possible human life; to that extent the sceptics' attitude is reminiscent of his. But there are still some notable differences. For one thing, the sceptics would not claim that their life was the *best possible* life, since that would itself be a dogmatic statement; they would simply claim to prefer it themselves, and would invite others to see whether they agreed.[29] For another, the reason why the sceptics preferred their life over others was because, they claimed, the holding of definite beliefs led to many kinds of emotional turmoil; their goal was freedom from worry (*ataraxia*), and they took freedom from belief to be the surest route to it. Such intellectual and practical disengagement would surely have been anathema to Socrates.

However, to deny that Socrates was a sceptic is not to deny that later sceptics could reasonably have found elements in Plato's portrait of Socrates, including his profession of ignorance, congenial to their own outlook. I mentioned Arcesilaus's reaction to Socrates' profession of ignorance. Even if, as I suggested, Arcesilaus misreads the letter of what Socrates says, it is not surprising, given the precedent provided by Socrates in the aporetic dialogues, that Plato's Academy would have moved in a sceptical direction a few generations after its founding.[30] But then, as has often been noted, virtually all the Hellenistic schools claimed, with some reason, to find in Socrates a significant

29 For some of the difficulties encountered by sceptics in this area, see Bett 2003.
30 On this topic, see further Annas 1994; Shields 1994.

precedent;[31] that is one measure of how many-faceted, and therefore also how elusive and puzzling, he turns out to be. I hope to have made clear that in this respect, the theme of Socratic ignorance is no exception.

WORKS CITED

Annas, J. "Plato the Skeptic." In *The Socratic Movement*, ed. P.A. Vander Waerdt. Ithaca, 1994, pp. 309–341.

Benson, H. *Socratic Wisdom: The Model of Knowledge in Plato's Early Dialogues*. New York, 2000.

Bett, R. "Rationality and Happiness in the Greek Skeptical Traditions." In *Rationality and Happiness: From the Ancients to the Early Medievals*, eds. J. Yu and J. J. E. Gracia. Rochester, NY, 2003, pp. 109–134.

Bett, R. "Socrates and Skepticism." In *A Companion to Socrates*, eds. S. Ahbel-Rappe and R. Kamtekar. Malden, MA/Oxford, 2006, pp. 299–316.

Brickhouse, T., and Smith, N. *Plato's Socrates*. New York, 1994.

Brickhouse, T., and Smith, N. *The Philosophy of Socrates*. Boulder, CO, 2000.

Burnyeat, M. "Socratic Midwifery, Platonic Inspiration." *Bulletin of the Institute of Classical Studies* 24 (1977): 7–16.

Dittmar, H. *Aischines von Sphettos: Studien zur Literaturgeschichte der Sokratiker*. Berlin, 1912.

Gulley, N. *The Philosophy of Socrates*. London, 1968.

Guthrie, W. K. C. *Socrates*. Cambridge, 1971.

Lesher, J. H. "Socrates' Disavowal of Knowledge." *JHP* 25 (1987): 275–288.

Long, A. A. "Socrates in Hellenistic Philosophy." *CQ* 38 (1988): 150–171.

Nehamas, A. *The Art of Living: Socratic Reflections from Plato to Foucault*. Berkeley/Los Angeles/London, 1998.

Shields, C. "Socrates among the Skeptics." In *The Socratic Movement*, ed. P.A. Vander Waerdt. Ithaca, 1994, pp. 341–366.

Tarrant, H. "Midwifery and the Clouds." *CQ* 38 (1988): 116–122.

Taylor, C. C. W. *Socrates*. Oxford, 1998.

Vlastos, G. "Socrates' Disavowal of Knowledge." In G. Vlastos, *Socratic Studies*, ed. M. Burnyeat. Cambridge, 1994, pp. 39–66. (Original version published 1985.)

Waterfield, R. "Introduction." In Xenophon, *Conversations of Socrates*, trans. H. Tredennick and R. Waterfield and edited with new material by R. Waterfield. Harmondsworth, 1990.

Woodruff, P. "Plato's Early Theory of Knowledge." In *Epistemology*, ed. S Everson. Cambridge, 1990. Rpt. in *The Philosophy of Socrates*, ed. H. Benson. New York, 1992, pp. 86–106.

FURTHER BIBLIOGRAPHY

Benson, H., ed. *The Philosophy of Socrates*. New York, 1992.

Beversluis, J. "Does Socrates Commit the Socratic Fallacy?" *American Philosophical Quaterly* 24 (1987): 211–223. Repr. in *The Philosophy of Socrates*, ed. H. Benson. New York, 1992.

Burnyeat, M. "Examples in Epistemology: Socrates, Theaetetus and G.E. Moore." *Philosophy* 52 (1977): 381–398.

31   On this, see especially Long 1988.

Geach, P. T. "Plato's *Euthyphro*: An Analysis and Commentary." *The Monist* 50 (1966): 369–382.

Irwin, T. H. *Plato's Moral Theory: The Early and Middle Dialogues*. New York, 1977.

Irwin, T. H. *Plato's Ethics*. New York, 1995.

Kraut, R. "The Examined Life." In *A Companion to Socrates*, eds. S. Ahbel-Rappe and R. Kamtekar. Malden, MA/Oxford, 2006, pp. 228–242.

Politis, V. "*Aporia* and Searching in the Early Plato." In *Remembering Socrates: Philosophical Essays*, eds. L. Judson and V. Karasmanis. Oxford, 2006, pp. 88–109.

Santas, G. *Socrates: Philosophy in Plato's Early Dialogues*. London, 1979.

Tarrant, H. "Socratic Method and Socratic Truth." In *A Companion to Socrates*, eds. S. Ahbel-Rappe and R. Kamtekar. Malden, MA/Oxford, 2006, pp. 254–272.

Vlastos, G., ed. *The Philosophy of Socrates: A Collection of Critical Essays*. Garden City, NY, 1971.

Vlastos, G. *Socrates: Ironist and Moral Philosopher*. Ithaca, 1991.

Vlastos, G., ed. M. Burnyeat. *Socratic Studies*. Cambridge, 1994.

Weiss, R. "Socrates: Seeker or Preacher?" In *A Companion to Socrates*, eds. S. Ahbel-Rappe and R. Kamtekar. Malden, MA/Oxford, 2006, pp. 243–253.

11 Reconsidering Socratic Irony

INTRODUCTION

On his way to court, as a defendant against the charges – of not wor-
shipping the city's gods; introducing new gods; and corrupting the
youth – which will lead to his conviction and execution, Socrates meets
his officious Athenian compatriot Euthyphro. Euthyphro is bringing a
prosecution of his own father for murder, an action that most Athenians
would regard with horror as violating the divine obligation of filial piety.
To Euthyphro's boast that he has knowledge of the divine, and of piety
and impiety, Socrates replies: "It is indeed most important, my admirable Euthyphro, that I should become your pupil, and as regards this
indictment challenge Meletus [one of the three citizen-prosecutors of
Socrates]...and say to him...that...I have become your pupil." (*Euphr.*
5a-b)

You may find it hard to believe that Socrates is sincere in his admiring desire to become Euthyphro's pupil. This is a prime instance of
the Socratic speeches in Plato's dialogues which many readers have
found it necessary, or desirable, to interpret as spoken ironically: in
this case, implying that the smug Euthyphro actually has nothing to
teach Socrates. For 'irony' is, in a representative definition, "saying
something with the intent that the message is understood as conveying
the opposite or an otherwise different meaning"[1] – although we must

For comments and advice on various aspects of this chapter, I thank Alex Long,
Donald Morrison, Emile Perreau-Saussine, Quentin Skinner, Karl Steven, and
Michael Trapp. I am also grateful for permission to see and cite pre-publication
proofs of an article by M. M. McCabe (McCabe 2006) in a volume edited by
Trapp. That volume is the first of two based on Trapp's 2002 King's College
London conference on 'The Uses of Socrates,' where I presented a paper that was
an antecedent both to Lane 2006 (this chapter's companion piece) and to this
chapter. (My eventual publication in the Trapp conference volumes examined a
different topic, Socrates in twentieth-century America: see Lane 2007.)

1   This definition is adapted from that in Opsomer 1998, p. 14. Compare
     the definitions in Brown 1993, I, "irony" q.v., among which figures "the

immediately ask, understood by whom? Sometimes, by an addressee who is expected to understand the irony, in which case irony can be a graceful and playful way of conveying meaning. At other times, when the addressee is expected to be obtuse to it and the irony is intended for reception by a third party, irony can be a mocking and even savage way of discriminating between those capable of understanding one's true meaning and those who are blind to it.[2]

Which is the case with Euthyphro? Most readers who discern Socratic irony toward Euthyphro assume that it falls into the latter camp: Euthyphro is not meant to understand it, the irony is meant to be understood only by Plato's reader. (In other dialogues, irony may be perceived as directed toward the understanding of a third character, such as the young boy Clinias in the *Euthydemus*, for whose benefit Socrates interrogates and comments on the destructive antics of two brother sophists.) The same is true of the candidate cases of Socratic irony that abound in the *Hippias Major*, where Socrates hails Hippias as "fine and wise" (281a1) and remarks on Hippias' success as a sophist:

That is what it is like to be truly wise, Hippias, a man of complete accomplishments: in private you are able to make a lot of money from young people (and to give still greater benefits to those from whom you take it); while in public you are able to provide your own city with good service (as is proper for one who expects not to be despised, but admired by ordinary people). (281b5-c3)

The implication that Hippias is "truly wise"; the suggestion that making money from teaching, which Socrates himself refused to do (*Ap.* 19d9-e1, 31c), is part of such wisdom; and the taking of "ordinary people" as the standard for admiration, are all aspects of Socrates' interaction with Hippias which can seem to demand to be read ironically. To these sorts of cases of 'Socratic irony' (we will discuss later why the conversations with Hippias and Euthyphro yield the most egregious

---

expression of meaning using language that normally expresses the opposite." While both these definitions focus on speech, we must expand them to include the possibility of other cases of ironic action (speech itself, of course, being a form of action).

2   In tragic or dramatic irony, the relevant intent is that of the author rather than that of the characters; knowledge imparted to or expected of the audience enables them to see that the characters' words and actions will in fact bring about a different meaning from that which they intend, although the characters do not themselves intend (to convey) this in what they do or say. This type of irony is relevant to the question of whether Plato is ironic as an author, a question (distinct from our present topic of whether Socrates is ironic as a character) that cannot be pursued here; for discussion of it, see Griswold 2002; Nehamas 1998.

candidates) can be added the broader stance associated with Socrates in the *Apology*, of the disavowal of knowledge. The idea that this should be read ironically had supporters already in the ancient world. Yet what it means to attribute irony to Socrates has been interpreted in many ways. When speaking ironically, does he (or anyone) simply mean the opposite of what his words literally say – so that, if he is ironically disavowing knowledge of human excellence and virtue (*Ap.* 20c3, 21b), he is really claiming to possess it? Or is irony a more mysterious and potentially all-embracing aspect of one's character, making the ironist essentially opaque? Further, is Socratic irony an occasional and incidental phenomenon, or does it permeate his very being and function as essential to his philosophy?

That Socrates is ironic is something that many people who know little else about Socrates believe. If this belief is rooted in ancient texts, they are likely to be thinking of Plato's and Aristotle's portraits of Socrates rather than those of Aristophanes and Xenophon, for two reasons. First, irony is absent from the features of Socrates lampooned in Aristophanes' *Clouds* (which treats him rather as an oblivious pedant), and while incidences of irony have been detected in Xenophon's writings about Socrates,[3] it has not been central to most interpretations of those writings or the portrait of Socrates they create. Second, neither Xenophon nor Aristophanes ever uses about Socrates the Greek word *eirōneia*, which is the only Greek term (sometimes) translatable as 'irony.' By contrast, Plato and Aristotle both use this word and its cognates about Socrates (though I argue later that it is not in fact translatable as "irony" in Plato), and this has played a key part in the formation of the tradition of "Socratic irony." The remainder of this Introduction will discuss Aristotle's role in forming this tradition, and those influenced by him, while Plato's Socratic dialogues will be the focus of the rest of the chapter.

Aristotle confines his central accounts of *eirōneia* to the special case of self-deprecation, conceived as the opposite extreme to boastfulness, both in contrast to a mean of truthfulness. As he explains:

The way self-deprecating people [*eirōnes*] understate themselves makes their character appear more attractive, since they seem to do it from a desire to avoid pompousness, and not for the sake of profit; most of all it is things that bring

---

3   Vlastos accepted in 1987 (quoted here in a further version of 1991) what he had earlier denied, that "there is an authentic streak of irony in Xenophon's depiction of Socrates" (1991, p. 31). But he insisted that in Xenophon – in contrast to Plato – this "contribute[s] nothing to the elucidation of Socrates' philosophy" (1991, p. 31). Morrison 1987 accepts and expands the list of Socratic ironies in Xenophon, while contending that irony is not philosophically central to either Xenophon's or Plato's portraits of Socrates.

repute that these people too disclaim, as indeed Socrates used to do. (*EN* 4.7, 1127b23–26)[4]

When Aristotle's *eirōneia* was transliterated into Latin as *ironia* by Cicero, it brought with it and reinforced this view of Socratic irony as modestly self-deprecating understatement. Aristotle's analysis has also been retrojected into Plato by many readers, including some of the ancient commentators, who thus came to take the characters in Plato who accuse Socrates of *eirōneia* as calling Socrates a self-deprecating ironist.[5]

An influential first-century imperial Roman rhetorician, Quintilian, significantly expanded upon the rhetorical tradition of *eirōneia* begun by Aristotle and continued by Cicero.[6] In his terms, the uses of irony that we have been so far discussing, in which ironic delivery changes the meaning of the words used (as in the examples from the *Hippias Major* earlier, where by calling Hippias wise for making money from his knowledge, Socrates might be taken to mean the opposite), is only one kind of irony – which Quintilian called a "trope," a rhetorical move in which the meaning of the words used changes (*Inst.*8.6.54–55). There was also, Quintilian posited, a broader and deeper rhetorical move of irony in the sense of a 'figure,' in which the meaning of the words used does not change, but the global effect is transparently that of a different meaning (*Inst.* 9.2.44–46) – for example, Jonathan Swift's *A Modest Proposal* of 1729, in which the point of any given sentence proposing that the English eat the Irish is not to convey the opposite meaning, but rather the work as a whole is intended ironically as a commentary on the hardheartedness of English attitudes. The figure may arise as the result of repeated use of the trope. However, whereas for the trope, "although it says something different from what it means, it does not *pretend* something different," by contrast for the figure, "the pretence involves the whole meaning" (*Inst.* 9.2.45, 46). And in the latter context, Quintilian remarked that "a whole life may be held to illustrate Irony,

---

4   Translation from Rowe and Broadie 2002.
5   Sedley 2002 shows that the Platonist commentators did not agree as to whether Socrates was in fact ironic; though this was the dominant tradition, most adhering to it were careful to distinguish the sorts of speakers toward whom Socrates used irony from those toward whom he did not. He also points out the need for a set of rules to enable us to decide whether or not a passage is to be read as ironic (41), and the fact that any such rules or assumptions will be imbued with specific interpretative prejudices (52).
6   In this brief chapter, it is not possible to touch on all of the intervening developments, such as the work of Theophrastus, on which see Diggle 2004 and Lane 2006, pp. 53–54, n.12.

as was thought of Socrates" (*Inst.9.2.46*).[7] This consolidated a new view of Socratic irony, as involving not simply the occasional self-deprecating remark, but a whole way of life, a global outlook and mode of interaction. This view would resonate powerfully in the portraits of Socrates and of irony produced by many of the medieval and Renaissance authors so deeply marked by Quintilian and other ancient authors (Knox 1989), and would be revived in the Romantic portrait of Socratic irony as the most important and deepest feature of Socrates' character.

As a result of Aristotle, Cicero, and Quintilian above all, a rich and internally diverse philosophical tradition of considering Socrates as ironic was born, a tradition that has often departed from these anchors to develop more general interpretations of what Socratic irony means. Some have read Socrates as globally ironic,[8] while others have insisted on delineating moments in which he is ironic from moments in which he is not.[9] Some have celebrated irony as one of the attractive and philosophically valuable aspects of Socrates;[10] others have taken it to be an index of both his achievement and his limitations;[11] still others have attacked it as a sign of his failure and the misconception of his project as a whole.[12]

PURPOSE AND AUDIENCE: DIVERSE VIEWS

Those holding such divergent attitudes on the value of Socratic irony divide in particular with respect to its purpose (why does he do it?) and its audience (who is able to understand it?). The dominant view of its

7   Translation from Russell 2001.
8   For a global account of irony as a species of consciousness, see Jankélévitch 1964, and for the Romantic irony that influenced him, see the brief discussion in Szlezák 1999, ch. 21. More recently a global account is defended in analytical terms by McCabe 2006.
9   For an interesting position distinguishing moments of "conditional irony" from moments of "reverse irony" in Plato's Socrates, see Vasiliou 1998 and 2002; I criticize aspects of this position however in Lane 2006, p. 50, n. 4.
10 For a modern argument that shares the view that irony and dialectic are closely related for Socrates, but evaluates both positively in line with the Quintilianic view of irony as part of the Socratic way of life, see Schaerer 1941: "Socrate pratique l'ironie comme le sceptique pratique le doute, et le Chrétien la charité" (196).
11 For all their differences, Hegel and Kierkegaard both saw Socratic irony as an achievement that was also starkly limited in its value and potential. Hegel saw the limitations as related to Socrates' place in the evolving dialectic of spirit, while Kierkegaard saw them rather as marking the limits of reason and the need for faith.
12 Socratic irony is interpreted as part of Socrates' failure as a teacher by Gagarin 1977, p. 36 and passim.

purpose, operating within an Aristotelian framework, has been shaped by Cicero, who in *De Oratore* (2.269–270) described irony as "serious play" (*severe ludas*), implying that it can go beyond self-deprecation, while retaining the playful and self-presentational purpose of Aristotle's conception. In his *Brutus* (292), the character Atticus says that *ironia* is used by Socrates in the books of Plato, Xenophon, and Aeschines, when "discussing wisdom, [he chooses to] deny it to himself and to attribute it playfully (*in ludentem*) to those who make pretensions to it."[13] On this account, the playful purpose of irony is tied to its transparency to its audience. The audience is meant to perceive the ironist's modesty and playfulness, and to perceive them as such. No one is intrinsically excluded from grasping this playful irony. Many writers associated with the Enlightenment movements of the eighteenth century adopted a similar approach in praising Socrates for his rhetorical adeptness in using irony.[14]

An opposing account of Socratic irony sees its purpose to lie in the philosopher's response to an inherently divided audience, of whom some are intended to perceive the irony while others are not. This is the view, for example, of Leo Strauss: "Irony is ... the noble dissimulation of one's worth, of one's superiority. We may say, it is the humanity peculiar to the superior man: he spares the feelings of his inferiors by not displaying his superiority" (Strauss 1964, p. 51). Irony for Strauss is not a rhetorical pleasantry; it is a political necessity. As he contended: "If irony is essentially related to the fact that there is a natural order of rank among men, it follows that irony consists in speaking differently to different kinds of people" (Strauss 1964, p. 51). Concomitantly, its intended audience is necessarily esoteric, limited to the philosophical few. For Strauss, Socratic irony is not just a graceful manner of speech. It is designed to make its true meaning accessible only to some, and to shield this meaning from those who are capable of understanding neither the irony nor the philosophy which it protects.[15]

13   The Latin text is from the Oxford Classical Texts, Cic. *Rhet.* vol. II, which uses a different paragraph scheme (in which this passage is 85). The translation is from Hendrickson 1971.

14   Fitzpatrick 1992, pp. 180–181, discusses the way that eighteenth-century philosophers who valued Socratic rationality dealt with elements in his persona that did not fit with that image. In particular, Socrates' talk of "knowing nothing" was understood by some to be irony, treated as a matter of elegance and modesty merely; but attackers of the Enlightenment such as Johann Georg Hamann took his confession of ignorance seriously, seeing it as a forerunner leading the way to Christian faith (Lane 2001, p. 22).

15   Allan Bloom broadly follows Strauss, arguing that one must read Socrates' political proposals in the *Republic* as involving irony (Bloom 1968, p. 411),

Whereas for Strauss irony functions to protect philosophy, for other writers irony was to be seen as inherent in philosophy – or the special case of Socratic philosophy – itself.[16] Again, for some, the purpose of such philosophical irony was to be celebrated, as being rooted in and revealing the intrinsically critical nature of philosophy. In his *Critical Fragments* of 1797, which was a paradoxical sort of founding text for German Romanticism, Friedrich Schlegel praised a thorough-going literary and philosophical irony as the exaltation of the subjectivity of the ego.[17] For others, however, the essentially ironic nature of Socratic thought was a sign of its limitations. In his *Lectures on the History of Philosophy* of 1805–06, G. W. F. Hegel criticized Schlegel for inflating Socratic irony too far, holding in contrast that it had limited but positive value in bringing out the actual subjective ideas of his interlocutors and so in "bringing the Notion into consciousness" (Hegel 1892, p. 400). Yet he held that this same irony was also a mark of the incompleteness of the Socratic stance, which needed a further and more positive integration into the dialectic.

The incompleteness of Socratic irony was stressed also by Søren Kierkegaard, both in his 1841 dissertation *The Concept of Irony with Continual Reference to Socrates* and elsewhere. But he rejected Hegel's progressivist resolution of it, arguing instead that the limits of Socratic irony testified to the need for a leap into religious faith (Kierkegaard 1989, 1998). Kierkegaard summed up the contrast thus: Socrates' "irony was not the instrument he used in the service of the idea [as Hegel had claimed]; irony was his position – more he did not have" (Kierkegaard 1989, p. 214). For their successor Nietzsche in his most scathing moods at the beginning and end of his writing career (which included throughout a wide spectrum of views of Socrates and Plato), irony was a sign of Socrates' knowledge of his own intellectual failure: a sign of the fear of pessimism in the 1872 *Birth of Tragedy* (1999, p. 4 [§1]), and arguably "an expression of plebeian *ressentiment*" in the 1888 *Twilight of the Idols* (2005, p. 164 [§7]).

Finally, there has been an influential debate as to the interpersonal as well as the philosophical significance of Socratic irony. The dominant view today is that Socratic irony serves at least some dialectical or argumentative purpose: for example, one historical dictionary defines

by which "the perfect city is revealed to be a perfect impossibility" (Bloom 1968, p. 409). See also Clay 2000.

16 That irony is inherent in Socratic philosophy is argued by Alexander Nehamas (1998) and Gregory Vlastos (1991), both discussed later.

17 See, for example, the *Critical Fragment* number 108, translated in Schlegel 1971, pp. 155–6, arguing that Socratic irony was the only literary attitude that could afford the Romantics total literary freedom.

it as "the pretence of ignorance practiced by Socrates as a step towards confuting an adversary" (Brown 1993, I, 'irony', q.v.) and as "a pose of ignorance by which a skilful questioner exposes the emptiness of the answerer's claims to knowledge" (Brown 1993, II, 'Socratic irony', q.v.). An innovative variant is to contend that by concealing Socrates' own beliefs, his irony serves to "tell us about the structure of wisdom, but not about its content," since each person must arrive at wisdom for him or herself (McCabe 2006, p. 31). But there has always been opposition to the line that Socratic irony is somehow pedagogically fruitful. The counter-claim that it is evasive and irresponsible in relation to what the philosopher owes his audience goes back to the Epicurean attack on Socrates.

Unlike the Sceptics and Stoics, the Epicureans declined either to idealize Socrates or to take him as the symbolic fount of their tradition, and a major reason for this refusal was his use of irony instead of direct philosophical instruction (Steven, unpublished manuscript). Cicero, an avowed anti-Epicurean, commented on Epicurus's approach to Socrates in the continuation of the *Brutus* passage quoted earlier:

Thus Socrates in the pages of Plato praises to the skies Protagoras, Hippias, Prodicus, Gorgias and the rest, while representing himself as without knowledge of anything and a mere ignoramus. This somehow fits his character, and I cannot agree with Epicurus who censures it. (*Brut.* 292)[18]

The Epicureans focused their criticisms on the claim that Socratic irony is pedagogically sterile: if Socrates had something to say, he should have said it, rather than hiding behind a veil of irony. To this sort of criticism, others have added the denunciation of Socratic irony as emotionally harmful, for example as humiliating for his interlocutors (Tarnopolsky 2004). This again has a precursor in Nietzsche: "dialectics lets you act like a tyrant; you humiliate the people you defeat" (2005: §7, p. 164).

The most developed view of this kind is that of Alexander Nehamas, for whom irony, including Socratic irony, is inherently wounding, asserting the superiority of the ironist and so akin to the cruder forms of sarcasm and mockery (1998, pp. 49, 58). The purpose of Socratic irony is however for Nehamas inherently mysterious. Because, as he points out, irony need not entail that one believes the opposite of what one says, but only imply that one believes something other than what one says, irony does not necessarily convey meaning. It does not make meaning transparent (1998, pp. 56, 67–69). (To borrow an example from the Wikipedia discussion of irony, the comedian Sacha Baron Cohen does not mean the

18   For text and translation, see n.13.

opposite of what he says when, in the guise of would-be rapper Ali G, he asks an informant from the National Poison Information Center, "Does Class A drugs absolutely guarantee that they is [sic] better quality?")[19] The ironist is, or can choose to be, mysterious, and this is how Plato portrays Socrates, perhaps (so Nehamas surmises) because he did not understand Socrates himself.

As if this contradictory range of interpretations of Socratic irony were not challenging enough, the task of judging these interpretations of Socratic irony is further complicated by the difficulty of proving any case of irony at all. Irony lies necessarily and notoriously in the eye of the beholder. In the absence of "irony marks" akin to question and exclamation marks (which the French pundit Jean Paul urged printers to invent), the question of whether or not Socrates is ironic in any given instance, or globally, is a matter of interpretation. There is no fixed point in the interpretation of Socratic irony. To understand Socratic irony requires us to discuss its complex history in the interpretation of the figure of Socrates and the texts of (above all) Plato; to disentangle aspects of it which are often confused; and ultimately to take a stand on the question of whether, where, and how Socratic irony arises.

In other words, the most fundamental fact about irony is its inherent elusiveness.[20] This makes it impossible to assemble a set of incontestable cases of Socratic irony for the reader to inspect. Debates about the meaning of Socratic irony cannot be distinguished from debates about what is to count as Socratic irony at all.[21] Therefore this chapter will now proceed by considering three distinct elements that have been incorporated into analyses of Socratic irony: (1) Socratic self-deprecation both as apparently exemplified in Plato and as described by Aristotle and Cicero; (2) the meaning of *eirōneia* as ascribed by Platonic characters to Socrates; (3) the apparent use by Plato's Socrates of what has been

---

19 http://en.wikipedia.org/wiki/Irony, last checked 28 November 2006.

20 As remarked in Morrison, 2007, p. 241: "There is no algorithm, no amount of brute force philology that will demonstrate the presence of irony to someone who doesn't see it, or the reverse."

21 Indeed, these questions are also linked to the debate over who is meant by "Socrates": the historical Socrates; the Socrates of the "early" Platonic dialogues, if these can be securely identified and their "Socrates" discovered to be significantly different from the "Socrates" of other dialogues, as argued by Vlastos 1991, pp. 45–80; the Socrates of both Plato and Xenophon; and so on. This chapter focuses on Socrates in Plato, as noted earlier, and does not assume any hard and fast lines between the Socrates of some of the dialogues and those of others, while acknowledging certain commonalities in the dialogues structured by the elenchus compared to those which are not, a position defended in Lane 2000.

called "ironic praise." In a sceptical spirit, it will be argued that none of these straightforwardly or necessarily supports the imputation of irony to Socrates.

SELF-DEPRECATION

The Aristotelian view that Socrates' irony, including his ironic praise of others, is closely related to his self-deprecation, has been extremely influential. Insofar as readers judge Socrates to be intellectually superior to his interlocutors, his praise of them as having something to teach him can seem to be ironically deprecating his own knowledge. When Socrates flatters others as having something to teach him, he seems thereby ironically to diminish his own claims to merit, since the irony-minded reader is likely to assume that it is far more probable that he has something to teach them. Yet does praising someone else always imply deprecating oneself?[22] Not necessarily: imagine the woman who wins her Wimbledon singles final one day congratulating the man who wins his the next. But when what is praised is someone's knowledge, the praise might seem to imply that one has something to learn from him, and thereby to imply a diminishment or deprecation of one's own merits.

A similar phenomenon occurs when in dialogues that he narrates, Socrates sometimes describes himself as having strong emotional reactions to his interlocutors. For example, he recounts that he was "afraid" of Thrasymachus's outburst and was only able to reply "trembling a little" (*Rep.*336d6, e1–2). Again, such reactions need not necessarily imply self-deprecation; they might flow naturally from the conversation's emotional currents without implying that Socrates has no basis for a considered response. But many readers find it difficult not to read such narrative asides ironically, as they find it difficult to believe that Socrates is really wrongfooted by such challenges.

Of course, Socrates in the *Apology* does explicitly make at least one self-deprecating claim: he recounts that when he heard that the Delphic oracle had proclaimed that no one was wiser than he, he averred that "I am very conscious that I am not wise at all" (*Ap.* 21b). Despite other instances in the dialogues where Socrates does claim to know something (e.g., *Ap.* 29b6–7: "I know that it is wicked and shameful to do wrong, to disobey one's superior, be he god or man"; *Smp.* 177d7–8: "the

---

22 Clay 2000, pp. 93–94, puts the issue well – "either he [Socrates] is insincere and, as a consequence, boastful and conceited; or he can be taken as sincere and as truly doubtful of his own knowledge" – although confounding *eirōneia* defined as "self-deprecation" with "irony."

only thing I say I understand is the art of love"), the self-deprecation of the *Apology* has been widely viewed as a disavowal of knowledge: a claim to know that he does not know. Interpreted as such, should it be read ironically?

The disavowal of knowledge certainly can seem to involve an ironic reversal. If Socrates alone knows that he does not know, then there is a sense in which he is (ironically) asserting himself to be wise, concomitant with a sense in which he (literally) asserting himself to be ignorant: "[T]he wise man who does not know that he knows is ignorant; and the ignorant man who knows only that he knows nothing is wise" (Mackenzie [now McCabe] 1988, p. 350).[23] Yet the question of how to understand the disavowal of knowledge, no less than the question of irony, requires settling a global interpretative framework for the dialogues. To take the disavowal of knowledge literally engenders one sort of reading of the dialogues, in which Socrates appears as the sceptical inquirer, genuinely seeking knowledge through elenchtic examination and collaborative inquiry. To take it ironically engenders a very different sort of reading, in which Socrates appears as the sphinx who does not share his knowledge, presenting an ironic face for reasons of his (or rather, Plato's) own; or in which his concealment of his knowledge serves some specific purpose, whether benign or sinister. What is certain is that the concept of Socratic irony offers no firm foundation for deciding between these different interpretations.

DOES *EIRŌNEIA* MEAN "IRONY"?

Yet surely, the reader may wish to object, there is a firm foundation for imputing irony to Plato's Socrates: the use of the term *eirōneia* about Socrates in the dialogues. Socrates is called an *eirōn* by three characters in Plato, all of them complicated and challenging figures: Callicles, the aggressive acolyte of power through rhetoric in the *Gorgias*; Thrasymachus, the belligerent defender of the claim that justice serves the interest of the stronger in the *Republic*; and Alcibiades, the glamorous and dangerous Athenian politician shown in the *Symposium* as a youth who has partially fallen under Socrates' spell. And in Plato's *Apology* (37e5–38a1), Socrates himself imagines that if he were to pursue a certain course of action, he would be called an *eirōn* by the Athenians. Does he mean that the Athenians would think him an "ironist," and do Callicles, Thrasymachus, and Alcibiades mean to say that he is? To answer this question fully would require detailed textual study of each

23   For further discussion of the disavowal of knowledge, see Woodruff 1990 and Irwin 1995, ch.2.

passage, but in brief, the view defended here is that they (and he) do not.[24] To see why not, we need to review the changing fortunes of the word *eirōneia*.

There are two fixed points in the career of this word. We have seen that from Aristotle's fourth-century treatment of *eirōneia* as self-deprecation grew a rhetorical tradition in which *eirōneia* could at least sometimes mean "irony." Equally, scholars agree that two generations earlier, in the fifth-century comic playwright Aristophanes, *eirōneia* and its cognates certainly did not mean "irony," but were rather best translated by a phrase like "concealing by feigning."[25] These two meanings must not be confounded: they are essentially different. The purpose of an Aristophanic *eirōn* (and hereinafter the Greek word will be restricted to its Aristophanic meaning) is to *conceal* what is not said, while the purpose of an ironist is to *convey* what is not said (to some audience, though not necessarily the addressee of the ironic statement). Thus someone accused of being an *eirōn* is accused of deception, whereas someone considered an ironist cannot be universally perceived as deceptive.[26] The ironist may simply be conveying his meaning in a playful and modest way, and even if he is concealing his meaning from those too obtuse to understand the irony, it could not be irony if there were not some audience who were intended to understand it as such.

Between Aristophanes and Aristotle, the only extant Greek author to speak of *eirōneia* is Plato. Debate has accordingly flourished as to whether the incidences of *eirōneia* in Plato are to be read in a backward-looking Aristophanic, or a forward-looking Aristotelian, way. Gregory Vlastos (1991) initiated the contemporary debate in work first presented in a Cambridge seminar paper in 1984. Vlastos acknowledged that Plato sometimes used *eirōneia* in its Aristophanic sense of dissembling or deceiving. But he contended that in the crucial contexts of the *Gorgias* (489e1) and the *Symposium* (216e2–5, 218d6–7) – where Callicles and

---

24 For fuller argument, on which the present chapter draws, see Lane 2006.
25 The most important uses in Aristophanes are *Birds* 1211 and *Wasps* 174; there is little context to go on in interpreting *Clouds* 449. Recent editions of Aristophanes concur that these uses do not signify irony (for example, Sommerstein 1983 on *Wasps*, Dunbar 1995 on *Birds*, both ad. loc.), and in the debate initiated by Vlastos as to when *eirōneia* came to mean "irony," it is taken as common ground that it did not do so in Aristophanes.
26 A may be perceived to be an *eirōn* by B (that is, to be concealing her true meaning), when A is actually addressing herself ironically to a third party, C. While such cases are theoretically possible, Plato presents the two phenomena in distinct contexts: *eirōneia* is carefully segregated as an accusation made by a certain type of character, whereas ironic praise and self-deprecation are (when properly interpreted) addressed to a different type.

Alcibiades respectively call Socrates an *eirōn* – he was inaugurating its new meaning of "irony" and doing so in relation to Socrates. Indeed, Vlastos went further to argue that Socrates is shown in Plato to have initiated a new form of "complex irony," in which what is said both is (in one sense) and is not (in another sense) what is meant.

Vlastos's aim was to show that Socrates was not a deceiver; his strategy was to show that neither Callicles nor Alcibiades, in calling him an *eirōn*, was accusing him of being so.[27] But this strategy is flawed. The question whether Socrates is a deceiver is different from the question whether Callicles et al. believe that he is. More importantly, Vlastos's argument that Callicles and Alcibiades should be translated as calling Socrates "ironic" does not do justice to the attacking quality of Callicles' accusation of *eirōneia*, nor to the context in which Alcibiades presents himself as unveiling something deceptively hidden in Socrates (contrasted with the communicative intention of irony). In accusing Socrates of *eirōneia*, both Callicles and Alcibiades, and indeed Thrasymachus as well, deploy a rhetoric of stripping away attempted concealment that fits far better with the Aristophanic than with the Aristotelian meaning of the term. Just like Aristophanes' characters, they use *eirōneia* to mean, roughly, "concealing by feigning," in a context of implied attempted deception. In sum, the fact that some of Plato's characters call Socrates an *eirōn* gives no warrant for the claim that he is an ironist.

IRONIC PRAISE

Even if *eirōneia* should not be translated as "irony" in Plato's texts, other evidence might show that Socrates is an ironist. The alert reader of (say) the *Gorgias* may feel that Socrates is clearly shown there and elsewhere, as in the *Euthyphro* and *Hippias Major* passages with which we began, to be engaging in ironic praise (Nightingale 1995, p. 115, 119). Many readers have felt that Socrates cannot possibly mean literally the compliments he pays to many interlocutors (for example, Socrates to Callicles: "you really do have good will toward me" (*Grg.* 487d2–3)), and so have surmised that he must mean them ironically instead.[28] Before we turn to a general consideration of such ironic praise, we need to consider a special category within it: 'friendship terms of address.'

27 Vlastos 1991, pp. 24–25, allowed that Thrasymachus used the term to mean that Socrates was a deceiver, rather than to call him an ironist; but Nehamas 1998, p. 58, argued that Thrasymachus, like Callicles and Alcibiades, should be taken to be calling Socrates ironic rather than deceptive.
28 Unless otherwise noted, translations of Plato are from Cooper 1997.

FRIENDSHIP TERMS OF ADDRESS

Like many other works of Greek literature, Plato's dialogues are full of expressions such as "o marvelous one," "stranger," and so on. These are "terms of address": ranging from the use of their name in whole or part, to an age or gender relationship, to terms specifically referring to aspects of a friendship relation (to which genre "o marvelous one" belongs). In Attic, as in other ancient and modern languages, such terms are used in culturally patterned ways which indicate and police the nature of the relationships they express. (In English, think of "howdy, pardner," "my good fellow," or "hello there, stranger.") The philologist Eleanor Dickey (1996) has made a study of the way terms of address function in ancient Greek in comparison with other languages, and the results are startling for the question of Socratic irony.

Most used in Plato's dialogues are friendship terms of address – that is, apostrophizing expressions that mean literally "o wonderful one," "o marvelous one," and so on. For modern readers, it is difficult to put aside the literal meaning of such phrases, but equally difficult to accept that literal meaning. The result is a strong inclination to read Plato's friendship terms of address ironically: to assume that when Socrates (who is the greatest, but not the only, user of such terms in Plato) calls someone "o marvelous one," he is being ironic. Insofar as readers judge most of Socrates' interlocutors to be of inferior intellectual standing to him, it is all the more tempting to assume that he cannot be serious in such positive terms of address.

Yet Dickey's analysis establishes that such epithets, including in particular the friendship terms, are (with only one exception) never in Plato to be read ironically.[29] Dickey's contention is that "[friendship terms] in Plato, rather than being complimentary to the addressee, show the dominance of the speaker" (Dickey 1996, p. 117). She argues that they are genuinely used as polite terms rather than insults or ironic put-downs. However, their politeness serves to demonstrate the speaker's control of the situation in a somewhat patronizing way (Dickey 1996, pp. 122, 126). An exchange of friendship terms, such as those batted back and forth by Socrates and Callicles in the *Gorgias*, is not an indication of irony; it is rather an indication of the tussle over conversational dominance that marks the dialogue as a whole. Friendship terms of address may appear to be cases of ironic praise, but in fact they are not.

---

29 Dickey 1996, p. 143, mentions only a single instance of a friendship term used in Plato as in other authors in a "usually ironic" way: this is *sophōtate*, used five times by Socrates in Plato. But her full evidence and analysis shows how rare is such an ironic use of a friendship term in Plato.

IRONIC PRAISE OUTSIDE TERMS OF ADDRESS

Excluding friendship terms of address, then, the most striking and extensive examples of ironic praise are Socrates' interactions with people such
as Hippias and Euthyphro.[30] He repeatedly praises Hippias as "fine and
wise" (punning on the *kalon* ["fine"] which is the main subject of the
Hippias Major), and praises Euthyphro as wise ("you are younger than
I by as much as you are wiser," 12a4–5), for example. Notice that those
who are most lavishly praised in this way are those whom we might call
the "complacent smug."[31] Socrates does not engage in anything like this
level of praise with any of the young men whom he leads in conversation; he reserves it for these mature older men who are uniformly self-
important. Moreover, none of those who are addressed with such lavish
praise ever gets angry with Socrates for so addressing them.[32] Euthyphro
and Hippias seem entirely impervious to any possibility that the praise
could be ironic, accepting it as their due. While ironic praise is offered
to a number of different kinds of interlocutors, from Agathon in the
Symposium to Callicles in the *Gorgias*, the case of the complacent
smug is the most developed and striking.

Why does Socrates flatter some of his interlocutors so egregiously?
Most answers, as we shall see, invoke a pedagogical purpose of some
kind or other. There could of course be other interpretations divorced
from any pedagogical framework. For example, ironic praise could be
held to indicate that Socrates (who is implied to know Euthyphro and
Hippias well already) knows that his encounters with them are doomed
to fail. He could be laying it on so thick out of bitter despair. Or ironic
praise could indicate the "savage" nature of Plato in his disdain for his
own contemporaries and those whom he believed had misunderstood
Socrates.[33] But the dominant lines of interpretation (we will consider

---

30 On the irony in Socrates' treatment of Euthyphro, in particular 5ab, see
    West 1993.
31 Compare Nehamas 1998, p. 48: "Plato populates his work with arro-
    gant innocents." But Nehamas implies that these are the majority of the
    interlocutors, toward whom "Socrates' attitude … is … almost unfailingly
    ironic," whereas I argue here that the complacent smug are a small and
    special case, and even toward them there may be less Socratic irony than
    we tend to think.
32 Callicles at *Grg.* 489e1 might seem to be an exception to this, but I argue
    elsewhere that Callicles' anger there is directed against Socrates for (as he
    believes) deceiving him, rather than for praising him (Lane 2006, pp. 62–64).
    His anger should be understood as registering Socrates' use of friendship
    terms not as praise but as condescension (Lane 2006, pp. 64–65).
33 Morrison 1987 remarks that "in both Plato and Xenophon, Socrates is much
    more savage and ironical when dealing with professional sophists and other

three of them) share the assumption that 'ironic praise' has a pedagogical purpose – to encourage at least part of its audience to engage in Socratic dialectic – although they disagree as to which is the audience to be so encouraged and just how the ironic praise is meant to accomplish the encouraging.

On the first line of this sort of interpretation, Socrates may be thought to *intend* his interlocutors to perceive irony in his flattery, because it is the perceiving of irony that will have a salutary pedagogical effect on them. Being wounded by Socratic irony will engage the pride of the interlocutors in a desire to prove it wrong. The sting of humiliation will prompt them into wishing to pursue philosophical discussion in order either to prove their worth and the worth of their current knowledge, or in order to learn what is true in order to better themselves. In this case, the relevant audience for the irony would be the interlocutors themselves (whether or not third parties or the reader of Plato also perceive it).

A second approach would be that Socrates is indifferent to whether his interlocutors perceive the irony or not (he probably expects that they won't), but he (that is, Plato in writing his character in the dialogues) intends the *audience* – third parties present, and the Platonic reader – to perceive it. That perception itself lulls them into a false complacency about their superiority, as Nehamas suggested in connection with his interpretation of Socratic irony (1998, p. 62). On Nehamas' account, if the reader is intended to perceive the irony in Socrates' praise of Hippias, she may not only be intended simply to believe that Hippias is fatuous; she may also be tempted to place herself in an equally fatuous position in believing that she is superior to Hippias in perceiving the irony about him.

The third interpretation argues that it is the praise itself, not any irony in it, that is intended to serve a pedagogical purpose. In this case, the praise would not be meant to be perceived as ironic by the interlocutors themselves. They are meant to hear it as real praise so that they are encouraged to engage.[34] The question of whether the audience perceives irony in this or not would be irrelevant to its pedagogical purpose: third parties, and the Platonic reader, may find such praise ludicrous, but that would not matter if it served its purpose of getting the smug to engage in philosophical debate. On this view, to ask whether

strangers" (p. 10); he also remarks on Plato's "savage" temperament as contrasted with Xenophon's (p. 14).

34 Compare Vlastos 1991, pp. 138–9, in the paper "Does Socrates Cheat?" arguing that such "extra-elenctic Socratic capers" do not deceive those falsely praised because they are "already wallowing in self-deceit"; instead, he claims that such ironic praise prepares them for "painful elenctic surgery."

such praise – assuming that it is false – is therefore dishonest risks being anachronistically moralistic.[35] Socrates' overriding ethical purpose, as Plato often explains, is to prompt his readers to examine their lives and to search for wisdom. Lying is certainly prohibited in the content of the Socratic elenchus, when interlocutors are enjoined to say what they believe, but if its use is intended to encourage interlocutors to *engage* in the elenchus, then it might well be justified.[36]

A RHETORICAL READING OF 'SOCRATIC IRONY'

We have just discussed a possible function of ironic praise as pedagogical: designed to encourage interlocutors to engage. This sort of pedagogical imperative is actually also and more deeply a rhetorical one, and as ironic praise has a rhetorical function, so too do the other purported elements of Socratic irony we have been discussing. Although detecting and interpreting irony (or the absence thereof) will depend on one's global approach to a text, our disaggregation of the possible elements of Socratic irony into *eirōneia*, ironic praise (separated off from the non-ironic case of friendship terms of address), and self-deprecation has uncovered related rhetorical functions among all of these otherwise very different phenomena.

Greek dialectical encounters, like Greek erotic encounters, involved the constant negotiation of who was on top and who on bottom. This dynamic interplay of balance was difficult to maintain in a situation where one person was inviting another to engage in dialectic. The inviter is in a superior position in virtue of his control over the initiation of the encounter. But the inviter has to risk that superiority if the engagement is to be a real one involving possible defeat, while at the same time maintaining sufficient control over the encounter to ensure that the rules of dialectic are observed. Conversely, the invitee has to risk his pride and any general sense of superiority that he may have to engage in the dialectic, while at the same time maintaining sufficient pride to defend his position with spirit.

There are different possible emotional routes to achieving this dynamic balance necessary to maintain an argumentative encounter.[37]

---

35 But contrast McCabe 2006, p. 18: "for Plato logic and morality are inseparable, and I think Plato may be right."

36 Plato's most extensive discussion of lying, in which it is commended in certain contexts, is found in the *Republic*; see the discussion in Schofield 2006: pp. 284–309, and that running throughout Rosen 2005.

37 These different emotional routes are independent of the question of what pedagogical purpose, if any, that encounter might be intended to serve.

One might invoke friendship on both sides and so pursue dialectic out of good will and a mutual desire for success. One might seek to enlist the pride of the invitee by asking him to show off his ability and argumentative wares, while having to temper it sufficiently that he is willing to unbend into the dialectical exchange rather than stiffly defending an assumed position. Or one might elicit the pride of the invitee to prove himself by showing that he can do it against the inviter's challenge that he can't. The difficulty is to enlist pride on the side of entering the dialectic, while avoiding any anger that might militate against continuing the encounter. In a competitive and agonistic culture like that of ancient Athens, this was especially tricky.[38]

This framework offers a new perspective on the purported elements of Socratic irony considered earlier. Those Platonic characters who accuse Socrates of being an *eirōn* do not (if the argument made above is correct) thereby call him an ironist. They are not indicating that they feel themselves to be the victims of his superior irony; instead, they are asserting a superiority of their own. The characters who make this accusation, after all, are not the hapless ones who are unable to cope with Socratic challenges (or at least at the point that they make the accusation, they still believe themselves well able to cope). Thrasymachus, Alcibiades, and Callicles are aggressive and self-confident, seeking not only to display their own knowledge but also to unmask what they take to be Socrates' feints and manoeuvres. They believe themselves to have penetrated Socrates' disguises and ferreted out a secret that he would wish to conceal – whether this is (as for Alcibiades) Socrates' genuine philosophical knowledge and virtue, or (as for Thrasymachus) Socrates' fear that he has no knowledge that could stand up to public examination. The vector of superiority in these accusations is entirely in their favour.

Contrast the very different characters, such as Euthyphro and Hippias, on whom Socrates seems to lavish ironic praise. They are complacent and smug, believing that they have great knowledge to display, but affable in their initial attitudes to Socrates. They are more interested in displaying their own merits than in attacking his, although they wish to do so on their own terms of public rhetorical display rather than elenchtic cross-examination. These characters are also self-confident, but they are not aggressive; they are at least initially secure in their conviction of their own superiority. Here, 'ironic praise' by Socrates serves

---

38   On the competitive nature of the Athenian speech context, see Allen 2000 and Ober 1989. My emphasis on the rhetorical situation is indebted to discussion with Karl Steven of his own views of Socratic irony in relation to dialectic.

to reinforce their sense of their own superiority, while subtly reshaping it to encourage a willingness to engage with him on his terms. To the extent that the 'ironic praise' is read by them or by the Platonic reader as self-deprecating, this self-positioning as inferior also reinforces the terms on which the complacent smug are willing to enter the debate. Once interlocutors are engaged in argument, however, the task is to keep them on the right track. For this purpose, Socrates sometimes needs to assert his own superiority, which he does in part by strategically deploying the friendship terms of address which (as we saw earlier) assert and signify dominance of the conversation. The conversation will only continue to flow if people are willing simultaneously to try to demonstrate their superiority by persisting in it, and to play by the conversational rules. Maintaining this balance sometimes requires that Socrates subordinate his interlocutors in order to keep them on track.[39]

Is the praise of the complacent smug in fact ironically spoken by Socrates? That is, it is certainly praise, but is it really ironic praise? On the reading just sketched, Socrates would not be praising them with the intention that they would understand the praise as ironic: the praise is intended to take them at their own evaluation while getting them to engage in conversation on Socratic terms, an elenctic interchange that will attempt to discipline them into revealing whether or not they have the knowledge that they claim. So far as they are concerned, the praise is meant literally: Socrates is not trying to convey another meaning *to them* other than what he is literally saying. But is Socrates' praise meant ironically with reference to Plato's reader? Are these passages written to convey to the reader that Socrates does not mean literally the praise that he bestows?

To read such praise as "ironic" is to make it quite heavy-handed in its literary function. It would be the prose equivalent of nudges and winks: here is Socrates purporting to take seriously someone who claims to know, as he claimed to have devoted his life to doing in the *Apology*, while surreptitiously signalling that he already knows that this person is a buffoon or ignoramus, not to be taken seriously at all. These dialogues would be over, from the reader's point of view, before they even begin; they would be autopsies of the fatuous rather than

---

39 Similar conversational dynamics are identified by Michelini 1998, p. 52 and *passim*, but she conflates *eirōneia* with irony, and ignores the moments when Socrates must take the upper hand: "Through his eironic [sic] pose of inferiority, Socrates plays the role of and speaks for the losers in argument; and his reassuringly low posture has a protreptic effect, since it lessens the danger that beginners may abandon philosophy before they begin to learn."

attempts to test their knowledge claims and to prod them to recognize whether or not they are deficient.

It is preferable to take our bearings from the fact that the praise of the likes of Euthyphro and Hippias is concentrated almost exclusively at the outset of each dialogue. It represents Socrates taking seriously and respecting the initial claims of these people to know, while encouraging them to engage in a dialectical encounter in which their knowledge claims will be tested and perhaps exposed. Even the expression of admiration for Hippias for charging for his teaching at the beginning of the *Hippias Major* need not be ironically intended. While Socrates objects in the *Apology* to people who charge fees for teaching while lacking knowledge of virtue, he nowhere condemns charging for teaching that genuinely merits the name. The praise that has made some readers so uncomfortable is the logical concomitant of the *Apology* project: "I go around seeking out anyone, citizen or stranger, whom I think wise" (23b4–6).[40]

This is not to deny that there are any moments of irony in the dialogues involving Socrates, either of Plato or of Xenophon. But it is to deny that 'Socratic irony' is a central organizing feature of Socrates as depicted by Plato. Each of the elements commonly associated with that phenomenon can be argued to be free of irony: Socrates' self-deprecation, such as it is, is not necessarily ironic; ascriptions of *eirōneia* in Plato do not mean irony; friendship terms of address in Plato do not function ironically; and ironic praise is not, at least in some central cases, best understood as 'ironic' at all. There is certainly a rhetoric to Socratic conversational interplay, and it is worth understanding, but it need not amount to irony. And if there is no textual basis for a systematic (as

---

40 In an unpublished book manuscript tentatively titled "Conversation and Self-Sufficiency in Plato's Dialogues," Alex Long observes that at 282e9-b3 Socrates calls making money a proof of wisdom, and takes this as evidence that Socrates' praise of Hippias must be insincere, though not ironic (because Socrates is not trying to convey any hidden meaning to Hippias). Long's distinction between insincerity and irony is instructive. It is however possible to read that passage as continuing a descriptive account of what ordinary people admire and despise (see 281c2-3): from there (and arguably from the opening of the dialogue) through 283b3, Socrates is articulating the widespread view, which Hippias shares, that making money is a sign of wisdom and of the superiority of the modern sophists over their intellectual predecessors. He is taking Hippias at his own estimation prior to investigating his claim to wisdom; and for his own part, it is possible for Socrates to believe that someone truly wise would indeed make money from his wisdom and be known to be wise by that: unlike Gorgias, Prodicus and Hippias, he does not charge (and indeed does not teach) because he claims to be ignorant (see *Ap.* 19d8–20c2).

opposed to occasional and casual) imputation of Socratic irony, then those traditions positing its philosophical significance – however one evaluates its purpose, audience, and worth – need to be reconsidered.

WORKS CITED

Allen, D. S. *The World of Prometheus: The Politics of Punishing in Democratic Athens.* Princeton, 2000.

Bloom, A. *The Republic of Plato,* trans. with notes and an interpretive essay. New York, 1968.

Brown, L., ed. *New Shorter Oxford English Dictionary on historical principles,* 2 vols. Oxford, 1993.

Clay, D. *Platonic Questions: Dialogues with the Silent Philosopher.* University Park, PA, 2000.

Cooper, J. M. with D.S. Hutchinson, eds. *Plato. Complete Works.* Indianapolis and Cambridge, 1997.

Dickey, E. *Greek Forms of Address: From Herodotus to Lucian.* Oxford, 1996.

Diggle, J., ed. and trans. *Theophrastus: Characters.* Cambridge, 2004

Dunbar, Nan, ed. and trans. *Aristophanes: Birds.* Oxford, 1995.

Fitzpatrick, P. J. "The Legacy of Socrates." In *Socratic Questions: New Essays on the Philosophy of Socrates and Its Significance,* eds. B. S. Gower and M. C. Stokes. New York, 1992, pp. 153–208.

Friedländer, P. *Plato,* vol.1. *An Introduction.* Trans. H. Meyerhoff. London, 1964.

Gagarin, M. "Socrates' hybris and Alcibiades' Failure." *Phoenix* 31(1977): 22–37.

Gordon, J. *Turning Toward Philosophy: Literary Device and Dramatic Structure in Plato's Dialogues.* University Park, PA, 1991.

Gordon, J. "Against Vlastos on Complex Irony." *CQ* 46 (1996): 131–137.

Gottlieb, P. "The Complexity of Socratic Irony: A Note on Professor Vlastos' Account." *CQ* n.s. 42 (1992): 278–279.

Griswold, C.L. Jr. "Irony in the Platonic Dialogues." *Philosophy and Literature* 26 (2002): 84–106.

Hegel, G.W.F. *Hegel's Lectures on the History of Philosophy,* 3 vols., ed. and trans. E.S. Haldane, vol.1. London, 1892.

Hendrickson, G.L., trans. *Cicero, Brutus.* In Cicero V: *Brutus and Orator.* Cambridge, MA, and London, 1971.

Irwin, T. *Plato's Ethics.* New York, 1995.

Jankélévitch, V. *L'Ironie.* Paris, 1964.

Kierkegaard, S. 1998. "On My Work as an Author", In *The Point of View,* vol.22 of *Kierkegaard's Writings,* eds. and trans. H. V. Hong and E. H. Hong Princeton, 1998, pp. 1–141.

Kierkegaard, S. 1989. *The Concept of Irony with Continual Reference to Socrates* [1841], ed. and trans. H. V. Hong and E. H. Hong. Princeton, 1989.

Knox, D. *Ironia: Medieval and Renaissance Ideas on Irony.* Leiden, 1989

Lane, M. "Gadfly in God's own country: Socrates in twentieth-century America." In *Socrates in the Nineteenth and Twentieth Centuries,* ed. M. Trapp. Aldershot, 2007, 203–224.

Lane, M. "The evolution of eironeia in classical Greek texts: why Socratic eironeia is not Socratic irony." *OSAP* 31 (2006): 49–83.

Lane, M. *Plato's Progeny: How Plato and Socrates Still Captivate the Modern Mind*. London, 2001.

Lane, M. "Introduction" [to Socrates and Plato section]. In *The Cambridge History of Greek and Roman Political Thought*, eds. C. Rowe and M. Schofield. Cambridge, 2000, pp. 155–160.

Mackenzie [now McCabe], M. M. "The Virtues of Socratic Ignorance." *CQ* n.s. 38 (1988): 331–350.

McCabe, M. M. "Irony in the soul: should Plato's Socrates be sincere?" In *Socrates, from Antiquity to the Enlightenment*, ed. M.B. Trapp. Aldershot, 2006, pp. 17–32.

Michelini, A. N. "ΠΟΛΛΗ ΑΓΡΟΙΚΙΑ: Rudeness and Irony in Plato's Gorgias" *Classical Philology* 93 (1998): 50–59.

Morrison, D. 2007. "The Utopian Character of Plato's Ideal City," In *The Cambridge Companion to Plato's Republic*, ed. G.R.F. Ferrari. Cambridge, 2007, pp. 232–255.

Morrison, D. "On Professor Vlastos' Xenophon." *Ancient Philosophy* 7 (1987): 9–22.

Nehamas, A. *The Art of Living: Socratic Reflections from Plato to Foucault*. Berkeley, 1998.

Nietzsche, F. *Twilight of the Idols*. In *The Anti-Christ, Ecce Homo, Twilight of the Idols, and Other Writings*, eds. Aaron Ridley and Judith Norman, trans. Judith Norman. Cambridge, 2005.

Nietzsche, F. *The Birth of Tragedy*. In *The Birth of Tragedy and Other Writings*, eds. Raymond Geuss and Ronald Speirs, trans. Ronald Speirs. Cambridge, 1999.

Nightingale, A. W. *Genres in Dialogue: Plato and the Construct of Philosophy*. Cambridge, 1995.

Ober, J. *Mass and Elite in Democratic Athens*. Princeton, 1989.

Opsomer, J. "The Rhetoric and Pragmatics of Irony/*Eirōneia*." *Orbis* 40 (1998): 1–34.

Roochnik, D. "Socratic Ignorance as Complex Irony: A Critique of Gregory Vlastos." *Arethusa* 28 (1995): 39–52.

Rosen, S. *Plato's Republic: A Study*. New Haven and London, 2005.

Rowe, C. J., (trans. and hist. intro.) and S. Broadie (phil. intro. and commentary). *Aristotle, Nicomachean Ethics*. Oxford, 2002.

Russell, D. A. *Quintilian: The Orator's Education*. 5 vols. Cambridge, MA, 2001.

Schaerer, R. "Le mécanisme de l'ironie dans ses rapports avec la dialectique," *Revue de Métaphysique et de Morale* 48 (1941): 181–209.

Schlegel, F. *Critical Fragments*, In *Friedrich Schlegel's Lucinde and the Fragments* [first published 1797], trans. with intro. by P. Firchow. Minneapolis, 1971.

Schofield, M. *Plato: Political Philosophy*. Oxford, 2006

Sedley, D. "Socratic Irony in the Platonist Commentators." In *New Perspectives on Plato, Modern and Ancient*, eds. J. Annas and C. J. Rowe. Washington, D.C., 2002, pp. 37–57.

Sommerstein, A. H., ed. and trans. *Aristophanes*: Wasps (*The Complete Works of Aristophanes*, vol. 4). Warminster, 1983.

Steven, K. Constructing Socrates: the creation of a philosophical icon. Thesis (Ph.D) – University of Cambridge, 2007.

Strauss, L. *The City and Man*. Chicago and London, 1964

Szlezák, T. A. *Reading Plato*, trans. Graham Zanker. London and New York, 1999. (Originally published as *Platon lesen*, 1993. Stuttgart: Verlag frommann-holzboog.)

Tarnopolsky, C. "Prudes, Perverts and Tyrants: Plato and the Contemporary Politics of Shame." *Political Theory* 32 (2004): 468–494.

Vasiliou, I. "Socrates' Reverse Irony." *CQ* 52 (2002): 220–230.

Vasiliou, I. "Conditional Irony in the Socratic Dialogues." *CQ* 49 (1998): 456–472.

Vlastos, G. *Socrates: Ironist and Moral Philosopher*. Ithaca, 1991.

West, E. J. M. "An Ironic Dilemma, or Incompatible Interpretations of *Euthyphro* 5a-b." In *Plato's Dialogues: New Studies and Interpretations*, ed. G. A. Press. Lanham, MD, 1993, pp. 147–167.

Woodruff, P. "Plato's early theory of knowledge." In *Epistemology*, ed. S. Everson. Cambridge, 1990, pp. 60–84.

12 Socratic Ethics and the Socratic Psychology of Action

A Philosophical Framework

In deciding what to do, people often work with a distinction between what is good as a means (to something else) and what is good as an end. If one does x for the sake of y, then one is taking x to be good as a means and y to be good as an end. Some ends – "intermediate ends" – are themselves means to further ends. But if we are to avoid an infinite succession of means to ends – since that would never allow us to act at all[1] – some ends will have to be final ends: single good things for the sake of which everything else in the relevant teleological (means/end) progression is ultimately desired. All three of Socrates, Plato, and Aristotle take this ball and run with it. They believe not only that every deliberate action is generated by a desire for a single final end, but, more strongly, that, for humans, this final end is the same in every case: happiness.[2]

Those seeking a more usual account of Socratic ethics and psychology of action will find useful all of the works of Annas, Dodds, Kahn, McCabe, McDowell, Morrison, Price, Rudebusch, Vlastos, and especially Irwin, listed in the Works Cited section of this chapter on pp. 291–292. I learn something every time I take up one of these works. I thank Don Morrison for a truly extraordinarily helpful set of comments on earlier drafts of this chapter.

1   Aristotle *Nicomachean Ethics* 1094A20–21, deriving, no doubt, from *Lysis* 219C1-D2.
2   The good as a single end to which every deliberate action whatever will be the relevant means: *Lysis* 219C-220B, *Gorgias* 466A-468E, and *Philebus* 20C-21A, *Nicomachean Ethics* I.1094a1–22, 1097a15–34. Happiness as that single good: *Symposium* 205A1–4, *Euthydemus* 278E3–6, 282A1–7, *Meno* 88C3, *Nicomachean Ethics* 1097a34-b21. That the good is happiness can also be inferred, on a certain plausible assumption, from *Protagoras* 355A-357E. (The assumption is that pleasure, if not limited to bodily pleasure, can be tantamount to happiness: see, for example, *Republic* IX.581Cff, esp. 582E-583E, 587E, where two of the three arguments that the just person is happier, including the one Plato says is "greatest and most decisive," are actually arguments that the life of the just person is "more pleasant.") That the good is happiness in the *Republic* will be obvious from the fact that the main point of the *Republic* is to show that each individual will be happier if he or she is just than if he or she is unjust.

True, Plato and Aristotle depart from Socrates in believing that there are some motivated actions which are not deliberate actions. Both believe there are such things as "akratic" actions, generated by irrational desires (for food, drink, sex, and the like). Both suppose that these irrational desires sometimes overwhelm (out-muscle) the deliberate desire for good which would otherwise have produced a quite different action.[3] But not Socrates. Socrates holds that all motivated actions whatever are deliberate actions – that is, actions generated by the desire for a final good or end, happiness, which lies at the top of a means/end structure running all the way down to the actual action done.

The resulting Socratic psychology of action is a belief/desire theory, treating every motivated action as determined by the mutual interaction of two elements. First, we have the generalized desire for good (that is, for happiness), which is the prime mover of every human action whatever, and which in that capacity takes the form of a desire to do whatever particular action is best – that is, whatever particular action turns out to be the best means available in the circumstances to the maximum of the good, or end, of happiness. We may call this a "whatever" desire. Second, we have a belief about which particular action will best produce this good or end. This belief results from a synthesizing of the agent's current beliefs and perceptions (about that final end, about the courses of action available in one's particular circumstances, and about what

---

3   I consider an action "deliberate" if it is taken as part of a means/end hierarchy leading to the agent's good overall. I do not require that the agent be self-consciously aware of a step-by-step deliberation. Those who believe that some acts are acts of akrasia hold that akratics see their irrational desires bringing them to act contrary to that means/end hierarchy (see *Republic* 438A1–4 with 439E5–440A4, 574D5–575A8, as well as *Nicomachean Ethics* III.2.1111b16–17). The desires causing those acts are, so to speak, totally unpersuadable by any considerations of what is better (554D1–3); rather they "drag" reason around (577E2, cf *Nicomachean Ethics* VII.2.1145b24). This Platonic-Aristotelian view is also the view of "the many" described at *Protagoras* 352C2 – a view which Socrates, in that Socratic dialogue, then proceeds to deny. (For Plato, Aristotle, and the many, what we have is an arena of contending forces, where rational and irrational desires each struggle to rule the other. For Plato, see *Republic* 558D4, 561B5, 560A1–2, 573D4–574A1, 587A4, 590C3–4. For Aristotle, see *Nicomachean Ethics* 1102a26–8, 1102b13–1103a3, 1111b10–16, 1147a10–24, 1148a4–10 with 1145b8–14, as well as *De Anima* 433a1–12, b5–10.) The reader should be aware that recently there has been some temptation to argue against this account of the *Republic* and to assimilate Plato's psychology of action to Socrates' (see the interesting Carone 2001) – somewhat implausibly contradicting the account of Socrates and Plato in the Aristotelian *Magna Moralia* I.i.7–8.

kinds of things are means to what). The deliberative process (whether consciously articulated or not) may be represented as follows: Starting with the final end, happiness, one initially wants whatever action is the best means available to the greatest amount of such happiness as turns out to be available in the circumstances. This "whatever-desire" is the generalized desire to do what will be best for gaining this end, present as starting-point in every action whatever. One then casts about in the situation to see what one can discern about (a) the particular circumstances, and also about (b) all those general priorities (health, safety, pleasures, food, the good of those one cares for, and other priorities for one's happiness) that become further relevant in those circumstances. Since these particular and general considerations tend to react on each other, this may lead to further inquiries into the particulars of the situation and the changing of both particular and general beliefs. (If it is necessary to act immediately, one simply goes with what one immediately takes to be best in the situation.) Usually, one settles soon enough on a particular course of action as the best available in the circumstances.

We may now return to the desire in question. Once having arrived at the belief as to which is the best course of action, the agent integrates that belief into the "whatever" desire which set the whole process in motion, by substituting this particular course of action for the "whatever" in the generalized desire. This in turn gives the generalized desire for good a particular concrete direction it did not have initially, a point of application in the actual world. This desire has now transformed itself, from a generalized, "whatever" desire into a desire to do a quite particular action. If there are no further changes of belief as one prepares to act, the generalized desire transforms itself (for this moment of action) into the "executive desire" (Aristotle's *prohairesis*, or choice) which then brings about the action "straightway."[4]

But it may also happen, just as one prepares to act, that there are further changes in belief either through (a) one's seeing new particular circumstances, or through (b) one's being struck with new beliefs about the relevance to just these circumstances of various general priorities for one's happiness. These changes of belief can redirect the generalized desire to another course of action, the merits of which can generate further inquiry. Obviously, deliberation will involve a constant up-and-down movement between (a) these general considerations (such

---

4   Aristotle, *Nicomachean Ethics* VII.3.1147a28, *De Motu Animalium* 7.701a14, 15, 17, 22. On Aristotle's impressive psychology of action generally, see *De Anima* III.9–12, *De Motu Animalium* 7–10. This, even though Aristotle, like Plato, supposes that at the last moment, an irrational desire may intervene, overwhelm the deliberate desire, and so hijack the action.

as health, safety, pleasure), and (b) particular available courses of action, as one assesses and reassesses circumstances and various priorities to which the circumstances come to seem relevant. When the costs of further inquiry come to seem too great, one settles on a belief that this particular course of action will be best, and then does the action. It can be seen how widely the course of these deliberations may range. Indeed, no limit can be set to which of one's vast stock of beliefs may turn out to be involved. After all, one wants, as far as is practical in the circumstances, to make an "all things considered" judgment.

We have now a sketch of how Socratic belief/desire offers an explanation for every motivated action whatever. A contrast should be noted between this Socratic belief/desire theory and modern belief/desire psychologies of action, wherein it is apparently enough to explain, say, this particular action of drinking from this glass of water, to refer to (a) a desire for drink, together with (b) the belief that there is a glass of water conveniently before me.[5] One wonders: why, on such theories, if one has six beliefs and seven desires in all, does one not simultaneously do as many as forty-one other actions at the very same time? For Socrates, this is not a problem since the one conclusion as to the best action in the circumstances is integrated into the single maximizing "whatever-desire" for happiness (which, appropriately transformed in any given case by the beliefs involved, generates every motivated action). Without some device such as this "whatever-desire," one will be reduced to mere co-occurrence of belief and desire to produce the action.[6]

Some might object to the thesis that only one desire, the desire for whatever is best, ever generates an action. For, they may ask, "Does desire for drink never generate an action? How can that be? Is it being denied that we have these desires?" No, the desire for drink does occur, but the way it gets us to act is to present itself to our desire for happiness, which turns to the belief-system to produce an estimate of the possible gains from various choices for fulfilling this desire. So the desire for drink operates not by its generating any action, but by leading to a belief

---

5   Davidson 1980 [1967], pp. 3–4.
6   This argument rules out the view that animal desires bring animals to act by mere co-occurrence. It also rules out the view that our 'animal desires' – those desires for food, drink, and sex we share with the animals, and which Plato and Aristotle make so much of – can bring us to act merely by the co-occurrence of one such desire with some one perceptual belief. Even with animals, some sort of 'whatever'-device, selecting and integrating perceptual features with desires, will be necessary for action to take place. See Penner and Rowe 2005, pp. 227–228, with n. 50, and 1990, p. 40, and esp. p. 61, n. 24.

as to the advantages of fulfilling the desire; that belief is then fed into one's all things considered judgment as to which particular action is best; that judgment is integrated into the "whatever" desire (by substitution); and the resulting executive desire to do this particular action then brings about the action. At this point, we see that it is, after all, as claimed, precisely this one desire for the good which generates the action.

As for "Everyone desires the good (happiness)," I understand the uniqueness of this final end as follows: What it is for us all to desire the same thing, happiness, is for me to desire my happiness, for you to desire your happiness, and so forth. This analysis of our all desiring the very same thing may surprise. ("Isn't my happiness one thing, your happiness another – two different happinesses rather than one?") But it shouldn't surprise. "There is some one thing everyone wants" – if the unmentioned something is a television set, surely says, in the general case, that I want a television set for me, you want one for you, and so forth. Just so, "There is one thing everyone standing here wants to do," if the unmentioned one thing is to run, says that I want that I run, you want that you run, and so forth.[7] No one should suppose that it says that you and I both want that everyone (in the world) runs, let alone that you or I want someone else to run.[8] Analogously, when Eudoxus is reported to have said (*Nicomachean Ethics* X.2.1172b9–15) that every living thing desires some one and the same thing – namely, pleasure – he is relying on the fact that donkeys desire the pleasure of eating hay (and not the pleasures of thinking), whereas humans desire, if anything, the pleasures of thinking and not the pleasures of eating hay. This is why there is nothing wrong with Aristotle's inferring, at the very beginning of the *Nicomachean Ethics* (1094a1–3, 18–19), that

7   The example of the television set is adapted from Michael Dummett's 1967 lectures. See further, Penner 2007, pp. 98–99.

8   Some scholars interpret the Socratic claim that, in the virtuous, happiness is the final end of every deliberate action as if it said that general happiness – the happiness of everyone, not necessarily one's own – can be the final end of one's every deliberate action. See, for example, Morrison 2003, esp. pp. 22–26; Rudebusch 2003, pp. 131–132, Annas 1993, pp. 127–128; as well as n. 17. But I cannot see how these scholars can get that "the virtuous desire happiness" (no passages I can think of) from anywhere but that "everyone desires happiness." Furthermore, I cannot see how anyone can get from the latter that everyone desires general happiness. McCabe 2005, pp. 189–191, 193, sees the fact that happiness and good are universals as excluding their being relevant to motivating individual agents (seeking their particular good or happiness) to good action – a worry that, if I am right, the remarks here about there being some one thing everyone wants to do [namely, to run] remove entirely.

since every action aims at some good, therefore there is some one and the same good which is what is aimed at in every action.[9]

When Socrates speaks of desiring happiness tout court, I take it that he is not saying that everyone desires, in every action, the maximum possible happiness anyone, anywhere, could have – that is, perfect or ideal happiness. (Too frequently, that is what Aristotle speaks of – as when he says that the life of contemplation is happiest.) For that surely sets the bar unrealistically high – since such perfect happiness is seldom, if ever, available to me in the circumstances I find myself in. What is needed here is surely the maximum of such happiness as is available to me – and over the rest of my life – starting from where I am now. Borrowing a term from Aristotle (Nicomachean Ethics I.7.1097a23), I shall speak (where Aristotle does not) of practicable happiness.

This understanding of happiness as practicable happiness in passages concerning action is strikingly confirmed by the resolution of an apparent contradiction in the Euthydemus (279C5–7, 280B2–4, 281B2–3). Here Socrates says that (a) wisdom is good luck – that is, success; that (b) we do not need good luck in addition if we have wisdom; and also that (c) wisdom brings us not only good luck but success (eupragia). What he must be saying in these apparently contradictory remarks is that (a) wisdom is practicable good luck – the most success you can plan on, given your circumstances (leaving out luck); that (b) we do not need any luck that is not practicable if we have wisdom; and that (c), if one notes the way in which blind luck can destroy success – a suggestion surely planted in everyone's mind by Socrates' affirmation of (a) – then we see that what wisdom brings us is practicable success.

As for the contrast with modern belief/desire psychologies, notice that if there is to be only one final end of all human desires that generate deliberate actions, then the agent's own happiness is the only realistic candidate for that unique end, since even if one were to grant what many moderns hold, and what Kant hoped was the case – namely, that:

M1a: people sometimes choose justice (morality, the good of others, the general good) over their own good,

no one (least of all Kant), would claim that

M1b: people will choose justice (morality, ...) over their own good in all cases where one might suppose[10] there is a conflict of justice(morality, ...) with their own good.

9   See Anscombe 1979, pp. 15–16, for the supposed fallacy; against there being a fallacy, see Penner 2003, pp. 207–210, with n. 32.
10 Thrasymachus is one who supposes there are such cases of conflict, since lying behind his view that injustice is a virtue (Republic I.348C), we can surely see his thought that (if one can get away with it) the life of injustice is the happy life.

With this much psychological apparatus in hand, I may now suggest that Socrates, in his famous ethical dictum:

S1:   Virtue is knowledge,[11]

is saying, not that such knowledge (science, expertise – Socrates uses such words interchangeably), which Socrates also calls wisdom, is good as a final end, but rather that this wisdom is good as a means to something else. If we wish to ask what is good as an end – what that is to which wisdom is a means – we need to turn to two other familiar psychological dicta;

S2:   Everyone desires the good, and
S3:   No one errs willingly [at getting the good].[12]

The good in question in these two dicta I take to be what is good as an end – indeed as the unique final end of all actions whatever, namely – one's own happiness.

One may be tempted to try to avoid these results by arguing that "Everyone desires the good" says merely that "Every person some-times generates their actions by means of this desire (but other desires may also generate their actions)."[13] But the move is fruitless. Take the

---

11   *Euthydemus* 281E, *Meno* 88B-89A. (Notice that 89A4 says, not, as many translations have it, that wisdom is either the whole or a part of virtue, but rather that virtue is the whole or a part of wisdom. Wisdom here is, as very often, used widely to include such other sciences as medicine, navigation, farming, and so forth: see n.28. For the identity of justice with wisdom, see *Republic* I. 350D, 351A-C, and esp. 353D3-E11 (on justice as the virtue of the human soul), *Lesser Hippias* 375DE.

12   I have used the standard convention of placing some of the words here within square brackets to indicate to the reader that there is no obvious equivalent to these words in the Greek text, the parentheses being placed here in a way that I view as explaining what is in the speaker's mind at this point. For my argument that the words in square brackets are correctly sup-plied, see my discussion on the "real good" below.

13   Of those tempted to avoid this account of virtue, Morrison 2003, pp. 19, 23, treats an agent's own happiness as "one reason-giving end, perhaps among others," citing the point agreed on by Meno and Socrates that everyone desires happiness as being compatible with agent's desiring others sorts of things – for example, the happiness of others when that involves sacrificing one's own. (This sort of reading of Socratic passages goes back at least to Vlastos 1969.) Morrison thinks of Socrates as a "rational eudaemonist" [i.e., utilitarian] who thinks people act well who promote not their own good but rather the good of everyone: promoting "the good as such" (21), "happiness tout court" (20), or what is "intrinsically" good. Others speak to the same effect of what is "good in itself" as opposed to what is "instrumentally"

dictum (S3) that no one errs willingly. The point here cannot be that sometimes people do not err willingly. It is surely that no one ever errs willingly in any of their actions. But this is just another way of saying that everyone desires the good in all their actions.

I have claimed that what it is for everyone to desire happiness is for me to want my happiness, you to want your happiness, and so forth. This does not imply that the virtue – knowledge, wisdom, or science – spoken of in (S1) is an egoistic science – a science of what is good for me. For nothing said so far implies that my wisdom (were I to possess it) would be wisdom about my happiness alone. For the content of all science and expertise is perfectly general.[14] As medicine can as easily cure your sickness as mine, the science of money-making will help you in making your investments, as well as me in making mine, and the expertise of shoemaking will make shoes for you and me as well as for the shoemakers themselves; so, too, if Socrates were to have the science of

good (Irwin 1995, pp. 66ff; Annas 1993, p. 127; McCabe 2005, pp. 190, 195, 199, 201–202, 208). Such views are designed to make Socrates' theory of motivation safe for morality, so that there can be an "independent" desire to be just (Morrison, p. 73), with justice evidently so conceived as to bring about actions intentionally contrary to an agent's best interest. But arguing from what is merely compatible with a text seems to me quite a different matter from what a text may reasonably be interpreted as saying. When Socrates argues that virtue is good (*Meno* 87Dff), this is explained solely in terms of benefit and harm, and the context, as I see it, makes it quite clear that, whatever may be compatible with the text, that this is benefit or harm to the possessor of virtue. So too at *Euthydemus* 279E-282C. See further discussion with n. 10.

The difficulty for those who wish to make it ethically good for people to act for what is good as such is that they will have to have a psychology of action will allow agents to have some desires for good are not desires for their own good. But that Socrates intended any such psychology of action has just been refuted in the treatment here of "No one errs willingly." The Socratic point is that it is inevitable that people do nothing which is not with a view to their own happiness. By these lights, what it is to seek the good of others can only be: to have the wisdom to see that one's own good is to be found in, amongst other things, bringing about the good of others. These matters are addressed more fully in Penner and Rowe 2005, ch. 12.

14 The point is that the objects a science studies are universals and not particulars. This is explicit in Aristotle's formulation of Plato's "Argument from the Sciences" (on which see Penner 1987, pp. 40–43, 2006b, passim), and it is implicit in the absolutely central Socratic view that virtue is teachable (*Meno* and *Protagoras*, passim). For the point of teaching medical science is surely so that the students will be able to cure not just the teacher's patients, but anyone who may later turn up as one of the student's patients. Hence it is health in general which the professor of medical science teaches the student – not simply the health of particular patients of the professor.

the good (or happiness), which is wisdom, he would be able to see what is good for your happiness quite as well as what is good for his own happiness. Socratic desire is egocentric in the way indicated here: Socratic wisdom is not. Desire is utterly particular; science and expertise are utterly general. (This point is important to many of Socrates' arguments in *Republic* I.)

But now, if the final end is happiness, so understood – and not wisdom – how is it that virtue, or human excellence, is wisdom, rather than being happy? If we note that Socrates does say that virtue (wisdom), rather than happiness, is the only thing "good in itself" (*Euthydemus* 281DE, *Meno* 88C), and does not say this of happiness, the question does not go away. If happiness is the unique final end of all actions, why is it not the only thing good in itself?

Here, an English speaker needs to distinguish between the human good and human good-ness.[15] It is human goodness that is virtue, while the human good is happiness. This will be clearer if we consider Socrates' general means/end theory of functions (*erga*, works), virtues, and goods. The function of a knife is given by its good or end, which is a clean cut, while the virtue of a knife is given by its good-ness at producing that clean cut – its providing the means to success in gaining that end. Socrates holds that this apparatus of function, virtue, and good applies to all artifacts, all bodily organs (such as eyes and ears), all athletic activities, and (most relevant for ethics, given that for Socrates virtue is a science or expertise) to all sciences or expertises. Each given science or expertise has a good or end proper to it, which it is the function of the science to provide; and the virtue of the practitioner of the given science consists in providing the means to the end of the given science.

With this distinction in hand, we are within striking distance of the central move of Socratic ethics – entirely original, if still largely

---

15 I am not saying that Socrates anywhere does anything equivalent to making the English distinction between good-ness and the good. After all, the Greek of Plato's time lacks the corresponding abstract noun *agathotês*. Plato uses *aretê* (virtue) not only for human goodness, but also for the goodness of knives, runners, archers, and so forth (*Lesser Hippias* 373C-375C, cf, *Republic* I.352E-354A). So it is easy for an English reader commenting on Plato's Greek to confuse being good (goodness) with being a good (or the good). Such a confusion would be entirely unlikely in Plato. Thus, when Plato has Socrates (or anyone else) speak of all humans desiring the good (n. 2), I take it that he is not saying that all humans desire human good-ness. (For example, at *Meno* 78C-D, Meno foolishly affirms that gold, silver, and high office are candidates for the human good; he surely doesn't think they are candidates for being what human goodness is.)

unrecognized. We are also within striking distance of the main reason why the psychology of action outlined at the beginning of this chapter is so central to Socratic thought. I refer to the fact that, for Socrates, ethics too is a science like any other. It is the science of the human good or end. This is the science of what is good for (that is, beneficial to) humans – the science of human happiness. Like any other science or expertise, what the end is, is a purely factual matter. It is not a matter of moral truth, or norms, or values, and not a matter of what is intrinsically good, good as such, good in itself, good simpliciter, or any such thing. It is simply what is good for humans. For Socratic ethics, in total contrast to most of modern moral philosophy, there are no further elements of the subject-matter of ethics involving any of the aforementioned norms, values, moral principles, intrinsic goods, and the like. There is just the science of what is good for humans and of the means to that good.

In this, the purely factual Socratic science of the good puts Socrates in stark opposition to Classical Greek culture generally, where the notions of responsibility, deserved punishment, and deserved blame are ubiquitous. So too, on the existence of "values" – what people "think good" without allowing the question "But is it really good?" to arise – Socrates and Plato are starkly at variance with the sophists, notably Protagoras (nn. 41, 44, 46). This in spite of the fact that Socrates was regularly treated by conservative Athenians as a sophist (on which more below).

If this reading of the "Socratic" texts in Plato's dialogues is right, then some considerable reorientation of modern ethical thought will be necessary if one is to grasp Socratic ethical thought from the inside. It is even worth considering whether such a reorientation might not be desirable from the point of view of our own thought. (This is of course a reorientation in strong contrast with that in Nietzsche's equally original *Genealogy of Morals*.) Noting the way in which the Socratic position appears to refrain from going beyond these purely functional and teleological considerations, all to be found in the natural world, we might be tempted to call this view "ethical naturalism." Unfortunately, the term has been given so many other uses by philosophers (for example, as a theory of values!)[16] that I shall not employ any other label than simply "Socratic ethics."

So too the other sciences or expertises each have their own purely factual subject-matter. As the science of medicine has as its good-and-end health (the imparting of health to the sick), and a doctor has the virtue of medical practitioners (is a good doctor) through his or her goodness at contriving the means leading to that end, so the science of ethics (the science of happiness) has as its end, or good, human happiness, and a

16   See, for example, Darwall 1998, pp. 28–30.

human being has the virtue of a human being, or is a good human being, through being good at contriving the means leading to that happiness (*Lesser Hippias* 373C-375D, *Republic* I.352D-354A).[17]

These features of human goodness in Socrates are sometimes said to flow from a "craft analogy," but this suggestion, while useful and thoroughly understandable, is doubly wrong. First, it is not an analogy. Virtue in Socrates isn't simply like a science or expertise; it is a science or expertise. Virtue is knowledge.[18] Second, Socratic expertises extend beyond crafts such as navigation, shoemaking, farming, shepherding, checkers-playing, and the like – all the way to arithmetic and geometry. If one asks what their good is, Socrates' answer is that the works (*erga*) produced by arithmetic are themselves used by dialecticians, who practice the science of working out means to human good (*Euthydemus* 290C, *Cratylus* 390C). What lies behind this suggestion, I think, is the thought (which I believe to be perfectly correct) that the practice of science is itself a teleological or means/end activity within the arena of human culture – so that its goals too are (ultimately) the ends of human beings. Looked at in this way, all sciences are teleological – sciences of some good. (One may, of course, affirm this thought without the utter misunderstanding of supposing that therefore the subject-matter of the sciences is determined by human ends or human concepts rather than being what it is quite independently of any human goals. For nothing less than the real truth – regardless of what humans may desire or believe – will serve human deliberations well, even about their own good.)

Back to our question earlier: why does Socrates on the present interpretation not say that happiness, rather than virtue, is the only thing

17   It is this anthropology, this theory of human nature and the human good (an extension of biology – the teleological biology of all three of Socrates, Plato, and Aristotle) – that, together with the Socratic psychology of action, brings it about, for Socrates, that "The good for each human being is his or her own happiness" is both a psychological truth about what we in fact desire and an ethical (though still factual) truth about what it is good for us to desire. There is no "ought to do" here over and above what it is good for us to do, and no "ought to have done." (Notice that "ought to have done" requires that one could have done otherwise than one actually did. But there is no room for this in Socrates if, as I argue later, Socrates is a determinist, and does not allow that one could ever have done otherwise than one's desire for good, and one's beliefs at the time, determine.)

18   For "craft analogy," see the influential Irwin 1977. Irwin himself speaks this way while still well aware that Socrates himself holds that virtue is a science. Presumably Irwin speaks of an analogy only because he himself thinks Socrates is wrong to affirm this identity between virtue and the science of the good.

good in itself? When Socrates says that virtue is the only thing good in itself, the context is a discussion of means to happiness (*Euthydemus* 279A1–4 with 278E3–6 and 282A1–7). So what Socrates is saying here, in this context of choice between rival candidates for being the best means to happiness, and in singling out wisdom as the only thing "good in itself," is not that wisdom is the only thing good in itself simpliciter – much as that will appeal to those anxious to find the intrinsic good or the moral good in Socrates – but that wisdom is the only thing good in itself as a means to happiness. He is presupposing that happiness is the final end, and so the good. Accordingly, when he says that wisdom is the one thing good in itself, he can only be saying that it is the one thing good in itself as a means. What, then, is the force of "in itself"? Well, remember that what is under discussion here is the choice among rival candidates for being the best means to happiness. The question is, then: what is it about the other supposed goods (let us call them "standard goods"), such as health, wealth, good looks, high office, cutting cleanly, shoes, and so forth that leads us to say that they are not good in themselves?[19] What Socrates says is that in some contexts, they may actually harm if not used with wisdom – as when my good health might lead me on a foolhardy mountain-climbing expedition; while if I have very bad asthma, even if I am foolish, I will be rather less tempted to join such an expedition. So since standard goods are not good in themselves because they are not always good (*Gorgias* 467E6–468C4, *Lysis* 220C4–5), I suggest that what it is for wisdom to be "good in itself as a means" is for it to be always good as a means to happiness.

Indeed, not only is wisdom always a means to happiness; it is an essential means to happiness, given that happiness needs to be achieved by action of one sort or other, and that all action has the deliberative means/end structure just described. For given the aforementioned complexity of the particular and general considerations involved in one's deliberative structures, any false beliefs in the belief-structure employed to get at what the best means is in the circumstances will risk forcing a misidentification of the best course of action available; and this misidentification will redirect desire to a quite different, suboptimal action. Since there is no antecedent limit that can be put on what considerations connected with means and end may be involved in the action, it will be clear that we cannot do without the knowledge

19   I understand "in itself" in this way not only at 281D4–5, D9-E1, but also at E3–5. Not so Irwin 1995, pp. 55–60, who like Vlastos 1991, ch. 8, and Annas 1999 passim, attributes to Socrates the astonishing thesis that virtue is sufficient for happiness. What? Socrates thinks that a virtuous person in constant screaming pain will be happy?

of what kinds of things and actions are good as means to what.[20] This is why wisdom (including perceptiveness) is also an essential means to happiness. It may indeed be this feature of being necessary and sufficient for the greatest happiness available, together with Socrates' simply taking for granted that happiness is the end, that accounts for Socrates' occasionally appearing to treat wisdom and happiness interchangeably, and feeling no compunction about saying that wisdom is the one thing good in itself.[21]

It is time to consider a number of other objections to interpreting Socrates in terms of the version of Socratic ethics I have been describing. The most obvious objection is that behind the theory of human goodness here attributed to Socrates lurks, in defiance of all accepted morality, that ravening Hobbesian beast, Selfish Egoism. This objection takes it that such a theory would give a free pass to every would-be Hitler and every bully in the schoolyard; it would allow a good person willingly to harm others whenever he thinks that it will be to his advantage to do so; and it would appear, implausibly, to align Socrates with a policy endorsed by both Thrasymachus and Callicles – that of *pleonexia* (literally "getting more": exploiting others, getting the better of them, getting one's own good by harming others or by taking their good away from them). Many will object: "Is not any such interpretation of Socrates

20   It is this complexity involved in figuring out which action will be the best available (in never-completely-known circumstances) that accounts for the way one may, from instant to instant, shift back and forth, in troubling circumstances, between different summary estimates of the upshot of the entire range of circumstances one faces in attempting to choose between possible courses of action. (Shall I take another oatmeal and raisin cookie, or not?) It is this kind of instability (*Protagoras* 356D3-357B6) that explains why Socrates thinks mere [true] belief will not suffice for effective action and for avoiding what the many call "being overcome by pleasure," but only knowledge – the science of measurement. This science, like all other sciences is, in its finished state, absolutely stable (*Protagoras* 356D3-E2, *Meno* 97C-98A, *Euthyphro* 15B-C).

21   If in the *Euthydemus*, Socrates identifies wisdom with (practicable) good luck, p. 265 above, he might well also have spoken as if he identified wisdom with practicable happiness. In the same way, there seems a case for identifying the "first friend" at *Lysis* 219C3ff both with happiness and with wisdom (so that the good is wisdom): see the apparently deliberately chosen Socratic example of wisdom at 218D2-B3, and Penner and Rowe 2005, 273–278, backed by the analysis at 143ff, esp. 148 (para. 3)-153. The basis of this strange talk of identification seems to reside in the fact that, in Socrates' view, to aim at maximum available happiness successfully is in the nature of things identical with aiming at this wisdom.

as a selfish, if science-based, egoist ruled out by Socrates' preoccupation with the moral rejection of *pleonexia*, which becomes central to Socrates' thinking once we get to the *Gorgias* and *Republic* I? Does this not show that Socrates, like any finer human being, appeals to certain rules of morality or justice that involve rules that occasionally override my individual happiness?"

I shall show that it does not. But it will be helpful first to address a related, Aristotelian objection. It may be put in terms of the following question: "Does not this account of human virtue as a science make Socrates foolishly confuse virtues with sciences and expertises in the way both Aristotle and Aquinas warn against?" Aristotle and Aquinas do both think that, unlike virtue, goodness at a science or expertise may show up in actions designed precisely to get the opposite of the good of the relevant science or expertise. This point is clearly correct for all sciences other than wisdom simpliciter.[22] In any case, the standard good aimed at by these sciences can turn out to be bad for us (as with health and the asthma example earlier). We may call this the problem of the ambivalence of sciences and expertises: since human goodness is not ambivalent in this way, must we not follow Aristotle and Aquinas and distinguish between human virtue on the one hand and sciences and expertises on the other?

Socrates appears to address this question in a dialogue in the *Lesser Hippias*, which I consider to be one of the greatest fruits of Plato's philosophical and dramatic genius. True, some interpreters[23] argue that Socrates in this dialogue is precisely reducing to absurdity the treatment of human goodness as a science or expertise. To say one knows how to make others (or even oneself) unhappy is not to say one will do it, they urge. So, on this interpretation, Socrates, anxious not to make this confusion of ability with motivation, is alleged to be reducing to absurdity the view that justice (virtue) is a science.

But this is a misreading. In brief, the context is this: Socrates is (mischievously) arguing that Odysseus, the wily liar, is a better man than the simple, true Achilles. The basis of his argument is the deliberately paradoxical claim (364Bff) that the false man (the man most able to tell successful lies) is also the true man – a claim which makes

---

22 Aristotle, *Nicomachean Ethics* V.1.1129a7ff, VI.5.1140b21–24, Aquinas, *Summa Theologiae* I-II, q.57, art. 4. Wisdom simpliciter: wisdom about the good. Ancient Greeks generally used "wise" of sculptors and builders just in virtue of their skill in their own expertise: see, for example, Aristotle, *Nicomachean Ethics*. VI.7.1141a9–17.

23 Kahn 1996, p. 225; also Gould 1955, pp. 42–44.

it appear that Socrates is confusing here what one is able to do with what one will do – that is, confusing ability with motivation. In support of his outrageous attack on the integrity of Achilles, Socrates points out (369E2), that Achilles too tells falsehoods! (He says he will leave Troy and fight the Trojans no more. Yet he stays and fights!) At 371E9–372A5, Hippias protests that Achilles tells such falsehoods unwillingly (that is, not realizing that they are falsehoods), whereas Odysseus willingly deceives people, being well aware that he is telling falsehoods. How, Hippias asks, can those who willingly harm others and[24] do injustice to them, be better than those who do so unwillingly? Is there not pardon when the harm is done unwillingly? And is not the law harder on those who do bad deeds and tell falsehoods willingly (371E9–372A5)?

Socrates, beginning an elaborate reply (372A6ff), allows that he knows nothing, being a simple fellow who is good in only one thing – namely, that he is persistent in questioning those who, like Hippias, are wiser. It must be the case that Socrates knows nothing on this point, since he disagrees with Hippias about it! True, sometimes, Socrates says, he does agree with Hippias about erring willingly and unwillingly. But for the moment, the argument that convinces him is that those who, like Odysseus, err willingly, are better than those who err unwillingly (372D7–373A8).

It is no small point on which Socrates departs from Hippias here. Not only is Socrates departing from the views of Hippias, but also from the (juridical) view of (legal and moral) responsibility, deserved punishment, and deserved blame which we find not only in classical Greek civilization but right through to the modern era. More grist to the mill of those interpreters who still suppose that Socrates could not have held this purely scientific ethics, and so the *Lesser Hippias* must, after all, be here reducing to absurdity the view that virtue is knowledge.

In replying to an impatient Hippias, Socrates looks at all of the following examples of things with functions, virtues, and ends: (a) various skills, expertises, accomplishments (comprising here running, wrestling, working out, dance, singing); (b) bodily parts (feet, eyes), tools or instruments (rudders, bows, lyres); and (c) "souls." (Souls comprise here – oddly, by modern lights, but foreshadowing the disguised climax of the dialogue – dispositions of soul or spirit in horses; expertises of archers, doctors, flute-players, and lyre-players; as well as souls of slaves.) From what is true in all these cases, Socrates infers that:

---

24 Probably the "and" here is an explanatory "and," equivalent to "i.e." Socrates often takes doing injustice to and harming to be the same thing. (I find the same assumption at *Crito* 46B-D.)

ERRING: If a person or expert of kind K, which kind has as its function doing actions of kind X, is discovered to err willingly at X-ing, then he or she will be a better expert of kind K and a better X-er than one who errs unwillingly at X-ing.

Those with the greatest expertise (*epistêmê*) and ability (*dunamis*) will be those who miss the mark willingly, not those who miss the mark unwillingly.

Socrates is now ready for the coup de grace (375D7ff). Turning to the human soul, he argues that justice, being the virtue (because the science and power) of the human soul, the better human soul (= the better person) will be the soul that brings about unjust deeds willingly – at least if there is such a person (376B5–6). Hippias is utterly flummoxed – not so much as suspecting the presence of a point Socrates may be making to those who can see that the if-clause here is vacuous. Hippias, the man of many expertises (of virtually all the expertises but the most important of all) has been deceived. But Plato has made it clear enough to the alert reader what Socrates' point is: of all the many kinds K, there is exactly one kind where the expert of that kind, though utterly and uniquely able to err willingly at doing actions fulfilling the function, never has a motive to do such actions, and so would never err willingly at them. That is the kind human being, whose function is living well or happily, and whose virtue is justice – justice here being a matter of being good at what human beings are for. For beings of this kind, the Socratic psychology of action described at the beginning of this chapter secures "no one errs willingly [at gaining their own good]" as a mere corollary.

Once more, this theory of the goodness of persons does not at all depart from the general theory of functional good introduced earlier, with its functions, virtues, and (standard) good ends for all sciences, all characterized in terms of the means/end distinction. As the science of medicine has a function (to heal patients), a virtue (being able to bring about health in patients), and a good at which the function aims (health), so too the human being has a function (to live a human life), a virtue (being good at gaining success in living), and a good (living well – a regular way of referring to happiness). Wisdom is the virtue of a human soul, and the end happiness. A remarkable, and purely factual, ethical theory![25]

25 At this point, some readers will ask, "How can this be an ethical theory?" I shall try to be clear. If we treat any theory committed to such notions as those of deserved blame or deserved punishment as a moral theory (n. 23), and any theory of human good and human goodness as an ethical theory, then Socratic ethics qualifies as an ethical theory, even though it makes no allowance for such moral notions. Williams 1993, pp. 5–9, works with

To return to the *Lesser Hippias*, is it really philosophically credible that a philosopher of Socrates' stature would have given up so fundamental and even essential a notion as responsibility? No wonder some scholars think Socrates must have been reducing to absurdity the idea of virtue as a science or as an ability or power (*dunamis*), to absurdity, and that he must have rejected any supposed functionalist confusion of virtues with sciences. Unfortunately, this view is implausible as an interpretation of the *Lesser Hippias*. For why on earth would Plato both want to reduce to absurdity the view that justice is an expertise (by showing that on this functionalist view, just people would do injustice willingly), and also want to show us how to avoid the conclusion that experts at justice would do unjust deeds (by using "no one errs willingly")? The interpreter must choose: Either (a) Socrates is attacking the idea of virtue as a science on the a priori grounds that Socrates could not possibly have identified virtues with sciences, or motivation with ability; or (b) Socrates is arguing that, with a correct theory of motivation (including "no one errs willingly") – that is, with the Socratic psychology of action – there is no problem with the idea of virtue as a science – or indeed as an ability or power (*dunamis*). One cannot affirm both (a) and (b). Anyone who takes the dictum "no one errs willingly" to be Socratic can hardly be in doubt that the second option is the one to choose.

But perhaps there is overriding textual evidence from elsewhere that Socrates could not have given up responsibility and its child, the moral good, for entirely non-moral notions of function, expertise, and good? Thus Vlastos, Price, and Annas,[26] relying in part on what they see as moral plausibility generally, would defend Socrates against supposing that he is a so-called selfish egoist. It is their view that (A) sometimes in these dialogues we encounter another end besides the agent's own happiness – namely what is just or moral – where that may lead an agent to choose courses of action which he is well aware do not lead to his overall greatest happiness.

An ingenious alternative realization of this view, built from a suggestion of Irwin 1977, 1995 (which Irwin finds in Plato and not in Socrates, though others have applied it to Socrates) is this. (B) Wisdom or justice is not a means to happiness (that is, an "instrumental" means) but is a part or component of happiness. The notion that justice (or moral goodness) is a "part" or "component means" is to be understood in the

a similar distinction between morality and ethics; but his notion of morality is somewhat narrower: he thinks morality is not present amongst the Ancient Greeks.

26   Vlastos 1991, pp. 179ff, 214ff; Price 1995, pp. 16–17; Annas 1999, p. 35.

following way: nothing will count as happiness that does not include the agent's being just (or moral).[27] Thus Interpretations (A) and (B) of Socrates stand in opposition to each other on the matter of whether justice or morality can conflict with one's happiness. Nevertheless, Irwin's suggestion (B) gains what proponents of (A) want – namely, that morality and "intrinsic goods" are, or are parts of, the highest good. But this gain is made without allowing that morality could force the sacrifice of our happiness on us. This is a definite advantage to (B), since the idea of happiness as final end is almost everywhere apparent in Socrates.

I shall not criticize (B) here except to note that it will function better for those wishing to find in Socrates a conception of morality (or of intrinsic goods over and above what is good for humans – that is, beneficial to them) than it will for those who find in Socrates the more purely functional conception of ethics on offer here. From the point of view of the purely functional conception, such devices as in effect redefining "happiness" as moral happiness will seem gratuitous. In any case, everything important about the supposed distinction between parts (ingredient means) and "instrumental" means is captured by the

27 For the supposedly Aristotelian distinction between instrumental means and parts, see Irwin 1995, chs. 5, 15, esp. pp. 65–67 with 89–90, 247–254; and for application to Socrates, Annas 1999, 33ff. For redefinitions of what happiness is, see the great deal of maneuvering on questions of what "conceptions" of happiness Callicles, Socrates, or Plato are employing, in various arguments at Irwin 1995, pp. 106, 117–121, 125 and esp. 244, 248, 250–251, 254; and see also p. 332 of Annas's *The Morality of Happiness* – aptly named, given her views of ancient "conceptions" of happiness – as well as her 1999, pp. 36–51. Something is an "instrumental" means in this view if it would be skipped provided that the end could be achieved in an alternative way. Something is a "part" or "component" of happiness if one will not be happy unless one has or does what is contained in the part. The difficulty with the (perhaps) Aristotelian notion of "parts" of happiness is that, once we distinguish between perfect happiness (not in fact to be found in this world) and the maximum available happiness (the happiness relevant to human action), it becomes clear that, for Socrates, there could be no "parts" of the happiness relevant to action other than simply wisdom. Take the Aristotelian example of contemplation, which, if anything, would be a "part" of happiness for Aristotle (since he is at this point thinking of ideal happiness). It is clear that the maximum available happiness of one able to contemplate will sometimes be best served by abandoning contemplation in order to earn money for an operation to save the life of that person's child, with whose happiness that person's own happiness is bound up. Similar considerations will surely apply to such supposed "parts" as acting morally, justly, or fairly even if that goes against one's own interests, in circumstances where, say, a child's very life requires stealing from those who can do without.

rather broader and less problematic distinction already introduced, between what is always a means to happiness, and what sometimes is, sometimes is not, a means to happiness – and this without reading morality into happiness and thus contaminating happiness with supposed truths "by definition." (I hold that happiness in Socrates is always simply natural happiness. That is, I reject what is common to both (A) and (B) – that Socrates held that there is this final end, the moral good, distinct from natural happiness, and that in order to be (properly) happy, one must be moral.)

It will be useful to pursue the objection that Socrates could not possibly be abandoning the notions of moral responsibility and deserved punishment by introducing an important passage from within the *Apology* itself. I refer to Socrates' mini-dialogue with Meletus at 25C-26A, which I paraphrase briefly as follows:

– Is there anyone who prefers being harmed to being benefited? – – Obviously not.

– Do I corrupt the young willingly, or unwillingly? – – Willingly.

– Am I so ignorant as not to realize that harming others leads to my harm? (For nothing else would lead me to commit this grave offense willingly.) You see, either I do not corrupt the young or I do so unwillingly, and either way your accusation is false. [Since you will reject the view that I don't corrupt the youth, I must be doing it unwillingly.] But if I do this unwillingly, then what I need from you, Meletus, is not to be dragged into court to be punished, but to be taken aside privately and instructed. What is needed here is not punishment (*kolasis*) but instruction (*mathêsis*).

What we see in this extraordinary but entirely characteristic Socratic argument is not only "No one errs willingly" [at getting what will make him happy], but also the obverse of our old friend "Virtue is knowledge" – namely "Vice is ignorance" – or, more precisely (in a characteristic bit of Socrates' teleological reductionism),

S1a So-called vice is actually nothing more than ignorance of what is good for me.

We also see here, generalizing from the case of Socrates in the passage, some quite astonishing new claims.
First:

S4a As a matter of fact, harming those around you [= those with whom you interact] will always end up harming you. So it will never be to your advantage, overall, to harm any of those around you. (If you think it will be to your advantage, then you are just ignorant.)

Second:

S4b Punishment is never a good or appropriate response when one person harms (does injustice to: n. 24) another,[28] since the action can only have flowed from ignorance of what was good for one.

And, therefore, third:

S4c If anyone ever harms another, since that will always be done in ignorance, the agent will not be culpable or responsible, just ignorant.

(We see here, how the accusation that this interpretation makes Socrates a selfish egoist actually confuses caring for no one but oneself (which is selfishness) with self-interest. People are fools if they suppose that not caring for the good of those around one will be in one's interest, or if they ignore the many happinesses of looking to the happiness of those one cares for.)[29]

Notice that Socrates is careful not to make explicit what he is plainly committed to: that his own case generalizes to all cases of harming anyone around one. That is, no one is ever responsible for harming others. Such actions are always based on ignorance, and so are to be excused. Socrates had good cause not to express himself any more explicitly than he does here. Upright, morally orthodox Athenians of the stripe of Anytus and Meletus knew in their bones that this man was a dangerous radical. That was why he was brought to trial. At the same time, they had no idea just exactly how dangerous. No wonder Socrates did not state his views upfront, but insisted always on dialogue to bring people to contemplate the whole picture for themselves. No wonder many Athenians confused him with the sophists.[30] No wonder he had

28   At Penner 2002, pp. 203–204, I note that the *Gorgias* (like the *Phaedo* and the *Republic*) is developing a view of punishment (see especially the Pythagorean-influenced myths) quite out of keeping with the one I have found in the *Apology*. If this is due to Pythagorean influence resulting from Plato's visit to Sicily more than ten years after Socrates' death (see Dodds 1959, pp. 20, 26–27, 303, 373–376), this treatment of punishment will not provide evidence against the account being presented here of Socrates' account of punishment.

29   The natural reply to the position I take up here is that the self-interest that cares for the welfare of others is, so to speak, a kind of depth selfishness, and so not genuine caring at all. This seems to be the view of Rudebusch 2003, pp. 131–132. It raises the Kantian question whether pure self-sacrificing altruism is really possible. Penner and Rowe 2005, ch. 12 suggest it is not.

30   On the Athenians confusing Socrates with the sophists, see *Apology* 19A–24B with Penner 2002, p. 198f.

little inclination toward legal proceedings, let alone toward practical politics.[31] And no wonder that the Athenians, given their occasional murderous instinct toward those they perceived to be dangerous, would put him to death. (So difficult is it to see just what he was up to, that I cannot think of any modern interpreters who have argued for these three generalized implications of Socratic thought about punishment, harm, and responsibility. On the other hand, they lie open before us in the passage – though of course they are hardly explicit.)

Nevertheless, this policy of almost never asserting his views explicitly (or telling people his answers to his own questions), but only asking questions and engaging in dialogue, involves a second, quite different consideration – one that is much more important to Socrates. This is his desire that people think things out for themselves, and accept nothing purely on Socrates' say-so (or anyone else's). Why was he so insistent on this? I conjecture that part of the reason for this desire may have been that people may assent to a sentence that is true and still be unable to exploit it correctly because it lies against a background of other sentences to which they also assent, but which are false. The result is that in understanding what a sentence says, and even more obviously applying this sentence, things will go wrong – even disastrously so. Only dialogue – especially the distinctively wide-ranging form of dialogue in which Socrates engaged – will explore not just the truth of individual sentences, but the entire background of views that will affect how the true sentences are understood and used.[32]

The claim that it is never to one's advantage to harm others should not be confused with a moral claim often – and in my view wrongly – attributed to Socrates at *Crito* 49B-E – namely, that:

31 *Apology* 17D, 31D-32A. That Socrates would sometimes eschew publicly standing up against injustices, because of this staying away from politics and the law, wins him little sympathy from Vlastos 1994, pp. 127–33.

32 This complexity makes it necessary for us to deal not just with what logically follows from a sentence that someone utters, say, "Piety is what is loved by the gods" (*Euthyphro* 6E), but with the entire context. Consider now the different sentence "Piety is what is loved by such beings as Zeus and Cronos." Neither of these two sentences follows from the other. Yet for all that, Euthyphro would surely have been equally happy using either sentence to express what he was saying. Appeals to what follows from something in the text, independently of the entire literary context, is not dealing with what the speaker is saying, but solely with a construct consisting of what the sentence says (according to logic). But Socrates and Plato are surely considering what the speakers are saying. See my "Death of the so-called 'Socratic Elenchus'" 2007.

M4   One ought not to harm someone, even in retaliation [since one has a moral obligation, regardless of the consequences for one's own happiness, not to harm anyone].[33]

For whatever we say about this passage in the *Crito* – and I find here only the same factual claim about harming others ending up harming oneself[34] – the argument here in the *Apology* is plainly not at the level of morality.

I want now to say a little more about the identity of virtue with knowledge or wisdom in Socratic ethics. First, we have seen that at *Lesser Hippias* 367D, Socrates treats virtue interchangeably with justice (as he does at *Republic* I. 353E-354A, 351A with 348E-349A, 350D). Second, in the passage in the *Meno* referred to earlier as parallel to the *Euthydemus* passage on which we have placed so much emphasis, Socrates adds something (88B3–8) that is not explicit in the *Euthydemus*. Take courage: will it harm us if not wisely used? Yes, says Socrates if it is not knowledge, but rather just a kind of daring (*tharros*). If it is mere daring, it will sometimes harm (when used ignorantly), and it will benefit only when used with sense (88A6-B5). And similarly for temperance and other mental attributes.

So what is courage? Is it knowledge (wisdom, science, expertise)? Or just a kind of daring? I have shown elsewhere[35] that just as *Protagoras* 351B-357E identifies temperance with the science of measuring goods or pleasures, so 358A-360E identifies courage with this same measuring science. It follows that courage, temperance, and wisdom are one and the same thing: the knowledge of good and bad. Putting this together with our earlier remarks about justice (and the fact that Socrates regarded piety as justice applied in theological areas), we have that courage, temperance, wisdom, justice, and piety are all one and the same thing – really just five different names for the same thing (329C6-D1, 332C8-333B6, 349A6-C5). This is the doctrine I call the unity of virtue.[36] Why then do we have five different words? In Penner 2005a, p. 34, I suggest that what

---

33   While this argument about harm is not a moral argument, it is nevertheless still an argument about ethics: see n. 25.

34   Especially if one applies the (non-moral) soul/body analogy 47A-48B to the soul as straightforwardly as Socrates does (and as Plato does at *Republic* IV.444E-445B, and does not read into "living well" at 48B anything such as "living in a way that is morally good' (Annas 1999, p. 50), instead of taking it in the ordinary (functional!) way as living happily (Annas 1999, p. 35 n. 20).

35   Penner 1996 (with 1973, 1992).

36   Contrast the plural in the title of Vlastos's 1973 paper, "The Unity of the Virtues."

we need here is no more than the idea that for historical reasons (or for reasons of communicating with others whose views are not Socratic), different words are used for the science of what is worth trading for what in situations of danger and in situations of temptation to pleasure. But in spite of different uses of words, it is the very same thing. (As, for historical reasons, we use "Morning Star" in the morning, "Evening Star" in the evening, but it is one and the same heavenly body in either case.)

It is time now to offer an absolutely crucial clarification to the account given earlier[37] of the desire for the good in the Socratic psychology of action – that is, the desire to do that action which is the best means available to the greatest good available. Is Socrates talking about the desire for what the agent thinks is the good – the apparent good – or is he talking about the real good?

Consider the powerful tyrant envisaged by Socrates at *Gorgias* 466A-468E (with 470Cff), who decides (let us say) to kill his prime minister as [the best] means [available] to the tyrant's own greatest good [that is, as a means to his own greatest available happiness over all]. Suppose further that, confident in his power, the tyrant does not take the trouble[38] to learn that this act he chooses as a means will actually bring about his own overthrow, torture, and execution: in short, a far worse life than he would have gained by not killing his prime minister. Yet that killing of the prime minister is just the action which the desire for the good brought about. It seems to follow, then – on pain of supposing that the tyrant wants both not to kill and to kill – that the desire for the good which brought about the tyrant's disastrous action could only have been, in the end, the desire to kill. But this, it appears, can only be a desire for what the tyrant thought was the real good – that is, a desire for the apparent good.

Certainly Aristotle thought it obvious that the apparent good was the right answer to the question[39] – as do most modern philosophers.[40]

---

37   In the first eleven paragraphs of this chapter.

38   It is this confidence and consequent insouciance in orators [and tyrants] that motivates Socrates' otherwise unmotivated talk of orators as ignorant (466E10).

39   Essentially the argument here is given at *EN* III.4.1113a15–19.

40   To say that the tyrant's act of killing is the apparent good is to say that he did the act of killing under the description "the real good." That is, although inside the tyrant's mind, so to speak, the killing was the real good, the actual truth, the truth outside of the tyrant's mind, is that the killing was not the real good. For this inside/outside, "under the description"

But Aristotle also thought that it was not the answer that Plato gave.[41] What is more, Aristotle is right about what the two thinkers believe. For, first, at *Gorgias* 468C2-D7, we see Socrates saying explicitly of this case where the tyrant acts mistakenly that, if the killing the tyrant chooses as a means to his good did in fact lead to the tyrant's good, then the tyrant did indeed want to do it. But if it does not lead to the good, Socrates says, then the tyrant didn't want to do it.[42] It merely "seemed best" to him.[43] Second, we find essentially the same view at *Republic* 577D: the claim that the tyrant does nothing that he wants to do plainly depends on this same idea, that if the action chosen does not lead to the good, the tyrant didn't want to do it. So it seems to me quite certain that Socrates and Plato do hold that if the action turns out badly, the agent did not want to do the action – and this, plainly, because the action done did not lead to the real good.

methodology, descended from the Aristotelian argument just described, and virtually universal in modern philosophy, see Anscombe 1957, pp. 28, 30; Davidson 1980, xii-xiii; and, for examples amongst important interpreters of Socrates, Plato, and Aristotle, Santas 1979 [1964], pp. 187–188, and Irwin 1977, pp. 145–147.

41 In the *Topics*, a playbook of arguments for the students in the Academy, Aristotle (revealingly) suggests that while the obviously correct answer to the question "What is the object of desire (*boulêsis*)?" is "the apparent good," believers in the Platonic Forms cannot give this answer, since they think there is no Form of the apparent anything, let alone of the apparent good (VI.8.146b36–147a11). Notice that this Aristotelian and modern "under the description" answer in effect raises the apparent good to the status of a natural kind which must be referred to in giving a universal account of the relation between desire for good and the good. Notice also that the supposed failure of Socrates and Plato to give this answer could not have been due to their unfamiliarity with this kind of answer – since the Protagorean position, described at length at *Theaetetus* 151E-183C, precisely does construe every attribute such as good, true, and real as the apparent good, the apparently true, and the apparently real. See also Aristotle, *Nicomachean Ethics* III.4, esp. 1113a33.

42 We should compare here, as Harry Nieves once pointed out to me, the wife who says to her overweight and dyspeptic husband about to stuff his face with yet another spicy beef taco, "You don't want to do that." Of course, proponents of the apparent good will immediately declare an ambiguity here, as do Dodds 1959, p. 236, and others, so that the wife is speaking of wanting "in a special sense." Such postulations of special senses to account for the strange-looking things Socrates and Plato sometimes say surely seem suspiciously easy (1991, sec. 13).

43 At Penner 1991, secs. 4, 7, I try to bring out the great pains which Socrates takes in making this, for him, important distinction between doing what one wants and doing what seems best to one.

But is Aristotle also right that Socrates and Plato are just flat wrong about the object of desire? He is not. For he has approached the question "How could the desire for the real good bring about the action which is not the real good?" too narrowly. He has in effect argued that since the means acted on is not in fact the means to the real good, therefore the desire for the end, the good which generated this action can only be desire for the apparent good. (Because he chooses the wrong means, his desire for the end would, by these lights, also be desire for the wrong end.) By these lights, no one who ever acts unwisely exhibits in those deeds desire for the real good. Perhaps many will suppose that this is right.

Let us try to see why this need not be so, so that we can see why Socrates and Plato would almost certainly have persisted in their view that all desire productive of deliberate action is desire for the real good.[44] Consider the way in which Plato has Socrates build to the conclusion that if the action turns out badly, the tyrant didn't want to do it. One thing we can certainly see here is that what Socrates has in mind is that the object of desire necessarily has a means/end structure along the lines suggested in the opening paragraphs of this chapter. In wanting to do what will bring about his own real or actual maximum available happiness, the tyrant should obviously also want to do whatever particular action is in fact the best means-to-that-further-end. That best means we know to be not killing. So we have the tyrant's desire directed (unbeknownst to him) at not killing. But we also know that the tyrant believes that the action to which his desire for his own real good directs him is this act of killing, which he actually brings about. So surely what has happened is that while he is, so to speak, proceeding from his desire for the particular action which in fact brings about his own real good, to the actual action he does, his beliefs lead him to misidentify the particular best action in question (the one he really does want to do – in fact, the not killing) with the disastrous killing. So, as a result of this false identity-belief (the action which is in fact best with the disastrous

44 Socrates and Plato will have been familiar with the Protagorean idea that desire must always be for the apparent good and not the real good (*Theaetetus* 151E-183C). Might this have been because they were unfamiliar with the idea that desire might be for the apparent good, not the real good? No, as the treatment of *Protagoras* at *Theaetetus* 151E-183C shows. Aristotle departed from Protagoras only in his refusal to accept the Protagorean position that, in addition, it is meaningless to speak of any (noumenal) real good. Hence Aristotle is careful to speak, with unnecessary obscurity, of what is "without qualification and in truth" desired as the real good: but this is only an expression of the point that when good people desire things their apparent good is the real good.

killing), the executive desire is hijacked and misdirected to the killing. This gets us that the object of the executive desire in this case is that action which is the really best means available [in fact, not killing] to the maximum of real happiness now available to me, where that act is identical with this act of killing the prime minister which leads to misery ever after.

But that is not the action the tyrant wanted to do. This account of this (incoherent) object of desire both explains why the tyrant did the killing because of his desire for his own real good, and also why he didn't in fact want to do the action he did. And this seems to me to be all that can be required of the Socratic/Platonic theory.

Notice how, in this account, the tyrant's mistaken action does not result from his desire for his own apparent happiness. The desired end remains his real happiness. The mistake in the action results from a mistake in the tyrant's beliefs: his beliefs about the best available means to his real happiness. He misidentifies the really best means whatever it may really be (which is really not a killing) with the killing, which is really only the apparently best means. There is no mistake in the end desired – the real good.

Can we make sense of this misidentifying, and so of this defective (and even incoherent) object of desire and the way it embodies a false identity belief?[45] That Plato would want to makes sense of this kind of psychological state embodying a false identity belief can be seen in the way he treats false belief in the Theaetetus. Suppose I think – or say to myself – "That guy is Theaetetus" when actually it is Theodorus.[46] If "that guy" is to refer, even inside my psychological state, to that guy, whoever he actually is, then my state is the incoherent state of thinking that someone, who is not Theaetetus, is Theaetetus. Here we have a choice: either (a) allow that at least some expressions occurring, so to speak, within psychological states, can refer to things in the real world, and so grant that our states may be in this way incoherent;[47] or (b) keep

---

45 The account in the next paragraph is slightly modified from Penner 1991, secs. 8–10, with Penner and Rowe 1994, pp. 1–8, and Penner and Rowe 2005, ch. 10, sec.4.

46 See the treatment of identity-beliefs at Theaetetus 192D-197a. I shall be treating elsewhere of masterful Fregean (sense/reference) treatments of this passage (e.g., McDowell 1973) which, while undoubtedly the best treatments so far, seem to me to fall short, through their failure to handle a problem analogous to that involved with desire for the real good. These treatments in effect have us doing something isomorphic with identifying the apparent "that guy" with Theaetetus.

47 This kind of move seems demanded by the treatment in recent philosophy of language of proper names and pronouns: see, for example, Perry 1997, with

our inner states self-consistent, and known with certainty to the agent.[48] This will involve representing the agent's thought in a way that entirely separates it from those actual things in the world that are there. For if not, one would not know with certainty the content of one's thought, since one does not know the actual objects in the real world in this way. The results in this second option are that our representation of the agent's thought will involve only the agent's descriptions of things – independently of whether or not they pick out anything.[49] I remember Gilbert Ryle remarking somewhere, in a related setting, "On this showing, solitude is the ineluctable destiny of the soul."

On the view here attributed to Socrates and Plato, we see (what I have elsewhere[50] called) Socratic/Platonic ultra-realism at work. This ultra-realism does not allow the essentially Protagorean view that we only ever succeed in referring to, or loving, or fearing things as they appear to us. Nor does it allow the modern view that we only ever succeed in referring to what our conceptions (or the meanings of our descriptions) determine in the real world. Thus, at *Cratylus* 387A1–9, with 385D2ff, 387C6–D9, Plato tells us, contra the Protagoreans, that when we want to cut, we don't want to cut in accordance with our beliefs about what cutting is, nor even in accordance with the conventions governing the use of our words. We want to cut in accordance with the real nature of cutting – and (implicit in this) even if that real nature differs from what

references there to Kaplan, Kripke, Donnellan, and, of course, the groundbreaking work of Frege. The resulting difficulties these treatments will find with coherence in the psychological state have been less emphasized.

48 If it were simply the apparent good which was the object of desire, then the object of desire would make a consistent whole – and be identical with what the agent thinks it is (so that the agent would know incorrigibly what he desires). Notice, however, that (as Mitsuyoshi Nomura has rightly emphasized to me) modern treatments using "under the description" (n. 40) also require a description that is actually false of the action that is being done. On incorrigibility, notice its early appearance in the Protagorean phenomenon/noumenon theory at *Theaetetus* 151D-152C, 178B5–7. I shall be treating this theme elsewhere, so close to the whole Fregean approach to objects of psychological states.

49 Alternatively, on this option we could allow the descriptions to refer to those things (and those things only) which the descriptions are true of. But what if our descriptions are inadequate, and even pick out an object we are not talking about? (Take Leonard Linsky's famous example, "Her husband is kind to her" – when actually it is her lover.) That this would also end up unsatisfactorily from the Socratic/Platonic perspective will become clear in the discussion immediately following of the real nature of cutting (as opposed to what our descriptions of cutting would be true of).

50 Penner 2005b.

our beliefs (or conceptions) or our linguistic conventions (or the meanings of our words) would determine cutting to be. Once again, we are invited to see our language and our beliefs and our conceptual schemes not as things determining what actions or things we refer to, but as things designed for us to look through (however imperfectly and inaccurately) to the real things that are there, as they are in themselves and with all their properties known and unknown.[51] Similarly, in Socrates' inquiries of the "What is X?" form – and also in what the "What is X?" inquiries become in later dialogues, namely, the search for the Forms as the objects of the sciences – the concern is not with our best scientific concepts (that is, with what current science delivers as the basic entities) but with what the basic entities really are, even if they differ from what our concepts deliver (now, or even in the indefinite future).

The metaphysics of the psychology of action that we get from the passages considered earlier – and in particular the requirement that what everyone desires is the real good, even if that is something different from what one thinks it is – is very simple and intuitive. It is also very much in accord with this Socratic/Platonic ultra-realism generally, as when Plato further argues that we do not want our words "cutting" ("burning," "naming," and the like) to name what we describe as "cutting" or "naming," or what is picked out by the supposed linguistic conventions for our use of those words.[52] Rather, we want them to refer to what cutting really is. (The implication is that at least sometimes we do. That is, we do succeed in referring to what cutting really is – through the fog of various false beliefs or misdirected linguistic conventions.) Just so, in the *Republic* (505E1–506A7, 505A1-B3), it is not what we believe to be best, or even suppose we know to be best, that we desire for ourselves and those we love, but what really is best, even though we do not know what that is. Similarly, what I want for those I care for is neither what I think is best, nor what they think is best, but what really is best, even though what that is be unknown to both me and them.

True, it might seem that since I cannot now distinguish between my real good and what I think my real good is, therefore it makes no sense to deny that what I now desire is what I think my real good is – that is,

---

51 At 385D2ff, Socrates identifies the view we know as "linguistic conventionalism" (words attach to things solely by virtue of our arbitrary convention) a form of Protagorean Relativism. This identification will seem a stretch unless one allows that, for a conventionalist, convention should also determine what the actual object is, the name of which is determined by convention only. This will hold for many who believe that we can only refer to what the conventions for our words pick out – who hold that "meaning determines reference" (Penner 2005a, n. 30 and passim.)

52 See *Cratylus* 387Bff.

my apparent good. But if I can worry that it will later appear that what I think is my real good is not my real good, then I can surely now want what will turn out to be my real good, and therefore want whatever my real good is, even if that differs from what I now think it is.

Two important implications of this Socratic/Platonic ultra-realism should be noted. First, on the politically centered notion of power, Socrates points out that orators and tyrants, to the extent they think that ability to win by persuasion alone (or by military and police force alone) guarantees power, actually have no power whatever (466D7-E1, 467A3). For suppose that power is the ability to do whatever you want, and that acting without knowledge of the real good is bound to end in disaster if, in reliance on persuasion and force, one ignores wisdom (n.38 above). For life, and our deliberative structures, are so complicated that acting in error is inherently likely to end badly. Then the orators and tyrants will not gain their real good, and so will have done nothing that they wanted.[53]

Second, this distinction between doing what one wants and doing what seems best parallels the odd-looking, but well-known Platonic distinction between true pleasures and false pleasures, true fears and false fears,[54] and that between true rhetoric, which is a science, and Gorgias-style rhetoric, which is not a science, and the like.[55] In that spirit, we might even speak of the tyrant who does what merely seems best as having a "false desire" to do that action. Socrates and Plato evidently think of desire, as they think of many emotions and many other experiences, as much more truth-involved (reality-involved) than do subsequent thinkers.[56]

In conclusion, I note two further consequences of this amazing combination of psychology of action with Socratic ethics that I have been urging. First, as soon as we notice that every motivated action whatever is determined by the generalized desire for good and the belief as to which

---

53 Thus neither Hitler nor Nixon, whatever their devastating effects on the lives of others, had any power at all.

54 *Philebus* 36Cff, *Republic* 583Bff.

55 Gorgias-style rhetoric not a science or expertise: *Gorgias* 449A-461 with Penner 1988. True rhetoric: *Gorgias* 517A, *Phaedrus* with 272D-Eff, esp 276A and 277B-278A. See also the contrast that shows up in the image of the slightly deaf shipmaster at *Republic* 487E-489C, who has the science of navigation, as opposed to what the raucous crew, at 488D10, declare to be a science. See also 493A-C.

56 In modern psychology and philosophy, there are some truth-involved or reality-involved psychological states – namely, knowing vs. falsely believing, and seeing vs mis-perceiving ("false seeing"!).

action is best, the thought must occur to us that both of these elements are themselves determined. For the desire for good holds of all of us in every motivated action by virtue of (what we would call) a law of nature. So at the level of desire for ultimate end, we could not have desired otherwise. Now subordinate ends appear only through the combination of this ultimate end with one's beliefs. But what one believes at any given time is presumably also determined – by one's encounters with both the perceptual environment, and the agent's mental history (including what discussions one has had with whom). The result: at any given moment one could neither have desired otherwise, nor believed otherwise than one did at the given moment. So, contrary to Aristotle and most later Western moral philosophers, no one ever could have done otherwise than he or she actually did. This (teleological or means/end) determinism also confirms the account of Socrates' attitude to punishment, and to standard legal and moral responsibility, as tools of ethics.[57]

Second, the differences between people who do bad things (things that are in fact bad) and people who do good things cannot reside in their generalized desire for good – if no one wants to be (really) miserable and unhappy, then no one desires (really) bad things: *Meno* 78A6 – for in this respect we are all alike. On Socratic belief/desire theory, the difference must therefore reside solely in people's beliefs.[58] This is also why, for Socrates, the only factor that is ever relevant to changing someone's conduct, or to educating someone in virtue, is changing his beliefs. It is also why discussion with others, every day, on the important questions of how to live, is the most important thing in one's life. For life is complex, and understanding limited. (As is well-known, Socrates holds that while he is the wisest person there is, he knows nothing of

57   I pass over Plato's determinist and heartless justification of punishment and his determinist species of responsibility in *Laws X* – in spite of his still endorsing "No one errs willingly." One result of the anti-Socratic belief that actions are caused by irrational desires alone is the Platonic/Aristotelian (and all too modern) belief in punishment and habituation (conditioning) as forms of moral education.

58   *Meno* 78A6–8. Notice that this is not so in Aristotle's theory. For Aristotle, good people do differ from bad people in their fundamental desires, since people do differ in what their apparent good is. By Aristotle's account of desire for the good, their false beliefs as to what the good is infect the fundamental desire. While in Socrates, the failure of the bad person is in his beliefs, not in the desire for good (the best end available in the circumstances); in Aristotle, as in modern treatments of desire of the under the description variety, the failure of the bad person also infects the desire for good which is the moving principle (*archê*) of action, resulting not in mere ignorance but in wickedness: see *Nicomachean Ethics* III.1.1110b28–1111a1 with 1113a16–17, 1140b19–20, 1151a15–20.

any importance about the good.) One cannot do it all by oneself. When Socrates says that the unexamined life is not worth living, what he has in mind is examination together – dialectic. Hence, indeed, not only the unexamined life, but even a life that is not examined in every waking hour, is not worth living.[59]

I can now also propose a possible answer to our earlier question[60]: "Why does Socrates think that harming others always ends up in harm to one-self?" To harm is to require that one also deceive others about what one is doing. But acting with the kinds of deception so graphically described in *Republic* I, IX, X, and elsewhere, is to cut oneself off from dialectic with those one harms or deceives (or those who care for them), since, without such deception, one may no longer expect such people to enter the dialectic with the kind of openness that alone enables one, together with them, to get to the bottom of what is being discussed. But with the deception, one cannot oneself be open. (From the deceiver's end, there may be no end to the auxiliary falsehoods forced on the deceiver to keep his or her story straight.) The consequences here will be fairly serious, since, as logicians from the time of Duns Scotus have rightly said, to add a falsehood to what one is saying is to imply everything whatever. And if one wants one's thoughts to refer to things as they are in the real world, there will be lots of falsehoods. In the end, the problem cannot be resolved except by withdrawal from communication of a sort that also bodes ill for the deceiver. This need for openness is often cited by those who advise on children, marriage, management, and even, sometimes government. Socrates would have found the advice not only good, but essential.

Socratic ethics, on my reading, is a simple corollary of this ultra-real-ist psychology of action, taken together with Socrates' functional theory of good (which involves teleological theories both of nature itself and of all the sciences or expertises). As for the theory of the sciences and the functional theory of good, they involve not just the means the function is to provide, but the end the function serves. In ethics, all means and ends are judged against the human good of maximum available real hap-piness. All questions here are purely questions of fact – however deeply hidden the answers (more deeply, no doubt, than those of particle phys-ics, another matter on which no one currently has final knowledge). For

59 Consider, by way of contrast, the view that the requirements on human goodness ("ethical principles") must be uncomplicated enough to be pub-licly promulgated and readily understood by the ordinary citizen. (Rawls 1971, p. 130–142.) Given the importance Socrates attaches to deliberation (just above), this is unlikely to be a view which would commend itself to Socrates.

60 See my discussion on pp. 287–289 above.

Socratic ethics too, then, there are no further non-factual, non-natural, evaluative, normative, moral, or conventional elements, no further Kantian principles, and no further "intrinsic goods." It is, I think, the one morality-free theory of objective good available to us that contains no elements of conventions of the sort Socrates or Plato would have regarded as unacceptable. The conjecture occurs to me that it may be virtually alone among non-conventionalist theories compatible with the Descent of Man from the higher primates. For I doubt that there could be a comparable evolution of a non-conventional categorical imperative.

WORKS CITED

Annas, J. *The Morality of Happiness*. Oxford, 1993.

Annas, J. *Platonic Ethics, Old and New*. Ithaca, 1999.

Anscombe, G. E. M. *Intention*. Oxford, 1957

Beaney, M., ed. *The Frege Reader*. Oxford, 1997.

Darwall, S. *Philosophical Ethics*. Boulder, 1998.

Davidson, D. "Actions, Reasons, and Causes." *The Journal of Philosophy* vol. 60, no. 23 (1963):685–700., repr. in *Essays on Actions and Events*. Oxford, 1980, pp. 3–20.

Dodds, E. R. *Plato: Gorgias*. Oxford, 1959.

Donnellan, K. "Reference and Definite Descriptions." *Philosophical Review* 75 (1966): 281–304.

Frege, G. 1892. "On Sinn and Bedeutung." tr. M. Black, in Beaney, 151–171.

Irwin, T. *Plato's Moral Theory*. Oxford, 1977.

Irwin, T. *Plato's Ethics*. Oxford, 1995.

Kahn,, C. H. *Plato and the Socratic Dialogue; The Philosophical Use of a Literary Form*. Cambridge, 1996.

Kant, I. *Groundwork of the Metaphysics of Morals*. In *Practical Philosophy*. Cambridge, 1996.

Kaplan, D. "Dthat." In *Demonstratives*, ed. P. Yourgrau. Oxford, 1990, pp. 11–34.

Kripke, S. "Naming and Necessity." In *Semantics of Natural Language*, eds. D. Davidson and G. Harman. Boston, 1972, pp.253–255.

Linsky, L. 1963. "Reference and referents." In *Philosophy and Ordinary Language*, ed. C. Caton. Urbana, 1963, pp. 74–89.

McCabe, M. M. "Out of the Labyrinth: Plato's Attack on Consequentialism." *Virtues, Norms, and & Objectivity: Issues in Ancient and Modern Ethics*, ed. C. Gill. Oxford, 2005, pp. 189–214.

McDowell, J., trans. *Plato: Theaetetus*. Oxford, 1973.

Morrison, D. "Happiness, Rationality, and Egoism in Plato's Socrates." In *Rationality and Happiness: From the Ancients to the Early Medievals*. eds. J. Yu and J. Garcia. Rochester, 2003, pp. 17–34.

Penner, T. "The Unity of Virtue." *Philosophical Review* 82 (1973): 35–68.

Penner, T. "Desire and Power in Socrates: the Argument of Gorgias 466a-468e that Orators and Tyrants Have No Power in the City." *Apeiron* 24 (1991): 147–202.

Penner, T. 1992. "Socrates and the Early Dialogues." In *The Cambridge Companion to Plato*. ed. R. Kraut. Cambridge, 1992, pp. 121–169.

Penner, T. "Knowledge vs. True Belief in the Socratic Psychology of Action." *Apeiron* 29 (1996): 199–230.

Penner, T. "The Forms, the Form of the Good, and the Desire for Good in Plato's Republic." *The Modern Schoolman* 80 (2003): 191–233.

Penner, T. "The good, advantage, happiness, and the Form of the Good: How continuous with Socratic Ethics is Platonic Ethics?" In *Pursuit of the Good*. eds. D. Carins, F. -G. Herrmann, and T.Penner. Edinburgh, 2007.

Penner, T., and C. Rowe. "The Desire for Good: Is the *Meno* consistent with the *Gorgias*?" *Phronesis* 39 (1994): 1–25.

Penner, T., and C. Rowe. *Plato's Lysis*. Cambridge, 2005.

Perry, J. 1997. "Indexicals and Demonstratives." In *A Companion to Philosophy of Language*. eds. B. Hale and C. Wright. Oxford, 1997, pp. 586–612.

Price, A. *Mental Conflict*. London, 1995.

Rawls, J. *A Theory of Justice*. Cambridge, MA, 1971.

Rudebusch, G. "Socratic Perfectionism." In *Desire, Identity and Existence*, ed. N. Reshotko. Kelowna, BC, Canada, 2003, pp. 127–141.

Santas, G. *Socrates: Philosophy in Plato's Early Dialogues*. London, 1979, chap.VI.

Vlastos, G. "Socrates on Akrasia." *Phoenix* 23 (1969): 71–88.

Vlastos, G. "The Unity of the Virtues in the *Protagoras*." In *Platonic Studies*. Princeton, 1973, pp. 221–264.

Vlastos, G. *Socrates: Ironist and Moral Philosopher*. Ithaca, 1991.

13   Socrates and Eudaimonia

I. INTRODUCTION

It has long been a commonplace that ancient ethical thought is characterized by its eudaimonism. The great nineteenth-century moral philosopher Henry Sidgwick, for example, remarks that "in the whole ethical controversy of ancient Greece ... it was assumed on all sides that a rational individual would make the pursuit of his own good his supreme aim." Sidgwick also thinks that its commitment to eudaimonism is one of the most important features that distinguishes ancient ethical reflection from that of the moderns from the time of Bishop Butler on.[1] Whether or not we accept Sidgwick's claims, *eudaimonia* (typically translated as "happiness") is a central concept in ancient Greek ethical and political philosophy. In this chapter, I shall examine the idea of *eudaimonia* or happiness in Socrates' thought and consider what place it has in his views about how to live and how to act, what content he gives it, and its relation to other important notions, such as virtue and knowledge.

But before turning to these substantive issues, I begin by marking out the territory that I shall be exploring. Many scholarly controversies surround any discussion of Socrates. For example, what evidence do we have for the views of the historical Socrates? How reliable are the depictions of Socrates by Plato, Xenophon, Aristophanes, and other "Socratic" writers? Can we reliably date Plato's dialogues so as to isolate those that are closest in time to his association with Socrates? Since other essays in this volume consider these disputes in greater detail, I shall simply state the limitations of my discussion without examining the arguments justifying them. My way of carving up this territory, although certainly not the only plausible one, is fairly common.

I would like to thank Corinne Gartner, Hugh Gorman, Eric Hutton, Christine Kim, Katy Meadows, and especially Don Morrison for their comments on this chapter.

1   Sidgwick 1981, p. 92, 404–405. For general discussions of happiness in the Greek tradition, see Annas 1993 and White 2002.

I shall confine my discussion exclusively to Plato, but I take no position on the relation between the views of the character named "Socrates" in these dialogues and the views of the historical Socrates. Plato's dialogues are standardly divided into three chronological groups: early, middle, and late. The early dialogues are sometimes called the "Socratic" dialogues in the belief that they especially reflect Socrates' influence on Plato. I take no position on this either, but I shall focus on the dialogues usually thought of as early.[2] Thus the relevance of my discussion for the views of the historical Socrates will depend on how these scholarly controversies are settled.

2. PRELIMINARIES

The adjective *eudaimôn* ("happy"), and its cognate forms such as the substantive *eudaimonia*, are compounds of *eu* and the noun *daimôn*: *eu* is the standard adverb of the adjective meaning "good" (*agathos*) and the noun *daimôn* denotes divine or semi-divine beings (or more generally the divine forces or powers) who influence what happens to humans. Being *eudaimôn* is thus, etymologically, to be well-off or successful or in a good way with respect to such beings or forces.

Eudaimôn first occurs in extant Greek literature in the early poet Hesiod, where it means "free from divine ill-will" or "being divinely favored."[3] For example, at the end of his poem *Works and Days*, Hesiod closes a discussion of which days are lucky and which unlucky with the comment:

That man is happy [*eudaimôn*] and prosperous in them who knows all these things and does his work without offending the deathless gods, who discerns the omens of birds and avoids transgression.[4] (lines 826–828)

2   I count as early, *Apology, Charmides, Crito, Euthydemus, Euthyphro, Gorgias, Hippias Major, Hippias Minor, Ion, Laches, Lysis, Menexenus, Meno,* and *Protagoras.* The stylometric evidence for putting these dialogues earlier than the rest is fairly strong and is accepted by some scholars who see no substantive philosophical differences between the early and middle dialogues (*Parmenides, Phaedrus, Republic,* and *Theaetetus*), see Kahn 1996, pp. 37–48, and Dorion's Chapter 1 in this volume. Although there is some stylometric evidence for placing the *Cratylus,* the *Phaedo,* and the *Symposium* after the early group and before the middle, my reasons for treating them as not belonging with the other early dialogues depend on substantive considerations about their content and thus are more controversial.

3   de Heer 1968, p. 26, is a helpful study of happiness in non-philosophical Greek thought.

4   Evelyn-White 1982. Here and elsewhere I have made occasional changes in the translation.

Similarly, in other archaic poets, such as Theognis and Pindar, its basic sense is "being divinely favored." And the result of being divinely favored is that I shall have and enjoy many things that are good for me and avoid bad things.

Two passages from these early writers are especially interesting in light of later developments. First, from Theognis:

> May I be happy and beloved of the immortal gods, Cyrnus,
> that is the only excellence or achievement I desire.[5] (lines 653–654)

This passage demonstrates the practical centrality of being happy; it is, for Theognis, the most important object of desire and perhaps even the only achievement desired. The second passage is the warning from Pindar that "it is impossible for one man to succeed in winning complete happiness."[6] This suggests that although happiness may be the primary object of desire, humans cannot completely or permanently attain it. We shall find related issues in Socrates.

There are two central lines of thought already implicit in these early non-philosophical claims about happiness that are especially important for the later Greek philosophical tradition. The first of these understands being happy and happiness in terms of well-being. As a first approximation, let us say that a person is happy or attains happiness if and only if he lives a life that is best for him, all things considered.[7] This characterization contains two basic ideas that, although requiring further specification, are intuitively fairly clear: (1) that of something being good (or bad) for a person, and (2) some notion of optimization, maximization or being best overall. (I shall leave aside, for now, some complications about whether happiness is a scalar notion – that is, comes in degrees, or is identified strictly with the optimal point.)[8]

Ancient Greeks, just as we, had a notion of something being good or bad for a person and the notion of taking various good and bad things into account in order to reach some overall judgment of how good or bad a person's state is. If we think of being *eudaimôn* in this way as attaining one's best overall condition, we might think that "happiness" is an inadequate translation, since "happiness" is commonly understood today to mean "feeling pleasure" or "feeling content." But there is no obvious better translation, and as long as we remember that it is

---

5   Edmonds 1968.
6   *Nemean* 7. 55–6; Race 1997.
7   For the idea that happiness is the state or condition of being happy, see *Euthd.* 289C6–8 with 291B4–7 and *Grg.* 478C3–7.
8   For further discussion, with references, see Bobonich 2002, pp. 210–213, and n. 10.

a substantive question whether one's best overall state consists in, or even involves, – for example, feeling pleasure, this translation should not mislead.[9] There may be some difficulty in understanding how a person could be mistaken about whether he is feeling pleasure or feeling content, but it is intuitively much more plausible that he might be mistaken about whether he is in his best possible state, and Greek philosophers standardly hold that people can, and often are, mistaken about whether they are happy.

The second line of thought starts from the idea that human actions and desires have purposes, goals, or ends, and goes on to suggest that happiness is the most important, or perhaps even the sole, end of human actions and desires. We saw something like this in the quotation from Theognis. This thesis, too, needs to be sharpened and made more precise, but we can note now one significant distinction. The primacy of happiness might simply be a fact about human action or desire: as a matter of fact, human beings do give such primacy to happiness in all their actions or desires. But Theognis's poem is a series of exhortations and counsels to Cyrnus, and simple declarative statements of how he acts and thinks are frequently implicit pieces of (supposedly wise) advice. So we might also understand this as a normative claim that it is wise or rational to make happiness the primary end of one's actions.

These two lines of thought are logically distinct. It would need further argument to show that if there is (or rationally should be) a primary end of one's actions and desires, then this is one's own happiness. Why might the end not, instead, be the happiness of all, the advancement of truth, or complete and perfect obedience to God's commands? Similarly, the very concept of the best state overall for an individual does not by itself include the claim that this state is, or rationally should be, the primary aim of each individual. We might think, for example, that it is sometimes rational to sacrifice my own well-being or happiness for some more important goal.

But bringing these two lines of thought together, we arrive at two theses that have often been attributed to Socrates.

The Principle of Rational Eudaimonism: It is rationally required that, for each person, his own (greatest) happiness is the decisive consideration for all his actions.

The Principle of Psychological Eudaimonism: Each person pursues (and tries to act upon) his own (greatest) happiness as the decisive consideration for all his actions.[10]

9   See Kraut 1979 and Vlastos 1991, pp. 200–209; this concern goes back at least to Sidgwick 1981, p. 92.

10   For further discussion, with references, of both principles, see Crisp 2003 and Irwin 1995, p. 52–5. In these principles, "greatest happiness" refers to

The Principle of Rational Eudaimonism is a normative principle; it tells us what we have to do to live up to the standard of acting rationally, but makes no claim about whether human beings do, in fact, act rationally. The Principle of Psychological Eudaimonism is a descriptive thesis; it purports to tell us how all human beings do, in fact, act. Stronger versions of rational and psychological eudaimonism hold that happiness is the only rational (or psychological) consideration relevant to pursuit and action: the only ultimate reason why I rationally should (or psychologically do) pursue anything is that it optimally contributes to my own happiness. I shall focus on the two principles as formulated (though I shall occasionally bring in the stronger ones). I do so both because the evidence is clearer with respect to the principles as stated and because what seems to be of the greatest practical importance is what rationally should, and what psychologically does, determine action.

In the rest of this chapter, I shall proceed to consider some of the basic issues surrounding Socrates' views on happiness.

(1) Does Socrates endorse either the Principle of Rational Eudaimonism or the Principle of Psychological Eudaimonism?
(2) What does Socrates think happiness consists of? What is the relation between happiness and virtue?
(3) What place does the notion of happiness have in Socrates' ethical thinking?

In the course of discussing these questions, I also argue that Socrates' views about happiness and its relation to virtue contain certain gaps and tensions that Plato's middle-period dialogues, such as the *Phaedo* and the *Republic*, try to resolve.

3. RATIONAL EUDAIMONISM AND PSYCHOLOGICAL EUDAIMONISM

For quite some time, a majority of scholars have held that the early dialogues espouse both psychological and rational eudaimonism. But in recent years, both parts of this consensus have come under criticism as has, more generally, the view that ancient Greek ethics is eudaimonist. The critics of the eudaimonist consensus with respect to Plato's

---

the optimal outcome on either the scalar or optimizing understanding of happiness. Note that the Principle of Psychological Eudaimonism does not say exactly what psychological facts about a person make it true that his desires aim at happiness, and it does not immediately entail that the person must have any particular conscious attitudes; cf. n.35.

early dialogues have pressed two worries. First, they claim that Socrates says things in the early dialogues that are inconsistent (or at least fit awkwardly) with eudaimonism. Second, they claim that the positive evidence for eudaimonism in the early dialogues is surprisingly thin.[11] Since I shall argue for a version of the consensus view, I begin by examining these concerns carefully.

Consider first the point about possible inconsistency. In some of these dialogues, especially the *Apology* and the *Crito*, Socrates makes what seems to be an unequivocal commitment to being virtuous or just and acting virtuously or justly. In replying to an objection in the *Apology*, for example, Socrates says:

> You are wrong, sir, if you think that a man who is any good at all must [*dein*] take into account the risk of life or death; he should look only to this when he acts, whether what he does is just [*dikaia*] or unjust, whether he is acting as a good [*agathou*] or a bad man [*kakou*].[12] (*Ap.* 28B6-C1)

While rejecting Crito's plan to escape from prison, Socrates reminds him of their previous agreements:

> Do we say that one must never in any way act unjustly willingly, or must one act unjustly in one way and not in another? Is acting unjustly never good [*agathou*] or fine [*kalon*] as we agreed in the past? ... Above all, is the truth such as we used to say it was ... that injustice is in every way bad [*kakon*] for, and shameful [aischron] to, the one acting unjustly? ... So one must [*dei*] never do injustice. (*Crito* 49A4-B7)

In these passages, Socrates claims that an individual must always act virtuously or justly. Such a commitment raises two concerns. First, if Socrates means that an individual must, from a rational point of view, always act

---

11   For discussions, with references, of eudaimonism see, Annas 1999, pp. 31–51; Brickhouse and Smith 1994, pp. 73–136; and Vlastos 1991, pp. 200–232. For criticism of the eudaimonist consensus, see Morrison 2003 and White 2002. More scholars are inclined to challenge psychological eudaimonism (especially on the basis of certain passages in the *Gorgias*) than rational eudaimonism. Brickhouse and Smith 1994 and Irwin 1995 both provide helpful references to the secondary literature on many of the issues discussed in this chapter; I shall often cite them in lieu of listing this literature. Gomez-Lobo 1999 is a useful account that is more accessible to the general reader.

12   Plato translations draw on those in Cooper 1997. *Dein* which is translated as "must" is from *deô* (B) in LSJ, i.e., "lack, miss, stand in need of," not, as is sometimes said, from *deô* (A) "bind, fetter." The LSJ entry for *dei* has the typographical error of "*deô* (A)" for "*deô* (B)"; also see Frisk 1960–72 and Goodell 1914.

justly even if doing so diminishes his happiness, this would be inconsistent with the Principle of Rational Eudaimonism. If this is Socrates'
meaning, and he also makes the reasonable assumption that in at least
some of these cases a person will do what he should do from a rational
point of view, then Socrates would also be committed to the denial of the
Principle of Psychological Eudaimonism. Second, even if virtue and happiness can never come apart – that is, even if the virtuous life must also
be the happy life – this does not settle which features of such a life the
individual takes, or rationally should take, as decisive. Is he choosing a life
for the sake of its happiness, its virtue, or some combination of them?

To begin with the first point, these passages do not claim or even suggest that the agent's happiness does or even can come into conflict with
what virtue requires. In fact, the *Crito* passage asserts that injustice is
"never good" and is "in every way bad" for the one acting unjustly. And,
indeed, this passage in context suggests that virtue is always consistent
with the agent's greatest happiness (see the later discussion of *Crito*
48B). Such a coincidence between virtue and happiness might obtain in
several distinct ways:

(1) Identity Claim. Happiness is identical with (or wholly consti-
    tuted by) virtue.
(2) Part/Whole Claim. Virtue is a part of happiness.
(3) Instrumental Claim. Virtue is only instrumental to happiness –
    that is, virtue is merely a causal means to the distinct end of
    happiness.

Clearly, if the identity claim is correct, there can be no conflict
between virtue and happiness. The part/whole claim does not by itself
guarantee a coincidence between virtue and happiness, but a version of
it that made virtue a sufficiently important part of happiness could. The
instrumental claim could sustain such a coincidence, but only if virtue
were a genuinely necessary instrument. I shall return to these options
later in this section and in Section 4. As I shall also go on to discuss, our
decision among these options will affect our answer to our second issue
– that is, what is the ultimate criterion on the basis of which people do,
or rationally should, pursue things and perform actions.

Critics of eudaimonism have not only pointed to passages such as the
ones from the *Apology* and the *Crito* we have noted that stress Socrates'
commitments to virtue, but have also suggested that eudaimonism is
not invoked at places in the early dialogues where we would expect to
find it. One skeptic about the eudaimonist interpretation, for example,
points to Socrates' engagement in questioning others as one thing that
is not explained by eudaimonism in the early dialogues:

When we look to his [Socrates'] own actual words for an account of why he makes such efforts to improve his fellow citizens' thinking, we find little to clarify what their place in his own *eudaimonia* might be. Suppose he were confronted with this question 'Are you better off by virtue of your educative activities, and is that the reason why you engage in them, or do you pursue them partly or wholly for themselves?' It does not seem to me – suspending the automatic unargued presumption that Socrates accepted a straightforwardly eudaimonist view – that Plato's early works really give us a basis for saying how he would answer.[13]

But in the *Apology*, Socrates does explain why he refuses to accept release on the condition that he keep silent in the future.

If I say that it is impossible for me to keep quiet because that means disobeying the god, you will not believe me and will think I am being ironical. On the other hand, if I say it is the greatest good for a man every day to discuss virtue and the other things about which you hear me conversing and testing myself and others, and that the unexamined life is not worth living for a man, you will believe me even less. (*Ap.* 37E5–38A7)

Socrates here provides an answer as to why he engages in questioning his fellow citizens, and that answer seems to give a decisive reason for acting in this way. It is sufficient, he thinks, to justify rationally his acting in the way that he does. (The context, I think, makes it clear that Socrates sees this as a rationally decisive consideration.) This passage certainly does not commit Socrates explicitly and unequivocally to any form of eudaimonism, but it suggests that we can explain his "educative activities" by the fact that they promote his happiness and, more generally, that considerations of one's own "greatest good" or happiness should have a central place in determining what to do. Socrates here gives two reasons for his practices: acting in this way is both to obey the god and also the "greatest" good for himself. He does not say that one has priority over the other.[14] But Socrates also does not suggest that they can come apart, and there is reason from the *Apology* itself to think that obeying the god conduces to happiness, at least in large part, because god is benevolent and points us toward what conduces to our happiness.[15] Similarly, Socrates does not explicitly say that these

13   White 2002, p. 181.
14   In the *Republic*, Plato tries to show that no matter what the gods' attitude, the just person is always better off than the unjust person. Since Plato recommends justice, it seems that he would give one's own happiness priority over obeying god's commands, in the counterfactual situation in which they come apart.
15   For example, *Ap.* 41C8-D7, 30D6–31A9, cf. *Rep.* 379B1-C7; Brickhouse and Smith 1994, pp. 176–212. *Ap.* 41C8-D7 suggests that engaging in the elenchus is good independently of being commanded by god.

criteria should guide all our choices and actions, but there is nothing special about this case except its importance.

Indeed, in two other places in the *Apology*, Socrates explicitly describes engaging in the sort of conversations he has about virtue – and in which he tries to get his fellow citizens to participate – as being what most contributes to the participants' happiness. Such participation is, Socrates claims, the "greatest benefit" for each individual: involving his fellow citizens in discussion of virtue is how Socrates makes them happy (*Ap.* 36B3-D10). Note that Socrates thinks that this fact about happiness gives his fellow citizens decisive reason to lead such a way of life, although they do not have Socrates' special reason of obeying the command of the god given by the Delphic oracle. (Thus we can resolve the possible ambiguity of *Ap.* 37E-38A quoted earlier.) Engaging in such conversation after one's death would, Socrates claims, be the greatest good – that is, it would be extraordinary happiness and this is the best possible afterlife fate (*Ap.* 40E4–41C4).

The happiness in these passages is the agent's own happiness, Socrates explicitly uses the language of optimization, and the fact that engaging in such conversation about virtue conduces to happiness, so conceived, is presented as justifying such a way of life. Although Socrates does not here state the Principle of Rational Eudaimonism as a fully general and formal principle, these passages strongly suggest that he holds it. Moreover, in these passages, Socrates does not even hint that there is some good distinct from happiness that could be added to happiness to improve it or that should be weighed against it or that there is some consideration besides happiness that a rational person should take into account. If Socrates thought that any of these possibilities held, we should expect him to mention it. These passages thus also offer support for attributing to Socrates a stronger form of rational eudaimonism such that one's own greatest happiness is the only ultimate reason for action.

In the *Crito*, we find a passage that provides further help:

> We must treat as most important not life, but the good life [*to eu zēn*] ... and the good life, the fine [*kalōs*] life and the just [*dikaiōs*] life are the same. (*Crito* 48B4–7)

Socrates here gives priority to leading the good life, and insofar as it is most important, it seems that it should at least trump other considerations from a rational point of view.[16] But what does "the good

16 Socrates does not explicitly say that happiness subsumes all other considerations. So, strictly speaking, this leaves open the possibility that if two courses of action are tied as highest with respect to happiness, there is

life" mean here? Given its context at the conclusion of an argument designed to show that justice is of the greatest benefit to its possessor (*Crito* 47A-48B), the good life should mean a life that is best for the one who lives it. If it merely meant the fine life, or the just life (i.e., the virtuous life), there would be no point to Socrates' further claim that the good life is the same as the fine and just lives. It is this coincidence that allows Socrates to proceed to settle the practical question of what to do in these circumstances by examining what justice requires (*Crito* 48B1off).[17] This passage, with its explicit claim that we must treat the good life as most important, shows that the decisive rational consideration in the evaluation of lives is their happiness and thus is yet stronger support for attributing the Principle of Rational Eudaimonism to Socrates.

What of the Principle of Psychological Eudaimonism? In the *Apology*, Socrates defends himself against the charge that he corrupts the youth by arguing that since corrupting one's associates will result in harm to oneself, he either does not corrupt them or does so unwillingly (*Ap.* 25D-26A). Although Socrates is not fully precise in this passage, doing X unwillingly seems to be a case in which one does X while falsely believing that refraining from X would be worse for oneself. If one learns the truth that doing X is, in fact, worse for one, one will then refrain from doing it. Such claims are justifiable if Socrates accepts the Principle of Psychological Eudaimonism. This principle is not the only logically possible way to justify these claims, but it is a plausible assumption in the context and, as we shall see later, Socrates in other early dialogues does accept the general principle that "no one does wrong willingly" on the basis of the Principle of Psychological Eudaimonism.[18] To sum

---

some other consideration that might rationally decide between them. But Socrates says nothing to suggest this possibility.

17   For the interchangeability of *eu zên* and being happy, see *Rep.* 353E10–354A2. The equivalent phrase *eu prattein* ("to do well") is also interchangeable with being happy, see *Euthydemus* 278E3, E6, 279A2 and 280B6–7; the evidence is well presented by Brickhouse and Smith 1994, p. 113. Aristotle thinks that the identification of *eu zên* and *eu prattein* with living happily is a commonplace, see *EN* 1095a18–20.

18   Socrates thinks that if one believes that doing X is bad for oneself (*Ap.* 25E4 may suggest that it is more than moderately bad, but this is not required), one will not do X. The conclusion is not just that one has some motivation not to do X, but that one will simply not do it. Socrates' defense would weaken if he allowed that he might corrupt the young – e.g., because of short-term pleasures – even if he knew it were bad for himself to do so and he claims that it is just obvious that if he learns it is bad, then he will act otherwise (*Ap.* 26A4–5). Strictly speaking, this passage does not commit Socrates to the idea that each person always acts in accordance with what

up: even in the early dialogues thought to provide some of the greatest
challenges for eudaimonism, the *Apology* and the *Crito*, we find very
strong support for the Principle of Rational Eudaimonism and strong
support for the Principle of Psychological Eudaimonism as well.

In some of the other early dialogues (especially the *Euthydemus*, the
Gorgias, the *Meno*, and the *Protagoras*), we do find connections between
eudaimonism and some more general normative and psychological
claims. It is controversial whether Socrates goes so far as to endorse
any general normative or psychological claims in the early dialogues
and, if he does, exactly what attitude he has toward them.[19] But there
are certain claims that we have good reason to think that Socrates took
especially seriously.

(I) The virtues are properly characterized in terms of knowledge of
the good.

(II) Akrasia (weakness of will or incontinence) is not possible – that
is, roughly, it is not possible for me to know or believe that one
course of action is overall better for me and yet do something
else.

(III) All wrongdoing is unwilling.

So I shall now turn to some of these connections.

(I) It is well-known that the early dialogues typically end in *aporia* – that
is, a failure to find a solution to the problem at hand. Paradigmatically,
in the early "dialogues of definition," Socrates fails to find adequate
accounts or definitions of the virtues: of courage in the *Laches*, of moderation in the *Charmides*, and of piety in the *Euthyphro*. Nevertheless,
in these early dialogues, Plato takes especially seriously the idea that
virtue should be defined in terms of knowledge of good and bad. In the
Laches, for example, the final definition of courage is one that the interlocutor, Nicias, endorses and claims is based on Socrates' views. (Nicias
thinks that his own definition comes close to following from something
Socrates has "often" said, *Laches* 194C7-D10.) According to this definition, courage is "the knowledge of what is to be dreaded or dared, in war
and in everything else" (*Laches* 194E11–195A1). Socrates shows that
such knowledge is only possible if one has knowledge of future goods
(*agatha*) and (*kaka*) bads (*Laches* 198B2-C4). (Although it is uncommon

he thinks has the greatest surplus, all things considered, of good over bad.
But the evidence that Socrates holds the Principle of Rational Eudaimonism
in a maximizing form makes it plausible that maximizing applies
here too.

19   See Penner's Chapter 12 and Griswold's Chapter 14 in this volume.

English, I prefer "bads" to "evils," since the latter may suggest that these are "moral evils," rather than simply things that are bad for their possessor.) This definition of courage is ultimately called into question on the grounds that, along with other apparently reasonable premises, it leads to the conclusion that courage is knowledge of all goods and bads, past, present, and future. This entails, it is claimed, that courage is the whole of virtue and, not as previously agreed, a proper part of virtue. There are disagreements over how Socrates thinks this puzzle should be resolved. But on most plausible views, Socrates is at least committed to the claim that every virtue is some form of knowledge of good and bad.[20]

What implications does this have for eudaimonism? To begin, does Socrates intend by knowledge of good and bad knowledge of what is good and bad for the possessor of the knowledge or what is good and bad in some other way? If this knowledge does not at least include knowledge of what is good and bad for its possessor, it seems to have little relevance to eudaimonism.

It is clear from the context that this knowledge of good and bad is knowledge of what is good and bad for human beings in the various complex circumstances of life (e.g., *Laches* 194E11–195A1). But what is the relation between this knowledge and its possessor's own good and bad? One of Socrates' concluding remarks in the *Laches* helps to answer this question.

[There is nothing] wanting to the virtue of a man who knows all good things and all about their production in the present, the future, and the past, and all about bad things likewise. [Such a man could not lack] moderation, or justice, or piety, when he alone can take due precaution, in his dealings with gods and men, as regards what is to be dreaded and what is not, and procure good things, owing to his knowledge of the right behavior towards them. (*Laches* 199D4-E1)[21]

According to this passage, the result of possessing this knowledge is that the individual will act to procure good things for himself and avoid bad things for himself in his actions. A person who possesses such knowledge will possess every virtue, and thus the virtue of wisdom. Indeed, this knowledge of what is good and bad for oneself is sufficient for all of virtue. No other specifically moral kind of knowledge is needed for virtue (although this knowledge of good and bad may well include knowing that acting in the way that is usually thought to be, for

20 See, with references, Brickhouse and Smith 1999, pp. 158–73, and Cooper 1999, pp. 76–117.
21 Strictly speaking, this is a question to which the interlocutor assents. Note that *porizô* at *Laches* 199E1 is in the middle voice.

example, just is good for you).[22] So we may infer that since acting so as to procure good things for oneself is the outcome of wisdom, this way of acting must be what reason recommends. Further, Socrates assumes that the one having such knowledge will in fact act in accordance with it, and thus assumes that people will pursue what they know to be good (this does not yet commit Socrates to thinking that people will act in accordance with their belief about what is good if they only have belief).

So an individual will act to obtain good things and avoid bad things, and this is what is required by reason. But this does not yet commit Socrates to either rational or psychological eudaimonism, since these claims concern what is good and are not yet explicitly concerned with the optimal or the best.

The Good and the Best

We have already seen evidence in the *Apology* and the *Crito* that Plato is committed to some form of optimizing. What of the other early dialogues? In the *Charmides*, Socrates remarks that if people attained the knowledge that is moderation, they would be happy:

For with error abolished, and correctness guiding, men in that condition [i.e. those who possess such knowledge] would necessarily fare finely and fare well [*eu prattein*] in their every action, and those faring well are happy. (*Chrm.* 171E7–172A3)[23]

This passage does several important things. First, it claims that if the individual has this knowledge, he will fare well and be happy. It is reasonable to infer from this that such knowledge is in fact aimed at happiness. So the end or goal aimed at by such knowledge is not merely some good, but it has the optimality of happiness (it also has the optimality

22   Socrates has just argued that genuine knowledge (*epistêmê*) of good and bad is general in form, so this person will also know general truths about what is good and bad for human beings. But since Socrates stresses that the outcome of this knowledge is acting so as to benefit oneself, it is reasonable to conclude that this is the goal of such knowledge.

23   Socrates might reject this proposed definition of moderation, but there is no reason to think that he rejects the idea that a person who had genuine moderation would be in the condition that he describes; cf. *Laches* 199D4-E1. This view seems to require that the virtues be at least inter-entailing, and for our purposes we do not need to settle the *Laches'* worry of whether there is some even stronger relation among them. That Socrates is trying to identify the knowledge that will make its possessor happy is also clear from *Chrm.* 173D6–174E2.

involved in the idea that all such actions are correct). Further, this is the goal for "every action", not just for some. So this passage helps to answer the question about optimality and thus, along with the other passages cited, supports the Principle of Rational Eudaimonism.

Moreover, Socrates thinks that the possession of such knowledge guarantees that the individual will fare well or be happy, and such an assumption is reasonable if Socrates holds the Principle of Psychological Eudaimonism: if it is possible that an individual might act against such knowledge of what is best, then it is not the case that he "would necessarily fare finely and fare well."[24]

The picture is the same and the context is less complicated in the *Meno*. In the *Meno*, Socrates begins with the claims that (a) everyone desires the good, and (b) no one desires the bad (77B2–78B4). The context makes it clear that the good and the bad involved here are the agent's own good and bad.[25] But these are in themselves fairly weak claims.

(i) Socrates does not say that these are our only desires and aversions or that they trump all other desires and aversions.

(ii) These are presented as facts about human nature with no explicit further assertion that these desires are rational. (Although if we are all by nature irrational, we would expect Socrates to comment on this.)

(iii) Socrates claims that we desire the good and not the bad, so once again, this claim does not yet commit him to a form of optimizing.

But later passages in the *Meno* provide some further evidence. At *Meno* 87C-89A, we find an argument designed to show that virtue is a kind of knowledge or wisdom. In it, Socrates makes two important claims:

(1) wisdom guides all external goods and all qualities of the soul towards the end of happiness and one who is guided by wisdom attains happiness (*Meno* 88C1–3),

(2) this guidance of wisdom is correct (*Meno* 88D6-E2, cf. 98E12–99A5).

24 For an argument that *Euthd.* 278Eff, along with an argument from the *Lysis* about the proper explanation of action entails psychological eudaimonism, see Irwin (1995, pp. 52–55).

25 *Meno* 77B6–78B8, especially 77C7–9, 77E5–78B2. Even those who do not think that Plato in the early dialogues endorses rational eudaimonism accept that the good and bad aimed at in this passage are the agent's own good and bad; e.g., Morrison 2003, p. 23.

These passages seem to resolve all three concerns, (i)-(iii). First, the claim that knowledge of the good guarantees happiness provides the same sort of argument for the Principle of Psychological Eudaimonism that we just noted in the *Charmides*. Second, since the end of wisdom is happiness, reason requires its pursuit, and thus we should accept the Principle of Rational Eudaimonism.[26] Indeed, the fact that it is the only goal mentioned strongly suggests a stronger form of rational eudaimonism such that happiness subsumes all other goals. Finally, the rational goal is said to be not just the good, but happiness, so the ultimate goal has the sort of optimality attaching to happiness. The same picture is found in a similar passage from the *Euthydemus*.[27]

I shall end this section by looking at the two early dialogues that provide the most explicit detail about Socrates' ethical psychology, the *Gorgias* and the *Protagoras*. These dialogues will also allow us to explore the connections between eudaimonism and Socrates' views about akrasia and the claim that no one does wrong willingly. In the *Gorgias*, Socrates, as part of his explanation of human action, divides existing things into the good, the bad, and the things that are neither good nor bad.

Things neither good nor bad [are] such things as sometimes partake of the good and sometimes of the bad and sometimes of neither, for example, sitting, walking, running, and sailing ... and anything else of that sort ... People do these intermediate things, whenever they do them, for the sake of good things, [they do not do good things for the sake of the intermediates] ... So it is pursuing the good that we walk, whenever we walk; because we think it is better [to walk]. And conversely, whenever we stand still, we stand for the sake of the same thing, that is, the good. [(I)] And so we put a man to death, if we do put him to death, or exile him or confiscate his property, because we think it better for us to do this than not ... So it is for the sake of the good that the doers of all these things do them ... Then we do not want to kill people or exile them from our cities or confiscate their property as an act in itself, but if these things are beneficial we want to do them, while if they are harmful, we do not want them.

26 Socrates clearly means to claim here that my wisdom guides all my external goods and the qualities of my soul so as to bring about my happiness, and that my lack of wisdom makes it the case that these same things harm me, *Meno* 88B1-8. As *Meno* 88B5-6 shows, this is what Socrates intends his argument (87E5-88D3) to prove.

27 *Euthd.* 278E-282A. *Euthd.* 280B8-281D2 makes it clear that my wisdom guides all my other goods so as to attain my own happiness, cf. *Euthd.* 288D6-E2. 282A1-7 tells us that we must (*dei*) in every way try to become as wise as possible because wisdom is necessary and sufficient for the agent's happiness. This is an overall verdict concerning what we are to do, so happiness at least takes priority over other ends.

For we want what is good ... but what is neither good nor bad we do not want, nor what is bad either ... (*Grg.* 467E6–468C7)

This passage commits Socrates to the claims that (1) every action is "for the sake of" the good, and (2) that every want is for the good. To see what implications this has for eudaimonism, we need to consider some further questions.

First, is the good for the sake of which the agent acts the good of the agent himself? This is what Socrates' argument requires. For example, the inference made at (I) in the passage cited earlier would simply be invalid, unless the claim that "People do these intermediate things, whenever they do them, for the sake of good things" means that "People do these intermediate things, whenever they do them, for the sake of good things for themselves" – that is, it must mean that the good for the sake of which X acts is X's own good.[28]

Second, granting that whenever X acts, X acts for the sake of X's own good, are we to understand this as X's own maximal good? We have already seen evidence for optimizing or maximizing in other early dialogues, and we shall find the most worked out statement of it in the *Protagoras*. But there is also some evidence from the *Gorgias*. For example, *Gorgias* 468B1–7 at least strongly suggests optimizing. Socrates presents choice here as a dichotomy: we can either do X or not do X, and we do the one that we think is better for us. Such comparisons involve options that are mutually exclusive and jointly exhaustive and thus give us a form of optimization. So since what is aimed at is the agent's own greatest happiness, and since Socrates seems to endorse this as a criterion of choice, this passage gives us good evidence for the Principle of Rational Eudaimonism.

Socrates claims that the one doing injustice is more miserable (*athlios*) than the one suffering injustice (*Grg.* 469A1-B6) because doing injustice is the worst thing (469B8–9). For this inference to be as obvious as Socrates and Polus suppose it is – Polus disputes the truth of the claim that the one doing injustice is more miserable, not the connection between my being miserable and my action being worst – worst

---

28   Morrison 2003, pp. 25–26, suggests that all that Socrates is committed to in this passage is that a person always acts for the sake of someone's good, not that the person acts for the sake of his own good. Morrison also thinks that at *Grg.* 468B, when Socrates makes this inference, he is assuming the tyrant's perspective and that in this case we must be acting for the sake of our own good. But the thesis about acting for the good is a perfectly general one in this section, and the claim about what we do is meant to state a truth about how all people act; *Grg.* 467D6-E1, 468B1–4 (cf. *Meno* 77E-78B).

must mean "worst for the agent." Socrates then comments that he would choose to suffer rather than to do injustice (*Grg.* 469C1–2) for this reason (note *ara* at 469B12). It is reasonable to take this both as a consequence of the general psychological claims that Socrates has just made and, since Socrates approves of this choice, as an endorsement of the rationality of choosing the less miserable option. Although Socrates does not work out a calculus for taking good and bad both into account in arriving at an overall judgment of how happy the person is, the claim that the happiest person is one without any badness in his soul suggests that such overall judgments are possible (*Grg.* 478C3-E5).

The position of the *Gorgias* on psychological eudaimonism is more complicated. The first complication arises from Socrates' apparent claim that we want (*boulomai*) only what is actually good – that is, what is best for us overall (*Grg.* 468C2–8).[29] On the traditional interpretation, Plato means that all people have at all times the attitude of wanting (*boulêsis*) toward what is actually good, but also at the same time have a positive desiderative attitude – for example, a desire (*epithumia*) for what they think best. Moreover, all people at all times act (or try to act) upon the desire for what they think to be best. Even without working out in detail the differences between wants and desires, this is straightforwardly a form of psychological eudaimonism, since the agent always acts so as to attain what he thinks best for himself.

A more recent line of interpretation takes the far more radical position that Plato holds that the only positive desiderative attitude we have is toward what is actually best. But on this interpretation as well, Plato is committed to what is reasonably seen as a form of psychological eudaimonism in that it attributes to him the claim that agent always acts in accordance with what he thinks best for himself.[30]

29 My discussion here explains why I think that the good as the object of want is what is best for the agent overall. This understanding is shared by both traditional interpretations and Penner's interpretation. On Plato's terminology, see Kahn 1987; for a survey of positions on these issues, see McTighe 1984.

30 I believe that this is an accurate account of Penner's position, see, e.g., his 1991. Penner 1991, pp. 201–202, n. 45, may allow for desires in the *Gorgias* for things that are not actually good (e.g., *Grg.* 491DE, 493D-494A) as long as they are not sufficient to bring about action. A concern for Penner's interpretation is whether it can explain actions that do not achieve the actual good. In the case of an action for what is actually best, Penner's interpretation explains the action in part by a desire for the actual good. When I make a mistake and do something that I wrongly think is best, why is not a desire to perform this action also needed to explain how I act? See also Penner's Chapter 12 in this volume.

A greater challenge to psychological eudaimonism in the *Gorgias* is that Socrates in his closing conversation with Callicles claims that a virtuous person must "rule himself" – in particular, must rule his own pleasures and desires and may suggest that the soul can contain desires that are "unrestrained" and "insatiable" (*Grg.* 491D7-E1, 493B1–3). It is these passages that provide perhaps the most serious threat to psychological eudaimonism in the early dialogues, since they have suggested to some that Plato goes so far as to allow that a person can act contrary to what he believes at that time is best for him overall ("clear-eyed akrasia").[31] But if Plato does allow clear-eyed akrasia in these later passages, this is inconsistent with the evidence already noted in the *Gorgias* for the Principle of Psychological Eudaimonism. Moreover, Socrates never commits himself in these later passages to the existence of clear-eyed akrasia. Fortunately, there are plausible ways of understanding these later passages so as to maintain the *Gorgias'* consistency: (a) Socrates might allow for the persistence of desires for something in the face of a belief that something else is best, but not allow such desires to move the agent to action, or (b) Socrates might allow such desires to move the agent to action, but only after they first change the person's judgment of what is best so that he does not act against his judgment of what is best at the time of action. Both (a) and (b) are consistent with the Principle of Psychological Eudaimonism, although not with the view that all of my desires or motivations are directed at my greatest happiness. So it is more reasonable to see the later *Gorgias* passages as compatible with the Principle of Psychological Eudaimonism than to attribute self-contradictory views to Socrates.

But even if Socrates were to allow for clear-eyed akrasia in the *Gorgias*, this does not undermine rational eudaimonism. Socrates claims that a moderate person will be self-controlled and possess all the virtues, and this must include wisdom. The upshot of acting in accordance with wisdom is that the virtuous person attains happiness (*Grg.* 507A5-C7). So for reasons similar to those considered here in connection with the *Charmides* and the *Meno*, we should see Socrates as also here committed to the Principle of Rational Eudaimonism.

A final reason for thinking that Plato holds to the Principle of Psychological Eudaimonism in the *Gorgias* is that he seems to draw some important consequences from it. In particular, Socrates explicitly endorses the claim that no one does wrong willingly (*hekôn*), and links this to his views about motivation by the good.[32] Near the end of the

---

31   See, e.g., Brickhouse and Smith 2007; Cooper 1999, pp. 29–75; Devereux 1995; and Irwin 1995, pp. 114–117.
32   See Brickhouse and Smith 1994, McTighe 1984, and Weiss 1985. For a related line of thought, see *Ap.* 25D9–26A8.

dialogue, Socrates claims that he and Polus had agreed that "no one does what is unjust because he wants to, but everyone who does injustice does so unwillingly" (*Grg.* 509E5–7). There is no prior place in this dialogue that states exactly this claim, but Socrates is probably referring to the claims about motivation that Polus previously agreed to and that we discussed earlier (*Grg.* 467C-468E).

As we saw, it is reasonable to interpret Socrates as claiming that:

Whenever I do X, I believe that doing X is overall best for me.[33]

So if I do injustice, I do this thinking that it is best for me. But this is, Socrates thinks, a false belief. So I only do injustice if I have a false belief that it is better for me to do so. What is it, precisely, that makes doing injustice an unwilling action? The simple fact that a person has a false belief about an action of his is too weak a condition to make the action unwilling. We might have false beliefs about a great many of our actions, but the bulk of these beliefs are irrelevant to our performing the actions.

The *Gorgias*, however, allows us to go further than this. Given Socrates' claims about motivation, it is also the case that if I were to believe that acting unjustly is worse for me, I would not do it. I would, rather, do what I would correctly believe to be better – that is, act justly. It is my false belief that explains why I act as I do: whenever I do X, I do X because I believe that doing X is overall best for me. This gives good sense to the claim that all wrongdoing is unwilling. (It may also be the case that all along I want to do what is actually best for me, and this would give us another way in which acting so as to do what is bad for me is unwilling.) The Principle of Psychological Eudaimonism thus can explain Socrates' view that all wrongdoing is unwilling.

The final dialogue I shall consider in this section is the *Protagoras*, in which Socrates famously denies the possibility of akrasia. At the beginning of this discussion, Socrates, on behalf of himself and Protagoras, endorses the following claim:

Knowledge is a fine thing, capable of ruling a person, and if someone were to know what is good and bad, then he would not be forced by anything to act otherwise than as knowledge commands. ... (*Prt.* 352C3–6)

This knowledge is knowledge not just of the good and bad, but knowledge of the best, and what Socrates and Protagoras think is impossible is that a person not do what he knows is best (*Prt.* 352D4–353A2).

---

33 I intend this to be neutral between the traditional interpretation and Penner's.

At the end of his argument, Socrates summarizes his conclusions:

No one who knows or believes that there is something else better than what he is doing that is possible, will go on doing what he had been doing when he is able to do what is better. To be weaker than oneself is nothing other than ignorance, and to be stronger than oneself is nothing other than wisdom. (*Prt.* 358B7-C3)

No one willingly goes toward the bad or what he believes to be bad; neither is it in human nature, so it seems, to want to go toward what one believes to be bad instead of the good. And when he is forced to choose between one of two bad things, no one will choose the greater if he is able to choose the lesser. (*Prt.* 358C6-D4)

These passages provide very strong support for attributing both the Principles of Psychological and Rational Eudaimonism to Socrates. They claim that every person will always choose and act to attain what he thinks is overall best and least bad for himself.[34] *Protagoras* 352C3-6 states the claim about a person who has knowledge; 358B7-C3 and 358C6-D4 generalize it so that action contrary to what one believes is best is also impossible. This is presented as a fact about human nature, and thus is sufficient for the Principle of Psychological Eudaimonism. But since this is action in accordance with knowledge (or a belief corresponding to knowledge), Socrates endorses the rationality of so acting and thus endorses the Principle of Rational Eudaimonism.[35]

The evidence of the *Protagoras* is controversial, however, because Socrates' specific argument against the possibility of akrasia (which we have not examined here) relies on a hedonistic conception of the good – that is, on the identification of a person's good with that person's pleasure. Many scholars hold, I think rightly, that Socrates rejects hedonism elsewhere in the early dialogues and also in the middle dialogues.[36] This makes it implausible that the *Protagoras* is the sole exception. So does Socrates have grounds other than hedonism for rejecting akrasia?

34 The good and bad at stake here are the agent's good and bad, e.g., *Prt.* 354A7-E2, 355D3-4, 358D1-4; for optimizing or maximizing overall, see *Prt.* 355B3-357E8.

35 Also even though the many here doubt only psychological eudaimonism, they do not hint at any doubts about rational eudaimonism. The Principle of Psychological Eudaimonism does not require that the agent's desire for the overall best that produces action always be fully available to his consciousness, and Socrates' analysis of apparent akrasia in the *Protagoras* may involve a desire for the overall best that is not fully available to consciousness; cf. Bobonich 2007. Kamtekar 2006 is helpful.

36 See Irwin (1995, pp. 78–94) for an interpretation that is sympathetic to finding hedonism in the *Protagoras*; for an alternate interpretation, see Zeyl 1980. For general discussions of hedonism in the early and middle dialogues, see Gosling and Taylor 1984 and Weiss 1989.

Fortunately, we find what we need to construct such an argument in the *Protagoras*'s own refutation of akrasia. At one point in the argument, Socrates claims that human beings do, as a matter of fact, pursue pleasure because it is good (*Prt.* 354C3–5). Thus it is the (perceived) goodness of an option that is motivationally fundamental: it explains why we pursue whatever it is that we pursue. On the basis of the assumption that the good is pleasure, Socrates further specifies this claim so that what the person pursues is not merely some pleasure, but what is overall most pleasant for him in the long run. But since we pursue what is pleasant just because it is good and not vice versa, Socrates is committed to the idea that we always pursue what we regard as overall best. This is sufficient for the Principle of Psychological Eudaimonism and thus for the rejection of the possibility of akrasia.[37]

Pursuing overall pleasure successfully requires using the "art of measurement" – which is our "salvation in life" – to calculate and compare the size and number of possible pleasures and pains (*Prt.* 356A-357B). Since the art of measurement directs us to maximize our pleasure because that is best for us, we get the Principle of Rational Eudaimonism (*Prt.* 356A-357E). Indeed, since Socrates thinks that all desire is for the good, and understands this in a maximizing way, he is committed to a stronger form of psychological eudaimonism – that is, to the claim that a person desires and pursues anything only insofar as it conduces to his own greatest happiness. Since this is what reason prescribes, Socrates is thus also committed to a stronger form of rational eudaimonism such that one's (greatest happiness) is one's only rational consideration in action.

4. THE CONTENT OF HAPPINESS

Both psychological and rational eudaimonism are formal theories: they specify what our attitude is (or rationally should be) toward happiness, but they do not give an account of what happiness itself consists in. Nor do we obviously get such an account in the early dialogues (especially if we do not think that Socrates endorses hedonism in the *Protagoras*). But there are two issues relevant to the nature of happiness that are explicitly discussed in the early dialogues. First, there is the issue of what the relation is between being virtuous and being happy. Second, Socrates, in certain dialogues, advances a Dependency Thesis according

37 Relying on the Principle of Psychological Eudaimonism to reject akrasia does not trivialize Socrates' argument: he does not simply make the immediate inference from this Principle to the denial of akrasia, but diagnoses in psychological detail why alleged cases of akrasia are not genuine.

to which the goodness of other goods, and thus the agent's happiness, depends on the his possession of virtue or knowledge of the good. Why does Socrates hold this thesis and what are its implications? Let us begin with the first question.

Virtue and Happiness

The three most important questions about the relation between happiness and virtue in the early dialogues are:

(A) Is virtue identical with happiness?
(B) Is virtue sufficient for happiness?
(C) Is virtue necessary for happiness?

So let us consider each. Rather than just proceeding by stating what conclusions are best supported by the evidence, I shall discuss in some detail the range of considerations that are relevant to deciding what positions we should attribute to Socrates.

A. There are passages in the early dialogues that some scholars have taken to suggest that virtue is identical with happiness:

We must treat as most important not life, but the good life [to eu zên] ... and the good life, the fine [kalôs] life and the just [diakaiôs] life are the same. (Crito 48B4–7)

I do not think it is permitted that a better man be harmed by a worse. (Ap. 30D1–2)

The Crito passage, which we discussed earlier, in claiming that the good life and the fine life are "the same," seems to suggest straightforwardly that happiness and virtue are identical.[38] The support provided by the Apology passage is less direct, but some have argued that, taken along with other things that Socrates believes, it suggests the identity thesis. This passage claims that a better man cannot be harmed by a worse man. Since the worse man can inflict all sorts of damage on a good man – to his body, his soul, his external goods, and on those close to him – except diminish his virtue, we might again think that only the thing bad for a person is vice or the diminishment of virtue, and thus that the only thing good for a person is virtue.

Yet before turning to the interpretation of these passages, we should consider the philosophical consequences of accepting the identity of

---

38   For discussion, see Brickhouse and Smith 1999, pp. 123–155; Irwin 1995, pp. 118–120; and Vlastos 1991, pp. 200–232.

virtue and happiness. As we have already seen, even carefully written texts often admit of more than one reading, and one important way of seeing what a particular passage means is by seeing how various interpretations and their consequences fit in with the rest of what Socrates thinks. Some have thought that if Socrates were to hold the identity thesis, this would have disastrous results for him. First, if happiness is identical with virtue, it would follow that virtue is the only non-instrumental good, and this is flagrantly in conflict with our intuitions. Surely, one might think, things such as pleasure and good health, even if they are not the most important goods, are good for us apart from their contribution to virtue. Second, Gregory Vlastos argues that if Socrates accepts the identity thesis, then

happiness is the final reason which can be given for any purposeful action, [and] hence for any rational choice between alternative courses of action. It follows that if identity were the true relation of virtue to happiness, we would have no rational grounds for preference between alternatives which are equally consistent with virtue – hence no rational ground for preference between states of affairs differentiated only by their non-moral values. And if this were true, it would knock the bottom from eudaimonism as a theory of rational choice. For many of the choices we make in our day-to-day life have to be made between just such states of affairs, where moral considerations are not in the picture at all.[39]

To begin our discussion, neither of these consequences, in fact, follows from the identity thesis. First, even if it were the case that in the happy life the only thing contributing to its happiness is its virtue, it would not follow that virtue is the only non-instrumental good. Even if happiness is an optimal state and optimality is attained by including virtue and no other good, other things could be non-instrumentally good. It might just be the case that no combination of them or no combination of them and a possible state of virtue could be as good as a life of optimal virtue.

What of the second concern that the identity thesis would undermine eudaimonism as a theory of rational choice? Vlastos's underdetermination worry may only be pressing if considerations of virtue typically leave open a very wide range of choices. But Socrates may not think that this is the case. In the *Apology*, for example, Socrates claims that he goes around "doing nothing but trying to persuade both young and old among [the Athenians] not to care for your body or your wealth in preference to, or as strongly as, the best condition of your soul" (*Ap.* 30A7-B2). This activity explains Socrates' great poverty (*Ap.* 31A-C), since it allows him little time to do anything else. So this requirement

39   Vlastos 1991, pp. 224–225, emphasis deleted.

on Socrates is highly demanding and sharply restricts his possible patterns of activity. Moreover, this does not seem to be simply a special requirement imposed on Socrates by the god, but is required or at least recommended by the nature of justice (e.g., *Ap.* 29D7-E3 and 32A1–2).

Although these two common objections to the identity thesis do not succeed, there is good reason to think that Socrates allows both that (i) there are non-instrumental goods besides virtue, and (ii) a person's optimal state includes more than virtue, and thus that Socrates rejects the identity thesis.

(1) On a textual level, there are ways of disarming the cited passages (*Ap.* 30D and *Crito* 48B) so that they are consistent with (i) and (ii). These passages may simply be asserting a certain primacy to virtue or justice – for example, that it is by far the most important non-instrumental good.

(2) There is a great deal of evidence that Socrates in the early dialogues is not (and does not recommend being) indifferent to all apparent goods and bads besides virtue and vice. The best explanation of this is that he accepts the Principle of Rational Eudaimonism and accepts (i) and (ii).[40]

(3) In a point related to (2), in the *Euthydemus* and the *Meno*, Socrates endorses a Dependency Thesis about goods (cf. *Ap.* 30B2–4 and *Chrm.* 173A-175A). Roughly, this is the claim that nothing is good for its possessor unless he is virtuous, but other things – such as health – can become good for their possessor if he is virtuous. The most reasonable interpretation of this thesis (which we shall discuss later) is that Socrates allows some things, such as health, to benefit a virtuous person apart from their contribution to that person's virtue.

So we do have good evidence that Socrates accepted (i) and (ii) in the early dialogues, and thus rejected the Identity thesis. Nevertheless, it is worth exploring what might motivate or follow from a denial of (i) and (ii). It is perhaps especially worth doing so, since in this way we can better see how Socrates' views about happiness are connected to other philosophical issues.

If all that is non-instrumentally good for me is my own virtue, this makes my well-being strongly self-confined. The only non-instrumental goods for me are my own states or activities. Such a view conflicts, or at least is in strong tension, with some of our basic intuitions and practices. Many of us seem to think that facts about the world can directly

40   On (1) and (2), see the literature cited in n. 38.

affect our own happiness.[41] Many people, for example, think that the happiness of their loved ones is good for themselves apart from its effect on their own virtue (or any other state of themselves). Confining what is non-instrumentally good for me to virtue also seems in tension with the related intuition that it can directly benefit me to bring about things in the world, or states of affairs, that possess genuine value. Why not think that if I am a cancer researcher, it would be good for me if my life-long efforts actually succeeded in producing a cure for cancer? This line of thought is especially tempting, if one holds a realist view about the non-relational value properties of things: if things objectively possess the property of goodness, why should bringing good things about not, at least sometimes, contribute to my happiness? More prosaically, it seems to be an obvious fact about human life that we can (and typically do), even after reflection, desire and aim at many things other than states of ourselves as ultimate ends. We might think that these considerations suggest either that (a) the ultimate ends of action include more than what is best for oneself, or (b) some of these aimed for and desired ends should count as parts of my happiness. Only option (b) retains a commitment to eudaimonism.

None of these conflicts or tensions shows that the identification of happiness with virtue is incoherent or patently false. Later in the Greek tradition, the Stoics – sometimes appealing to Socrates as an early proponent of this view – explicitly held that the only non-instrumental good was virtue and that the only non-instrumental bad was vice. But they did respond to these tensions by developing deep and controversial theories of human nature and of the nature of the world that supported the identity thesis.

Perhaps one plausible way to support the identity thesis is by means of identifying the happiness or well-being of a creature with the full realization or perfection of its natural characteristic capacities and holding that this full realization or perfection is constituted by virtue.[42] Such an identification of virtue with the full realization of a human being's natural capacities might obtain in more than one way. If human nature, at bottom, were to consist in a single capacity (or a set of capacities in which the lower ones simply subserve the higher), virtue could be a single thing insofar as the realization of that single capacity is itself unitary. Alternately, if human nature, at bottom, were to consist of several distinct capacities (which do not all merely subserve a single highest

41 For a start on contemporary discussions, see Parfit 1984, pp. 493–502.
42 I leave aside here this claim's relation to the idea that virtue is what enables a thing to realize its nature or what makes it a good instance of the kind to which it belongs.

one), then virtue and thus happiness could still have a certain kind of unity insofar as the full realization of these capacities were co-realizable or, more strongly, interdependent.

Yet even if we accept the identification of virtue with the full realization of capacities in either of these ways, we cannot yet tell how plausible it is to identify the individual's well-being with a full realization of his capacities. If, for example, the nature of a creature essentially involved the disposition to detect and predate a certain kind of animal, say sheep, it is hardly clear that such a creature would be well-off, no matter how finely honed these dispositions were, if there were no sheep in the environment. The problem is not that it would starve (since this would involve a failure to realize its capacities), but rather that if there are no sheep around, a sheep detector is just a waste.[43] We might try to meet this problem by describing the characteristic capacity as, for example, an ability to detect prey that might be instantiated in different ways in different environments. But although Plato and Aristotle are sensitive to the idea that the same virtue can be expressed in different actions in different circumstances, both seem to think that human virtues involve fairly specific and determinate capacities and activities.

But the simplest and philosophically most fundamental reason for rejecting the identity thesis is that once we keep in mind how Socrates understands virtue in the early dialogues, we can also see that the identity thesis must be highly implausible. It is easy to slip into thinking that by "virtue" Socrates means knowledge of what is morally right or wrong or knowledge of moral principles. Such a view, although it is sometimes found in the scholarly literature, is a mistake. As we have seen, there is reason to think that Socrates takes especially seriously, or is moving toward, an account of virtue as knowledge of good and bad – that is, knowledge of what is good and bad for the agent (such knowledge might come along with or be based on knowledge of what is good for human beings in general). On such an account of virtue, there is an obvious concern about how it could be identical with happiness. A thesis identifying virtue with happiness on this conception of virtue would require that such knowledge all by itself constitute what is best for the individual.

Middle-period dialogues, such as the *Phaedo* and the *Republic*, give accounts of human nature that emphasize the centrality to it of the rational capacity to possess an understanding of reality and value. On this conception of human nature as essentially directed toward knowing fundamental truths about reality and the goodness of reality, we can

---

43   Cf. Copp and Sobel 2004.

see why such knowledge, even if not the sole constituent of happiness, could be a primary component of it. Socrates, however, understands knowledge of the good as knowledge of what is good for its possessor. It is extremely hard to see how any theory of human nature could ground the identity of happiness and this kind of knowledge (or even the primacy of such knowledge in happiness).[44]

B. Is virtue sufficient for happiness? There are passages in the early dialogues that suggest that virtue is sufficient for happiness. These include *Crito* 48B4–7 quoted earlier, as well as the following:

It is very necessary that the moderate person, because he is just and courageous and pious … is a completely good person, and that the good person does well and finely whatever he does, and that the person who does well is blessed and happy, while the corrupt person, the one who does badly, is miserable.[45] (*Grg.* 507B8–C5, cf. 470E4–10 discussed later.)

The exact relation between the sufficiency thesis and the identity thesis is complicated.[46] But one way in which the sufficiency thesis has been interpreted so as to be distinctive is this: being happy is a threshold or scalar notion, not an optimizing one. There is a range of lives somewhat below the optimal life, all of which are very good lives, that count as happy. On this view, it could be true that A is happier than B, while it is also the case that A is happy and B is happy. The most straightforward way to flesh out this idea is to see happiness as a composite of distinct goods and the degree to which one is happy as a function (not necessarily a simply additive one) of the goods that one possesses. Virtue is a sufficiently important good that by itself – without any other goods and despite any bads – its possession makes one's life very good or happy. The addition of further goods, or a reduction in bads, could increase one's surplus of good over bad and thus make one happier.

The sufficiency thesis would have two quite striking implications:

(A) Since the agent's virtue is within the agent's control, his happiness or well-being is within his control.[47]

44 Alternately, one might think that the knowledge required is something like knowledge of god's will or plan for things. Sharing in god's will or plan could then be seen as a full realization of human nature. The knowledge required to share in god's plan, unlike the sort of contemplation of the *Phaedo* or the *Republic*, perhaps need not involve the grasp of an elaborate theory. Related questions will become important in the Stoics.

45 Cf. *Rep.* 353D-354A and n.38.

46 For discussion with references, see Bobonich 2002, pp. 209–215.

47 This is especially the case if there are no non-rational motivations that could prompt an agent to clear-eyed akrasia. I leave aside here worries

(B) The world is supportive of virtue. Many moderns find that there is a conflict, or at least a tension, between the individual's virtue and his well-being. If the sufficiency thesis is true, then the world – including human nature – is such that virtue guarantees happiness.

If Plato does hold the sufficiency thesis, then he accepts both of these claims. Nevertheless, they are easily misinterpreted by a modern reader. As a point of comparison, consider the following two passages, the first in which Augustine describes the turmoil surrounding his conversion, and the second from Kant:

During this agony of indecision I performed many bodily actions, things which a man cannot always do, even if he wills to do them ... I tore my hair and hammered my forehead with my fists ... But I might have had the will to do it and yet not have done it, if my limbs had been unable to move in compliance with my will. I performed all these actions, in which the will and the power to act are not the same. Yet I did not do that one thing that I should have been far, far better pleased to do than all the rest and could have done at once, as soon as I had the will to do it, because as soon as I had the will to do so, I should have willed it wholeheartedly. For in this case, the power to act was the same as the will. To will it was to do it.[48]

Ask [a man] whether, if his prince demanded it, on the pain of ... immediate execution, that he give false testimony against an honorable man whom the prince would like to destroy under a plausible pretext: he would consider it possible to overcome his love of life, however great it may be. He would perhaps not venture to assert whether he would do it or not, but he must admit without hesitation that it would be possible for him.[49]

Augustine realizes in his period of struggle that it is open to him at any moment to follow god, and that by doing so he will bring himself into a good condition of soul and a condition that is good for him. Both the good condition of soul and benefit for himself are fully within his control; they require only that he will appropriately. (I leave aside complexities arising from Augustine's views about the role of grace.) In the passage from Kant, any rational person must admit that it is possible for him to act on the moral law and thus for his action to have moral worth. Kant does not claim that the person's happiness is within his

---

about, e.g., determinism or circumstantial luck. The identity thesis would, of course, also have these same implications.

48 *The Confessions*, Book 8, Chapter 8: Pine-Coffin 1983, pp. 171–172.
49 *Groundwork of The Metaphysics of Morals*, Book 1, Chapter 6, Problem II, Remark 5:30: Gregor 1996, p. 163.

own control, but acting on the moral law is within the person's control, and simply depends on the manner of his willing.

For Socrates, in contrast, virtue is within the person's control only insofar as it is a state of an individual's soul and does not additionally require that anything in particular be true of the person's body or of the external world. If virtue is sufficient for happiness, this is also true of happiness. But if virtue requires knowledge, it is not ensured by any choice or decision open to the person at any given time: attaining knowledge will require much more than deciding to do so and, indeed, Socrates does not guarantee that it is possible for everyone (and later I shall discuss whether he thinks it is possible for anyone).

As for (B), moderns tend to see possible conflicts between individual well-being and morality insofar as morality involves a commitment to, for example, promoting the well-being of all or to acting in a way that reflects an impartial point of view. But neither of these ideas is immediately relevant to the sufficiency thesis as Socrates would understand it. Taking virtue as knowledge of good and bad for the agent, what the sufficiency thesis comes to is the claim that knowing what is good and bad for oneself is sufficient for happiness.[50] As I have suggested, it is not clear that this line of argument succeeds, but it does seem to be the line of argument that underlies Socrates' claims that virtue is sufficient for happiness in the passages we have discussed from the *Charmides*, and will discuss later from the *Euthydemus*. Note that Socrates' rationale for the sufficiency thesis does not seem to rely on any further substantive assumption about what virtue requires beyond the idea that it requires knowledge of what is good for its possessor. Although Socrates appears to think that there is a considerable – but not full – overlap between what a conventionally virtuous person and what a Socratically virtuous person would do, the line of thought supporting the sufficiency thesis does not require this, and Socrates does not in the early dialogues explain fully why there should be such an overlap.[51]

50 If Socrates accepts the Principe of Psychological Eudaimonism, a person with such knowledge would act (or try to) act upon it; if he recognizes the existence of non-rational motivations that can irrationally change the agent's judgment of what is best, then it would be natural for Socrates to recognize the existence of virtues that would inhibit such non-rational motivations.

51 Perhaps the most specific defenses of practices are those of Socrates' political obligations in the *Crito* and those of his elenctic activities in the *Apology* and *Gorgias* (which have a clear political dimension insofar as these activities are intended to improve his fellow citizens; e.g., *Ap.* 30D-32A, 36BE; *Grg.* 521D-522A: Socrates may be the only true statesman in Athens). The "do not harm" principle is asserted in the *Crito* (49AE) and receives some

The sufficiency thesis, however, may be called into question by other passages that suggest that some degree of ill health could not only deprive a virtuous person of happiness, but in fact make his life not worth living. In the *Crito*, for example, as part of an argument stressing the importance of justice understood as the healthy condition of the soul, Socrates seems to suggests that life is not "worth living with a body that is in a bad condition and corrupted" (*Crito* 47E4–6, cf. *Grg.* 505A and 512AB).

But despite these passages, Socrates may very well accept the sufficiency thesis as the passages quoted at the beginning of this section suggest. *Crito* 47E4, *Grg.* 505A, and 512AB might mean only that a corrupted bodily condition can render a virtuous person unhappy only insofar as such ill health undermines his virtue. Constant excruciating pain, for example, could undermine whatever knowledge one has.[52] Further, if the loss of goods, such as health, and the suffering of bads, such as disease, can make even the virtuous person's life not worth living, then these goods and bads must have considerable weight in determining the individual's overall balance of good and bad. If so, it becomes increasingly difficult to justify Socrates' frequent claims that being virtuous or acting virtuously always takes priority over other goods and bads.

This concern is especially acute if the dividing line between being virtuous and not being virtuous is such that the non-virtuous person can approximate the virtuous person closely. If such approximation is possible, then it is hard to justify the priority of virtue. Why should the non-virtuous person who approximates the virtuous person as closely as possible, and who has all other possible goods and no bads, be worse off than the virtuous person who has no other goods and all other possible bads? The idea that the virtuous person is always better off and that one is always better off acting virtuously seems to require that there be a great divide between virtue and anything that falls short of it. What it would go well with is, for example, the sort of discontinuity that is found between an action's having moral worth or lacking it in Kant's system, or that between knowledge and belief in Plato's middle-period epistemology.

Finally, given an understanding of virtue as knowledge of the good, there are problems for the sufficiency thesis that are related to those I have considered in connection with the identity thesis. Merely knowing

defense in the *Gorgias*, but this principle is surprisingly unspecific until we receive what we do not get in the early dialogues – that is, an account of what is really good and bad for people.
52   Brickhouse and Smith 1999, pp. 139–140; Kraut 1984, pp. 37–39; and Vlastos 1991, pp. 200–232.

what is good and bad for oneself does not, it seems, guarantee that one in fact obtains the good and avoids the bad (and perhaps it is not even necessary for it, since one might obtain the requisite goods without having such knowledge). If, for example, I know that what is good for me is an overall balance of pleasure over pain, such knowledge seems to fall far short of ensuring that I obtain such a surplus. Here, too, unless such knowledge has great value in itself, it is implausible to think that it is sufficient for happiness. But this seems to require that such knowledge be more than simply knowledge of what is best for oneself.

C. Is virtue necessary for happiness? It has seemed to many that the answer to this question is obviously, yes. Consider, for example, the following passage from the *Gorgias*:

Polus: It is clear, Socrates, that you will not even claim to know that the Great King is happy.

Socrates: Yes, and that would be true, for I do not know how he stands in regard to education and virtue.

Polus: Really? Does happiness depend entirely on that?

Socrates: Yes, Polus, so I say anyway. I say that the fine and good person, man or woman, is happy, but that the one who's unjust and wicked is miserable.[53]
(*Grg.* 470E4–10)

The necessity of virtue for happiness also follows immediately from the Dependency Thesis (which I shall discuss later). But if virtue is necessary for happiness, we then face serious concerns about the possibility of happiness. If knowledge is necessary for virtue, then Socrates is not happy, and perhaps no human can be happy.

To begin, it is not clear that these are unacceptable results. Especially if happiness is an optimal state, it is not obviously counter-intuitive or a disaster for Socrates' ethical theory to hold that no one, not even Socrates himself, is happy.[54] What would be more worrisome, however, is the possibility that without virtue, no one could have a life worth living (and it would be an especially unattractive consequence for Socrates if no one could improve with respect to well-being, if he did not become virtuous). If this were the case, how could Socrates' claim in the *Apology* that he confers the "greatest benefit" on his fellow citizens and makes them happy be true (*Ap.* 36B3-D10)?

On the account of virtue as knowledge of good and bad, it seems quite plausible that one could live a life well worth living without such knowledge and it is certainly plausible that one could improve with

53 Cf. Brickhouse and Smith 1999, pp. 147–149.
54 Cf. *Ap.* 40CE and de Heer 1968, pp. 38–67.

respect to well-being without having such knowledge. A person might have many goods other than virtue and many true beliefs about good and bad without possessing knowledge. Why think that such a person's life would not be worth living and why deny that improvements to his well-being might accrue if he gained more true beliefs and lost false ones (especially if these are important beliefs)? Indeed, this line of argument calls into question the necessity of virtue for happiness. If happiness is not an optimal state, why would it be impossible for such a person to be happy? Although as we saw, for example, in our discussion of the *Apology* and the *Crito*, Socrates asserts the centrality of virtue in choice and life, we do not yet have an account of virtue that would ground such a claim. I thus turn to Socrates' most radical and philosophically interesting defense of the importance of virtue.

The Dependency Thesis

In the *Euthydemus* and the *Meno*, Socrates advances a thesis about the dependence of all other goods upon wisdom or knowledge of the good.[55] Let us introduce some terminology:

x is a Dependent Good if and only if x is good for a wise person and x is bad for an unwise person.

x is a Dependent Bad if and only if x is bad for a wise person and x is not bad for an unwise person.

Dependent Goods include such things as wealth, health, beauty, and strength, but also some purely psychic goods such as a keen memory. Dependent Bads are the natural contrast class, and include things such as poverty, sickness and so on. Corresponding to this account of Dependent Goods and Bads, we can give an account of Independent Goods and Bads:

G is an Independent Good if and only if G is good for a person regardless of what else he possesses.

B is an Independent Bad if and only if B is bad for a person regardless of what else he possesses.

Wisdom is an Independent Good and lack of wisdom an Independent Bad.

In the *Euthydemus* and the *Meno*, Socrates holds that all goods that are entirely distinct from wisdom are Dependent Goods (I shall call this

---

55 *Euthd.* 278E-282E, *Meno* 87D-89A. For discussion, see Annas 1999, pp. 40–51; Bobonich 2002, pp. 123–145; Brickhouse and Smith 1994, pp. 103–136; Ferejohn 1984; and Irwin 1986, 1995, pp. 55–58.

the "Dependency Thesis.") So why does he think that this is true? The line of thought suggested by some of the examples in the *Euthydemus* (280B-281B) is this:

(1) Right use of a Dependent Good is a necessary (and sufficient) condition of its possessor benefiting from a Dependent Good.

(2) Wisdom is a necessary (and sufficient) condition of the right use of a Dependent Good.

Therefore,

(3) Wisdom is a necessary (and sufficient) condition of its possessor benefiting from a Dependent Good.

Carpenters, for example, are not benefited by possessing tools and raw materials, unless they know how to use them, and carpentry provides knowledge of how to use means to bring about beneficial ends (e.g., *Euthd.* 280C4-E2). More generally, the goodness of Dependent Goods for their possessor is dependent on knowledge of the good because such knowledge is necessary and sufficient for using Dependent Goods correctly. If you do not know how to use the resources available to you, you will not be able to use them rightly, and if you do not use your resources rightly, they will not benefit you. If, on the other hand, you do know how to use your resources, you will use them rightly and they will benefit you.

The Dependency Thesis can help justify some of Socrates' views about the intimate connection between virtue and happiness. If it is true, the necessity of virtue (understood as wisdom) for happiness quickly follows, since the person lacking virtue or knowledge can have nothing good. What is the relation of the Dependency Thesis to the claim that the virtuous person is always better off than the unvirtuous and that virtue is sufficient for happiness? First, on the Dependency Thesis, it will be the case that nothing benefits the person lacking knowledge. On the other hand, the person with knowledge possesses the Independent Good that consists in having such knowledge. This, however, does not settle the comparative question, since the Dependency Thesis allows that Dependent Bads, such as sickness, are bad for the virtuous person. The comparative thesis would only be plausible if knowledge of the good were an especially weighty good in itself and the corresponding lack of knowledge an especially weighty evil. Understanding happiness as a threshold concept, the sufficiency of virtue for happiness would require that knowledge of the good by itself (and despite the presence of any Dependent Bads) is a weighty enough good to push the person over the threshold of happiness.

The Dependency Thesis thus has important implications for Socrates' views about the relations between virtue and happiness. But it is not clear that Socrates really has good reason for accepting the Dependency Thesis. The natural line of thought suggested by the *Euthydemus* and the *Meno* passages is that the relevant wisdom is the knowledge of good or correct use – that is, it consists in the knowledge of how to use Dependent Goods in order to produce a good for their possessor. But such a justification of the Dependency Thesis faces serious problems. First, there is the problem of bad luck. Such knowledge does not seem sufficient for benefiting from Dependent Goods, since accidental misuse and unexpected external circumstances may disrupt normally correct use and cause it to misfire.

There are also problems with good luck. Why should such knowledge be necessary, if a person can accidentally use the Dependent Good correctly or do so under the guidance of others without possessing knowledge himself? The latter possibility should be especially troubling to Socrates. Throughout the early dialogues, Socrates emphasizes the great practical importance of examining one's own views about the good. In the *Apology*, for example, he claims that "the unexamined life is not worth living" (*Ap.* 38A5–6). If a person can use his Dependent Goods correctly by relying on the guidance of others, there seems to be no further need for knowledge or self-examination. But more important for our questions about happiness, such an account of the Dependency Thesis does little to suggest that this sort of knowledge of the good (and thus virtue understood in this way) is of more than instrumental value. Once again, Socrates does not develop a worked-out justification for thinking that virtue understood in this way is of such extraordinary value, and we can see Plato's middle-period metaphysics, epistemology, and psychology as offering the resources to provide some grounding for this claim.[56]

5. CONCLUDING ISSUES

In conclusion, let us consider some of the attractions of Socrates' views on happiness, as well as some of their problems.

1. The Principle of Rational Eudaimonism claims that there is a single, decisive rational consideration for all of a person's actions and choices – that is, the person's (greatest) happiness. Indeed, we have found good evidence from the early dialogues that Socrates holds a

---

56   For example, Bobonich 2002, chs. 1 and 2.

stronger form of rational eudaimonism such that one's own happiness is the only rational consideration. This gives Socrates a clear strategy for justifying the choice to develop the virtues and act virtuously: he can provide such a justification by showing that this most conduces to the individual's happiness. Moreover, the Principle of Rational Eudaimonism sharply restricts the possibility of irresolvable rational conflicts for an individual agent by providing a single goal for action – that is, the agent's own (greatest) happiness. (If there are ties for first place, it seems reasonable to allow that any of these actions is rational.)

2. The fact that reason recommends the course of action that most conduces to the agent's own happiness does not entail that reason recommends that considerations of happiness ought to guide the agent's actual practical deliberations. It might be the case that happiness is best achieved by focusing on other considerations in one's deliberations. But Socrates does not seem to think that such a possibility in fact obtains. He seems to think that attaining happiness is best achieved by taking it as an explicit target in one's own deliberations. This is why, for example, he stresses the pressing need for each of us to acquire knowledge of what is good and bad for us.

Since we all wish to be happy, and since we appear to become so by using things and using them correctly, and since knowledge was the source of correctness and good luck, it seems that every man must prepare himself by every means to become as wise as possible.[57] (*Euthd.* 282A1–6)

Thus, along with his commitment to rational eudaimonism, Socrates has a theory of what ideal practical deliberation should be like. In light of Socrates' lack of knowledge in the early dialogues of what virtue is and what is good, non-ideal deliberation will take the form of relying on claims that have been examined and not yet refuted (*Crito* 46BC and 49AB).

As argued in Section 3, Socrates' repeated emphasis on the need to be guided in one's deliberations by the thought of what is virtuous or just is perfectly consistent with the idea that the agent's deliberations should be guided by the thought of his own happiness. Acting virtuously is

---

57 The Dependency Thesis also constrains the form of practical deliberation. Insofar as one should aim at what is best for oneself, and nothing benefits a person lacking virtue or knowledge of the good, practical deliberation should be carried out in light of whatever psychological states are required for virtue or knowledge of the good.

always better for the agent (and the virtuous agent is aware that this is the case), and thus the person can, as Socrates does at *Crito* 47A-48D, deliberate about what is just as a way of deliberating about what is best for himself.

> 3. Rational eudaimonism provides a formal specification of our proper concern with others: we should take account of and be concerned with others in the way that most conduces to our own happiness. This does not, however, tell us how far we should be concerned with others. But it does provide a natural way of further specifying that concern. Such concern could, for example, be manifested by respecting the rights of others or helping to advance their preferences. But it is natural for a rational eudaimonist to think that the proper target of concern for others is advancing their happiness. Rational eudaimonism may thus allow us to fix the way in which we should show concern for friends and for others more generally.[58]

A rational eudaimonist should also want to explore whether happiness can help give content to other important ethical (and political) ideas. As our analysis of virtue showed, happiness gives content to the notion of virtue since my action is just if and only if it is best for me overall. As just noted, happiness can also give content to the notion of benefiting others. But might it also, for example, help give content to the notion of a just or correct law or institution? The most straightforward way, but not the only way, it might do so is via the principle that a just law or institution is one that makes the city and its citizens as happy as possible.[59] Further, a rational eudaimonist should consider whether happiness can help give content to the notion of treating another person justly (insofar as this is distinct from treating him in accordance with a just law or institution). Must such an action affect the person's happiness in any special way? In particular, is it a necessary or sufficient condition (or perhaps both) of a person's being treated justly that this treatment aims at (or perhaps is just consistent with) that person's (greatest) happiness? This is, of course, a stronger requirement than that of simply doing no harm.

---

58   See, e.g., *Euthd.* 282E and *Lysis* 208A. For an interesting modern discussion, see Darwall 2002.

59   For the idea that Socrates aims at benefiting all, see *Ap.* 36BC. The *Gorgias* claims that this makes him the only one to practice the art of statesmanship truly (521D6-8) and that this is the task of the good citizen (*politês*, 517C1-2); more generally, see *Grg.* 515BD, 517B-518C, and 521D-522B.

4. The Principle of Psychological Eudaimonism provides Plato with the basis of a theory of ethical education and training. If people always act to try to bring about what seems best to them, ethical education and persuasion should focus on their beliefs about what is good. It does not need to take into account the possibility that desires and emotions might lead the person to act contrary to what he thinks best at the time. The Principle of Psychological Eudaimonism does not, however, entail that people's only motivations are for their own happiness. There could be reason for special training if there are desires and emotions that might cause an irrational change in the person's judgment of what is overall best, or if these desires and emotions merely persist in the face of an overall best judgment, without leading to clear-eyed akrasia or irrational judgment changes, but cause some psychic turmoil. But we also have seen that there is good evidence that Socrates accepts a stronger form of psychological eudaimonism in which the only motivations are for happiness.

5. Finally, rational eudaimonism may be attractive to us for reasons that Socrates himself does not clearly articulate and may not share. We might think that eudaimonism has the potential to provide a rational goal that is less contested and more compatible with naturalism than many other options. It may be possible to come to some more widely shared agreement about what benefits human beings or makes them flourish than to agree about what the Form of Justice requires or what a rational agent can will as a universal law. Such agreement may rest on our ability to develop an account of human nature and understanding happiness in terms of that nature.[60]

But there are also important concerns about Socrates' eudaimonism and certain gaps and tensions in his views. I shall start by mentioning two that have been especially prominent:

1. Significant lines of thought in modern moral philosophy reject the idea that the single ultimate goal of practical reason is the agent's own happiness. Kant, for example, holds that practical reason takes an interest in acting from the moral law, and Sidgwick accepts the "dualism of practical reason" according to which the principle of rational egoism and the principle of rational benevolence are both equally authoritative, obligatory, and rational.[61] Rational eudaimonism will need a response to these views.

60 Cf. Foot 2001 and Hursthouse 1999. Note that this does not entail that such theories of human nature would be entirely non-normative.
61 For a discussion of Sidgwick, see Frankena 1992.

2. A related objection is that rational eudaimonism is unacceptably egoistic. Some have argued that if my ultimate end is my own (greatest) happiness, then I can take an interest in other people or things, such as virtue or the well-being of others, only instrumentally – that is, only insofar as they are causal means to the distinct end of my own happiness or well-being. This concern has generated and continues to generate a lively controversy. A reasonable response to this objection is that rational eudaimonism can allow that these things are not (merely) instrumental to my own happiness, but are themselves part of my happiness. So I do not choose, for example, virtue as a means to my happiness, but rather because a virtuous life is in itself part of what it is for me to live happily. Objectors still worry (a) whether choosing virtue in this way is really compatible with choosing it "for its own sake," and (b) that even if it is compatible, rational eudaimonism still has the unattractive consequence that if virtue is not optimally conducive to my happiness, I should not rationally choose it.[62] But even apart from these concerns, Socrates in the early dialogues does not provide a detailed description of how we should take the interests of others into account.

I shall close by noting what I think are perhaps the two most serious gaps in Socrates' views that mark issues to which Plato and the rest of Greek ethics were sensitive. First, as we have noted, Socrates does not provide a detailed account of what is good for human beings. Without some such account, it is very hard to tell whether happiness captures all that is of rational interest to us. Almost all of the succeeding writers in the Greek ethical tradition attempt to provide such an account via an analysis of human nature along with the claim that the realization of that nature is central to happiness. Although Socrates does offer some important claims about human nature, such as psychological eudaimonism, these are not sufficiently detailed to provide a substantive account of the human good. Moreover, without such a substantive account, it is quite difficult to see why (as Socrates clearly expects) a person seeking happiness would follow, at least in large part, ordinary judgments about what is and is not virtuous.

Finally, as we have seen, Socrates in the early dialogues both insists on the priority of virtue and seems to be moving in the direction of an account of virtue as knowledge of good and bad. Yet, as we have also seen, it is unclear that such a conception of virtue can sustain the priority claim, the necessity or sufficiency of virtue for happiness, or the

---

62   For a discussion of these issues with references to the literature, see Bobonich 2002, pp. 450–479.

Dependency Thesis. We can see Plato's middle-period view of human beings as fundamentally rational creatures, his understanding of rationality as involving love and knowledge of the truth, and his conception of knowledge as requiring a grasp of Forms as providing one response to this gap. On this conception of human nature and an account of virtue as involving knowledge of Forms, the priority claim, the necessity and sufficiency of virtue for happiness, and the Dependency Thesis are much more plausible.[63]

In the Stoics, who perhaps have more in common with Socrates than do any of the other Greek ethical thinkers, we also find a response to this gap in their development of detailed theories of human nature as rational, the connection of human nature to the nature of the rest of the universe, and a conception of the knowledge that constitutes virtue as a form of knowledge of the goodness and order of the universe itself. It would be a fruitful approach to the consideration of Greek ethics to see how each of the traditions responds to the questions we need to resolve in order to evaluate Socrates' views.

WORKS CITED

Annas, J. *The Morality of Happiness.* Oxford, 1993.

Annas, J. *Platonic Ethics, Old and New.* Ithaca, 1999.

Augustine, trans. Pine-Coffin, R. *The Confessions.* Harmondsworth, 1983.

Bobonich, C. *Plato's Utopia Recast: His Later Ethics and Politics.* Oxford, 2002.

Bobonich, C. "Plato on *Akrasia* and Knowing Your Own Mind." In *Akrasia in Greek Philosophy: From Socrates to Plotinus*, eds. C. Bobonich and P. Destrée. Leiden, 2007, pp. 41–60.

Bobonich, C. and Destrée, P., eds. *Akrasia in Greek Philosophy: From Socrates to Plotinus.* Leiden, 2007.

Brickhouse, T. C., and Smith, N. D. *Plato's Socrates.* Oxford, 1994.

Brickhouse, T. C., and Smith, N. D. *The Philosophy of Socrates.* New York, 1999.

Brickhouse, T. C., and Smith, N.D. "Socrates on *Akrasia*, Knowledge, and the Power of Appearance." In *Akrasia in Greek Philosophy: From Socrates to Plotinus* eds. C. Bobonich and P. Destrée. Leiden, 2007, pp. 1–18.

Cooper, J. ed. *Plato: Complete Works.* Indianapolis, 1997.

Cooper, J. *Reason and Emotion.* Princeton, 1999.

Copp, D., and Sobel D. "Morality and Virtue: An Assessment of Some Recent Work in Virtue Theory." *Ethics* 114 (2004): 514–544.

Crisp, R. 2003. "Socrates and Aristotle on Happiness and Virtue." In *Plato's and Aristotle's Ethics.* ed. R. Heinaman. Aldershot, 2003, pp. 55–78.

Darwall, S. *Welfare and Rational Care.* Princeton, 2002.

Devereux, Daniel T. "Socrates' Kantian Conception of Virtue." *Journal of the History of Philosophy* 33 (1995): 381–408.

---

63 This is not to say that all these claims obviously follow (and there are particular concerns about the sufficiency thesis). For further discussion, see Bobonich 2002, chs. 1–2.

Edmonds, J. *Greek Elegy and Iambus I.* Cambridge, MA, 1968.

Evelyn-White, H. *Hesiod: The Homeric Hymns and Homerica.* Cambridge, MA, 1982.

Ferejohn, M. "Socratic Thought-Experiments and the Unity of Virtue Paradox." *Phronesis* 29 (1984): 105–122.

Foot, P. *Natural Goodness.* Oxford, 2001.

Frankena, W. 1992. "Sidgwick and the history of ethical dualism." In *Essays on Henry Sidgwick* ed. B. Schultz. Cambridge, 1992, pp. 175–198.

Frisk, H. *Griechisches etymologisches Wörterbuch.* 3 vols. New York, 1960–1972.

Gomez-Lobo, A. *The Foundations of Socratic Ethics.* Indianapolis, 1999.

Goodell, T. "XPH and DEI." *The Classical Quarterly* 8 (1914): 91–102.

Gosling, J., and Taylor, C. *The Greeks on Pleasure.* Oxford, 1984.

Heer de, C. 1968. [*Makar-Eudaimôn-Olbios-Eutuchês*] *A study of the semantic field denoting happiness in ancient Greek to the end of the 5th century B.C.* Crawley, Western Australia, 1968.

Heinaman, R., ed. *Plato's and Aristotle's Ethics.* Aldershot, 2003.

Hursthouse, R. *On Virtue Ethics.* Oxford, 1999.

Irwin, T. "Socrates the Epicurean?" *Illinois Classical Studies* 11 (1986): 85–112.

Irwin, T. *Plato's Ethics.* Oxford, 1995.

Kahn, C. "Plato's Theory of Desire." *Review of Metaphysics* 41(1987): 77–103.

Kahn, C. *Plato and the Socratic Dialogue.* Cambridge, 1996.

Kamtekar, R. "Plato on the Attribution of Conative Attitudes." *Archiv für Geschichte der Philosophie* 88 (2006): 127–162.

Kant, I., trans. and ed. Gregor, M. 1996. *Practical Philosophy.* Cambridge, 1996.

Kraut, R. "Two Conceptions of Happiness." *The Philosophical Review* 88 (1979): 167–197.

Kraut, R. *Socrates and the State.* Princeton, 1984.

McTighe, K. "Socrates on desire for the good and the involuntariness of wrongdoing: Gorgias 446a-468e." *Phronesis* 29 (1984): 193–236.

Morrison, D. 2003. "Happiness, Rationality, and Egoism in Plato's Socrates" In *Rationality and Happiness: from the Ancients to the Early Medievals.* eds. J. Yu and J. Garcia. Rochester, NY, 2003, pp. 17–34.

Nehamas, A. 1999. "Socratic Intellectualism." In *Virtues of Authenticity: Essays on Plato and Socrates.* Princeton, 1999, pp. 27–58.

Parfit, D. *Reasons and Persons.* Oxford, 1984.

Penner, T. "Desire and Power in Socrates: The Argument of Gorgias 466A-468E that Orators and Tyrants Have No Power in the City." *Apeiron* 24 (1991): 147–202.

Race, W. *Pindar Nemean Odes Isthmian Odes Fragments.* Cambridge, MA, 1997.

Schultz, B. ed. 1992. *Essays on Henry Sidgwick.* Cambridge, 1992.

Sidgwick, H. *The Methods of Ethics.* 7th ed. Indianapolis, 1981.

Vlastos, G. *Socrates, Ironist and Moral Philosopher.* Ithaca, 1991.

Weiss, R. "Ignorance, Involuntariness and Innocence: A Reply to McTighe." *Phronesis* 30 (1985): 314–322.

Weiss, R. "The Hedonic Calculus in the Protagoras and the Phaedo." *Journal of the History of Philosophy* 25 (1989): 511–529.

White, N. *Individual and Conflict in Greek Ethics.* Oxford, 2002.

Zeyl, D. "Socrates and Hedonism – Protagoras 351b-358b." *Phronesis* 25 (1980): 250–269.

14   Socrates' Political Philosophy

> I believe that I'm one of a few Athenians – so as not to say I'm the
> only one, but the only one among our contemporaries – to take up the
> true political craft and practice the true politics. This is because the
> speeches I make on each occasion do not aim at gratification but at
> what's best.
>
> Socrates[1]

Especially in the modern age, Socrates is sanctified as a defender of free
speech, honest and relentless inquiry, and the love of truth. Other philosophers too have shared these commitments. But Socrates stood up
for them at the cost of his own life. In enacting his commitments as he
did, Socrates became more than a theorist: in some sense, he was also
an actor on the political stage.

In light of the enormous difficulties inherent in the effort to locate
either the philosophy of the historical Socrates, or a Socratic philosophy about whose content the major ancient authors on Socrates
agree, in this chapter I will confine myself principally to the Platonic
"Socrates."[2] When referring to "Socrates," I mean the Socrates of Plato's
dialogues. I have taken note of several interesting and relevant points of
contact with other portrayals of Socrates where doing so is useful to my

---

I am grateful to Jeffrey Henderson, David Konstan, Marina McCoy, Don
Morrison, Josh Ober, and Jay Samons for discussion of this chapter.

1   From Plato's *Gorgias* 521d6–9. All of my quotations from Plato's works are
    from translations contained in Cooper and Hutchinson 1997. For the Greek
    text of the *Republic*, I have used the edition of J. Burnet. For the Greek
    text of the *Euthyphro, Apology,* and *Crito,* I have used the revised *Platonis
    Opera,* Vol. I, eds. E. A. Duke et al.

2   For a critique of the view that the *Apology* is even "a historically reli-
    able source for the *reconstruction* of Socrates' character and opinions" see
    Morrison 2000 (the quotation is from p. 236, emphasis added). Nobody any
    longer defends the view that even Plato's *Apology* seeks merely to *report*
    what the historical Socrates said at his trial; the dialogue is the product of
    Plato's literary and philosophical genius.

discussion. While confining myself mainly to the Platonic Socrates, I shall, unless otherwise noted, suspend judgment about the relation between Plato and Socrates. The Socratic views I elicit from several Platonic dialogues may or may not represent Plato's own views; an entirely different, and certainly much more detailed, discussion of the dialogues would be required to establish the point either way. I shall also range across several dialogues in which Socrates takes active part; this approach is not confined by the early/middle/late interpretive schema.[3] Dialogues such as the *Statesman*, which are obviously of relevance to political philosophy, will receive little attention here, for Socrates barely participates in the discussion.[4] And the *Laws*, in which Socrates makes no appearance, will also not be discussed here.

In one sense, all of the Platonic dialogues in which Socrates participates are relevant to assessing his character as an actor in the polis, as well as some aspect or other of his political philosophy. No chapter-length treatment of both issues could hope to take into account every one of those twenty-two dialogues.[5] I shall therefore pick and choose relevant passages from the dialogues that scholars would most readily grant as basic to understanding the political philosophy of Plato's Socrates – in particular the *Euthyphro*, *Apology*, *Crito*, *Gorgias*, and *Republic*.

Socrates is portrayed by Plato – and especially in his defense speech, Socrates portrays himself – as active in his polis. In Section 1 of this chapter, I will discuss this "dramatic" portrayal and self-portrayal. While Socrates was not a "statesman" in any ordinary sense, he suggests in the passage from the *Gorgias* that heads this chapter that he alone undertakes to be the true statesman of his time (a genuine leader who holds no office, in effect). Socrates also contrasts an ideal community

3   For critical assessment of that schema, see the papers collected in Annas and Rowe 2002, in particular Annas's paper (Annas 2002, "What are Plato's 'Middle' Dialogues in the Middle Of?") and my "Comments on Kahn" (Griswold 2002; this is a commentary on Charles Kahn's "On Platonic Chronology," included in the same volume). On the general issue of the organization of the Platonic corpus, see Griswold 1999(a) and also the follow-up exchange between Kahn and Griswold cited there.

4   My views on the *Statesman* may be found in Griswold 1989. Along the same general lines, see Miller 1980.

5   The Platonic dialogues in which Socrates actively participates are the *Apology*, *Charmides*, *Cratylus*, *Crito*, *Euthydemus*, *Euthyphro*, *Gorgias*, *Hippias Minor*, *Ion*, *Laches*, *Lysis*, *Menexenus*, *Meno*, *Phaedo*, *Phaedrus*, *Philebus*, *Parmenides*, *Protagoras*, *Republic*, *Symposium*, *Theaetetus*, and *Timaeus*. He appears and speaks in the *Sophist* and *Statesman*. The authorship of the *Hippias Major*, *Clitophon*, and *Alcibiades I*, is disputed; Socrates is active in all three. The *Critias* is a fragment.

with extant communities, and especially in Section 2, I shall examine briefly some relevant passages from the *Republic*.

A common theme at both levels – that of Socrates' interactions with others and that of his political philosophy – concerns the relation of the philosopher to the polis, of philosophy to politics (taking the latter term in the broadest sense).[6] This theme will therefore be central in what follows.

1. SOCRATES AS POLITICAL ACTOR

We often think of Socrates as philosophizing in the agora, as a "public philosopher" very much involved in the intellectual and cultural debates of the period. That Socrates had become an extremely well-known and controversial figure is clear from the fact that Aristophanes and other comic poets lampooned him, and that democratic Athens viewed him as enough of an irritant to warrant putting him to death. No other major intellectual was put to death by the Athenian polis in the fourth or fifth century.[7]

The picture of Socrates as philosophizing in the agora comes to us more from Xenophon's *Memorabilia* (I.1.2) than from Plato (cf. Diogenes Laertius 2.21). We know the geographical boundaries of the agora, and it is safe to say that Plato rarely portrays Socrates as engaging in philosophical conversation in its open byways.[8] To be sure, at *Apology* 17c Socrates refers to his customary conversations in the agora, and the implication of his descriptions of his interrogations of the poets (22b) and craftsmen (23a) is that there are quite a few bystanders present, presumably because the conversations were held in a public place (cf. *Apology* 21c3–7, d1–2). The *Euthyphro* takes place on the porch of a Court, also in the agora. And yet aside from the *Apology*, the other dialogues in which he appears take place in private homes, outside of the walls of the city, or in public places such as gymnasia, wrestling schools, or jail (if one may call such a place "public"). Further, by and large Plato does

---

6   The term "political" is potentially misleading in the context of Plato's philosophy, because the contrast with "social" – so natural for us – is never made by Plato. The modern distinction carries with it a set of presuppositions about the scope of "the political" that are arguably foreign to Plato. When referring to "politics" or "the political," then, I shall, unless otherwise indicated, have in mind a sense broad enough to encompass what we would call the social.

7   On the question of the persecution of intellectuals in ancient Greece, see Dover 1976 and Wallace 1994. The full roster of targets of comedy can be found in Sommerstein 1996. See also *Protagoras* 316c5–317c5.

8   For a useful discussion of the Athenian agora, see Millett 1998.

not portray Socrates as picking up conversations with the "common man." His interlocutors tend to be young men of promise from noted families, sophists and rhetoricians, established public figures (including generals), philosophers (Zeno and the aged Parmenides), and figures positioned to exercise political influence (such as Charmides, Critias, and Alcibiades). Some are Athenian and some not. Plato's Socrates is unquestionably a public figure, then, but not quite in the sense often imagined.

Plato's Socrates is neither just the practically involved Xenophontic figure who wanders the agora, nor the apolitical Thales-like theoretician (compare Aristophanes' portrait of Socrates in the *Clouds*, and *Theaetetus* 173d-175e). His Socrates is a considerably more complex "political" figure and correspondingly more difficult to characterize concisely.

Socrates performed his civic duties, such as serving in the armed forces on military campaigns (see the start of the *Charmides*, *Apology* 28e, and *Symposium* 219e5-7 and context) and in required political office. Yet he was not a seeker of public office and civic responsibility. However much he contrasted a political "ideal" with the unsatisfactory reality of the historical polis, he did not otherwise agitate for the radical reformation of his polis by, say, proposing measures in the Assembly or organizing reform movements. We tend to think of him as a political radical, but it is important to remember that he did not refuse to fight in Athens' wars abroad; he was not a pacifist. Further, he never takes direct aim at them in the Platonic dialogues, asking an "applied political philosophy" question [such as, "is our] country's expedition to Sicily just?" although he certainly provides a basis for launching a scathing philosophical critique of the pursuit of power and wealth, as well as of every extant political regime. He did not say, and certainly did not act as though it were the case, that it is the duty of a conscientious person to oppose publicly every immoral political act. For example, there is no record of Socrates' publicly having criticized Athens' decision to kill all adult Mytilenean males, even though a debate about the matter was held in 428/427BCE, or of his publicly having opposed Athens' expedition to Sicily in 415BCE. In the *Crito*, he explains (in an argument whose intentions and defensibility are much debated in the secondary literature) that he will not – that one ought not – break the law, for example by escaping from prison.[9] He was not an "individualist" who trumpeted without qualification the rights of conscience over positive law, as we might put it today.

9   A sample of the debate will be found in Kraut 1984, ch. III.

Yet he was not a quietist, and he made it clear that he refused to carry out orders from the polis that he deemed illegal or immoral. He provides two examples. The one took place in the period of the democracy: as a member of the Council, Socrates alone voted against the cruel (and later much regretted) decision to condemn the ten generals who were unable (because of conditions at sea) to rescue the survivors of the battle of Arginusae in 406BCE. Socrates deserves kudos for this risky and brave opposition. His other example is more ambiguous: when the oligarchy ordered him to help in the arrest of Leon of Salamis, in order to execute him unjustly, Socrates simply "went home" while four others obeyed the order. He rightly notes that he risked death in thus resisting (see *Apology* 32a4-e1). Yet he did not, as far as we know, make any attempt to save Leon or others who were similarly mistreated, or indeed either to leave the city (along with many anti-oligarchs) during this period or to actively take up arms against the oligarchy.

Socrates' statement that he is not a quietist ("I have deliberately not led a quiet life," *Apology* 36b5-6; cf. 38a1) is supported by his insistence that not even the threat of death would prevent him from philosophizing in his customary fashion, and that he is on a life long, god-given mission to improve the virtue of his fellows (*Apology* 29d7-30b4, 30d6-31a2).[10] In the *Laches*, he is portrayed as leading two generals (Laches and Nicias) to reflect critically on their conceptions of virtue, and of courage in particular. In the *Symposium* and elsewhere, we learn that Socrates had also tried hard to turn Alcibiades, one of the key players in the catastrophic expedition to Sicily, from his love of fame and power to the love of wisdom and virtue. Dialogues such as these chime with Socrates' insistence in the *Apology* that he actively sought to induce his fellows – including politically important people – to reflect on their lives and thereby to emend their ways. While Socrates famously claimed only to possess human wisdom or awareness of his ignorance (*Apology* 20d7-e3), he was not immobilized by this recognition, for it clearly is not at all equivalent to ignorance *simpliciter*, let alone ignorance of one's ignorance. Indeed, that recognition motivated a peculiar kind of engagement with the citizens of his community.

Socrates' main mode of participation – or perhaps one should say, intervention – in the polis was that of oral conversation. He did not

---

10 On the issue of Socrates' alleged quietism, see Ober 1998, ch. 4. Ober argues that while Plato chose "the quietist path" (p. 186), the politically active Socrates of the *Apology* (unlike that of the *Gorgias*) did not (p. 212). He also argues that the Socrates of the *Republic*, resolves the tension between the two, but in the context of the ideal polis (p. 237). By contrast, the present chapter attempts to locate an outlook that is consistent across the *Apology*, *Gorgias*, and *Republic*.

write philosophy, and so chose not to act politically through that medium. He stresses that he was not a "teacher," meaning that he did not accept tuition (*Apology* 33a-b). That he did in other senses teach others (sometimes by "teaching them a lesson," other times by showing them that a philosophical question exists and how to pursue it) is however undeniable. Socrates makes it perfectly clear that he has had great influence on the young (*Apology* 23c, 33c, 37d6-e2, 39d) and enjoys wide fame (*Apology* 34e2-4, 38c1-5). Socrates both was and was not a political actor; he modeled, so to speak, a highly unconventional practice of political engagement.

It was also a deeply controversial practice. The most striking and famous chapters of Socrates' life are his trial and execution. He appeared before 501 fellow citizens to answer the charges brought against him and, in effect, to justify the philosophical life. Socrates' defense stresses that the antagonism his public practice of philosophy generated is of long standing, and the Court's verdict confirms that reconciliation between himself and the polis – indeed, a democratic polis – is not to be. The relation of Socrates to his community is decisively (though of course not entirely) characterized by sustained antagonism.[11] Indeed, Socrates' statements, both here and elsewhere, suggest that on his own view, the conflict is deep and permanent:

Be sure, gentlemen of the jury, that if I had long ago attempted to take part in politics, I should have died long ago, and benefited neither you nor myself. Do not be angry with me for speaking the truth; no man will survive who genuinely opposes you or any other crowd and prevents the occurrence of many unjust and illegal happenings in the city. A man who really fights for justice must lead a private, not a public, life if he is to survive for even a short time. (*Apology* 31d6–32a3)

When Socrates comments on the possibility of his going into exile, he says that he would "be driven out of one city after another," the hostility to his philosophizing recurring again and again (*Apology* 37d4-e2). By choosing examples from both the oligarchic and democratic periods of recent Athenian history to illustrate his resistance to collaborating with injustice, he implies that malfeasance is endemic to politics as such.

11   This is not to say that Socrates lacked friends, or to deny that they are in evidence at his trial. As Plato records it, Socrates states that "a switch of only thirty votes would have acquitted me," i.e., given him a simple majority (*Apology* 36a5-6). The vote was surprisingly close. For a different view about the relationship of Socrates to democratic Athens, see Ober's Chapter 7 in the present volume. Cf. Callicles' vivid polemic at *Gorgias* 484c4–486d1.

In the *Republic*, Socrates paints an equally dire picture of the dangerous ignorance of the polis and of its hostility to the one who truly knows how to guide the ship of state (488a2–489a2). The most revolutionary and famous argument of the *Republic* is quite probably that "Until philosophers rule as kings or those who are now called kings and leading men genuinely and adequately philosophize, that is, until political power and philosophy entirely coincide, while the many natures who at present pursue either one exclusively are forcibly prevented from doing so, cities will have no rest from evils, Glaucon, nor, I think, will the human race" (473c11-d6; recapitulated at 499b1-c5). Short of that extraordinary ideal, the antagonism between politics and philosophy seems deep and permanent, as books V, VI, and VII of the *Republic* argue in detail. Socrates states what very likely remains true today: namely, that not a single actual city is worthy of a philosophical nature (*Republic* 497b1–2). Indeed, it would take "divine dispensation" for a philosopher to grow to maturity uncorrupted (493a1–2). What is a philosopher to do, should he or she manage to escape the destructive forces inherent in any this-worldly community? Socrates' answer clearly ties into the passages of the *Apology* to which I have already referred, and indeed he cites his own decision (backed up by his "daemonic sign," also referred to in the same context in the *Apology* (31c4–32a3)) not to enter politics. Socrates goes on to comment on the rare souls who have

tasted how sweet and blessed a possession philosophy is, and at the same time they've also seen the madness of the majority and realized, in a word, that hardly anyone acts sanely in public affairs and that there is no ally with whom they might go to the aid of justice and survive, that instead they'd perish before they could profit either their city or their friends and be useless both to themselves and to others, just like a man who has fallen among wild animals and is neither willing to join them in doing injustice nor sufficiently strong to oppose the general savagery alone. Taking all this into account, they lead a quiet life and do their own work. Thus, like someone who takes refuge under a little wall from a storm of dust or hail driven by the wind, the philosopher – seeing others filled with lawlessness – is satisfied if he can somehow lead his present life free from injustice and impious acts and depart from it with good hope, blameless and content. (*Republic* 496c5-e2)

It would be hard to imagine a more extreme statement of the hostility between philosophy and politics as they exist in the non-ideal world. The same thought is vividly echoed in the simile of the cave, which represents imprisoned cave dwellers who are "like us" (515a5) as wanting to kill the philosopher who had miraculously escaped to the regions above (517a3–6). And the philosopher is presented as preferring to be a miserable landless serf than to live again as a cave dweller (516d4–7).

What is at the heart of that antagonism? Let us return to Socrates' startling statement in the *Gorgias* that he alone – and not such celebrated figures as Pericles – takes up the true *techne* and practice of politics. As he there explains, "the speeches I make on each occasion do not aim at gratification but at what's best" (521d6-9; on Pericles, see 516d2-3 and context). In effect, he demands that politics be based on knowledge of what is best for the community, and this means what is best for the "souls" of the citizens. Statecraft ought to be based on a philosophically defensible understanding of what is best for human beings. Socrates was famous, correspondingly, for leading every question back to an examination of his interlocutor's way of living (e.g., *Apology* 36c3-d1, 39c6-d2, *Laches* 187e6–188a5, *Symposium* 215e6–216c3), and for being concerned above all about how he should live his own life. One of the key methods Socrates used to raise the question of the justifiability of an individual's or community's *modus vivendi* was the paradigm of expert knowledge. We would surely grant that, say, in such areas as military strategy, horse training, or ship building, the relevant expert should dictate what is to be done. By analogy, must we not search for expert knowledge (*techne* or *episteme*) about what we should do in politics; would it not be irrational and deleterious to settle for anything less?

Socrates is, in effect, demanding that we seek to guide ourselves by knowledge of what is best. This is not of course to say that we actually possess the requisite knowledge, only that we ought to pursue it both relentlessly and in a particular manner – namely, through the give and take of Socratic dialogue (I am not claiming that Socrates had or thought he had the knowledge at issue). The controversial metaphysical and epistemological assumptions built into this view of knowledge are scarcely evident in the *Apology* and *Gorgias*, but emerge in books V-VII of the *Republic* (among other places). In spite of the debatable character of those assumptions, and of the deeply difficult problem of what it would mean to be guided by an unrealized ideal of knowledge, the motivation for Socrates' questions is difficult to resist.

Consider his conversation with Euthyphro. It is a splendid example of the type of exchange that fueled the antagonism against Socrates. The setting is the steps of the courthouse, where Socrates has gone to receive the indictment against him. Euthyphro is there in order to prosecute his own father on charges of impiety. The context, then, is politically and morally charged. Socrates remarks that nobody would take such an extraordinary step against kin unless he were wise about the matter in question – in this case piety – lest he be rightly accused of acting impiously himself. And who could disagree? Euthyphro responds that as a matter of fact he does have accurate knowledge of the nature of piety (*Euthyphro* 4e4–5a2). But the remainder of the dialogue demonstrates that Euthyphro simply cannot answer the famous "what is it?" question. When Socrates reminds him that he surely would not proceed with so drastic an action without having a coherent account of piety and begs him to provide that account, Euthyphro flees and the dialogue ends.

Socrates is especially interested in the topic of piety because of Meletus's indictment against him. Certainly Meletus too must pretend to be wise in this as well as the other matters referred to in the indictment he has brought against Socrates (*Euthyphro* 2c2-d1), and he cannot avoid the implication that if he is unable to defend his claim to wisdom, he has no business bringing the indictment. Socrates' dialogue with him in the *Apology* is just long enough to support serious doubts about Meletus's ability to give any such account of himself. The consequences of his ignorance are as obvious as they are unjust.

Euthyphro is a sort of fanatic, not only in claiming explicitly what so many assume implicitly – knowledge of what piety is – but also in asserting without qualification that if an act is wrong (impious), then whoever did it should be prosecuted to the full extent of the law, even if the wrongdoer is your own father (4b7-e3). Meletus is in his own way a fanatic. He is taking drastic steps in the absolute certainty that he is in a position to assess whether or not someone is corrupting the youth or acting impiously, and yet he is without a rationally defensible account of the very concepts he himself is employing. Neither Euthyphro nor Meletus discharges adequately the heavy responsibilities they have shouldered. They hubristically pretend to have knowledge they do not possess. This is in effect Socrates' indictment of them and of many others, and it is, quite understandably, not a charge they appreciated, especially when its validity was demonstrated publicly. By contrast, Socrates comes off not as a fanatic but as moderate precisely (if paradoxically) because of his zealousness for philosophical discussion, as well as humble in his admission that he does not know the answers (cf. *Theaetetus* 210c5-d4). This is the ethical and political dimension of the great divide Socrates sees between himself and just about everyone else, as he tells the jury:

> And surely it is the most blameworthy ignorance to believe that one knows what one does not know. It is perhaps on this point and in this respect, gentlemen, that I differ from the majority of men, and if I were to claim that I am wiser than anyone in anything, it would be in this, that, as I have no adequate knowledge of things in the underworld, so I do not think I have. I do know, however, that it is wicked and shameful to do wrong, to disobey one's superior, be he god or man. (*Apology* 29b1-7)

Socratic politics – or better, his applied political philosophy, if one may so put it – is premised on the tenet that ignorance corrupts, that the (philosophical) pursuit of knowledge saves the soul (to use Socrates' term), and that bettering the soul ought be our chief pursuit in life.

Socrates' compatriots rarely care about that pursuit. Instead, they devote themselves to the cultivation of the body and the accumulation of wealth and power (perhaps we are not altogether unlike them), whereas for Socrates these cannot be beneficial things unless guided by knowledge of the good (for example, see *Apology* 30a7-b4). Socrates' disinterest in the pursuit of wealth, power, and adornment of the body mark him off starkly from most of his fellow citizens, and help constitute the unconventional persona for which he became famous. Enacting his principles would revolutionize the community from the inside out, so to speak, for it would turn each soul in a direction that would cause a drastic shift of individual and collective priorities. Socrates is quite explicit that he aims for nothing less (e.g., *Apology* 29e3–30b4). His is fundamentally the politics of self-transformation.

Does Socrates recommend that everyone ought to strive to become a philosopher? The *Apology* certainly suggests an affirmative answer. In principle, everyone should focus primarily on self-knowledge and the perfection of his own soul. As we have seen, the *Apology* also makes perfectly clear that this is extremely unlikely to happen, and dialogues such as the *Republic* assert that few will ever in fact become philosophers in the full sense of the term. Is Socrates therefore recommending the impossible, and acting on that recommendation? In the next section I will say something more about that subject, but by anticipation note that it would not be irrational to believe that some philosophical self-awareness is better than none at all. Given, however, that most people will not become philosophers in any full sense (including that modeled by Socrates) and that their lives communally and individually will therefore depend on beliefs for which they lack defensible philosophical reasons, the antagonism – or at least the tension – between philosophy and political life would seem irresolvable. A comprehensive understanding of politics would include the recognition that this antagonism or tension is likely to be permanent.

If that is true, however, why does Socrates engage in political life at all? Why not retire behind a "little wall" somewhere, and like the Thales he sketches in the *Theaetetus* (173d–175e), contemplate the unchanging patterns of things, or conduct dialogues with philosophical friends in private, and focus on perfecting one's own soul?

The form that Socrates' answer takes in the *Apology* – to the effect that his philosophical quest was coeval with his political involvement, following an event he narrates – is unconvincing. As he tells the story, when his impulsive friend Chaerephon (well known to the jury, and as Socrates is careful to underline, a partisan of the democracy) took it upon himself to ask the Oracle at Delphi whether any man was wiser than Socrates, the Pythian replied that "no one was wiser." Naturally, Socrates was puzzled, and hit upon a way of attempting to "refute" the Oracle – namely, that of cross-examining those who claimed to be wise (*Apology* 21a, c1). If any were such, then the Oracle erred. The impulse to test by refutation is paradigmatically Socratic, suggesting that Socrates had long since understood what it means to philosophize (further, nowhere else in the dialogues does he suggest that his philosophical quest began with the Oracle's pronouncement). This task of examining others is one he sets himself. The Oracle at Delphi never sent Socrates on any mission, never pronounced him the god's gift to humankind, and never gave any directive whatever (contra *Apology* 23b5, 30d6–31a2). Socrates quite accurately remarks, after the guilty verdict, that "if I say that it is impossible for me to keep quiet because that means disobeying the god, you will not believe me and will think I am being ironical" (37e5–38a1).

Socrates examines others so as to learn something about himself – that part of his *Apology* self-presentation seems right, incomplete though it is. He cannot simply talk to himself; he needs to work out various claims, especially claims about how best to live, through dialogue with others who are attracted to their own views of the subjects in question (consider *Gorgias* 486d2–7 and context, and 487a; *Charmides* 166c7-d6; and *Protagoras* 348c5-e4). The exchange may be beneficial for his interlocutor, as Socrates asserts in the *Apology*. There is no reason to doubt that Socrates also wished philosophy to benefit others, including in a non-ideal state of affairs when philosophers do not rule. His political involvement, however, is not primarily altruistic. To live one's *own* life virtuously is an axiomatic imperative of his enterprise, one to which all else is subservient. He is above all (but not exclusively) concerned with self-knowledge (*Phaedrus* 229e4–230a7) and the perfection of his own soul. His willingness to intervene politically, even when his life might be placed in danger, is governed by those axioms.

If one keeps in mind his radical position that "the unexamined life is not worth living" (*Apology* 38a5–6) and therefore that one's chief duty is to improve one's own soul, the minimalism of Socrates' political involvements (putting aside his philosophical interventions) shows itself as part of a moral life conceived along the lines of a perfectionist moral outlook.[12] He was willing to die rather than give it up; if ordered to prevent you from pursuing the examined life, he would refuse; and he would assist you in the pursuit insofar as doing so forms part of his own. Whether he would die in order to protect your pursuit of self-perfection

12 On the meaning of "perfectionist moral outlook," see Griswold 1999(b).

is questionable. Socrates' political philosophy is deeply tied to a perfectionist conception of the individual's moral life, and therefore also to the "transcendentalist" metaphysics on which he claims it rests.

2. RECONCILING THE IDEAL AND THE ACTUAL

The intentions of the *Republic* have been a matter of controversy for millennia. Aristotle read the dialogue as proposing a program of political reformation (see n. 23). Other readers down to the present day have also, in effect, read the dialogue as setting out a blueprint that Plato's Socrates or Plato meant to put into practice.[13] Another school reads the dialogue as "ironic" and as warning us *against* any effort at radical political reform guided by a heavenly "blueprint" (they cite *Republic* 592b2–5); the tensions internal to Socrates' "perfect" polis, and between it and any non-ideal polis, are taken to yield a sort of secondary political theory that meshes with Socrates' practice of staying out of politics as far as possible in order to pursue philosophy.[14] Yet other readers emphasize the "literary" or dialogical dimension, seeing the dialogue as evolving in a way that successively opens up new horizons for reflection on ethics as well as politics. The dialogue is here viewed as structured in ways that indicate Plato's intention that the closed regime of the middle books of the *Republic* be read as open to question.[15]

The ancient Platonists and Stoics, and at least one prominent modern scholar, deny that the dialogue is primarily about politics; rather, they claim, it is primarily an ethical treatise.[16] After all, books II through X are an effort to answer the famous challenge put by Glaucon and Adeimantus to Socrates: show us that justice is in and of itself good for the soul that possesses it (367d2–5). The "political" discussions are introduced as a means of understanding the soul and what is best for it (cf. 611e1–612b5). The city being the soul writ large (see 368e-369a) – the "greatest

13 For example, Popper 1966, vol. 1, pp. 153–156. For an argument that while not a "blueprint," the *Republic's* ideal city is intended to be a practicable (and desirable) possibility, see Burnyeat 1999. Some of the material at the start of this section is taken from Griswold 1999(b).

14 This reading is offered by Leo Strauss and his followers. See, for example, Bloom's "Interpretive Essay" appended to his translation of the *Republic*: "Socrates constructs his utopia to point up the dangers of what we would call utopianism; as such it is the greatest critique of political idealism ever written" (Bloom 1968, p. 410). See also Strauss 1964, p. 65: "Certain it is that the *Republic* supplies the most magnificent cure ever devised for every form of political ambition." I criticize this approach in Griswold 2003, Section I.

15 See Clay 2002.

16 See Annas 1999.

of all reflections on human nature," to borrow Madison's phrase – a problematic city/soul analogy guides much of the discussion, but is not (according to this view) to be mistaken for a political philosophy.[17]

These interpretive debates have been accompanied by mostly negative responses to the political proposals Socrates puts forward in the dialogue. The critique began almost immediately with Aristotle. In the modern age, luminaries of the liberal Enlightenment, such as Jefferson, Madison, and Adams, were pointed in their criticism of Plato.[18] The most famous recent polemic is undoubtedly that of Karl Popper, while I. F. Stone's much discussed book presented an attack at a more popular level.[19] For Popper, Plato's views were "totalitarian" and prepared the way for Nazism and Stalinism (certain Nazi theorists did in fact take themselves to be continuing the program of Plato's Republic).[20] Even though Popper's interpretation of Plato has been subjected to a great deal of critical assessment,[21] it remains difficult to free oneself from the long-standing judgment that Socrates' political proposals in the Republic are deeply flawed.

The specific accusations against the political philosophy presented in the Republic are fourfold in nature. First, Socrates' "beautiful city" (Republic 527c2; cf. 497b7) is accused of being unfair because it is not committed to a notion of the moral equality of human beings. Socrates' theories seem inegalitarian at their core, and the social and political schemes he sets out are, to our sensibilities, offensively hierarchical. Correspondingly, we hear nothing here about "natural rights" or their equivalent.[22] Second, Socrates' proposals seem illiberal to the extreme. Especially as presented in the Republic, they seem to leave very little

17 Madison wrote, in Federalist no. 51: "But what is government itself but the greatest of all reflections on human nature? If men were angels, no government would be necessary. If angels were to govern men, neither external nor internal controls on government would be necessary." See Hamilton et al. 1961, p. 322.

18 In his semi-retirement, Thomas Jefferson wrote to John Adams that "It is fortunate for us that Platonic republicanism has not obtained the same favor as Platonic Christianity; or we should now have been all living, men, women and children, pell mell together, like beasts of the field or forest." Jefferson to Adams, July 5, 1814; in Cappon 1988, p. 433.

19 I refer to Stone 1988. For discussion of Stone's book, see Griswold 1991, Burnyeat 1988, and Schofield 2002.

20 See Popper 1966, vol. I, p. 87 et passim. On the appropriation of Plato by Nazi theorists, see Hoernlé 1967, pp. 32–35.

21 For a sample of the debate, see the essays collected in Brambough 1967 and in Thorson 1963; also Robinson 1969, ch. 4, and Klosko 2006.

22 Averroes, an otherwise sympathetic reader of the Republic, objects to the Republic's view that the Greeks are best suited by nature to perfection. See Averroes 1974, pp. 13–14 (section 27.1–13).

room for political liberties. And this too strikes us as unjust. Third, they are accused of being tied to complex and doubtful metaphysical doctrines that just about nobody wants to defend.

A fourth set of criticisms alleges that the political proposals presented in the *Republic* are simply unworkable or fail to produce the results intended. Aristotle's arguments to the effect that abolishing private property does not remove either strife or the desire for accumulating property fall into this class.[23] James Madison took it to be a crucial axiom of statecraft that "a nation of philosophers is as little to be expected as the philosophical race of kings wished for by Plato."[24] Locke's pragmatic criticisms (in the *Letter Concerning Toleration*) of a civic religion that is coercively implemented are echoed over and over again in the liberal Enlightenment by thinkers such as Rousseau, Adam Smith, and Voltaire, and are implicitly directed against the *Republic*. The dialogue's infamous censorship of the poets (many of whom are advocating conventional Greek religion) has also been roundly criticized (for its final statement in the dialogue, illuminated by the "ancient quarrel between it [poetry] and philosophy," see 606e-608a).

To these points about the impracticality of Plato's scheme we may add the objection, articulated by Rawls (without specific reference to Plato), that since there exists no popular consensus as to the truth of a single notion of the human good, a "city in speech" such as that put forward in the *Republic* would be politically irrelevant even if its truth could be established philosophically. Modern democratic republics are characterized by wide, even extreme, disagreement about the human good in the sense Plato's dialogues speak of that good.[25] This characteristic of modern liberal societies is a cause of lament for some, and of celebration for others. In either case, Rawls takes it to be a basic fact that must orient any realizable theory of justice. As Rawls puts it, a theory of justice must be "political" and based on an overlapping consensus rather than be "metaphysical." And "the conception of justice should be, as far as possible, independent of the opposing and conflicting philosophical and religions doctrines that citizens affirm."[26]

Seemingly every aspect of the *Republic* is, then, the subject of controversy. Yet we may venture to observe that the dialogue is continuous with the *Apology* in the sense that it insists that a form of expert knowledge

---

23 See *Politics* 2.1261a37–1264b25, where this and other of the *Republic*'s proposals are criticized.

24 See Hamilton et al. 1961, no. 49, p. 315. For a similar point, see Hume 1987, p. 514.

25 See Rawls 1999, pp. 290–291, 214–215; and 1996, pp. xli, 134.

26 Rawls 1996, pp. 10, 9.

is required if individuals and communities are to live well. That knowledge turns out to be the dialectical or philosophical knowledge of the Forms, in particular, the Form of the Good, "the most important thing to learn about" and that thanks to which "just things and the others become useful and beneficial." Without knowledge of the Good "even the fullest possible knowledge of other things is of no benefit to us" (505a2-b1). We will not become "perfect" (499b3) either individually or collectively until the philosopher (hence, the knower of the Good) rules. The *Republic* presents much more fully than do the other dialogues we have mentioned the perfectionist basis of Socrates' political philosophy. One might say that Socrates' politics is theological in the sense that it is premised on a notion of the divine understood as the Good and the other Forms.[27] Strangely, though, the achievability of knowledge of the Good at the political level – the achievability of the "ideal" state – is in severe doubt. Partly because the institution of philosopher–rulers is unlikely, the attainability of perfect wisdom by the individual is also in doubt (see *Republic* 499a11-c5). And if this is right, then the *Republic* ultimately harmonizes with the *Apology's* insistence that human, not divine, wisdom is all that we are likely to attain.[28] I note that we are also told that were the perfect city to come into being, it would soon die; it seems to carry the seeds of its own destruction (546a-e).

Perhaps this is one reason why at the end of book IX, Socrates asserts that the best polis will come to be only by "divine good luck," absent which the person of understanding will not take part in the politics of his fatherland (592a7-9). Instead, as Glaucon puts it, one will "take part in the politics of the city we were founding and describing, the one that exists in theory (*en logois*), for I don't think it exists anywhere on earth." Socrates adds that perhaps "there is a model (*paradeigma*) of it in heaven, for anyone who wants to look at it and to make himself its citizen on the strength of what he sees. It makes no difference whether it is or ever will be somewhere, for he would take part in the practical affairs of that city and no other" (592a10-b5).[29] The best city must be

27 The word "theology" is used (apparently for the first time in the history of philosophy) at 379a5–6, as Socrates drastically revises conventional Greek religion in a way that effectively turns the gods into his conception of the divine (the Forms).

28 Is this consistent with Socrates' statement in the *Gorgias* quoted at the start of this essay? I think the answer is affirmative, if one emphasizes the verb "take up" (*epicheirein*, at *Gorgias* 521d7); Socrates does not there actually claim to possess the political art, only to be one of the few to attempt it and thereby to practice (no doubt imperfectly) the "true politics." Cf. *Gorgias* 517a1–3.

29 This passage echoes a much earlier description at 500b8-d2. Cf. 611e1–612a6.

writ small in the soul; the "constitution within" (591e1) alone matters in this, our non-ideal world. The emphasis at the end of the *Republic* is on the individual's formation of self, and thus of a way of life. This is a major theme of the myth with which the dialogue concludes.

The *Republic*'s famous descriptions of the perfected constitution nevertheless come to serve a crucial purpose, whether or not perfection of self or polis is realizable. They provide the telos, and therewith the standard to which everything – including the politics of the day – should aspire. They help one to understand the respects in which the non-ideal is lacking, and to realize that the non-ideal cannot (thanks to the sort of thing it is) ever become ideal (no soul will ever *be* a Form, no created being, including a polis, will ever last, and so forth). What is the political upshot? The phrases from the end of book IX just quoted might suggest quietism. But that would be a mistake. To begin with, as we have already seen, the aspiring dialectician – the Socratic philosopher, in short – cannot but live and participate in a community. The character of the community cannot but matter to him, and the philosopher will affect it in turn.

But what sort of community precisely? Governed by what sort of constitution? What would its economic, social, and political structure look like? Plato's Socrates does not provide firm and detailed answers to such questions, and in that sense he does not have a "political theory." His views about self-perfection do have political consequences, however. As already mentioned, certain regimes would be unacceptable (e.g., one that requires its citizens to commit great injustices, such as arresting Leon of Salamis) and others would come in for philosophical critique (ancient democracy and tyranny come to mind). More positively, it would seem that in a non-ideal world, a polis that avoids injustice, makes possible the pursuit of wisdom, allows for the voicing of demands to the effect that wisdom ought to rule, encourages debate, and tolerates the tension between philosophy and the demands of the non-philosophical majority would be better than a polis that does otherwise. Reflections such as these at least narrow the scope of acceptable regimes, even though they leave the assessment of the character of the alternatives to judgment.

Some interpreters have suggested that of the next-best regimes Socrates sketches in the *Republic*, a slight and surprising preference for democracy might be indicated for the sorts of derivative considerations just sketched. Democracy is characterized by its liberty (including freedom of speech, 557b5), license (557b5), the leave given to each to arrange his private life as he judges best (557b4–10), and therewith its permissiveness with respect to the pursuit of wisdom as well as luxury and decadence. Strikingly, even the democratic soul is said to be attracted to "philosophy" at times (561d2). Socrates at one point remarks that democracy is "a convenient place to look for a constitution" for the reason that "it contains all kinds of constitutions on account of the license it gives its citizens. So it looks as though anyone who wants to put a city in order, as we were doing, should probably go to a democracy, as to a supermarket of constitutions, pick out whatever pleases him, and establish that" (557d1–9). If one were to have the sort of conversation that is the *Republic*, one should do so in a democracy where the requisite variety of regimes are advocated. This is a non-trivial, though hardly conclusive, suggestion about the relative worth of a specific regime in a non-ideal world.[30]

3. CONCLUSION

The *Crito* may seem to offer a counter-example to the proposition that Socrates has no political theory properly speaking, no specific political outlook with a worked-out notion of political obligation. The particular issue before Socrates is whether or not to heed Crito's urgent plea that he flee from prison in order to save his life. As Socrates frames it, the issue is "whether it is just for me to try to get out of here when the Athenians have not acquitted me" (48b10-c1). Notably, the case for staying put is voiced by the (Athenian) "laws," not by philosophical rationality as such (and not by Socrates in his own name). And Socrates also enunciates an important principle that constrains the reach of the argument: "I think it important to persuade you before I act, and not to act against your wishes" (48e3–5). The argument is very much directed to Crito, who is a loyal friend and decent man but not even remotely a philosopher. The laws conclude with an injunction that Socrates not let Crito persuade him. Socrates strikingly adds: "these are the words [those of the laws] I seem to hear, as the Corybants seem to hear the music of their flutes, and the echo of these words resounds in me, and makes it impossible for me to hear anything else. As far as my present beliefs go, if you speak in opposition to them, you will speak in vain. However if you think you can accomplish anything, speak" (54d3–8). Crito must yield (and indeed, his final and resigned response is simply "I have nothing to say, Socrates").

30 For a cautious statement of Socrates' preference for democracy all things considered, see Roochnik 2003, ch. 3.1. See also Kraut 1984, ch. 7, and his exchange with Orwin (Kraut 2002 and Orwin 2002); Euben 1996; Mara 1988; de Lattre 1970; Versenyi 1971; and Griswold 1999(b). Consider as well the appraisals of Ober 1998, pp. 245–247; Reeve 1988, ch. 4 (esp. pp. 231–234); Saxonhouse 1996, ch. 4; Monoson 2000; and chs. 2 and 3 of Schofield's outstanding *Plato: Political Philosophy* (2006).

Correspondingly, whether or not the speeches of the laws purporting to prove that it would be unjust to escape from prison are endorsed by Socrates without qualification is the subject of a great deal of scholarly controversy.[31] For the sorts of reasons just indicated, among others, I would argue in favor of the view that Socrates is here presenting an argument that is designed to encourage adherence to the laws of the (democratic) polis by non-philosophers. For Socrates, this is a wiser course than to encourage the Critos of the world to break the law whenever their free-thinking "philosophy" persuades them that it is just to do so. The *Crito* brings its addressee to the same conclusion Socrates has, for different reasons, arrived at (namely, not to escape from prison). The laws are made to say:

You must either persuade it [the city] or obey its orders, and endure in silence whatever it instructs you to endure, whether blows or bonds, and if it leads you into war to be wounded or killed, you must obey. To do so is right, and one must not give way or retreat or leave one's post, but both in war and in courts and everywhere else, one must obey the commands of one's city and country, or persuade it as to the nature of justice. (51b4-c1)

The "persuade" proviso both limits the sort of regime under discussion to one in which avenues for persuasion exist (the laws are those of democratic Athens) and provides an alternative to *merely* obeying *whatever* the laws enjoin. At the same time, the striking statement just quoted seems patently at odds with Socrates' critiques of majority rule (for example, he holds that the truth is not determined by a vote; see *Laches* 184d5–185a9), as well as with his corresponding invocation, made here (*Crito* 48a5–7; cf. 44c6–7, "My good Crito, why should we care so much for what the majority think?"), in the *Apology* (29d3–4), and in the *Republic*, of higher principles that serve as the measure of that claimed by one's community. They turn out to include the Form of the Just, and ultimately of the Good.[32]

31   For the view that Socrates endorses the arguments put in the mouth of "the laws," see Kraut 1984. For the view that the *Crito* presents an argument designed to give Crito reasons to obey the law, rather than reasons endorsed without qualification by Socrates, see Weiss 1998, Harte, 1999, and Miller 1996.

32   See also Socrates' remarkable praise in the *Gorgias* of "a philosopher who has minded his own affairs and hasn't been meddlesome in the course of his life" (526c3–4), and his proclamation that "I disregard the things held in honor by the majority of people, and by practicing truth I really try, to the best of my ability, to be and to live as a very good man, and when I die, to die like that" (526d5-e1).

If this line of interpretation is correct, Socrates is not committed without qualification to the proposition that the truth shall make you free, as though every soul were by nature prepared to understand the truth and to act on that understanding wisely. His politics – and the conversation that is the *Crito* exhibits his politics at work – is moderated by the recognition that in this non-ideal world, philosophers in his particular sense of the term are few and far between. In the *Phaedrus*, Socrates argues that the philosophical rhetorician both knows the truth and the soul of his interlocutor, such as to be able to present the subject in a way that the interlocutor is capable of grasping without being harmed (*Phaedrus* 271c10–272b2, 272d2–273a1, 276e4–277c6). This may well entail that a particular interlocutor (or kind of soul) is best addressed with a discourse that communicates some but not all of the truth about the subject. Even in the *Republic*, Socrates states that the "ideal state" (in our phrase) requires the telling of a "noble falsehood" as well as the therapeutic use of "falsehood and deception" (414b8–c7; 459c2-d2). Many people suspected that Socrates knew more than he let on (*Apology* 23a3–5), his famous irony being an instance thereof. At work in the political realm, Socratic philosophy inevitably takes on a rhetorical dimension (which does not mean that he is simply an ironist, let alone an esotericist, but that he must proceed like the good rhetorician he describes in the *Phaedrus*).

But if the speeches of the laws do not explain why Socrates refused to escape from prison, what does? Certainly, he does not take death in and of itself to be evil (*Apology* 40c1–2). Socrates' dream recounted at the start of the *Crito* (44a5-b5), the invocation of god in the last sentence of the dialogue, and the remark in the *Apology* that his "daimonion" or inner voice had not diverted him from his course of action (40a2-c4) together suggest that he had decided that the time to die had arrived (cf. *Apology* 41d3–5: "it is clear to me that it was better for me to die now and to escape from trouble"). It is not irrelevant that Socrates was already an old man (see Xenophon's *Apology of Socrates* 6–7). Further, if he were to escape death either by persuading the jury through debasing means (say, by appealing for pity; *Apology* 34c1-d10, 38d5-e2) or by escaping from prison, his moral standing and reputation would have been fatally compromised (*Apology* 34e1–35a3, 28d9–29a5). After all, Socrates publicly insisted that he was not afraid of death; either of those courses of action would have made him a mockery forever. Socrates is explicitly attempting to define and justify a new human possibility – the "philosopher" understood in a distinctive and innovative way – and the manner of his death was an inherent part of his enactment of that deeply controversial life. Socratic politics aimed to establish publicly and persuasively, and therefore in deed as well as word, that the philosophically examined life is best.

WORKS CITED

Annas, J. "What are Plato's 'Middle' Dialogues in the Middle Of?" In *New Perspectives on Plato, Modern and Ancient*, eds. J. Annas and C. Rowe. Cambridge, MA, 2002, pp. 1–23.

Annas, J. "The Inner City: Ethics without Politics in the *Republic*." In J. Annas, *Platonic Ethics, Old and New*. Ithaca, 1999, pp. 72–95.

Aristotle. *The Politics*, trans. C. Lord. Chicago, 1984.

Averroes. *Averroes on Plato's Republic*, trans. R. Lerner. Ithaca, 1974.

Bloom, A. *The Republic of Plato*. Commentary and Translation. New York, 1968.

Bambrough, R., ed. *Plato, Popper, and Politics*. New York, 1967.

Burnet, J., ed. *Platonis Opera*. 5 vols. Oxford, 1900–1907.

Burnyeat, M. "Cracking the Socrates Case." *New York Review of Books* 35.5 (1988): 12–18.

Burnyeat, M. "Utopia and Fantasy: The Practicability of Plato's Ideally Just City." In *Plato 2: Ethics, Politics, Religion, and the Soul*, ed. G. Fine. Oxford, 1999, pp. 297–308.

Cappon, L. J., ed. *The Adams-Jefferson Letters*. Chapel Hill, 1988.

Clay, D. "Reading the *Republic*." In *Platonic Writings/Platonic Readings*, ed. C. Griswold. New York, 1988; rpt. University Park, PA, 2002, pp. 19–33.

Cooper, J. M., and Hutchinson, D. S. eds. *Plato: Complete Works*. Indianapolis, 1997. Includes an Introduction by Cooper.

de Lattre, A. "La Liberté Socratique et le Dialogue Platonicien." *Kant Studien* 61 (1970): 467–495.

Dover, K. J. "The Freedom of the Intellectual in Greek Society." *Talanta* 7 (1976): 24–54.

Duke, E. A. et al., eds. *Platonis Opera*. Vol. 1. Oxford, 1995.

Euben, J. P. "Reading Democracy: 'Socratic' Dialogues and the Political Education of Democratic Citizens." In *Dēmokratia: A Conversation on Democracies, Ancient and Modern*, eds. J. Ober and C. Hedrick. Princeton, 1996, pp. 327–359.

Griswold, C. "*Politikē Epistēmē* in Plato's *Statesman*." In *Essays in Ancient Greek Philosophy*, vol. III, eds. J. Anton and A. Preus. New York, 1989, pp. 141–167.

Griswold, C. "Stoning Greek Philosophers: Platonic Political Philosophy and the Trial of Socrates." *Classical Bulletin* 67 (1991): 3–15.

Griswold, C. "E Pluribus Unum? On the Platonic 'Corpus.'" *Ancient Philosophy* 19 (1999a): 361–397. (For C. Kahn's response to that piece, as well as Griswold's response to the response, see *Ancient Philosophy* 20 (2000): 189–197.)

Griswold, C. "Platonic Liberalism: Self-Perfection as a Foundation of Political Theory." In *Plato and Platonism*, ed. J. M. van Ophuijsen. Washington, DC, 1999b, pp. 102–134.

Griswold, C. "Comments on Kahn." In *New Perspectives on Plato, Modern and Ancient*, eds. J. Annas and C. Rowe. Cambridge, MA, 2002, pp. 129–144.

Griswold, C. "Longing for the Best: Plato on Reconciliation with Imperfection." *Arion* 11 (2003): 101–136.

Hamilton, A., Jay, J. and Madison, J. *The Federalist Papers*. With an introduction by C. Rossiter. New York, 1961.

Harte, V. "Conflicting Values in Plato's Crito." *Archiv für Geschichte der Philosophie* 81(1999): 117–147.

Hoernlé, R. F. A. "Would Plato have Approved of the National-Socialist State?" In *Plato, Popper, and Politics*, ed. R. Bambrough. New York, 1967, pp. 20–36.

Hume, D. "Idea of a Perfect Commonwealth." In his *Essays Moral, Political, and Literary*, rev. ed., edited E. Miller. Indianapolis, 1987, pp. 512–529.

Kahn, C. *Plato and the Socratic Dialogue: The Philosophical Use of a Literary Form.* Cambridge, 1996.

Klosko, G. *The Development of Plato's Political Theory.* Oxford, 2006.

Kraut, R. *Socrates and the State.* Princeton, 1984.

Kraut, R. "Reply to Clifford Orwin." In *Platonic Writings/Platonic Readings*, ed. C. Griswold. New York, 1988; rpt. University Park, PA, 2002, pp. 177–182.

Madison, J. see Hamilton, A.

Mara, G. M. "Socrates and Liberal Toleration." *Political Theory* 16 (1988): 468–495.

Miller, M. *The Philosopher in Plato's* Statesman. The Hague, 1980.

Miller, M. "'The Arguments I Seem to Hear': Argument and Irony in the *Crito*." *Phronesis* 41 (1996): 121–137.

Millett, P. "Encounters in the Agora." In *Kosmos: Essays in Order, Conflict and Community in Classical Athens*, eds. P. Cartledge, P. Millett, and S. von Reden. Cambridge, 1998, pp. 203–228.

Monoson, S. *Plato's Democratic Entanglements.* Princeton, 2000.

Morrison, D. "On the Alleged Historical Reliability of Plato's *Apology*." *Archiv für Geschichte der Philosophie* 82 (2000): 235–265.

Ober, J. *Political Dissent in Democratic Athens.* Princeton, 1998.

Orwin, C. "Liberalizing the *Crito*: Richard Kraut on Socrates and the State." In *Platonic Writings/Platonic Readings*, ed. C. Griswold. New York, 1988; repr. University Park, PA, 2002, pp. 171–176.

Popper, K. *The Open Society and its Enemies*, 5th ed. (revised). Princeton, 1966.

Rawls, J. *Political Liberalism.* New York, 1996.

Rawls, J. *A Theory of Justice*, rev. ed. Cambridge, 1999.

Reeve, C. D. C. *Philosopher-Kings.* Princeton, 1988.

Robinson, R. "Dr. Popper's Defence of Democracy." In Robinson's *Essays in Greek Philosophy.* Oxford, 1969, pp. 74–99.

Roochnik, D. *Beautiful City: the Dialectical Character of Plato's* Republic. Ithaca, 2003.

Rowe, C. See Annas, J., 2002.

Saxonhouse, A. *Athenian Democracy: Modern Mythmakers and Ancient Theorists.* Notre Dame, 1996.

Schofield, M. "Socrates on Trial in the USA." In *Classics in Progress: Essays on Ancient Greece and Rome*, ed. T. P. Wiseman. Oxford, 2002, pp. 263–283.

Schofield, M. *Plato: Political Philosophy.* Oxford, 2006.

Sommerstein, A. H. "How to Avoid Being a *komodoumenos*." *Classical Quarterly* 46 (1996): pp. 327–356.

Stone, I. F. *The Trial of Socrates.* Boston, 1988.

Strauss, L. *The City and Man.* Chicago, 1964.

Thorson, T. L. ed. *Plato: Totalitarian or Democrat?* Englewood Cliffs, NJ, 1963.

Versenyi, L. G. "Plato and his Liberal Opponents." *Philosophy* 46 (1971): 222–237.

Wallace, R. W. "Private Lives and Public Enemies: Freedom of Thought in Classical Athens." In *Athenian Identity and Civic Ideology*, eds. A. L. Boegehold and A. C. Scafuro. Baltimore, 1994, pp. 127–155.

Weiss, R. *Socrates Dissatisfied: an Analysis of Plato's* Crito. Oxford, 1998.

FURTHER BIBLIOGRAPHY

Bobonich, C. *Plato's Utopia Recast: His Later Ethics and Politics*. Oxford, 2002.

Brickhouse T., and Smith, N. *Plato's Socrates*. Oxford, 1994.

Brickhouse, T., and Smith, N. *The Trial and Execution of Socrates: Sources and Controversies*. Oxford, 2002.

Brown, E. "Justice and Compulsion for Plato's Philosopher-Rulers." *Ancient Philosophy* 20 (2000): 1–17.

Carter, L. B. *The Quiet Athenian*. Oxford, 1986.

de Strycker, E. *Plato's Apology of Socrates: a Literary and Philosophical Study with a Running Commentary*. Revised S. R. Slings. Leiden, 1994.

Griswold, C. "Relying on Your Own Voice: An Unsettled Rivalry of Moral Ideals in Plato's *Protagoras*." *Review of Metaphysics* 53 (1999): 283–307.

Griswold, C. "Philosophers in the Agora." *Perspectives on Political Science* 32 (2003): 203–206. (Commentary on M. Lilla's *The Reckless Mind: Intellectuals in Politics*.)

Hansen, M. H. *The Trial of Sokrates – from the Athenian Point of View*. Royal Danish Academy of Sciences and Letters. Historisk-filosofiske Meddelelser 71. Copenhagen, 1995.

Howland, J. *The Republic: The Odyssey of Philosophy*. Philadelphia, 2004.

Kamtekar, R. "The Politics of Plato's Socrates." In *A Companion to Socrates*, eds. S. Ahbel-Rappe and R. Kamtekar. Malden, MA, 2006, pp. 214–227.

Kraut, R. *Plato's Republic: Critical Essays*. Lanham, MD, 1997.

Lachterman, D. "What is 'The Good' of Plato's *Republic*?" *St. John's Review* 39 (1990): 139–171.

Mara, G. *Socrates' Discursive Democracy*. Albany, 1997.

Morrison, D. "Some Central Elements of Socratic Political Theory." *Polis* 18 (2001): 27–40.

Morrison, D. "The Happiness of the City and the Happiness of the Individual in Plato's *Republic*." *Ancient Philosophy* 21 (2001): 1–24.

Morrison, D. "The Utopian Character of Plato's Ideal City." In *The Cambridge Companion to Plato's* Republic," ed. G. R. F. Ferrari. Cambridge, 2007, pp. 232–255.

Nails, D. *Agora, Academy, and the Conduct of Philosophy*. Dordrecht, 1995.

Rowe, C. "The Place of the *Republic* in Plato's Political Thought." In *The Cambridge Companion to Plato's* Republic," ed. G. R. F. Ferrari. Cambridge, 2007, pp. 27–54.

Schofield, M. "Plato and Practical Politics." In *Greek and Roman Political Thought*, eds. C. Rowe and M. Schofield. Cambridge, 2005, pp. 293–302.

Smith, N. "How the Prisoners in Plato's Cave are 'Like Us.'" *Proceedings of the Boston Area Colloquium in Ancient Philosophy* 13 (1999): 187–205.

Vlastos, G. *Socrates, Ironist and Moral Philosopher*. Ithaca, 1991.

Vlastos, G. "Socrates and Vietnam." In *Socratic Studies*, ed. M. Burnyeat. Cambridge, 1994, pp. 127–133.

Vlastos, G. "The Historical Socrates and Athenian Democracy." In *Socratic Studies*, ed. M. Burnyeat. Cambridge, 1994, pp. 87–108.

15 Socrates in Later Greek Philosophy

INTRODUCTION

Socrates is a philosopher whose world historical importance and renown are largely due to three remarkable facts.[1] First, his life and especially his trial and death, though cardinal to his posthumous influence and standing, were relatively minor events for the majority of his contemporary Athenians and their immediate descendants. During the first years after his death, he was still the controversial figure he had been throughout his later life. He had written nothing, and it was just a few of his companions, Plato, Antisthenes, Xenophon, and the other Socratic authors, whose writings in his defense and teachings began, though only gradually, to turn this eccentric and disturbing Athenian into an intellectual and moral icon. He had hardly achieved that status even fifty years after his execution; for he is mentioned in only one context by Isocrates (*Busiris* 4.3; 5.9), but once by the orator Aeschines (*Against Timarchus* 173), and never by Demosthenes.

Socrates, then – and this is the second salient fact – owes his philosophical significance to the diverse ways he was interpreted, lauded, and sometimes even criticized by authors who, thanks to their *own* intellectual and educational creativity, made Greek philosophy the major cultural presence it had not yet become during his own lifetime. With the founding of official schools of philosophy – the Academy, the Lyceum, the Garden of Epicurus, the Zenonian Stoa – and with less formally organized philosophical movements, especially the Cynics, contexts emerged for Socrates to return to live a life far more wide-reaching and various than anything he could have imagined for himself. Because each school or movement had its own quite distinct identity, their interpretations of Socrates followed suit. Yet, even if there had been more unity between them, the question of what exactly Socrates stood

---

[1]   In writing this chapter, I draw selectively on material presented in Long 1996a, ch. 1, and I go beyond it in discussing the role of Socrates in Epictetus and in Platonist and Christian authors of the Roman Empire.

for would have remained as open and intriguing as it still is for us. Just like us, the generations of thinkers after Plato, Xenophon, Antisthenes and the other Socratics were faced with a record of multifaceted and far from fully consistent images of the man. They had to decide, as we do, whether their Socrates was a radical and austere moralist (the Stoic Socrates), a caustic and exhibitionist preacher of asceticism (the Cynic Socrates), a self-confessedly ignorant dialectician (the Socrates of the Academic skeptics), someone with theological doctrines (as in Xenophon), or a philosopher with strong interests in inductive arguments and definition (as in Aristotle).

The third fact I want to mention about Socrates' world historical importance takes us well beyond philosophy in the strict sense. Evidence for his cultural presence in antiquity gets increasingly larger the later we go, right up to the third century of the Christian era. In the Roman Imperial epoch, Socrates becomes a rhetorical topos and exemplar, a constant subject for anecdotalists, a name on which to hang numerous moral apothegms, and an author of fabricated letters and lectures. And for a few early Christian writers, most notably Justin Martyr, he is an authentic harbinger of Jesus.[2] In this material, the principal focus is on Socrates' unjust indictment, trial, execution, and equanimity in the face of death. These biographical details had long been treated as educational models, especially among Stoic authors, but for the rhetoricians of the Roman Empire, such as Dio of Prusa, Aelius Aristides, and Libanius, they, and little else, are what their audiences expect to hear about Socrates. At this time, too, reflecting the zeitgeist, we find special interest being taken in Socrates' divine sign (*daimonion*), and mention of him as a sage in company with Pythagoras, Plato, and Heraclitus.

This later literature on Socrates, extensive though it is, tends to repeat the same biographical details time and again, drawn principally from Plato's *Apology*. Whereas the Socrates of Aristotle and the Hellenistic philosophers, taken collectively, is a highly complex figure, derived from many of Plato's dialogues and other early Socratic authors, the Socrates of later antiquity has been largely reduced to an exemplary victim of human wickedness, his irony, eroticism, and exploratory dialectic forgotten. Occasionally we hear about his confession of ignorance, largely in Christian contexts, but even his ethics has acquired the musty air of platitude. Yet for all its tedium, the sheer volume of material on Socrates at this time attests to an iconic figure of unparalleled

2   SSR provides a splendid collection of the testimonies on Socrates, starting with the comic poets other than Aristophanes and with Aristotle, and concluding with the Christian Fathers. I refer to his work only for the more recondite passages that I note.

significance and diffusion; and so he would be transmitted into the medieval world and beyond.

Given the wealth of data and the interpretive complexity that much of it presents, my treatment of Socrates' afterlife has to be selective and cursory. What I shall do, rather than presenting an encyclopaedic or chronological survey, is to focus on the following points: (1) the doxographical tradition and its principal sources; (2) fundamentals of Socratic ethics; (3) Socratic ignorance, dialectic, and irony; (4) criticism of Socrates; (5) Epictetus on the Socratic *elenchus*; and 6) Socrates' divine sign.

DOXOGRAPHICAL TRADITION AND
PRINCIPAL SOURCES

Looking back at the history of philosophy in the Hellenistic epoch, the authors of doxographical handbooks viewed Socrates as the central defining figure. On the one hand, because he was reputed to have studied physics in his youth, he could be seen as the last of the "Ionian" thinkers, starting with Thales. On the other hand, as the supposed originator of ethics, he stood at the head of a bifurcated succession.[3] One branch of this went from Plato down to the Academic skeptics; the other passed from Antisthenes via the Cynics to Zeno and his Stoic successors.

Because our modern Socrates is primarily the figure who dominates discussion in the Platonic dialogues, we regularly pose questions about Plato's historicity; we try to distinguish Socrates' specific and authentic voice from distinctively Platonic accretions to it. Most modern scholars doubt whether the flesh and blood Socrates can anywhere be fully detached from Plato's brilliantly creative pen. Nonetheless, there is broad agreement that what we have traditionally taken to be the "early" Socratic dialogues, starting with the *Apology* and stopping before the *Republic*, provide the best Platonic evidence for authentically Socratic discussions and interests.

The scholars of antiquity did not pose our Socratic problem. Yet, so far as Plato is concerned, the Socrates they took from him is the same as our Socrates, at least for the most part. Cicero (106–43 BCE) was well aware that Plato credited Socrates with what he calls "Pythagorean" doctrines (*Rep.* 1.15–16), and everything that Aristotle attributes to Socrates can be referred to the early dialogues. Epicurean polemic against Socrates concentrated on the following dialogues, all of them, except perhaps the last, taken to be early – *Euthyphro, Lysis, Gorgias,* and *Euthydemus*. In Diogenes Laertius' *Life of Socrates*, all of these, except for the *Gorgias*,

---

3   D.L. 1.13–15.

are cited, and in addition, Diogenes (fl. 200 CE) refers to *Apology, Meno, Phaedo, Symposium,* and *Theaetetus* – the last four all for biographical and not doctrinal data. For Epictetus (c. 55–135 CE), whose remarkable recourse to Socrates I shall discuss later, the favorite dialogues are *Gorgias* and *Apology;* and, like others in later antiquity, he draws on Socrates' lengthy protreptic speech from the *Cleitophon.*[4]

While Plato's early dialogues, especially the *Apology,* were fundamental to all images of Socrates, the doxographical tradition (by which I mean standard pen-portraits starting in the early Hellenistic era) is strongly marked by a single passage from Xenophon's *Memorabilia* 1.1.11–16. Defending Socrates against the charge of impiety, Xenophon emphasizes Socrates' distance from "useless" and "contentious" inquiry into nature (what we call Presocratic cosmology), his single-minded investigation of ethical concepts, and his taking knowledge of the latter to be the essence of human excellence. Readers of Plato's *Apology* could find more nuanced statements to the same effect there, as Xenophon himself probably did; but it is Xenophon's pithy reprise that largely encapsulated Socrates' philosophical significance for later generations, as we can see from the following doxographical report:

The original philosophers opted only for the study of nature and made this the goal of their philosophy. Socrates, who succeeded them much later, said that this was inaccessible to people ... and that what was most useful was investigation of how best to conduct one's life, avoid bad things and get the greatest possible share of fine things. Believing this more useful, he ignored the study of nature ... and focused his thought on the kind of ethical disposition that could distinguish good and bad, and right and wrong.[5]

Socrates is standardly represented, as here, in being both the founding father of philosophical ethics and as someone who repudiated the branch of philosophy later called physics.[6] Was he, then, regularly regarded, in the words of Vlastos, as "exclusively a moral philosopher"?[7] In some quarters, certainly. Of his immediate followers, Aristippus is said to have repudiated mathematics, dialectic, and physics; the Cynics,

4   Epictetus 3.22.6; cf. Plutarch, *De lib.* 4e; Dio of Prusa 13.16.
5   ps.-Galen, *History of Philosophy* 1 = I C 472 SSR.
6   Cicero, *Tusc. disp.* 5.10, *Rep.* 1.16; Sextus Empiricus, *M.* 7.8; Themistius 34.5 = SSR IV A 166; Aulus Gellius 14. 3, 5–6, who cites Xenophon and contrasts his report of Socrates with Plato, 'in whose discourses Socrates discusses physics, music, and geometry'; Lactantius, *Div.inst.* 3.13, 6. Diogenes Laertius makes Socrates the founder of ethics (2.20), but questions his repudiation of physics (2.45), citing Socrates' discourses on providence in Xenophon.
7   Vlastos 1991, p. 47.

taking their lead from Antisthenes, fit Vlastos's description, and that pertains very clearly to the early Stoic philosopher Aristo (see n. 21). All of these figures, we may presume, took themselves to be following the lead of Socrates. However, even the truncated reports in the doxographical tradition also credit Socrates with formidable rhetorical skills or expertise in dialectical arguments, and Socrates' irony is sometimes remarked on.[8]

More spasmodic are references to his logical or metaphysical interests and his confession of ignorance. Aristotle, after endosing the standard image of Socrates as an ethicist who ignored physics, notoriously says that he "sought the universal in the domain of ethics and was the first to focus thought on definitions".[9] The later Platonists followed Aristotle's lead, with Proclus (410–485 CE) contradicting Aristotle by even imputing "separately existing Forms" to Socrates.[10] Antisthenes seems to have reduced Platonic forms to concepts; and the Stoics, in acting similarly, may well have thought they were being true to Socratic doctrine.[11] But a logical or metaphysical Socrates is not a mainstream feature of the tradition.

As for Socrates' repeated confessions of ignorance in Plato, these first come to the fore with Arcesilaus and the Academic skeptics. When they are mentioned elsewhere, as in some Christian authors, we may assume the influence of the Academics' representation of Socrates as their skeptical forerunner.[12]

Thus by the time of Cicero anyone interested in Socrates had a great range of authors to consult. These included Comic poets, Hellenistic biographers, Peripatetic and Epicurean polemicists, and the Academic and Stoic philosophers, who, in their different ways, pointedly advertised their allegiance to Socrates. Diogenes Laertius cites more than twenty authorities in his *Life* of Socrates, only a few of whom stem from the Roman Imperial period. Yet the predominant influences on the Socratic tradition were always the immediate Socratic authors, Plato, Antisthenes, and Xenophon. It was from these authors that the later Greeks and Romans drew their favorite Socratic sayings and stories,

---

8 Cicero, *Tusc. disp.* 5.11; Aristocles ap. Euseb., *PE* 11.3.2 = I C 460 SSR; ps-Galen (n. 5 above); D.L. 2.19 quoting Timon.

9 *Met.* 1.6, 987b1–3; cf. *Met.*13.9, 1086a37-b5 and 13.4, 1078b17–32.

10 Proclus, *In Plat. Parm.* 3.4 = SSR I C 461; Aristotle, *Met.* 13. 9, 1086b1–6; cf. also Aristocles (n. 8).

11 See Long 1996a, p. 19.

12 Justin, *Cohort. ad Graec.* 36 = SSR I G 11, who takes Socrates' ignorance to have been sincere; and Augustine, *Civ. dei* 8.3, who speaks of Socrates' concealing his knowledge or beliefs.

finding in that material, rather than in doctrinal statements, their sense of the great man's cultural and intellectual significance.

May we conclude that no one living after Plato and Xenophon was in a position to know more about Socrates than any of us today is able to infer from reading them? My answer is affirmative for the most part; but we should not forget that we have virtually lost the dialogues of Antisthenes, whom Xenophon, in his *Symposium*, presents as perhaps Socrates' leading disciple. Although the record of Antisthenes' work is exiguous, what survives of it tallies strikingly with basic doctrines of Stoic ethics. The Cynics were the primary recipients of Antisthenes' work, and via the Cynics, and probably directly too, it influenced Zeno of Citium (334–262), the founder of Stoicism. All of Antisthenes' ethical theses are consistent, I think, with Socratic propositions in Plato or Xenophon. Their importance for us, like the doxographical tradition on Socrates, is their snappy formulation of doctrines that were generally taken to be Socratic.

FUNDAMENTALS OF ETHICS IN THE SOCRATIC TRADITION

Here now is a selection of Antisthenes' reported claims:[13]

1. Virtue is sufficient for happiness.
2. The wise man is self-sufficient.
3. Only the virtuous are noble.
4. The virtuous are friends.
5. Good things are morally fine (*kala*) and bad things are base.
6. Male and female virtue is identical.
7. Practical wisdom (*phronesis*) is a completely secure fortification.
8. Virtue is an irremoveable armor.
9. Nothing is alien or beyond resource for the wise man.
10. Defenses are needed to make one's reasoning impregnable.

We do not know how Antisthenes supported these propositions. Stated in this bald form, they are very distant from Socrates' subtle dialectic in Plato. Yet when scholars today try to extract the core of Socratic ethics from Plato's dialogues, they operate quite similarly, emphasizing especially propositions 1 and 5.[14] The most distinctive features in Antisthenes' formulations are, first, his explicit focus on the wise man and, second, the military metaphors with which he invests the power of

13 Drawn from D.L. 6.10–13.
14 See Vlastos 1991, esp. ch. 8, and Irwin 1995, esp. ch. 4.

virtue or wisdom. Plato's Socrates had stated in the *Apology* (41d) that no harm could come to the good man in life or in death; and Xenophon (*Mem.* 1.2.1) had emphasized Socrates' extraordinary self-mastery. However, neither Plato nor Xenophon lays Antisthenes' stress on the way virtue arms the wise man against all vicissitudes. Here we have the embryo of the Cynic and Stoic sage with his impregnably rational disposition.

The Greeks, of course, had the concept of a wise man before Socrates, as exemplified by the likes of Solon and Thales. The earliest Socratic literature, building on that concept, not only promoted Socrates to the status of paradigm sage but also in that process modified the criteria of exemplary sagacity. Solon was renowned for his legislative skill and Thales for his practical ingenuity. Socrates, instead, was taken to instantiate a new model of wisdom, the hallmarks of which were intellectual and moral integrity, and self-mastery.[15] Although his most recognizable inheritors were the Cynics and Stoics, Pyrrho (c. 365–270) and Epicurus (341–271), though without allegiance to Socrates, also took on that mantle for their followers. The Academic skeptics modeled their ideal of complete suspension of judgment on Socrates, and the hedonistic Cyrenaics posited their own wise man. Even Aristotle, who hardly heroized Socrates, fits the pattern in as much as he frequently cites the 'wise man' (*phronimos*) as his ethical standard.

Socrates, then, as the ancients saw from their Hellenistic perspective, symbolized a radical shift in human values and possibilities, much of it already captured in Plato's *Apology*: the downgrading of bodily and conventional goods, the focus on ethical excellence as a quality of soul, the identification of rationality as both the only proper criterion of judgment and the secure source of mental and emotional strength.

One of the first, and certainly the most dramatic, representatives of this Socratic legacy was the Cynic Diogenes, reputed to have died in the year 323 BCE, and supposedly described by Plato as "Socrates gone mad."[16] While it is difficult to extract an authentic portrait of this notorious figure from the largely anecdotal evidence, the following account may be regarded as plausible enough.[17]

Diogenes sought to undermine *nomos* (convention) as the foundation of values and replace it with *physis* (nature). Taking the essence of human nature to be rationality, he made it his aim, by shocking instances of exhibitionism, to isolate this conception from social practices and evaluations that could not be justified in the light of reason.

15 See Long 1993 and 1999.
16 D.L. 6.54.
17 For a more detailed treatment, see Long 1996b.

Happiness, conceived as freedom and self-mastery, was a viable objective for anyone prepared to identify its necessary and sufficient conditions with rigorous training of body and mind. Persons so fortified would be able to live as reason requires, indifferent to wealth, luxury, social status or pleasure, contemptuous of public opinion, and impervious to changes of fortune. Wisdom and wisdom alone was the proper basis for genuine wealth, status, and power.

No genuine writings from Diogenes, if he did put stylus to papyrus, have survived. But we have a number of sardonic poems composed by his follower Crates (fl. 300 BCE), which exemplify the salient ideas I have attributed to Diogenes. Here are two instances:

Hunger puts an end to lust; if not, time does; but if you can't use these, a rope will do. (fr. 14 Diehl)

I don't have one country as my refuge, nor a single roof, but every land has a city and house ready to entertain me. (fr. 15 Diehl)

The Socrates of Plato and Xenophon is hardly a cosmopolitan. What the Cynics, and, under their influence, the earliest Stoics did, was cast the Atheno-centric Socrates, or what they took to be his ethical message, into pan-Hellenic and distinct forms of discourse and teaching – popular and proseletyzing with the Cynics, systematic and analytical in the case of the Stoics.

From Zeno to Epictetus and Marcus Aurelius (Roman Emperor from 161 to 180) – that is to say, throughout the history of the Stoa as a living institution – Socrates is the philosopher whom the Stoics took as their primary inspiration and model. Epictetus' recourse to Socrates merits special attention; here I shall focus on the role of Socrates in the earliest phase of Stoicism.

According to the biographical tradition, Zeno's decision to devote himself to philosophy was generated by his reading and inquiring about Socrates. In one version of the story, when he had started to read book two of Xenophon's *Memorabilia* in an Athenian bookshop, the shopkeeper pointed to Crates, and told Zeno to follow the Cynic as a latter-day Socrates.[18] Cynicism was certainly the most potent influence on the beginnings of Zeno's philosophy. We know this from the fragments of his *Republic*.[19] With its rejection of such dominant social conventions as marriage, coinage, and temples, Zeno's *Republic* reflected Diogenes' antinomian stance. As such, it was far more radically subversive than Plato's *Republic*, and probably deliberately written to be so. But, while

18   D.L. 7.2–3.
19   See Schofield 1991.

Zeno's philosophy, taken as a whole, had many anti-Platonic features, Zeno was positively influenced by Plato as well, especially in regard to the Socrates of Plato's early dialogues. As a young man, he studied with Polemo, head of the Platonic Academy at the end of the fourth century BCE. What he may have learned specifically from Polemo does not concern us here. The relevant point is that Zeno had a Platonic mentor, as well as Xenophon, Antisthenes, and the Cynics, to facilitate his understanding of Socratic ethics.

The most fundamental doctrines of Stoic ethics were (1) the unqualified restriction of goodness to ethical excellence; (2) as a corollary to (1), the indifference of all bodily and external advantages or disadvantages (conventionally deemed good or bad respectively); (3) the necessity and sufficiency of ethical excellence for complete happiness; and (4) the conception of ethical excellence as a kind of knowledge or craft. There can be no doubt that, in defending these doctrines, the Stoics took themselves to be authentically Socratic, and litte doubt that, in doing so, they drew especially on Socrates' main argument in Plato's *Euthydemus* 278e-281e.[20]

There, Socrates attempts to convince his interlocutor that the foundation of happiness is simply and exclusively knowledge or wisdom. All other so-called goods, such as wealth, health, and honor are beneficial and superior to their opposites if and only if they are correctly – that is, wisely and knowledgeably – used. Otherwise they are more harmful than their opposites. Neither do wealth and the like, just by themselves, have any positive value, nor do poverty and the like, just by themselves, have any negative value. Socrates concludes:

Of the other things (i.e. everything except wisdom and ignorance), none is either good or bad, but of these two things, one – wisdom – is good, and the other – ignorance – is bad. (*Euthd.* 281e-3–5)

This argument provided Zeno not only with Socratic authority for the doctrines I outlined here. More specifically, it offered him support for his concept of "intermediate" or "indifferent" things, neither good nor bad in themselves, but materials for wisdom or ethical knowledge to use well. Moreover, it is highly probable that a crucial ambiguity or equivocation in the argument helped to feed the great disagreement between Zeno and his leading disciple Aristo (fl. early third century. BCE).[21]

20 For a much fuller treatment of what follows, see Long 1996a, pp. 23–32, and for further study of the Stoics' interest in the *Euthydemus* argument, see Striker 1996b.
21 For the evidence on Zeno and Aristo, see Long/Sedley 1987, ch. 58. For Aristo's cynicizing restriction of philosophy to ethics and his other

According to Zeno, although only ethical excellence is strictly good and constitutive of happiness, and only ethical failings are strictly bad and constitutive of misery, such indifferent things as health and wealth have positive value and their opposites corresponding disvalue. Aristo disagreed. He rejected Zeno's categories of "preferred" and "dispreferred" indifferent things, holding that the grounds for selecting one of these over the other was nothing intrinsic to the value of the items themselves, but solely a wise or knowledgeable decision. Aristo's position was heterodox (as was his restriction of Stoic philosophy to ethics, in imitation of Socrates). However, he could say that it was exactly true to the letter of Socrates' argument in the *Euthydemus*, where no intrinsic value is attributed to things like wealth and no intrinsic disvalue to things like poverty. Zeno, on the other hand, could say that, notwithstanding Socrates' statement to that effect, Socrates had also said that wisely used wealth and the like were greater *goods* than their opposites. As formulated, Socrates' argument equivocates between the position that health and the like have no intrinsic value (Aristo's doctrine) and the position that they are greater goods than their opposites if they are well used. Zeno's solution to the equivocation was to deny that they are ever good, but to credit them with "preferential value."

There are other Socratic contexts in Plato that the Stoics very likely drew upon in elaborating their own ethics.[22] For the sake of brevity, I offer this one example, choosing it because it shows that they were creative as well as imitative in their appropriation of Socrates.

SOCRATIC IGNORANCE, DIALECTIC, AND IRONY

For us moderns, who have all too many examples of heroic victims of injustice, Socrates is most widely known for giving his name to a method of teaching – asking questions instead of feeding answers, eliciting students' opinions, and subjecting their responses to criticism – that is to say, the Socrates of aporetic Platonic dialogues such as the *Euthyphro* and *Laches*. The post-Platonic philosopher in antiquity who pushed the aporetic Socrates to its limits was Arcesilaus, head of the Academy from c. 273–242, and the originator of the skeptical stance that prevailed in Plato's school down to Philo of Larissa in the early first century BCE.[23]

disagreements with Zeno, seemingly motivated by his wish for a still closer alignment with Socrates, see Long 1996a, pp. 22–23 and Porter 1996.

22 See Sedley 1993 (on the *Crito* and *Phaedo*), Vander Waerdt 1994b (natural law), Striker 1996b (on the *Clitopho*).

23 For the main evidence on Arcesilaus, see Long/Sedley 1987 chs. 68–9, and for further discussion, see Schofield 1999 and Cooper 2004a.

Arcesilaus and his followers became known as "those who suspend judgment about everything." He pinned his credentials for this stance and his dialectical practice on Socrates, claiming that Plato's dialogues should be read as vehicles for inducing radical skepticism. Cicero, speaking as an Academic skeptic himself, outlines Arcesilaus' position as follows (*De oratore* 3.67):

> Arcesilaus, the pupil of Polemo, was the first to derive this principal point from various of Plato's books and from Socratic discourses – that there is nothing that the senses or the mind can grasp ... He is said to have belittled every criterion of mind and sense, and begun the practice – though it was absolutely Socratic – not of indicating his own opinion, but of speaking against what anyone stated as his (i.e. the speaker's) opinion.

Cicero was almost certainly correct to emphasize Arcesilaus' originality in this way of reading Plato and interpreting Socrates. It is true, as we have seen, that Xenophon's Socrates (followed by the Cynics) repudiates any interest in physical science, and there are occasional fourth-century references outside Plato to Socrates' confession of ignorance.[24] But there is no reason to think that, prior to Arcesilaus, Socrates was chiefly associated with this characteristic, and strong positive evidence to the contrary. At the beginning of the Hellenistic period, as we can see from Stoicism and the doxographical tradition, Socrates most typically stood for the thesis that ethical excellence is knowledge and ethical badness is ignorance. Those who accepted these doctrines could not be comfortable with the thought that their leading proponent was a self-confessed ignoramus and therefore, by implication, a bad person.

We should suppose that Arcesilaus's skepticism was actually motivated, at least in large part, by his reading of Plato's Socrates – a fundamentally new reading, not one that he foisted on Socrates and Plato because he was already a skeptic. In another context (*Academica* 1.44–5), Cicero presents Arcesilaus's skepticism as a response to the obscurity of the things that had led Socrates and earlier philosophers to "a confession of ignorance." Cicero goes on to say that Arcesilaus took Socrates to have had knowledge of just one thing – his own ignorance. The nearest the Platonic Socrates comes to saying this is at *Apology* 21b4–5: "As for myself, *I am not aware* of being wise in anything, great or small." What Socrates probably means in saying this is simply that he does not take himself to have any wisdom. But Arcesilaus, we may suppose, interpreted Socrates as making the strong cognitive claim that

24   Aeschines Socraticus frs. 3–4 Krauss (on which see Long 1996a, p. 11, n. 25) and Aristotle, *Soph. El.* 183b6–8.

he *knew* that he knew nothing, and then proceeded to deny that he himself knew even that much.

The best evidence on Arcesilaus indicates a single-minded intent to model himself on this rigorously skeptical interpretation of Socrates – his declining to write books, his dialectical virtuosity, his playing the role of questioner rather than respondent, his destructive criticism of other philosophers, and, quite generally, a life seemingly devoted to discussion with anyone he thought worth talking to. Arcesilaus must have intended his close alignment with Socrates to mark a radical reorientation of the post-Platonic Academy, away from the doctrinal focus on Plato's metaphysics that had chiefly occupied his immediate successors, Speusippus and Xenocrates, toward a reinvigorated Socratic posture. And in that endeavor, he was so successful that it would take two hundred years before a doctrinal Plato reemerged.

One would like to know the identity of the "various" Platonic texts Arcesilaus invoked to justify his wholesale skepticism. Unfortunately, we have no specifics to work from apart from the *Apology*, but it is a fair guess that he drew heavily on the *Theaetetus*, with its failure to define knowledge, as well as the numerous aporetic conclusions and *ad hominem* argument of earlier dialogues.[25]

The question all this most starkly raises is, of course, what Arcesilaus made of Socrates as the father of ethics? We should presume that he drew attention to such Platonic contexts as *Gorgias* 508e6–509a7, where Socrates, after endorsing the thesis that it is worse to do wrong than to suffer it, insists that, for all its seeming cogency, he does not *know* it to be true. Rather than taking Socrates to have been the propounder and teacher of firmly held moral doctrines, as the Stoics did, Arcesilaus viewed him as the authority for his own dialectical practice – advancing ethical propositions as steps toward exploring and undermining the dogmatic claims of other thinkers, especially the Stoics. What we have here is a fascinating debate over the Socratic legacy, with the two sides each appealing one-sidedly to its own selection from the record in Plato and elsewhere.

At issue was the main question debated by the Hellenistic schools – the nature of philosophical wisdom and the disposition of the wise man. The Stoics, from their interpretation of Socrates, derived an ideal of ethical perfection, grounded in infallible craft knowledge, which they defended as being humanly possible and the aim of every would-be good person. Arcesilaus, inspired by Socrates' frequent

---

25 How Arcesilaus may have justified his imputation of scepticism to Socrates and Plato, and how we ourselves should assess his strategy, are questions well explored by Annas 1994, Shields 1994, and Cooper 2004a.

cognitive disclaimers, emphasized instead the wisdom of freedom from error, taking his cue from the Socratic idea that nothing is worse than thinking that you know something when you do not. In reporting Arcesilaus's skepticism, Cicero attaches the highest moral commendation to suspension of judgment, stating it to be the only right and honorable response to the impossibility of knowledge.[26] Here, then, we have our best clue to the way Arcesilaus positioned himself in relation to Socratic ethics.

By putting Socrates at the head of his skepticism and dialectical method, Arcesilaus not only corrected the record as he saw it; he also reclaimed Socrates for the Academy. He clearly wanted to detach Socrates from the upstart Stoa, but in this he was not successful. By the end of the second century BCE, Socrates has become so Stoically entrenched that we find Panaetius, as head of the Stoa, defending Socrates against Peripatetic detraction and establishing a canon of the 'truthful' Socratic literature.[27]

To undermine the Academics' skeptical Socrates, the Stoics could retort that his confessions of ignorance were no more than a dialectical manifestation of his notorious irony. Thus Antiochus (fl. 80 BCE), speaking as a virtual Stoic in Cicero, says:

From the list of those [alleged by Arcesilaus to have denied the possibility of knowledge] we must remove both Plato and Socrates – the former because he bequeathed a most splendid system ... while Socrates, depreciating himself in discussion, used to assign greater weight to those he wished to refute. Thus in saying something other than he thought he liked to make use of the dissembling that the Greeks call irony.[28]

For later antiquity in general, Socrates was an ironist rather than a sincere skeptic. In fact it was probably the Academics' skeptical characterization of him that chiefly promoted, as its antidote, a positive evaluation of Socratic irony. The Stoics, who officially disapproved of irony, are unlikely to have advertised this Socratic trait unless they were responding to the Academics. However, as early as Epicurus, those who sought to discredit Socrates made irony one of the many charges against him.[29] To the negative reception of Socrates I now turn.

26   See Cicero, *Academica* 2.77, where the context is a dispute between the Stoic Zeno and Arcesilaus over the wise man's cognitive disposition.
27   D.L. 2.64.
28   *Academica* 2.15.
29   Cicero, *Brutus* 292. By contrast, Aristotle's single reference to Socrates' irony is dispassionate (*EN* 4.7, 1127b25).

CRITICISM OF SOCRATES

Socrates was not a comfortable figure to encounter. So we would say even from reading Xenophon, and comfort zone is the last place in which to situate Plato's Socrates, whom modern students often find arrogant and disingenuous. Cynics, Stoics, and Academics were all inspired by Socrates' challenging style of discourse, whether to mock conventional values or to urge rigorous reflection on the foundations of authentic happiness or to refute all philosophical claims to certainty. Yet, although the philosophical tradition heroized Socrates for the most part, he also had strong detractors, especially in the early Hellenistic period. We may begin our study of this negative reception with Aristotle.

As Plato's prize pupil, Aristotle could not have overlooked his master's philosophical indebtedness to Socrates and the extraordinary honor paid to Socrates in the Platonic dialogues. In spite of that, Aristotle accords little explicit attention to Socrates. The names of Empedocles, Democritus, and Plato himself occur many times more frequently in the Aristotelian corpus. Outside the brief references in the *Metaphysics*, to which I have already alluded, Aristotle makes a few positive and critical remarks on Socrates in his ethical treatises, and that is more or less all. Taking Socrates, as he did, to have disclaimed any interest in the physical sciences, Aristotle's reticence about him may appear unsurprising. Plausible though that reaction would be, I think that more is at stake. Temperamentally, if I may engage in armchair psychology, Aristotle with his cool intellect had nothing in common with the passionate missionary zeal that Socrates exhibits in Plato's *Apology* and elsewhere. A single sentence by Plutarch does more to explain the Socratic legacy than all of Aristotle's comments on the man: "Socrates was the first to show that life accommodates philosophy at every time and part and in all states and affairs without qualification."[30] It was this Socrates that fired the imagination and allegiance of the first generation of his followers, and that of their Cynic and Stoic successors.

Aristotle did not make a point of disparaging Socrates; that much seems certain. No less certainly, however, he refrains, in his surviving works, from eulogizing him or giving him premier status as a philosopher, and he did allude to criticisms of Socrates by others.[31] Aristotle's followers in the Lyceum were either silent about Socrates, as Theophrastus appears to have been, or determinedly malevolent. Aristoxenus, according to Porphyry, is said to have written a life of Socrates that was more vicious than the accusations of Meletus and Anytus.[32] It made out Socrates to

30 *An seni resp. ger.* 26, 796d = SSR I C 493.
31 D.L. 2.46.
32 Fr. 51 Wehrli = 1 B 41 SSR.

be a bigamist and the boyfriend of the Macedonian king Archelaus. The charge of bigamy, repeated by other Peripatetics, acquired sufficient currency to provoke the Stoic Panaetius into writing what Plutarch calls an adequate refutation.[33] Such tittle tattle, if it were confined to the scandalmongering Aristoxenus, would merit no further comment. The fact that it became a common Peripatetic practice suggests a studied attempt to undermine the integrity of Socrates' life. We may conclude that many Peripatetics sought to combat Socrates' growing status as the paradigm of the way a philosophical life should be lived. The more Socrates' exclusive concentration on ethics was emphasized, the less at home he could be in the research environment of the Lyceum.

Peripatetic disparagement of Socrates appears to have been long on gossip and short on precise engagement with texts of Plato and Xenophon. Not so the Epicureans' attack. In the case of Epicurus, we hear only about his criticism of Socrates' irony (n. 28). If he himself was fairly restrained in his comments on Socrates, his followers were not.[34] From his immediate disciples down to the middle years of the Roman Empire, the Epicureans displayed a hostility to Socrates that is virulent even by the extreme standards of ancient polemic. In their writings, Socrates was portrayed as the complete anti-Epicurean – a sophist, a rhetorician, a braggart, a skeptic, a credulous purveyor of false theology, in sum – a figure whose inconclusive ethical inquries and neglect of natural science turned human life into chaos.[35]

From our modern perspective, such unmitigated hostility is hard to fathom; for both Socrates and Epicurus were in the business of curing people's souls. Xenophon's Socrates especially could have given the Epicureans excellent support for much of their ethical precepts and practice, including their focus on frugality, self-sufficiency, and control of vain and unnecessary desires. That they chose instead to attack aspects of Socrates' ethics and to present him as a thoroughgoing skeptic indicates that their immediate target was the image of Socrates transmitted by the Stoics and the Stoics' Academic rivals.

As I have already mentioned, Epicureans wrote books against several of Plato's Socratic dialogues. Two of these dialogues, the *Gorgias* and *Euthydemus*, were texts that the early Stoics seem to have particularly

33 Plutarch, *Aristides* 335c-d.
34 Kleve 1983 gives an excellent conspectus of the Epicurean view of Socrates.
35 The Epicureans were quite precise in their attacks. For instance, Colotes (fl. third cent. BCE) fastens upon Socrates' statement (*Phaedrus* 230a) that he does not even know himself, citing Plato's text exactly (Plutarch, *Adv. Col.* 21 1119b); and Philodemus (fl. first cent. BCE) rejects Socrates' argument (*Prt.* 319d) that virtue cannot be taught (*Rhet.* I 261, 8ff.).

drawn from, and the *Gorgias* was the favorite dialogue of Epictetus.[36] In attacking Plato's representation of Socrates in these works, the Epicureans almost certainly took themselves to be indirectly criticizing the Stoics and their Socratic paradigm. This suggestion, or rather the probability that Epicurean polemic against Socrates had a contemporary focus, is strongly confirmed by what Colotes, an Epicurean coeval with Arcesilaus, made of Socrates in his books against the *Lysis* and *Euthydemus*. There he maintained that Socrates ignored self-evidence – the hallmark of Epicurean criteria of truth – and suspended judgment.[37] Here, in quite precise language, Socrates is being presented as the prototype of the skeptical Arcesilaus.

There is much more to the Epicurean attacks on Socrates than I shall discuss here, including a lengthy criticism by Philodemus of Socrates' discussion of household management in Xenophon's *Oeconomicus*.[38] Right from the beginning, Socrates' eccentricities had made him an obvious target for mockery by the Greek comic poets, and Lucian much later continued that game most entertainingly.[39] But few traces of humor lighten the Epicureans' efforts to derail his reputation and significance. What we have there is a sustained and thoroughly serious strategy of self-promotion – to wean their would-be converts from the figure whom their main rivals had elevated to a position threatening the quasi-divine status and salvational message of Epicurus himself. Of those rivals, the Stoics, according to Philodemus, actually "want to be called Socratics."[40]

EPICTETUS ON THE SOCRATIC ELENCHUS

The Stoics' strong allegiance to Socrates, as we have seen, began with Zeno the founder of the school. From nearly all the leading Stoics thereafter down to Panaetius and Posidonius (late second to mid-first century BCE) there are testimonies to their specific interests in Socrates. That fact is significant because so little verbatim evidence survives for this formative period of Stoicism. The material, though piecemeal, shows that the early Stoics drew heavily on Socratic literature, not only in formulating their ethics but also in seeking support for their interests

---

36   See Long 2002, ch. 3, and later.
37   See Krönert 1906, 163–170, and Kleve 1983, 231.
38   For Philodemus' treatment of Socrates, see the edition, with translation and commentary, of Méndez/Angeli 1992, and Kleve 1983, pp. 238–142.
39   See the passages of Lucian excerpted in SSR, I A 31–5.
40   *De stoicis* col. 12 = SSR V B 126.

in dialectic, law, prophecy, and moral progress.[41] To which I think may be added divine teleology and providence.[42]

From Cicero we can infer that Stoic philosophers were in the habit of attaching Socrates' name to some of their central ethical theses. For instance, they took from Socrates the view that "all who lack wisdom are insane" (*Tusculan Disputations* 3.10) and supposed that "everything goes well for great men if the statements of our school and Socrates, the leader of philosophy, are adequate concerning the bounty and resources of virtue" (*Natura Deorum* 2.167). We can presume that it was also common practice to cite salient instances of Socrates' life and character, representing him as the next best thing to the elusive and ideal Stoic sage. The exemplary Socrates – unflinching victim of a supremely unjust prosecution and sentence – became so popular with Roman moralists that Cicero and Seneca mention him in the same breath as such home-grown Roman saints as Regulus and Cato.

In the extensive discourses Arrian ascribes to Epictetus, Socrates is all this, but he is also much more.[43] Epictetus canonizes Zeno and the Cynic Diogenes (3.21.18–19), but it is Socrates who primarily authorizes everything he seeks to give his students in terms of philosophical methodology, self-examination, and a life model for them to imitate. The special and quite distinctive interest of Epictetus's Socrates, or rather of Epictetus's reflection of Socrates, consists in the way his discourses appropriate and adapt Socratic dialectic. His Socratic procedures include question-and-answer dialogue, closely modeled on Plato. Here the point I want to develop is Epictetus's recourse to the Socratic *elenchus*.

Plato's Socrates in the *Apology* maintains that recognizing one's own ignorance and practising self-examination are fundamental starting-points for anyone who wants to live well. Epictetus echoes these famous Socratic principles repeatedly. The first job of one who philosophizes, he says, is to cast off the illusion that one knows (2.17.1), and to be aware, from the outset, of one's weakness and impotence concerning absolute essentials (2.11.1). Epictetus even thanks a certain Lesbius for proving (*exelenchein*) every day that "I know nothing" (3.20.19). If he is being ironical here, as I suspect, that is a further mark of how his recourse to Socrates is directly Platonic rather than simply a feature of

---

41 For details, see Long 1996a, pp. 16–17.
42 In Long 1996a, pp. 20–21 (originally published as Long 1988, pp. 162–163), I propose that the early Stoics drew on Xenophon, *Mem.* 1.4.5–18 and 4.3.2–18, where Xenophon credits Socrates with these theological doctrines. My proposal is endorsed and expanded by De Filippo/Mitsis 1994, 255–260.
43 My treatment of Epictetus draws selectively on Long 2002, ch. 3.

the Stoic tradition. Socrates in Plato's *Gorgias* (458a) had commented on the value of having one's false beliefs refuted. For Epictetus, the essence of meeting a philosopher is a mutual exchange of beliefs with a view to testing or refuting one another (*exelenchein* again: 3.9.12–14).

In Epictetus's use of the word *exelenchein*, we can be quite sure that he is taking Socrates as his authority because he characterizes Socrates as divinely appointed to hold the elenctic position (3.21.19), and he associates this position with Socrates' protreptic expertise (2.26. 4–7). By deploying these skills in conversation, Socrates (he says) revealed to his interlocutors their involuntary ignorance and their inconsistency in acting contrary to their real interests. Socrates' refutative methodology had inspired the Academic skeptics in their project of advocating suspension of judgment about everything. Epictetus, to the best of our knowledge, is the only Stoic who made the *elenchus* a *positive* instrument of his own teaching method.

The main key to understanding the rationale underlying Epictetus's use of the *elenchus* is his doctrine of 'innate (*emphytoi*) preconceptions' (*prolepseis*). The early Stoics had proposed that human beings 'naturally' acquire certain concepts, but they took the mind to be a *tabula rasa* at birth. Instead, Epictetus holds that people have innate preconceptions of universally valid and consistent ethical notions (2.11.1–8). The general basis of error, according to him, is ignorance of how to apply and articulate preconceptions (4.1.42–3). Because this endowment is too rudimentary to guide particular judgements in difficult cases, philosophical training and *elenctic* argument are needed to show people that a particular judgment – for example, Medea's terrible decision to punish Jason by killing her own children – may be radically incompatible with their innate preconception of the long-term happiness they really want for themselves.

The Platonic dialogue that resonates most deeply in Epictetus is the *Gorgias*. Although Plato's Socrates does not have the concept of innate preconceptions, there is a striking similarity between his claims for the *elenctic* method in that dialogue, as interpreted by Vlastos, and Epictetus's procedure.[44] Vlastos explains Socrates' confidence in the *positive* outcomes of his *elenctic* arguments in the *Gorgias* by a twofold assumption: first, that any set of entirely consistent beliefs must be true, and second: that whoever has a false moral belief will always have latent true beliefs entailing the negation of that false belief. Socrates finds that his own beliefs, because their consistency has been exhaustively tested, satisfy the first assumption; and in the *elenchus*, he elicits from his

44   See Vlastos 1983 and 1984, ch. 1.

interlocutor true beliefs that cohere with Socrates' own judgments and contradict the beliefs originally proffered.

Vlastos's interpretation of positive *elenchus* has not convinced all scholars.[45] What matters for my purpose is not its correctness as the interpretation we moderns should adopt regarding the Platonic Socrates, but its affinity to Epictetus's methodology, and therefore the likelihood that he interpreted Socrates in much the same way that Vlastos did. As a Stoic philosopher, Epictetus takes himself to have a set of true moral beliefs that he can employ as premises, and he appeals to his interlocutors' innate preconceptions as resources equipping them to endorse those beliefs and thereby recognize the inconsistency infecting the particular desires and judgments with which they started.

Epictetus's interest in closely aligning his methodology with the Platonic Socrates is also indicated by a discourse (2.12) in which he praises Socrates both for using ordinary language, as distinct from technical terms, in his *elenctic* conversations, and for his patience in dealing with his interlocutors. In advising his students to follow suit, he is also commenting reflexively on his own discourses. His language is largely free from the technical jargon of Stoicism. Instead, he uses the everyday terms that he can expect to engage his students, and he also imitates Socrates in his readiness to drive his points home by craft analogies and other straightforward appeals to experience.

These affinities between Epictetus and the Platonic Socrates are creative rather than simply imitative. While Epictetus includes interpersonal dialogue in his discourses, he is chiefly concerned with urging his students to practise the *elenchus* on themselves, as he says that Socrates did in his concern with self-examination (2.1.32–3), and he also associates Socrates with his favorite injunction "to make correct use of impressions" (*phantasiai*, 3.12.15). As a committed Stoic, Epictetus does not use the Socratic *elenchus* for purely negative purposes, as in such exploratory dialogues as Plato's *Euthyphro*. He adapts it to his role as a paternalist instructor of the young men who form his audience.

If Epictetus, as seems probable, was largely original in his appropriation and adaptation of Socratic dialectic, how should we account for his procedure? By his time, Stoicism had become notorious for its technical refinements, especially in the domain of logic. Epictetus constantly warns his students against mistaking expertise in Stoic scholarship for moral progress. We may best explain his intense focus on Socratic methodology as a very deliberate intention to return Stoicism to its primary goal of radically reshaping people's values and goals. The Socratic impulse had been characteristic of Stoicism from the outset, but

45   See Kraut 1983 and Benson 1995.

Epictetus gives it his own special trademark. In his use of the *elenchus*, associated with his doctrine of innate preconceptions, he cleaves more closely to the Socrates of Plato's early dialogues than any later philosopher from antiquity. Instead of imposing elaborate doctrines on his students, he prefers to offer them leading questions and answers that they are competent to examine, on the basis of their own mental resources, and use as material for making progress under his direction but their own volition.

SOCRATES' DIVINE SIGN

One of Socrates' most celebrated peculiarities was his experience of an intermittently and purely admonitory voice that Plato and Xenophon call his "divinity" (*daimonion*), generally rendered in English by divine sign or divine voice. Along with Socrates' respect for the Delphic oracle, the divine sign gave the Epicureans material to charge Socrates with pandering to superstition,[46] and it has troubled those modern scholars (and at least one ancient spokesman), who would like to discount all traces of religiosity or departures from rationality in the hard core of his outlook.[47] The fact is, however, that such an approach presents us with a Socrates who is much too sanitized to do justice to all the oldest Socratic literature, where we find him taking dreams and prophecies seriously. Just as the mathematical genius Newton believed in astrology, so criteria of rationality are always relative to salient cultural factors. The rationalistic Stoics took divination seriously because they believed that cosmic reason, the all-pervading *logos*, presents signs of causal connexions that expert augury can detect. Unsurprisingly, one leading Stoic, Antipater, collected instances of Socrates' experiences of his divine sign.[48] Epictetus refers to it (3.1.19), and tells a would-be Cynic to consult his *daimonion* (3.22.53). It is highly probable that the later Stoics' use of the term *daimon*, to refer to the mind's normative rationality, has a deliberately Socratic resonance.[49]

Epictetus was an exact contemporary of the Academic philosopher and biographer, Plutarch. In Plutarch's voluminous essays, most of them on ethical topics, Socrates is a ubiquitous presence. He characterizes Socrates, along with Pythagoras and Plato, as "resplendent in soul";[50]

46 See Kleve 1983, pp. 242–243.
47 I am thinking especially of Vlastos 1991 ch. 6, who is skilfully answered by Brickhouse/Smith 1994, pp. 193–195, and by McPherran 1996, ch. 4.1.
48 Cicero, *Div.* 1.123, where the context is the need for authentic augury to be practised by a 'pure mind'.
49 See Long 2002, pp. 166–167.
50 *De lib.* 2c.

and, in hagiographical vein, he refers to numerous instances in Socrates' life and conversation where he displayed this quality. The keen attention Plutarch pays to Socrates is episodic and unsystematic except for the essay entitled *On Socrates' divine sign*. In devoting a whole work to this topic, Plutarch reflects his own strong interests in religious experience and, more discursively, the culture of his epoch. His essay, written mainly as a reported dialogue, is interesting enough to warrant a full summary of its Socratic part.[51]

A group of Thebans, recently returned from exile, has gathered together, some twenty years after Socrates' death, to discuss findings at the excavation of a tomb. They learn that an Italian Pythagorean is about to arrive, on a mission inspired by dreams and apparitions, to collect the remains of a certain Lysis, "unless forbidden by some *daimonion* in the night" (579f). Hearing this, Galaxidorus protests about the prevalence of superstition, and contrasts it with Socrates' philosophical allegiance to unadorned truth. His rationalistic retort provokes Theocritus to ask him about Socrates' divine sign, which he claims to have observed giving a salutary warning to Socrates when the latter was engaged in discussion with Euthyphro.

Galaxidorus scornfully retorts that Socrates only acted upon the promptings of his divine sign when he needed some purely chance factor to turn the balance if confronted with the equipoise of two contrary reasons.[52] This prompts another party to the discussion to report the proposal that the divine sign was nothing more than a sneeze, though he declines to believe that a man as resolutely rational as Socrates could have given a sneeze that elevated name! Galaxidorus then agrees to listen to what Simmias (the character from Plato's *Phaedo*) heard Socrates say about the matter himself.

According to Simmias, Socrates declined to answer directly. However, because Socrates was known to have completely rejected anyone's claims to visual experience of the divine, but to have shown interest in those who said they had heard such a voice, he and his companions arrived at the following conjecture:

Socrates' divine sign was perhaps no vision but the perception of a voice, or the conceiving of a discourse, that made contact with him in a strange way, just as

---

51   I discuss Plutarch's essay more fully in Long 2006b.
52   580f. Plutarch (*Stoic. rep.* 1045b-1045f) was aware of the philosophical debate on this issue: Epicureans had argued that deciding between such equally balanced alternatives is settled by a random swerve of the soul's atoms; to which the Stoic Chrysippus responded that the decision has a cause that simply illudes our awareness.

in sleep, without actual utterance, people grasp the meanings of statements and think that they are listening to conversation. (588d)

Ordinary people, because they are distracted by their passions and needs when awake, hear the higher powers better if they are asleep. Socrates, on the other hand, thanks to his soul's virtual independence from the body, was always hypersensitive to such aural visitations:

What he experienced, one may suppose, was not spoken language but the voiceless discourse of a daimon, that made contact with him purely semantically. (588e)

Simmias now launches into an account of the soul's structure, borrowed from Plato's *Laws* (644d-645b): equipped with numerous cord-like motions, the soul, when rationally contacted, is able to respond to the object of thought. Just as reason can move the body without spoken language, so we may believe that a higher and more divine intellect can, without language, make contact with our understanding, illuminate it, through the medium of air, and "indicate to divine and outstanding men" the content of its thought.

Did Plutarch invent this account of Socrates' divine sign? Probably not, for we find the gist of it repeated by Calcidius, the fourth-century CE commentator on Plato's *Timaeus* (255). Fascinating in itself, as an account of what we would probably call intuition, it is also a skilful rejoinder to those who want Socrates to be either an earth-bound rationalist or an airy mystic. His divine sign, as represented by Plutarch, was the voice of reason, or rather it was a purely semantic communication from objective reason (a more than human intellect) as such.

While Platonists found no difficulty in accommodating the divine sign within their polytheistic theology, it naturally troubled many Christian authors. Augustine (354–430 CE) praised Socrates for his ethical integrity and for being a virtual monotheist (*Civ. dei* 8.3), but he was unhappy about what the Platonist Apuleius (fl. CE) had said about the divine sign in his work "On Socrates' god" (*De deo Socratis*).[53] The point at issue was Augustine's understanding of the term *daimon(ion)*. According to Plato, as interpreted by Apuleius, a *daimon* is a being intermediate between gods and humans. Apuleius, says Augustine, notwithstanding his title "On Socrates' god," actually took the divine sign to issue from a *daimon*, and should have entitled his work accordingly; but if Socrates had association with such a being, he is not to be felicitated because *daimons* are actually the abhorrent creatures that we moderns, following the Christian anathematization of them, call demons.

53 *Civ. dei* 8.14. For Apuleius's comments, which are too jejune to be worth excerpting, see SSR I C 413.

In striking contrast to Augustine and some three hundred years earlier, with Christianity still in its infancy, Justin Martyr praised Socrates for being an enemy of demons. Justin wrote:

When Socrates by his truthful and inquiring discourse was striving to publicize these [proto-Christian] doctrines and banish the demons from human beings, the demons themselves were stirred up by people who rejoice in wickedness to kill him as someone godless and impious, claiming that he was introducing new *daimonia*. (Justin Martyr, *First Apology* 5.3.)

Justin's expression "new *daimonia*" comes directly from Socrates' encounter with Meletus in Plato's *Apology* (26b). It is regularly and rightly supposed that Socrates' divine sign was the basis for this indictment, but Justin, if he knew that, declines to say so. Rather, drawing on Socrates' dismissal of the poets from the ideal state of Plato's *Republic*, Justin takes this act to have been tantamount to the expulsion of "the evil demons" described by Homer and other Greek poets. In so behaving, Socrates was seeking to convert people, through rational inquiry, into recognizing the divinity unknown to them. Justin supports his judgment of Socrates by citing words spoken by Timaeus in Plato's dialogue of that name (28c): "It is not easy to discover the father and maker of the world, nor, having made that discovery, is it safe to broadcast it."[54]

Justin's Christianized Socrates is an appropriate place at which to draw this survey toward its conclusion. What it illustrates, like so much else I have discussed, is a virtual paradox attaching to the legacy of Socrates. On the one hand, the early Socratic literature presented its readers with a strikingly unique and incomparably remarkable figure. They could find no one else whose biography was as firmly, vividly, and charismatically characterized as his. His hagiographical defenders presented him as a model of consistency, moral courage, and mental strength. No doubt the real Socrates was all of that, but he was also much more, as Plato especially had the genius to recognize and record – ironic, fun loving, unremittingly disputatious, promiscuously if Platonically homo-erotic, and so forth. On the other hand, this complexity, though a great part of Socrates' uniqueness, made any attempt to capture the essence of the man extraordinarily difficult, and that difficulty was compounded both by the great range of roles and contexts in which Plato has him appear and by Socrates' cognitive disclaimers. Hence the virtual paradox: you would never mistake anyone else for Socrates but the virtuosity and

---

54 For other Christian commentators on Socrates, see Frede 2004. In monasticism, Epictetus's *Manual* was adapted to Christian use, with the name of St. Paul being substituted for that of Socrates; see Long 2002, p. 261.

even plasticity of Socrates the literary figure made it inevitable that his philosophical significance would always be highly contested.

More positively, it meant that future generations would repeatedly interpret Socrates in their own image, draw support for their own philosophies and paradigms from him, elide what did not suit them, or even turn him into their own antithesis, as the Epicureans did. Can we do better? Probably not, and that is just as well. For whatever we make of Socrates, these words from Epictetus ring true:

Now that Socrates is dead, the memory of what he did or said when alive is no less beneficial to people, or rather it is even more so. (4.1.169)

What matters most about Socrates is the fact that we never tire of him or stop wanting to talk to him and get mad with him.

WORKS CITED

Ahbel-Rappe, S. and Kamtekar, R. eds. *A Companion to Socrates*, Oxford, 2006.

Algra, K., Barnes, J., Mansfeld, J., and Schofield, M., eds. *The Cambridge History of Hellenistic Philosophy*. Cambridge, 1999.

Annas, J. "Plato the Skeptic", In Vander Waerdt 1994a, 309–40.

Benson, H. H. 1995. "The dissolution of the problem of the elenchus," *OSAP* 13 (1995): 45–112.

Branham, B. and Goulet-Cazé, M.-I. eds. *The Cynics. The Cynic Movement in Antiquity and its Legacy.* Berkeley/Los Angeles, 1996.

Brunschwig, J. and Nussbaum, M., eds. *Passions and Perceptions. Studies in Hellenistic Philosophy of Mind.* Cambridge, 1993.

Carratelli, G. V. ed. *Suzetesis. Studi sull' Epicureismo Greco e Romano offerti a Marcello Gigante*, vol. 1. Naples, 1983.

Cooper, J. "Arcesilaus: Socratic and Sceptic", In Cooper 2004b, ch. 4, pp. 81–106.

Cooper, J. *Knowledge, Nature, and the Good. Essays on Ancient Philosophy.* Princeton, 2004b.

Crönert, W. *Kolotes und Menedemus.* Leipzig, 1906, repr. Amsterdam 1965.

De Filippo, J. G. and Mitsis, P. "Socrates and Stoic natural law," In Vander Waerdt 1994a, 252–271.

Frede, M. "The early Christian reception of Socrates." In Karasmanis 2004, 481–90.

Giannantoni, G. ed. *Socratis et Socraticorum Reliquiae*, vol. 1. Naples, 1990.

Green, P. ed. *Hellenistic History and Culture.* Berkeley/Los Angeles, 1993.

Irwin, T. *Plato's Ethics.* Oxford, 1995.

Karasmanis, V., ed. *Socrates 2400 Years since his Death.* Delphi, 2004.

Kleve, K. "Scurra Atticus. The Epicurean view of Socrates," In Carrattelli 1983, 227–253.

Kraut, R. "Comments on Gregory Vlastos, 'The Socratic elenchus,'" *OSAP* 1 (1983): 59–70.

Long, A. A. and Sedley, D.N. *The Hellenistic Philosophers*, 2 vols. Cambridge, 1987.

Long, A. A. "Socrates in Hellenistic Philosophy," *CQ* 38 (1988): 150–171; repr. with postscript as ch. 1 of Long 1996a.

Long, A. A. "Hellenistic ethics and philosophical power." In Green 1993, 138–156; repr. with postscript as ch. 1 of Long 2006a.

Long, A. A. *Stoic Studies*. Cambridge, 1996a; repr. Berkeley/Los Angeles, 2001.

Long, A. A. "The Socratic Tradition: Diogenes, Crates, and Hellenistic Ethics," in Branham/Goulet-Cazé 1996b, 28–46.

Long, A. A. "The Socratic legacy." In Algra et al. 1999, 617–641.

Long, A. A. *Epictetus. A Stoic and Socratic Guide to Life*. Oxford, 2002 [2004].

Long, A. A. *From Epicurus to Epictetus. Studies in Hellenistic and Roman Philosophy*. Oxford, 2006a.

Long, A. A. "How does Socrates' divine sign communicate with him?" In Ahbel-Rappe/Kamtekar, 2006b, 63–74.

McPherran, M. L. *The Religion of Socrates*. University Park, PA, 1996.

Méndez, E. A. and Angeli, A. eds. *Filodemo Testimoniane su Socrate*. Naples, 1992.

Porter, J. I. "The Philosophy of Aristo of Chios", In Branham/Goulet-Cazé 1996, 156–189.

Schofield, M. *The Stoic Idea of the City*. Cambridge, 1991.

Schofield, M. "Academic epistemology", In Algra et al. 1999, 323–351.

Sedley, D. N. "Chrysippus on psychophysical causality", In Brunschwig/Nussbaum, 1993, 313–331.

Shields, C. "Socrates among the Skeptics," In Vander Wardt 1994a, 341–366.

Striker, G. *Essays on Hellenistic Epistemology and Ethics*. Cambridge, 1996a.

Striker, G. "Plato's Socrates and the Stoics", in Striker 1996a, 316–324.

Vander Waerdt, P. A., ed. *The Socratic Movement*. Ithaca/London, 1994a.

Vander Waedt, P. A. "Zeno's *Republic* and the origins of natural law," In Vander Waerdt 1994a, 272–308.

Vlastos, G. "The Socratic elenchus," *OSAP* 1 (1984): 27–58 and 71–4; repr. in Vlastos 1994, ch. 1, pp. 1–28.

Vlastos, G. *Socrates. Ironist and Moral Philosopher*. Cambridge, 1991.

Vlastos, G., ed. M. Burnyeat. *Socratic Studies*. Cambridge, 1994.

FURTHER READING

Caizzi, F. "Antistene," *Studi Urbinati* 38 (1964): 24–76.

De Luise, F., and Farinetti, G. *Felicità socratica: Immagini di Socrate e Modelli Anthropologici Ideali nella Filosofia Antica*. Hildesheim/Zürich/New York, 1997.

Du Toit, D. S. *Theios Anthropos. Zur Verwendung von theios anthropos und sinnverwandten Ausdrücken in der Literatur derKaiserzeit*. Tübingen, 1997.

Döring, K. *Exemplum Socratis. Studien zur Sokratesnachwirkung in der kynisch-stoischen Popularphilosophie der frühen Kaiserzeit und im frühe Chistentum*. *Hermes Einzelschrift* 42 Wiesbaden, 1979.

Ferguson, A. *Socrates. A Source Book*. London, 1970.

Hadot, P. *Philosophy as a Way of Life*, tr. M. Chase. Oxford, 1995.

Nehamas, A. The Art of Living. Socratic Reflections from Plato to Foucault. Berkeley/Los Angeles, 1998.

Socrates Bibliography

I. BIBLIOGRAPHIES

Dorion, L.-A. "Les écrits socratiques de Xénophon. Supplément bibliographique (1984–2008)," in M. Narcy and A. Tordesillas (eds.), *Xénophon et Socrate*, Paris, 2008, pp. 283–300.

McKirahan, R. D. *Plato and Socrates: a comprehensive bibliography, 1958–1973.* New York, 1978.

Döring, K. "Bibliographie zum zweiten Kapitel: A. Sokrates," In *Die Philosophie der Antike*, vol. 2, pt. 1. ed. H. Flashar (Basel, 1998), pp. 323–364.

Morrison, D. *Bibliography of Editions, Translations, and Scholarly Commentary on Xenophon's Socratic Writings, 1600-present*. Pittsburgh, 1988.

Navia, L. E., and E. L. Katz. *Socrates: an annotated bibliography*. New York, 1988.

Patzer, A. *Bibliographia Socratica: die wissenschaftliche Literatur über Sokrates von den Anfängen bis auf die neueste Zeit in systematisch – chronologischer Anordnung*. Freiburg, 1985.

Two surveys of Socratic scholarship over recent decades provide extensive guides to important bibliography. Although their topics overlap, the first focuses more on Plato, and the second on the other Socratics.

Notomi, Noburu, et al. "'Socratic Dialogues.'" *Plato* (*The Internet Journal of The International Plato Society*) 9 (2009).

Stavru, A., "Introduction" to *Socratica 2008*, Bari, 2010, pp. 11–55.

II. TEXTS AND TRANSLATIONS

II.A Aristophanes

Dover, K.J., trans. and ed. *Aristophanes' Clouds*. Oxford, 1968.

Henderson, J., trans. *Aristophanes' Clouds*. Newburyport, 1992.

Mastromarco, G., ed. 1983. *Commedie di Aristofane*, vol. 1. Turin, 1983.

Meineck, P., trans. *Aristophanes: Clouds*. Indianapolis, 2000.

Wilson, N., ed. *Aristophanis Fabulae*. New York, 2007.

II.B Plato

Brisson, L. ed. *Platon, Oeuvres complètes*. Paris, 2008.

Burnet, J. ed. *Platonis Opera*. Oxford, 1903.

Cooper, J.M., and D.S. Hutchinson, eds. *Plato: Complete Works*. Indianapolis and Cambridge, 1997.

Reale, G. *Platone. Tutti gli scritti*. Milan, 1991.

II.C Xenophon

Bartlett, R. C., ed. *Xenophon. The Shorter Socratic Writings: Apology of Socrates to the Jury, Oeconomicus, and Symposium*. Ithaca, 1996.

Bonnette, A. L., *Xenophon: Memorabilia*. Ithaca, 1994.

Bowen, A. J., *Xenophon: Symposium*. Warminster, 1998.

Dorion, L.-A., and M. Bandini. *Xénophon: Mémorables, vol. 1: Introduction générale et Livre I*. Paris, 2000.

Pucci, P. *Xenophon. Socrates' Defense*. Amsterdam, 2002.

Radspieler, H., and J. P. Reemtsma. *Xenophon: Sokratische Denkwürdigkeiten*. Frankfurt, 1998.

Santoni, A. *Senofonte. I memorabilia*. Milan, 1989.

Xenophon. *Conversations of Socrates*, trans. H. Tredennick and R. Waterfield, Harmondsworth, 1990.

Zaragoza, J. *Jenofonte:Recuerdos de Sócrates, Económico, Banquete, Apología de Sócrates*. Madrid, 1993.

II.D Socratic School

Decleva Caizzi F. *Antisthenis fragmenta*. Milan, 1966.

Dittmar, H. *Aischines von Sphettos*. Berlin, 1912.

Döring, K. *Die Megariker*. Amsterdam, 1972.

Giannantoni, G., ed. *Socratis et Socraticorum Reliquiae*, 4 vols. Naples, 1990.

Johnson, David. "Fragments of Aeschines of Sphettus, *Alcibiades*," in *Socrates and Alcibiades: Four Texts*. Newburyport, MA, 2003, pp. 91–98.

Mannebach, E. *Aristippi et Cyrenaicorum fragmenta*. Leiden and Cologne, 1961.

II.E Other Ancient Texts

Calder, W. et al. *The Unknown Socrates*. Wauconda, IL, 2002. (Translations of texts by Diogenes Laertius, Libanius, Maximus of Tyre, and Apuleius.)

Diogenes Laertius. "Life of Socrates." In *Lives of Eminent Philosophers*, vol. 1, trans. R.D. Hicks. Cambridge, MA, 1972.

Ferguson, A. *Socrates. A Source Book*. London, 1970.

Giannantoni, G. et al., ed. and trans. *Socrate. Tutte le testimonianze: da Aristofane e Senofonte ai Padri cristiani*. Bari, 1971.

Méndez, E. A., and A. Angeli., eds. *Filodemo Testimoniane su Socrate*. Naples, 1992.

Plutarch. "On the Sign of Socrates." In *Moralia VII*, trans. P.H. De Lacy and B. Einarson. Cambridge, MA, 1959.

III. COMPREHENSIVE STUDIES

III.A Books and Monographs

Brickhouse, T. C., and N. D. Smith. *Plato's Socrates*. Oxford, 1994.

Brickhouse, T. C., and N. D. Smith. *The Philosophy of Socrates*. Boulder, 2000.

Döring, K. "Sokrates, die Sokratiker und die von ihnen begründeten Traditionen." In *Grundriss der Geschichte der Philosophie: Die Philosophie der Antike*, Band 2/1. ed. H. Flashar (Basel, 1998), 141–364.

Dorion, L-A., *Socrate*. Paris, 2004.

Gigon, O. *Sokrates. Sein Bild in Dichtung und Geschichte*. Bern, 1947.

Grote, G. *Plato and the Other Companions of Sokrates*. vol. 1. London, 1865.

Gulley, N. 1968. *The Philosophy of Socrates*. London: Macmillan.

Guthrie, W.K.C. *Socrates*. Cambridge, 1971.

Hadot, P. *Éloge de Socrate*. Paris, 2002.

Kahn, C.H. *Plato and the Socratic Dialogue: The Philosophical Use of a Literary Form*. Cambridge, 1996.

Santas, G.X. *Socrates: Philosophy in Plato's Early Dialogues*. London, 1979.

Strauss, Leo. 1989. "The Problem of Socrates: Five Lectures." In *The Rebirth of Classical Political Philosophy*, ed. Thomas Pangle. Chicago, 1989, 103–183.

Taylor, A.E. *Socrates*. London, 1932.

Taylor, C.C.W. *Socrates*. Oxford, 1998.

Vlastos, G. *Socrates: Ironist and Moral Philosopher*. Ithaca, 1991.

Vlastos, G. *Socratic Studies*. Cambridge, 1994.

Wolff, F. *Socrate*. Paris, 1985.

III.B Collections of Articles

Ahbel-Rappe, S. and R. Kamtekar, eds. *A Companion to Socrates*. Malden, MA, 2006.

Benson, H., ed. *The Philosophy of Socrates*. New York, 1992.

Boudouris, K. J., ed. *The Philosophy of Socrates*. 2 vols. Athens, 1991/1992.

Giannantoni, G., and M. Narcy, eds. *Lezioni Socratiche*. Naples, 1997.

Gower Barry, S., and M.C. Stokes., eds. *Socratic Questions: New Essays on the Philosophy of Socrates and Its Significance*. New York, 1992.

Judson L. and V. Karasmanis. *Remembering Socrates: Philosophical Essays*. Oxford, 2006.

Karasmanis, V., ed. *Socrates: 2400 Years since his Death*. Delphi, European Cultural Centre of Delphi, 2004.

Laks, A., and M. Narcy, eds. *Philosophie Antique 1: Figures de Socrate*. Villeneuve d'Ascq (Nord), 2001.

Prior, W. J., ed. *Socrates: critical assessments*. 4 vols. New York, 1996.

Romeyer Dherby, G., and J.-B. Gourinat., eds. *Socrate et les Socratiques*. Paris, 2001.

Rossetti, L., and A. Stavru, eds. *Socratica 2005*. Naples, 2008.

Rossetti, L., and A. Stavru, eds. *Socratica 2008*. Bari, 2010.

Rossetti, L., and A. Stavru, eds. "Introduction" to *Socratica 2008*. Bari, 2010, pp. 11–55.

Vander Waerdt, P.A., ed. *The Socratic Movement*. Ithaca, 1994.

Vlastos, G., ed. *The Philosophy of Socrates: A Collection of Critical Essays*. Garden City, NY, 1971.

IV. STUDIES OF PARTICULAR AUTHORS

IV.A Aristophanes

Adkins A. W. H. "Clouds, Mysteries, Socrates and Plato." *Antichthon* 4 (1970): 13–24.

Berg, S. "Rhetoric, Nature, and Philosophy in Aristophanes' *Clouds*." *Ancient Philosophy* 18 (1998): 1–19.

Dover, K. J. "Socrates in the *Clouds*." In *The Philosophy of Socrates*, ed. G. Vlastos. Garden City, NY, 1971, pp. 50–77.

Edmunds L. "Aristophanes' Socrates." *Proceedings of the Boston Area Colloquium in Ancient Philosophy* 2 (1986): 209–230.

Havelock, E. A. "The Socratic Self as It Is Parodied in Aristophanes' *Clouds*." *Yale Classical Studies* 22 (1972): 1–18.

Konstan, D. *Greek Comedy and Ideology*. New York, 1995.

Marianetti, M. C. "Socratic Mystery-Parody and The Issue of Asebeia in Aristophanes' *Clouds*." *Symbolae Osloenses* 68 (1993): 5–31.

Nussbaum, Martha. "Aristophanes and Socrates on Learning Practical Wisdom." *Yale Classical Studies* 26 (1980): 43–97.

Segal, C. "Aristophanes' Cloud-Chorus." *Arethusa* 2 (1969): 143–161. Repr. in C. Segal, *Aristophanes und die alte Komödie*. Darmstadt, 1975.

Strauss, L. *Socrates and Aristophanes*. Chicago, 1966.

Tarrant, H. "Midwifery and the Clouds." *CQ* 38 (1988): 116–122.

Vander Waerdt, Paul A. 1994. "Socrates in the Clouds." in *The Socratic Movement*, ed. Paul Vander Waerdt. Ithaca, 1994, pp. 48–66.

Whitman, C. H. *Aristophanes and the Comic Hero*. Cambridge, 1964.

IV.B Plato

A short, separate bibliographical guide to Plato's Socrates is not feasible. Most of the scholarly literature on "Socrates" is about Plato's Socrates. Thus, most of the books and articles elsewhere in this bibliography (e.g., in III. "Comprehensive Studies" and V. "Studies of Particular Topics") in fact concern Plato's Socrates. Furthermore, since Socrates is the dominant character in most of Plato's dialogues, much of the enormous literature on Plato is also about Plato's Socrates. For the question, "What is distinctive about *Plato's* Socrates, in contrast to our other sources?" the best place to look is the literature on "the historical Socrates" (see V.A). A useful recent survey of attempts to distinguish "Socratic" elements from "Platonic" ones in Plato's writings is:

Notomi, Noburu et al. "'Socratic Dialogues'." *Plato (The Internet Journal of The International Plato Society)* 9 (2009).

IV.C Xenophon

Cooper J. M., "Notes on Xenophon's Socrates." In *Reason and Emotion. Essays on Ancient Moral Psychology and Ethical Theory.* Princeton, 1999, pp. 3–28.

Danzig, G. "Apologizing for Socrates: Plato and Xenophon on Socrates' Behavior in Court." *Transactions of the American Philological Association* 133 (2003): 281–321.

Delatte, A. *Le Troisième Livre des Souvenirs Socratiques de Xénophon.* Liège and Paris, 1933.

Dorion, L.-A., "*Akrasia* et *enkrateia* dans les *Mémorables* de Xénophon." *Dialogue* 42 (2003): 645–672.

Dorion, L.-A., and L. Brisson. Eds. "Les écrits socratiques de Xénophon." *Les Études philosophiques* 2 (2004): 137–252.

Gera, D. "Xenophon's Socrateses" in M. Trapp, ed. *Socrates from Antiquity to the Enlightenment.* Burlington, VT, 2007, pp. 33–50.

Gigon, O. *Kommentar zum ersten Buch von Xenophons* Memorabilien *(Schweizerische Beiträge zur Altertumswissenschaft,* Heft 5). Basel, 1953.

Gigon, O. *Kommentar zum zweiten Buch von Xenophons* Memorabilien *(Schweizerische Beiträge zur Altertumswissenschaft,* Heft 6). Basel, 1956.

Gray, V.J. *The Framing of Socrates. The Literary Interpretation of Xenophon's* Memorabilia *(Hermes Einzelschriften,* Heft 79). Stuttgart and Leipzig, 1998.

Huss, B. *Xenophon's Symposion. Ein Kommentar (Beiträge zur Altertumskunde,* Band125). Stuttgart and Leipzig, 1999.

Joël, K. *Der echte und der xenophontische Sokrates,* 3 vols., Berlin, 1893–1901.

Johnson, D. M. "Xenophon's Socrates on Law and Justice." *Ancient Philosophy* 23 (2003): 255–281.

Johnson, D. M. "Xenophon at his most Socratic *(Memorabilia* 4.2)," *Oxford Studies in Ancient Philosophy* 29 (2005): 39–73.

Morrison, D. "On Professor Vlastos' Xenophon," *Ancient Philosophy* 7 (1987): 9–22.

Morrison, D. "Xenophon's Socrates on the Just and the Lawful." *Ancient Philosophy* 15 (1995): 329–341.

McPherran, M. "Socrates on teleological and moral theology." *Ancient Philosophy* 14 (1994): 245–262.

Narcy, N., and A. Tordesillas, eds., *Xenophon et Socrate.* Paris, 2008.

Pangle, T. L. "The Political Defence of Socratic Philosophy: A Study of Xenophon's *Apology of Socrates to the Jury.*" *Polity* 18 (1985): 98–114.

Pomeroy, S. B. *Xenophon, Oeconomicus: A Social and Historical Commentary.* Oxford, 1994.

Strauss, L. *Xenophon's Socratic Discourse: An Interpretation of the Oeconomicus.* Ithaca, 1970.

Strauss, L. *Xenophon's Socrates.* Ithaca, 1972.

Vander Waerdt, P.A. "Socratic Justice and Self-Sufficiency. The Story of the Delphic Oracle in Xenophon's *Apology of Socrates.*" *OSAP* 11 (1993): 1–48.

IV.D Other Socratics

Billerbeck, M., ed. *Die Kyniker in der modernen Forschung.* Amsterdam, 1991.

Brancacci, A. *Oikeios logos: la filosofia del linguaggio di Antistene.* Elenchos 20. Naples, 1990.

Branham, R. and M.-O. Goulet-Cazé, eds. *The Cynics. The Cynic Movement in Antiquity and Its Legacy.* Berkeley, 1996.

Caizzi, F. "Antistene." *Studi Urbinati.* 38 (1964): 48–99.

Desmond, William D., *Cynics.* Berkeley, 2008.

Döring, K. *Der Sokratesschüler Aristipp und die Kyrenaiker (Abhandlungen der Akademie der Wissenschaften und der Literatur Mainz. Geistes- und sozialwissenschaftliche Klasse).* Wiesbaden and Stuttgart, 1988.

Döring, K. *Die Philosophie der Antike,* vol. 2 pts. 1st. ed. H. Flashar (Basel, 1998), Sections 16–21: 201–365.

Goulet-Cazé, M.-O., *L'ascèse cynique.* Paris, 1981.

Kalouche, F. "Antisthenes' ethics and theory of language." *Revue de Philosophie Ancienne* 17 (1999): 11–41.

Mann, W.-R. "The life of Aristippus." *Archiv für Geschichte der Philosophie* 78 (1996): 97–119.

Rossetti, L. *Aspetti Della Letteratura Socratica Antica.* Chieti, 1977.

Rossetti, L. "Logoi Sokratikoi anteriori al 399 a.c." In *Logos e logoi,* ed. L.Rosetti. Naples, 1991, pp. 21–40.

Tarrant, D. "The Pseudo-Platonic Socrates." *CQ* 32 (1938): 167–173. Repr. in *Der historische Sokrates,* ed. A. Patzer. Darmstadt, 1987, pp. 259–269.

Tsouna, V. *The epistemology of the Cyrenaic school.* Cambridge, 1998.

Vander Waerdt, P.A., ed. *The Socratic Movement.* Ithaca, 1994.

V. STUDIES OF PARTICULAR TOPICS

V.A Question of the "Historical Socrates"

Beversluis, J. "Vlastos's Quest for the Historical Socrates." *Ancient Philosophy* 13 (1993): 293–312.

Brickhouse, T. C., and Smith, N. D. "Apology of Socratic Studies." *Polis* 20 (2003): 108–127.

Deman, T. *Le Témoignage d'Aristote sur Socrate.* Paris, 1942.

Döring, K. "Der Sokrates der Platonischen Apologie und die Frage nach dem historischen Sokrates." *Würzburger Jahrbücher für die Altertumswissenschaft* 14 (1987): 75–94.

Dorion, L.-A., "A l'origine de la question socratique et de la critique du témoignage de Xénophon: l'étude de Schleiermacher sur Socrate (1815)," *Dionysius* 19 (2001): 51–74.

Gigon, O. *Sokrates. Sein Bild in Dichtung und Geschichte.* Bern, 1947.

Graham, D. W. "Socrates and Plato." *Phronesis* 37 (1992): 141–165.

Kahn, C. H. *Plato and the Socratic Dialogue.* Cambridge, 1996.

Magalhães-Vilhena, V. de. *Le problème de Socrate: le Socrate historique et le Socrate de Platon,* Paris, 1952.

Montuori, M. *Socrates: Physiology of a Myth.* Amsterdam, 1981.

Morrison, D. "On the Alleged Historical Reliability of Plato's *Apology.*" *Archiv für Geschichte der Philosophie* 82 (2000): 235–265.

Patzer, A. *Der historische Sokrates.* (The standard collection of classic essays on this topic, with a substantial introduction and bibliography.) Darmstadt, 1987.

Ross, W. D. "The Problem of Socrates." *Proceedings of the Classical Association* 30 (1933): 7–24.

Taylor, A. E., *Varia Socratica,* London, 1911.

Vlastos, G. *Socrates: Ironist and Moral Philosopher.* Ithaca, 1991.

V.B The Trial and Death of Socrates

Brickhouse, T. C. and Smith, N. D. eds., *The Trial and Execution of Socrates: Sources and Controversies.* Oxford, 2002.

Brickhouse, T. C., and N.D. Smith. *Socrates On Trial.* Oxford, 1989.

Connor, W. R. "The other 399. Religion and the trial of Socrates." In *Georgica. Greek studies in honor of G. Caldwel,* eds. M.A. Flower and M. Toher. London, 1991, 49–56.

Gill, C. "The Death of Socrates." *CQ* 23 (1973): 25–58.

Mossé, C. *Le procès de Socrate.* Brussels, 1987.

Ober, W.B. "Did Socrates die of hemlock poisoning?" *Ancient Philosophy* 2 (1982): 115–121.

Reeve, C. D. C. *Socrates in the Apology.* Indianapolis, 1989.

Stone, I. F. *The Trial of Socrates.* Boston, Toronto 1988.

Waterfield, R. *Why Socrates Died: Dispelling the Myths.* New York, 2009.

V.C Religion

Beckman, J. *The Religious Dimension of Socrates' Thought.* Waterloo, IA, 1979.

Burnyeat, M. F. "The Impiety of Socrates." *Ancient Philosophy* 17 (1997): 1–12.

Cohen, S. M. "Socrates on the Definition of Piety: *Euthyphro* 10a–11b." In *The Philosophy of Socrates,* ed. G. Vlastos. Garden City, NY, 1971, pp. 158–76.

Destrée, P., and N.D. Smith., eds., *Socrates' Divine Sign. Religion, Practice, and Value in Socratic Philosophy. Apeiron.* Kelowna, BC, 2005.

Garland, R. *Introducing New Gods.* Ithaca, 1992.

Jackson, B.D. "The Prayers of Socrates." *Phronesis* 16 (1971): 14–37.

McPherran, M. L. *The Religion of Socrates.* University Park, PA, 1996.

Mikalson, J. D. *Athenian Popular Religion.* Chapel Hill, NC, 1983.

Morgan, M. L. *Platonic Piety.* New Haven, 1990.

Parker, R. *Athenian religion: a history.* Oxford, 1996.

Smith, N. D., and Woodruff, P., eds., *Reason and Religion in Socratic Philosophy.* Oxford, 2000.

Vlastos, G. "Socratic Piety." In *Socrates, Ironist and Moral Philosopher*. Ithaca, 1991, ch. 6, pp. 157–178.

Weiss, R. "Virtue Without Knowledge: Socratic Piety in Plato's *Euthyphro*." *Ancient Philosophy* 14 (1994): 263–282.

Yunis, H. *A New Creed: Fundamental Religious Belief in the Athenian Polis and Euripidean Drama*. Hypomnemata 91. Göttingen, 1988.

Bruit Zaidman, L. and Schmitt Pantel, P. (trans. P. Cartledge). *Religion in the Ancient Greek City*. Cambridge, 1992.

V.D Method

Benson, H. "The Dissolution of the Problem of the Elenchus." *OSAP* 13. (1995): 54–112.

Benson, H. H. *Socratic Wisdom: The Model of Knowledge in Plato's Early Dialogues*. New York, 2000.

Bolton, R. "Aristotle's Account of the Socratic Elenchus." *OSAP* 11 (1993): 121–152.

Ioppolo, A. M. "Vlastos e l'elenchos socratico." *Elenchos* 6 (1985): 151–162.

Kraut R. "Comments on Gregory Vlastos' 'The Socratic Elenchus'" *OSAP* 1 (1983): 59–70.

Nozick, R. "Socratic Puzzles." *Phronesis* 40 (1995): 143–155.

Patzer, A. "Τί ἐστι bei Sokrates?" in *Dialogos. Für H. Patzer zum 65. Geburtstag* (Wiesbaden 1976): 49–57.

Robinson, R. *Plato's Earlier Dialectic*. Oxford, 1953.

Scott, G.A., ed. *Does Socrates Have a Method?: Rethinking the Elenchus in Plato's Dialogues and Beyond*. University Park, PA, 2004.

Vlastos, G. "The Socratic Elenchus." *OSAP* 1 (1983): 27–58. Repr. in *Socratic Studies*, ed. M. Burnyeat (Cambridge, 1994) 1–33.

Wolsdorf, D. "Socrates' Pursuit of Definitions." *Phronesis* 48 (2003): 271–312.

V.E Self-examination

Annas, J. "Self-knowledge in early Plato." In *Platonic Investigations* (Studies in Philosophy and the History of Philosophy, vol. 13), ed. Dominic J.O'Meara. Washington, DC, 1985.

Benson, H. H. "A Note on Socratic Self-Knowledge in the *Charmides*." *Ancient Philosophy* 23 (2007): 31–47.

Brunschwig, J. "La déconstruction du 'Connais-toi, toi même' dans *l'Alcibiade Majeur*." *Recherches sur la philosophie et la langage* 18 (1996): 61–84.

Griswold, C. *Self-Knowledge in Plato's Phaedrus*. New Haven, 1986.

North, H. *Sophrosune: Self-Knowledge and Self-Restraint in Greek Literature*. Ithaca, 1986.

Rappe, S. L. " Socrates and Self-Knowledge." *Apeiron* 28 (1995): 1–24.

Tsouna, V. "Socrate et la connaissance de soi: quelques interprétations." *Philosophie Antique* 1 (2001): 37–64.

V.F Ignorance

Fine, G. "Does Socrates Claim to Know that He Knows Nothing?" *OSAP* 35 (2008): 49–88.

Forster, M. "Socrates' Profession of Ignorance." *OSAP* 23 (2007): 1–35.

Lesher, J. H. "Socrates' Disavowal of Knowledge." *JHP* 25 no. 2 (1987): 275–288.

Tarán, L. "Platonism and Socratic Ignorance." In *Platonic Investigations*, ed. D.J. O'Meara. Washington, D.C., 1985.

Vlastos, G. "Socrates' Disavowal of Knowledge." *The Philosophical Quarterly* 35 (1985): 1–31.

V.G Socrates as Teacher

Blank, D. L. "Socrates versus Sophists on Payment for Teaching." *Classical Antiquity* 4 (1985): 1–49.
Euben, J. P. *Corrupting Youth: Political Education, Democratic Culture and Political Theory.* Princeton, 1997.
Jaeger, W. *Paideia*, vol. II, New York, 1943 [cf. pp. 27–76: "Socrates the teacher"].
Morrison, D. "Xenophon's Socrates as a Teacher." In *The Socratic Movment*, ed. P.A. Vander Waerdt. Ithaca, 1994, pp. 181–208.
Nehamas, A. "What did Socrates Teach and to whom did he Teach it?" *The Review of Metaphysics* 46 no.2 (1992): 279–306. Repr. in *Virtues of Authenticity: Essays on Plato and Socrates.* Princeton, 1999.
Nehamas, A. "Meno's Paradox and Socrates as a Teacher," OSAP, 3 (1985): 1–30. Rpt. In A. Nehamas, *Virtues of Authenticity: Essays on Plato and Socrates.* Princeton, 1999, pp. 3–27.
Rossetti, L. "The Rhetoric of Socrates." *Philosophy and Rhetoric* 22 (1989): 225–238.
Scott, G. A., *Plato's Socrates as educator.* Albany, 2000.

V.H Irony

Bouchard, D. "L'ironie Socratique." *Laval Théologique et-Philosophique*, 57 no. 2 (2001): 277–289.
Edmunds, L., "The practical irony of the historical Socrates," *Phoenix* 58 (2004): 193–207.
Gourinat, M. "Socrate était- il un ironiste?" *Revue de Métaphysique et de Morale* 91 (1986): 339–353.
Lane, M . "The Evolution of Eironeia in Classical Greek Texts: Why Socratic Eironeia Is Not Socratic Irony." *OSAP* 31 (2006): 49–83.
Nagley, W. E. "Kierkegaards' Early and Later View of Socratic Irony." *Thought: Fordham University Quarterly* 55 (1980): 271–282.
Scott-Taggart, M. J. "Socratic Irony and Self-Deceit." *Ratio: An International Journal of Analytic Philosophy* 14 (1972): 1–15.
Vlastos, G. "Socratic Irony." In *Socrates, Ironist and Moral Philosopher.* Ithaca, 1991, ch. I, pp. 21–44.

V.I Ethics and Moral Psychology

Devereux, Daniel T. "Socrates' Kantian Conception of Virtue." *Journal of the History of Philosophy* 33 (1995): 381–408.
Ferejohn, M. "Socratic Thought-Experiments and the Unity of Virtue Paradox." *Phronesis* 29 (1984): 105–122.
Gomez-Lobo, A. *The Foundations of Socratic Ethics.* Indianapolis, 1994.
Irwin, T. *Plato's Ethics.* Oxford, 1994, chs. 2–9.
Irwin, T. "Socrates the Epicurean?" *Illinois Classical Studies* 11 (1986): 85–112.
Penner, T. "The Unity of Virtue." *Philosophical Review* 82 (1973): 35–68. Rpt. in *Essays on the Philosophy of Socrates*, ed. H. Benson. New York, Oxford 1992, pp. 162–184.
Santas, G. *Goodness and Justice: Plato, Aristotle, and the Moderns.* Oxford, 2001. Ch. 2.

Segvic, H. "No One Errs Willingly: The Meaning of Socratic Intellectualism." *OSAP* 19 (2000): 1–45.

Vlastos, G. "Happiness and Virtue In Socrates' Moral Theory." *Topoi* 4 (1985): 3–22.

Young, C. M. "First Principles of Socratic Ethics." *Apeiron:* 30 no. 4. (1997): 13–23.

Zeyl, D. "Socratic Virtue and Happiness." *AGP* 64 (1982): 225–238.

V.J Political Thought

Kraut, R. "Socrates, Politics, and Religion." in *Reason and Religion in Socratic Philosophy.* Oxford, 2000, p. 13–23.

Kraut, R. *Socrates and the State.* Princeton, 1984.

Morrison, D. "Some Central Elements of Socratic Political Theory." *Polis* 18 (2001): 27–40.

Ober, J., "Living freely as a slave of the law. Notes on why Sokrates lives in Athens," in P. Flensted-Jensen et al. (eds.), *Polis and Politics.* Copenhagen, 2000, pp. 541–552.

O'Connor, D. K., "Socrates and political ambition: the dangerous game," in J. J. Cleary & G. M. Gurtler (eds.), *Proceedings of the BACAP,* XIV (= 1998). Leiden, 1999, 31–52.

Pangle, T. *The Roots of Political Philosophy: Ten Forgotten Socratic Dialogues. Translated with Interpretive Studies.* Ithaca, 1987.

Villa, D. *Socratic Citizenship,* Princeton, 2001, ch. 1: 1–58.

Vlastos, G. "The Historical Socrates and Athenian Democracy." *Political Theory* 11 (1983): 495–516.

V.K Legacy

Calder, W. M. *The unknown Socrates: translations, with introductions and notes, of four important documents in the late antique reception of Socrates the Athenian.* Wauconda, IL, 2002.

Kierkegaard, S. *The Concept of Irony with Continual Reference to Socrates* [1841], ed. and trans. Howard V. Hong and Edna H. Hong. Princeton, 1989.

Lane, M. *Plato's Progeny: How Plato and Socrates Still Captivate the Modern Mind.* London, 2001.

Montuori, M. *De Socrate iuste damnato. The Rise of the Socratic Problem in the Eighteenth Century.* Amsterdam, 1981.

Montuori, M. *Socrates: An Approach.* Amsterdam, 1988.

Montuori, M. *The Socratic Problem. The History, the Solutions.* Amsterdam, 1992.

Trapp, M. ed. *Socrates from Antiquity to the Enlightenment.* Burlington, VT, 2007.

Trapp, M. B. ed. *Socrates in the Nineteenth and Twentieth Centuries.* Burlington, VT, 2007.

Index of Names and Subjects

Index of Passages

OTHER VOLUMES IN THE SERIES (continued from page iii)

Lightning Source UK Ltd.
Milton Keynes UK
UKHW022016070720
366165UK00014B/236